Ezekiel in Context

Princeton Theological Monograph Series

K. C. Hanson, Charles M. Collier, D. Christopher Spinks,
Robin Parry, and Rodney Clapp, Series Editors

Recent volumes in the series:

William A. Tooman, Michael A. Lyons, editors
*Transforming Vision:
Transformations of Text, Tradition, and Theology in Ezekiel*

Lowell K. Handy, editor
Psalm 29 through Time and Tradition

Thomas J. King
*The Realignment of the Priestly Literature:
The Priestly Narrative in Genesis
and Its Relation to Priestly Legislation*

Sara M. Koenig
*Isn't This Bathsheba:
A Study in Characterization*

Julie Woods
Jeremiah 48 as Christian Scripture

Aaron B. Hebbard
Reading Daniel as a Text in Theological Hermeneutics

Scott A. Ellington
*Risking Truth:
Reshaping the World through Prayers of Lament*

David Rhoads, David Esterline, and Jae Won Lee, editors
*Luke-Acts and Empire:
Essays in Honor of Robert L. Brawley*

Ezekiel in Context

Ezekiel's Message Understood in Its Historical Setting of Covenant Curses and Ancient Near Eastern Mythological Motifs

BRIAN NEIL PETERSON

◆PICKWICK *Publications* • Eugene, Oregon

EZEKIEL IN CONTEXT
Ezekiel's Message Understood in Its Historical Setting of Covenant Curses and Ancient Near Eastern Mythological Motifs

Princeton Theological Monograph Series 182

Copyright © 2012 Brian Neil Peterson. All rights reserved. Except for brief quotations in critical publications or reviews, no part of this book may be reproduced in any manner without prior written permission from the publisher. Write: Permissions, Wipf and Stock Publishers, 199 W. 8th Ave., Suite 3, Eugene, OR 97401.

Pickwick Publications
An Imprint of Wipf and Stock Publishers
199 W. 8th Ave., Suite 3
Eugene, OR 97401
www.wipfandstock.com

ISBN 13: 978-1-60899-524-0

Cataloging-in-Publication data:

Peterson, Brian Neil.

    Ezekiel in context : Ezekiel's message understood in its historical setting of covenant curses and ancient Near Eastern mythological motifs / Brian Neil Peterson.

    Princeton Theological Monograph Series 182

    xviii + 416 pp. ; 23 cm. — Includes bibliographical references and index.

    ISBN 13: 978-1-60899-524-0

    1. Bible—O.T.—Ezekiel—Criticism, interpretation, etc. 2. Blessing and cursing in the Bible. 3. Myth in the Bible. I. Title. II. Series.

BS1545.52 P100 2012

Manufactured in the U.S.A.

Scripture quotations marked (NASB) are taken from the New American Standard Bible® Copyright © 1960, 1962, 1963, 1968, 1971, 1972, 1973, 1975, 1977, 1995 by The Lockman Foundation. Used by permission. (www.Lockman.org)

I would like to dedicate this book
to Sandra (Sandie) Dawn Martin,
a longtime friend who encouraged me to begin
this journey in biblical studies.

Her endless encouragement and support over my
many years of intense study brought a degree of sanity
to an otherwise crazy period of my life.

Sadly, Sandie did not live to see the completion
of my twelve-and-a-half years of study.
She lost her battle with ovarian cancer on
October 26, 2008.

Although she is absent in body,
I can still hear the echo of the gentle and kind words
of my dear friend saying, "You can do it."
I have faith that someday we will meet again.

Contents

Preface / ix

Acknowledgments / xi

Abbreviations / xiii

Introduction / 1

1. Methodology and Literary Technique / 3
2. God's Glory Revealed: The Awesome Deity Departs (Ezekiel 1–3, 8–11) / 97
3. The Awesome Deity's Judgment (Ezekiel 16 & 23) / 173
4. The Awesome Deity's Love: The Covenant Curses Reversed (Ezekiel 37 juxtaposed with 38–39) / 226
5. The Awesome Deity Returns (Ezekiel 43; 48:35) / 291
6. Conclusions and Implications / 331

Appendix: Ezekiel and Apocalyptic / 341

Bibliography / 357

Scripture Index / 393

Preface

THE BOOK OF EZEKIEL STANDS OUT AMONG THE PROPHETIC WORKS as not always fitting the mould of prophecy in the clearest sense of the genre. Any attempt to better understand this book and its complexities can only be seen as beneficial to the scholarly community. In this book I will attempt to show the unity of thought of the author(s)[1] of the book of Ezekiel as it has come down to us in its final form. While no one study perhaps will ever satisfy all the critics concerning message, literary style, background influences, and later borrowed motifs, it still is my hope to shed some light on a book that has often been dissected to the point of unrecognizability.[2]

The literary methodology undertaken in this work will not reflect source and text-critical approaches, but rather will focus on a rhetorical analysis of the final form and the possible reasons the book of

---

1. I use the term "author" in the sense of the final form of the book. Part of my contention is that the organization of the final form is vital to the message the "original" author intended (be it the prophet himself or a later disciple who lived close to the time of Ezekiel himself). Therefore, for ease of argument and for general flow of thought I will use the term "author" in its most general sense whether he is from the sixth century or beyond. Also, I will refer to the author as "Ezekiel" in the same sense, whether that is the original prophet himself or the compiler(s) of the later form under the pseudonymity of the original author, cannot be proven. The purpose of this work is not to debate the authorship issue of each section, although the implications and outcome of the findings here may lead in that direction, but rather to look at the unity of the final form and try and understand what literary and theological methodology the author used to shape the book in the fashion as we have it today. For cogent debates on the multiple authorship issue where Ezekielian authorship is primarily concluded see Collins, *The Mantle of Elijah*, esp. 93 and Greenberg, "The Design and Themes," 115. For a discussion on the book of Ezekiel as a literary unity see Davis, *Swallowing the Scroll*, and Davis, "Swallowing Hard," 217–37.

2. Speaking of Zimmerli's work which exemplifies the historical critical approach to Ezekiel over the past century, Boadt states that Zimmerli's conclusions have "left the ordinary reader of Ezekiel bereft of a single, coherent message from the text, and made the reading of the entire book as a unitary whole extremely difficult." Cf. Boadt, "Rhetorical Strategies," 183.

Ezekiel has been preserved with this arrangement intact.[3] Again, while authorship debates and dating of certain portions of the book often dominate any discussion on Ezekiel as a whole, one cannot overlook the possibilities that these and other prominent questions and issues will be indirectly affected by the outcome and conclusions of this study. It is my hope that the insights and conclusions gleaned from this work by those who read it will affect their understanding and appreciation of this colorful work by Ezekiel and in doing so cause a greater respect for the man, the message, and the motifs behind the final form.

---

[3]. Block gives the following outline to show the process that books such as Ezekiel went through to get to their final form, (Block, *Ezekiel 1–24*, 18).

1. The prophetic event: the prophet receives a message from God.
2. The rhetorical event: the prophet transmits that message to his or her audience.
3. The transcriptional event: the oracle is written down.
4. The narratorial event: the account of the circumstances of the prophetic event are added to the transcribed oracle, creating a complete literary unit.
5. The compilation event: the literary units are gathered.
6. The editorial event: the collection is organized and the individual oracles are stitched together by means of connective and correlative notes, resulting in a more or less coherent book.
7. The nominal event: a formal heading is added to the book, identifying the prophet, the circumstances of the ministry, and the genre of the collection.

He concludes that after this process is complete, the literary work on a text is more "text-critical rather than compositional" (18). In Ezekiel's case, Block states that there is no reason not to assign many, if not all, of these steps to the prophet himself. He quips that this position is no more speculative than the "elaborate evolutionary and often contradictory schemes proposed by those who dissect the text into numerous layers of tradition." Cf. Block, *Ezekiel 1–24*, 23.

Acknowledgments

I WOULD LIKE TO THANK THOSE WHO HAVE AIDED ME THROUGHOUT the process of writing this monograph. Foremost I would like to thank my director, Dr. J. Glen Taylor for the numerous hours of discussion and encouragement he gave me over the last several years. He has not only been my PhD director; he has also become a good friend. His patience with my often-stubborn temperament, as well as his godly example has been a blessing. I would also like to mention Dr. Marion Taylor, for whom I have had the privilege of being a TA for several years. She gave me the opportunity to experiment with my hypothesis in a classroom setting. She also agreed to be one of my readers, and caught many of my typos as well as offered helpful suggestions for the thesis as a whole. I would also like to thank my other readers, Dr. Mark Boda (McMaster Divinity College), Dr. Brian Irwin (Knox College), and Dr. Paul-Alain Beaulieu (Department of Near and Middle Eastern Civilizations at the University of Toronto), who all gave of their time and their expertise to this project. Moreover, Dr. John McLaughlin (University of St. Michael's College) and the late Dr. Brian Peckham (Regis College) were invaluable in the proposal stage of the process. Finally, I would like to thank my lovely wife, Christine Curley, for her patience over the past four years. Her encouragement, love, and support were unconditional. Her willingness to aid in the editing process to bring this work to fruition was indeed a blessing.

Abbreviations

AB	Anchor Bible
ABD	*Anchor Bible Dictionary*
AfO	*Archiv für Orientforschung*
AJIL	*American Journal of International Law*
AJSL	*American Journal of Semitic Languages and Literatures*
ALGHJ	Arbeiten zur Geschichte des antiken Judentums und des Urchristentums
AMWNE	*Apocalypticism in the Mediterranean World and the Near East*
AnBib	Analecta biblica
ANET	*Ancient Near Eastern Texts Relating to the Old Testament*
AnOr	Analecta orientalia
AnSt	*Anatolian Studies*
AOAT	Alter Orient und Altes Testament
AR	*Archiv für Religionswissenschaft*
ArBib	The Aramaic Bible
AS	Assyriological Studies
ASOR	American Schools of Oriental Research
ASTI	*Annual of the Swedish Theological Institute*
ATANT	Abhandlungen zur Theologie des Alten und Neuen Testaments
ATSAT	Arbeiten zu Text und Sprache im Alten Testament
BA	*Biblical Archaeologist*
BapQ	*Baptist Quarterly*
BAR	*Biblical Archaeology Review*
BASOR	*Bulletin of American Schools of Oriental Research*

BEATAJ	Beiträge zur Erforschung des Alten Testaments und des antiken Judentums
BETL	Bibliotheca ephemeridum theologicarum lovaniensium
BHT	Beitrage zur historischen Theologie
Bib	*Biblica*
BibInt	*Biblical Interpretation*
BibOr	Biblica et orientalia
BJRL	*Bulletin of the John Rylands University Library of Manchester*
BJS	Brown Judaic Studies
Bsac	*Bibliotheca Sacra*
BWANT	Beiträge zur Wissenschaft vom Alten und Neuen Testament
BZ	*Biblische Zeitschrift*
BZAW	Beihefte zur Zeitschrift für die alttestamentliche Wissenschaft
CAD	*The Assyrian Dictionary of the Oriental Institute of the University of Chicago*
CahRB	Cahiers de la Revue Biblique
CANE	*Civilizations of the Ancient Near East*
CAT	*The Cuneiform Alphabetic Texts from Ugarit, Ras Ibn Hani, and Other Places*
CBOTS	Coniectanea Biblica Old Testament Series
CBQ	*Catholic Biblical Quarterly*
CBQMS	Catholic Biblical Quarterly Monograph Series
CC	Continental Commentaries
CHJ	*Cambridge History of Judaism*
ChrCent	*Christian Century*
CJ	*Classical Journal*
Con	*Concilium*
COS	*The Context of Scripture*
COT	Commentary on the Old Testament
DDD	*Dictionary of Deities and Demons in the Bible*
EBC	Expositor's Bible Commentary
EF	Erträge der Forschung

EHB	*Ezekiel and His Book*
Enc	*Encounter*
EncApoc	*Encyclopedia of Apocalypticism*
EncDSS	*Encyclopedia of the Dead Sea Scrolls*
EncJud	*Encyclopaedia Judaica*
EncRel	*Encyclopedia of Religion*
ErIsr	*Eretz-Israel*
EstBib	*Estudios Biblicos*
EvJ	*Evangelical Journal*
EvQ	*Evangelical Quarterly*
ExAud	*Ex Auditu*
ExpTim	*Expository Times*
FB	Forschung zur Bibel
FOTL	Forms of the Old Testament Literature
GRBS	*Greek, Roman, and Byzantine Studies*
HAR	*Hebrew Annual Review*
HAT	Handbuch zum Alten Testament
HSM	Harvard Semitic Monographs
HSS	Harvard Semitic Series
HTR	*Harvard Theological Review*
HUCA	*Hebrew Union College Annual*
HUCM	Monographs of the Hebrew Union College
IB	*Interpreter's Bible*
ICC	International Critical Commentary
IEJ	*Israel Exploration Journal*
Int	*Interpretation*
ISBE	*International Standard Bible Encyclopedia*
ITC	International Theological Commentary
JANESCU	*Journal of the Ancient Near Eastern Society of Columbia University*
JAOS	*Journal of the American Oriental Society*

JBL	*Journal of Biblical Literature*
JCS	*Journal of Cuneiform Studies*
JESHO	*Journal of the Economic and Social History of the Orient*
JET	*Jahrbuch für Evangelische Theologie*
JETS	*Journal of the Evangelical Theological Society*
JFSR	*Journal of Feminist Studies in Religion*
JHScr	*Journal of Hebrew Scriptures*
JITC	*Journal of the Interdenominational Theological Center*
JNES	*Journal of Near Eastern Studies*
JNSL	*Journal of Northwest Semitic Languages*
JPS	Jewish Publication Society
JPSTC	Jewish Publication Society Torah Commentary
JSJ	*Journal for the Study of Judaism in the Persian, Hellenistic, and Roman Period*
JSNT	*Journal for the Study of the New Testament*
JSOT	*Journal for the Study of the Old Testament*
JSOTSup	Journal for the Study of the Old Testament: Supplement Series
JSP	*Journal for the Study of Pseudepigrapha*
JSPSup	Journal for the Study of the Pseudepigrapha: Supplement Series
JTC	*Journal for Theology and the Church*
JTS	*Journal of Theological Studies*
KAT	Kommentar zum Alten Testament
KHC	Kurzer Hand-Commentar zum Alten Testament
LBC	Layman's Bible Commentary
LHB/OTS	Library of Hebrew Bible/Old Testament Studies
ML	*Mennonite Life*
NAC	New American Commentary
NIBC	New International Bible Commentary
NIBCOT	New International Biblical Commentary: Old Testament Series

NICOT	New International Commentary on the Old Testament
NR	*Nova Religio*
NSKAT	Neuer Stuttgarter Kommentar Altes Testament
NTS	New Testament Studies
OBO	Orbis biblicus et orientalis
OBT	Overtures to Biblical Theology
OIUC	Oriental Institute of the University of Chicago
OLZ	*Orientallistische Literaturzeitung*
OTG	Old Testament Guides
OTL	Old Testament Library
OTM	Old Testament Message
OtSt	Oudtestamentische Studiën
PEQ	*Palestine Exploration Quarterly*
RB	*Revue Biblique*
RevExp	*Review and Expositor*
RevQ	*Revue de Qumran*
RHR	*Revue de l'histoire des religions*
RHPR	*Revue d'histoire et de philosophie religieuses*
RIMA	The Royal Inscriptions of Mesopotamia, Assyrian Periods
RIME	The Royal Inscriptions of Mesopotamia, Early Periods
RSR	*Recherches de science religieuse*
SAA	State Archives of Assyria
SBB	Stuttgarter biblische Beiträge
SBL	Society of Biblical Literature
SBLit	Studies in Biblical Literature
SBLBSNA	Society of Biblical Literature: Biblical Scholarship in North America
SBLDS	Society of Biblical Literature Dissertation Series
SBLMS	Society of Biblical Literature Monograph Series
SBLSP	Society of Biblical Literature Seminar Papers
SBLSS	Society of Biblical Literature Semeia Studies

SBLSymS	Society of Biblical Literature Symposium Series
SBS	Stuttgarter Bibelstudien
SBT	Studies in Biblical Theology
Sem	*Semitica*
SHR	Studies in the History of Religions
SWBA	The Social World of Biblical Antiquity
TBT	*The Bible Today*
TCS	Texts from Cuneiform Sources
TDOT	*Theological Dictionary of the Old Testament*
Them	*Themelios*
ThSt	Theologische Studien
TLZ	*Theologische Literaturzeitung*
TOTC	Tyndale Old Testament Commentaries.
TQ	*Theologische Quartalschrift*
TynBul	*Tyndale Bulletin*
TZ	*Theologische Zeitschrift*
UCOIS	University of Chicago Oriental Institute Seminars
VAB	Vorderasiatische Bibliothek
VE	*Vox evangelica*
VT	*Vetus Testamentum*
VTSup	Supplements to Vetus Testamentum
WBC	Word Biblical Commentary
WMANT	Wissenschaftliche Monographien zum Alten und Neuen Testame
WMAT	Wissenschaftliche Monographien zum Alten Testament
WUNT	Wissenschaftliche Untersuchungen zum Neuen Testament
WTJ	*Westminster Theological Journal*
WW	*Word and World*
ZA	*Zeitschrift für Assyriologie*
ZAW	*Zeitschrift für alttestamentliche Wissenschaft*

Introduction

THIS STUDY CONCLUDES THAT THE BOOK OF EZEKIEL IS NOT AN amalgam of visions and oracles compiled with no particular literary strategy but rather is a purposeful literary work, which betrays Ezekiel's rhetorical intent. The book of Ezekiel shows a masterful literary mind behind the framework of visions and metaphors closely linked to ancient Near Eastern covenant curses, symbolism, and motifs. Ezekiel's visions and extended metaphors appear at key junctures forming the "peaks" of the framework of the work. The chariot-throne vision of chs. 1–3 sets the tone for the ensuing prophecies. In Exodus fashion, Yahweh, the offended Suzerain, appears in theophanic glory as the one who will enact the covenant curses of the Law against his wayward vassal, Judah. Thus, it is no surprise that the reappearance of the chariot-throne vision in chs. 8–11 marks the enactment of the greatest covenant curse—temple abandonment. This first curse opens the floodgates for the outpouring of the covenant curses upon the "rebellious house" of Judah (chs. 13–24). These covenant curses find their nexus in the extended metaphors and covenant language of chs. 16 and 23 where Judah is judged by the "standards"/"customs" of the nations.

However, the "house of Israel" is not forever abandoned to the enacted curses as was the fate of most unfaithful vassals of the ANE. Yahweh tempers his justice with his *ḥesed* manifested by the reversal of the curses in chs. 25–48. Curses once placed upon "the house of Israel" are now turned against her enemies. The vision of the valley of dry bones in ch. 37, a picture of a much-feared ANE curse, stands at the heart of the restoration chapters as a testimony to the plan of Yahweh to reverse the curses. The final destruction of chaos in chs. 38–39 paves the way for the vision of the new temple and the ultimate curse reversal. Ezekiel's message comes full circle as the glory of the Lord, which had once abandoned the covenant people, returns to its earthly abode and the rebuilt city of Jerusalem is renamed "Yahweh is there."

I

Methodology and Literary Technique

Introduction

SCHOLARS HAVE LONG RECOGNIZED THE INHERENT DIFFICULTIES IN interpreting Ezekiel's visions.[1] The book's seemingly random visions and sign acts have often been interpreted independently of each other as oracles for a particular time and purpose with questions concerning multiple authorship often stemming from the debate (as per Hölscher).[2] However, when viewed in light of the ancient Near Eastern setting within which Ezekiel ministered, a better understanding of his message and purpose becomes clear. In an era when covenant treaties (viz., Hittite, Babylonian, and Assyrian) dominated political alliances between ruling countries and their vassals, Ezekiel steps onto the prophetic scene in Babylon with a message rooted in a similar covenant treaty format which had been established between Israel and her God.[3] Hillers comments, "Although the Pan-Babylonian School was

---

1. Norris points out that Jerome noted in the fourth century CE that the rabbis had a strict policy on the reading of certain parts of Ezekiel. The reading of the opening chapters of Ezekiel dealing with the cherubim and the final chapters on the building of the temple were to be "held back till last of all" when reading the Bible. In fact readers were required to be at least thirty years of age. See Norris, *Song of Songs*, 1–2; and Carley, *Book of the Prophet Ezekiel*, 8.

2. Hölscher, *Hezekiel*. For a completely opposite view, see Kaufmann, *Religion*, 429–30. Kaufmann (430) notes, "A few obvious marginal notes and later expansions have entered the text, but nothing that warrants the assumption of an extensive and continuous process of revision and supplementation." For a critique of Hölscher, see Freedy, "Literary Relations," 47–63.

3. Wong, *Idea of Retribution*, 31, notes that "the word 'covenant' (ברית) occurs 12 times in Isaiah, 24 times in Jeremiah, 18 times in Ezekiel, and 15 times in the Twelve," thus showing the importance of the concept in Ezekiel.

guilty of ridiculous excesses in claiming that everything worthwhile in Hebrew literature was derived from Mesopotamia, it is still generally recognized that certain elements in biblical literature are related to Mesopotamian prototypes. Innumerable instances of Canaanite influence on the Old Testament have already been pointed out, and new examples are constantly being discovered. Since this is so, it is not *a priori* far-fetched to propose . . . that passages in the Hebrew prophets may show dependence on originally foreign treaty-curses."[4]

From this perspective, one can pose the argument that Ezekiel may have chosen to formulate his prophetic announcements using treaty-curse language. Interestingly, according to Hillers, of all the prophetic books, Jeremiah contains the most occurrences of the treaty curse parallels.[5] Now beyond the obvious fact that Ezekiel and Jeremiah were contemporaries, Ezekiel appears to have also adopted this form of prophetic address by embracing his new exilic setting. Using the symbolism and mythological motifs readily available in Babylon,[6] the heart of ANE politics and culture at this time, Ezekiel fashioned his message of warning, doom, and future hope for the exiles in Babylon and those left in Jerusalem.[7] Judah had broken covenant with her Suzerain, Yahweh, and as Yahweh's spokesman (cf. 3:1–3), Ezekiel painted an intricate but unified picture of the nation's

---

4. Hillers, *Treaty-Curses*, 6.

5. Ibid., 77. Hillers presents numerous examples of occurrences of treaty-curse language not only in Ezekiel, but also in Hosea and Isaiah 1–39. He goes on to point out that the appearance of the treaty curses and the closest word-for-word parallels to ANE treaty curses are found almost half of the time in the oracles against the foreign nations (78).

6. I do not mean to suggest that Ezekiel used the imagery and mythological symbols of Babylon and other ANE cultures in the same way that these cultures had, but rather that in most cases he reinterpreted them and invested them with new meaning for his message and his audience. See Russell, *Method & Message*, 186; Lewis "CT 13:33–34," 28–47; and Cook, *Apocalyptic Literature*, 96, for examples of ANE mythological parallels to Ezekiel.

7. I will attempt to establish that Ezekiel's message was more than the spoken words of the text and the content of the visions presented to the people. While I believe that these were the primary means by which the prophet conveyed his message (contra Davis, *Swallowing the Scroll*), the symbols themselves, reflective of Babylonian images and import, became an effective means of communicating the gravity of the situation the house of Israel found themselves in. The multifaceted nature of the prophet's verbal and nonverbal communication is brought to the fore in Robson's, *Word and Spirit*, esp. ch. 2, which will be addressed further below.

covenant breaches. His use of oracles, allegory, and covenant lawsuit language, shrouded in symbols and imagery, helped shake a lethargic people into the stark reality of what was ahead for Jerusalem and why many were already in exile in a foreign land. By understanding this methodological approach of Ezekiel as a literary artist in his own right, one can better appreciate the wake-up call that the prophet delivered to his nation.[8]

In this monograph I will contend that Ezekiel's visions and extended metaphors have to be seen through the interpretive lens of the covenant lawsuit format (viz., treaty curses) placed within a literary framework that many times reflects ANE mythological coloring. From this perspective it is possible to understand the book as a relatively coherent work in which one can discern the indictment of Yahweh and the cry of the prophet's heart to his people.

General Approach

Because I will focus on a broad approach to the issues of the rhetorical strategy of Ezekiel coupled with the motifs of covenant, curse, and Mesopotamian influences, a typical history of scholarship will not be undertaken.[9] Rather, a history of pertinent scholarship as it applies to my topic will be addressed in particular sections as needed. In this vein, the purpose of this opening chapter is to introduce the reader to the main issues handled in subsequent chapters. These issues include: 1) methodological factors including historical setting for the book, cross-cultural textual and motif analysis, motif/metaphor blending, the rhetorical strategy of the prophet, and the theological purpose of the message; 2) the possible evidence of direct Mesopotamian influence on Ezekiel; 3) the plausibility that Ezekiel was reeducated and had access to Mesopotamian literature and/or art[10] from which he bor-

---

8. Contra Siegman, *Ezechiel*, 1:7, who posits that Ezekiel lacked "originality," his sermons were "monotonous," and his visions were "overdone" and "almost bizarre."

9. For a general presentation of the history of scholarship on Ezekiel, see Pohlmann, *Das Buch*, 23–27. For a critique of Pohlmann, see Renz, "Review of Pohlmann," 182–84. For a brief overview of the history of study on the coherence of Ezekiel, see Kutsko, *Between Heaven and Earth*, 5–9. For an overview of the changing tide of Ezekielian scholarship since the 1960s, see Joyce, *Ezekiel*, 13–16.

10. The massive work of Bruce Power, "Iconographic Windows to Ezekiel's World" has traced the influences of Mesopotamian art/iconography on the book of Ezekiel and will be referenced throughout this book.

rowed; and 4) how Ezekiel used covenant curses from ANE and OT covenant(s) and law. Note, however, that the final three issues will all be handled under the appropriate methodological sections.

Methodology Defined

As I analyze the message of Ezekiel, I will incorporate five different methodological approaches. These include 1) historical, 2) cross-cultural textual and motif analysis, 3) motif/metaphor blending, 4) rhetorical/literary, and 5) theological. While at points these approaches will appear well-defined, most of the time they will be blended, with the exception of the theological aspect which may have a separate section assigned to it in a given chapter where necessary. Also, while some scholars seek to reconstruct certain texts for their discussions, I will assume a literary coherency and integrity for each unit as I address them unless there is overwhelming evidence to warrant emendation. Thus, I will quote and base my work upon the text of the BHS as it stands.

Historical

Before we can discuss any of the main issues of the book of Ezekiel as they relate to Babylonian influences, cross-cultural borrowing of literature and motifs and the like we need to determine the possibility of an actual Babylonian setting for the book. Furthermore we need to decide whether Ezekiel ministered solely in Babylon or whether he had a split ministry between Judah and the land of his exile.[11] Methodologically, it is important to scrutinize the main arguments in this regard and determine if we can proceed within a solid consensus of scholarship.

Thomas Renz has summarized the heart of the historical debate by formulating two questions that need to be answered. First, "was the book meant for a specific audience, and if so was this audience an exilic one? Secondly, does the book portray the ministry of a prophet who was (exclusively) active in Babylonia, or, more precisely, . . . is

---

11. Some scholars go beyond the debate of the mere historical provenance of the book of Ezekiel and try to determine how the prophet presents history itself. For example, see Krüger, *Geschichtskonzepte*.

the picture drawn by the book accurate?"[12] Scholars have approached these questions from various perspectives and presuppositions and have argued for a particular position based on literary content, possible historical setting, and prophetic perspective.[13] In an effort not to reinvent the proverbial wheel I will summarize the meticulous work of Renz and update his research from the date of his publication in 1999. Renz highlights the six prevailing stances and their proponents.[14]

1. The majority of scholars at present view the book of Ezekiel as being written in Babylon with minor revisions in the post-exilic era. This position is held not only by Renz himself but also by scholars such as, Cooke, Fohrer, Wevers, Eichrodt, Freehof, Greenberg, Zimmerli, Maarsingh, Hals, Allen, Block, Kutsko, Mein, Wright, Odell, Joyce, and Launderville.[15]

---

12. Renz, *Rhetorical Function*, 28. For a review of Renz's book, see Bultmann, Review of Thomas Renz, 419–20. Bultmann points out Renz's emphasis on the rhetorical unity of the book to the relative exclusion of the structural aspects. He also correctly notes the need for further debate concerning the blending of the message of the individual parts and the unity of the book. Indeed, as I will seek to demonstrate throughout, the message highlighted by each "peak" or structural high point of Ezekiel stresses a particular curse from the ANE and/or the OT. While these structural markers are a vital part of the overall structural and rhetorical presentation of Ezekiel, they serve primarily as a framework or backbone to which the rest of the prophet's message adheres. For a more favorable review of Renz, see Mein, Review of Thomas Renz, 733–55.

13. Some scholars bypass these questions all together and start from the assumption that Ezekiel was a prophet of the exile; that he wrote most of the book that bears his name; and that the text is coherent as it stands. For example, see Kamionkowski, *Gender Reversal*, 10, 16.

14. The following list and relevant sources have been adapted from Renz, *Rhetorical Function*, 28–31.

15. Cooke, *Ezekiel*; Fohrer, *Hauptprobleme*; Wevers, *Ezekiel*, 23–6; Eichrodt, *Ezekiel*, 8–9. Also, Freehof, *Ezekiel*, 8, suggests that the book was written by Ezekiel in Babylon and edited mostly by the prophet himself; Greenberg, *Ezekiel 1–20*, 15–20; Zimmerli, *Ezekiel 1 & 2*, has adopted the concept of an Ezekielian "school" with a long tradition of "extrapolation." Maarsingh, *Ezechiël*, 1:14, suggests that Ezekiel was in fact with the exiles but traveled by the Spirit to Jerusalem in chapter 8 as the text suggests; Hals, *Ezekiel*; Allen, *Ezekiel 1–19*, xxxvi, suggests the book was compiled by Ezekiel or his disciples in Babylon. Block, *Ezekiel* (2 vols); Kutsko, *Between Heaven and Earth*, 14–15; Mein, *Ethics of Exile*, 258. Wright, *Message of Ezekiel*, 39, proposes that the book was basically complete and edited by the second generation of the exile shortly after the death of Ezekiel. Odell, *Ezekiel*, 4; Joyce, *Ezekiel*, 6–7. Joyce (16) avers that the book was essentially completed by the end of the sixth century with much of the literary influence coming from the prophet himself. One of the latest books to

2. Ezekiel ministered in Jerusalem before being taken into exile in 597 BCE (e.g., Spiegel, Auvray, Robinson, Mays, and Steinmann).[16] This explains some of the problematic material in the first half of the book that deals with Jerusalem in detail. This view had some following in the 1930s to the 1950s but has since lost much of its appeal, although a few scholars are still willing to suggest at least small portions of the book may have been written by Ezekiel in Judah (e.g., Fuhs, Blenkinsopp, Rabinowitz).[17]

3. Next, some posit that Ezekiel did in fact minister in Babylon. However, while the book might have had its beginnings in Babylon with the prophet, since then, the bulk of the book has had a Palestinian reworking. This stance was taken by Hölscher in 1924 and adapted by Irwin in 1943.[18] Hölscher actually propounded that only sixteen passages along with five short sections of prose (i.e., 150–170 verses of a total of 1270)[19] could be positively attributed to Ezekiel in Babylon.[20]

---

be published dealing with aspects of Ezekiel and his message is that of Launderville, *Spirit and Reason*, 14, who holds a similar position as stated here.

16. Spiegel, "Toward Certainty in Ezekiel," 145–71, esp. 170, and his review of Bertholet, 403–8, esp. 407–8. Auvray, "Le Problème," 503–19 and idem, *Ezéchiel*, 13–15. Robinson, *Hebrew Prophets*, 75–79, and Mays, *Ezekiel*, 51–53, aver that Ezekiel was in Palestine until 586 BCE. On the other hand, Steinmann, *Le* Prophète, 16, suggests that Ezekiel ministered in Jerusalem until 597 BCE when he was taken to Babylon.

17. Renz, *Rhetorical Function*, 28–29. Fuhs, *Ezechiel 1–24*, 13, (as cited by Renz, *Rhetorical Function*, 29); Blenkinsopp, *Ezekiel*, 27, suggests portions of the first half of the book may have been written in Jerusalem. Rabinowitz, *Da'ath Sofrim*, ii, proposes that chapters 2 and 17 may have been written by Ezekiel while in Jerusalem.

18. As pointed out by Stalker, *Ezekiel*, 20.

19. Stalker, *Ezekiel*, 20. Pohlmann, *Das Buch*, 25, notes that Hölscher's conclusion had a maximum of 170 verses attributed to Ezekiel.

20. Hölscher believed that Ezekiel was written by an early fifth century Zadokite redactor in Jerusalem. However, Davis, *Swallowing the Scroll*, 13, rightly points out that Hölscher's methodological approach was inconsistent. He would often assign portions (e.g., 32:1–16) of the poetic style (which he claimed was the hallmark of a prophet's work) to a redactor while arguing that the prose section in 8:1—11:25 was from the prophet himself. For further critiques of Hölscher see Kittel, *Geschichte des Volkes Israel* vol. 3 part 1, 144–80, and Herntrich, *Ezechielprobleme*, 7–30. Kittel (146) defends the differences in the book of Ezekiel based upon the catastrophe of the prophet's exile to a foreign land and of his somewhat conflicting role as an impassioned prophet and a teaching priest. Cf. also comments by Renz, *Rhetorical Function*, 29 n. 5.

Methodology and Literary Technique 9

4. The ministry of the prophet was only in Jerusalem and the book bearing his name had no affiliation with Babylon.[21] It was a later reworking of the original Palestinian book by a redactor in the post-exilic period in Palestine that incorporated Babylonian motifs and setting. Variations of this position were suggested by Berry[22] and Herntrich[23] in the 1930s but were mostly abandoned when Howie, Mullo Weir, and Fohrer published pivotal works pushing for a Babylonian setting.[24]

5. The book of Ezekiel is a Palestinian pseudepigraph from a much later period and the prophet, Ezekiel, never existed.[25] In this vein, Leopold Zunz (1794–1886) was perhaps the first to suggest a redating of Ezekiel to at least the Persian period[26] while others

---

21. As of 1983 Brownlee still maintained this position in his 1986 posthumously published volume on Ezekiel 1–19. Cf. Brownlee, *Ezekiel 1–19*, xxiii.

22. Berry, "Was Ezekiel in the Exile?" 83–93, propounded that most of the book was written late during the Persian or Greek period. Ezekiel himself was an exilic prophet but did not go to Babylon during the exile.

23. Herntrich, *Ezechielprobleme*. For a concise critique of Herntrich's position, see Freedy, "The Literary Relations," 64–67.

24. Renz, *Rhetorical Function*, 29–30. Cf. also, Howie, *Date and Composition*; Mullo Weir, "Aspects," 97–112; Fohrer, *Hauptprobleme*. While the works of these scholars returned the focus of Ezekiel to a Babylonian setting, there still remained scholars in the 1950s who held to some form of a "Babylonian" or "Palestinian" Ezekiel, see Frost, *Old Testament Apocalyptic*, 96.

Interestingly, Freedy seems to be paradigmatic of Ezekielian scholarship during this turbulent time. Freedy upbraided the work of earlier literary-critical scholars for their presuppositional approach to the text of Ezekiel. Freedy complained that they emended and/or reduced the text and "genuine" words of Ezekiel to a skeleton of the original (e.g., Hölscher) for no good reason. However, Freedy himself turns around and tries to recover the "original" words of the prophet by excising portions of the text that are in his words, "intrusive," "make no sense," or are "later expansions" (to list a few). Cf. Freedy, "Literary Relations," 194–95 n. 3. Freedy goes on to meticulously reproduce the entire text of Ezekiel (i.e., chapters 1–24) and then eliminate, in some cases, over fifty percent of the text as secondary or glosses (233–99).

25. Renz, *Rhetorical Function*, 30.

26. Zunz, *Gottesdienstliche* as noted by Freehof, *Ezekiel*, 3. For a discussion of Zunz's position (with bibliographic data) during the years of 1832–73, see Feist, *Ezechiel*, 104–15.

opted for the Greek period. In the past, Torrey[27] and Becker[28] adhered to this position. More recently, Pohlmann, and Feist[29] have adopted variations of this position.[30]

6. While Ezekiel may have worked predominantly in Babylon, he may have had an early ministry in Jerusalem.[31] The book has undergone a long history of redaction with some even suggesting that there may have been a "Deutero-Ezekiel."[32] Some scholars have taken a middle position between the first position above and this final position. These include Simian,[33] Hossfeld[34] and Sedlmeier.[35]

The range of opinions as to whether or not Ezekiel and/or his book is of Palestinian or Babylonian origin is telling of the scope of

27. Torrey, *Pseudo-Ezekiel*. Torrey propounded a date of 230 BCE as being the time when the Babylonian content was added to the book. For a brief rebuttal of his position based on archaeological finds, see Albright, "King Jehoiachin," 54–55.

28. Becker, "Erwägungen," 137–49, and idem, "Ez 8–11," 136–50. Becker postulates that Ezekiel was written during the post-exilic era (perhaps by a priestly hand) when apocalyptic was taking shape. Renz, *Rhetorical Function*, 30, points out that Becker saw some of the Babylonian framework as original.

29. Feist, *Ezechiel*, as noted by Sedlmeier, *Das Buch*, 55.

30. Renz, *Rhetorical Function*, 30 n. 11, goes on to give an extensive list of those who held this position prior to Torrey. Since the work of Renz, Pohlmann has written a monograph on Ezekiel from a theological perspective in which he continues to present the pseudepigraphical perspective. See Pohlmann, *Der Stand*, 48–51.

31. Renz, *Rhetorical Function*, 31.

32. Cf. Schultz, *Das Todesrecht*, 163–87. Schultz (187) concludes that for him, the Deutero-Ezekiel layer is based upon a sacral source resembling Lev 18–20. Garscha, *Studien zum Ezekielbuch*, 303–5, also suggests a "deutero-Ezekiel layer" to the book. Joyce, *Ezekiel*, 14, points out that Garscha closely follows the conclusions of Schultz; yet assigns different passages to the same "Deutero-Ezekiel." Garscha tries to make a clear distinction between the work of a "Deutero-Ezekiel" and a "*sakralrechtlichen*" layer (305). Garscha propounds that Ezekiel is the work of a systematic revision in which the Babylonian setting was fictionalized. The prophet Ezekiel may have only written about thirty verses himself and a redactor did the rest between 485 and 460 BCE.

33. Simian, *Die theologische*, 58–65, defines his methodology as one that focuses on the small units in order to decide when and how they were developed in stages. Simian's focus is on three chapters of Ezekiel (i.e., 6, 35, 36).

34. Hossfeld, *Untersuchungen*.

35. Renz, *Rhetorical Function*, 31. Sedlmeier, *Das Buch*, 55–56, notes his position as being between that of Allen and Hossfeld. See also Sedlmeier's early work on Ezekiel, *Studien zu Komposition*, as noted by Renz, 31 n. 17.

scholarly perspective and presuppositions.[36] While I will argue for position number one above, those holding to the Palestinian stance, at first glance, appear to have legitimate reasons for adopting such a view.[37] Their arguments include the following: 1) Ezekiel's ministry appears to have been directed at those in Jerusalem and the "community of faith" which would have had to include more than the small exilic community. Furthermore, it would only make sense for Ezekiel to be in Jerusalem to address their sin especially if he was called by Yahweh to do so.[38] 2) Jeremiah seems to suggest that the exiles were actually the "moral" minority (cf. chs. 24 and 29). Therefore, Ezekiel's harsh message would be better suited for the "rebellious house" of Jerusalem rather than the exilic community. 3) Next, the hardships of exile in Babylon are not given nor is the traumatic exile of 597 mentioned. Furthermore, the author appears to be pro-Babylonian, something one would not expect from someone in exile.[39] 4) Finally, the prophet appears to have first-hand knowledge of the "moral, political, and military conditions in Judah."[40] For example, Ezekiel knows of the "sentiments of the people" there[41] and of Zedekiah's failed escape and his blinding (cf. 12:3–12). Also, he has an intricate knowledge of the conditions in the temple in chs. 8–11 (note especially the plight of Pelatiah) as well as knowledge of the themes addressed by Jeremiah (who ministered from Jerusalem).[42]

---

36. Due to Renz's detailed and somewhat up-to-date presentation of the arguments I will only present a summary of Renz's work here. Cf. Renz, *Rhetorical Function*, 32–33. See also Brownlee, *Ezekiel 1–19*, xxiii–xxv.

37. Those who argue that Ezekiel ministered in both locations note that Ezekiel's message appears to fluctuate between the exiles and the entire nation.

38. See Fohrer, *Hauptprobleme*, 209–12, for a discussion of the appearances of identifying terms for Israel in Ezekiel. These arguments stem from Ezekiel's apparent distinction in his use of the phrases "house of Israel" (i.e., the exiles) and the "whole house of Israel" (i.e., Jerusalem as well). For example, compare Ezekiel's address to the exilic community in 3:15 and 37:11 with the prophet's call by Yahweh to declare to Jerusalem her abominations in 16:2 and 22:2. Scholars suggest that Ezekiel would need to be present in Jerusalem to perform the latter command. Moreover, they insist that Ezekiel's use of "rebellious house" would have had to include the entire nation not just those in exile.

39. Renz, *Rhetorical Function*, 32.

40. Brownlee, *Ezekiel*, xxiv.

41. Cf. 11:15; 12:21–28; 20:32; 33:23–29.

42. Renz, *Rhetorical Function*, 33.

While these concerns and apparent discrepancies do appear to have validity, careful analysis of these issues from another perspective helps alleviate some of the suggested problems. Over the past half-century, select scholars have addressed these particular concerns. In this vein, the arguments in favor of a Babylonian setting and against the Palestinian hypothesis have been discussed in whole or in part by Fohrer, Mullo Weir, and Renz and need not be repeated in detail here. Therefore I will summarize the conclusions of the more recent work of Renz.[43] Renz, building upon the work of Fohrer and Mullo Weir, presents fourteen rebuttal statements to the above arguments. I will present some of his conclusions and add my own analysis where merited.

1–2. The idea that the prophet is only addressing Jerusalem and Judah when he uses the phrases "house of Israel" or "rebellious house" does not prove that his message was only to the nation and not those in exile. First, "rebellious house" as will be demonstrated in ch. 2 below, is a vital part of the rhetorical and literary strategy of the author when speaking to *both* groups in chs. 1–12. To suggest that the prophet's message was that narrowly focused or that he could not address the nation without being physically present in Jerusalem is to exclude the stylistic license of the author. Moreover, few would suggest that the prophets had to be present in a foreign land when delivering oracles against them (cf. Ezek 25–32, 35; Amos 1–2 etc.).[44] Also, the language of Ezekiel often moves between first, second, and third person address in a single oracle for style and effect (cf. 29:6b–9a; 33:23–29; 34:17–31).[45] As Renz notes, "A particularly clear distinction is made between those the oracle is concerned with (the Jerusalemites) and those who actually hear it (the exilic community cf. 2:4–3:11 note especially 3:15) in 12:1–11; 14:12–23 and 24:15–24."[46] In this regard, it is my belief that the oracles against the exilic community and their kindred in Jerusalem are being fashioned with the intended purpose of condemning their

---

43. Fohrer, *Hauptprobleme*, 203–15; Mullo Weir, "Aspects," 97–112; and Renz, *Rhetorical Function*, 33–8.

44. Brownlee, *Ezekiel 1–19*, xxv–xxxiii, does indeed suggest this very thing; however, Joyce, *Ezekiel*, 6, rightly notes the implausibility of such a stance.

45. Renz, *Rhetorical Function*, 34

46. Ibid., 33–34.

(i.e., *the exiles'*) disbelief in the fall of Jerusalem and a prolonged exile. At the same time this does not negate the possibility that portions of the prophet's message may have reached Jerusalem before its fall.

3. The message of Jeremiah in chs. 24 and 29 is in no way reflective of a "moral" community in the exile but rather reflects a message looking forward to a future time (cf. ch. 24 see especially vv. 6–7 and 29:12–14). This message also includes a sharp rebuke for their lack of spiritual insight (ch. 29 see especially vv. 15, 29–32 and 36:20). It was this spiritual blindness that caused the exiles to believe in the lie that the exile would be short. Both Ezekiel and Jeremiah make it clear that the exile will be long (Jer 29:29–32).[47] Finally, the salvation of the remnant in the exile was not based on merit and religious purity but rather on the grace of God alone and his holy name (36:20–38 esp. v. 22). Again, Renz correctly points out that the misplaced trust of the exiles in Jerusalem was evidence of their rebellious nature and their failure to realize that Yahweh was punishing them for their sin.[48]

4. As will be further demonstrated below, the pro-Babylonian sentiments of Ezekiel are founded upon the premise that Babylon is Yahweh's instrument of judgment against Judah.[49] Also, there is no definitive evidence that the exiles had excessive hardships early on in the exile other than what would be associated with a forced migration. For example, the free movement of the elders appears to betray a somewhat normal existence in Tel-abib (cf. 8:1; 14:1; 20:1).

5. The exile of 597 BCE is in fact mentioned in 11:15–16 but is not the focus of the prophecy of Ezekiel. While it does act as a harbinger for what is to come in 586, it is not *the* watershed moment when Yahweh will be vindicated for the nation's breach of covenant. Furthermore, the ultimate fulfillment of Yahweh's

---

47. Ezekiel's prophecy of the fall of the city of Jerusalem and that its inhabitants would go into exile flew in the face of those in exile who assumed that they would soon return to their homeland and re-inhabit their cities especially Jerusalem. Ezekiel's prophecy concerning the destruction of Jerusalem made it clear that the exile would be longer than they had anticipated.

48. Renz, *Rhetorical Function*, 34.

49. Ibid., 35. So too Newsom, "Maker of Metaphors," 190–91.

plan is in his restoration of the entire exilic community, both north and south, as noted in 37:11–23.

6–7. Ezekiel's "firsthand" knowledge concerning the issues "on the ground" in Jerusalem need not be a reason for assuming he was present when the events took place. Ezekiel was a resident of Jerusalem for some time before he was taken into exile and, as an up-and-coming priest, would have been fully aware of the spiritual depravity of the nation. As for the details surrounding the death of Pelatiah (11:13), some have posited that the event is not meant to be seen as a historical account (e.g., Howie and Renz) but rather parabolic. However, we should not rule out the possibility that it was indeed an actual prophetic event. The details seem to suggest that this is the case although news from Jerusalem may have been used to flesh out the prophecy at a later date. There is clear evidence in Jeremiah 29:24–28 that correspondence between the exiles and those in Jerusalem did in fact take place.

8. The prophecy of Ezekiel is not directed at the city of Jerusalem and Palestine as much as it is towards the exiles. In 2:5, 7; 3:7, 11, the prophet is called to the exiles to address their rebellious behavior. The tenor of the entire book of Ezekiel is one that suggests that the destruction of Jerusalem is unavoidable and a foregone conclusion. If in fact the prophecy was directed at Judah and Jerusalem, one would expect the hope of salvation for the city if repentance came; however, chs. 8–11 seal the fate of the doomed city. Indeed, the message serves as a warning (as will be developed further in chs. 2–3, below) to the *exilic* community to repent of sin and rebelliousness.

9. While scholars such as Becker suggest the dating system of Ezekiel is not to be trusted, there is no sound reason to accept this position especially in light of the lack of reference to Zedekiah in the dating system.[50] It would be more acceptable for the exiles of 597 to see Jehoiachin as the rightful heir to the throne and not Zedekiah who was the puppet king of Nebuchadnezzar.[51] It

---

50. Renz, *Rhetorical Function*, 36.

51. Archaeological evidence of the past century has shown that indeed Jehoiachin did go into exile and may have been partially supported by his estates back in

would therefore make sense that Jehoiachin (and not Zedekiah) would be used to date the events of the exile as we see in Ezekiel. Furthermore, the dates appear to be reflective of actual dateable events of the period in question.[52]

10-11. If in fact Ezekiel was prophesying in Jerusalem before the fall of the city, he would have been in more danger than even Jeremiah had been due to his harsh indictments, especially of Zedekiah.[53] At the same time he in no way appears to address issues leading up to the immediate fall of the city.[54] Apart from the possible visionary experience of ch. 8, Ezekiel's knowledge of the events appears to come from secondhand accounts (e.g., 33:21). Ezekiel does not dwell on the hardships of the siege as one would expect of a prophet in the city, but rather speaks in terms reflective of an individual standing afar off and viewing (whether in the spirit or not is a debate all of itself) the events and casting judgment.

12. The language of the sign acts (4:1-3; 5:1-3; and 12:1-11) reflects a Babylonian locale.[55] For example, digging through mud or clay walls (cf. 12:5) would have been possible in the region of Babylon where mud or clay bricks were the common building materials.[56] Also, the reference to the art of belomancy in 21:26 (Heb) is only found in Ezekiel and reflects a Babylonian means of divination.

Palestine. Cf. Albright, "Seal of Eliakim," 79-106 esp. 79-80, 102-3. Furthermore, tablets found in Babylon from Nebuchadnezzar's thirteenth year note the food rations for king "Yaku-kinu" (i.e., Jehoiachin) of the land of "Yahudu" (i.e., Judah). Cf. Sweeney, *I & II Kings*, 459; Wiseman, *Nebuchadrezzar and Babylon*, 81; and Noth, *Laws in the Pentateuch*, 265-66. For notations on the actual archaeological finds see Albright, "King Jehoiachin," 49-55 (Albright also argues for the historical veracity of Ezekiel); Weidner, "Jojachin, König von Juda," 2.923-35; May, "Three Hebrew Seals," 146-48; and Malamat, "Jeremiah and the Last Two Kings of Judah," 81-87.

52. Lemaire, "Les formules," 359-66. See also, Kutsch, *Die chronologischen*, esp. 33-69; Finegan, "The Chronology of Ezekiel," 61-66; and Fohrer, *Hauptprobleme*, 105-22.

53. Renz, *Rhetorical Function*, 37.

54. Ibid., 36-37.

55. Ibid., 37.

56. Ibid. Stones were the common building material for fortification walls in Judah during Ezekiel's day. See Brownlee, *Ezekiel*, xxiii.

13. As will be developed in greater detail below, the imagery and symbolism is best suited to a Babylonian provenance. Ezekiel's use of Babylonian art, architecture, literature, and the like is evident throughout his prophecy.[57]

14. Finally, the ministry of a "Palestinian Ezekiel" only, seems suspect if such a ministry was "suppressed" and not recorded as was Jeremiah's.[58] There is no plausible reason for the suppression of a prophetic ministry in Jerusalem especially if many in the exile would have known of the actual prophet who delivered such scathing indictments.[59] Furthermore, the complete fabrication of a Babylonian setting along with all the Babylonian imagery and symbolism would make little sense centuries after the fact especially during the Maccabean or Greek period when efforts were being made to distinguish Jew from foreigner. Ezekiel's pro-Babylonian message (as was Daniel with Persia) suggests that he accepted Babylonian hegemony over Judah. A later period for such a message seems highly unlikely for a prophet of Yahweh.

Having assessed the divergent theories about Ezekiel's setting, Eichrodt's conclusion seems appropriate. He states, "All these widely divergent theories serve to illustrate the danger of throwing away what this book testifies to in regards to itself, because it only leads to fleeting speculations which, in spite of all their cleverness, cannot arouse any confidence in the results."[60] It seems that beginning from the standpoint of a sixth-century Babylonian provenance for the setting of the book of Ezekiel and its author places one within a solid scholarly consensus. Indeed, the arguments of Eichrodt, Renz, Fohrer, Mullo Weir, and others for such a position appear well-founded. In light of a scholarly consensus and the historical setting it suggests, it is logical to conclude that Ezekiel was written and compiled in Babylon especially in light of the clear Babylonian influences within the book (we will return to this shortly). Therefore, as a book set in the land of

---

57. The study of the Babylonian influences on the author of Ezekiel has a long history in the scholarly debate of Ezekiel, e.g., Jirku, *Altorientalischer Kommentar*, 209–13.

58. Renz, *Rhetorical Function*, 37.

59. Ibid., 37.

60. Eichrodt, *Ezekiel*, 11.

Babylon with a Hebrew author, we need to determine what outside influences may have shaped the author's thinking. Furthermore, we need to determine what criteria we will use for determining how to assess the possible influence of cross-cultural literature and motifs on the final form.

Cross-cultural Textual and Motif Analysis

Perhaps one of the most difficult challenges in any endeavor involving the relationships between literature from various cultures is determining the criteria that will be used to decide what is, or what is not, a valid comparison. In the case of Ezekiel we are left in the dark as to what texts he had available to him. Furthermore, we are not certain he could even read cuneiform. For this reason I will devote a portion of this section discussing the possibility of Ezekiel's "reeducation" in the language and literature of Babylon and the possible availability of Mesopotamian literature to the prophet. However, before I do that I will need to lay out the criteria I will use for determining the possibility of inter-textual and motif borrowing by Ezekiel.

As we move forward, I will note several scholars who suggest that Ezekiel may have used different Mesopotamian texts as a pattern to fashion either sections of his prophecy or his entire book (e.g., Bodi, Frankena, T. Lewis, Astour, Petter). However, the problem with this approach is that there is no way of proving an argument that rests upon one particular text (e.g., Bodi's use of the *Poem of Erra*). In this book, I will not adopt one text in particular but rather I will focus on motifs that are ubiquitous across a wide range of cultures, especially those that dominated the ANE for extended periods of time (e.g., Babylon, Sumer, Assyria, Hatti, and Egypt). If in fact a motif has wide appeal then there is a greater possibility that Ezekiel may have been familiar with it (e.g., temple abandonment and particular curses). Second, if the date of a text is close to the time of Ezekiel, especially if it is from Babylon or Assyria, preference will be given to that particular text. This is due mainly to proximity and the actual interaction between Israel and these two dominant powers during the eighth–sixth centuries BCE. Third, priority will be given to curses from ANE treaties if they are directly relateable to a proposed curse motif in Ezekiel (we will develop this more in the next methodological section). Finally, motifs that appear only in Ezekiel and are not found in other OT books will be given closer scrutiny as to where they may have originated (e.g., the *Sebetti* in Ezekiel 9—see ch. 2 below). In situations where themes and motifs appear both in the OT and across the ANE, the OT connection will be given priority (e.g., theophanic appearances). With these criteria in place I will now discuss the likelihood of Ezekiel's reeducation, the possible ANE influences on Ezekiel, and the availability of Mesopotamian literature for use by the prophet.

Was Ezekiel Reeducated?

Writing seems to find a long history among the leadership of Israel (cf. Josh 8:32–35; 24:26; Isa 8:1; 30:8).[61] We also know that at least a portion of those in exile were literate (cf. 2 Kgs 24:14–16). Recent archeological finds dating to the monarchial period appear to support this latter conclusion.[62] Moreover, the fact that Ezekiel, as a priest, was literate finds ample textual support (cf. Num 5:23; Deut 17:18; 31:24–26; Jer 30:2; Ezek 24:2; 37:16, 20; 43:11).[63] In this vein, Stephen Cook notes that Ezekiel, as a Zadokite priest, "was well educated and thoroughly familiar with Israelite and general Near Eastern lore and mythic poetry. Ezekiel's priestly, cosmopolitan training strongly informs the literary character of his book, which frequently uses rich metaphors and mythic images to portray and interpret the times."[64] If this was the case for Ezekiel as a resident of Judah and a member of the priestly class of Jerusalem, how much more would his new surroundings in Babylon

---

61. For a discussion on the literacy of pre-exilic Israel see Davis, *Swallowing the Scroll*, 41–45.

62. Demsky, "Literacy in Israel," 117–32, as cited by Davis, 42–43. See also Demsky, "Education," 6:381–98 (esp. 383, 391–97). Demsky posits that the seemingly late age of 25 and 30 for Levites and priests (respectively) to enter service in the temple may be due in large part to their extended period of education and apprenticeship (396). See also Naveh, "A Paleographic Note," 68–74. Naveh postulates that based upon "recent" (as of 1968) archaeological finds there seems to be clear evidence that Judah was a literate society as of the late seventh and early sixth centuries BCE. According to a recent inscriptional find at Khirbet Qeiyafa in the Elah Valley, 20 miles southwest of Jerusalem, an ostracon shows scribal work in the fortress from the period of David.

63. Davis, *Swallowing the Scroll*, 40. Even though Jeremiah may have employed Baruch to write many of his oracles does not mean that he was illiterate. Paul was literate yet often used an amanuensis.

64. Cook, *Apocalyptic Literature*, 96.

have added to his understanding and use of Near Eastern imagery to frame his message to those in the new land of exile?

From a literary perspective, J. H. Tigay has pointed out that authors of the ANE many times formulated their literary works in uniform ways. He notes that ". . . this involved the use of standard formulas, similes, epithets, and the like. But beyond this, ancient writers drew extensively upon larger components, such as topoi, motifs, groups of lines, and episodes, which had their original settings in other compositions. Sometimes they composed passages imitating such elements, and at other times they simply transferred such elements verbatim into their own compositions . . . by the standards of the ancient Near East, these phenomena reflected a highly valued reliance on tradition."[65] Indeed, one need only peruse portions of the OT to find texts lifted from one author and placed upon the pen of another.[66] Furthermore, parallels, often verbatim, between the OT and ANE texts have been pointed out by numerous scholars.[67] While it is highly likely that Ezekiel also relied on standard works, symbols, motifs, and themes from his period, methodologically it is problematic to simply assume that the prophet did so while in his land of exile. We must therefore examine the probability of Ezekiel's access to (and ability to read) texts from outside of his culture.

Scholars generally agree that some form of reeducation process took place during the period of the exile especially for the religious and political elite.[68] Norman Porteous posits that beyond the expected

---

65. Tigay, *Evolution of the Gilgamesh Epic*, 162.

66. Compare Isa 2:2–4 to Mic 4:1–3 and portions of Isa 36–39 to 2 Kgs 19–20. One can also note Ps 29 and the parallel motifs attributed to Baal and the motif of the Divine Warrior present throughout the OT and the ANE literature. Cf. also, Cross, "Divine Warrior," 11–30.

67. For example, Matthews and Benjamin, *Old Testament Parallels* or Arnold and Beyer, *Readings from the Near East*.

68. Goldingay, *Daniel*, 16, points out that education in the Chaldean language "refers not merely to the Babylonian language itself, a dialect of Akkadian (though they would also need to know that), but to the script and contents of the cuneiform texts preserved among the 'Chaldean' sages . . ." In this regard, Clifford, "The Roots of Apocalypticism," 1:21, avers that the official language of Levantine scribes during the late second and early first millennium was Akkadian, a fact that adds to the prospect of an exchange of thoughts and motifs between Levantine cultures from earliest times. Clifford also notes that the influence of the creation and flood myths of the ANE on the Bible may be attributed to this proximity of thought and the training of both Israelite and Canaanite scribes in canonical literature from the Levant.

"Neo-Babylonian language of the court" the selected exiles would also have probably learned "the sacred Sumerian language along with the highly complicated cuneiform script and the sacred myths and rituals and omen texts characteristic of Babylonian religion."[69] It is my contention that part of the main influence on Ezekiel, aside from the obvious role pre-exilic prophecy played in his message, is directly attributable to ANE customs, mythology, and imagery that surrounded and influenced Ezekiel, especially written works. Scholars have often noted the high level of education that priests and scribes would have had to gain in order to teach the law and copy texts. In this vein, due to the fact that Ezekiel was among some of the first exiles to be taken in 597 BCE,[70] he could very possibly have been "reeducated" in the ways and literature of the Chaldeans.[71] Therefore, we can postulate that many of the literary works of Babylon would have been available to Ezekiel as part of his reeducation. Furthermore, Tigay's concept of uniformity in literary techniques throughout the ANE does fall within the uniform presentation of much of Ezekiel's literary technique as will be demonstrated below.

Another factor supporting the plausibility of Ezekiel's reeducation is directly connected to his obvious leadership position in the community[72] and his previous role as a member of the cultic hierarchy in Jerusalem.[73] W. Sibley Towner comments that "like Pharaoh in the days of Joseph, the king needs dream interpreters and sages; and his

---

See also Albright, "King Jehoiachin," 53, and his comments about the possibility of the sons of Jehoiachin receiving a Babylonian tutor for the purpose of Babylonian indoctrination. See further, Stevenson, *Vision of Transformation*, 102; and Wiseman, *Nebuchadrezzar and Babylon*, 81, 84–86.

69. Porteous, *Daniel*, 27.

70. Josephus, *Ant.* 10:98. Josephus tells of Ezekiel's deportation in the first exile in the reign of Jehoiachin. See also comments by Zimmerli, *Fiery Throne*, 52. See further inter-textual notations in Jer 52:28–30.

71. This understanding is not at all farfetched especially if one is to take Daniel 1:4 as a valid picture of the practice of the Neo-Babylonian Empire.

72. In Ezek 8:1; 14:1 and 20:1, we see the leadership role Ezekiel played in giving spiritual advice and direction.

73. Ezekiel's age plays a key role in this assumption. Scholars are uncertain as to how old Ezekiel was when he went into exile. Even if he were relatively young, he would have been familiar with the cultic management of the Jerusalem temple. Furthermore, his education would have been closely connected to the temple and the priestly class of which his family was a part.

search for them among the exiles of Judah seems perfectly legitimate among all parties."[74] This not only explains Nebuchadnezzar's desire for learned members of Israel's elite (e.g., Daniel and his three friends), but also the likelihood that Ezekiel would have been subject to some form of reeducation.

It also is probable that the reeducation of the exiles was formatted much like that of other Babylonian scribes and elite, which included exposure to a wide array of texts. We know that from earliest times in Mesopotamia, priestly guilds were taught in divination and "omen interpretation."[75] Erica Reiner posits that the scribes of Babylon "learned their craft by first copying vocabularies, then standard works of the literary tradition . . ."[76] She goes on to point out that the vast array of genres discovered at the private library of Sultantepe (Huzirina near Harran) was surprising to many archeologists but also insightful as to the dissemination of varied genres of literature across the farthest reaches of the Assyro-Babylonian Empire.[77] Thus, if in fact a wide variety of genres was prevalent before the period of Ezekiel in the farthest reaches of the kingdom, it only stands to reason that the center of the Babylonian kingdom, namely Babylon, would also have had a wide and varied range of genres and literature at the disposal of the deportees during their reeducation process. We can therefore posit, as M. Astour does, that the prophet also had similar access. Astour concludes that, "there is little wonder that Ezekiel had access to Babylonian literature or some of its works. He spent at least a quarter of a century in the heartland of Babylonia, was politically extremely pro-Babylonian, was receptive to foreign myths, and knew about the Babylonian practice of haruspicy (Ezek 21:26). He could hardly have failed to learn the official language of the country and to absorb some of its ancient culture."[78] This understanding seems logical in light of the many literary parallels

74. Towner, *Daniel*, 23.

75. Collins, *Daniel*, 138.

76. Reiner, "Fortune-Telling," 23. See also the work of Sparks, *Ancient Texts*, 22–33, for a discussion on the development of writing and literacy in the ANE.

77. Reiner, "Fortune-Telling," 23. Reiner's comments concern the private library of a *langu*-priest family from Sultantepe from the Neo-Assyrian period of the eighth to seventh centuries BCE in southern Turkey.

78. Astour, "Ezekiel's Prophecy of Gog," 579. Toy, "The Babylonian Element," 62, also noted the long period of Ezekiel's stay in Babylon and pointed to the only appearance in the Bible of the common Babylonian divination technique of belomancy which, not surprisingly, appears in Ezek 21:26 [Heb].

between the OT and ANE literature that we find not only in Ezekiel but also the entire OT. However, beyond the obvious literary parallels cultural influences, which included art, architecture, and the like, would have played a vital role as well. Savignac notes the role that this new culture had on the Jewish elite. He states, "Assurément il est impossible que le long séjour de Jéhojachin et des siens auprès de la cour royale à Babylone, attesté non seulement par la Bible mais aussi par plusieurs documents babyloniens, n'ait pas amené une connaissance des grands monuments de la littérature babylonienne dans l'élite juive."[79] The closeness of the settlements of the exiles to the Babylonian heartland (e.g., Tel-abib—3:15) and the reeducation program by Babylon solidifies this understanding even more.[80] Finally, S. P. Garfinkel comments, "A priest in the exile, such as Ezekiel... might well have been exposed to local literary works, as are the religious and intellectual leadership of any age. The *literati* somehow find common grounds despite political or social pressures toward segregation."[81]

The realm of possibilities that these observations lay out is interesting when looking at the life of the prophet-priest, Ezekiel. Even if one were to discard Cook's Israelite-based knowledge of the ANE (see above), it is also conceivable that Ezekiel could just have easily relied on the daily, oral "education" and visual stimuli of architecture, statues, and reliefs and the like to gather and increase his understanding of mythology and knowledge of symbolism and imagery of the ANE.[82] However, if one is to add to the mix of this "homegrown" and "osmosis-style" of learning, the actual likelihood of a structured reeducation of Ezekiel in his new home in Babylon, then the level of

---

79. Savignac, "La sagesse du Qôhéléth," 321. Cf. also Bodi, *Poem of Erra*, 22 n. 46.

80. Petter, "The Book of Ezekiel," 148–49, also convincingly argues that Ezekiel may have lived within a half mile or so from Nippur, the great cultic center where religious culture and learning flourished. So too Power, "Iconographic Windows," 12.

81. Garfinkel, "Akkadian Influences," 10, as noted by Bodi, *Poem of Erra*, 315.

82. Although I will focus mainly on Mesopotamian and Assyrian influences on Ezekiel throughout this book, it does not diminish the role played by other ANE cultures. This can be seen in the mythological symbols borrowed from Canaanite literature via the pre-exilic prophets and the psalms. An example of this can be seen in Kvanvig's parallel of the "Daniel" of the Ugaritic tale of Aqhat with Ezek 14:14 (see also Ezek 28:3). Cf. Kvanvig, *Roots of Apocalyptic*, 482. Kvanvig, as do many scholars, posits that due to the spelling of the name in Ezekiel, it cannot be the Daniel of the later biblical text. However, see my comments concerning Dressler and Day's perspectives on page 180 n. 26.

Ezekiel's understanding of the mythology of Babylon and ANE literary works increases significantly.

Even before many of the archeological discoveries of the last century, Herrmann had pointed out that Ezekiel "made a conscious adoption of Babylonian manner of speech."[83] And beyond this, Ezekiel's Aramaisms and Akkadianisms[84] point to the Babylonian provenance of the book and the influence of this new homeland on the prophet.

From this vantage point there is a strong probability, if not certainty, that Ezekiel was reeducated in some fashion, or at least learned the language of Babylon over his lifetime. But this also begs the question as to the extent these influences had on the prophet's written work. While there can be little doubt that he did glean from some earlier motifs and symbols present in Hebrew writers' material, we still need to explore the extent that his setting may have had on his writing.

Influences on Ezekiel: The ANE Exchange of Literature and Culture

The roots of the vision sequences of the book of Ezekiel along with its sometimes bizarre imagery has been studied by scholars from diverse theological and educational persuasions (e.g., psychoanalytical)[85] with numerous explanations, interpretations, and background influences being offered. While this study does not seek to present radically new explanations for every one of the visions (i.e., independent of each

---

83. Herrmann, *Ezechiel*, 20, states, "Ez liebt die Bezeichnung בית ישראל statt בית יהוה sie ist ihm eigentümlich; man wird das schwerlich anders erklären können denn als bewußte Übernahme babylonischer Redeweise, . . ." While the context of Herrmann's comments fall within the purview of Ezekiel's use of the term "house of Israel" (what Block notes as reflective of designations for Mesopotamian states in their documents where *byt* plus the geographic name was used to identify a particular area, Block, *Ezekiel 1–24*, 31–32) instead of the "house of Yahweh" his comments are pertinent to the overall tenor of Ezekiel's Babylonian style of message—a position that I will develop throughout. Block argues simply for the use of בית ישראל as a means by which Ezekiel showed "family solidarity" of the nation's eponymous founder.

84. Garfinkel, "Studies in Akkadian Influences," notes that Ezekiel contains 24 definite links to Akkadian speech with 14 more being probable, and possibly 12 others, as cited by Block, *Ezekiel 1–24*, 40.

85. For example, cf. Jaspers, "Der Prophet Ezechiel," 1–9. Jaspers argues that Ezekiel was a schizophrenic. Cf. also, Stiebert, *Prophet's Wife*, 84–108; Bloome, "Ezekiel's Abnormal Personality," 277–92; and Halperin, *Seeking Ezekiel*. For a brief overview of this approach, see Kamionkowski, *Gender Reversal*, 74–78.

other) and the background influences on them, it does attempt to pull together, in a new way, the general tenor of scholarship in this regard and add a unifying didactic framework. Ezekiel's visions are not the result of random ecstatic experiences with clouded symbolism and bizarre imagery, but rather are the product of a thoughtful literary construction based upon known and borrowed images and symbols.[86] Now that is not to preclude divine involvement, for we know throughout the prophetic corpus that God used the prophets' experiences, setting, and literary abilities to fashion dynamic prophetic messages of impending doom, judgment, and restoration (e.g., Amos).

Ezekiel's new home offered a ready opportunity for a diverse range of genres and culturally specific motifs. But was it possible while living only in Babylon, to be influenced by Assyrian, Sumerian, Persian, and other surrounding literature and cultures as well?[87] To answer this question one must establish the fact that Babylon and Assyria (as well as the surrounding region) shared much of their literature and culture from earliest periods. To begin, Peter Machinist points out that during the Old Babylonian Period (2000–1595 BCE) Assyrian inscriptions, royal epithets, and official literature were written in the Babylonian dialect. He is quick to comment, however, that a pan-Babylonian concept is not to be adopted for this time. Assyria still had distinct culture and cultic aspects that were not Babylonian inspired. An example of this cultural specificity is reflected in their use of Assyrian rooted personal names. Nevertheless, aside from specific examples such as this, we can be confident in asserting that the interchange definitely started earlier than later.[88]

Literarily, the similarity in languages and the use of cuneiform betrays the close links these two empires shared. As early as the Middle Assyrian period with the reign of Tukulti-Ninurta I (1243–1207 BCE) literature tells of this borrowing. It was at this time that Assyria sub-

---

86. So too Power, "Iconographic Windows," 5. It is also important to note that these visions came through the inspiration of the Spirit of Yahweh himself. Yahweh inspired Ezekiel's visions using symbolism relevant to the prophet and his audience.

87. Obviously some of the cultures would have been long "dead," (e.g., Sumerian), but their literature survived.

88. Machinist, "Literature as Politics," 468–70. Machinist (470) concludes his discussion on cultural tensions by noting that the period of Aššur-uballit marked the defining moment when the clear issues of cultural and geographic independence began to come to the forefront of Assyrian-Babylonian relations. He goes on to assign the term *KulturKampf* as best fitting this period.

jugated Babylon for the first time and established Assyrian hegemony over the region.[89] Interestingly enough, the *Tukulti-Ninurta Epic* tells of the conquest of Babylon and the booty carried from Babylon to Assyria. Among this spoil, the account lists literature as part of the items removed from Babylon and taken to Assyria.[90] Scholars feel that this was the clear beginning of the cross-culturalization of the two regions.

Turning to the text itself, the pertinent parts dealing with the plunder of Babylon shed light on this cultural exchange (i.e., VI obverse B lines 2–9). The author of this account makes it clear that the plunder of Babylon by Tukulti-Ninurta I (ca. 1220 BCE) included the acquisition of many clay tablets which he returned to adorn "the temples of the Assyrian gods."[91] Lambert avers that this points to a very early cross-cultural awareness and borrowing by Tukulti-Ninurta and, as such, challenges the later claim of Ashurbanipal that he was "better versed in all kinds of literature than any of the kings who went before him."[92] The fragmented Tukulti-Ninurta text reads,

2. Treasu[re . . .
3. Tablets of [. . .
4. . . .[. . .
5. The art of incantation [. . .
6. The Eršaḫunga prayers according [to . . .
7. The craft of the seer [. . .] . . .
8. Medical texts, rituals of banda[ges . . .

---

89. Ibid., 471.

90. Ibid., 471–74. Machinist posits that the Epic itself, written in a Babylonian format, was proof that literary style, like the earlier Babylonian epics, was now a part of Assyrian culture. He further notes that the sacking of Babylon and the mentioning of the literary works as spoils of war was to show everyone who read the Epic that the positive cultural exchange and upgrading was to be credited to Tukulti-Ninurta and his conquest of Babylon. Also, the building projects in Assyria after Tukulti-Ninurta's defeat of Babylon reflected Sumerian names for the palaces in Ashur and Kar-Tukulti-Ninurta (*Elugalumunkurkurra*—"house of the king" and *Egalmešarra*—"palace of the universe" respectively) along with several other buildings.

91. Lambert, "Three Unpublished Fragments," 41. See also comments by Lambert in *Babylonian Wisdom Literature*, 19–20.

92. Ibid., 42. The hegemony of Aššur-uballit (1363–1328 BCE) over Babylon was not as complete and decisive as Tukulti-Ninurta's due to the fact that Aššur-uballit had to secure the hegemony by a marriage and not conquest alone.

9. The former inspections of his fathers which [...

10. ... scepters and soldiers [...

11. There was not left any [...] in the land of Sumer and Akkad [...[93]

Although propagandistic, the text attests to the acquisition of literature (and cultural aspects) from Babylon by Assyria. Medical practice, divination methods, art, and literature all are part of the spoil returned to Assyria. From this one text alone we can conclude that Assyrian booty of war (no doubt over a long period of time) included literary works and cultural ideas. Moreover, the exchange in the opposite direction and throughout ANE empires must have been a common occurrence as well. Texts such as these seem to imply explicitly that Ezekiel and the exiles would have been inundated with cultural influences from several societies of the region. The free exchange of these cultural specifics, albeit through conquest, made available to Ezekiel a ready pool of literary, cultic, and state material. Therefore it is likely that Mesopotamian cultural material was available to the prophet, but what, if any, influence did the region of Persia play on Ezekiel's thought processes? To this we now turn.

The Possibility of Persian Influence on Ezekiel Examined

Most Ezekielian scholars will concede Mesopotamian influence on Ezekiel through cultural contact and blending. However, there are others who also posit Persian influences for certain motifs such as the prophet's interpreting angel in chs. 40–48 and the apparent Zoroastrian connection in Ezekiel 37:1–14.[94] But can Persian influence be conclusively demonstrated in Israelite texts as early as the sixth century? Most scholars are not willing to concede Persian influence on Hebrew writers until the later period of Greek and Persian dominance of the fifth–third centuries BCE.[95] Most recognize the Achaemenid Empire

---

93. Ibid., 44–45.

94. Reddish, *Apocalyptic Literature*, 33, notes the possible Zoroastrian themes which contributed to apocalyptic thought as including: 1) resurrection, 2) dualism, 3) the periodization of history, and 4) "eschatological judgment followed by rewards and punishments." See also Lang, "Street Theater," 297–316.

95. Cf. Collins, "Early Jewish Apocalypticism," 1:284–85. For a full discussion on the background history and the motifs present in Persian influences on Jewish and Christian apocalypticism, see Hultgård, "Persian Apocalypticism," 1:39–83. For the

and especially the rule of Alexander the Great and his generals as the watershed era that opened the free flow of thought and culture between the east and west. While Greek thought definitely influenced later writers such as Philo (a contemporary of Jesus), Persian thinking is believed to have played a vital role in the development of dualism, demonology, angelology, etc. within the literary world of the Jewish apocalyptists three centuries *after* Ezekiel. But can we assume, for example, that Ezekiel's use of cherubim (e.g., chs. 1–3; 8–11) and an otherworldly attendant (chs. 40–48) constitutes the same thing as Persian angelology? Perhaps it is more appropriate to turn to Ezekiel's land of exile for answers as opposed to Persian influence in this case.

One need only look at the Akkadian myth, *The Descent of Ishtar to the Netherworld* [96] (found in both Assyria and Babylonia), to find examples of otherworldly attendants in a dream or mythic sequence. This connection could very easily explain Ezekiel's earlier use of the interpreting angel motif. As for the Zoroastrian link in Ezekiel 37 and the vision of the valley of dry bones, this too appears tenuous in light of the dominant curse language and imagery of Ezekiel's era.[97] As will be demonstrated in ch. 4, below, this vision is perhaps best explained in light of the curse motif.

Another key issue when dealing with Persian literature is the problem of dating texts with these motifs. Most Persian literature of

---

background and origins of Iranian apocalypticism cf. Hultgård, "Forms and Origins," 385–411. Hultgård (407) is not clear in his dating of Persian apocalyptic texts but does note references in the fourth century BCE work of Plutarch quoting Theopompus as the earliest reference to this literature. He seeks to trace the later Persian literature back through the Sasanian period (i.e., mid third century CE to the mid seventh century CE) to the "dark age" of the Parthian period (i.e., mid-third century BCE to mid-third century CE).

96. See "The Descent of Ishtar to the Netherworld," translated by Stephanie Dalley (*COS* 1.108:381–84). This text has a long history before the time of Ezekiel and is present across cultures in various renditions.

97. Lang, "Street Theater," 297–316, seeks to make the Zoroastrian connection with ch. 37 on the basis of Zoroastrian burial practices and their hope for a resurrection. This belief included allowing their dead to lie exposed on the ground for the sun to bleach their bones, which would allow for an easier reunification of the body and soul at the resurrection. However, beyond the obvious problem of dating Persian material lays the issue of when Israelite belief in a bodily resurrection actually began. Based on these two issues alone, it is perhaps best to move away from Lang's position and look for an explanation elsewhere.

this bent dates after the ninth century CE.[98] There is some agreement, however, that certain elements of Persian thought did in fact predate the later Jewish writers and perhaps influenced them in some ways. Just the same, the definite dating and pinning down of the particular influences remains elusive. It is for this reason that most scholars in this field have suspended hard and fast judgment in the matter until further evidence can be uncovered.

Therefore, Persian influence on Ezekiel on any large scale must be seen as unlikely due to the lack of Persian world domination and control during the early sixth century BCE. Furthermore, most scholars who do posit Persian influence on Jewish writers do so most emphatically for the later apocalyptic works. Even in this setting there is continued debate as to what degree of influence is to be attributed to these works. It seems logical to conclude that if we are to look to any cultural milieu for mythological influences on Ezekiel it must be west of Persia in the region of Mesopotamia and the Levant.

Examples of Mesopotamian Influence in Ezekiel[99]

Based on our earlier presentation of the historical and geographical setting for Ezekiel we can concur with John Kutsko, of the "likelihood of a Mesopotamian setting for the book and the prophet's conscious interaction with Assyro-Babylonian traditions in exile."[100] Furthermore, we must conclude that to deny the Babylonian influences on Ezekiel would be to deny the unique "color" Ezekiel adds to the prophetic corpus. As I hope to demonstrate here, various themes found in Ezekiel can be directly related to his interaction with Babylonian culture and literature. Apart from those examples of ANE influences specifically targeted in the following chapters, it seems appropriate to examine briefly a few of these common Mesopotamian thematic and literary links in order to demonstrate our basic methodological approach throughout.

98. Collins, "Early Jewish Apocalypticism," 1:284–85.

99. The scope of this book does not allow me to go into detail on the extensive history of research as it relates to the Babylonian influence on the book of Ezekiel. However, Bodi gives an extensive, yet concise look at the history of scholarship in this field as it relates to philological, iconographic, and thematic studies. See Bodi, *Poem of Erra*, 35–51.

100. Kutsko, *Between Heaven and Earth*, 5.

Ezekiel 32:5–6 and the Annals of Tiglath-pileser I and the Prism of Esarhaddon

In Ezekiel ch. 32 we find some interesting mythological motifs that have parallels with other ANE texts. For example, in 32:5–6 we find a striking parallel with a text from the Annals of Tiglath-pileser I. Ezekiel 32:5–6 reads,

⁵ וְנָתַתִּי אֶת־בְּשָׂרְךָ עַל־הֶהָרִים וּמִלֵּאתִי הַגֵּאָיוֹת רָמוּתֶךָ ⁶ וְהִשְׁקֵיתִי אֶרֶץ צָפָתְךָ מִדָּמְךָ אֶל־הֶהָרִים וַאֲפִקִים יִמָּלְאוּן מִמֶּךָּ

"And I will place your flesh upon the mountains and I will fill the valleys with your refuse[101] and I will cause the land, even to the mountains, to drink the out-flow from your blood and the ravines will be full of you."

From the Annals of Tiglath-pileser I, column III on lines 25–27 the text reads,

"Like a storm demon I piled up the corpses of their warriors on mountain ledges (and) made their blood flow into the hollows and plains of the mountains."[102]

The parallels in this example are close, but we can find these motifs even closer to Ezekiel's day during the reign of Esarhaddon. In the Prism of Esarhaddon we find a similar picture of carnage in his dealings with defeated foes. One line reads, "their blood like a broken (dam) I let flow on the slopes of the mountains"[103]

In these three texts the similar picture of bloodshed and carnage is striking. While perhaps these specific Assyrian texts may have not been available to Ezekiel, the ubiquitous nature of the motif of carnage

---

101. I follow the NASB which renders רָמוּתֶךָ as "your refuse." Holladay, *Hebrew and Aramaic Lexicon*, 340, suggests "rubbish" for this rendering in Ezekiel, which seems to imply one's inner organs/entrails.

102. Grayson, RIMA 2/17, col iii lines 25–27a. See also Grayson, RIMA 2/14, col i lines 75–82. In this latter text, we read of Tiglath-pileser I's bloody conquest of the kings of Alzu. The text reads, "like a storm demon I piled up the corpses of their warriors on the battlefield (and) made their blood flow into the hollows and plains of the mountains." See also ibid., 14–15, col ii lines 12–15; and ibid., 18, col iii lines 53–55. Later, during the reign of Aššur-bēl-kala we find the same phrasiology for the defeat of his enemies. See ibid., 92, col iii lines 5–14.

103. Thompson, *Prisms of Esarhaddon and Ashurbanipal*, 23, col. v line 14.

and bloodshed surely was. Beyond this type of thematic content lies the even greater possibility that Ezekiel may have in fact patterned his prophecy, at least in part, upon other literary works readily available to him.

Ezekiel 32 and the Labbu Myth

T. J. Lewis has also looked at ch. 32 and pointed out that the ancient Akkadian Labbu myth (CT 13:33–34) depicting the battle between the great sea monster and Tishpak (chief god of Eshnunna) may have had some influence on Ezekiel 32:2–6 (esp. v. 2).[104] The Labbu story features the great beast as both lion-like[105] (perhaps likened to the rage of a lion or in physical features, i.e., feet) and as serpentine/dragon-like (i.e., elongated neck or body). This coincides with the picture found in Ezekiel 32 depicting pharaoh and the mythological proportions of the battle scene.

Ezekiel's use of the perplexing lion and dragon-like features for pharaoh does make more sense in light of the Labbu myth. Further, Lewis points out that the translations and commentaries of the past have tried to explain, often unsuccessfully, why the lion and the dragon of the seas are used together in this portion of Ezekiel. Lewis has answered these plaguing questions by finding the mythological links in the Labbu myth. He insists that Ezekiel's Mesopotamian milieu perhaps explains this mythological picture in the prophetic text.

In the text itself, the battle ends with the slaying of the great leviathan-like monster, which is 50 miles long and 1 mile wide.[106] The blood is said to flow for three years and three months. The picture presented in Ezekiel 32:6 is that of a similar bloody outcome of Egypt/pharaoh (probably Hophra when he challenged Nebuchadnezzar as noted in Jer 37:5 and 44:30).[107] We can see that the discharge of blood

---

104. Lewis, "CT 13:33–34," 37–40. For another translation see also Foster, *Before the Muses*, 581–82.

105. For a series of pictures of reliefs from the ANE depicting this dragon monster, see Lewis's article for reproductions and drawings.

106. Various dimensions are given for the sea creature Labbu. In Cohn's account he notes that it was 300 miles long and 30 miles high. See Cohn, *Cosmos*, 44.

107. Feinberg, *Jeremiah*, 610, 644. Similarly, Herodotus 2:161 and 4:159, notes the bloody civil war between the Egyptian pharaoh Apreis and his people and later the bloodbath Egypt suffered at the hands of the Greeks during the rule of Apreis.

is reflective of the Labbu myth. It is obvious that this type of exaggerated imagery was a common feature of ANE writing.

We can also find further links between Ezekiel 32 and other ANE texts. For example, in the Ugaritic text KTU 1.83:3–7 one can see similar language describing the churning of the waters by the dragon as in Ezekiel 32:2b.[108] Also, the concept of catching the dragon in a net in 32:3 finds parallels in the battle scene of Marduk and Tiamat (*Enuma elish* table IV 41, 95, 112).[109] Lewis concludes by noting that attempts to link the account of Ezekiel 32 to Egyptian motifs have been unsuccessful.[110] For Lewis those who fail to take into account the cultural setting of the prophet Ezekiel fail to understand the links he would have made with his surroundings.[111]

On a side note of interest, scholars date ch. 32 to March 3, 585 BCE. Because we know that Ezekiel went into exile in 597 BCE. we can posit with Lewis that "Ezekiel surely drew upon Mesopotamian art and literature to illustrate his work for his audience. The historical background underlying Ezekiel's literary activity (between 593 and 571 BCE, to judge by the dates given in the book) falls within the reign of Nebuchadrezzar II (604–562 BCE), whose achievements include the rebuilding of the Ishtar Gate, itself replete with reliefs of the *mušhuššu*-dragon."[112] While I am cautious, as is Lewis, in trying to push for an exact one-to-one connection between the Labbu Myth and Ezekiel 32, I do see the possible mythological allusions that were common "cur-

---

108. For a brief discussion on the chaos monster motif in the OT, see Angel, *Chaos and the Son of Man*, 210–12.

109. Lewis, "Lion-Dragon Myths," 39. Lewis goes on to point out that "the use of the slain carcass as food for birds and beasts in 32:4 (see also 29:5) finds a direct parallel in the *tannîn*/Leviathan in Psalms 74:13." See also Leviathan and Rahab references in Job 3:8; 7:12; 26:12–13; 41:1–34; Isa 27:1; 51:9; Rev 12:3; 17:1–14; 19:20; 21:1; 2 Esd 6:49–52. For a translation of the creation myth see the "Epic of Creation," translated by Benjamin R. Foster (*COS* 1.111:397–98).

110. Block, *Ezekiel 1–24*, 17, notes that Ezekiel "takes special care to imbue [particular oracles against foreign nations] with local coloring, reflecting the culture of the person or country addressed." While Block points out passages such as chapters 27, 28, 29, and 30:20–26 as likely examples, Lewis's point noted above concerning chapters 32 and 29 as having Mesopotamian and not Egyptian motifs challenges Block's assumption. This being said, it seems that sometimes the "local coloring" may be more reflective of Mesopotamian motifs that may very well have been known in Egypt and other locales.

111. Lewis, "Lion-Dragon Myths," 46.

112. Ibid., 46.

rency" when Ezekiel wrote. These allusions are possibly reflected in Ezekiel's work as, what Lewis calls, "raw material" and "images" that served as a backdrop for his visions.[113]

While Lewis concludes that the work of Ezekiel reflects predominantly West Semitic motifs he also recognizes the possible influence from the east as well. In this regard he states that "one need only look to the composite images in Ezekiel's opening visions to recognize his dependence on motifs found in Mesopotamian art and literature."[114] This dependence will be developed in more detail in ch. 2, below.

The Poem of Erra and Miscellaneous Cases

Beyond the cases like those stated above, scholars have produced works on particular chapters and verses of Ezekiel pointing out possible Mesopotamian literary and thematic ties. Beyond the insightful work of Bodi who has effectively observed possible links between the *Poem of Erra* and Ezekiel (e.g., the sword motif or the *sebetti* "the Seven")[115] several scholars have seen literary links with the poem or general ANE motifs.[116] For example, B. Maarsingh[117] compared the sword motif that appears in both the *Poem of Erra* and Ezekiel 21 while M. Anbar[118] focused on Mesopotamian similarities with Ezekiel 22:24. Moreover, Jean-Georges Heintz, in three separate works, looked at motifs of the "Devouring Fire" and "Song of the Sword" and how they may have been influenced by or connected to ANE art and images.[119] Also, O.

---

113. Ibid., 46–47.

114. Ibid., 47.

115. Bodi, *Poem of Erra*, 55, notes the difficulty in dating the text of the poem because of its appearance across so many centuries. He points out that the poem is mentioned in texts as early as the second millennium BCE and as late as the time of Esarhaddon (680–669 BCE).

116. I am indebted to the work of Bodi, *Poem of Erra*, 50–51, for pointing out the research of these particular scholars.

117. Maarsingh, "Schwertlied," 350–58. See also Bodi's treatment of it in *Poem of Erra*, 231–57.

118. Anbar, "Une nouvelle allusion," 352–53. Anbar points out that there must have been an influence on Ezekiel literarily because of his sojourn in Babylon.

119. Heintz, "Le 'Feu Dévorant,'" 63–78, as noted by Bodi, *Poem of Erra*, 51. See also, Heintz, "De l'absence," 427–37, and idem, "Langage métaphorique," 55–72 (note esp. 63–64). Here Heintz looks at several motifs and artifacts of the ANE depicting the sword and insists that Ezekiel 21:14–22 (as with elsewhere in the prophets, e.g.,

Lortez briefly discussed possible parallels between Ezekiel 23:20 and a Sumerian proverb.[120] Finally, Kutsko suggests that major thematic aspects of Ezekiel may in fact be built upon the common ANE motifs of divine temple abandonment, repair of the images of the gods, and restoration of the gods to their temples.[121] These few examples noted here and above, along with numerous others that will be discussed below, add support for the argument that Ezekiel used Mesopotamian motifs and symbols to fashion his message. The findings of scholars like Lewis, Bodi, and Kutsko help bring new meaning to difficult imagery in the book of Ezekiel.

The Book of Ezekiel as a Key Shift in Literary Style of the OT Prophets

There can be no doubt that Ezekiel was influenced not only by his immediate historical milieu but also by a long prophetic, legal, and cultic witness that preceded him. Some of the images used by the prophet also flowed from Ezekiel's understanding of poetic and prophetic material, which he reinterpreted in light of his Mesopotamian provenance for the purpose of formulating a new message.[122] Moreover, legal material, whether written or oral, had to have been present in some form and readily available to Ezekiel as a priest (we will return to this shortly).

The reason for the dramatic change in prophetic presentation from the classical prophets of the pre-exilic period to Ezekiel can be summed up in three points. First, the increased detail and symbolic presentation of the prophet rests upon the assumption that Ezekiel required more forcefulness in his oracles in order to prove that Yahweh was indeed speaking through him outside of the land of Israel. Second, Ezekiel's historical setting was key in determining the shape and style of the final form of his prophecy. Third, at this particular period in

---

Amos) must be understood in light of the ANE mindset of destruction by the metaphorical "sword."

120. Loretz, "Eine sumerische Parallele," 126. Loretz points to the Sumerian proverb "One does not marry [i.e., have sexual relations with?] a three-year-old female like donkeys do" and suggests that this may have influenced the statement by Ezekiel in 23:20 based on the incessant "sexual activity" of a donkey.

121. For a further discussion of Kutsko's work see chapter 5, below.

122. For example, cf. Zimmerli, "Special Form," 515–27.

Israel's writing history, a new trend was emerging that began to focus almost exclusively on the written text as opposed to oral tradition.[123]

Ezekiel's Uniqueness

The primary reason for the birth of this book is directly related to the uniqueness of Ezekiel's style in fashioning his message. When it comes to his use of ANE imagery, symbolism, and mythological ties, Ezekiel stands head and shoulders above the prophets before and after him. Block correctly comments, "In my view, no other prophet is so creative in his presentation of his message, and none is as forceful. The rhetorical strategies reflected in this collection are both visual and aural, all designed to penetrate the hardened minds of his hearers."[124] It is obvious that the methodological approach of Ezekiel allowed him the leeway to fashion his prophecy in such a way as to get the attention of those who listened to, or read his oracles. As I have demonstrated above and will continue to point out in the following chapters, Ezekiel's uniqueness stems from his location in the heart of Babylon. Because Ezekiel lived among the exilic community in the heart of ANE literature and culture, we have a ready explanation as to why Ezekiel stands out among the prophets. René Dussaud helps move this assumption along when he opened his article on the message and visions of Ezekiel by noting that "Le theme est celui des prophètes antérieurs; mais la forme a des saillies toutes nouvelles dues au milieu dans lequel vivait l'auteur. Les monuments qui l'entouraient l'ont vivement frappé et lui ont fourni le fond de ses visions et de ses descriptions. Son imagination ajoutant ou retranchant aux figures initiales, les mêlant peut-être, les a rendues quelque peu confuses. Le symbolisme qui s'y rattache rend encore plus difficile la recherche du prototype."[125] It appears that Ezekiel even used the architectural techniques of the Babylonians as a means to fashion his map of the city of Jerusalem on a brick in 4:1.[126] In essence the daily interaction with the people and the rich culture of the

---

123. Davis, *Swallowing the Scroll*, 29–30, follows this similar line of argument. She correctly points out that although there probably would have been some written forms of the earlier prophets and perhaps the Torah, this period is generally agreed to be the era when consolidation and organization of texts was undertaken.

124. Block, *Ezekiel 1–24*, 15.

125. Dussaud, "Les Visions," 301.

126. Ibid.

land, made available through both literature and architecture, shaped the very essence of Ezekiel's message and vision sequences.[127] Finally, in his assessment of D. H. Müller's work, *Ezechiel-Studien*,[128] Dussaud points out that Müller concluded "Puisqu'on trouve . . . des traces de littérature assyro-babylonienne dans les écrits bibliques, on ne doit pas tenir pour hasardé d'en rencontrer dans Ézéchiel qui a vécu en Babylonie."[129] Clearly scholars have long recognized that the literature, location, architecture, and the people of Babylon had a great influence on Ezekiel which comes to bear in his literary work.

Finally, Ezekiel's location and its influences may also go far in explaining why Ezekiel departs radically from his predecessors. A brief exploration of these differences will help support our ongoing discussion on the influences on Ezekiel and his historical setting.

Ezekiel and the Prophetic Corpus

The work of Ezekiel, although often building upon earlier prophetic motifs,[130] stands in stark contrast to many of the pre-exilic prophets' literary presentations. At the same time, Ezekiel functions somewhat independently of later prophetic works such as Zechariah, Haggai and Malachi. I believe that the differences between these two literary groups can be best explained by the bridging effect, which the book of Ezekiel plays between these two eras. The book of Ezekiel stands at a crossroads in the prophetic period and offers key answers to how these changes came about—changes that can only be accounted for by looking at the setting of Ezekiel in a foreign land.

This being noted, the writers of prophecy during the period leading up to the exile have long been recognized for their familiarity with, and use of, ANE motifs. In this regard, as early as the beginning of the twentieth century D. B. Stade[131] pointed to the late Assyrian and

127. Ibid., 312–13.

128. Müller, *Ezechiel-Studien*.

129. Dussaud, "Les Visions," 313.

130. This is commonly recognized within scholarship. See Zimmerli, *Fiery Throne*, 79; Childs, *Introduction*, 364–65, who suggests several areas of inter-textual borrowing by Ezekiel; Carley, *Ezekiel among the Prophets*, 13–47, 69–71; Kutsko, *Between Heaven and Earth*, 10–11; and Davis, *Swallowing the Scroll*, 61–62.

131. Stade, *Biblische Theologie*, 53. Stade insists, contra Gunkel, that the first real influence of Babylonian concepts on Hebrew writers came in the eighth century and

early Babylonian period as the most fertile time for the introduction of Mesopotamian myths and influence into the literary style of the Hebrew writers. Later Mowinckel,[132] who averred that the primeval history of Genesis had definite Mesopotamian influences, corroborated this assumption for other parts of the OT. Most scholars[133] have adopted and propagated this position, a fact rarely challenged today.[134] Further, Gunkel[135] and Gressmann[136] connected the eschatological imagery of the prophets to foreign mythology.[137]

Apocalyptic scholars have also made this connection especially in light of their study of Ezekiel. Cook,[138] along with most other scholars in his field (see Appendix for a discussion on these connections), acknowledge that the mythological concepts of many of the prophetic texts and the psalms lay within the ANE setting in which Israel and its writers lived.[139] One need only look to the creation, flood, and divine

not earlier. Ibid., 53, "Erst vom 8. Jahrh. An lässt sich in Israel sicher und in erheblichem Umfange ein Eindringen babylonischer Vorstellungen beobachten."

132. Mowinckel, *Two Sources*, 72–84. Even though Mowinckel's discussion focuses on the Mesopotamian influence on the primeval history and certain pre-Abrahamic stories (e.g., the flood and Nimrod), he concludes that Mesopotamian influence may have started much earlier than believed. Nevertheless, he does express the belief in a later influence on the Hebrew writers when Judean scribes would have had knowledge of Assyro-Babylonian culture and myth.

133. Cf., for example, Frost, *Old Testament Apocalyptic*, 72.

134. There are two main opinions as to the nature of ANE influence on the Hebrew writers: 1) they borrowed mythological concepts directly from their neighbors with very little being "original" to the Israelites (e.g., see Friedrich Delitzsch's lectures on Babel und Bibel in 1902), and 2) they did not borrow directly but wrote from a similar conceptual worldview which enables us to draw parallels. See for example, Walton, *Ancient Near Eastern Thought*. I tend to agree more with the latter whereas many scholars during Mowinckel's era adopted the former.

135. Gunkel, *Schöpfung und Chaos*, 122, argues that the influence of Mesopotamia can be seen in the prophetic corpus as evidenced in "second Isaiah" and the prophet's presentation of Yahweh as superior over the gods of the surrounding nations, viz., Babylon.

136. Gressmann, *Der Ursprung*.

137. Peake, *Roots of Hebrew Prophecy*, 14.

138. Cook, *Apocalyptic Literature*, 31–32.

139. Cross argues that in order to understand the transition of the sixth-century writers of Hebrew literature one must trace their use of mythic lore throughout the history of Israel to old Canaanite mythic forms. Cf. Cross, *Canaanite Myth*, 346 n. 13. At the same time, in all fairness, Cross does point out the possible Mesopotamian, Persian, and Greek mythical borrowings (no doubt of more influence to the later period of apocalyptic imagination). At its fundamental premise, this position does

warrior myths to see similarities and possible conceptual parallels between cultures.[140] Consequentially, we can posit that if the influences of eastern culture were prevalent prior to the exile, how much more during and after the exile?

For example, the combat myth was one of the longest lived of the ANE genres. It spanned centuries influencing writers into the full-blown apocalyptic era. Clifford is correct to caution however, for a direct one-for-one parallel of the genre of the combat myth because there is no "ideal form" where all the key aspects of the myth can be found in a given text.[141] However, even where mythological influences may occur in the OT, whether the flood, creation, or combat myths, they were demythologized to reflect a clear Hebrew understanding of Yahweh and the theological perspective to which they adhered.

As for Ezekiel and the pre-exilic prophetic use of the mythical motifs, depth of detail seems to set Ezekiel apart. This is reflected in the somewhat grotesque and colorful imagery with which he delivers his message and uses motifs such as this divine warrior myth, which reflects apocalyptic tendencies (e.g., chs. 38–39). Once again what is clear is that the Babylonian setting of his work seems to have affected

---

seem relevant here especially as it relates to Canaanite mythology, but the proverbial, "which came first the chicken or the egg," still comes into play. If one says that the Deuteronomistic history and the Pentateuch was edited in its final form during the late sixth century and after, at what point did the mythological aspects get added? Was it of old, as Cross assumes, or was it much later as scholars such as John Van Seters (*Prologue to History*) posits? The issue here for me is not one of whether mythological parallels are present in Hebrew texts prior to Ezekiel but to what degree Ezekiel relied *only* or predominantly on the earlier Hebrew forms of them. It is my contention that the position of Cross is a valid one (contra Van Seters's late date) but that one must go beyond the traditional stance and see a wider influence, even more so from Mesopotamia, in the book of Ezekiel. Cross is correct in his scrutiny of the sixth century for the radical shift in OT prophecy, but appears to fail in his presentation of just how important a Mesopotamian setting played in this radical shift. The Hebrew writers did not write in a cultural vacuum, but rather were influenced by it in numerous ways, one of which is evident in the new literary forms present in Ezekiel.

140. For a detailed analysis of the influence Mesopotamian and Canaanite combat myths (e.g., *Lugal-e, Anzu, Enuma elish*, and the Baal Cycle) had on Israel, see Clifford, "Roots of Apocalypticism," 1:3–38.

141. Clifford, "Roots of Apocalypticism," 1:3, 28. Clifford lists the four stages of development in the influence of the combat myth on Hebrew literature: 1) early poetry (i.e., Exodus 15), 2) liturgical poetry of the monarchic period, 3) second-temple literature such as Isaiah 40–66 and Zechariah 9–14, and 4) fully developed apocalyptic literature such as Daniel 7 and Revelation 12.

the form that his oracles took on (we will discuss the mythological features of chs. 38–39 in ch. 4). As Frost reminds us, it is the "unknown . . . Babylonian-Ezekiel who is the father, if any one man can claim that title, of the apocalyptic genre of thought and writing."[142] While debate may rage around the validity of a "Babylonian-Ezekiel" and a "Palestinian-Ezekiel" (see above), Frost has correctly noted the obvious shift and has assigned it closer to that of the later apocalyptists, an implication that will be dealt with in ch. 6.

Also, Ezekiel's use of literary features such as allegories, imagery, color, and symbolism reflects the oriental flavor of Babylon.[143] Frost concludes that "this is just what might be expected of a people newly introduced to artistic forms, which are themselves of immense antiquity and tradition, and which the newcomers attempt to take over and make their own but which they can never use with the sureness of the native."[144] Despite the differences between Ezekiel and the pre-exilic prophets, few have taken the step to trace this change in style. Cross echoes this sentiment when he notes the obvious differences between early prophecy and the later writers. He comments, "The evolution of late biblical religion has not been adequately traced: the decline and transformation of prophecy, the recrudescence of mythic themes stemming in part from decadent royal ideologies and from archaic lore preserved in the wisdom schools, and the new synthesis of these elements which should be designated 'proto-apocalyptic.'"[145] Cross's perspective is not new when it comes to the "transformation of prophecy," but it is in the sense of recognizing the revival of mythic themes in a "proto-apocalyptic" form.[146] While one may not necessarily agree with the preservation of the mythic elements in "wisdom schools" only, there is validity in Cross's stance that the mythic themes are brought out in a rediscovered form in later works.[147] Cross has already noted that

142. Frost, *Old Testament Apocalyptic*, 85.

143. Russell, *Method & Message*, 90.

144. Frost, *Old Testament Apocalyptic*, 85, notes that Babylon of the captivity period was a "Renaissance Babylon" and he states (quoting Goodspeed—footnote 10 on page 86) that the "artificiality of form and grotesqueness of conception" found in the style of Ezekiel and Zechariah are Babylonian.

145. Cross, *Canaanite Myth*, 343.

146. See further, Osten-Sacken, *Die Apokalyptik*.

147. Von Rad has posited the connection of apocalyptic to the wisdom tradition, albeit somewhat less convincing than that of Gunkel and Rowley who push for the

the "transformation of classical prophecy into proto-apocalyptic takes place in the oracles of Ezekiel before one's eyes, coinciding with the fall of the house of David."[148] Thus one can easily begin to recognize the unique role that Ezekiel plays in this discussion of literary change. For Cross, prophecy as seen in pre-exilic texts ceased in its classical form with the death of the monarchy.[149] Ezekiel therefore acts as the lodestar of exilic style, prophecy, and later apocalyptic.

Nevertheless, caution must be taken when suggesting an exact moment in time when the transition between prophecy and later apocalyptic took place. It appears that the transition was gradual.[150] What I am suggesting here is that Ezekiel reflects many of these transitional features that cause one to take note of the technique of the author. For example, Ezekiel, while prophetic in the fundamental understanding of the term (i.e., as exemplified in his calling and oracles of woe), houses his prophecies in visions and imagery more attuned to the apocalyptic era. At the same time, Ezekiel's eschatological outlook is linear in that he sees the fulfillment of God's restoration of the nation and land being enacted within a historical time frame—a key position of classical prophecy. Conversely, for the apocalypticists of the third century BCE and beyond, God would not act *within* history but would rather supercede and do away with the linear historical framework.

---

connection with the prophetic tradition, mythology, and Babylonian-based notions. See von Rad, *Theologie des Alten Testaments*, as noted by Collins, *Apocalyptic Imagination*, 20. For a concise critique of von Rad's position, see Lambert, *Background of Jewish Apocalyptic*, 4–5. Also, Preuss, *Jahweglaube*, 212, argues against an exclusive connection of apocalyptic with wisdom literature. He suggests that the influence of the entire OT tradition, especially the prophetic corpus, is the basis of apocalyptic eschatology. For further discussion on mythological influences on the Hebrew writers, see Gunkel, *Schöpfung und Chaos*; Gunkel, *Creation and Chaos*, 152–53; and Rowley, *Relevance of Apocalyptic*. For a concise essay discussing these traditions and influences on apocalyptic, see Knibb, "Prophesy," 155–80.

148. Cross, *Canaanite Myth*, 223 n. 15. See also Clifford, "Roots of Apocalypticism," 1:30. Clifford also points out the discernable change in sixth-century prophecy as it relates to the latter chapters of Ezekiel and Isaiah 34–35, 40–55, especially as they relate to the "democratizing and eschatologizing of classical prophetic themes and forms."

149. Cross, *Canaanite Myth*, 343. Cross points out that "classical" prophets focused on the "royal oracles, war oracles, oracles of legal judgment against king and people." Cross does however acknowledge the brief flicker of the old school in Haggai and Zechariah under the reign of Zerubbabel whom he labels a "pretender to the royal office."

150. Peake, *Roots of Hebrew Prophecy*, 14.

One final aspect of the book of Ezekiel that causes it to stand out in this transitional period is the author's use of the covenant format especially as it relates to the curses found in both biblical and extra-biblical treaty forms. In the following chapters discussion will focus on the presence of implicit and explicit covenant curse motifs. Ezekiel's use of covenant curse forms, while not necessarily new to Ezekiel's period (Jeremiah uses curse more than any other prophet)[151] is, nonetheless, uniquely presented in his work. As will be pointed out below, covenant forms from both the Neo-Assyrian and the Neo-Babylonian periods would have been known by Ezekiel. Ezekiel exploits these forms unlike any prophet before or after him.

Ezekiel's Pro-Babylonian Stance

Another unique characteristic of Ezekiel is his apparent pro-Babylonian stance in the presentation of his message, which is radically different than even his contemporary Jeremiah (cf. Jer 51). Many have suggested that this pro-Babylonian position influenced his message, which helps explain his favorable treatment of his new country of exile (e.g., 30:24–25).[152] It is true that the oracles against the nations found in chs. 25–32, 35, 38–39 do not explicitly implicate Babylon in any way.[153] However, this needs to be viewed through the lens of Ezekiel's intended message. Cooke summarizes the reason best by noting that although Babylon is ". . . the chief aggressor, [it] stood apart from the rest, as being the instrument of Jahveh's justice, ordained, in the prophet's eyes, to punish Israel."[154] Clearly the focus of Ezekiel's message was first and foremost the punishment of Judah for their covenant infidelity (see especially Ezek 16 and 17).[155] Further, this had to

---

151. Hillers, *Treaty-Curse*, 77.

152. An example of this can be seen in the work of Hölscher, *Hesekiel der Dichter*, 8.

153. It is possible that the enemies from the "north" in chapters 38–39 may have served as a veiled indictment of Babylon indirectly, especially in light of the nebulous call of the armies of the north and the phrase, and "many people with you" (עַמִּים רַבִּים אִתָּךְ) found in 38:6.

154. Cooke, *Ezekiel*, 281. So too Bodi, *Poem of Erra*, 317.

155. Contra Stevenson, *Vision of Transformation*, 104, who posits that Jeremiah and Ezekiel were "better political analysts" than the leaders of Judah when both prophets "favoured" Babylon over Egypt. This simplistic view of the role of the prophet as no more than a prognosticator removes the spiritual element completely.

be placed within the context of the curses of that same covenant (cf. Lev 26 and Deut 28). The fact that Ezekiel found himself living within the borders of the very country that Yahweh was using to fulfill these curses, would have, in some ways, endeared his host country to him.[156] In the same way Joseph embraced the land of Egypt as the instrument of Yahweh to preserve his family until they became a nation, so too Ezekiel seems to have embraced the nation of his exile as the preserver of the remnant.

At the same time, the message of Ezekiel calls one to listen not from a pro-Babylonian position but rather from a predominantly anti-Israelite perspective on account of their abominations (תּוֹעֵבוֹת), even greater than the nations around them (cf. 5:7–8).[157] Therefore, Ezekiel's message had one primary goal and that was to set before the people the indictments of Yahweh and the reality of the curses. While chs. 25–32 would have offered the opportunity for anti-Babylonian sentiment, the purpose in these chapters seems more focused on the inter-relationship of those countries in immediate proximity to Judah and how they had treated Israel throughout its history. Ezekiel chose nations well known to Israel or covenantally linked to them as a means to enact the reversal of the covenant curses from Israel to her enemies (see discussion in ch. 4).

To summarize then, the book of Ezekiel is indeed different from the earlier prophetic texts in its presentation of prophecy. This difference in turn is perhaps best attributable to its setting and Ezekiel's use of Mesopotamian motifs and possibly its literature. Ezekiel's use of varied motifs in visionary and metaphorical form, colored by ANE symbolism, caused his message to take on this marked shift. Nevertheless, can we find unity in such a diversity of motifs presented over the entire career of the prophet? I believe the answer is in the affirmative.

The issue is not one of "accommodating" one nation over another as a suzerain, but rather the prophets' focusing on Yahweh's choice for punishing Judah for their covenant violations.

156. So also Zimmerli, *Fiery Throne*, 90–91.

157. The references to Judah's "abominations" may be found in 5:9, 11; 6:9, 11; 7:3, 4, 8–9, 20; 8:6 (2x), 9, 13, 15, 17, 9:4; 11:18, 21; 12:16; 14:6; 16:2, 22, 36, 43, 47, 50–51, 58; 18:12–13, 24; 20:4; 22:2, 11; 23:36; 33:26, 29; 36:31; 43:8; 44:6–7, 13.

Motif/Metaphor Blending

Throughout the following chapters I will argue for the unity of Ezekiel based upon the placement of the four visions and extended metaphors in the final form. As such, I will present a variety of motifs/metaphors as possible unifying factors. These motifs may appear on the surface to be unrelated; however, it is my intent to demonstrate that the one underlying unifying element rests in curse language of not only Deuteronomy 28 and Leviticus 26 but also of ANE treaties and daily life. Therefore when dealing with temple abandonment (ch. 2); the punishment of unfaithful wives and prostitutes (ch. 3); the curse of unburied dead (ch. 4); the (re)building of temples, giving of law, and the return of gods to their temples (ch. 5), the common thread is to be found in the dominant curse language and social, religious, and political policies of the ANE during Ezekiel's period. More specifically, in the ANE it was believed that temple abandonment (cf. Ezek 8–11) was the result of a nation or a king's "sin" against not only their deity but also a sworn oath to an earthly suzerain. In the case of Judah, deity and suzerain happened to be one-in-the-same. Second, the punishment of unfaithful wives and/or the curse of being treated as a prostitute (in both cases the punishments were similar viz., public humiliation and possible mutilation, cf. Ezek 16 and 23) finds numerous examples in marriage contracts of the period and can be attested in at least one treaty curse example (we will return to the marriage metaphor versus suzerain/vassal motif shortly). Third, the curse of being left unburied (cf. Ezek 37:1–14; 38–39) is a prevalent curse in the OT and ANE literature, especially in treaties. It should not be surprising that the author of Ezekiel uses this curse as an effective means to warn of Yahweh's wrath not only against Judah, but also the nations. Finally, the rebuilding of temples, the return of the gods, and the establishment of order (i.e., the giving of laws) served as a fitting full-circle conclusion to the destruction unleashed by an earthly suzerain. For example, one could note the kind actions of Esarhaddon towards Babylon after its destruction by Sennacherib (see ch. 5) or the decree of Cyrus in 539 BCE that allowed the exiles to return to Judah. These acts demonstrate this common restoration/reversal motif. It appears that it was an unwritten policy that once a suzerain/conqueror had established relative peace in his kingdom acts of restoration and beneficence ensued—a strikingly similar picture presented in Ezekiel 40–48.

Returning to the marriage metaphor of 16 and 23, some rightly contend that the marriage metaphor and the suzerain/vassal motif appear to be at odds with one another. However, in the context of Israel's relationship with Yahweh the conflict perhaps is not as great as one would suspect. The underlying issue appears to be how one defines the nature of Israel's covenant with Yahweh, namely, a family-based marriage covenant versus a suzerain/vassal covenant/treaty. In our discussion below I will argue for the latter but this in no way precludes the possibility of the former being used in specific cases. For example, Hosea, as does Ezekiel, uses the marriage metaphor as a means of invoking a desired emotive response in his hearers, yet the use of the marriage metaphor in Hosea does not necessarily mean that that metaphor is in fact the nature of Israel's covenant. Indeed, the marriage metaphor can explain away neither the dominant theme of the covenant lawsuit found within the prophetic corpus nor the treaty-style curse lists of Leviticus and Deuteronomy (not to mention the very shape of the book of Deuteronomy itself—see below). Furthermore, many scholars who propose the suzerain/vassal motif as the defining structure of Israel's relationship with Yahweh also see the use of the marriage metaphor in the prophets as a legitimate means of defining the intimate relationship between Israel and Yahweh.[158]

In the case of Ezekiel, whereas the marriage metaphor served as an effective means of indicting the nation for covenant "infidelity" while serving the prophet's emotive purposes, the curses allowed for a direct link to the Sinai covenant and ANE political norms. Thus, the curse language of ANE treaties and the Sinai covenant appears to have influenced Ezekiel's message (something readily accepted by many scholars in this field e.g., Fensham-1963, Frankena-1965, Hillers-1969, Niehaus-1995, Block-2000), even more than the family/marriage model.

Finally, we must accept the fact that the book of Ezekiel is presented within a given historical setting and cannot be divorced from the influences of culture and political realities exerted on its author. Because I believe Deuteronomy 28 and Leviticus 26 are part of these

---

158. I personally know of two specific scholars (i.e., G. P. Hugenberger and J. J. Niehaus) who hold to the suzerain/vassal motif and yet accept the marriage metaphor as a legitimate means of defining the close relational aspects of that same covenant motif.

"influences" on Ezekiel and because the suzerain/vassal motif has been debated for decades, a brief discussion of these issues may be helpful.

The Historical Reality of Treaty and Covenant for Israel and Judah

Israel and Judah were all too familiar with the ANE treaty forms and the consequences (i.e., the curses) of breaking their oaths to their earthly suzerains. Both had been subjected at some point in their history to one of the dominant powers of the ANE (e.g., Egypt, Assyria, or Babylon) especially in their later years of nationhood. This fact also finds attestation in extra-biblical records (e.g., the Assyrian Annals).[159] At the public ceremonies that marked the conclusion and ratification of these treaties, they were read aloud and the curses were often enacted.[160] Knowledge of the dangers inherent in these treaties by means of the curses offered an excellent deterrent to any breach thereof. However, Judah's breaking of their oath to Yahweh had brought no immediate result for generations and as such they had continued in their rebellious ways confident in the inviolability of Jerusalem and the temple (cf. Jer 7:4). Ezekiel's message was to change that misunderstanding.

---

159. Frankena, "Vassal-treaties," 152. Frankena asserts that the presence of copies of vassal-treaties in Jerusalem between Judah's kings and Assyria and Babylon (e.g., Nebuchadnezzar and Zedekiah—Ezek 17:9; Hezekiah and Sennacherib—2 Kgs 18:7; and Manasseh and Esarhaddon—Annals of Esarhaddon, see Borger, *Asarhaddons*, 60, §27: Nin. Episode 21 line 55b "*Me-na-si-i* šàr ᵘʳᵘIa-ú-di") lends credence to the possibility that the editors of both Ezekiel and Deuteronomy would have had access to, and did in fact use them to add blessings and curses to their works.

On the other hand (contra Frankena), I see no reason not to believe that Ezekiel could have gained access to the curse material from an earlier biblical source like Deuteronomy or Leviticus (or both) or that he may have simply borrowed forms from the ANE. The latter is possible because all the curses that are covered in chapters 2–6 below have parallels in the ANE. However, the former is perhaps the most valid in light of the indictment style that Ezekiel used. In light of earlier prophetic tradition, it would only stand to reason that Ezekiel would have needed to have some basis for the indictments and curses which he used to fashion his message and create a framework for the overall book. Frankena's suggestion that they were added "later" does not make sense of the overall framework of Ezekiel that will be argued below.

160. Ibid., 139. This was often done with a sheep or another animal where the suzerain said something along the line of, "may the head of vassal X be as the head of this sheep" as it is severed from its body. Another example from an eighth-century Aramaic treaty reads, "just as this calf is cut up, so may Matiʾel be cut up"; see "Inscriptions of Bar-gaʾyah and Matiʾel from Sefire," translated by Joseph A. Fitzmyer (*COS* 2.82:214) and Hillers, *Covenant*, 41.

Warning signs had loomed for generations, none so blatant as the deportation of the Northern Kingdom in 722 BCE, for their breach of covenant with Shalmaneser V (726–722 BCE) and as a result of their broken covenant with Yahweh.

On the international level, these formats became stock-in-trade for the way the leadership of Israel and Judah saw themselves in the ANE world during the final two centuries of their existence. Vassalage was understood as a way of life and in many cases, their desire to free themselves from the oppressive rule of their suzerain was a common topic of discussion. They violated treaties and broke covenant with their suzerains while forging forbidden alliances to better position themselves against their suzerain (e.g., Hezekiah seeking the help of Egypt against Assyria—Isa 36:7, Zedekiah rebelling against Nebuchadnezzar—Ezek 17, Hoshea shunning Shalmaneser V—2 Kgs 17:4).

From just a cursory reading of the OT one can easily see that the concept of covenant and suzerainty was a prevalent topic in the period between the eighth and sixth centuries BCE. There is little doubt why the prophets often adapted this motif when defining the relationship between Israel and her God. However, prophets seldom, if ever, addressed the treaty form on a secular level where the prophet took the side of the foreign oppressor as seen in Ezekiel 17. Ezekiel's message would change this and, furthermore, would be the basis upon which he would formulate his message to the nation in exile and those left in Jerusalem. Ezekiel was all too willing to point out the failures of the nation in this regard.[161] One need only look to the message of the prophet to recognize this emphasis. In 17:11–21, 21:23–29 (Heb), and 29:14–16, Ezekiel focuses on the failure of Judah and her rulers to keep their treaties with Babylon and their penchant to forge alliances with Egypt. As Tsevat correctly comments, "The problem of political perjury of vassals was uppermost in his [i.e., Ezekiel's] mind, . . ."[162] Yet at the same time these passages beg the question as to why Ezekiel focused in this manner on aspects of foreign covenants (beyond the obvious Sinai covenant) that other prophets refused to mention? Once again, Ezekiel's setting and literary style is key to answering this query.

---

161. Tsevat, "Vassal Oaths," 201.
162. Ibid., 201.

The Responsibility of the Leadership

The tension between individual and corporate responsibility (i.e., leadership) for covenant violation in the OT is evident. While normally the leadership/king of the nation was responsible for covenant fidelity (e.g., Exod 32; 1 Kgs 12:28–33; 14:15–16; 2 Kgs 21:8–11), we also see how the individual could cause the judgment of Yahweh to fall upon the nation for covenant violations (e.g., Achan in Josh 7; see also Num 16:24–26). In Ezekiel it appears that the prophet covers both aspects equally. While at points he narrows his focus primarily to that of the leadership and king (cf. chs. 13, 14, 17, 34), he also spends time indicting the individual for covenant violations (cf. chs. 14:6–9, 18, 20). Nevertheless, responsibility for the nation ultimately fell on the shoulders of the leadership who were responsible for keeping the oaths of the nation and conversely, the breaches as well.[163]

In chs. 16 and 17 of Ezekiel, the indictment of leadership finds its most vivid portrayal. In ch. 17 especially, Ezekiel's indictments move away from previous prophetic attitudes of ambivalence concerning secular treaties to a solemn indictment of Zedekiah as unable to keep oaths of any kind, even the one with Nebuchadnezzar.[164] There can be little doubt that the plan of Ezekiel was to draw a parallel between covenant infidelity on both the secular and cultic/divine level. Scholars have suggested that this is due to Ezekiel's use and affinity with the law of oath-taking as found in Leviticus, especially Lev 5:4.[165] As Tsevat suggests, "Ezekiel's strictness in legal matters and his close affinity with the law of Leviticus and, on the other hand, the inclusive and explicit language of the law provide an obvious explanation of his position regarding desecration of any sort of oath, the imposed oath

---

163. Greenberg, *Ezekiel 1–20*, 322.

164. Scholars have noted the tension of chapters 16 and 17 when it comes to covenant loyalty and violation. In chapter 16 it appears that Yahweh is punishing Judah for making alliances with Babylon, yet in chapter 17 Zedekiah is chastised for trying to break the very covenant he is accused of trying to enter into in chapter 16. The tension is alleviated, however, when we understand that Zedekiah, while guilty of making covenants against Yahweh's will, was still responsible for that treaty because Zedekiah had sworn in Yahweh's name to keep it (cf. 17:19). Therefore, contra Levenson, "The Last Four Verses in Kings," 358–59, Ezekiel is not "sanctioning" the foreign covenant; he is criticizing Zedekiah's endemic unfaithful behavior.

165. Tsevat, "Vassal Oaths," 203.

not excepted."[166] The indictment of ch. 17 (suzerain/vassal language is implicit) is laid at the feet of Zedekiah and is placed within the literary context of covenant infidelity of the previous chapter (see discussion in ch. 3, below). On the secular level, it was the actions of the leadership that often brought the wrath of the foreign suzerain on the helpless masses—indeed the reality facing Jerusalem on account of Zedekiah's stubbornness. Corporate responsibility of the leadership as defined by the vassal treaty in the ANE was to be expected, as was the onus Yahweh placed upon them for not adhering to the Sinai covenant.

Biblical Covenant Forms as a Legal Basis for Ezekiel

It is impossible to prove with one-hundred-percent certainty what legal and cultic material Ezekiel had at his disposal during the exile. Ezekiel's indictments while at first glance appearing to be based upon the covenant curses as found in Leviticus 26 and Deuteronomy 28 must have had some basis in legal tradition within Israel. It seems legally invalid for the prophets to indict the nation for covenant offenses if, in fact, Israel did not understand her relationship with Yahweh in a covenantal sense that had curses as deterrents and blessings as rewards.[167] However, scholars are sharply divided as to how and when this motif first entered Israel's theological understanding. Some posit an early Hittite influence (thirteenth century BCE) while others suggest a much later period (sixth century BCE) for the adoption of ANE treaty formats by the Hebrew writers. The period from the early second millennium to the middle of the first millennium saw very little

---

166. Ibid., 203. Tsevat goes on to point out that this was due to Ezekiel's concept of individualism contra a more corporate concept elsewhere. His use of the law in Lev 5:4, while focused on the individual, is also valid for the community—the nation must keep its oaths. Thus Tsevat (204) sees that what applies to the individual also applies to the community. The former separation of the individual and the community now is blended in Ezekiel's message (I will deal with this concept more in ch. 3, below).

167. Hillers, *Covenant*, ch. 6, esp. 138–41, gives a strong argument for the prophets writing from a covenant curse-and-treaty perspective. He concludes that the lack of the use of the actual word "covenant" may in fact have been due in part by the association of the word with the kingship of Israel as opposed to the actual relationship of the nation with her God. Hillers points out, however, that the curse motif became a particularly effective means of speaking to the people about their sin and as a means of indicting the nation based upon their previous oaths to Yahweh in a treaty format.

change in curse language[168] and how the treaty forms were presented especially as they relate to OT forms.[169] This being noted, one can still appreciate the dating issues from both sides of the scholarly divide.[170] Advocates of an early date often note Hittite formulary parallels between Deuteronomy, Exodus 20–24, and Joshua 24 (and aspects of Leviticus). On the other hand, many scholars seek to connect the covenant language of the Pentateuch (e.g., blessings and curses), the Deuteronomistic History, and the prophets, with the later Neo-Assyrian vassal treaties where curses predominated.[171] In this latter case, some scholars explain the presence of the covenant language in "earlier" texts as an anachronistic interpolation. Due to the validity of many of the arguments on both sides of the debate, the trend for most scholars has been to interpret the "evidence" and make a final decision based upon a particular presupposition or bias.[172] Due to the apparent

---

168. For a few examples, see Sefire I and Ashurnirari V of Assyria (754 BCE); both treaties note the loss of the sound of music and joy as one of the curses which can also be found in Ezek 26:13 and Jer 7:34; 16:9; 25:10; 33:11. One of Esarhaddon's treaties of the seventh century mentions the loss of the sound of the millstone, which is also mentioned in Jer 25:10. In the treaty of Baal of Tyre with Esarhaddon and Sefire I the breaking of the bow of the warrior is mentioned as a curse which can also be seen in Hos 1:5; Jer 49:35 and Ezek 39:3. In the Ashurnirari Treaty people are cursed with the reality of eating their own children, which can be seen in Deut 28:53–57, Lev 26:29, Jer 19:9, and Ezek 5:10. In the Esarhaddon treaties the phrase, "the earth is like iron and the sky as copper" is close to that found in Lev 26:19 and Deut 28:23. Cf. Hillers, *Covenant*, 132–37.

169. Fensham, "Maldictions and Benedictions," 1, comments, "It is obvious from a comparison of these treaties [i.e., ANE and Israel's] that the form and even the language are closely related, which shows that from Late Bronze into the Iron Age, from the second half of the Second Millennium to the first half of the First Millennium the form and language of Near Eastern and Old Testament vassal-treaties or covenants were, with a few minor differences, similar." See also Hillers, *Covenant*, 66. On the other hand, Kitchen, *Reliability*, 283–94, forcefully argues for marked shifts in the treaty form from its earliest inception in the third millennium until the late Iron Age.

170. For a concise unbiased presentation of the two perspectives, see Walton, *Ancient Israelite Literature*, 95–109.

171. For a detailed analysis of Deuteronomy 28 and the Esarhaddon succession treaties, see Steymans, *Deuteronomium 28*.

172. My assertion of a presuppositional or "biased" decision in this matter rests upon my research of a wide range of scholars on this topic. Those scholars coming from more traditional/conservative backgrounds and perspectives have a tendency to interpret the data from that perspective. For example, those who hold to the Mosaic authorship for the bulk of Deuteronomy tend to opt for Hittite treaties as a paradigm for the Israelite covenant at Sinai (e.g., Hugenberger and Niehaus). On the

scholarly deadlock, a brief history of scholarship in this regard seems in order.

History of Research

Most scholars now recognize that the old Wellhausenian view, which suggested that the religious life of Israel was based upon an evolutionary model moving from the simplest relationship with her God to that of a complex covenant-based religious format, is too simplistic and is no longer valid in light of what is known of the ANE.[173] The discoveries of a complex literary society in Mesopotamia centuries before Israel's birth as a nation bears record to at least the possibility that Israel may have understood her relationship with her God in a more sophisticated manner than Wellhausen proposed. Based on the early development of other nations Hillers asks the simple question, "why should the Israelites have been incapable of drawing on a political analogy to express religious ideas?"[174] Indeed, this question must be a part of the debate, and is one that is often invoked in the discussion for an early covenant formulary date.

Much of the debate that raged around the topic took place a generation ago and has since subsided with no clear winner. It appears that each side still takes a position from either a late date based on Neo-Assyrian and Neo-Babylonian treaties (e.g., McCarthy and Baltzer)[175] or an earlier covenant form based on the Hittite formulary (e.g., Kline, Hillers, and Kitchen). One need only open any modern commentary on Deuteronomy to see the ambivalence in the modern debate on the subject. When commentators do deal with the covenant issue they tend to only briefly address the subject and then choose either a late or early covenant date depending on the presuppositions of the author.

---

other hand, those who adopt a seventh-century date for Deuteronomy tend to look to the Neo-Assyrian period for predominant parallels (e.g., Patrick Miller). See further comments below.

173. Hillers, *Covenant*, 67. Cf. Wellhausen, *Prolegomena*, 11–12, 429–40, 464–65.

174. Ibid., 68.

175. Lothar Perlitt takes it one step further and argues for an exilic construction of the covenant as a means to offer hope to a people in need of encouragement in the face of the trials of exile. He argues that the earliest appearance of *bĕrît* is in Ezekiel 16 and the Deuteronomistic History in Joshua 24. Cf. Perlitt's *Bundestheologie*. McCarthy and others have effectively argued against Perlitt's position.

Rarely does the debate go further than a mere mentioning of previous scholars' work on the topic before a presuppositional choice is made and the author moves on with his/her commentary. Thus, date seems to be of little debate today due to the hardened positions of the two sides. Nevertheless, some generally accepted position does need to be established especially if one is to use the covenant formulary as a basis for defending a vital aspect of a hypothesis. It is for this reason that a quick survey of the most prominent scholarly positions over the past fifty years needs to be given as a basis for the position, which will be adopted here.

Space does not allow for a thorough study of the history of research in the once ubiquitous field of covenantal and vassal treaty studies. Therefore I will survey some of the key scholars from Mendenhall forward in order to glean from their works the development of thought on this topic. Because the bulk of research on covenant forms took place during the period from the 1950s to the early 1970s, a few key scholars covering these decades will be mentioned concluded by a more recent evaluation by Kenneth Kitchen in 2003.[176]

---

176. I am not suggesting by this gap in the history of scholarship that the issue of covenant is no longer debated but rather that the issue of covenant as it relates to treaty formats (i.e., Hittite versus Neo-Assyrian) seems to have subsided during the three decades since the work of Weinfeld and his contemporaries. Recently, some scholars have returned to the family model (e.g., marriage covenants) as a basis for the covenant between Israel and Yahweh. However, a large segment of scholarship still adheres to the suzerain/vassal motif as the best explanation for Israel's covenant. For further study on recent covenantal studies, see Hugenberger, *Marriage as a Covenant*; Cross, "Kinship and Covenant"; Sohn, "I will Be Your God," 355–72; McKenzie, *Covenant*; and Hahn, "Covenant in the Old and New Testaments," 263–92. I am grateful to Mark Boda for pointing out these bibliographic entries. Cf. also, Williamson, *Sealed with an Oath*; and Hafemann and House, *Central Themes*.

One of the most recently published articles on the topic of covenant is Niehaus's "Covenant: An Idea in the Mind of God," 225–46. In this article Niehaus discusses the nature of covenant as rooted in the social and relational attributes of God that were passed onto humankind in the Garden of Eden. Niehaus contends that looking to family or civil institutions as the incipient motivation for covenant is incorrect. One must go back even further to the very nature of God. Humanity has used certain institutions to define relationships (e.g., marriage, treaties, covenants) but in essence they all rest on a much earlier reality. Therefore in the same way Plato saw an ideal example in "heaven" of everything that appears on earth, so too the idea of relationships finds their ideal in "heaven" viz., in the mind of God. This being noted, however, Niehaus still sees the suzerain/vassal motif as the most logical understanding of Israel's covenant.

George E. Mendenhall: Law and Covenant[177]

Mendenhall is attributed with being the first scholar to draw unique parallels between Hittite treaties and the covenant of the Decalogue in Exodus 20. He pointed out that the apodictic forms found in the Decalogue were very much like the Hittite treaty form of Muršilis to Kupanta-Kal where the term "Thou shalt not desire any territory of the Hatti" resembled that found in the Ten Commandments. Mendenhall tempered his treaty comparisons by pointing out that Exodus 20 is not a complete Hittite parallel because it lacked the last three aspects of the form, i.e., 1) the place of deposit, 2) public reading and 3) the list of witnesses.

On issues of the law codes, Mendenhall also drew comparisons between the case law of the Covenant Code of Exodus 21–23 (which he dated as pre-monarchial),[178] and the case and apodictic laws of the Hittite covenant form. He went on to point out that the case law of Israel had even earlier roots in Mesopotamian law codes. These earlier case law codes, as early as the third millennium, were much older than those found in the Law of the Hammurabi. Mendenhall insisted that because the law codes were not used (i.e., quoted/referenced) in judicial cases in other ANE settings it is doubtful that they were used in Israel in the same way. Therefore he saw the lack of reference to the Covenant Code and other laws in the earlier writings of Israel as proving nothing of their prior existence before the historical books and the prophets. Finally, he insisted that the Canaanites were not the source of the Hebrew laws because there is no archeological evidence pointing to the existence of any Canaanite laws even resembling the Hebrew law codes.

---

177. Mendenhall, *Law and Covenant*. See too idem, "Ancient Oriental," 46; idem, "Covenant Forms," 50–76. In 1950 Wright, *Old Testament against Its Environment*, 42–76, esp. 62, argued against a late date of the covenant formulary. For him, even though the term "covenant" may not appear in "early" material, he opted for at least the concept of covenant terminology for Israel and Yahweh's relationship in the wilderness period.

178. He asserts that this was when the code was "codified." See "Biblical Law," 37.

Meredith Kline: Treaty of the Great King[179]

The work of Mendenhall opened the floodgates for covenant and treaty study over the next two decades. Meredith Kline was one scholar who based his work on Hittite parallels and opted for an early date for much of the law forms in the Pentateuch. Kline asserted that the basis of understanding the covenant in the complete book of Deuteronomy (with the exception of the epilogue containing Moses' death account) and that found in Exodus 20, was to see the parallels of the two with the Suzerain-vassal treaty format of the Hittites. He used the actual ANE Hittite treaty between Muršilis and his vassal Duppi-Teššub as the basis for his argumentation. While Mendenhall did not see a treaty oath being taken by the Israelites, Kline pointed out that when the elders of the people ate the meal on the mountain (Exod 24:11) they were, by the very nature of the act, ratifying the covenant. The differences between the covenant in Exodus and that in Deuteronomy, according to Kline, could be accounted for by the need for updating it for the next generation, a fact common to other ANE treaty settings.

Unlike Mendenhall, Kline saw in the Exodus account Mendenhall's three "missing" aspects of the Hittite formulary, viz., the public reading, storage, and witnesses. Kline noted that Exodus 24:7 handled the public reading clause while 25:16 made provision for the covenant's storage in the Ark of the Covenant. The common practice of placing the treaty in the temples of both the vassal and the suzerain was not possible in the case of Israel. For this reason the two (duplicate?) tablets of the covenant were placed in the tabernacle within the Ark of the Covenant. Hence both the people and Yahweh had the same tabernacle and therefore both copies were stored in the same place and served the same purpose. Finally, because the Israelites were to have no other gods, Yahweh served as both suzerain and witness to the covenant.

Kline also noted that the blessing/curses section of the covenant was the basis of the indictments of the later prophets as seen in their oracles of woes and weal. As for chs. 33 and 34 of Deuteronomy, Kline pointed out that notations concerning dynastic succession were vital in covenants of the ANE. Esarhaddon's Nimrud treaty stated that the

---

179. Kline, *Treaty of the Great King*. So too Harrison, *Introduction*, 648–50. Here Harrison presents an evaluation of Kline's work.

crowned prince Ashurbanipal would succeed him at his death. At this point the covenant had to be renewed between the vassals and their suzerain in the same way Moses' successor, Joshua, stood before the people and renewed the covenant at Ebal and Gerizim (Josh 8).

Finally, besides the visible absence of the historical prologue, the differences between first and second millennium treaties is most obvious in the stressing of the curses in the later forms with few or no blessings at all (e.g., Sefire and Esarhaddon). Because of this, Kline argued that the presence of the historical prologue and the curse *and* blessing sections of the Sinai covenant proved the Sinai covenant was closer to the earlier Hittite formulary. Moreover, he insisted that Deuteronomy 4:2a supports the ANE treaty provisions of not altering the text of the treaty in any way. For Kline, this flew in the face of modern critical methods, which asserted that Deuteronomy was a slow amalgam of laws altered at will.

Dennis McCarthy: Treaty and Covenant[180]

McCarthy, while not eliminating the role that the Hittite treaties played as a generally uniform formula, sought to focus on the late Assyrian treaties of Esarhaddon and stress the elongated list of curses found in these texts. These lists, he felt, matched best the curse list found in Deuteronomy 28. He moved away from the perspective of Mendenhall and Albright, which suggested clear distinctions between first and second millennium texts. McCarthy saw them as more unified in theme and form (i.e., treaties forged under oaths with stipulations, invocation of gods, and curse formulae). Furthermore, he saw no reason for eliminating *a priori* the possibility of Israel's writers (late in their history) using an old covenant formula which was so prevalent in the ANE between the eighth and sixth centuries (e.g., Esarhaddon treaties with Hittite vestiges). He agreed with the general consensus that the bulk of Deuteronomy (chs. 5–28) represented this (late) treaty format. He posited that the Sinai covenant had no blessings and curses (Kline would disagree with this) and Joshua 24 had only reminiscences of it. As for Exodus 19–24, he saw most of the old covenant form as being lost to history and transmission. He concluded that while the idea of covenant may be behind these chapters it was the ritual which

180. McCarthy, *Treaty and Covenant*; and idem, *Old Testament Covenant*.

"looms larger than the verbal and contractual."[181] Thus, McCarthy saw the Sinai covenant as the earliest form of covenant found in Israel but opted for a parallel closer to the Bedouin treaty contracts where the stronger party joined the family of the weaker. Israel became a "family" member of Yahweh and as such fostered a relationship, which was later developed into a formal covenant after the period of the prophets. He therefore concluded that Deuteronomy was a mixture of old Hittite and later Assyrian treaty forms.

R. E. Clements: Prophecy and Covenant and Prophecy and Tradition[182]

The work of Clements in 1965 focused primarily on the role of the prophets as the harbingers of punishment and destruction for covenant violation. For Clements, the covenant was to be linked to the earliest period of Israel's history in the wilderness (i.e., the Sinai tradition), the basis upon which the prophets fashioned their messages of woe and weal.[183] As the prophets moved away from their connections to the cult shrines and spoke directly to the people concerning covenant violations (e.g., Amos and Hosea) they began to function as the mediator of the covenant curses. Clements insisted that the prophets by and large were the "voice of covenant tradition"[184] and could not be understood apart from the early covenant relationship of Israel and her God.[185] In his later work in 1975, while not rejecting the influence of covenant on the prophetic voice, Clements did move beyond his original proposal of an "all-encompassing covenant theology." Here he suggested that the idea of covenant mediator was not necessarily present in full force from a much earlier period, but rather developed over time especially in the period of the Deuteronomic tradition.[186] He rejected Mendenhall, Hillers, and Baltzer's idea that early suzerainty treaty formats (i.e., Hittite) were behind the earlier traditions of Israel's covenant understanding and cautiously conceded that perhaps seventh-century treaty forms may have informed Israel's tradition

---

181. McCarthy, *Treaty and Covenant*, 163.
182. Clements, *Prophecy and Covenant*; and idem, *Prophecy and Tradition*.
183. Clements, *Prophecy and Covenant*, 23.
184. Ibid., 128.
185. Ibid., 126.
186. Ibid., 13–23, esp. 23.

at a later date. He asserted that treaty-curses *may* have informed the pre-exilic and exilic prophets but it was not necessarily a foregone conclusion. He concluded that common ANE motifs of punishment and dread from the prophetic period may be the simplest explanation for the similarities between the prophetic indictments and the treaty curses.

E. W. Nicholson: Deuteronomy and Tradition[187]

Nicholson focused much of his work around the dating of Deuteronomy. On this he followed the scholarly consensus by dating the bulk of the work in the time of Josiah's reform (ca. 621 BCE) but noted that the traditions reflected in it must be older. He concluded that the book was used to fuel only part of the Josianic reforms after the death of Ashurbanipal in 633 BCE in light of the fact that Josiah had already begun the political reforms before the book was "discovered" (2 Chr 34; 2 Kgs 22–23). He saw only chs. 5–26 and much of 28 as the "original" book while going on to defend both the early and late aspects of the book. He also recognized that the covenant format was close to that suggested by Kline, only from a later period. He noted the provenance of the book was from the Northern Kingdom promulgated by the prophetic circle there. This group of prophets and priests from the Northern Kingdom, he posited, fled to Judah after the fall of Samaria in 721 BCE. Once in Jerusalem they formulated their plan for reformation in Judah where they felt the future of Israel lay. They made some concessions to the Jerusalem cult and helped foster the reform of Josiah through the influence of their writings. Nicholson suggested that the actual writing of the book happened during the reign of Manasseh when a hope for future reformation was needed.

Delbert Hillers: Covenant: The History of a Biblical Idea[188]

Hillers focused on the parallels between the covenant of Exodus 19–24 and those found in the Hittite forms, as pointed out by Kline and Mendenhall. He argued for an early vassal treaty form in Israel's history (pre-prophetic period) as the basis for prophetic indictments.

---

187. Nicholson, *Deuteronomy and Tradition*.
188. Hillers, *Covenant*.

His analysis of the curse lists of Deuteronomy 28 and Leviticus 26 focused on the later period of Israel's history when the Assyrian and Sefire treaties may have been instrumental in shaping the final form of the biblical texts.

Lothar Perlitt: Bundestheologie im Alten Testament[189]

Perlitt belittled scholars' assumptions of Hittite and Assyrian covenant forms in Deuteronomy. He argued that the earliest possible date for the idea of a covenant *per se* came during the period of the eighth to seventh centuries, most likely, during the reign of Josiah. He saw in Joshua 24 the possibility of the earliest form of a covenant ceremony but argued against the Exodus 19–24 passages as being covenantal in nature. For Perlitt, the Exodus tradition was based on the "promise to the fathers." He rejected the connection between covenant and treaty and saw *běrît* as an obligation taken upon oneself and not a relationship as such. The covenant did not have its roots in the old Sinai, patriarchal, and prophetic traditions, but rather was borrowed from the seventh-century international treaties as a means of giving a hopeless people some solid connection to Yahweh. This "hope" he asserted was generated by fabricating a past rife with covenant promises and treaty obligations. He contended that wherever the idea of covenant appeared in the OT outside of the Deuteronomistic writings, it must be attributed to the later Deuteronomistic hand. Perlitt asserted (as with Wellhausen) that the prophetic writers birthed the concept of *běrît*.[190]

---

189. Perlitt, *Bundestheologie*. For critiques of Perlitt's work see Buss, Review of Lothar Perlitt, 210–12; Kearney, Review of Lothar Perlitt, 524–28; and McCarthy, Review of Lothar Perlitt, 110–21.

190. Today there are those who follow Perlitt's lead and point to the period in Israel's history when Deuteronomy was found (ca. 621 BCE) as the plausible incipient moment for the concept of covenant in Israel. For example, McKenzie, *Covenant*, 24, 57. On the other hand, Kapelrud, "The Prophets and the Covenant," 176, critiques this position by noting that "this must be characterized as a one-sided view which disregards facts in the Old Testament itself." Kapelrud goes on to note James Barr's response to the same issue as, "Yet with all the will in the world it is a little hard to believe that the covenant of YHWH with Israel became significant only so late . . . A current of tradition that used *berit* in one kind of linguistic context might use other terminology in another, without this being evidence of a basic theological conflict." Cf. Barr, "Some Semantic Notes, 37. One could also add that McKenzie's position does not take into account the earlier *rîb* formula that appears in prophetic literature earlier than 621 BCE (e.g., Isaiah 1, Micah 6, or Amos 3) or the possibility that

Klaus Baltzer: Covenant Formulary[191]

Baltzer noted the binding nature of the older treaties (i.e., Hittite) when established in a written form. He pointed out that the Hittite treaties did not become binding (i.e., come into being) until they were written down. The treaty was recited to the vassal by the great king and then the vassal assented to the stipulations by an oath (e.g., as found in Joshua 24). He therefore saw no reason not to identify Joshua 24 as an early covenant formulary that was patterned after the Hittite form. Contrary to Alt's view of a late Canaanite influence on Israel's Book of the Covenant,[192] Baltzer insisted that the formulary was therefore old and came before its later use in Chronicles, the prophets, and the psalms, not vice versa. He hypothesized that the form had to be passed on by the worship format of the people. Thus, it was reiterated frequently and remembered by the constant use in worship settings. Baltzer noted that in the process of the borrowing of the treaty form over centuries it was the curse and the blessing section that was the most reworked to serve the purpose of the authors. Thus, when things were going well the blessings were stressed with the curses presented as being a futuristic aspect of the covenant, but when disaster came, the curses became present tense with the blessings reflecting a futuristic period.

Moshe Weinfeld: Deuteronomy and the Deuteronomic School[193]

Weinfeld saw the date of Deuteronomy and its covenant format as late (i.e., seventh century). He noted that the covenant format was to be

---

the sources used by the Deuteronomistic Historian may have reflected covenant at a much earlier date.

191. Baltzer, *Covenant Formulary*. See also McCarthy's summary of Baltzer's work in McCarthy, *Old Testament Covenant*, 24–25.

192. Alt, *Essays on Old Testament History*, 81–132. Note esp. 97–101 where Alt argues that the casuistic laws of Israel came into existence only after their entry into the Promised Land where Canaanite law codes informed Israel's. Conversely, Alt does hold to an early origin (i.e., during the desert wandering) for the apodictic laws of the Book of the Covenant perhaps as early as the time of Moses (cf. 130–32). These laws he sees as distinctly Israelite in origin. However, Alt's understanding of a distinctively Israelite origin of the apodictic law has fallen into disfavor. For a critique of Alt's view see Mendenhall, "Biblical Law," 20–31; and Phillips, "Prophecy and Law," 217–32.

193. Weinfeld, *Deuteronomy and the Deuteronomic School*.

identified with that of the later Mesopotamian and Assyrian treaties. He rejected the concept that Joshua 24 and Exodus 19–24 were representative of the treaty form. He argued that the reason the Assyrian treaties lacked a historical prologue and blessing section was because of the arrogance of the Assyrians. He propounded that there was no need for these sections because the Assyrians were rulers of the then-known world. Weinfeld did note that the historical prologue of Deuteronomy was close to the Hittite and Mesopotamian forms especially that of Muršilis to Duppi-Teššub. He made a distinction between the treaty form and the royal land grants and went on to posit that the Hittite treaties and Deuteronomy were basically a combination of both of them. He presented Deuteronomy as being linked to the Patriarchal promises by this land grant. The land grants were thus a reward for loyalty while the treaty was an inducement for loyalty. Weinfeld thus contended that scribes borrowed the curse sequence of Deuteronomy from the Esarhaddon and Sefire treaties. He saw the Sinai covenant as a covenant of law much like the laws of the Hammurabi while the Shechem treaty was more of a vassal treaty. Deuteronomy, on the other hand, was a mixture of both placed within the vassal treaty format in a homiletic style.

Kenneth A. Kitchen: On the Reliability of the OT[194]

Kitchen, an Egyptologist, argued that the Hittite treaty style best resembled that of Deuteronomy and the Sinai covenant as found in Exodus—Leviticus and Joshua 24. He pointed out that there are thirty Hittite inspired documents that lend credence to this conclusion. Although there are some variances in the Hittite forms the main order remains the same. Kitchen critiqued the work of McCarthy (1963, 1973, and 1978) and Weinfeld (1972) on Hittite treaties and argued against many of their conclusions. Kitchen pointed out that there were major changes in the treaties over the centuries, a fact that Weinfeld later admitted. Further, Kitchen refuted their claim that a historical prologue is present in the seventh-century Assyrian treaty of Ashurbanipal with the Arabs of Qedar.[195] Kitchen also addressed

---

194. Kitchen, *On the Reliability of the Old Testament*, 283–94.

195. For a historical summary of the battles and intrigues between Ashurbanipal and the Arabs of Qedar see Eph'al, *Ancient Arabs*, 142–69.

the issue of those scholars who suggest that the curses of the Assyrian period are closer to those found in Deuteronomy than any other period. He maintained that this position could not be sustained because curses and their format was one area that remained fairly consistent over a long period of time, even from the second millennium until the sixth century BCE. Also, he noted that there are only seven curses from the Esarhaddon treaties that could be matched up with those in Deuteronomy 28 while there are fifteen links to those of the early second millennium (cf. Hammurabi [10] and Mari [5]) and six more from the late second millennium. He averred that these facts help tie Deuteronomy with the second millennium more so than the seventh century. Kitchen concluded that all totaled, there were 43 parallels between Deuteronomy and ANE treaty and law codes from the eighteenth to seventh centuries BCE (30 of which are before 1200 BCE) and only six in the seventh century. Kitchen concluded his argument by noting various linguistic terms found in Deuteronomy that he asserts further point to a second millennium date.

Modern Commentaries

The relative silence of scholars over the past 40 years on issues related to treaty and covenant does not mean that one side or the other has "won the day." Perlitt's work was a radical appraisal of the use of covenant in the OT, but it has not changed the overall tenor of scholarship. Modern commentaries on books like Deuteronomy where covenant forms are sure to be addressed generally take one of three positions: 1) either the late date of the treaty form based on the treaties of Esarhaddon (e.g., Miller),[196] 2) the early date for Deuteronomy based on the Hittite form (e.g., Peter Craigie, *The Book of Deuteronomy*; Christopher Wright,

---

196. Miller, *Deuteronomy*. In his commentary Miller asserts, as do most critical scholars, that the dating of Deuteronomy is to be placed in the seventh century. However, he points out that there were older strands in Deuteronomy that came, no doubt, from a northern tradition as Nicholson suggests. He sees the war motif of Deuteronomy as being read back into the history as a reflection of the way the people felt in Josiah's day. The use of the Moses figure is, according to Miller, a means to speak authoritatively to the writer's own day. He also notes McCarthy and Weinfeld's work on the covenant formulary. He acknowledges the influence of the treaty formulary on Deuteronomy but opts for the Neo-Assyrian treaties as the best means of comparison.

Deuteronomy; Earl S. Kalland, *Deuteronomy*),[197] or 3) total ambivalence (e.g., Jeffery Tigay, *Deuteronomy*).[198]

The focus on Deuteronomy, while not the sum total of the treaty debate, does offer a good overview as to where scholarship is presently situated. Further, its importance becomes relevant to our discussion due to the possible connections between the extensive curse and blessing lists found in Deuteronomy 28 and Ezekiel's possible use of them. While the date and earliest form of Deuteronomy may never be proven conclusively, it appears that most agree on the vassal treaty format in Deuteronomy from at least the seventh century onward.[199]

Finally, in light of our assessment above it appears that sound scholarship lies on both sides of the debate. It seems valid when considering the final form of Ezekiel that the author must have had legal material available to him that reflected curse and blessing content in some form from Deuteronomy 28 (Leviticus 26 will be dealt

---

197. Craigie, *Deuteronomy*. Craigie sees the very fact that a treaty form was used to frame Deuteronomy as proof that it was fashioned as such in the second millennium. If Israel just came from being under Egyptian bondage it would only make sense to present the nation as a vassal not to another earthly kingdom but rather to their God, Yahweh. He also notes that the greatest advantage of using the treaty form was that it gained its binding power by being written down and agreed to by the people. The very nature of the covenant renewal would give the proper *Sitz im Leben* for such a work.

Wright, *Deuteronomy*. Wright barely touches on the covenant issue in his introduction. While he lists the key parts of the formula and notes it as a means of establishing the structure, he does not assign it to either a first or second millennium date. Wright does see the dating of the book to Josiah's reform as problematic. This is mainly due to many of the historical features that would allow portions of it to have been written much earlier than 621 BCE. He says that the dating of the book to Josiah's reform is more of a "habit" as opposed to a reliance on the facts. He therefore places it predominantly within the period it suggests, the Mosaic era.

Kalland, *Deuteronomy*. Kalland jumps immediately to a Hittite form between the fourteenth and thirteenth centuries BCE. He points out that suggested dates for Deuteronomy in the historical critical field range from the mid-eighth century to 400 BCE.

198. Tigay, *Deuteronomy*. Tigay writes his commentary from a Jewish perspective. He opts for a date during the reign of Hezekiah, with Deuteronomy written by prophets and priests who fled the Northern Kingdom and came south to promulgate their reforms. They wrote the book during the reforms of Hezekiah and thereafter it lay dormant during the evil reign of Manasseh. When Josiah's reform started, it was ready for the "discovery" and introduction. He does not deal with the covenant format at all in the introduction of his book but rather the dating issue.

199. Frankena, "Vassal-treaties," 152.

with shortly). Whether this came in an early Hittite-type form or in the Neo-Assyrian period or thereafter may never be agreed upon. Nevertheless, the fact remains that as for the question related to the dating of the bulk of Deuteronomy, most scholars adopt a date at least as early as 621 BCE (well before Ezekiel's time). For this reason, I will proceed with the understanding that this is indeed the case and follow the conclusions of the consensus of scholarship.

Ezekiel's Use of Biblical Curse Lists as a Basis for His Indictments

Deuteronomy 26–28

Many scholars have pointed out the role that Deuteronomy or at least the basic knowledge of a "Deuteronomic School" played in the shaping of Ezekiel's thought process. Because we have already noted above that scholars generally seek to present Deuteronomy in its basic shape at least as early as 621 BCE there is no reason not to equate many of Ezekiel's clear references to breach of covenant and the curses with those presented in Deuteronomy.[200] Moreover, it is clear in Deuteronomy 28:15 and 29:27 that the punishment for breaking covenant with Yahweh would bring the "curses" (הַקְּלָלוֹת) of "this book" upon the children of Israel and that the curses would "overtake them" (Deut 28:45). In the case of Ezekiel, one can sense the tenor of judgment from the beginning of the book on account of Judah's covenant violations. Immediately after the vision of ch. 1 Yahweh sends Ezekiel to a rebellious nation to speak of coming judgment on sin (2:3, 5–8).[201] Judgment would take the form of the covenant curses while restoration would incorporate the blessings. Beyond these general parallels the following list helps provide evidence of other more specific intertextual dependencies.

---

200. Stuart, *Hosea-Jonah*, xxxii–xl, gives a detailed list of the curses of the Law, as found predominantly in Deut 28 and Lev 26, which the prophets drew upon in their indictments of Israel and Judah.

201. Fishbane, "Sin and Judgment," 132; or idem, *Interpreting the Prophets*, 170–87, esp. 171.

1. Ezekiel 6:6; 18:6=Deuteronomy 12:1–4: destruction of pagan and idolatrous high places[202]

2. Ezekiel 11:16=Deuteronomy 4:27; 28:49: curse of exile promised

3. Ezekiel 11:20; 36:27=Deuteronomy 6:5; 26:16: restoration promised

4. Ezekiel 5:11; 6:9; 8:10=Deuteronomy 6:10–15; 7:1–5; 8:17–20; 11:16–17: idolatry cursed

5. Ezekiel 16:40; 23:47=Deuteronomy 22:21: stoning of harlots

6. Ezekiel 40–48 present a central sanctuary with the nation dwelling in harmony and close proximity with their God. This in effect is reflective of a Deuteronomic program

7. Ezekiel 20:32=Deuteronomy 28:36, 64: worshipping wood and stone forbidden

8. Ezekiel 20:33, 34=Deuteronomy 4:34; 5:15; 26:8: "With a mighty and outstretched arm"

While this short list is by no means complete, it does show direct connections between Deuteronomy and Ezekiel. The prophet's familiarity with some form of an established law code that is reflected in Deuteronomy seems to be valid. Moreover, terms and motifs that connect the two books (as pointed out by Carley, Fohrer, and more recently Kohn) suggest some general dependence or tradition.[203]

This naturally ties with how the oft-cited priestly law code plays a role in Ezekiel. Many of the indictments overlap between Deuteronomy and Leviticus thus making any attempt to pinpoint the exact origin of a particular indictment difficult. Nevertheless, the "Holiness Code" (i.e., Lev 17–26) and especially ch. 26 does offer another legal foundation for Ezekiel's message.[204]

---

202. Kohn, *New Heart*, 94–95, and Carley, *Ezekiel among the Prophets*, 58, also have seen this connection. Carley, (57–66), discusses the influences of both the Holiness Code and Deuteronomy on Ezekiel.

203. Carley, *Ezekiel among the Prophets*, 57–62; Fohrer and Galling, *Ezechiel*, 61–62, 112; and Kohn, *New Heart*.

204. For a detailed discussion on Ezekiel and the Holiness Code, see Zimmerli, *Ezekiel* 1:46–52. Zimmerli sees "P" and Ezekiel as drawing from a similar tradition (52). Cf. also Lyons, *From Law to Prophecy*.

Leviticus 26 and the "P" Source[205]

The debate over Ezekiel's use of a priestly source has never reached a complete consensus and I will in no way attempt to solve the issue here. Rather, I am seeking to show that a consensus of scholars is beginning to form concerning an early date for the priestly source. Some scholars such as Haran argue that because Ezekiel was a priest, he shared a common "heritage" with the priestly writers.[206] Similarly, Fohrer insisted that both used a common earlier written source.[207] Scholarship of the past two decades has begun to shed new light on this debate and offer more conclusive linguistic evidence that the priestly source/material indeed predates Ezekiel. The extensive debate centered on inter-textual dependence between Ezekiel and the priestly source has tried to answer several plaguing questions. For example, did Ezekiel and the priestly source develop independently of one another? Did Ezekiel rely on the priestly source or was it vice versa? Did both rely on a common older source? Did both develop apart from each other and during later "editorial" work begin to influence each other by editorial insertions?[208] More recently, Risa Levitt Kohn has worked extensively on the parallels between Ezekiel, the priestly source, and the Deuteronomistic school. Her research goes a long way towards clarifying the tensions between the three sources.

In 2002, Kohn undertook a study in which she presents "97 terms, expressions and idioms common to Ezekiel and P" and "27 terms common to Ezekiel and D/Dtr."[209] In her third and fourth chapters (pages 30–95) she examines these connections by doing an inter-textual analysis of terms and concepts such as: Yahweh's relationship to Israel, the covenant, the land, social structure, law, holy days, tabernacle/temple and priesthood, ritual, humans, animals, plants, and legal citations. As for Ezekiel's use of a "P" source she concludes that while it is virtually

---

205. For a detailed and forceful presentation of Ezekiel's use of Lev 26 and the rest of the "Holiness Code" cf. Wong, *Idea of Retribution*, 78–119, 120–95.

206. Haran, "Law Code of Ezekiel," 45–71.

207. Fohrer, *Hauptprobleme*, 144–48. So too the conclusion of Freedy, "Literary Relations," 207 n. 18.

208. Hurvitz, *Linguistic Study*, 14–18, gives a good summary and the pitfalls of these different methodological approaches to Ezekiel and the priestly source. See also idem, "Evidence of Language," 24–56.

209. Kohn, *New Heart*, 4. Cf. also, idem, "Ezekiel, the Exile, and the Torah," 501–26.

impossible to be definitive on which source came first, based on her analysis, Ezekiel must have been "familiar with a Priestly Source . . . [he] knows P, quotes P, but also modifies it at will, adding and deleting material as suits his personal agenda and the current circumstances of his audience."[210]

While Kohn's conclusions are informative and thorough, many times language assigned to a particular source is no more than common expressions in anyone's writing repertoire (e.g., "griddle" [מַחֲבַת]—Ezek 4:4=Lev 2:5; 6:14; 7:9, "turban" [מִצְנֶפֶת]—Ezek 21:31=Lev 8:9; 16:4, or "locks" of hair [פֶּרַע]—Ezek 44:20=Lev 10:6; 13:45).[211] Thus, it is perhaps best to proceed with caution and examine only those expressions that appear germane to our discussion viz., those occurrences where law and covenant seem to find common expression in "P" and Ezekiel.

In 1982 Hurvitz published a detailed literary analysis of these two books/sources in which he adapted a synchronic approach to both sources. While he in no way jettisoned the belief in the "obvious" layers in both sources proposed by the historical critical approach, he did see the futility in developing a theory based upon reconstructed texts and purely hypothetical theories. Hurvitz instead opted for a linguistic approach ("Lower Criticism") that examined the texts in their final forms to see what could be determined about inter-dependence based on purely literary grounds as opposed to stylistic nuances.[212] His linguistic analysis thus rested upon the following three criteria:

1. Elements present in P, for which no parallels at all exist in the corresponding passages of Ezekiel
2. Elements present in Ezekiel, for which no parallels at all exist in the corresponding passages of P;
3. Elements found in one of the two, for which there are alternative elements in the corresponding passages of the other[213]

210. Kohn, *New Heart*, 84–85. Her conclusions about D and Dtr are similar as well, ibid., 95.

211. Ibid., 60–63.

212. Hurvitz, *Linguistic Study*, 146. Hurvitz compares grammatical links between, common lexical terms related to sacrifice, kingship, temple, covenant and oath, anthropomorphisms, and oaths.

213. Ibid., 25. Hurvitz's primary focus is on the differences as opposed to similarities.

Hurvitz concluded that on purely linguistic grounds based on the final form of the texts, Ezekiel appears to have been written *after* the priestly source. He drew this conclusion based upon the late (i.e., exilic) linguistic patterns found in Ezekiel and absent in P. He goes on to postulate that lack of evidence for direct borrowing one way or the other leads him to believe that the common elements in both must have derived from a common earlier source or tradition.[214]

The conclusions of Hurvitz exemplify only one of the varied approaches to the study of Ezekiel and the priestly source, whether that entails the general priestly material or more specifically, the Holiness Code (Lev 17–26) is harder to determine. Nevertheless, his conclusions for an early "P" source are in line not only with Kohn, but also Jacob Milgrom,[215] Mark Rooker,[216] and Menahem Haran[217] and seems to be growing in popularity.[218]

Finally, Haran's work on Ezekiel 40–48 is helpful in bolstering a conclusion for an early P source. Haran stands within the group of scholars who support an Ezekielian provenance for these chapters. He comments, "surely Ezekiel did not compose his code in a vacuum, by

---

214. Ibid., 150. Hurvitz acknowledges the limits of his linguistic analysis by noting the argument that the absence of "late" linguistic elements may have been due in part to a priestly propensity to write in "classical Hebrew" even into the exilic or post-exilic period. Other scholars have put forward the following perspectives: Clements, "Ezekiel Tradition," 128–33 esp. 130, suggests the two traditions may have developed side by side during the exile. Wilson, *Prophecy and Society*, 283–84, sees the influence of pre-exilic Deuteronomic and "Ephraimite" thinking in Ezekiel's prophecies that were shaped by the prophet for his own use. Driver, *Introduction*, 146–47, sees the priestly material, in some form, as before Ezekiel and influencing him; and Kaufmann, *Religion of Israel*, 434–35, suggests that Ezekiel used material from "ancient collections of priestly writings" but "P" and Deuteronomy were still being shaped in the time of Ezekiel.

215. In Milgrom's review of Hurvitz's work he concurs with his final conclusions of an early "P" source noting that they are "irrefutable." See Milgrom, Review of Avi Hurvitz, 118–19. Cf. also idem, *Studies in Levitical Terminology*; idem, *Studies in Cultic Theology*, esp. ix; idem, *Leviticus* (2 vols); idem, *Ritual and Ethics*.

216. Rooker, "Ezekiel and the Typology," 133–53; and idem, *Biblical Hebrew in Transition*.

217. Haran, "The Law Code of Ezekiel," 66, asserts that the "P" source is from the pre-exilic period and was a product of the late first temple period (i.e., some time "preceding Josiah"). This bodes well with the presentation here of cultic laws and covenant codes that were broken by the nation leading to the exile.

218. Zimmerli, "Special Form," 524, points out the possibility of Ezekiel's reliance on earlier priestly traditions and language.

creating something *ex nihilo*, but rather availed himself of a certain heritage."[219] Ezekiel could then take the "ready-made" legal material and adapt it for his composition.[220]

According to Haran the "P" source is very similar to the cultic presentation of Ezekiel—Ezekiel is thus virtually a "miniature" "P" source.[221] Therefore the material of Leviticus 17–26 (i.e., the "Holiness Code")[222] must have been known in at least some incipient form before Ezekiel's prophetic ministry even though it may not have been written in the form as we see it today. Haran concludes,

> the visions in the law-code are the fruit of prophetic imagination (cast in precise architectural moulds), though they are imbued with the priestly ideology and the Jerusalem temple tradition is clearly impressed on them. The laws, by contrast, are based on the priestly legal-cultic heritage, though in this code they are displayed in a prophetic wrapping. The visions are Ezekiel's personal creations, the product of his ecstatic fantasy, and were set down by his own pen. The laws, to be sure, were written by the same hand but they are not merely products of imagination—they relate to certain material; some of them were apparently taken up ready-made, and were adapted by the prophet-priest to his composition.[223]

Based upon the scholarly consensus, I will adopt the conclusions of Kohn, Hurvitz, Haran, Milgrom and Rooker. Ezekiel, as a priest, certainly must have known some form of a cultic Levitical code, which

---

219. Haran, "Law Code of Ezekiel," 47.

220. Ibid., 53.

221. Ibid., 61. While similarities are abundantly clear, Haran goes on, however, to point out the glaring differences between the two (i.e., Ezekiel's law-code and P). He sees these two as dependent upon a similar tradition but not each other per se. He comments, "Ezekiel's code is merely a late and epigonic outgrowth of that same school, the exemplary manifestation of which is exhibited by P" (63).

222. On the argument of the primacy of H versus Ezekiel, see Fohrer, *Hauptprobleme*, 148 n. 67. Fohrer notes "Da die Hälfte der angeblichen ezechielischen Parallelen erst von Redaktorenhand stammt, geht man vielleicht in der Annahme nicht fehl, daß eine Redaktion des Buches Ezechiel durch dieselben Kreise vorgenommen wurde, in denen H entstanden ist." Despite this belief, even though Fohrer assigns at least half of the parallels to later authors, as Carley correctly notes, even this does not lessen the "significance of the relationship" (Carley, *Ezekiel among the Prophets*, 64). It is assumed here that based on the linguistic parallels with that of Leviticus, some form of the Holiness Code was understood at the time of Ezekiel.

223. Haran, "Law Code of Ezekiel," 53.

had to have included some form of Leviticus 17–26. Thus I find the conclusion of Greenberg appropriate to our ongoing discussion. He states, "as when dooming Israel Ezekiel used the language of the covenant curses found at the end of the Book of Leviticus (ch. 26), so when describing their future happiness he uses the idiom of the blessings found there."[224] Thus it is safe to assume that Ezekiel used some form of a pre-existent law code. His indictments had to have rested upon a pre-understanding that Israel was indeed under covenant and cultic law that governed the nation's interaction between itself and its Suzerain.

While the above comments focus on the general nature of the content of the material in Leviticus, a few examples will help highlight some of the specific parallels.[225]

1. Ezek 18:6c; 22:10=Lev 18:19: approaching a menstrual woman
2. Ezek 34:25–31= Lev 26:4–13: peace and blessing promised
3. Ezek 14:8; 15:7=Lev 26:17: Yahweh will set his face against Israel
4. Ezek 24:21; 30:6, 18; 33:28=Lev. 26:19: pride of her power removed
5. Ezek 5:12, 17; 6:11–12; 7:15; 12:16; 14:21=Lev 26:25–26: famine and sword as punishment
6. Ezekiel 6:3–6=Leviticus 26:30: altars and high places destroyed
7. Ezek 22:26=Lev 10:10: priests are upbraided for failing to make a distinction between the holy and profane
8. Ezek 16:60=Lev 26:42, 45: "Remember the covenant"
9. Ezek 16:60, 62=Lev 26:9: "Establish a covenant"
10. Ezek 34:25; 37:26=Num 25:12: "Covenant of peace"
11. Ezek 18:19, 21; 36:27=Lev 26:3; 25:18: "keep" and "observe" the statutes and ordinances of Yahweh

224. Greenberg, "Design and Themes," 182.

225. I am indebted to Kutsko's and Kohn's works (*Between Heaven and Earth*, 11–12, and *New Heart*, 35–37, 42–47 respectively) in pointing out many of these parallels. Cf. also the detailed list of parallels between Ezekiel and Lev 26 by Driver, *Introduction to the Literature of the OT*, 147; Wong, *Retribution*, 80–86; and the comments of Kaufmann, *Religion of Israel*, 440, who links Lev 26 and Ezekiel. Wong's chart is by far the most detailed and extensive.

12. Ezek 20:18; 36:27=Lev 26:3; 20:23: following the statutes of the Lord

13. Ezek 16:37; 22:10; 23:10, 18, 29=Lev 18:6–19; 20:19–21: "uncovering someone's nakedness"

14. Ezek 5:10, 15; 11:9; 16:41; 28:22, 26; 30:14, 19=Exod 6:6; 7:4; 12:12 (designated as a part of the "P" source)

15. Ezek 18:13; 33:5=Lev 20:9, 11–13, 16: "His/Their blood upon Him/Them"

16. Ezek 4:4–6; 14:10; 18:19–20; 44:10, 12=Lev 5:1, 17; 10:17; 16:22; 17:16; 19:8; 20:17; 22:16; Num 5:31; 9:13; 14:18, 34; 18:1, 23; 30:16 and Exod 28:38: "To bear guilt"

17. Ezek 14, 18, 20=Lev 26:39: Those who follow in the sins of their fathers will bear their own sin and the sin of their fathers

As we can see from the above discussion it appears that Ezekiel must have had some legal material available to him. Moreover, in light of Ezekiel's propensity to rely on covenant terminology and curses, it seems appropriate at this juncture to look briefly at both the ANE and Ezekiel's use of covenant terminology.

Terminology[226]

In the discussions of covenant, treaty, and curses a wide range of meanings and implications are present in the definitions and nuances presented by different scholars. Terms such as "treaty," "covenant," and "law" have different nuances in a particular setting. For us, the concept of covenant and treaty needs to be clarified when discussing treaty curses and covenant language in Ezekiel, especially in light of ANE treaties.[227]

---

226. For a detailed discussion on blessing and curse terminology in inscriptions from Syria-Palestine during the Iron Age, cf. Crawford, *Blessing and Curse*, esp. ch. 2. Crawford lists nine important scholars who have contributed to this field of study. These include: Pederson, *Israel*; Mowinckel, *Psalms in Israel Worship*; Hempel, "Die israelitische Anschauungen," 30–113; Westermann, *Blessing in the Bible*; Wehmeier, *Segen*; Scharbert, "ארר," "אלה," and "ברך," in vols. 1 and 2 of the *TDOT*; Brichto, *Problem of "Curse"*; Thiselton, "Supposed Power of Words," 283–99; and Mitchell, *Meaning of BRK*. For a further discussion of the "conditionality" aspects in OT covenants, see Waltke, "Phenomenon of Conditionality," 123–49.

227. See also Fensham, "Maledictions," 2–9, for clarification of terms.

Akkadian and Hebrew Covenant/Treaty Terms[228]

The Akkadian term *adê* (i.e., "treaty"—lexical form *adû*) in vassal-treaty contracts was common throughout the ANE.[229] The *Chicago Assyrian Dictionary* defines *adû* in the context of a treaty/agreement as an "agreement drawn up in writing between a partner of higher status (god, king, member of the royal family) and servants or subjects. It was typically made sure by magic and religious means (ceremonies, curses and oaths)."[230] It appears that the *adû* agreement was primarily a "unilateral" or "imposed" agreement placed upon a vassal by a king.[231] In many cases the *adû* "agreement" included clear reference to curses if the agreement was broken. For example, in a text from the reign of Ashurbanipal we read, "Aššur, Sin (and the other gods) (quickly) inflicted upon them all the curses that have been inscribed in (the tablet of) their *adû* agreement."[232] The concept of coupling oaths and curses with an agreement is a common feature in ANE treaties.[233] In the case of Israel's "agreement" with Yahweh, curses played a fundamental part in the covenant stipulations as well (cf. Lev 26 and Deut 28).

228. For a discussion of the Akkadian and Near Eastern terms for covenant making see Tadmor, "Treaty and Oath," 130–40. For a detailed discussion on the multiple terms and their nuances connoting covenant in the OT, see Kalluveettil, *Declaration and Covenant*, esp. 7–57.

229. The eighth-century Neo-Assyrian term *adê* took the place of the earlier *riksu u mamītu* (lit. "bond and oath"). Cf. Tadmor, "Treaty and Oath," 132.

230. *CAD*, A 1, page 133. Also, Tadmor, "Treaty and Oath," 135, avers that the western Semitic practice of killing a dog (*mīrānum*) and a she-goat (*ḫazzum*) was commonly used to solemnize an oath. Tadmor insists that the meaning of *ḫazzum* is "she-goat" and not "lettuce" as suggested previously by Mendenhall. Cf. Mendenhall, "Puppy and Lettuce," 26–30.

231. Frankena, "Vassal-treaties," 134. Frankena gives several examples from Assyrian and Akkadian to define the interrelationships between suzerain and vassals (see esp. 134–40).

232. *CAD*, A 1, page 132. Text in *CAD* from M. Streck, Ashurbanipal, 76 ix 60 in Harper, *Assyrian and Babylonian Letters 7*.

233. So important were the oaths of their vassals to ruling kings that severe measures would be taken to enforce the curses of the oath when and if they were broken. During the period of Esarhaddon, one of his vassals who ruled Shubria, north of Assyria, apparently aided some of Esarhaddon's enemies. When Esarhaddon attacked the unfaithful vassal, the latter proposed an unconditional surrender and begged for clemency. Esarhaddon would not hear of it. He insisted that the "rebellious vassal who harboured Esarhaddon's enemies should bear the full onus of his betrayal of the loyalty oaths" (cf. Tadmor, "Autobiographical Apology," 43). For reference to the text itself, see Borger, *Inschriften*, §68 I:3.

Nevertheless, in the case of Israel, the use of the concept of "treaty" (as defined in *CAD*) does not define Israel and Yahweh's relationship in the best manner. The definition presented in *CAD* focuses on a unilateral arrangement while Israel's covenant was mutually agreed upon (e.g., Exod 24:7–8). That is perhaps why "covenant" is the best choice when defining the relational aspect between Yahweh and his people.[234] We will return to this distinction below. What is important to note here is that the curses of the covenant, as invoked by the prophet Ezekiel, were a well-known feature not only in ANE "agreements" but also in the agreement between Israel and her God.[235] The people had no excuse or recourse for what befell them in the exile.

Next, the language for establishing a covenant is consistent across cultures from the Akkadian period until the Roman period.[236] This can be seen in a wide range of terms found in languages of the ANE. Here we will focus on Hebrew, Akkadian, and some Aramaic (in the footnotes).

In Hebrew, the use of the phrase "to establish/make (lit. "to cut") a covenant" (כָּרַת בְּרִית)[237] shows that covenant formulary is in play. Also the concept of formally concluding a covenant, namely "entered into a covenant," (בּוֹא בִבְרִית)[238] had the same force as the former aspect (cf. Jer 34:10; Ezek 16:8; 17:13; 20:37; Neh 10:30; 2 Chr 15:12). Similarly, the terminology for breaking a covenant has cognate terms across Hebrew and Akkadian usage: Hebrew—הֵפֵר בְּרִית "to break/shatter a treaty"

---

234. Cf. also Walton, *Ancient Israelite Literature*, 95.

235. Even later at Qumran, the curses of the covenant were a means of keeping its members loyal to the community. Cf. Nitzan, "Blessing and Cursing," 95–100, esp. 96. For further thematic and textual comparisons between Ezekiel and Qumran material, cf. Eybers, "The Book of Ezekiel," 1–9.

236. Cf. Weinfeld, "Covenant Terminology," 190–99.

237. In Aramaic and Akkadian several forms of covenant establishing terminology are attested: 1) *śym bryt*—Hebrew for "make a covenant" (2 Sam 23:5) and in Akkadian *adê šakanu*, and Aramaic *śym 'ady'* (Sefire I A:7). 2) *ntn byrt*—Hebrew "give a covenant" (Gen 9:12; 17:2; Num 25:12) in Akkadian—*riksa nadānu*. 3) *hyqm bryt*—Hebrew "establish a covenant" (Gen 6:18; 9:9, 17; 17:7, 19; Exod 6:4; Lev 26:9; Deut 8:18; 2 Kgs 23:3; Jer 34:18). Cf. Weinfeld, "Covenant Terminology," 196–97. Also Tadmor, "Treaty and Oath," 136, points out the corresponding Aramaic phrase *gzr 'dn* (גזר עדן) to the Hebrew *krt bryt*. Tadmor, "Treaty and Oath" 137, goes on to aver that the concept of "cutting" a covenant was primarily a west Semitic concept where the eastern Mesopotamian concept of covenant solemnizing was more rooted in the idea of "binding" a party to a treaty and "establishing" a covenant with them.

238. Akkadian—*ina adê erebu*.

(cf. Ezek 17:15, 19) and Akkadian—*māmīta parāṣu*.[239] This is further delineated by terms such as: 1) עָבַר ("to trespass") and Akkadian—*māmīta etēqu*; 2) עָזַב בְּרִית ("to abandon the covenant"—cf. 1 Kgs 19:10) and Akkadian—*riksa wuššuru*, and 3) שֶׁקֶר בְּרִית ("to be false to the covenant"—cf. Pss 44:18 and 89:34).[240] Finally, the Hebrew terms for violation of a covenant or "negligence/disrespect" to it are מָאַס and בָּזָה ("to despise"), terms that are found in 2 Kgs 17:15; Ezek 16:59; 17:16, 19.[241] The Ezekielian passages will be dealt with shortly.

In examining the basic covenant terminology for making and breaking covenants in the Hebrew and Akkadian languages we find common literary links between the OT and Mesopotamian usage. Weinfeld places the date of the origin of these links, among others, to the mid-second millennium which is expressed in the Egyptian and Hittite treaties along with Egyptian and Assyrian contacts. He concludes that the origins of the terms must be in the East and early.[242] In agreeing with Weinfeld's perspective that covenant and treaty forms were early, there is good reason to assume that Israel's relationship with her God was defined in similar terms.

Covenant Language in Ezekiel

In the case of Ezekiel, beyond the clear use of covenant terminology in chs. 16, 17, 20:37, 44:7, 34:25, and 37:26 (the latter two focusing on the new covenant), there are several other terms and phrases that point to vassalage and the broken oaths of secular treaties and/or the covenant with Yahweh. Moreover, treaty terminology describing the relationships between Judah and the nations can be found in Ezekiel as well (e.g., 17:11–21; 21:23–29 [Heb]). We see the covenant concept of vassalage in the following instances: 1) "vassal kingdom" (מַמְלָכָה שְׁפָלָה literally, "a weak kingdom") in 17:14 and 29:15, 2) the concept of "the remembrance of guilt" (מַזְכִּיר עָוֹן) through perjury against the treaty in 21:28 (Heb) and 29:16, and 3) "being captured in" (וְנִתְפַּשׂ בְּ) the snare of

239. Weinfeld, "Covenant Terminology," 197. Also, Fensham, "Maledictions," 5, notes the similarities between the Hebrew verb *prr* and the Akkadian equivalent, *parāru*.

240. See Fitzmyer, "Aramaic Suzerainty Treaty," 450–51, for a similar rendering found in the Sefire III stele.

241. Weinfeld, "Covenant Terminology," 197.

242. Ibid., 197–99.

deception related to the broken oaths of vassaldom (cf. 17:20).[243] Block also observed that the term *bĕrît* appears 17 times in Ezekiel (six of these in ch. 17 to refer to Zedekiah's covenant with Nebuchadnezzar) whereas *'ammî* ("my people") occurs 25 times in the book.[244] He goes on to point out that,

> The covenantal basis for his [i.e., Yahweh's] relationship with the nation is evident not only in the prophet's designation of Israel as *'ammî*, "my people," but also in numerous citations of and allusions to the covenant formula "I will be your God, and you shall be my people" (11:20; 14:11; 34:24, 30–31; 36:28; 37:23) and explicit references to the covenant itself. Because his compatriots treated Yahweh's covenant promises to Israel as unconditional guarantees of security, the prophet spends chs. 1–24 seeking to debunk this illusory conviction. Apart from faith in the covenant Lord and obedience to the terms of the covenant, there is no safety either from human enemies or from Yahweh himself. Israel is a "rebellious" family (*bêt mĕrî*), whose wickedness exceeds the abominable practices of the heathen nations (5:5–7; 16:44–53). Because the nation has rejected his covenant standards (*mišpāṭîm*) and ordinances (*ḥuqqôt*), Yahweh will impose upon them the covenant curses spelled out in Lev. 26 and Deut. 28. The people's rebellion has become so intense that no screaming for help will move him to pity (Ezek. 8:18; 9:10; 24:14).[245]

Block has delineated the key factors of the argument that are present in Ezekiel's indictments of Yahweh's people. It is vital to understand that the prophecies in the book of Ezekiel are indeed based upon the premise that the nation *is* in covenant with Yahweh. Also, the covenant indictments (i.e., the *rîb* formula)[246] of earlier prophets appear to pre-

243. Tsevat, "Vassal Oaths," 201.

244. For a discussion on the use of *'am* for Israel in the Hebrew Bible, see Speiser, "'People' and 'Nation,'" 157–63, esp. 157–60.

245. Block, *Ezekiel 1–24*, 48–49.

246. See Cross, "Council of Yahweh," 274–75 n. 3 for a brief discussion on the *rîb* formula. Harvey, *Le Plaidoyer*, 119–28, 170–72, looks at the covenant lawsuit format in the *Tukulti-Ninurta Epic* and establishes sound structural parallels between it and the biblical *rîb* form. See also the work of Huffmon, "Covenant Lawsuit," 285–95, for biblical evidence. Huffmon argues that the calling of heaven, earth, and the mountains as witnesses against a guilty party is not a reference to the "divine council" as per Cross, "Council of Yahweh," 274–77, and Wright, *Old Testament against Its Environment*, 36, but rather a direct reference to the actual earthly elements which

suppose a covenantal relationship between Israel and her God (cf. Isa 1:41–46 and 48; Mic 1:2–7; 6:1–8 and Amos 3).[247]

Finally, Block is correct in noting that the indictments in the book of Ezekiel are not to be seen as an abandonment of the covenant by Yahweh but rather the "strict adherence to its fine print. Israel has brought on itself the covenant curses by trampling underfoot the covenant grace of Yahweh (16:15–43)."[248] Israel had to come to the knowledge that the covenant was not unconditional as presented in the erroneous belief in the inviolability of Jerusalem, but rather was rooted in the fact that both Yahweh *and* the people had to remain faithful to the covenant. It is obvious that the hope of Ezekiel was to show the exiles that the false hopes of an early return and the inviolability of Jerusalem were ill founded. Yahweh had kept his part of the covenant but Israel had rescinded on her end. While they may have misunderstood the demands of the covenant, not from lack of warning but rather from voluntary "ignorance," they were in no way exculpated from the awaiting punishment of the covenant curses.

With a high degree of certitude we can conclude that Ezekiel was well aware of covenant formulary and used it in his indictments of Judah. However, beyond the slight nuances of treaty and covenant, law also plays a role in our understanding of Ezekiel. For the sake of my argument, I will follow Kitchen's definitions and distinctions as they relate to these three concepts while keeping in mind the Hebrew

---

are part of the phenomena invoked in the blessings and curses (291–92). He gives evidence of this from the Hittite treaties of the second millennium and Deut 4:26; 30:19 and 31:28.

247. See also the discussion about these and other indictment passages by Phillips, "Prophecy and Law," 217. I cannot, however, agree with Phillips's rejection of the possibility of the prophets' use of curse motifs from much earlier suzerainty formats. The *rib* formula seems to rest upon just such a prehistory; whether written or oral, one cannot be certain. Moreover, Phillips's exclusion of covenant offences such as idolatry as "redactional" in the indictments of Isaiah 1, Amos 3 and Micah 6, while affirming only the indictments of injustice and antihumanitarianism, appears arbitrary and unsupported (cf. 222). Indeed, the entire notion that a lack of direct reference to "covenant" and legal terms implies a lack of the covenant understanding at an earlier period appears to be an "argument from silence." Also, his oversight of the clear covenant language of Hos 6:7 and 8:1, which again he credits to the hand of a "redactor" (226), appears to reflect "special pleading." Interestingly, Wright, *Against its Environment*, 60, argues that Israel's special role in promoting proper humanitarian response arises from the very moral nature of the covenant itself.

248. Block, *Ezekiel 1–24*, 49.

and Akkadian cognate parallels and the technical definitions in *CAD*. Thus, Kitchen points out that what took place at Sinai was neither "law" nor "treaty" but was a "confluence of these two, producing a further facet in group relationships, namely, social-political-religious covenant. Law, treaty, and covenant in this context are three parts of a triptych. Law regulates relations between members of a group within the group. Treaty regulates the relations between the members of two groups politically distinct (or, with vassals, originally so). Covenant . . . regulates relations between a group and its ruling deity."[249] Because covenant was the means by which a nation had relationship with its deity and law was a means of regulating relations between individuals, covenant appears to define most appropriately the relational aspects between Yahweh and Israel on the whole. Treaties between a person of higher status and a vassal would also have been well known to Israel based upon clear references to treaties in the OT and the ANE but fail to paint a true picture of the relationship between Yahweh and Israel.[250] As for law and its relationship to covenant, many are now recognizing its expanded role both inside and outside of the covenant formulary.[251] Law does indeed regulate relations between members of society, both ancient and modern; however, in the context of covenant it served as stipulations (enforced by the curses) from the suzerain to the vassal—in our case, Yahweh to his people.

Summary

To summarize, both prior to and during Ezekiel's ministry, treaties were a common trend in cross-cultural relations. This reality could easily have influenced Ezekiel's ministry especially in light of the numerous extant and fragmented Neo-Assyrian and Neo-Babylonian treaties. It appears that the latter borrowed from the former with the

249. Kitchen, *Reliability*, 289. Compare also the definition of Lundquist, "Temple, Covenant, and Law," 293. Lundquist defines law, covenant, and temple as such: "the temple founds (legitimizes) the state; covenant binds the foundation; law underlies the covenant." See also the discussion by Niehaus, *Ancient Near Eastern Themes*, 56–57.

250. Cf. 1 Kgs 15:19; 2 Chr 16:3; Josh 9; 1 Sam 11:1; 2 Sam 21:2; 1 Kgs 5:12; 20:34; Ezek 17; Hos 12:1 etc. Note also in the Annals of Esarhaddon where Manasseh is mentioned as bearing gifts/tribute to the new king of Assyria after the death of Sennacherib. See Borger, *Asarhaddons*, 60, §27: Nin. Episode 21 line 55b "*Me-na-si-i šàr^{uru}Ia-ú-di*").

251. Walton, *Ancient Near Eastern Thought*, 287–302.

strong possibility of both finding their roots in earlier treaty formats between a suzerain and his vassal (e.g., Hittite). The vassal-treaty was the means by which suzerain nations controlled vassal nations. Sometimes the formation of a treaty created friendship between the parties, but in most cases the imposed treaty caused resentment and severe consequences if the binding oath (i.e., Akk. *māmītu*) was broken.[252] Frankena puts it well when he states, "After its being sworn the oath becomes something solid, a thing having power over the person who has sworn the oath. When the oath remains unbroken, it will stay without danger for him, but the oath automatically changes itself into something dangerous, when the oath is not guarded. The curse inherent in every oath (*adê, māmītu*)[253] or the curse in action (*arratu*)[254] becomes immediately effective and hits the person who breaks his oath."[255] In the OT, the curses of the covenant had long been delayed due to Yahweh's longsuffering nature but they were not forgotten (cf. 2 Kgs 22:19–20). After the deportation of Ezekiel, the prophet recognized that the curses had finally begun to be enacted as promised by God in earlier times. It was in the reality of the exile that the prophet Ezekiel became a unique spokesman of Yahweh to reveal the curses of the covenant. Thus, one should not be surprised to find his prophecy laden with curse imagery and containing covenant language.

Moreover, with so many possible parallels between Ezekiel and the books of Leviticus and Deuteronomy we may safely conclude that Ezekiel must have had some understanding of legal material and the use of covenant indictments. His organization of these warnings and indictments in a visionary and metaphorical framework helped highlight the general tenor of his message. The prophet's rhetorical technique is second to none and requires further study in order to

---

252. Frankena, "Vassal-treaties," 137–38.

253. These are parallel to the Hebrew terms for "oath" שְׁבוּעָה and אָלָה; cf. Josh 9:15 and Gen 26:28 respectively. Also note that when שְׁבוּעָה and אָלָה are used together אָלָה can be interpreted as "curse," cf. Dan 9:11 and Neh 10:30. For a detailed linguistic study of these and many other terms related to taking oaths and effecting a curse, see Brichto, *Problem of "Curse,"* note esp. 22–39, 215–18.

254. These are parallel to the Hebrew term for "curse" קְלָלָה. Frankena points out an important difference between the biblical parallels and the ANE use of the concept of cursing. He avers that "contra-magic" i.e., magic to counter the curses of treaties, was common in the ANE and was thus banned by the suzerain. In the OT contra-magic is never mentioned explicitly (Frankena, "Vassal-treaties," 138).

255. Ibid., 137.

appreciate the full impact of the message. It is to this rhetorical agenda that we now turn our attention as a part of our methodological approach.

Rhetorical/Literary[256]

My fourth methodological approach will focus on the possible rhetorical strategy of the compiler of the final form of Ezekiel.[257] I will begin by examining the recent trends within Ezekielian scholarship to study the book in its final form as well as the benefits of such an endeavor. (I must admit at the outset that the most "fruit," for the Church and the academy, seems to be gained from literary approaches that take seriously the canonical shape of the book.) Next, I will examine the visionary and extended metaphor framework to determine if there was a deliberate attempt by the compiler to deliver an overarching message apart from its constituent parts. Finally, I will examine the oft-held assumptions about the structure of the book and then propose my own structure along with the proposed framework and "peaks" that will be argued throughout.

Recent Trends in Ezekielian Scholarship: A Return to the Past?

The history of Ezekielian scholarship has been varied in relation to the unity and literary value of the final form. In this vein, Smend in 1880 commented that the book of Ezekiel was a well thought-out and systematic unity that would be destroyed if one part was removed.[258]

---

256. See Moore, "Rhetorical Analysis," as noted by Enns, "Abstracts," 362. For a helpful study on prophetic rhetoric, see Fox, "Rhetoric of Ezekiel's Vision," 1–15, esp. 1–10.

257. I must stress at the outset that there is strong evidence based on the unity of the book that the "compiler" may very well have been the prophet himself.

258. Smend, *Prophet Ezechiel*, xxi. Smend states, "The whole book is the logical development of a series of ideas according to a well-considered and to some extent schematic plan: no part could be taken away without destroying the whole ensemble. Just observe the correspondence between ch. 1 and chs. 8–11 . . . as well as the strict logical connection and advance in the several divisions of the book . . . which, moreover, is also characterized by the recurrence and fuller exposition of the same images . . . and the same significant turns of phrase. Thus it is highly probable that the whole book was written down all of a piece." As cited by Stalker, *Ezekiel*, 19. See also Gunkel

Near the end of the nineteenth century S. R. Driver also commented that "no critical question arises in connection with the authorship of the book, the whole from beginning to end bearing unmistakably the stamp of a single mind."[259] However, the position of scholars such as Smend and Driver was not to last as source and literary critics turned their focus on Ezekiel. While much of critical scholarship of the late nineteenth century and beyond concerned itself with trying to isolate and identify the "original" words of the prophet, little consensus has arisen. This impasse has no doubt contributed to the more recent trend towards studying the book in its present, final form (i.e., a canonical or "holistic" approach).

In the past four decades, there has been a refocusing on how to best approach the study of the Old Testament. Indeed Muilenburg's landmark address to the Society of Biblical Literature in 1968 and his subsequent article in 1969, "Form-Criticism and Beyond," opened the door for rhetorical approaches to the text in which larger sections of a given book could be scrutinized for linguistic patterns that helped shape the final form of the text.[260] Muilenburg and others realized that intense historical-critical approaches, while valid at times, often left the reader with more questions than answers. Since this refocusing some four decades ago, the historical-critical approaches to the text have given way, to a certain degree, to the new canonical approach.[261]

Brevard Childs led this charge noting the need to understand a text as it appears before us in its final form and in its position in the canon.[262] Thus we can safely say that Childs (1923–2007) is to the ca-

---

and Gray who held to the unity of the text as well. Cf. Gray, *Critical Introduction*, 198; and Gunkel, "Israelitische Literatur," 82. Interestingly, Joyce, *Ezekiel*, 7, points out that Gunkel asserted that Ezekiel was "the first prophet who wrote a book."

259. Driver, *Introduction*, 279.

260. Muilenburg, "Form Criticism and Beyond," 1–18. Muilenburg's focus on the larger sections of text within a given book paved the way for the focus on the book as a whole, i.e., the entire book and how it is made up of constituent rhetorical parts.

261. The general trend in German scholarship (e.g., Pohlmann, Becker, Sedlmeier, Hossfeld, Krüger) appears still to be focused on a diachronic approach as opposed to a synchronic approach adopted by many North American scholars of the past few decades. A similar conclusion is reached by Robson, *Word and Spirit*, 8 n. 22, and Boadt, "Mythological Themes," 211.

262. Childs, *Introduction*, 355–72. Childs's assessment of biblical books from a canonical perspective revolutionized the way in which scholars looked at not only this book, but the entire OT. While Childs still embraced much of the form-critical and

nonical approach as Hermann Gunkel (1862–1932) was to the form critical approach. Indeed many are coming to the conclusion that this form of textual analysis is meritorious and valid especially when approached with a systematic methodology. As Joyce aptly notes "This position is by no means necessarily a flight into naïve conservatism; its proponents are generally skilled in the use of historical-critical methods but believe them no longer adequate to the task, and instead resort to other critical methods, sometimes including structural analysis and rhetorical criticism."[263] Studies in Ezekiel have been no different as numerous scholars are beginning to look at the book as a unified whole with an intended ordering of chapters as opposed to a divided hodgepodge of stories, oracles, sermons, sign acts, and visions. Today, even those scholars who reject an exilic date for Ezekiel and argue for a series of redactions in the post-exilic period recognize the merits of such an approach.[264] Pohlmann even goes so far as to say that there is no doubt that the final form of the book as we have it should be regarded as a well-planned composition.[265]

It was Moshe Greenberg who championed the "holistic" perspective by viewing Ezekiel as a unified whole that needs to be read as it appears before us.[266] He proposes, as did many a century ago, that Ezekiel is the "product of art and intelligent design."[267] He insists that in order to gain a full appreciation of the text and the message one must listen to the book the way the final author(s) handed it down to us.[268] He

---

historical-critical tenets, the methodology employed and conclusions often drawn by such approaches were inadequate in his mind to really address the needs of the biblical exegete. For example, he saw in the final form of Ezekiel the accruence of Israel's "experience" that became a vital part of the canonical whole.

263. Joyce, *Ezekiel*, 15.

264. Pohlmann, *Ezechiel*, 32, notices the possibilities of studying the text synchronically but is quick to point out that a diachronic approach has its benefits.

265. Pohlmann, *Das Buch*, 26. Pohlmann goes on to qualify his statement by noting that just because the final form may be ordered and coherent does not prove that the earlier forms were such (27).

266. Greenberg has written two volumes on Ezekiel, the first appeared in 1983 (chs. 1–20), the second in 1997 (chs. 21–37) and the final volume was written by Jacob Milgrom prior to his passing in 2010.

267. Greenberg, *Ezekiel 1–20*, 26.

268. Greenberg does lean toward Ezekielian authorship for the majority, if not all, of the book. However, not all scholars who adhere to a "holistic" approach go this far. For example, Clements, "Chronology," 288–89, sees validity in Greenberg's holistic approach but rejects the position that attributes the majority of the book to the

also upbraids modern critical scholarship for their arbitrary and *a priori* assumptions about what is authentic and inauthentic to the text of Ezekiel.[269] For Greenberg, thematic, stylistic features, and literary patterns used by the author point to a unity many times overlooked or purposely sidestepped by strict historical critical approaches.

This synchronic or "holistic" approach to Ezekiel has found favor among scholars of the past thirty years. These include, among others, Boadt, Niditch, Davis, Matties, Bodi, Galambush, Stevenson, Renz, Kutsko, Levitt Kohn, and more recently, James Robson. While some of these authors have written focused articles on the use of rhetorical strategies in Ezekiel, others devote entire monographs to Ezekiel, or portions of it, using the approach.

Boadt has adopted the approach by looking at the appearance of word pairs and repetition throughout the oracles of Ezekiel.[270] He suggests that these word pairs and repetitions point to a rhetorical strategy of the author that reflects unity within the text. Later he argued that the rhetorical approach to larger blocks of material in Ezekiel (e.g., chs. 15–19 and 25–32) could also help prove the unity of the overall book.[271] Boadt again looked to repetitions and similarity in theme and content to bolster his position.

Similarly, Niditch also applied the holistic approach to her analysis of the rhetorical system of Ezekiel as found in chs. 40–48.[272] She noted continuity in language and theme with the rest of the book (esp.

---

prophet himself. Clements insists that the presence of hope oracles mixed with oracles of doom prove that they were reworked for a later purpose (290–91). However, are we to assume by Clements's assertion that a sixth-century audience (or later) could not grasp a message of doom and hope in one oracle?

269. Greenberg, "Valid Criteria," 123–35. Greenberg (134–35) does list a few possible areas where editorial work may have occurred in Ezekiel. However, even these he approaches with caution based upon the unexplainable inclusion of glaring historical inconsistencies in the final form dealing with the lack of fulfillment of Ezekiel's prophecies (e.g., the pattern of the temple construction which never materialized and the lack of cult reform).

270. Boadt, "Textual Analysis," 489–99. See also Cassuto, "Arrangement," 1:227–40, and Duguid, *Ezekiel and the Leaders*, 142–43, who both argue for the unity of Ezekiel in a similar vein.

271. Boadt, "Rhetorical Strategies," 182–200. See also his similar presentation dealing with the oracles against Egypt in *Ezekiel's Oracles*.

272. Niditch, "Ezekiel 40–48," 208–24.

chs. 38–39) and thus argued for the possible inclusion of these oft-contested chapters in the overall book of Ezekiel.

Perhaps one of the most helpful literary approaches to the book of Ezekiel came in 1989 with the work of Ellen Davis.[273] She builds upon the work of Ewald (1841) and Orelli (1896) and highlights the uniqueness of Ezekiel's literary presentation. Her methodology is anchored in the assumption that the text as we have it, while perhaps modified over time, was not far from the form of the original composition. Any additions to the text were of minor consequence while the message of the original prophet remained intact. Thus, for Davis, Ezekiel was not so much a prophet who delivered oral pronouncements but was rather a literary prophet. The completed book was a literary work that functioned in and of itself as a prophecy in the same way the oral pronouncements of the classical prophets did before they too became codified in a written form. She avers that the act of swallowing the "scroll" (cf. 3:1) reflected the ingestion of the written record (i.e., the book of Ezekiel itself) that contained the ensuing judgments that Yahweh was going to pour out upon Judah.[274]

While I can concur with Davis on many points in her assessment of the literary techniques of the prophet, I am unwilling to suggest with Davis that the first presentation of the prophecy was merely in a written form especially in light of Ezekiel 20:49 and 33:30–33.[275] I would

---

273. Davis, *Swallowing the Scroll*. See also Becker, "Erwägungen," 139, who propounds that Ezekiel is entirely a "prophetic interpretation developed at the desk" during the Greek period. Jong, "Literary Figure," 1–16, follows the work of Davis and Becker by suggesting a literary as opposed to a historical setting for much of the book. He concludes that the book is, "by and large, a compositional unity" (15).

274. The issue of the exact role the scroll plays in defining Ezekiel's message finds a wide range of interpretations among scholars. However, it is perhaps the interpretation of Odell that best fits Ezekiel's presentation. Odell "You Are What You Eat," 244, asserts that the scroll is not representative of a fixed written word per se but rather represents the "fixed and unchanging," pronouncement of Yahweh. Thus, judgment is coming upon Jerusalem with no means of escape. She concludes, "Ezekiel cannot avert the judgment, and so he is left with a bellyful of inchoate mourning and pain (3:14–15)" (245). This conclusion resonates with my position that the covenant curse (i.e., judgment) is being enacted without reprieve.

275. Wilson, *Prophecy and Society*, 285, suggests that as Ezekiel's message became more and more unpopular, he resorted to writing his message as a means of "expressing his views." He further notes that the complexity of the oracles makes it more probable that they were delivered in a written form. While Wilson's views can perhaps be assumed for some final form of the text, we can still, quite soundly, propose that many of the visions and sign acts were indeed part of a public, oracular ministry

Methodology and Literary Technique 81

admit, however, that the final, completed, written form would have had more prophetic punch than earlier individual oracles.[276] While many have critiqued Davis's work, most notably the analysis of K. P. Darr,[277] it still seems appropriate at this juncture to point out a couple vital flaws in Davis's proposed hypothesis.[278]

First, the basis of Davis's argument rests upon the assumption that Ezekiel's "dumbness" (אָלַם) in 3:26, while metaphorical,[279] was proof that Ezekiel did not prophesy to the exiles until after his "speech" is reinstituted in 33:22. He therefore wrote the entire prophecy *before* he ministered using it as a means to declare Yahweh's words. Now at first glance it does appear that Ezekiel was mute during this period but it was more than metaphorical. The address by Yahweh in 3:26 has to be understood within the context of v. 27. Verse 27 makes it clear that when the word of the Lord would come upon Ezekiel, Yahweh would open his mouth to speak ("but when I speak to you I will open your mouth"—וּבְדַבְּרִי אוֹתְךָ אֶפְתַּח אֶת־פִּיךָ).[280] Therefore, the exiles would understand it was Yahweh speaking and not the prophet because at all other times Ezekiel would be mute. We see this bolstered by the oft-cited phrase, "the word of the Lord came to me" which appears at the beginning of every prophecy in the book.[281] Interestingly, this phrase is

---

(cf. 33:30–33). One need only look to the distress of the prophet directed to God in 20:49 where the people were mocking him for his prophetic style as one who spoke in parables. So too the conclusion of Streane, *Ezekiel*, xxiii.

276. For a similar conclusion see Boadt, "Mythological Themes," 215.

277. Darr has critiqued Davis's essay "Swallowing Hard," in the compendium of essays titled *Signs and Wonders*, edited by J. C. Exum. This essay by Davis follows many of the tenets of her book *Swalowing the Scroll*. For the critique, see Darr, "Write or True?" 239–47.

278. For a further critique of Davis, see Odell, "You Are What You Eat," 242–43.

279. Davis, *Swallowing the Scroll*, 49.

280. So too Robson, *Word and Spirit*, 40–66, esp. 59. See also Greenberg, *Ezekiel 1–20*, 120–21. Greenberg sees the prophet's confinement in his house as a part of the silence he was to keep. He interprets Ezekiel's "dumbness" as a command from Yahweh not to speak words of warning unless directed by the Lord. This restriction is lifted after the fall of Jerusalem and the prophet is free to speak. Greenberg's association of *piṯḥon pe* ("opening of the mouth") with Mishnaic Hebrew is insightful but perhaps beyond the straight forward interpretation suggested by the text itself which we will adopt here. Cf. also Wilson, "Interpretation," 91–104.

281. Cf. 3:16; 6:1; 7:1; 11:14; 12:1, 8, 17, 21, 26; 13:1; 14:2, 12; 15:1; 16:1; 17:1, 11; 18:1; 20:2, 45; 21:1, 8, 18; 22:1, 17, 23; 23:1; 24:1, 15, 20; 25:1; 26:1; 27:1; 28:11, 20; 29:1, 17; 30:20; 31:1; 32:1, 17; 33:1, 23; 34:1; 35:1; 36:16; 38:1. Robson, *Word and*

excluded from the beginning of the sign acts of chs. 4–5[282] and the extended visions of chs. 8–11, 37, and 40–48, which one would naturally expect from these types of visual "prophetic words." Also, the promise of the future removal of Ezekiel's dumbness in 24:27 itself served as a sign to the people that Ezekiel's words were from the Lord. This further reinforces a literal interpretation of the physiological condition rather than a mere metaphorical state reflecting Ezekiel's commission as only a *writing* prophet.

Second, Davis argues that after 33:22 Ezekiel is now free to prophesy a message of hope, which he was unable to do before because the scroll which he swallowed in 3:2 contained only oracles of doom.[283] This may hold true if it were not for the numerous examples of messages of hope within the woe oracles of chs. 1–24.[284] We also

---

Spirit, 28, notes that some form of this "word event formula" appears fifty times in Ezekiel. For a discussion on the formula in Ezekiel and the prophets, see Robson, *Word and Spirit*, 28–35. See also Zimmerli's comments about this formula, "Special Form," 516. For a discussion on the use of the "son of man" motif in Ezekiel, see Houk, "Literary Criteria," 184–90.

282. Davis, *Swallowing the Scroll*, 71. Others have held a similar view citing the "physical impossibility" of the acts and the complexity of the text as evidence that they were not actually performed but rather only written. Cf. Wilson, *Prophecy and Society*, 283. Interestingly, Davis remains an "agnostic" as to whether the sign acts were actually performed and not a mere literary device. It seems that the whole purpose of the sign acts contextually was to teach the people something by the visual actions, rather than a mere literary telling of a fictional event. On the other hand, Odell, "You Are What You Eat," 232–34, sees the sign acts of chapters 4 and 5 as part of the prophet's call in chapters 1–3 much the same way Moses' calling to lead his people was vindicated by visible sign acts (cf. Exod 4:8–9). She espouses the perspective that they were performed within his house concurrently and it was only after their fulfillment that he begins to speak (cf. 6:1). Odell's perspective is thought provoking but has a couple of problems. First, her equating of the sign acts of Moses' call with those of Ezekiel does not seem to coincide as she proposes. Moses' sign acts were performed before the people in order to bring credibility to his call. In Ezekiel's case, if they were performed within the confines of his house, no legitimacy for such acts could be gained. Secondly, a straightforward reading of the text seems to suggest that the people were observing the sign acts especially when the acts are followed by a series of "Thus says the Lord Yahweh" (כֹּה אָמַר אֲדֹנָי יְהוִה) clauses as we find in 5:5–17. This seems to be directed in an oracular fashion against the people. For a critique of Odell's interpretation of Ezekiel's swallowing of the scroll, see Robson, *Word and Spirit*, 61–62.

283. Davis, *Swallowing the Scroll*, 58. So too Wilson, "Ezekiel's Dumbness," 91–104.

284. Cf. 11:14–21; 16:42, 51–63; 17:22–24 and 20:39–44. So too Robson, *Word and Spirit*, 64. Many scholars reject the notion that all of these are later additions to the text. For example Zimmerli, *Ezekiel* 1:62–63, suggests 11:14–21 may be original.

see in 33:24–33 and ch. 34 a continuation of rebuke oracles. If we follow Davis's theory it seems unlikely that immediately after Ezekiel's dumbness is gone that he would continue in this vein of retributive prophecy. One would expect prophecies of hope immediately after his tongue is loosed; however, this is not the case. Finally, if the first telling of the prophecy came after the fall of Jerusalem in 33:23 then Ezekiel's message of rebuke found within chs. 1–24 are given well after the fact and would be of no immediate use. Moreover, Ezekiel would have had to wait for more than eight years to speak the word of the Lord,[285] a highly unlikely proposition (cf. Jer 20:9).

While I have issues with Davis's basic premise and approach to Ezekiel, her analysis of the text in a final form used to convey a distinct message has merit.[286] It is for this reason that part of my argument will rest upon the belief that the original final form (whatever that may have entailed) served not only as the ultimate rebuke but also an encouragement to those who found themselves in exile.

Next, in his published dissertation, Matties adopted a rhetorical methodology from a synchronic perspective when analyzing ch. 18 and the "moral discourse" of the prophet (viz., his ethical stance).[287] While he uses traditional critical methods for his exegetical work, his approach to the text is more synchronically focused. After his exegetical assessment of ch. 18, he uses it as a paradigmatic grid to interpret the ethical perspective of the prophet in other parts of the book.

Galambush also approached her study of Ezekiel 16 and 23 synchronically.[288] While her work focuses on a close analysis of the female metaphor found in chs. 16 and 23, she does, nonetheless, apply the metaphor across the entire book of Ezekiel, especially in chs. 1–24,

---

Also, Joyce, *Divine Initiative*, 27, 113–15, posits that 11:14–21 is a self-contained unit that was an early oracle before the destruction of Jerusalem. See also the comments by Boadt, "Salvation Oracles," 3. Ganzel, "Descriptions of the Restoration," 1–22, argues that all of the oracles of hope in Ezekiel play a vital role in the prophet's message. See further, Raitt, *Theology of Exile*, esp. 106–73. For the opposite position, cf. Clements, "Ezekiel Tradition," 127, who offers 16:53–55 and 20:33–35 as exemplars of later additions.

285. So too Gottwald, *Hebrew Bible*, 486.

286. Power, "Iconographic Windows," 355, suggests that the iconographic evidence/argument points to the fact that we do have the "original text."

287. Matties, *Ezekiel 18*, 5, esp. 22 n. 59. For a critique of Matties's work see, Allen, Review of Gordon Matties, 523–25.

288. Galambush, *Jerusalem in the Book of Ezekiel*.

in her fifth chapter. Her methodology is not one of detailed text or form-critical applications but rather is a literary analysis of the use of metaphor first inter-textually and then historically. Her approach, nonetheless, has shed light on the use of metaphor in the final form of Ezekiel.

Bodi[289] and later, Kutsko,[290] address the book of Ezekiel from a textual and motif-comparative perspective respectively. Both adopt a more synchronic approach to the text using literary and thematic parallels as a means of explaining the prophet's rhetorical choice of the ordering and presentation of his material. Bodi focuses on the literary parallels between the *Poem of Erra*[291] and Ezekiel (e.g., the use of the sword motif and anger of the god[s]). On the other hand, Kutsko suggests that the ANE motifs of temple abandonment, exile, repair, and return of the gods to their rebuilt temples was the paradigm that Ezekiel adopted for his prophetic message (we will discuss Kutsko's thesis further in ch. 5). Kutsko uses his paradigm as a grid which he places over the text of Ezekiel showing parallels between ANE examples of "exiled" pagan idols and the house of Israel. Methodologically Kutsko sees coherence in the final form but admits that the "accretion" that took place in the text of Ezekiel "occurred between and around the text . . ."[292]

Next, Renz (cf. also Stevenson[293]) has adopted a synchronic approach that allows him to argue that the author/compiler of Ezekiel had a rhetorical argument in mind aimed at the second generation of exiles.[294] Renz approaches the book from a more "holistic" perspective suggesting that the book was completed before 538 BCE. He makes a distinction between the audience of the author (i.e., the prophet Ezekiel) who may have first heard the oracles and the intended audience of the finished compiled oracles (i.e., the second generation of exiles). Thus the written text that was delivered to the second generation would have been close to what we have today in our canonical book of

289. Bodi, *Poem of Erra*.
290. Kutsko, *Between Heaven and Earth*.
291. For a full translation of the *Poem of Erra* see also Foster, *Before the Muses*, 880–911.
292. Kutsko, *Between Heaven and Earth*, 9–10.
293. Stevenson, *Vision of Transformation*. I will address Stevenson's work in ch. 5, below.
294. Renz, *Rhetorical Function*.

Ezekiel. This rhetorical presentation would then have allowed the final compilation to influence the second generation of exiles to move away from their previous generation's past and sinful patterns and adopt the new perspective as presented in Ezekiel's book.

Renz's approach, while valid at many points, fails to account for the meaning of the structure as we have it today. Furthermore, if the final form was indeed for the second generation, who is to say that it may not just as easily have been fashioned for the first generation?[295] This seems more fitting seeing how much of the message in chs. 1–24 addresses those from the first exile of 597 BCE and circumstances before the fall of Jerusalem in 586 BCE. Either way, we must concur with Renz that the message does appear to be primarily for the exilic community.

In 2002 Risa Levitt Kohn undertook a lexicographical study in which she convincingly demonstrated the parallels between Ezekiel and the priestly source, Deuteronomy, and the Deuteronomistic History. Her analysis cuts across the entire book of Ezekiel bypassing the historical critical approach as it relates to the compositional history of the text of Ezekiel itself.[296] Her starting point is a synchronic understanding of the final form of Ezekiel. She looks to the early exilic period for the beginning of the developmental process of Ezekiel and the compilation of the final forms of the other Deuteronomistic and priestly sources. For Kohn, Ezekiel served as a "new Moses" reinterpreting older laws for the needs of the new situation "on the ground" during the exile.[297] Thus, Ezekiel expected a new exodus in which his prophetic writing would be the guide.[298]

---

295. Collins, *Mantle of Elijah*, 92–94, avers that the "first edition" of Ezekiel had to have been written very close to the time of the oral pronouncements it describes. Collins proposes a date of 570–560 BCE as the most likely time of compilation with a *terminus ante quem* of 515 BCE, after the completion of the second temple.

296. Kohn takes the second chapter of her book (6–29) to address the history of scholarship on the P and D influence on the book of Ezekiel. In subsequent chapters she applies her analysis to the entire book of Ezekiel.

297. Cf. also Wilson, *Prophecy and Society*, 283, who suggests that Ezekiel was following in the steps of an "Ephraimite Mosaic prophet" and Kaufmann, *The Religion of Israel*, 436, who suggests Ezekiel saw himself almost as an equal to Moses in prophetic utterance, temple construction, and law giving. McConville, "Priests and Levites," 28, suggests that Ezekiel, as a second Moses, is describing in miniature the giving of the Law, the establishing of the cult, and the settlement of the land in chapters 40–48.

298. Kohn, *New Heart*, 117–18.

Finally, and by this brief survey I am in no way attempting to be exhaustive,[299] in 2006 James Robson did a detailed study of the use of "word" (דָּבָר) and "spirit" (רוּחַ) in Ezekiel. His approach was synchronic although he admits the final form of the text most likely has a "redactional unity."[300] Robson studied the intricacies of how speech is delivered and received by an audience.[301] Methodologically, he followed many of the tenets that Davis, Renz, and Stevenson espoused in their rhetorical studies of Ezekiel in his effort to determine the "communicative intent" of the author of Ezekiel. Thus, his first goal focused on the interrelationship between the delivered "word" of Yahweh (i.e., the "speech event") and how the "spirit" of Yahweh worked within that event to effect a response in its audience.[302] And secondly, to determine whether the book of Ezekiel in and of itself was intended as a "word event" from Yahweh by the "implied author," as per Davis, or rather only contained "words" from Yahweh (i.e., a series of oracles) that were compiled into the final form.[303]

We may conclude from this brief survey that studying the book of Ezekiel in its final form for its "literary artistry" has been fruitful and has validity. While we may never return to a consensus position, which caused H. Ewald in 1841 to suggest that the book of Ezekiel "arose almost entirely out of literary effort"[304] there is interpretive importance in returning our focus to the final form. At the same time, I also want to reiterate that I do not agree with the assumption set forward by scholars such as Davis and E. Reuss that Ezekiel was only an "author" and did not address the public with his message.[305] This

299. Donna Petter has written a dissertation on Ezekiel from a rhetorical perspective as well. In it she contends that the book of Ezekiel is fashioned according to a Mesopotamian city lament in which the nine features of the typical lament are present. We will discuss aspects of her proposal throughout. Cf. Petter, "Book of Ezekiel."

300. Robson, *Word and Spirit*, 6.

301. Ibid., 14.

302. Ibid., 67. Apóstolo, "Imagining Ezekiel," 14, points out the possibility of a wide range of interpretations for Ezekiel's original audience based upon the "reader's definition of *reality* and *imaginary*." (italics his)

303. Robson, *Word and Spirit*, 67.

304. Ewald, "Jeremia und Hezeqiel," 2.207, as cited by Bodi, *Poem of Erra*, 15.

305. Reuss, *Bible*, 3:10, states, "Il n'y a pas, dans tout ce livre, une seule page nous devrions supposer avoir été lue ou débitée publiquement. Ézéchiel n'a pas été orateur; il est écrivain. Ce qu'il nous donne, ce sont des élucubrations littéraires, le produit d'un travail de cabinet, le fruit de recueillement et de la contemplation" (as cited by

seems too narrow a claim in light of the fact that Ezekiel is explicitly described as a divinely appointed prophet to his people (Ezekiel 2), many of whom may have been illiterate (cf. Jer 52:15).[306] It seems most likely that some interaction with the general populace of the exile did take place for the purpose of instruction especially in light of the sign acts of chs. 4, 5, 12, and 24.[307]

Taking into account the scholarly shift in the study of Ezekiel in its final form and for its rhetorical value, we find ourselves in the mainstream of Ezekielian scholarship. It seems the most helpful to study the book as it now appears in an attempt to answer the question as to why Ezekiel arranged it as such and what exactly his rhetorical strategy was. Furthermore, in the book of Ezekiel it is virtually impossible to divorce the author's rhetorical argument from the structure of the book.[308] As I examine Ezekiel's rhetorical argument in the following chapters we will see that the unity and deliberate inclusion of certain visions and motifs support an approach that takes seriously the structural whole as opposed to focusing on the constituent parts.

Why Study the Structure of a Biblical Text?

When it comes to the study of the structure of any biblical book there is always a wide and varied set of opinions. Nevertheless, any attempt to understand the intended structure of the biblical text and the intent of the author is a valuable point of departure in any literary study of the final form of a book.[309] The need for coherent structural analysis of

---

Bodi, 15). Zimmerli, *Fiery Throne*, 76–77, opts for a variation of this assumption by suggesting that Ezekiel's work was compiled by a school of followers who met in his house for instruction.

306. While the exile of 597 may have included a proportionately large number of literate individuals because they were from the ruling class, the later exile of 586 included a large portion of the lower class (cf. Jer 52:15).

307. These acts present, in a nutshell, the heart of the message of woe found in Ezekiel (i.e., deprivation, exile, and mourning). They also highlight the message of Ezekiel much like underlining a word for emphasis. Yet, even these acts do not present the full message of hope and restoration that play out in chapters 33–48.

308. Davis, *Swallowing the Scroll*, 86.

309. Apóstolo, "Imagining Ezekiel," 19–20, correctly notes the difficulty in determining the "intent of the author" due to the potential of there being a long history of transmission and editing. *Who* exactly is the "author" and what was his/her "intent?" While Apóstolo prefers the phrase the "intention of the text," I still feel that the author(s) of the final form had a unified "intent" as I hope to demonstrate throughout.

books enables one to focus on the "forest" as opposed to the common tendency to get lost in the proverbial "trees."[310] Dorsey notes, "At the very least, the re-discovery of a well-conceived, thoughtful arrangement of a particular text enables the modern reader to appreciate the artistic skill and care that went into the composition of that text. Books in the OT that were formerly considered chaotically arranged are increasingly being seen as masterpieces of literary architecture as a result of structural investigation . . . The growing awareness of the high level of literary skill employed by biblical writers serves as a corrective to our earlier and incorrect impressions of structural carelessness."[311]

The Framework (see diagram on next page)

With a book as complex in imagery as that of Ezekiel, a structure that reflects the big picture can only serve to clear the way for a better understanding of the possible message Ezekiel hoped for his audience to hear. As noted in the section above, many are coming to recognize this holistic approach as a valid means of understanding and analyzing the book. Kutsko's perspective becomes paradigmatic of this trend when he notes that any investigation of the book of Ezekiel as a basically integrated and coherent text—indeed, with an articulated, artful design—reflecting the context of the exile is a defensible critical position when textual and redactional issues are carefully weighed.[312]

In the light of this importance, my use of the concept of a structural "framework" for the curse motif seems logical when understanding the way in which the OT authors, and those of the ANE for that matter, related their message to their audience. It is generally accepted that many cultures during this period, including Israel, were both oral and aural.[313] In this case, the audience would have needed aural hooks

---

310. Dorsey, "Can These Bones Live?" 15.

311. Ibid., 15.

312. Kutsko, *Between Heaven and Earth*, 5. Kutsko (5–9) gives a concise history of scholarship on the structural debate of the book of Ezekiel.

313. Porter, *Images*, 114–15, esp. 114, points out that there are numerous accounts in the ANE where reading written accounts aloud to the populace was the norm. These included public documents such as royal decrees, treaties, and edicts. She quotes a passage from a second millennium Hittite treaty between Muwatalliš and Alaksandus of Wiluša. The text reads, "Moreover let someone read thee this tablet

The Rhetorical Structure of Ezekiel: *The Peaks of the Framework*

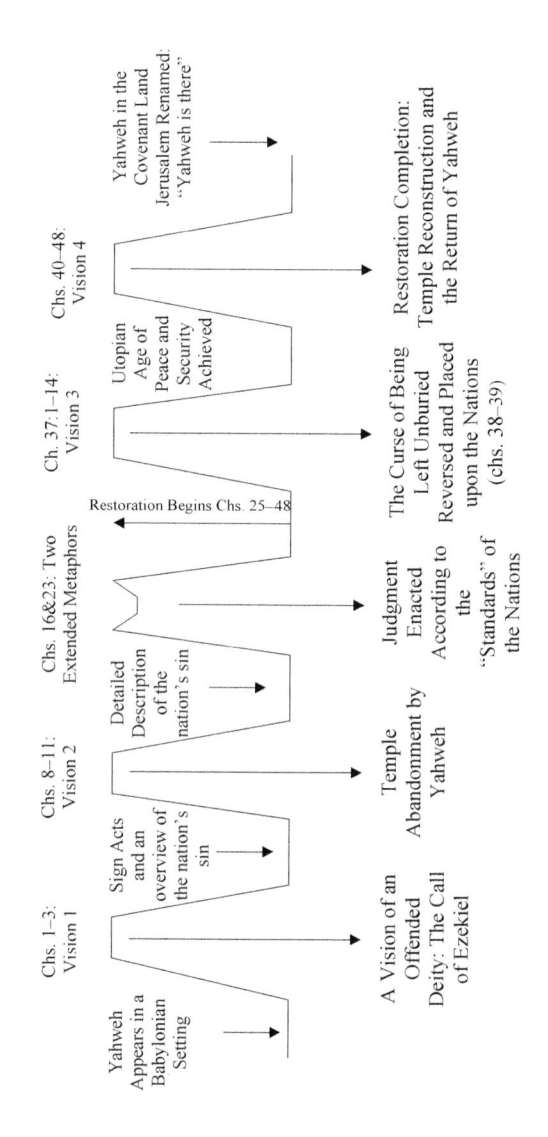

Chs. 1–3: Vision 1	Chs. 8–11: Vision 2	Chs. 16 & 23: Two Extended Metaphors	Ch. 37:1–14: Vision 3	Chs. 40–48: Vision 4
Sign Acts and an overview of the nation's sin	Temple Abandonment by Yahweh	Detailed Description of the nation's sin	Utopian Age of Peace and Security Achieved	Yahweh in the Covenant Land Jerusalem Renamed: "Yahweh is there"
Yahweh Appears in a Babylonian Setting	A Vision of an Offended Deity: The Call of Ezekiel			

Restoration Begins Chs. 25–48

- Judgment Enacted According to the "Standards" of the Nations
- The Curse of Being Left Unburied Reversed and Placed upon the Nations (chs. 38–39)
- Restoration Completion: Temple Reconstruction and the Return of Yahweh

---

which I have made for thee three times a year." Cf. also a similar practice in the OT: Exod 24:7; Deut 31:11; Josh 8:34–35; 2 Kgs 23:2; 2 Chron 34:30; Ezra 4:23; Esth 3:14; Neh 8:3, 8, 18; 13:1; Jer 36:6–23; 51:61. This final passage in Jer 51:61 makes it clear that the prophetic word was to be read aloud to the general populace.

to enable them to remember the message being presented, especially in a longer treatise.[314] Rhetorically, the visual hook, through the mind's eye, was Ezekiel's means of formatting and structuring his message to his audience especially in light of the memorable horrors associated with covenant curses. This message became somewhat drawn out over the course of Ezekiel's ministry and at the point of organizing his oracles into a formal, written presentation some form of a structural tool would have been needed to package the vast quantity of material. On the issue of the mental organization of material, Beekman, Callow and Kopesec point out that "the human mind cannot handle large quantities of information unless it applies the 'packaging' principle . . . It would seem that there are certain general characteristics of the mind which are shared by all people and which determine when a quantity of information has reached a point at which it should be organized into separate packages rather than continue on."[315] I propose that the "packaging principle" employed by Ezekiel was none other than the strategically placed visions and extended metaphors.

Based upon our diagram above, it appears that Ezekiel used curse-based visions pregnant with imagery and symbolism as mental pictures and as a means to "package" and to "hook" his audience.[316] These visions, along with the extended metaphors, served as an effective tool to shock the house of Israel out of their lethargy.[317] This framework served as both a literary device and as a mental picture that was vital to the presentation of his message. As can be seen in the diagram, the "peaks" or "highpoints" of the book are linked to the visionary sequences and the two extended metaphors placed at key junctures in the book. The paired visions in particular, placed at both ends of the book, serve as focal points for the messages of judgment and cursing (chs. 1–3 and 8–11) followed by restoration and blessing

---

314. Both Davis, *Swallowing the Scroll*, 45, and Cassuto, "The Arrangement of the Book of Ezekiel," 228, come to the same conclusion when considering the vast amount of material in Ezekiel's prophecy.

315. Beekman, et al., *Semantic Structure*, 14–15, as cited by Dorsey, "Can These Bones Live?," 11.

316. For example, Boadt correctly points out that "the images often involve whole narrative incidents or allegories that become the primary vehicles for the message." Cf. Boadt, "Rhetorical Strategies," 186.

317. Casson, "When Israel Loses Its Meaning," 225, also points out that part of the "prophet's rhetorical strategy" is to shock his audience with his visions and language.

(chs. 37 and 40–48). At the same time, the metaphors serve as an effective means of highlighting exactly how the nation would be judged and the reasons for it.

In a similar vein, Terence Collins, following the work of Van Dyke Paranuk,[318] focuses on the "framework" of the "Glory of the Lord" visions in chs. 1–3, 8–11, 43:1–5.[319] His assertion is that throughout the literary development of the book these three visions remained the backbone of the book around which other material accrued.[320] Both Collins and Van Dyke Paranuk note the possible redactional history of the book but assert that it is the visions that are the vital structural element that give the final form validity as a cohesive unit. As I have already noted, these visions do indeed play a key role as the framework/backbone of the book, however, my proposal adds to this framework the vision of ch. 37 and the extended metaphor and allegory of 16 and 23 respectively.[321] Finally, the visions also depict covenant curses and curse-reversal motifs whereby the first 24 chapters focus on judgment and the last 24 chapters present a picture of curse reversal. It is to this structure we now turn.

---

318. Paranuk, "Literary Architecture," 61–74.

319. Collins, *Mantle of Elijah*, 88–89. Cf. also Apóstolo, "Imagining Ezekiel," 13, who includes 37:1–14 with the *kābôd* visions as a part of "Ezekiel's fantastic dimension." Robson, *Word and Spirit*, 36, suggests that 3:22–5:17 should be seen as a separate or "fifth" vision. Nevertheless, while the language of 3:22 does suggest this distinction, the context best reflects a continuation of the earlier vision with a distinct series of sign acts following it. Wevers, *Ezekiel*, 12, points out the decisive role the four visions play in Ezekiel's overall message as "four critical points in the prophet's life and thought." Joyce, *Ezekiel*, 42–43, also avers that the visions of 1:1–3, 8:1–3 and 40:1–2 are like "great landmarks" within the book. He also asserts that chapters 16, 20, and 23 serve a vital role in the book as historical presentations of the nation. I will argue that chapters 16 and 23 stand out even from chapter 20 because of their metaphorical nature. Also, Kaufmann, *The Religion of Israel*, 437, has noted that the visions serve as "a framework for the revelation of the divine message." Finally, Odell, *Ezekiel*, 1, also notes the role the visions of chapters 1; 8–11; and 40–48 play in the structural ordering of the text. See further, Odell, "You Are What You Eat," 231.

320. For example Collins, *Mantle of Elijah*, 90–91 insists he can easily see the later additions to the text in places such as 23:1–35 and 16:53–63.

321. Zimmerli, *Fiery Throne*, 59, comes very close to my understanding of the structure of Ezekiel as being centered around the visions of Ezekiel. Zimmerli does not, however, pinpoint the metaphors of 16 and 23 as a central focus in the oracles against the house of Israel.

Structural Divisions

Open any commentary on Ezekiel and structural divisions can range from two major sections to multiple divisions ordered around thematic or content-driven indicators.[322] Also, the thirteen dated headings throughout Ezekiel offer a chronological structure to the book.[323] Some scholars even suggest that these dates reflect a larger "autobiographical" structure of the book that highlights key events in the life of the prophet.[324] Apart from this chronological concept, however, the fourfold thematic structural division of Ezekiel appears to hold a consensus.[325] Yet, it perhaps fails to reflect the best understanding of the rhetorical perspective of the compiler.

It is my belief that the fourfold "thematic" structural breakdown of Ezekiel, namely, chs. 1–3 (the call of the prophet); 4–24 (the oracles

322. Generally the structure is presented as follows, 1–24, 25–32, 33–48 as exemplified by Davis, *Swallowing the Scroll*, 11 and Driver, *Introduction*, 279. On the other hand, some scholars such as Clements, "Ezekiel Tradition," 127; and Childs, *Introduction*, 365, divide it into four sections (e.g., 1–24; 25–32; 33–39; 40–48). There are also those who use a five-fold division (e.g., 1–3; 4–24; 25–32; 33–39; 40–48), cf. Biggs, *Ezekiel*, xiv.

323. Cf. Ezek 1:1–3; 8:1; 20:1; 24:1; 26:1; 29:1, 17; 30:20; 31:1; 32:1, 17; 33:21; 40:1. Becker, "Ez 8–11," 136, suggests that the dating scheme in Ezekiel is artificial and has been added after the fact. This is a similar position taken by Spiegel, "Toward Certainty," 170. However, Freedy and Redford, "Dates in Ezekiel," 462–85, present a forceful argument for the validity of the dates in Ezekiel based on Babylonian and Egyptian chronologies. They conclude that there is no reason to assume that these dates are later editorial insertions. They aver that they aid in our understanding of the exact historical situations on the ground at the time of the prophet's writing. So too, the conclusion of Miller, "Thirtieth Year," 499–500, who suggests that this dating schema serves structurally as a "chronological skeleton" for the entire book. See also Malamat, "Last Kings," 137–56, for a detailed historical analysis of the dates and the political intrigue from Josiah to Zedekiah.

324. Odell, "You Are What You Eat," 238–41, following the work of Miller, posits, I feel correctly, that this refers to Ezekiel's age for entering the priesthood. So too, Betts, *Ezekiel the Priest*, 50–53. Therefore, the last date in 40:1 (i.e., 25th year of the captivity and 20 years after Ezekiel began to minister) would correspond with Ezekiel's fiftieth year when priests retired from ministry. However, Miller, "The Thirtieth Year," 499–503, bases his understanding of the beginning and end dates of Ezekiel's prophecy on Num 4:3, 23, 30 along with the seven-day "incubation" period of priestly initiation (Num 8=Ezek 3:15–16). He explains away the date of 571 in 29:17 as a later prophecy by Ezekiel, but not important to the structure of the book. For further discussion, cf. Mein, "Ezekiel as a Priest," 199–213.

325. For a study on the structure of Ezekiel focused on selective passages, see Talmon and Fishbane, "Structuring of Biblical Books," 129–53.

against Judah); 25–32 (the oracles against the nations) and; 33–48 (the restoration of the nation) is not the best way to understand the compiler's structural strategy especially in light of the rhetorical scheme.[326] Based upon my findings below dealing with Ezekiel's rhetorical argument, I posit that while chs. 1–3 definitely concern the "call of the prophet," they should be combined with chs. 4–12 based upon imagery, common language, and content. Thus, the first block of material extends from chs. 1–12 (see the beginning of ch. 3 below for a detailed analysis).[327] Second, chs. 13–24 show the unfolding of the curses and indictments against Judah as outlined in chs. 4–12. Third, the oft-held assumption that the book divides smoothly at the beginning of ch. 25 and then again at the end of ch. 32 fails to account for the appearance of the oracles against the nations again in chs. 35 and 38–39.[328] The oracles against the nations (i.e., chs. 25–32) should be seen as a key part of the restoration chapters especially in light of the continued oracles against the nations in chs. 35 and 38–39 which appear in the midst of the "restoration" chapters of 33–48. The indictments and judgment against the nations reflect similar motifs and terms used earlier to describe the "rebellious house" of Israel but are now reversed.[329]

---

326. Adapted from Daniel Block's structural presentation. Block, *Ezekiel 1–24*, 23. Kutsko, *Between Heaven and Earth*, 1, presents an interesting chiastic structure of Ezekiel based on the divine *kābôd*:

A—From Divine Presence to Divine Absence (1:1—11:25)
  B—Preparation for Destruction (12:1—24:27)
    C—Oracles against the Nations (25:1—32:32)
  B'—Preparation for Restoration (33:1—39:29)
A'—From Divine Absence to Divine Presence (40:1—48:35)

327. In ch. 3, below, we will discuss the role that ch. 12 plays as an inclusio to the opening twelve chapters. For this reason I see it as part of the opening chapters and not necessarily fitting into the second half of the oracles against Judah.

328. Cf. Boadt, "Salvation Oracles," 11. Because of the apparent lack of continuity between chs. 33–34 and 35:1–15 Boadt correctly notes the tendency within scholarship to see 35:1–15 as the work of a later hand. For example, Wevers, *Ezekiel*, 264–65. However, I will argue for their literary and thematic unity in ch. 4 below.

329. Interestingly, Freehof, *Ezekiel*, 13, suggests the same division as I do here for chapters 25–48 by noting the completely different "tone" of these later chapters. He also suggests a two-part aspect to the book in which he includes all of chapters 1–24 together. Also Galambush, *Jerusalem in the Book of Ezekiel*, 127, notes that the oracles of "promise" begin in ch. 25 and build toward the final vision of 40–48. She does go on to note that chapters 25–39 belong to one section dealing with "oracles of promise"/ "restoration" (129).

To summarize, I suggest then, that the book should be divided into three main parts: 1) chs. 1–12 (the call of Ezekiel to the "rebellious house" of Israel, an overview of sins, the departure of the deity and the exile promised); 2) chs. 13–24 (the covenant curses enacted against the "rebellious house"); 3) chs. 25–48 (the reversal of the covenant curses; the curses removed from the house of Israel and placed upon the nations; Israel restored).[330] On a final note, it needs to be pointed out that the general consensus is not necessarily incorrect in noting the different sub-divisions, but rather that these sub-divisions often mask the apparent strategy of the author.

Therefore, Ezekiel must have found his greatest ability to persuade his audience by means of the rhetorical argument of the final form. Indeed, the trend in Ezekielian scholarship betrays a desire to take seriously this fact. This rhetorical argument, however a particular scholar views it, was in turn used to promote a clear theological message to a people in exile.

Theological

My final methodological approach will include a theological perspective. The study of the book of Ezekiel from a theological viewpoint has been revived even more so since scholars have returned to a focus on the final form. As recent as 2008, Pohlmann in his work, *Ezechiel: Der Stand der theologischen Diskussion*, focuses on this very perspective. Baltzer also approached the book from this stance spending little time focusing on text-critical concerns.[331] There have also been entire anthologies of essays on Ezekiel whose primary focus is on the theological perspective of Ezekiel. One such anthology is that edited by Odell and Strong, which studies both the theological and anthropological

---

330. There is the possibility that chapters 40–48 could be placed within a section of their own based upon the return of the glory of the Lord to the new temple. This section does present a utopia far beyond any envisioned by the prophets before. However, the presence of common thematic motifs of restoration such as those found in chapters 38–39 (e.g., a utopian military defeat of Israel's enemies) caused me to place chapters 40–48 within the restoration material. Also, chapters 12 and 33 function as transitional chapters within their larger blocks of material (see discussions below).

331. Baltzer, *Ezekiel und Deuterojesaja*. Baltzer does an inter-textual analysis of several key theological features in Ezekiel and "Deutero-Isaiah" to identify commonalties and differences. Se also Simian, *Die theologische Nachgeschichte*, 58.

bents of the book.[332] Other scholars have given concise evaluations of Ezekiel's theology and the theological importance of the message he delivered.[333]

When arguing for a particular rhetorical agenda for Ezekiel, one also needs to consider the author's desired effect(s) on his audience. Indeed, it is virtually impossible to divorce one from the other without destroying the intended message of the prophet. If in fact the final form of the book reflects a deliberate attempt to persuade readers of some action, then some exploration of that agenda needs to be undertaken. In the case of Ezekiel, a priest, one can assume that a theological/cultic agenda is in play. Therefore, in my theological approach to Ezekiel, I will adopt the concept of audience reaction as presented by Robson. Robson suggests that because Yahweh is seen as effecting both the destruction and restoration of the house of Israel, the book "asks of its readers not a plan of action, but a change in belief."[334] It is my contention that this "change in belief" was the most critical rhetorical function and outcome desired from the message of Ezekiel. For example, the reference to the departure of the deity in ch. 11 would likely have sent a strong theological message to its intended audience. To be left alone to the wrath of the deity would have sent a clear message of the impending doom for those who were still in Jerusalem while quashing the false hope of a quick return of the exiles to Jerusalem (Ezekiel 13). Conversely, by ch. 37 the theological implications of a restored Israel and the presence of Yahweh in chs. 43–48 would, no doubt, have sent a message of hope in the midst of despair and exile. Furthermore, Ezekiel's constant use of the recognition formula (i.e., "then you will know that I am the Lord") betrays a desired ontological shift in his readers/hearers (we will return to this in ch. 4, below). Thus, while many times the theological message is explicit as is natural of prophetic speech, at select points throughout I will discuss the possible implicit theological message. As noted in our previous section, nowhere is the implicit message more evident than in Ezekiel's use of structure and visionary motifs/framework to house his message.

---

332. Odell and Strong, *Book of Ezekiel*.
333. For example, Gowan, *Theology of the Prophetic Books*, 121–37.
334. Robson, *Word and Spirit*, 13.

Conclusion

In light of our discussions throughout this chapter, we may conclude then that Ezekiel was indeed a prophet of the exile who had ample opportunity to avail himself of Mesopotamian literature, art, and culture in general. The symbolism and imagery so radically different throughout his message is best attributed to his setting in Babylon. These peculiarities have made Ezekiel a transitional prophet between the classical prophets of the pre-exilic era and the visionaries of the post-exilic period. Moreover, his message presupposes a pre-existent law code of some form and the covenantal relationship of Israel with her Suzerain. Ezekiel's knowledge of the covenant curses found in the law codes of the OT and ANE treaties, especially those of the Late Iron Age, allowed for a ready pool of punishments appropriate to the indictments that he would set forth as instructed by Yahweh. The stage was now set for the unfolding of what would be perhaps the most vivid presentation of symbolism and covenant curses that Israel had seen or heard to date. Indeed, Yahweh was their King and Suzerain against whom they had rebelled. The message of Ezekiel would make that clear once and for all. It is perhaps for this reason that Ezekiel's own words are best applied as we move forward to unpack the message of the prophet. "And that which comes into your mind surely it will not come to pass, when you are saying: 'We will be like the nations, like the tribes of the lands, serving wood and stone.'" "As I live," declares the Lord God, "with a strong hand and with an outstretched arm and with wrath poured out, I will be king over you" (Ezek 20:32–33).

Ezekiel's message here is clear. Israel's covenant with Yahweh will be upheld and he, as the mighty God of the throne vision, will see that it unfolds as he declares. The wrath about to come upon the nation will indeed be from Yahweh, even though Babylon appears to be in control. Because Judah had broken covenant with both Yahweh and Babylon (cf. Ezek 17), the curses of both covenants would now fall upon a rebellious nation. The latter is clear from the siege, destruction of the city, and the deportation of Judah in 586 BCE by Nebuchadnezzar due to Zedekiah's treachery. The former is evidenced by the desolation of the country and city and the deportation of the people as promised in Deut 4:27 and 28:29.

2

God's Glory Revealed

The Awesome Deity Departs (Ezekiel 1–3; 8–11)

> No prophet was endowed with such vision—no other vision was as extreme. No man has shed such light on the future, for no other light was as forceful in tearing darkness apart. But, then, no one had ever seen such darkness, the total darkness that precedes the breaking of the dawn.[1]

Introduction

IN THE PREVIOUS CHAPTER WE LOOKED AT A VARIETY OF ISSUES RANGing from Ezekiel's literary technique and the setting of his prophecy to his use of covenant language and earlier OT traditions and texts. We also concluded that it was very probable that Ezekiel was reeducated in Babylon and had access to at least some of the literature of his new homeland and/or the great monuments of Babylon. In this chapter we will build upon these foundations and begin to unpack various aspects of Ezekiel's message especially those related to his first two visionary sequences, which I have identified in my structural chart in ch. 1 as the first two "peaks" of the framework of the prophet's rhetorical argument. I will devote the majority of this chapter to studying these first two visions and the possible messages inherent in the symbols which were adopted by the prophet as well as the possible sources, both literary and iconographic, where Ezekiel may have found such rich images to utilize in fashioning his prophetic visions.[2] Because of

---

1. Wiesel, "Ezekiel," 167.
2. I do not mean to imply by this statement that Ezekiel's visions were fabricated without the aid of Yahweh's Spirit but rather that Yahweh could have used common motifs and images present in Ezekiel's new homeland as the "material" for the visions

the similarities of the visions of chs. 1–3 and 8–11, I will handle them as though they are the same except where differentiation is needed to clarify the message or rhetorical technique of the prophet. Finally, we will examine a series of ANE texts that help to demonstrate that Ezekiel's message and vision of chs. 8–11 are anchored to the ANE curse of temple abandonment. While this curse may not be explicitly noted in the curse lists of Leviticus 26 and Deuteronomy 28, it can be argued that this particular curse is nonetheless present in prophetic warnings both before and during Ezekiel's era. It is to these texts we will now turn to begin our study.

"I Will Hide My Face from You"—A Warning Ignored

The words of the prophets long before the time of Ezekiel had carried the harsh warning that Yahweh would abandon his people on account of their continued sin (cf. Hos 5:4–6).[3] Often this took on the anthropomorphic nuance of Yahweh turning his face (פָּנִים) from Israel (a concept also common in the ANE)[4] or removing his "hand" (יָד) of protection.[5] For example, Isaiah, in his opening covenant lawsuit (i.e., *rîb*)[6] against Judah, threatens that Yahweh's eyes would be hidden (אַעְלִים עֵינַי) from his people if they continued in their sin (cf. Isa 1:15) and that he would turn his hand toward them in judgment (cf. Isa 1:25).[7] Similarly, in Isaiah 8:17 when speaking of Yahweh, the prophet

---

he gave to the prophet. Throughout the prophetic corpus God constantly employs the imagery and the language of a particular prophet when fashioning a prophetic oracle (e.g., Amos as a farmer uses a lot of agricultural imagery and language cf. 7:14). We should not expect any less when trying to understand Ezekiel's visions set within a Babylonian context.

3. Ps 51:11 records the anguished plea of King David for Yahweh not to remove his Spirit from him (as he had from Saul, cf. 1 Sam 15:23). David recognized the danger that could befall not only a nation but an individual when Yahweh decided to reject or turn from a person and leave them to their own devices.

4. Balentine, *Hidden God*, 22–44.

5. This is the direct opposite posture we see in the Aaronic blessing (Num 6:25–26) where Yahweh is invoked to look favorably upon Israel by allowing his face to shine upon them (יָאֵר יְהוָה פָּנָיו אֵלֶיךָ) and lifting his face toward them (יִשָּׂא יְהוָה פָּנָיו אֵלֶיךָ). So too, Block, *Ezekiel 25–48*, 483.

6. For a detailed discussion of the lawsuit format, see Niehaus, "Amos," 1:318–22.

7. Balentine, *Hidden God*, 45, lists every occurrence of the phrase סָתַר פָּנִים ("hide the face") in the OT. Balentine (44) argues that this phrase may have its roots in other ANE contexts and often is associated with "divine wrath operating as punishment for sin." See also his comments on p. 77.

uses an analogous phrase "the one who hides his face" (הַמַּסְתִּיר פָּנָיו) to warn of abandonment.[8] Later, he also warns of Yahweh removing his "hedge" (מְשׂוּכָה) of protection from his unfaithful "vineyard" (cf. Isa 5:5) and bringing a distant invader against his own people (cf. Isa 5:26–30).

Other prophets of the classical prophetic period also forewarned of the destruction of Judah, Jerusalem, and Israel for their continued sin. Amos warned of judgment and destruction on Judah for her unfaithfulness to Yahweh (cf. Amos 2:4–5) but also noted that Yahweh would warn his prophets ahead of time (Amos 3:7), as also can be seen with the "watchman" motif in Ezekiel (Ezek 3:17; 33:2–7). Micah also forewarned of coming judgment and destruction upon Israel on account of her covenant violations (cf. Mic 1:8–16; 6:16). Interestingly, Micah's terminology is perhaps closest to that of Ezekiel's in his warning of abandonment. Micah notes that Yahweh would indeed "hide his face from them" (וְיַסְתֵּר פָּנָיו מֵהֶם) for their sins (Mic 3:4) especially the sin of presumption as defined in Micah 3:11.[9] With the exception of the fluctuation between the third and first person address, this phrase is mirrored in Ezekiel 39:24 as the reason for Judah's judgment (וָאַסְתִּר פָּנַי מֵהֶם, see also Ezek 5:11; 7:22). Finally, Jeremiah picks up on this theme and develops it by paralleling the cursed outcome of Shiloh to that of Jerusalem and her rulers (Jer 7:8–15). He even goes so far as to declare outright that Yahweh would "abandon" (נָטַשׁ) his people and city (Jer 23:33; cf. also 24:8). Therefore it should be no surprise that Ezekiel adopts this hidden-face/abandonment theme and develops it into a full-blown visionary motif.

---

8. Only here with the hiphil participle. See also Isa 54:8; 59:2; 64:6 for passages with this phrase in the context of divine wrath. The same phrase appears in 50:6 and 53:3 but both appear to have a messianic context. Balentine, *The Hidden God*, 77, points out that this phrase is used primarily in the context of the prophetic corpus with the connotation of judgment from God for Israel's sin. However, in the psalms they usually appear in the form of a lament as a means of protesting one's innocence in the face of trials. For the range of appearances of the phrase in the Psalms, cf. Pss 10:11; 13:2; 22:25; 27:9; 30:8; 44:25; 51:11; 69:18; 88:15; 102:3; 104:29; 143:7.

9. Block, *Ezekiel 25–48*, 484, notes that in every case where this idiom is used in the OT; with the exception of the two times it is used in Job (i.e., 13:14; 34:29), it is used as "God's reaction to covenant betrayal." However, Balentine, *Hidden God*, 76–77 suggests the appearances of the phrase in the lament psalms is one of petition to God asking "why" Yahweh has left the individual. Thus, it appears not always to be one of "covenant betrayal" in the strict sense of the term. Cf. also Ps 51:11 as another example of a "neutral" reference.

Ezekiel's choice of divine abandonment also appears to rely on ANE motifs and treaty forms. Aside from the warnings in the prophets just mentioned, we can search in vain to find such a curse within the curse lists of Deuteronomy and Leviticus.[10] Because of this lacuna perhaps one needs to look to the literature of the ANE to find the precedent for this OT prophetic usage in both the classical and exilic periods. However, at the same time, a note of caution needs to be given when applying the motif equally between Ezekiel and the ANE texts. Ezekiel, as a priest of the exilic era, would have been repulsed not only by the multiplicity of the gods of the ANE but also by their capricious nature.[11] Ezekiel sets out to make it clear that the acts of Yahweh, as sovereign over all gods, were purposeful and just. Yahweh, and not the gods of Babylon, was to be feared and revered above all. Indeed, the only reason the covenant people found themselves at odds with their Suzerain was due to their covenant violations and because Yahweh had hidden his face from them as noted above (cf. 7:22; 39:23–24).

The practical application of the Lord "hiding" his face from his people equates to his departure from their presence (cf. Ezekiel 8–11). As a result of this act Israel would be vulnerable to her enemies on every side both in international intrigues and in direct confrontation in battle. Therefore, as in other cultures of the period and earlier, the defeat of an army or a king often proved to the people of that land that their deity was not with them or that they had offended their

---

10. Block, "Divine Abandonment," 17, correctly points out that we do not find the curse of abandonment in the curse lists of Deuteronomy and Leviticus. Nevertheless, judgment in the form of exile (cf. Lev 26:33, 38, 39, 43; Deut 28:64–65), the Lord setting his face against Israel (Lev 26:17, 24), and the Lord causing Israel's enemies to invade her (cf. Deut 28:25, 48, 49) do appear. Note also Deut 31:16–18 for the common motif of Yahweh turning his face from his people.

11. For a brief discussion on the development of monotheism in Israel, see Lang, *Monotheism and the Prophetic Minority*; idem, "No God but Yahweh!," 41–49; and idem, "Zur Entstehung," 135–42. In this last work, Lang gives a brief overview of the religious history of Israel from pre-monarchial times to the post-exilic period. He asserts that in essence monolatry began only in Hosea's era (135). In *Monotheism and the Prophetic Minority*, 54–56, Lang posits that the birth of monotheism involved a rapid revolution starting with the battle against Phoenician Baal in the ninth century to the Yahweh-alone movement of the eighth century to the monolartic system of the seventh century. For those of the sixth century and beyond, monotheism "is the answer to the political emergency, in which no solution is to be expected from diplomatic maneuvering or foreign military help. There is but one saviour: the only true God" (54).

god(s) in some way.¹² For the people of Judah, this offense was primarily wrapped up in their unwillingness to remove idolatry from their midst. The first eleven chapters of Ezekiel serve to address just such a setting. The nation had rebelled against their Suzerain (3:9) and was now in a fearful state. The unfolding of these first few chapters sets the tenor of what is to follow. The house of Israel had broken covenant and because of that, Yahweh would indeed hide his face from them, but what that would fully entail was, up to that point in their history, never completely realized in the lives of those who lived in Judah.¹³ Yes, they had experienced privation and attack from foreign powers in the past, but what was about to unfold was far from what anyone could possibly imagine. Total destruction and exile had never crossed their minds. The inviolability of Jerusalem and the temple based upon a strong Zion theology and the Lord's presence had been a long-held assumption that was about to change (cf. Jer 7:4).¹⁴

The inhabitants of Judah were about to encounter through the visions of Ezekiel, the majesty and power of the deity they had offended.¹⁵ This was no mere carving on the wall or stone god; this was their living and all-powerful Suzerain who would manifest himself in the storm theophany of chs. 1–3. Indeed, Ezekiel's visions and message were clear: Yahweh was no longer to be taken for granted; judgment was on its way.

The sign that this was a reality can be seen in four aspects of Ezekiel's opening visions and oracles. First, Yahweh would reveal his glory to the nation as he had done generations earlier in the wilderness prior to their ratification of the covenant (Exod 20:18). At the

---

12. Speiser, "Ancient Mesopotamia," 56, notes that the end of a dynasty of a particular king was a sign of divine displeasure with that king. The dynasty of David ended for all intents and purposes with the exile of Zedekiah.

13. See Balentine, *Hidden God*, for a discussion of this motif.

14. The salvation of Jerusalem from Sennacherib's invasion during the time of Hezekiah appears to have been the watershed moment when this perception became a reality (cf. 2 Kings 18–19 and Isa 36–37).

15. In her dissertation on Ezekiel's similarity to a Mesopotamian city lament, Petter notes that the motif of the god(dess) becoming angry with his/her city is paralleled here in the opening chapters of Ezekiel. Furthermore she points out that once the word went forth it was irrevocable (such as we see in Ezekiel). As examples she notes the actions of Enlil in *The Lament over the Destruction of Ur*, 150–51; *The Lament over the Destruction of Sumer and Ur* 57, 163–64, 365; *The Curse of Agade*, 99; and the *Uruk Lament*, 3:27; 12:38. See Petter, "Book of Ezekiel," 104–9, esp. 109 n. 24.

inception of the Sinai covenant the people had recognized their insignificance and sinful nature before Yahweh and, out of fear for Yahweh's awesome power, had asked Moses to speak on their behalf (Exod 20:19).[16] Sadly, however, the nation had forgotten this healthy fear. As a result, this time the divine revelation would not be for the purposes of drawing the nation into covenant, but rather as a sign that they had failed to remember the awesome nature of their God. Yahweh's longsuffering had run its course and now the house of Israel would suffer the consequences of their repeated sin, especially that of idolatry. Second, Ezekiel would enumerate and present the sins of the people as the reason for their impending doom (chs. 4–8). Third, they would witness the most feared sight possible from an ANE perspective: their God would abandon his temple. Finally, the full implications of that reality would be made known to the people by what was to follow. The abandonment of his temple and the hiding of Yahweh's face from the people meant one thing, destruction of the nation was inevitable and exile was a foregone conclusion (cf. ch. 12).

The Call of the Prophet[17]

The sudden appearance of Yahweh in all his glory sets the stage for what is to follow—the calling of Ezekiel to a ministry much the same as Isaiah's and Jeremiah's (Isa 6:9–11; Jer 13:10). As with most of the great prophets before and after him, only a brief introduction precedes an immediate vision from Yahweh. The urgency of Ezekiel's message is heightened by the terse movement of the narrative from the introduction to the first vision. Although Ezekiel sets out on his prophetic voyage to a people that will, for the most part, refuse to hear his message, Yahweh will have the last word. The message to the inhabitants of Jerusalem and the exilic community is clear: when Yahweh departs from his temple, all the curses spoken of in the Law will fall upon them and their beloved city (chs. 4–6). While their misplaced trust in the ever-abiding presence of the Lord was echoed in the common

---

16. Muilenburg, "Ezekiel," 569, avers that Ezekiel is "overborne by his awful sense of the holiness of Yahweh, and feels himself and his people involved in the absolute Either-Or of the holy and the profane, the sacred and the common, the clean and the unclean."

17. For a discussion of the theological and thematic issues of Ezekiel's call, cf. Wilson, "Prophecy in Crisis," 157–69.

refrain of the day, "the temple of the Lord, the temple of the Lord, the temple of the Lord" (Jer 7:4), Ezekiel would remove this façade of protection by predicting through this visionary sequence the departure of Yahweh's glory, and thus, by association, the presence of Yahweh (11:23). Note, however, that in the vision of chs. 8–11, Ezekiel is careful to point out that it is the same vision of the awesome deity he saw in chs. 1–3. Yahweh who was now leaving through the eastern gate and departing the city was the same one who had revealed his glory in chs. 1–3. The people were left to the fate of a nation who had not only broken covenant with their suzerain but also their god. As a wronged deity, Yahweh would abandon his temple because of this inexcusable sin of worshipping other gods (cf. Ezek 8), a breach of the first two stipulations of the Ten Commandments (cf. Exod 20:3–4). At the same time, Yahweh's abandonment would also remove his protection as their "suzerain." In this vein, Yahweh would lead the armies of Babylon as a means of bringing ultimate physical judgment to Judah (we will return to this below).

Ezekiel 1–3—A Vision of the Offended Deity[18]

The vision of the chariot-throne of Yahweh is perhaps the best known, but most confusing of all of Ezekiel's visions.[19] It is at once full of color, light, and the grandeur of Yahweh and at the same time full of mystery. Scholars now recognize the clear Mesopotamian influence and the need to understand Ezekiel's geographical context when studying this vision.[20] The vision is steeped in symbolism and meaning which can only be appreciated by comparing Ezekiel's vision with other comparable ANE literature and iconography. Indeed, one does not have to look too far from Tel-abib to find parallels with Ezekiel's vision.

---

18. For a discussion on the textual difficulties in Ezekiel 1, see Block, "Text and Emotion," 418–39.

19. Wiesel, "Ezekiel," 170–71, points out that in the Mishnah one finds in the *Treatise of Hagiga* the following: "'one must not debate with three students questions about intimate relations between men and women' . . . 'nor the mysteries of creation with two students' . . . 'nor the mystery of the *Merkavah*, the chariot, with just one student.'"

20. E.g., Koch, *Prophets*, 2:88–89.

An ANE Precedent for the Vision

Before delving into the symbolism of Ezekiel's vision and the parallel aspects between it and similar ANE imagery, it seems relevant to present an example of a similar vision with a long history even into the time period of Ezekiel. In the Assyrian text, *A Vision of the Nether World*, graphic detail is given of the gods living in the underworld. While this vision is clearly a picture with an opposite setting (i.e., Sheol) to that seen by Ezekiel, the symbolism and detail remain strikingly similar. This ancient account, found in several recensions even in the library of Ashurbanipal (668–627 BCE—only 30 or so years removed from Ezekiel's era) in Nineveh, offers clues to the visionary genre used by Ezekiel. Visionaries in Babylon and Assyria seemed to have had similar experiences when it came to dream visions and other-worldly encounters. The text describes fifteen gods in similar fashion as Ezekiel describes the four living beings accompanying Yahweh's throne. The text tells of a man named Kumma[21] who saw the images in a night vision.

> 1. [Kum]ma lay down and beheld a night vision in his dream: "... I held and I saw his awe-inspiring splendor ...
>
> (*for relevance sake I have skipped this section*)
>
> 4b. Alluhappu (had) the head (of) a lion, four human hands (and) feet.
>
> The upholder of evil (had) the head of a bird; his wings were open as he flew to and fro,
>
> (his) hands (and) feet were human.
>
> 'Remove Hastily,' the boatman of the nether world,
>
> (had) the head (of the) Zu-bird; his four hands (and) feet ...
>
> 5 ... (had) the head (of) an ox, four human hands (and) feet.
>
> The evil Utukku (had) the head (of) a lion, hands (and) feet (of) the Zu-bird.
>
> Shulak was a normal lion stand[ing] on his hind legs.

---

21. Kummâ here is assumed to be a pseudonym of an Assyrian prince. Cf. The introduction of the text "A Vision of the Nether World," *ANET*, 109.

6. [Ma]mitu (had) the head (of) a goat, human hands (and) feet,

Nedu, the gatekeeper of the netherworld, (had) the head (of) a lion, human hands, feet (of) a bird.

'All that is Evil' (had) two heads; one head was (that of) a lion, the other head [...].

7 ... (had) three feet; the two in front were (those of) a bird, the hind one was (that of) an ox; he was possessed of awesome brilliance.

Two gods—I know not their names—one (had) the head, hands (and) feet (of) the Zu-bird; in his left ... ;

8. The other was provided with a human head; the headgear was a crown; in his right he carried a Mace; in his left ... In all, fifteen gods were present. When I saw them I prayed [to them].[22]

Further along in line 13 of the same text, we also see the concept of being caught away by the lock of one's hair, as Ezekiel experienced in 8:3. This part of the text states, "The nether world was filled with terror; before the prince lay utter st[ill]ness ... took me by the locks of my forehead and dre[w me] before him."[23]

One can discern from this brief introduction that visions depicting figures with an inter-mingling of animal and human traits were not at all foreign to individuals of this time period. Indeed, Ezekiel does not stand alone in this regard when it comes to the use of these particular motifs and images. Where Israelite literature had been devoid of such colorful depictions, other cultures had experienced them for centuries. These types of texts give credence to the notion of Babylon's literary influence on Ezekiel as we discussed in ch. 1. In light of this probable Mesopotamian influence we can begin to unpack the meaning behind Ezekiel's first vision.

22. Ibid., 109.
23. Ibid., 110.

The Meaning of the Theophanic Vision for the House of Israel

The Vision as an Interpretive Grid

The complexity of the meaning of the chariot-throne vision is matched only by its popularity throughout the centuries. For example, when highlighting the prophets of old, the second century BCE Jewish author, Ben Sirach (49:8) opted to highlight this introductory vision as a means of identifying the great prophet Ezekiel. Understandably, beyond its memorable qualities it's the complexity of the vision which has opened the door to a plethora of meanings. It must be pointed out, however, that Ezekiel's message here in the opening chapters is fused with the vision itself. The prophet's message cannot be heard apart from the symbolism that houses the message within the vision. It is for this very reason that any exposition of the text must begin by taking seriously the meaning of the vision and its symbolism for those who heard it.

On a surface level, the theophanic depiction of Yahweh in chs. 1–3 had a foreboding tone, which could not be overlooked by Ezekiel's audience. As previously noted, covenant curse issues were indeed in play.[24] These covenant curses are heightened by the visionary depictions of Yahweh especially in the imagery accompanying the storm theophany. Niehaus comments that in "Ezekiel's visions by Kebar and after, one fact is paramount: what he saw was disastrous. Yahweh appears in an awesome storm theophany as covenant judge [. . .] he comes in theophanic judgment. The revelation of his glory portends not covenant blessings but covenant curses—disaster for his people, who have long broken their covenant. As he visited and filled his tent, tabernacle, and temple with his glory, he will now depart his temple as a sign of disapprobation of a sinful people."[25] As I hope to demonstrate

---

24. Even after making an in-depth analysis of the parallels between Ezekiel and the Mesopotamian city laments, Petter admits that it is the curse motif that serves as the covenantal "framework" behind the prophecy of Ezekiel. Cf. Petter, "Book of Ezekiel," 169–70.

25. Niehaus, *God at Sinai*, 255. Petter, "The Book of Ezekiel," 143 n. 8, points out that the use of *sĕ'ārāh* appears in the prophets predominantly associated with the "stormy presence of God coming to destroy either Israel or her foes. This storm is always associated with God's presence or his voice (Isa 29:6; Jer 23:19; 30:23; Zech 9:14)." Keel, *Jahwe-Visionen*, 252, also picks up on the importance of theophany to Ezekiel's message.

throughout this chapter this is exactly the picture Ezekiel is seeking to relay to his audience.

At the same time, one could argue that Ezekiel's use of specific words help anchor his message to earlier theophanic appearances. For example, the use of סְעָרָה ("storm wind") in v. 4 appears to hark back to Elijah's encounter with the theophany of the chariot of Yahweh in 2 Kings 2:11. However, while similar terminology may exist between these two, there is not necessarily a direct one-to-one connection between each chariot appearance.[26] In this regard, Niehaus correctly points out that the theophany of Ezekiel "surpasses in awesomeness and detail any other in the OT."[27] There can be no doubt that the theophanic imagery of previous Israelite writers did play a role in Ezekiel's description of what he saw, but it should in no way be limited to these surface linguistic and historical references and explanations. Also, one must contend with the fact that for the average person of Ezekiel's day, knowing the minutest linguistic details of the Hebrew text (e.g., 2 Kings 2) concerning theophanic appearances is improbable. Even though we can assume that a prevailing oral tradition of the past must have been known, there appears to have been more behind the vision than a simple recollection of Elijah's chariot theophany. Could it be that Ezekiel's audience recognized in the vision sequence a deeper meaning that was elicited from the imagery and symbolism present around them in their exilic setting? I believe the answer is in the affirmative. Again, that is not to say that oral tradition could not have informed the populace about the great appearances of Yahweh in the past. At the very least, it is probable that they would have been familiar with the language of the Sinai theophany, but to what degree Ezekiel is relying solely on it, one cannot be certain.

These concerns being noted, if we assume, as with Niehaus, that (at least some of—parenthesis mine) the people knew about earlier Hebrew texts and tradition, then even the terminology, in a general sense, found in the first chapter plays a vital role in presenting Ezekiel's message as to the coming judgment. Niehaus succinctly points out

---

26. Niehaus, *God at Sinai*, 256. The picture presented here is much like that of Dan 7:9–10. Two possible conclusions can be drawn from the similar language used here and in Daniel: 1) Daniel may very well be borrowing theophanic language from Ezekiel to describe his dream-vision of God, or; 2) Ezekiel may be having an independent revelation that is described in similar terms to that of 2 Kings 2.

27. Ibid., 264.

that, "The phraseology, moreover, sadly anticipates the disastrous judgment Yahweh intends. The phrase "sound of a great storm" (קוֹל הֲמֻלָּה) occurs elsewhere only in Jeremiah 11:16 ... where it characterizes Yahweh's judgment on Judah. The combination of "roar" (קוֹל) and "many waters" (מַיִם רַבִּים) recalls the portrayal of Yahweh enthroned above the judgment waters of the Flood (Ps 29:3, 10). The sound of the creatures' wings is like that of an army, and God will bring an army against Judah. Against such an ominous background, Ezekiel hears Yahweh's 'thunderous voice.'"[28] Thus, one could argue that there is a strong possibility that Ezekiel is adopting judgment language from other Hebrew texts in an effort to harmonize his message with his contemporary Jeremiah and those who came before.

On a similar note, Charles Walmesley in 1778 also noticed the ominous tone of the vision. For Walmesley, the use of the whirlwind and the imagery in the vision has the primary purpose of "expressing something terrible and threatening."[29] He goes on to posit that the amber and fire that Ezekiel saw in the vision points to the wrath of the Lord and presents Yahweh in all his anger about to take vengeance on Israel for their sin of idolatry and crimes against him.[30] The presence of the word מַחֲנֶה for "army" or "host" in 1:24 again reflects the imagery of military activity and the ominous threat of invasion that awaited the nation of Judah.

Walmesley's and Niehaus's observations of foreboding along with Niehaus's assumption that literary hooks are being used by Ezekiel to evoke mental pictures from both present and past Hebrew writers seems to be what is in play here. Cross also posits the possibility of an earlier Canaanite influence from the storm god myths where the sound that Ezekiel hears in 1:25 and later in 10:5 is the thunder/voice of Yahweh (i.e., *Šadday*) accompanying the theophany.[31] Cross's link also seems likely as it relates to the concept of theophany due in part to the reality that Hebrew texts do indeed appear to reflect specific Canaanite borrowing (e.g., Ps 29). Nevertheless, beyond these types of general parallels a more refined understanding of the symbolism appears to be in play.

28. Ibid., 259.
29. Walmesley, "Ezechiel's Vision Explained," 17. Cf. also ibid., 3–73.
30. Ibid., 57–59.
31. Cross, *Canaanite Myth*, 58.

To summarize then, we can adduce that Ezekiel did not attempt to depict the visionary presence of Yahweh from a strictly Neo-Babylonian context without an anchor to the past. His use of the storm theophany (i.e., from the Sinai tradition) and the chariot imagery (i.e., from Elijah's ascension) served as the foundation for the highly symbolic message that followed. At the same time, Ezekiel did not work in a vacuum regarding his Babylonian setting, but rather built upon the theological principles of the past all the while housing his message in imagery relevant to his contemporary audience in Babylon.[32] This would make for a perfect balance of the past and the present as a means to deliver a message for the future of Jerusalem and to those in exile. Judgment was coming and in every way, linguistically, symbolically, and practically, the people of Judah needed to recognize the sad state of affairs in which they found themselves.

The Indictment

As noted above, the most prominent indictment against Judah, while not the only, is that of idolatry.[33] The sequence of visions and indictments in this section sets the stage for the rest of the book when it comes to understanding the reason *why* Yahweh is punishing his people and bringing the covenant curses upon them.[34] In this vein, Kutsko has opted to focus on this idolatry motif in the book of Ezekiel. He points out numerous passages that develop idolatry as the primary cause of the exile.[35] From as early as the call of Ezekiel (1:28—3:27

---

32. Many scholars point to the link between the sapphire pavement in Exod 24:10 and that in Ezekiel's vision in Ezek 10:1. See for example, Berry, "Glory of Yahweh," 117. The use of both Babylonian and former Hebrew literature is apparent throughout the book of Ezekiel. It is not my desire to belittle the place the former literature played in Ezekiel's arsenal of literary symbols and motifs. What is important is to identify unique motifs and symbolism from Babylon that served a particular purpose in the message of the author.

33. So too Petter, "Book of Ezekiel," 114–18.

34. Ibid., 119. Although Petter argues for a parallel between the laments found in Mesopotamian city laments and Ezekiel's "lament" for Jerusalem, she nonetheless sees the validity in the theory that Judah has fallen under the curses of the covenant because of their sin.

35. Kutsko, *Between Heaven and Earth*, 29, has developed a detailed chart wherein he lists no less than 50 instances in the book of Ezekiel where improper worship or idolatry of some kind is presented.

especially 2:3, 5–8; 3:9, 26–27), idolatry is referenced as a reason for judgment. It is developed further in chs. 5 (vv. 6–11), 6 (vv. 4–6, 9, 13), 8 (vv. 3, 5, 10–12, 14), 14, 16, 18, 20, and 23. There can be little doubt that idolatry is in fact the epitome of Judah's failures.

The indictment of the prophet moves from the general to the specific as the book progresses.[36] It is important to notice this deductive principle in the development of the rhetorical structure of the book. For example, in the case of idolatry, Ezekiel uses general indictments beginning in ch. 4 and continues to get more specific as the text gets closer to the departure of the glory of the Lord in ch. 11. As Ezekiel's presentation of the oracles gets closer to this key change (i.e., the second vision sequence in the proposed framework), more precise details begin to emerge. One can discern that tension is building within the text which culminates with the first covenant curse of divine abandonment. As this literary movement takes place, Ezekiel, through the word of the Lord, begins to be more and more specific as to the reason behind the departure of Yahweh. This departure was primarily due to the accumulation of specific intolerable idolatrous activities.[37]

Incessant idolatry does appear to be the proverbial "straw that breaks the camel's back" in this section of Ezekiel. The oppression of Judah by the Babylonians did not drive the nation to their Suzerain; instead they adopted the belief that they needed to return to their old practices of idol worship (cf. Jer 44:15–23). Nowhere is this more pronounced than in ch. 8.[38] In 8:3 the "idol of jealousy" (סֶמֶל הַקִּנְאָה) is presented but this, the text notes, is not the greatest of Judah's idolatrous abominations. In v. 10 Ezekiel is confronted with the images of

---

36. Ibid., 25–27.

37. Fishbane, "Sin and Judgment," 135–36, suggests that the reforms of Josiah should have stamped out the practices delineated here in ch. 8. He suggests that they reflect more accurately the time of Manasseh and may have served as a basis for the indictments based on past performance. However, he goes on to point out that the residual effects of the sins of Manasseh may have remained in the cultic worship up to Ezekiel's day. Similarly, Kaufmann, *Religion of Israel*, 430, suggests that ch. 8 is only a "proverb" that reflects the "shadows" of the distant past from the time of Manasseh. He sees in this vision a call for retribution that "still clamors for satisfaction" (cf. 435–36). There can be no doubt that the remembrance of many of the sins of Manasseh are reflected in the visions of the temple in Ezekiel. Nevertheless, to suggest that the sins of the people during the exile and immediately before, were not idolatrous fails to take into account the obvious idolatrous nature of the people even after the fall of Jerusalem (cf. Jer 7:17–18, 33; 44).

38. See Ackroyd, *Exile and Restoration*, 40–41.

animals and detestable things that are present in the temple which are depicted as carvings on the walls of the house of the Lord. Here Ezekiel sees the elders burning incense and worshiping these images "in the dark" (בַּחֹשֶׁךְ). Next, Ezekiel is shown even "greater abominations" (תּוֹעֵבוֹת גְּדֹלוֹת) than these, continuing with the worship of Tammuz by the women.[39] From here (i.e., v. 16) the prophet is taken to the inner court between the porch and the altar where 25 men are seen bowing down (מִשְׁתַּחֲוִיתֶם) to the sun (שֶׁמֶשׁ) with their backs to the Holy of Holies.[40]

---

39. In the introduction of the text "Descent of Ishtar to the Netherworld," Dalley links the annual Assyrian celebration of the return of Dumuzi (Tammuz=June/July) found at the end of the myth with Ezek 8:14. Apparently this was a mourning period when the statues of Dumuzi in Nineveh, Assur, Arbela and Kalah were bathed and anointed and then laid in state. For a description of the role Tammuz played in the Babylonian pantheon, see Jeremias, *Alte Testament,* 114–21; Alster, "Tammuz," *DDD,* 828–34; and Jacobsen, *Toward the Image of Tammuz,* 73–101. Jacobsen points out that Tammuz was the "intransitive" god of food. This entailed being the power of sap that rises in trees and plants—Damu; of grain and beer—Dumuzi of the Grain; of milk—Dumuzi the Shepherd; and the power in the date palm and its fruit—Dumuzi Ama-ushumgal-anna. This would make sense if the people were facing food shortages due to famine (one of the curses sent by Yahweh cf. 5:16, 17; 6:11; 7:15 etc.). Jacobsen, 90–91, also points out that the occurrence of the Tammuz cult in Ezekiel truly depicts the cult as one moderated by women and largely adhered to by the female populace in Mesopotamia. Block also suggests that the people's misconception that Yahweh had abandoned his people may have been the catalyst for the women using the Tammuz lament and adapting it into a lament for Yahweh's return. Cf. Block, "Divine Abandonment," 37, and Block, *Ezekiel 1–24,* 297–300. So too Petter, "Book of Ezekiel," 127.

40. May, "Departure," 309–21, is no doubt correct when he makes the assumption that what is being viewed by Ezekiel is worship of the sun and the festivals associated with the equinoxes. He posits that the vision of ch. 8 was Ezekiel's own recollection of the ceremonies in the temple at Jerusalem. May's article, while informative, places too much emphasis on Ezekiel's reliance on the probable practices of sun worship in Jerusalem as opposed to the tenor of Ezekiel's message. Ezekiel clearly is belittling the practice, but is not using it as *the* means of supporting his message against idolatry. See also, Hollis, "Sun Cult," 87–110. Hollis suggests that Solomon's temple construction was based upon an oracle (i.e., 1 Kgs 8:12–13) concerning the sun god because on May 22, 948 BCE there was an eclipse of the sun (a harbinger of bad things). Further, the orientation of Solomon's temple was in such a way that as the sun rose over the Mount of Olives, it would shine into the holy of holies.

Taylor, *Yahweh and the Sun,* 147–58, deals specifically with Ezek 8:16–17. Taylor has shown, what I feel correctly, that the practice of solar worship played a key part in the Jerusalem cult until the period of the exile. He also has noted the parallels between Ezek 8:16 and those found in 1 Kgs 8:12. The directional motif is definitely being played upon as Solomon turns his back on the temple to bless the people before the presence of Yahweh *enters* the temple whereas the 25 men are actually turning their back on Yahweh to worship the sun before Yahweh's *kābôd departs* (italics mine).

As a result of these blatant covenantal infractions, the closing verse of ch. 8 spells out clearly the fury of the Lord, which will be poured out upon the land. In light of what the prophet has seen, a picture long before prophesied by Isaiah (2:8–9), Yahweh will act; Jerusalem and the temple will not be spared. This idolatrous picture is the setting and the focal point, which elicits the first and greatest covenant curse, the departure of the Lord.

On a side note, G. R. Berry propounded that the vision of the glory of the Lord (1:1a, 4–28a) was originally placed just before 43:4.[41] He asserts that the throne imagery in chs. 3, 8, 9, and 10 was a later addition to the text. He further comments that these additions to the text were added "without any great significance."[42] It is here that I must disagree with Berry's conclusions. In the light of the final form, which Berry dates to a third-century-BCE redactor, the throne vision played the *defining* structural role in the entire book. It is the foundation for the message of covenant curses and a vital part of the structural framework that holds the entire work together (see ch. 1, above). Furthermore, it is the appearance of the glory of Yahweh in ch. 43 that gives the final form its cohesiveness and serves as a fitting bookend to the overall prophecy. In the consummation of the age of restoration, the reversal of all the curses once enacted upon the nation would be finalized. The book had begun with the greatest curse of all, the departure of Yahweh's presence,[43] but now ends with the reversal of that first enacted curse, namely the return of Yahweh to his temple and people. This is especially forceful in light of the final phrase in the book, "Yahweh *is* there" (יְהוָה שָׁמָּה).

Theological Message

There are valuable theological principles communicated in the *kābôd* (i.e., glory) visions of this section of Ezekiel. The mobility of the char-

---

41. See Berry, "Title of Ezekiel," 54–57. Berry, 56, argues that the text containing the vision was removed from before 43:4 and placed at the beginning of the book (to which vv. 1–3 were added to fill the gap). He insists that this was done by the redactor(s) in order to have an inaugural vision like those found in Isaiah and Jeremiah.

42. Berry, "Glory of Yahweh," 116.

43. Cf. Niehaus, *Ancient Near Eastern Themes*, 32, where he notes that "temple abandonment is the most profound curse and can bring a host of others."

iot-throne sent a clear message to the exiles—Yahweh's presence was mobile—as it had been in the wilderness.[44] Even though they were in exile in Babylon, the presence of Yahweh was not restricted to borders.[45] Kutsko stresses the importance of three key concepts of Ezekiel's theological presentation to the exiles. He asserts that any exilic theology had to: 1) "account for the exilic experience"; 2) "maintain God's transcendence in order to provide the vehicle for God to trespass borders"; and 3) "employ an image of God's proximity whose sentient quality the prophet can communicate to those who have no vision."[46]

To a certain degree, Kutsko is perhaps correct in his theological assessment of the *kābôd* visions. Offering hope and an explanation for the exiles are key aspects of the message that Ezekiel was presenting. However, as will be demonstrated here and below, the tone of Ezekiel, at least for the first 24 chapters, is one of foreboding focusing on covenant indictment and curses. It appears that a greater theological message is being presented by the use of these visions—the house of Israel is in serious trouble with their Suzerain. Other theological messages at this point are merely ancillary.

Now, that is not to downplay ancillary theological factors present in the chariot-throne vision for these too had a role to play in

---

44. Petter, "Book of Ezekiel," 138, posits that the *kābôd* of Yahweh is actually "hovering" over the cherubim with free movement on its own.

45. Kutsko, *Between Heaven and Earth*, 28, lists several OT passages as examples of Israel's belief in a locally restricted deity e.g., Deut 4:28; 28:64; Judg 11:24; Mic 4:5; 1 Sam 26:19; 1 Kgs 20:23, 28; 2 Kgs 5:17; and Ps 137:4. However, with the exception of Ps 137:4 (even this is asking a question not stating a fact), most, if not all, do *not* support the concept of a God restricted to the confines of Israel but rather a *perception* of an individual in a given situation.

Koch, *Prophets*, 2:88, also notes the omnipresent nature of Yahweh as presented in this vision. Kutsko suggests that this is pointing directionally to the exiles in Babylon. He asserts that Ezekiel is seeing the glory of the Lord depart from Jerusalem and head toward the land of Babylon to the east. This concept is noted in Jewish literature by Morgenstern, "Gates of Righteousness," 7. However, this seems forced in the context and most likely only represents the movement of the presence of Yahweh out the eastern gate of the temple complex to the Mount of Olives from where Yahweh can then view the destruction of the city (so too Brownlee, *Ezekiel*, 165). Further, this was the gate of the king/prince's entrance (1 Chr 9:18). Therefore, it is fitting that this was the gate of the "King's" departure. For a full discussion on the history of the eastern gate, see Morgenstern, "The Gates of Righteousness," 1–37. For a discussion of the east gate in Ezekiel's vision, see Turner, "Gate, East," 409.

46. Kutsko, *Between Heaven and Earth*, 152. Cf. also the comments by Wilson, "Prophecy in Crisis," 164–65.

the overall message to the exiles. For example, theologically Ezekiel needed to stress that while the earthly temple would be destroyed by the Babylonians, the heavenly presence and throne of Yahweh were beyond the reach of the Babylonian war machine.[47] The earthly temple was only a temporary dwelling but Yahweh's heavenly throne was eternal (see Ps 115:2–3).[48] Even in the midst of the turmoil of the exile and the destruction of Jerusalem, Yahweh still could reach out to those in Babylon. For those who may have lost hope in the power of their God Yahweh promised to be their "sanctuary for a little while" (לְמִקְדָּשׁ מְעַט) while they served their sentence in exile (cf. Ezek 11:16).[49] Thus, Yahweh is not "in the sanctuary; he is their sanctuary."[50]

The fact that Yahweh was using Ezekiel as a prophet was further evidence of the presence of the Lord with those in exile. This is another means by which the prophet's message receives the direct approval of Yahweh before the people. The vision of the destruction of Jerusalem and the warnings to those remaining in Judah pointed to the truthfulness of Ezekiel's message. The people needed to change their understanding of their God. A building or national borders could not confine him. He could use Ezekiel in a foreign land and he could reach out to those in exile. Moreover, no matter where they lived, as an omnipresent God he could see their sin. Hence, the people needed to listen to Ezekiel, as the mouthpiece of Yahweh. In this regard, Ezekiel's message was correct. The exile would not be short lived as the false prophets in Babylon were prophesying (13:16). Moreover, those who had remained in Jerusalem may have felt that they were the chosen of God because they had not been exiled (33:24), but the real "truth" was soon to be revealed in their destruction and/or exile as well.

---

47. Levey, *The Targum of Ezekiel*, 3, 11.

48. Ps 115:2–3 states, "Why should the nations say, 'Where, now, is their God?' But our God is in the heavens; He does whatever He pleases" (NASB). This passage reflects the message Ezekiel was trying to get across to the exiles. Yes, they were away from their homeland, and yes, they were away from the temple, but soon even those in Jerusalem would not have the temple for their safety. They and the exiles needed to realize the omnipresent nature of their God and his role as sovereign over all nations and gods.

49. Wiesel, "Ezekiel," 169, suggests this "little sanctuary" was actually a reference to the first synagogue.

50. Kutsko, *Between Heaven and Earth*, 2–3. See also Rendtorff, "Concept of Revelation," 37.

The Message behind the Symbolism

Apart from those theological insights mentioned above, the theological message present in Ezekiel's message and vision sequences served to promote both new and renewed theological ideas over the course of Israel's later history. While the immediate theological insights were important, they could serve an even greater function over time as the Israelites looked back on their texts and studied the various character traits of their God and his interaction with his people. However, beyond the overarching theological facets of the chariot-throne vision, the message behind the symbolism and imagery played an even greater role in the immediate historical context.

According to the dating of the second vision (i.e., chs. 8–11— Aug/Sept 592 BCE), Jerusalem had not yet fallen to Babylon. It is my contention that apart from the obvious theological dimension of the visions, Ezekiel was painting a graphic picture in the mind's eye for all his readers and hearers to understand clearly what was about to befall Jerusalem. The message advanced by the symbolism and imagery of these and later visions of Ezekiel were the basis of Ezekiel's rhetorical strategy and framework. As I have argued in ch. 1 above, the Babylonian setting of the prophet helps to explain the uniqueness of his presentation. But that unique presentation rests in Ezekiel's choice of symbols and an understanding that they were pregnant with meaning for the exilic community.[51] Thus, it is not at all farfetched to recognize Ezekiel's purpose in choosing certain images to present his message. Yes, the first and greatest covenant curse was unfolding before the readers'/hearers' eyes, but the vision held more information than a mere telling of the curse; it told of the *how*, *who*, and *why* through specific symbols adopted by Ezekiel from his immediate surroundings. The cultural "garden" of Babylon offered rich and ripe images ready for the picking. Ezekiel would take every advantage of the geographical location in which Yahweh had placed him.

---

51. Betts, *Ezekiel the Priest,* 66–68, and Sweeney, "Ezekiel: Zadokite Priest," 735–36, suggest that the key to interpreting the symbolism of the chariot throne is in the tabernacle of Moses and the Solomonic temple. Betts notes especially the cherubim over the Ark of the Covenant. This position may have merit on a basic level, however, the detailed imagery and the multi-faced beings seem to move beyond the realm of the past temple experiences of the prophet-priest.

The Living Beings/Cherubim: (Akkadian—Kuribu=כְּרוּב)[52]

From before the turn of the twentieth century scholars have noted the Babylonian imagery present in Ezekiel's vision of ch. 1 especially as it relates to the four living beings in ch. 1 and the cherubim in ch. 10[53] (e.g., Dussaud,[54] Jeremias,[55] Meissner,[56] Dhorme and Vincent).[57] First and foremost, the thing to note from these scholars' work is that the concept of multi-faced cherubim easily predates Ezekiel in ANE art

---

52. Dhorme and Vincent, in "Les chérubins," 336, state, "Nous n'hésitons point à reconnaître au mot כרוב la même racine qu'au mot *karibu* des Babyloniens." See also Bodi, *Poem of Erra*, 37 n. 13, and Meissner, "Bemerkungen," 474–77, esp. 476–77.

53. For a discussion on how the early church fathers interpreted ch. 1, see Christman, *"What Did Ezekiel See?"* A common understanding of the vision of Ezekiel at this period in church history was to read and interpret them in light of the New Testament and Christological issues. For example, the vision of the four cherubim and their four faces represented the four gospel writers (i.e., Matthew, Mark, Luke, and John). For an in depth discussion of the history of this perspective, see Fromaget, *Symbolisme des Quatre Vivant*. Also, the Targum of Ezekiel interprets the text by suggesting the creatures each had 16 faces and 64 wings. Cf. Levey, *The Targum of Ezekiel*, 20–21, esp. 21 n. 5.

54. Dussaud, "Visions d'Ézéchiel," 308. Dussaud sees in this ANE parallel a borrowing from depictions of Shamash. Dussaud acknowledged the Babylonian and Assyrian imagery that inspired Ezekiel in the vision of the chariot-throne and the radiant presence of the glory of Yahweh above the cherubim. He asserts that this imagery was prolific in both Assyrian and Chaldean art and stretched well into the Persian period as a common symbol for divinity. He describes one common depiction in the ANE as a winged disk containing a human figure that appears over the heads of cherubim. This is perhaps a glimpse into the mindset of Ezekiel as he expounded this vision in available symbols and images.

55. Jeremias, *Alte Testament*, 580–85. Also, Layard, *Nineveh and Its Remains*, 70, gives a clear picture of an eagle-headed cherub/being from the ruins of Nineveh (ca. first century BCE). He also presents several pictures of reliefs from ancient Babylon and Assyria that clearly depict the eagle-headed cherub, the man-faced cherub, the copious lion-faced cherub, and the bull-faced cherub.

56. Meissner, "Bemerkungen," 474–77, esp. cols. 476–77. He notes, "Dass die Keruben, die Wächter zum Eingang des Paradieses, die Träger des göttlichen Thronwagens, sachlich auf die assyrischen Stier-und Löwenkolosse zurückgehen, war immer schon behauptet worden." He goes on to point out that the depictions of the cherubim under the chariot-throne in Ezekiel (and those guarding the entrance to paradise in Genesis) are directly related to the colossal bull and lion reliefs found in Assyria from the period of Esarhaddon. See also Bodi, *Poem of Erra*, 37; Meyers, "Cherubim," 899–900, esp. 900; and Collon, "Mesopotamian Iconography," 4315–17.

57. Dhorme and Vincent, "Les chérubins," 257, offer pictures from Assyrian reliefs, which show two-headed cherubim (man and lion) with wings and in various poses.

and architecture and could have been developed to suit his particular needs. It is upon this reality that we will proceed to unpack Ezekiel's chariot-throne vision.

When we look to Israelite literature it is clear that cherubim were indeed a part of the normal makeup of temple artistry. In 1 Kings 7:27–39 lions, bulls, and cherubim appear in Hiram's artisan work in the temple.[58] Lions, oxen, and cherubim definitely were common figures even in Hebrew art; however, in 1 Kings 7 the lions and the oxen do not appear *as* cherubim but merely accompany them. Even Ezekiel's temple vision in 41:18–19 presents only two-faced cherubim, that of a man and lion. There seems to be a better explanation for the four living beings/cherubim of Ezekiel's vision which have human bodies but the heads of different beasts—one closer to the ANE vision noted above in the opening of this chapter.[59]

---

58. Keel, *Jahwe-Visionen*, 162–63.

59. M'Fadyen, "Ezekiel," 504, suggests that the human, lion, ox, and eagle faces represent "intelligence, dignity, strength, and speed" respectively. So too, Siegman, *The Book of Ezechiel*, 1:11. Moule, *Notes on Ezekiel* 10, suggests (without explanation) that the faces represent the four tribal groupings around the tabernacle in the wilderness in Num 2; viz., Reuben—a man; Judah—a lion; Ephraim—an ox; and Dan—an eagle. Other scholars, such as Douglas Stuart and also Moshe Greenberg ("Ezekiel's Vision," 164–65) argue for a non-mythological perspective in the symbolism of these cherubim. Stuart feels that they are representative of the four main categories of created life forms. The ox represents the greatest of the domesticated animals, the eagle as the greatest of the birds of the air, the lion as the king of wild beasts and the human face an image of the dominion of all created earthly creatures. "Intelligence, strength, ferocity, freedom, etc. were all wrapped up in one of these special angelic creatures." Cf. Stuart, *Ezekiel*, 32 (as noted by Niehaus, *God at Sinai*, 257 n. 49). See a similar position given by Walmesley, "Ezechiel's Vision Explained," 26–30. This interpretation is also common in rabbinic Judaism (*Exodus Rabba* 23:13). One problem exists with this understanding. In Ezekiel's vision all the faces appear equal in importance. This would make the human face depicting the "dominion" of mankind over the other three, not as convincing.

However, it is possible that a double entendre may be in play here in the text. As a priest familiar with the creation account of Genesis, Ezekiel's use of the imagery may very well have sought to show Yahweh's dominion over all creation. For a further discussion on Ezekiel's use of creation imagery, see, Petersen, "Creation in Ezekiel," 490–500. On the other hand, within the Babylonian context, it appears that Ezekiel had taken into account the threat and terror that these images would evoke in the minds of his listeners. The faces depicted on the cherubim are the same as the guardians of Babylonian and Assyrian temples (cf. Dussaud, "Les Visions d'Ézéchiel," 306). The awesome nature of the vision seems to conjure terror more than that of passive acknowledgement of Yahweh's supremacy over all creation. In this regard, the natural inclination of the exiles in a land inundated with similar symbolism would

The groundbreaking work of Lorenz Dürr in 1917 took a close look at chs. 1 and 10 of Ezekiel and the iconography related to the throne vision. In Dürr's study he was "decisive in demonstrating that the models for Ezekiel's visions should be sought in Babylonian iconography."[60] While Bodi downplays the findings of Dürr by concluding that nowhere is a four-faced figure found in ANE iconography such as is found in Ezekiel,[61] there is no reason not to assume that concepts could have been borrowed and reworked for Ezekiel's own purposes.[62] Interestingly, when speaking of Ezekiel's adaptation of ANE material, Bodi himself points out that "the material has been used in a creative way, being thoroughly reworked and fully adapted to the specific points which the Book of Ezekiel makes."[63] Therefore, by Bodi's own admission, limiting Ezekiel to an exact one-to-one parallel would in essence, tie the creative hands of the author. Toy's assumptions further this conclusion. He notes, "It is not necessarily true that the cherub-forms were bodily copies of Babylonian figures—the prophet may have got from these only the suggestion of composite creatures, and fashioned his material to suit the symbolism he had in mind. But the whole conception of this symbolism seems to be

---

naturally have been to draw parallels with the images of their new homeland as well. Interestingly, Greenberg (ibid., 163) also notes that the "composite nature of Ezekiel's creatures accords entirely with Mesopotamian and Syrian iconography. Composite deities and mythological beings are common in Egypt and Mesopotamia." Greenberg (164) does point out, however, the difficulties in finding a one-to-one parallel for the four-faced images described in Ezekiel's vision.

60. Bodi, *Poem of Erra*, 43, commenting on the work of Dürr, *Ezechiel's Vision*. For a critique of Dürr, see Vogt, "Vier 'Gesichter,'" 327–47, as noted by Bodi, *Poem of Erra*, 45 n. 42.

61. Bodi, *Poem of Erra*, 44. However, Keel, *Jahwe-Visionen*, 222–29, and Power, "Iconographic Windows," 356–57, give iconographic evidence of four-faced figures from Egypt and Mesopotamia although all four are the same face. Power notes the four-faced images found at the temple Ischali in the city-state of Eshnunna in ancient Ur proves that the concept existed in Mesopotamia. Further, Power (355) suggests that while no exact matches can be found, the similarities in ancient Near Eastern art betray Ezekiel's reliance on his surroundings.

62. In his monograph *Baal Tetramorphos*, Landerdorfer asserts that this four-faced image seen by Ezekiel was inspired by a four-faced Baal image that he links to the graven image set up by Manasseh (2 Kgs 21:7).

63. Bodi, *Poem of Erra*, 310.

Babylonian in form, though lofty moral and religious ideas attached to it by the prophet are the product of Israelitish thought."[64]

Thus we are left to determine what message Ezekiel was actually trying to portray by his use of these Babylonian symbols. The work of Egyptologist Jaroslav Černý may shed light on the message behind the symbolism. Černý, when studying Egyptian animal-headed gods with human bodies, pointed out that composite figures, at least in Egypt, often reflected the nature of the deity being represented. The animal trait (e.g., the falcon head for Horus) was seen as representative of the trait of the god. He comments, "thus the anthropomorphized gods were given a human body, but only seldom a human head, this mostly replaced by that of the animal in whose form the god originally used to appear."[65] This concept is helpful in understanding the message behind the symbols of Ezekiel. Isaac Matthews's conclusion is helpful when he suggests that "the four living beasts were the common symbols throughout Babylonia for 4 of their chief deities. Huge figures . . . cut in stone, stood in front of palaces and temples, and were symbols of the guardian deities. The bull colossus, with ox-face, was the symbol of Marduk; that with the lion-face was Nergal, the god of the underworld and of plague; that of the eagle was Ninib, god of the chase of war; while the human face represented Nabu, the announcer or revealer. Each one of these in Babylonia had a long and varied history . . . These 4 were chief in their pantheon at this time, and may be considered representing all the gods of the empire."[66] Matthews seems to have a clearer picture than most when it comes to Ezekiel's rhetorical strategy, although he neither teases out the implications of his connections nor does he point out the importance of the covenant curse angle.

---

64. Toy, "Babylonian Element," 64. See also Lenormant, *Origins*, 121–24. Lenormant also struggles with the many differences between the Babylonian and Assyrian reliefs depicting the cherub-like figures and those of Ezekiel but also recognizes (as of his time in 1880) that perhaps new evidence would be discovered to better understand Ezekiel's visions.

65. Černý, *Ancient Egyptian Religion*, 29.

66. Matthews, *Ezekiel*, 5. Even though Matthews assumes this section is to be attributed to a "scribal interpretation" of the preceding vision, this in and of itself does not take away from the imagery that is present. The author clearly had an intended focus in mind based upon the imagery in play as noted above. The thematic unity of this section and the detailed description lends itself better to a unified whole as opposed to a piecemeal presentation by several hands.

It seems possible that Ezekiel incorporated these symbols representative of the Babylonian gods into his vision, but lowered their stature to the level of mere attendants to the greater deity, Yahweh.[67] It is clear that scripturally the cherubs do play a subservient role in relation to the throne of God (cf. 2 Sam 6:2; 22:11; 2 Kgs 19:15 see also Ps 18:11[Heb]) but here the imagery presents a more nuanced picture.[68] Matthews comments, "to build the symbols of Babylonian deities into the old pattern of Hebrew religion was a natural and easy task for an exile."[69] In this vein, part of Ezekiel's intent may very well have been, as noted in ch. 1 above, to theologically "educate" those in exile who may have been illiterate. Černý posits that at least in Egypt the portrayal of these gods as such in artwork was a common way to present, in a concrete fashion, the deity before the people who were largely illiterate.[70] As in the case of Ezekiel, we can assume the same level of illiteracy for most of his audience, especially for those of the second wave of exiles in 587 BCE (cf. Jer 52:15). Therefore, the use of real-life iconography adapted to an aural and/or literary setting seems to be a possibility when "educating" the exilic community about the nature of their offended God, especially if the vision/prophecy was read aloud in a public place (cf. Ezek 3:11; 11:25; 12:23; 14:4; 24:19; Jer 36:6; 51:61). This would have been an effective teaching tool both *before* the fall of Jerusalem as a warning of impending doom and *after* as a means of educating the exilic community about the sovereignty of their God.

---

67. Matthews, *Ezekiel*, 5–6.

68. Ezekiel as a priest would have been well aware of the cherubim in the temple as would any "pious" Hebrew (1 Kgs 6:23–35; 8:6–7).

69. Matthews, *Ezekiel*, 6. Matthews argues that Ezekiel saw these images as real and representative of the Babylonian deities that were actual living gods. He posits that Ezekiel is endowing life upon these stone deities of Babylon as a means to show that they were in some way real deities to be feared, what Matthews calls a natural assumption for a Jewish person viewing the colossal statues after having been defeated and placed in exile. However, in light of Ezekiel's priestly heritage and his clear monotheistic thrust, especially in the chariot-throne vision, it is unlikely that Ezekiel saw these figures as any more than available symbols to represent all that the Hebrews had come to hate and fear in their new land of exile. Moreover, Matthews's interpretation does not fit with the overall tenor of Ezekiel. It is better to see in the description of the cherubim a symbolic expression of Babylonian thought without attributing a polytheistic perspective to Ezekiel. This is especially true in a period of a quickly developing Jewish monotheistic world-view. See further the comments of Lang on monotheism in the exile in footnote 11, above.

70. Černý, *Ancient Egyptian Religion*, 40.

God's Glory Revealed 121

This pedagogical bent being noted, the symbolism behind the creatures is striking when one looks at what they stood for in Babylon. Ezekiel here is divesting them of their role as "gods" (contra Matthews)[71] while keeping aspects of their representative status intact.[72] Numerous texts from the ANE not only attribute these particular animal/human traits (i.e., the ox, lion, eagle, man) appearing in Ezekiel's visions to the Babylonian gods but also help identify the gods' function within the cosmos. For example, throughout ANE literature we find references to Nergal as the god of the underworld/death and plague,[73] Ninib as the god of the chase of war,[74] Nabu as the announcer or revealer[75] and Marduk as the chief deity and representative of Babylon.[76] Ironically,

71. Power, "Iconographic Windows," 360, also notes the intended subordination of the "creatures" to the "exalted One."

72. Collins, "Apocalyptic Genre," 91, correctly notes, albeit in relation to mythical allusions in Daniel, yet relevant to our discussion of Ezekiel, that "scholars who identify mythological images do not claim that they have the same meaning or reference in their new contexts." It is this position that appears to be relevant here in Ezekiel. In light of the overall tenor and message of the prophet, it makes no sense for Ezekiel to present a pantheon of gods on par with Yahweh or even in a henotheistic manner. To suggest that Ezekiel would have thought that the Babylonian gods were real (as perhaps many of the exiles may have assumed) would have been to fly in the face of his message that Yahweh was sovereign over all nations and, by extension, their gods. So too Brownlee, *Ezekiel*, 11–12.

73. Cf. Foster, *Before the Muses*, 706–8. In several of the brief texts presented in *Before the Muses* from various regions of Mesopotamia, Nergal, also known as Erra, is presented as the warrior god of the underworld and as a lion. Cf. Foster, *Before the Muses*, 506–24 (esp. the introduction on 506) and references to the *Poem of Erra and Ishum* below.

74. Also known as Ninurta or Ningirsu. In the *Cylinders of Gudea*, Ningirsu is depicted as an eagle circling to enter his temple. The text reads, "The warrior, Ningirsu, was entering into the temple; the king of the house came. Being (like) an eagle gazing at a wild bull; the warrior, his entering into his temple being (like) a storm roaring into battle, Ningirsu was coming into his temple." Cf. "Cylinders of Gudea," COS 2:155:431. Interestingly, Ninurta, when being described in battle, is also given the title "wild bull" and the "lion-headed one" cf. Cooper, *Return of Ninurta*, 75, 87, respectively. Cf. also Steymans, *Deuteronomium 28*, 94–100, esp. 94–95. Steymans (95) points out that Ninurta is represented by both the bird and "double lion cub." It appears that many of these particular animal designations had a wide usage for several gods over time. Note too that Ezek 17:3 uses the metaphor of the eagle for Babylon and Egypt.

75. Foster, *Before the Muses*, 702–3, deals with a section titled "The Names of Nabu" in which Nabu is called the "Bearer of the Tablet of Divine Destinies." In ANE iconography, Nabu is generally depicted in human form carrying a tablet and stylus.

76. The name Marduk in Akkadian is ᵈAMAR.UTU, "calf of the sun." Gaebelein, "Marduk," 3:244. However, Abusch, "Marduk," 543, spells it ᵈAMAR.UD in Akkadian and amar.uda.ak in Sumerian. He also notes that "calf of the storm" is to be preferred

the eagle symbolism of Ninib (the god of war) aligns very closely to the symbolism found in the curse passage of Deuteronomy 28:49. The text reads, "And Yahweh will raise up against you a nation from the far reaches of the earth, like a swift-flying *eagle*, a nation whose language you do not know (italics mine)."[77] One could argue that Ezekiel is playing off Deuteronomic language as a means of warning his people of exactly *who*, in an earthly sense, would be responsible for the coming destruction.

Thus we can preliminarily conclude from the imagery in the chariot-throne vision that Babylon, whose chief god was Marduk, would be the means by which Yahweh would fulfill several curses of the Law. Some of these curses that were coming upon the people of Jerusalem can be seen in the primary roles attributed to these four Babylonian gods. For example, death (Lev 26:24) and plague (Lev 26:21) could be equated to Nergal while the curse of war could be connected to the god Ninib (Lev 26:17). Furthermore, all the horrors of being conquered were being "announced" and "revealed" symbolically by Nabu's presence in the imagery. Ezekiel goes on to explicitly announce these curses to the people in 5:12, 17; 6:11; 7:15.

The irony is unmatched. Ezekiel is using the very symbols of the enemy to present a message against his own people, yet the message itself was not at all new. Jeremiah had also warned of Yahweh's use of the surrounding nations to punish Israel (Jer 1:1, 14, 15; 4:6; 5:15; 6:1, 22; 10:22; 15:12; 25:9; 47:2; 49:5; 50:3; see also Ezek 28:7; Joel 2:20).[78] The difference is, however, that Ezekiel is drawing upon the symbolism of the Babylonian gods as a means of identifying the specific nation which would enact this judgment.

One final note of clarification, however, needs to be made regarding Ezekiel's use of Babylonian imagery in the chariot-throne visions of chs. 1–3 and 10–11. Linguistically there is support for the position

---

over "calf of the sun" because Marduk was not a solar deity (some would dispute this however).

77. Cf. also the language of the eagle (נשר) in Jer 48:40 and 49:22 in the oracles of judgment against Moab and Edom at the hands of Babylon (Hab 1:8 and Hos 8:1 has similar imagery). In the Hosea passage, covenant transgression is in view as a reason for the judgment of Israel.

78. Even the later judgment on Babylon is to come from the north, cf. Jer 50:3, 9, 41; 51:48. See also Tyre's judgment in Ezek 26:7. Moreover, in chs. 38–39 God draws all the nations of the north to his judgment (cf. 38:6, 15; 39:2).

that Ezekiel used Babylonian imagery in chs. 1–3 but changed the wording in chs. 10–11 in order to accommodate a Hebrew theological perspective for the event of temple abandonment in the second vision. In Ezekiel's description of the throne bearers in ch. 1 he notes that they are in the "likeness of four living beings" (דְּמוּת אַרְבַּע חַיּוֹת). However, in ch. 10 he identifies these same throne bearers/living beings as "cherubim" (כְּרֻבִים). This is not a mere oversight or an editorial error.[79] Ezekiel's use of "living beings" (חַיּוֹת) in his first vision of the chariot-throne in chs. 1–3 and "cherubim" for the throne bearers in ch. 10 serves a rhetorical function within his presentation of judgment. As just noted above, in the first vision the symbolism of the living beings reflected that of the gods of Babylon. This same interpretation would not have served Ezekiel's purposes in chs. 10–11 when the glory of Yahweh departs. Ezekiel is making it clear that Yahweh was not being removed by other gods such as Marduk or by the Babylonians but rather was being born along by "cherubim" and leaving on his own accord.[80]

In this vein, missing among the "faces" of the four living beings mentioned earlier in ch. 1 and reintroduced here in ch. 10 is the face of the "bull" (שׁוֹר cf. 10:14).[81] It was Marduk who was the "Bull/calf of

---

79. Contra Cooke, *Ezekiel*, 113–14; and Power, "Iconographic Windows," 411, who argue that the cherub description in ch. 10 and the bull-faced creature of ch. 1 are to be equated and that Ezekiel is just realizing this in his second vision. Also, Greenberg, "Ezekiel's Vision," 163, makes a similar assumption but concludes that the reason for the differences between chs. 1 and 10 "eludes" him. While the confusion of the images is understandable, the conclusions of these scholars do not make sense of Ezekiel's priestly status. First, it is unrealistic to think that a priest would not be able to make the connection between the creatures in his first vision and the temple cherubim. Second, the conclusion that the bull face seen in the first vision is now a cherub does not make sense based upon earlier descriptions of the temple adornments and later in Ezek 41:18–19. In 1 Kings 7, the adornments of the temple included lions, oxen, *and* cherubim. There is no equating of the bull and cherubim in 1 Kings 7, nor do we see them equated in Ezek 41:19. Therefore, the actual change in appearance in the latter vision seems more in line with a change in the function and message of the symbolism as embraced here.

80. Petter, "Book of Ezekiel," 130–40, esp. 130–31, argues that the movement of the *kābôd* of Yahweh is independent of the cherubim. She also posits that based upon the verbs of movement in this passage (i.e., עָלָה [9:3] רוּם [10:4, 16] יָצָא [10:18] עָמַד [10:18; 11:23]) the avian imagery of the vision reflects a similar motif in Mesopotamian laments.

81. Block, "Text and Emotion," 431, suggests that the faces in this second vision are the same as the first vision but have been "rationalized" by the author. While this

heaven" and the head of the Babylonian pantheon as well as the patron god of Babylon. Ezekiel makes sure Marduk's image/face is not in any way associated with the removal of Yahweh. Yahweh was sovereign and no earthly god or army had power to remove him from his throne.[82] It should not at all be surprising to see Ezekiel identify this particular face as that of a cherub thus divesting the god imagery of chs. 1–3 and reinvesting the imagery with cherubim status, a role closer to that of Hebrew religious custom.[83] This would have been a fitting Hebrew understanding especially in light of the cherubim flanking the ark of the covenant along with similar depictions as seen in 1 Kings 6:23–35; 7:29; 2 Chronicles 3:13; 5:7; and later in Ezekiel's concluding vision where the cherubim have only two faces (cf. 41:18–20). Thus, it is possible that Ezekiel took the original symbolic vision, given to him over a year earlier, and reinterpreted it in the second case to fit a Hebrew theological perspective.

---

is possible, it does not seem likely due to the fact that only one face is "rationalized." On the other hand, it is possible that the inclusion of the eagle face/imagery in the second vision of ch. 10 may find support within the descriptions of Yahweh himself during this period (cf. Deut 32:11). Also, the lion seems to have played an important role as a descriptor for Yahweh (Isa 31:4; Jer 25:38); Judah's kingship (Gen 49:9; Num 24:9; Prov 19:12; 20:2; Ezek 19); Israel (Jer 12:8); and even the tribe of Gad (Deut 33:20). Moreover, textually Yahweh is often described as having a human face (Num 6:25). Finally, while in Ezek 41:19 the face of the man and lion are associated with the cherubim of the new temple, never do we find the term "bull" (שׁור) used as a descriptor for Yahweh. However, in ANE literature it is indeed used for Marduk.

82. So too Petter, "Book of Ezekiel," 141, 163.

83. Here I must cautiously agree with Zimmerli, *Ezekiel* 1:256; Cooke, *Ezekiel*, 119; Freedy, "Literary Relations," 252; and Joyce, *Ezekiel*, 106–7, that vv. 20–22 are no doubt a later addition/clarification by a redactor/editor who was trying to harmonize this vision with ch. 1. However, the redactor has missed the rhetoric behind the symbolism here in Ezekiel's second vision. While 10:15b also identifies the cherubim with those of the living beings in ch. 1 here it appears only as a means to bring continuity between the general depictions of the two visions especially due to the different depictions of the faces immediately preceding in v. 14. Thus, in essence these visions are the same but have a different theological message. Block, *Ezekiel* 1–24, 324–25, harmonizes the bull and the cherub faces in 1:10 and 10:14. He bases his harmonization upon the fact that the description of the faces of cherubs in Israelite literature is not given and thus may very well have been a bull (contra rabbinic belief in human-faced cherubim). However, while Block appears to be correct about the ambiguity for other biblical appearances of cherubim, in Ezekiel we see the prophet describing the cherubs in 41:19 as human and lion-faced.

The Chariot-throne of the Deity

Finding exact ANE parallels for Ezekiel's vision of four cherubim carrying the chariot-throne has proven futile to date. The most that can be found on reliefs are two images attending a deity. However, this "problem" may not be as difficult to solve as one may expect. Keel rightly points out that by their very nature, reliefs and seal iconography are two-dimensional. Thus, these depictions only show two cherubs carrying a throne. Keel argues that if the three-dimensional aspect were to be viewed all four[84] cherubs would be seen.[85]

Also, while four-faced (i.e., of different animals)[86] throne bearers in ANE iconography have not been found as of yet, there is ample evidence of the two-faced, four-winged, throne bearers throughout the ANE.[87] One such example hails from the fourteenth century in Megiddo where an ivory carving depicting multiple tiers of various-faced creatures are presented holding up or bearing the sky. This appears to show the role these creatures had in separating the holy from the profane.[88] This also helps elucidate the role played by the cherubim on the lid (i.e., footstool) of the Ark of the Covenant. They too separated a holy God from the common/profane of the earthly realm. In Ezekiel's case, the living beings/cherubim appear not as carved, lifeless, images but rather as they truly were, alive and separating the holiness

---

84. Keel, *Jahwe-Visionen*, 248, sees in the number four (i.e., wings, faces, and wheels) the completeness of the power of Yahweh over the four corners of the world.

85. Ibid., 168. Keel also gives copious examples of this concept from both Assyrian and Babylonian sources (169–75).

86. Ibid., 241–43. Based upon late Egyptian art, Keel suggests that perhaps the four creatures are directionally situated to represent the four winds due to the note on the direction in 1:10. Thus the lion would be looking south, the bull north, the eagle to the east, and the human face to the west. Block, *Ezekiel 1–24*, 324–25, arranges them based upon the fact that the original vision of ch. 1 came from the north and therefore the first face appearing to Ezekiel would have been the human face looking to the south. Thus it would follow that the eagle would have been looking north, the bull to the east, and the lion to the west. Regardless of the exact orientation of the faces, this particular aspect of the directional motif appears moot in light of the overall northerly motif as will be discussed below.

87. Keel, *Jahwe-Visionen*, 231.

88. Ibid., 233. Keel posits, "Ihre Omnipräsent dient der Scheidung des Heiligen vom Profanen."

of Yahweh from the profane while he appeared in the lands of Israel and Babylon (11:16).[89]

Next, depictions of two and four-wheeled carts and chariots used for carrying the gods in the ANE are ubiquitous from the second millennium in Babylon into the Neo-Assyrian period.[90] Keel has also given ample evidence in artwork from Anatolia, northern Syria, and Mesopotamia where divine thrones are sitting on a fundament, which in turn is supported by cherub-like creatures.[91] Parallels can also be seen in Phoenician iconography where winged creatures bear the seat/throne of Astarte. In an Assyrian rock-relief from Maltaia cherubim are pictured carrying Ishtar's throne.[92] The difference between these and the vision seen by Ezekiel according to Kvanvig is that normally a static throne with attendants is depicted as opposed to Ezekiel's mobile chariot with attendants. Kvanvig does note that the combination of the static throne and the movable chariot can be seen in the relief from Khorsabad which "depicts the royal procession of Sargon . . . [however] . . . the chariot does not roll, but is carried by attendants."[93] We are therefore left with a mixed bag of iconographic evidence in this regard. This however should not deter us from drawing the conclusion that the ubiquitous nature of chariot-throne iconography could very easily have influenced Ezekiel's visionary experience.

To summarize, divine beings are either depicted on a static throne sitting on a fundament being borne up by cherubim or sitting in a chariot or cart without attendants. The only chariot-throne and deity with attendants is the Khorsabad occurrence but here the chariot-throne is carried by attendants and the wheels apparently do not move. Interestingly, the wheels in Ezekiel's vision do not move either (cf. 1:17; 10:16) but appear to be pushed forward or borne along by the storm wind and the cherubim.

In light of these findings a few points can be made. First, the clear ANE iconographic evidence for a deity on a throne on a fundament

---

89. Bodi, *Poem of Erra*, 45 n. 47.

90. Keel, *Jahwe-Visionen*, 183. He points out examples of Anatolian, Babylonian, Neo-Assyrian, Urartian, and Elamite seals showing the two and four-wheeled carts. Also, the concept of the four-winged cherubim/creatures can be found in the period of Sargon II (722–705) (ibid., 194).

91. Ibid., 168–77.

92. Eichrodt, *Ezekiel*, 56.

93. Kvanvig, *Roots of Apocalyptic*, 510. Cf. also Steinmann, *Ézéchiel*, 103.

and being borne up by numerous cherub-like creatures is too close to that depicted in Ezekiel to dismiss. Second, while some want to see the wheels of Ezekiel's chariot-throne as a later addition to the text, based upon other ANE depictions, there is no textual reason for following this suggestion. Third, as already noted, nowhere in the OT do we find a depiction as we see here in Ezekiel. However, if in fact Ezekiel did use some literary creativity thus enabling his chariot-throne to be mobile as depicted in other OT texts (e.g., 2 Kings 2) why should this creativity be questioned? Finally, it is apparent that the throne imagery and theophanic picture with cherubs/attendants does appear more prevalent in the ANE material than in any biblical text. Thus once again we can conclude that Ezekiel no doubt borrowed this imagery either in whole or in part from his surroundings and refashioned it to meet his intended needs.

The Radiance of the Lord (1:27–28)

Setting aside, for a moment, the imagery and symbolism of the living beings and the description of the chariot-throne we need to examine the appearance of Yahweh, himself. Besides the flashing lightning and the sound of thunder mentioned in 1:26–28 Yahweh's appearance is described as glowing metal and as emitting a radiance like a rainbow. This theophanic depiction of Yahweh here in ch. 1 is unlike any found in the OT although aspects of it do resemble that of Yahweh's appearance when he initiated the covenant at Sinai (Exod 19:16). To further compound the problem, nowhere in ANE literature is a theophanic description given as we see here. In certain respects, Ezekiel appears to have experienced a unique vision unlike any before. Nevertheless, there is evidence in ANE literature of the gods being attributed theophanic phenomena such as radiant faces with light surrounding them. They are also presented as thundering forth from their cosmic abodes with lightning flashes and beaming light, a picture that is also reflected in Ezekiel's description of Yahweh.

During the days of Sargon I (2329–2274 BCE) it is believed that his daughter (i.e., Enheduanna) composed a hymn called the "The Exaltation of Inanna"; the hymn reads,

> 1 Lady of all me's[94] [i.e., "divine attributes" in Sumerian], resplendent light,
>
> 2 Righteous woman clothed in radiance... beloved of Heaven and Earth,...
>
> 5 Whose hand has attained [all] the seven me's...
>
> 9 Like a dragon you have deposited venom on the land
>
> 10 When you roar at the earth like Thunder, no vegetation can stand up to you.
>
> 11 A flood descending from the mountain,
>
> 12 Oh foremost one, you are the Inanna of heaven and earth!
>
> 13 Raining the fanned fire down upon the nation
>
> 14 Endowed with me's of An, lady mounted on a beast,
>
> 15 Who makes decisions at the holy command of An.
>
> 16 [You] of all the great rites, who can fathom what is yours?[95]

In this hymn, characteristics of the theophany of radiant light, thundering forth, and raining fire all appear. While this particular hymn comes from a much earlier period, it is, nonetheless, an early example of theophanic phenomena attributed to deities, a reality present in many of the biblical appearances of Yahweh.[96]

The concept of radiant faces also appears in Neo-Assyrian literature from at least the ninth century onward. In a text from Shalmaneser III's reign we read that his enemies were, "overwhelmed by fear and the radiance of Aššur (and) the god Marduk, they [i.e., the enemies of Shalmaneser] abandoned their cities and ascended a rugged mountain."[97] From later in the same century in the annals of Adad-nirari III, the grandson of Shalmaneser III, we see some of the closest language to that found here in Ezekiel's vision. In the account

---

94. For a discussion of this Sumerian term, see "Inanna's Descent to the Nether World," *ANET*, 53 n. 11.

95. Hallo and van Dijk, *Exaltation of Inanna*, 14–17.

96. For a detailed discussion of this development and for examples, see Niehaus, *God at Sinai*, 125–36.

97. Grayson, RIMA 3/71. See also page 8, lines 26–29a; page 14, line 22; and Grayson, RIMA 2/18, col. iii lines 69–71.

the attributes of luminescence and brilliance are attributed to the god Adad. The text reads, [Adad] "who is bedecked with luminosity, who rides the great storms (and) is clothed with fierce brilliance, ... who makes the lightning flash."[98] Later in the seventh century Ashurbanipal (668–627 BCE) describes his gods as follows, "With their bright countenances and lifting their beautiful eyes through which they view the world, Aššur and Ninlil looked joyfully upon Aššurbanipal, the delight of their hearts."[99] In similar fashion, from the Neo-Babylonian period, Nebuchadnezzar II (604–562 BCE) prays, "[O Shamash] look with your radiant countenance, your happy face joyfully upon the precious work of my hands, my good works, [and] my royal statue and inscription."[100]

These few examples of the radiant features attributed to the gods are not new in light of OT attestations with the same type of language (e.g., Exod 34:25—Moses' face shone because of Yahweh's radiance and the glory of the Lord shone upon the earth, his people, and temple—cf. Num 6:25; Deut 33:2; Pss 50:2; 67:1; Dan 9:17; Ezek 43:2). However, when we look at the general concept of theophanies in literature from the ANE this motif is still the dominant feature as it is here in Ezekiel. Truly, the authors of ANE theophanies desired to present their gods in splendor and power in order to elicit respect, worship, and fear— Ezekiel 1 reads as intending no less.

The Accompanying Storm Wind

Due to the ubiquitous nature of the presence of the storm wind (סְעָרָה) within Mesopotamian literature one need not spend too much time trying to prove the parallels. For example, in the Babylonian creation myth, *Enuma elish*, we find the four winds accompany Marduk when he travels in his divine chariot (tablet II starting at line 105 and tablet IV starting at line 113).[101] Also in "the Old Babylonian Susa Version of the Myth of Anzu" (table III) Ninurta is also accompanied by the

---

98. Grayson, RIMA 3/208 lines 1–5, esp. 3–5.

99. Niehaus, *God at Sinai*, 123. Cf. *CAD* vol B, page 320 (Thompson, *Esarhaddon*, pl. 18 vi. 12). The text reads, *Aššur u Ninlil . . . ina bu-un-ni-[šu-n]u namrūti ina nīš i[nī]šunu damqāti ša ibar[rû] kibrāti RN migir libbišunu . . . ḫadîš [it]taplasu*.

100. Langdon, *Neubabylonischen Königsinschriften*, 258, ii.21, as noted by Niehaus, 124.

101. "Creation Epic," *ANET*, 62, 66.

four winds.¹⁰² Because Babylonian literature is full of concepts related to the "four regions of the world" ((*kibrāt erbetti(m) arba'i(m) arbai(m)*))¹⁰³ and "the four winds" (*šārī erbetti*), it was only natural for this concept to have been adopted by the later writers such as Jeremiah (49:36) and Ezekiel (37:9).¹⁰⁴ On the other hand, the concept of the סְעָרָה is also found in biblical texts (e.g., 2 Kgs 2:1, 11) and therefore need not necessarily rely on a Mesopotamian origin.¹⁰⁵ However, it is the combination of motifs within the vision of the chariot-throne that suggests that Ezekiel did indeed borrow concepts from his surroundings. It is noteworthy that in Daniel 7 the author of the text appears to have either borrowed from Ezekiel (or vice versa depending on one's perspective on the dating issue of Daniel) or adapted material from the ANE as well. The former seems most logical.¹⁰⁶

The Eyes

The theories surrounding the meaning of the eyes and exactly how other cultures may have influenced Ezekiel in this regard are numerous. Pettazzoni has studied the concept of the omniscience of the gods throughout the ANE and has presented several distinct examples that may help us understand this aspect of Ezekiel. As noted in ch. 1, the

102. "Myth of Zu," *ANET*, 517.

103. So too Black, et al., *Concise Dictionary of Akkadian*, 156.

104. Greenberg, "Ezekiel's Vision," 166–67. Greenberg concludes by belittling the role Babylonian art and symbols played on Ezekiel's vision in favor of an Israelite provenance for most of the parallels. However, he has spent a good portion of the article showing Mesopotamian and ANE parallels in the presentation of Ezekiel's visions. While it is no doubt true that Ezekiel's visions are based upon foundational and theological concepts from Hebrew thought and literature, the imagery and symbolism still appear to find closer parallels to that of Babylonian mythology and iconography than to that of Hebrew texts.

105. Cf. 2 Kgs 2:1, 11; Job 38:1; 40:6; Pss 55:8 [Eng]; 83:15 [Eng]; 107:25, 29; 148:8; Isa 40:24; 54:11; Amos 1:14; Jon 1:4, 12; Jer 25:32. So too Petter, "The Book of Ezekiel," 143 n. 8, who also lists Isa 29:6; Jer 23:19; 30:23; and Zech 9:14 as containing similar imagery. Note also the use of סְעָרָה in Isa 41:16 which is in the context of Yahweh's giving Israel power to judge its enemies.

106. Rowland, *Open Heaven*, 55, notes that it is the first chapter of Ezekiel that inspired Dan 7:9–28. It is possible that the author of Daniel may have used Ezekiel's symbolism and imagery and embellished them in an apocalyptic fashion. Understandably, it is for this reason that many have come to recognize the vision sequences in Ezekiel as in some way proto-apocalyptic even though they fail to use this term. This latter argument is addressed further in the appendix.

dating of Persian material is difficult and the likelihood of it having a direct influence on Ezekiel is small; however, a couple of points can be made from their literature.

First, some scholars suggest that Persian concepts of omniscience date at least to the time of Ezekiel if not before.[107] Ahura Mazdāh (i.e., the chief deity of Zoroastrianism) is described in literature as the all-seeing god. In Yašt, i:8b the text reads "My seventeenth name is the All-Seeing One."[108] This idea is followed in lines 12–13 with similar notations on the all-seeing nature of the deity. Pettazzoni goes on to note that even the lesser deity Mithra is attributed with the all-seeing nature of Ahura Mazdāh. This is presented in Yašt x:82 in more depth. This texts reads, "To whom [i.e., Mithra parallel with the Vedic Mitra] Ahura Mazdāh gave thousand senses and ten thousand eyes to see. With those eyes and those senses, he watches the man who injures Mithra, the man who lies unto Mithra. Through those eyes and those senses, he is undeceivable, he of the ten thousand spies, the powerful, all-knowing, undeceivable god."[109] Clearly the omniscient nature of the god is being presented here. Interestingly, the granting of all-seeing characteristics to a lesser deity like Mithra is not a developed Israelite concept when it comes to the angelic hosts in later Judaism and Christianity. Nevertheless, we see in Ezekiel the possibility for this concept of omniscience being attributed to the living creatures through the imagery of the multiple "eyes" on the wheels and cherubim. However, if one sees in the vision a picture of Yahweh in totality (i.e., all-encompassing imagery of the presence of Yahweh) then the omniscience motif is in no way compromised by the presence of the eyes on the cherubim and wheels.

In this vein, Russell suggests that when one looks at the imagery from the perspective of the ANE the connection of the eye imagery in Ezekiel's vision of the chariot-throne becomes clearer. He asserts that the "ubiquitous eye of Horus symbolizes the fertilizing power of the sun, but in apocalyptic usage it becomes a potent symbol of God's om-

---

107. The dating of the Iranian Yašt of the Avesta texts is not easy to do as noted in ch. 1. The relatively late dating of the literature does not necessarily create a disconnect with earlier thinking. As a matter of fact, most scholars recognize the earlier concepts in the Iranian tradition and the close parallels with the Vedic material.

108. Quoted from Pettazzoni, *All-Knowing*, 132.

109. Ibid., 136. The repetition of the thousand and ten thousand, according to Pettazzoni, is for the purpose of stressing the ubiquitous nature of the eyes.

nipresence as in the eyes on the rims of Ezekiel's chariot (Ezek. 1:18) or in the four living creatures of the Book of Revelation . . ."[110] Thus, one can begin to recognize the proto-apocalyptic flavor of Ezekiel and appreciate why his imagery was later adopted by the apocalyptic writers for Yahweh's omnipresence.

In Ezekiel's second vision of Yahweh we see the proliferation of the "eyes" (עֵינַיִם) from being not only in the wheels in 1:18, but also throughout the bodies of the cherubim as well (cf. 10:12). Many have posited explanations for the prevalence of the eyes with a general consensus agreeing that they represent, in one way or another, the omniscience of Yahweh.[111]

It is also intriguing that the eyes appear in relation to the cherubim. Walmesley posited that the eyes in this vision within the wheels are none other than the administrative angels that watched over the entire world for God. Thus, it was a way of presenting the omnipresent nature of God.[112] While this is possible, it is not likely. This is due mainly to the fact that it is only in later literature (viz., The Similitudes 71:7; 61:10)[113] that the wheels (*ôpannîm*)[114] become angelic figures themselves. Furthermore, it was not at all common at this period in Israelite thought to see angelic administration in this fashion.

---

110. Russell, *Method & Message*, 186. Also we see the all-seeing nature of the Egyptian god Re by means of his temple in the text *The Divine Nomination of Thut-Mose III*. The text states "Re (is) the lord of Karnak, and his glorious eye which is in this land (is) Hermonthis" [which is the cult site of the sun god in the district of Thebes]. Cf. "Divine Nomination of Thut-Mose III," *ANET*, 447.

111. For example, Kaufmann, *Religion of Israel*, 437.

112. Cf. Walmesley, "Ezechiel's Vision Explained," 45, and Streane, *Prophet Ezekiel*, xxxiii.

113. See also *b. Hagigah* 12b, 13a and *b. Roš Haššanah* 24b. as noted by Zimmerli, *Ezekiel* 1:129 n. 113.

114. Russell, *Method & Message*, 241. Also, Keel, *Jahwe-Visionen*, 273, comes to the same conclusion. He comments, "Die Räder in Ez 1,15-21 sind in Kap. 10 zu selbständigen Wesen mit Flügeln, Gesichtern usw. ausgebaut worden. Sie erscheinen als Ophannim neben Kerubim und Serafim schon im äthiopischen Henoch [. . .] um 100 v. Chr. als eigenständige Engelswesen. Ein solcher Ophan könnte mit dem ungewöhnlichen geflügelten Rad gemeint sein, das auf einer persischen Münze der Provinz Judäa aus der Zeit zwischen 350 und 332 v. Chr. eine dem Zeus ähnliche Gottheit trägt . . . ." See also ibid., 270 fig. 195.

Some scholars (e.g., Zimmerli)[115] have suggested that the "eyes" were actually the copper rivets that held the wheels together.[116] However, while this is a possibility for the first vision it is not at all tenable for the appearance of the eyes on the cherubim in the second vision. Thus, most still admit that in the context, the all-seeing nature of God appears to be the thrust of the imagery.

Returning to the distinct Mesopotamian context, many of the Babylonian deities were also attributed the trait of omniscience. These included, Marduk, Nabu, Nergal, and Ninib (i.e., Ninurta), the same four noted by Matthews above. Pettazzoni points out the omniscient characteristics of Marduk in the *Enuma elish* myth,[117] while those of Nabu are represented in appellations such as the "all-knowing" (*mūdū kalāma*) and "he who knows everything" (*mūdū mimma šumšu*).[118] Concerning Nergal we find texts addressing him as a god "of wide understanding, knower of all things, omniscient, of penetrating intelligence, very intelligent."[119] Finally, in reference to Ninib, Pettazzoni makes a general note pointing to the role that the eyes of this deity played in the concept of omniscience.[120]

---

115. Zimmerli, *Ezekiel* 1:129.

116. Keel, *Jahwe-Visionen*, 268–69. Copper rivets also are seen in Egyptian art of the god Bes, where the rivets/nails are used as accents to the appearance of the deity. See Keel, 270, fig. 193. Siegman, *The Book of Ezechiel*, 11, suggests the eyes are stars. Also, from the period of Psammetikos I (664–610 BCE) a statuette of Bes full of eyes can be found. At this time Assyrian domination of Egypt was prevalent and interaction between the two countries could have easily transferred this concept to Mesopotamia almost 100 years prior to Ezekiel's day. Interestingly enough, some of these figurines of Bes contain up to eight heads of animals (including the lion, bull, and various other animals). The figure of Bes was often used as a talisman to protect from the bite of these animals depicted in the image of the Bes figurine. If this was the case, when Egyptians traveled to a new region like Mesopotamia, these talismans could easily have been a part of their luggage. See Pettazzoni, *The All-Knowing God*, 58–61.

117. Tablet 1 line 80 "most able and wisest of gods" and tablet 2 line 116 "who knowest all wisdom." "Creation Epic," ANET, 62, 64. Cf. also, Arnold and Beyer, *Readings from the Ancient Near East*, 33, where the *Enuma elish* text reads, "Four were his eyes . . . and the eyes . . . scanned all things."

118. See Tallqvist, *Der assyrische Gott*, 86, 382, as noted by Pettazzoni, *All-Knowing God*, 84.

119. Tallqvist, *Der assyrische Gott*, 86, 395, as noted by Pettazzoni, *All-Knowing God*, 84.

120. Pettazzoni, *All-Knowing God*, 78.

These characteristics being noted, it again appears possible that the omniscient characteristics attributed to these gods are subverted by Ezekiel and brought under the authority of the one true Israelite deity, Yahweh. It is Yahweh alone who knows the thoughts and intentions of all people and while other nations may have claimed this characteristic for their gods, in Ezekiel's mind they must fall to the ultimate authority of Yahweh—a fact noted in later texts (cf. Job 1:7; 2:2; Zech 4:10 and 2 Chr 16:9). Moreover, in light of our previous discussion on the living beings/cherubim, it seems best not to suggest that the Babylonian deities are in view in ch. 10. The proliferation of the eye motif to include the cherubim appears only in the second *kābôd* vision and as such seems best associated with Yahweh's omniscience alone.

There is also the possibility that the use of the "eyes" motif, beyond representing the omniscience of Yahweh, may have been an allusion to the "all-seeing" nature of the ANE suzerain by means of the vassal treaty and its adherents. In the Neo-Assyrian period, vassal states and their leaders became the "eyes" ("to see"—*amāru*) and "ears" ("to hear"—*šemû*) of their suzerain and were to report any potential crime against the king such as rebellion and treachery (i.e., treaty violations).[121] Thus, the suzerain was "all-knowing" concerning what went on in his empire. In a similar vein, Yahweh exhibited the same ability through the symbolism of the eyes in the vision by knowing all of the sins and treachery of his vassal, Judah. Apart from the obvious omniscience of Yahweh, one could also argue, that Yahweh "knew" of Judah's treachery through his "vassal" Babylon (i.e., through Nebuchadnezzar's invoking of the gods to fulfill the curses of the treaty). Indeed, Babylon was the instrument of Yahweh's wrath (cf. Ezek 21) and because Israel had broken covenant not only with Yahweh but also with Babylon (cf. Ezek 17) Yahweh was well "informed" of the nature of Israel's repeated crimes against her suzerain both earthly and heavenly.[122]

---

121. Cf. Tadmor, "Treaty and Oath," 148–49; and Oppenheim, "Eyes of the Lord," 172–74. Tadmor (149) notes that this policy of policing the empire became prevalent during the reigns of Esarhaddon and his son, Ashurbanipal.

122. The fact that ch. 17 delivers such a scathing indictment against Zedekiah for covenant infidelity against Nebuchadnezzar may be proof that the Babylonian king had invoked the gods (including Yahweh) against Judah. While Yahweh would in no way need the permission of Babylon to punish his treacherous vassal Judah, the prevalent understanding of faithful vassals reporting crimes against the suzerain coupled with the clear vassal treaty nuances in the symbolism of Ezekiel's vision bolsters this conclusion. So too the conclusion of Freedy, "Literary Relations," 159–60.

Finally, looking at the symbolism of the eyes from a perspective of judgment may also add to our understanding of the vision. In a land grant from Adad-nerari III (806–783 BCE) to the god Aššur, a threat is issued to anyone who tries to take away the land given to the god. The text reads on lines 6–8. "Whoever takes away from [Ašš]ur any of the t[owns th]at [I have given] t[o Aššur], [may] Aššur, the great lord, [cast] a furiously angry eye u[pon him]. Do not remove any of the towns of Aššur, (but) [add] to the towns [of Aššur]. [Aššur, the great lord], will hear your prayer."[123]

Here we see the use of the eye motif in the context of casting an angry or "furious" gaze upon those who wronged the deity by stealing that which belonged to the god (i.e., the land used for raising offerings for the god). In Ezekiel's case Yahweh had been wronged by the misdirected affections of the people and the "stolen" offerings that had been given to other deities. Furthermore, as in the land grant above, the temple and the city of Jerusalem had been "removed" from its rightful owner, Yahweh, and given to foreign gods (see my treatment of chs. 16 and 23 in ch. 3). Thus in the ANE text the people brought upon themselves the anger and curse of Aššur as well as the reality that the god would not hear their prayers (implied). Interestingly, this was also the case with Yahweh and his people (cf. Jer 11:11, 14). Therefore, in Ezekiel's vision the multiplication of the eyes could possibly demonstrate the multiplication of the fury of Yahweh. This bodes well with the tenor of the book up until ch. 25, which begins to shift to the restoration motif.

To summarize then, the ubiquitous presence of the eyes perhaps plays multiple roles here in Ezekiel. First, it is very hard to pinpoint the exact connections and influences from one culture to another. What is clear, however, is that throughout the ANE, even before Ezekiel's day, the idea that the multiplication of eyes denoted omniscience seems a foregone conclusion. Persian, Egyptian, and Mesopotamian cultures display this perspective. Ezekiel was merely adopting it and using it as a means to show the nation of Israel that it was Yahweh, and not the foreign gods, who possessed the true power of omniscience. The motif of the eyes elevates Yahweh's omniscience concerning all of Israel's evil and covenant shortcomings. The need for stressing Yahweh's omniscience finds support in various ways. First, the phrase spoken by the

---

123. Kataja and Whiting, *State Archives*, 7.

elders in 8:12: "Yahweh is not seeing us," (אֵין יְהוָה רֹאֶה אֹתָנוּ) is an allusion to the misconception of the people while they performed idolatrous acts (cf. 9:9)—Yahweh did indeed see them. Second, it may have had a vassal treaty connection where the earthly suzerain was "all-seeing" over his empire looking for any vassal infractions. Third, as noted in the land grant curse, the presence of the eyes may also have been a means of invoking a curse against the people for the "stolen" land of Jerusalem and the temple. Whatever perspective one takes, curse and punishment are at the heart of the vision; this becomes particularly pertinent in the directional motif of the vision in 1:4.

Coming from the North [124]

Attacks on Israel and especially on Jerusalem coming from the north have been the plight of Israel and its capital for centuries. Apart from the simple fact that most of Israel's enemies hailed from the northern regions of the ANE, the topographical layout of the city also made it most conducive for foreign invaders to attack from this direction (e.g., Pompey in 63 BCE).[125] For the average Israelite living in or around Jerusalem, to hear about "trouble" from the north would have meant one thing, possible invasion: both of the land and the city. Not surprisingly, it is for this reason that the Antonia Fortress was built on the northern approaches of the city during Herod the Great's reign. Vulnerability to attacks in this area of the city had always been a problem. In Ezekiel's day the threat of northern invasion was not diminished as can be seen in Jeremiah's numerous prophecies in this regard (e.g., Jer 1:13–15; 4:5–8, 13–22, 27–31; 6:1–8, 22–26; 8:14–17; 10:22; 25:9; 46:24 etc.). Some scholars even postulate that the final breech of the walls of Jerusalem during the siege of Nebuchadnezzar in 587/6 happened on the northern side.[126] Whatever the case may be,

124. For a classic discussion on the realm of possibilities for the "northerly" invaders, see Gressmann, *Ursprung*, 174–92; Hyatt, "Peril from the North," 499–513; and Childs, "Enemy from the North," 190–95.

125. Cf. also, Moule, *Notes on Ezekiel*, 8, and Vawter and Hoppe, *New Heart*, 26.

126. Malamat, "Last Kings of Judah," 155. Malamat suggests the meeting place (i.e., the "Middle Gate" situated in the northern wall) noted in Jer 39:3 may be an indication of this fact. Furthermore, Zedekiah is noted as perhaps situating himself near the fight during the siege at the "Gate of Benjamin" (Jer 38:7) prior to the fall of the city. This aligns with his escape (in the opposite direction) from the southern end of the city (cf. Jer 39:4).

here in the chariot-throne vision sequence the directional motif takes on an interesting twist in relation to the impending doom, which the prophet was proclaiming.

The first appearance of the chariot-throne vision takes place in Babylon by the river Chebar (1:3). In v. 4 Ezekiel notes that the theophany he sees is coming from the north (צָפוֹן). Ezekiel here envisions the revelation of the awesomeness of Yahweh and the imagery depicting the impending doom coming upon Judah even though he is in Babylon. This first vision must be understood in the same directional context as that in 9:2 when judgment starts to be meted out on Jerusalem. In this passage the executioners are summoned from the northern reaches of the temple mount to begin the annihilation of the wicked.[127] Also, in 8:3 the divine attendant takes Ezekiel to Jerusalem and through the "north gate" of the temple where Ezekiel was shown the "altar of jealousy,"[128] a key factor in Yahweh's indictment of his people. The directional movement noted in these verses is instrumental in helping us understand the coming judgment from that direction. Indeed it appears that "nothing positive" comes from the north in the book of Ezekiel.[129]

The approaching theophany from the north stands out here as somewhat odd due to the fact that Yahweh was generally seen as coming from the south in the OT (Judg 5:4; Deut 33:2; Hab 3:3; Ps 68:8; Zech 9:14–15).[130] Cross notes that "In early Israel the language of the storm theophany was taken over and applied to Yahweh in his role of divine warrior, marching from the south."[131] In this case Cross sees the Sinai event and the "divine warrior" motif as both reflective of Canaanite motifs; however, Ezekiel has moved beyond this older directional motif for a greater purpose. The concept of the divine war-

---

127. We will return to this below.

128. For a linguistic discussion on the use of the verbal forms קָנָא "to be jealous" קָנָה and "to create" here in 8:3, see Odell, *Ezekiel*, 108.

129. Petter, "Book of Ezekiel," 144. Petter lists 23:23–24; 26:7; 38:6, 15; 39:2 and 36:30 as further evidence of this fact.

130. In the psalms we find an occasion where the city of Zion is seen as being in the north (Ps. 48:3 [Heb.]). This may be a reflection of the dwelling place of the gods in ANE lore as noted in the allusion found also in Isaiah 14:13. For a discussion on this passage as it relates to possible Canaanite roots, see Cross, *Canaanite Myth*, 38–39.

131. Ibid., 58.

rior marching from the south was most often used for the purpose of showing Yahweh's protection of Israel, the covenant people. However, in the case of Ezekiel's vision, if one couples it with the Babylonian imagery noted above and the northerly direction of the approach, then a different message emerges. Yes, Yahweh, the "divine warrior" was the deity being seen, and yes, he was the deity over all creatures and gods, but he was also the one behind Babylon's advancements from the north on his own people.[132]

As early as 1937, Berry recognized this directional motif in the opening vision of Ezekiel and commented, "this manifestation came from the north, 1 4, a common expression for coming from the region of Babylon."[133] However, rarely do scholars draw the connection between the northerly approach of the vision and the judgment motif of a foreign invader from the north which is ubiquitous in the prophetic corpus. In this first vision we see that the normal appearance of Yahweh from the south to protect his people from external harm (e.g., Hab 3:13) and to manifest his glory and goodness (Ps 68:8), is absent. Instead, for the first time in the OT, the northern directional motif, normally reserved for northern aggressors, is now linked to Yahweh himself. Yahweh, in the guise of Babylon, would be the one responsible for the punishment of Judah.[134] Interestingly, we find out later in the prophecy that Nebuchadnezzar is presented as the servant of Yahweh (e.g., Ezek 30:25) when passing judgment on Egypt.[135]

This connection of Yahweh with the northern aggressor motif is also interesting in light of the fact that many times in the ANE if the gods abandoned their own nation they are often presented as being a part of the opposing army's vanguard, a point that will be developed in greater detail below. Here this factor becomes strikingly clear as Yahweh is seen not only in Babylon but also above its gods, in representative form, coming in the vanguard of the attack—Yahweh is about to destroy his own city (cf. Lev 26:17 and Ezek 5:8; see also Exod

---

132. So too Petter, "Book of Ezekiel," 144.

133. Berry, "Glory of Yahweh," 117.

134. Driver, *Introduction*, 280, comments that Yahweh's abode was "no longer in the city of his choice . . ." However, it seems to be clear in Ezekiel that Yahweh is in complete control of his coming and going as well as his abode.

135. Nebuchadnezzar is actually called "my servant" by the prophet Jeremiah (עַבְדִּי–Jer 43:10).

23:27–30).¹³⁶ Indeed, the "enemy" Ezekiel is seeing is Yahweh!¹³⁷ As Bruce Power correctly notes, "It is as if the king of the world has been on campaign, and while he is gone his palace, his very throneroom has been usurped—and the citizens of his capital have allowed his rule to end within the city! Another has taken his place. And they are prepared to die rather than surrender to their rightful ruler. Now he has returned to capture the city, with his invincible army comprised of multinational units. The emperor has besieged the city and declares 'I myself, am coming against you; I will execute judgments among you in the sight of the nations' (5:8). YHWH is to be taken literally, and while he watches and waits, enthroned above the city, his international army, under the direction of his field commander Nebuchadnezzar will destroy the city."¹³⁸

To help bolster the assumption that ANE god(s) led attacks against their enemy, a couple of examples from ANE iconography may help to clarify things. In Assyrian reliefs from the ninth century BCE (now housed in the British Museum) one relief depicts the god Aššur flying above and ahead of Assur-nasir-pal II as the king attacks his enemy with his bow drawn and firing. In the same relief Aššur is depicted in the vanguard of the attack with his bow drawn and firing at the enemy.¹³⁹ In another relief depicting the return of Assur-nasir-pal II from a victorious battle, again both the victorious ruler and the god are depicted with bows at their side undrawn.¹⁴⁰ The message is clear; the god of the nation led both the attack and the victory parade and is one and the same with the state.¹⁴¹ For Judah, this reality would have been well known. The taking of the Ark of the Covenant into battle with the armies of Israel (e.g., Josh 6; 1 Sam 4) would have been, in

---

136. This avenging motif also appears in other prophetic texts. For example, Nahum 1:2 pictures Yahweh as the one who takes vengeance on his enemies. Nahum uses the participial form of the verb נקם ("the one who avenges") three times in one verse. See further, Mendenhall, *Tenth Generation*, 69–104.

137. Petter, "Book of Ezekiel," 141, 146.

138. Power, "Iconographic Windows," 385–86.

139. See Mendenhall, *Tenth Generation*, 46, for a picture of the relief. In the Annals of Shalmaneser III, son of Assur-nasir-pal II, we also find a note where Shalmaneser speaks of the might of "the divine standard which goes before me" as he attacks his enemies of Ḥaiiānu. Cf. Grayson, *Assyrian Rulers*, 9, line 58.

140. See Mendenhall, *Tenth Generation*, 47, for a picture of the relief.

141. Ibid., 47.

essence, the reality of what is depicted in these Assyrian reliefs. The difference, however, was that now Yahweh was against his own nation.

Finally, in 43:2, when the glory of Yahweh returns to the temple, the directional motif focuses on the eastward return of Yahweh. Yahweh had appeared in the first vision coming from the north, in judgment, had departed through the eastern gate of the city in the second appearance and now, in his third appearance in similar grandeur, is returning from the east. In the closing restoration chapters the judgment from the "north" is now complete and the restored city and nation is under divine blessing and not a curse.[142]

Conclusion

We may conclude then from these brief studies concerning the symbolism and language of Ezekiel's vision of the chariot-throne that the entire purpose of this first vision (apart from the original oracular presentation of it) was to set the tone for the rest of the book. The people were witnessing, in literary form (and no doubt verbally as well), the awesome presence of a deity who would be their judge. This was not an advent to initiate a covenant; this was an appearance to punish those who had broken covenant. During the Sinai experience the people had feared for their lives when Yahweh appeared to seal the covenant (Exod 20:18–19); now they were to fear for their lives because Yahweh was about to enact judgment in the form of the covenant curses.

Ezekiel 4–7 Buildup to the First Curse: The Impending Doom of Jerusalem Prophesied

The chapters between the call of Ezekiel and the departure sequence of chs. 8–11 serve to alert the audience about the gravity of their sin and punishment that will befall Judah and Jerusalem specifically. The sign-acts of chs. 4–5 serve as an overview of what is to come upon the land and the people. Moreover, they embody Ezekiel's message in miniature. Fishbane comments that "chapters 4–5 sound those dark cords of fatality which echo consistently from shortly after the commission theophany in July 593 (1:2–3) until the commencement of the siege of

---

142. We will return to this final insight in ch. 5, below.

Jerusalem in January 588 (24:1)."[143] At the same time one can see in these opening chapters the highlighting of the curses that will unfold in the rest of the book. For example, in 5:10 the curse of cannibalism reflects the language of Deuteronomy 28:53–57 and Leviticus 26:29.[144] Curses of the covenant are peppered throughout the book and push the oracles along to their natural conclusion, viz., the destruction of the nation and exile.

In ch. 6 the sins of the people, both cultic and civil, are listed in general terms. False religion is addressed (6:2–3, 6) to which entire chapters will be devoted later (e.g., chs. 8; 16; 23), and the motif of unburied bodies is presented in 6:5, 7, which will be developed in 37:1–14 and 39:3–20. We also find a message of hope for the individual and the nation within this chapter (6:8–10 compare to chs. 9; 18; 37)—a message that will dominate the second half of the book. Fittingly, following immediately on the heels of this mini oracle of hope comes a final warning of doom (6:11–14).

Chapter 7 begins in a similar fashion with general warnings of doom which are about to be enacted.[145] Verse 8 sets the tone and warns of the soon-coming judgment: "Now I will shortly pour out my indignation on you, and complete my anger against you, and I will judge you according to your ways, and I will bring on you all your abominations" (NASB). The use of the imperfect tense in the first verbal sequence sets the tone of the verse for a future expectation of judgment. Again, the verses in ch. 7 point forward to the coming judgment and add to the general tone of foreboding in these chapters. Verse 19 also speaks of that coming doom as being "in the day of the wrath of Yahweh" (בְּיוֹם עֶבְרַת יְהוָה). Interestingly, this phrase is found elsewhere only in Zephaniah 1:18 where Zephaniah is also warning of impending judgment on Jerusalem.[146] The chapter ends with a warning of invasion by an oppressor and the horrors linked to such an event (7:18–27). These intermediate chapters thus build the tension which began with the prophet's call in chs. 1–3 and continue until the pivotal moment of the

143. Fishbane, "Sin and Judgment," 133.

144. We find a similar curse in various places throughout the prophetic texts (e.g., Isa 9:19–20; 49:26; Jer 19:9; Lam 4:10; Zech 11:9).

145. See also Bogaert, "Deux Rédactions, 21–47, for a discussion on the primacy of the LXX over the MT with a special focus on Ezekiel 7.

146. Ezek 13:5 and 30:3 speak of the "Day of the Lord" but not with the use of "wrath" (עֶבְרַת) in the clause.

entire book unfolds, that being the vision of the temple in Jerusalem and the departure of the glory of God (chs. 8–11). It is in these chapters that general indictments and cultic impropriety turn into specifics thus fleshing out the sins enumerated in the previous chapters.

Ezekiel 8–11—The First and Greatest Treaty Curse Enacted[147]

An Exposition of Chapters 8–11: Temple/Divine Abandonment[148]

From the beginning of the book of Ezekiel and the prophet's first vision of the glory of the Lord, the narrative gains intensity toward the departure scene of ch. 11. As we have just pointed out, the indictments become more and more pronounced until ch. 8 at which time they take on a marked specificity. In chs. 8–11 the prophet delineates in painstaking detail the profane cultic practices that caused the ultimate covenant curse to be enacted, i.e., divine abandonment of the temple. In this regard, Kutsko points out that this "self-exile" by the deity was common in the ANE. He asserts that it was very common for the gods who imposed exile on themselves to go to the land where their people had been exiled.[149] On one level this theoretically explains Yahweh's presence in Babylon with the exiles there (11:16) but theologically falls short of the picture Ezekiel was attempting to portray.

---

147. Petter, "Book of Ezekiel," 121–23, presents a detailed literary framework for these chapters arguing for their internal coherency and purposeful ordering.

148. I am indebted to Niehaus's work in *God at Sinai*, 268–76 for many of the insights on the terminology and concepts used here in these chapters, many of which reflect my position in this book.

149. Kutsko, *Between Heaven and Earth*, 108. This "self exile" and migration of the gods to the land where their people were exiled is a natural phenomenon for pagan gods seeing how the invading armies carried away both the people and the statues of the deit(y/ies). However, with Yahweh and Israel there is a distinct difference. Babylon had been able to carry away only the cult objects from the temple (along with the people). Ezekiel's visions make it clear that Yahweh was not a stone or wooden idol that a foreign army could carry off to exile, but rather the all-powerful God of heaven who was sovereign over all nations and was not controlled by any foreign invader.

Chapter 8: The Sin of Idolatry

Ezekiel's vision of chs. 8–11 graphically describes Judah's sin of idolatry in the temple at Jerusalem. Ezekiel is given a detailed picture of the sins of the people and of the dire straits they are in spiritually. In ch. 8 the picture is revealed in all its defiling and explicit truth. The event is at once heart-breaking and breath-taking as the prophet witnesses not only the sins that cause Yahweh's departure, but the departure itself. Niehaus notes, "How ironic that Ezekiel now sees God's glory in the temple—that same glory that filled the temple during Solomon's dedication of it. For Yahweh is there in theophany not to show Ezekiel how he dwells there (faithful to the Davidic promises of long ago) but to show him the cause that will drive him "far from [his] sanctuary" (v.6)—namely, Israel's sin. Ezekiel is about to witness not only the sin that causes Yahweh to leave but also the departure itself."[150] The sad state of affairs unfortunately, rested upon the hardened attitude of the people in Jerusalem (and even the exile). The people had refused to acknowledge their sin of idolatry and evil practices but instead blamed it on the supposed absence of Yahweh (cf. 8:12; 9:9). Instead of recognizing that the impending doom of their city was due to their own sin (as most cultures in the ANE would have) they opted to use Yahweh's apparent silence as justification for their sinful practices.[151]

Therefore one could say that the key to Israel's demise and ultimate cursing by God was their incessant penchant for *going after* other gods. Niehaus notes that the concept of "walking after" (הֹלֵךְ אַחֲרֵי) other gods of the land played a vital role in their soon-to-come judgment (compare Deut 13:4 with 8:19).[152] Interestingly, the ANE understanding of a vassal's loyalty to his suzerain was also described in similar terms. Frequently, the Akkadian idiom *alāku arki* is used in covenant formats where a vassal is to "walk after" their suzerain in order to avoid punishment and the curses of treaties.[153] For example, a letter from Itun-Asdu to King Zimri-lim (1782–1759 BCE) of Mari reads,[154]

---

150. Niehaus, *God at Sinai*, 268.
151. Block, "Divine Abandonment," 36.
152. Niehaus, *God at Sinai*, 270.
153. Ibid.
154. Ibid.

24 There is no king who is strong (enough) for himself

25 10–15 kings walk after Hammurapi, king (lit. "man") of Babylon

26 likewise after Rim-[S]in king of Larsa

27 likewise after Ibapil king of Eshnunna

28 likewise after Amutpil king of Qatanim

29–30 kings walk after Iarimlim king of Iamh[a]d[155]

Similarly, the biblical parallel related to this form of covenant fidelity can be seen in Yahweh's warning to Israel not to "walk after" other gods in Deuteronomy 11:28;[156]

וְהַקְּלָלָה אִם־לֹא תִשְׁמְעוּ אֶל־מִצְוֹת יְהוָה אֱלֹהֵיכֶם וְסַרְתֶּם מִן־הַדֶּרֶךְ אֲשֶׁר אָנֹכִי מְצַוֶּה אֶתְכֶם הַיּוֹם לָלֶכֶת אַחֲרֵי אֱלֹהִים אֲחֵרִים אֲשֶׁר לֹא־יְדַעְתֶּם

"[You will have blessing if you follow Yahweh] and a curse if you do not listen to the commandments of the Lord your God, but turn from the way which I am commanding you today to *walk after* other gods which you do not know" (italics mine).

Truly, part of the curse of the Law was a direct result of Judah's unfaithfulness to Yahweh which was displayed in their constant idolatrous acts and covenant violations. Yahweh would punish Judah for their sin of "walking after" other gods; in this case the curse would take on the form of divine abandonment, one of the greatest curses of the ANE.

On a similar note, the very breaking of a covenant constituted a "sin" not only in the relationship between Yahweh and Israel but also in the covenantal world of the ANE. In the Annals of Sennacherib, the term *ḫi-iṭ-ṭu* in Akkadian, often translated as "rebelled," can also stand for "sin" as paralleled in the Hebrew cognate חטא ("to sin").[157]

155. Dossin, "Archives," 117 (II.24–29) as noted in Niehaus, *God at Sinai*, 270.

156. Niehaus, *God at Sinai*, 270.

157. Luckenbill, *Annals of Sennacherib*, 70, line 26. See also, *CAD*, page 211 vol. 6, where "sin" or "offense" is a valid definition. One text given as an example reads, *ḫi-iṭ-ṭu dannu ana DN aḫṭu*—"I committed a grave sin against DN." Note also Black et al., *A Concise Dictionary of Akkadian*, 118, under the Akkadian word *ḫitu(m)* where "sin" is an accepted definition. Cf. Tadmor, "Treaty and Oath," 145, where he gives several examples of similar renderings of sinning against an *adê* agreement during the Neo-Assyrian period.

The idea is that if a vassal broke covenant and rebelled, he in essence sinned against his suzerain and by association his god. Beyond the obvious parallels in Ezekiel, this is clearly reflected in Exodus 32:30, 31, 33 where Israel rebelled against God in the wilderness. In this situation Aaron caused the people to "sin" a "great sin" (חֲטָאָה גְדֹלָה) by breaking covenant with Yahweh and worshipping the golden calf. Here, Israel in their earliest test of covenant loyalty had sinned in essence by *walking after* another god. In this one act they had offended both their suzerain and their god. It is perhaps this act of covenant infidelity that caused Ezekiel to proclaim in 20:23 that even while the nation of Israel was still in the wilderness they had amassed enough guilt to merit being exiled among the nations. Sadly, even now the nation refused to take the prophets' (i.e., Jeremiah and Ezekiel) messages to heart. What Ezekiel was witnessing leading up to the departure of Yahweh's presence in ch. 11 was a steady downward spiral. This spiral would become more acute as Yahweh pronounced judgment on the city at the hands of the executioners. The vision Ezekiel sees in ch. 9 is one of dread containing Mesopotamian symbolism as seven "men" take their place to effect judgment on Jerusalem.

Chapters 9–10: The Seven Executioners

Two options have been posited for the seven figures presented in ch. 9: 1) they represent the seven astral deities of the ANE and 2) they parallel the seven warrior gods also called the *Sebetti* (the "Seven Gods").[158] As for the first option, as early as 1898 Gunkel suggested this parallel between Ezekiel's vision and ANE literature. Both Gunkel[159] and Alfred Jeremias[160] averred that the seven men were a reflection of the mythological figures/gods (viz., Shamash, Sin, Nergal, Marduk, Nebo, Ninib,

---

158. "Erra and Ishum," COS 1.113:405. On page 405 n. 5, Dalley points out that this term "can be regarded as a singular and as a plural deity." See also Foster, *Before the Muses*, 963, for a text describing the role of the "Seven." On the other hand, Odell, *Ezekiel*, 115, argues that by the time of the seventh to sixth centuries BCE, these deities were seen as "beneficent" and were often carved into doorways and entrances. She notes the Palace of Ashurbanipal as an example. However, even here she comments that they are depicted as "undifferentiated warriors." It is still very possible that there was a terrifying side to these deities especially if they are invoked over doorways to protect or ward off enemies who may seek to enter.

159. Gunkel, "Schreiberengel Nabû," 294–301.

160. Jeremias, *Alte Testament*, 589.

Ishtar) representing the seven astral planets found within the lore of Babylon and the surrounding region. Niehaus notes that these figures carried weapons, which was a common depiction for deities of Assyria and Babylon.[161] In this vein, most of the gods had specific weapons of choice. For example, Marduk had a bow and net, Hadad the lightning bolt and ax and Sin, the moon-god, had a crescent-shaped scimitar.[162] Interestingly enough, the seven astral gods of Mesopotamian mythology included Nabu (or Nebo), the secretary for the seven, a possible parallel with the seventh "man" in Ezekiel's vision in 9:3.[163]

The second position is supported by the prolific use of the *Sebetti* in ANE texts.[164] For example, on the *Senjirli Stele* found in 1888 in northern Syria these deities appear as "the Seven, the warrior gods, who overthrow my foes." On the *Dog River Stele*, commemorating the defeat of Egyptian pharaoh, Tirhakah, they appear in the opening list of gods who protect and fight for Esarhaddon.[165] In the god-list of the Treaty between Ba'alu of Tyre and Esarhaddon the text states, "may the Seven, the warrior-gods, defeat you with their arms"[166]

Finally, in the account of "Erra and Ishum" (also called the *Poem of Erra*) the seven warrior deities also appear as gods who do battle for the divine council.[167] As with the texts we noted immediately above,

---

161. Niehaus, *God at Sinai*, 272.

162. Ibid.

163. So too Langdon, *Semitic*, 160. For a discussion on the Sumero-Akkadian pantheon, see Langdon, 88–165. See also comments by Niehaus, *God at Sinai*, 272 and Brownlee, *Ezekiel 1–19*, 143–44. Brownlee notes the oft-held opinion of Babylonian mythological borrowing here but also suggests that they may simply be "angel-warriors." He struggles with the *Sebetti* link because of the more passive role played by the man dressed in white linen. However, as will be pointed out below, Ezekiel seems to be modifying this mythological feature for his own purposes. See also May, "Departure," 320 and Spiegel, "Ezekiel or Pseudo-Ezekiel?" 305.

164. Langdon, *Semitic*, 138, lists the seven "fates" that are assigned to the *Sebetti*. These include: 1) "On high appear and go without rival"; 2) "Be like the god Mes the furious great bull"; 3) "The appearance of a lion has been provided for thee . . . carry out the order"; 4) "When thou liftest thy raging weapons let the mountains perish"; 5) "Rush like the wind and spy out the regions"; 6) "Enter above and beneath and spare no thing"; 7) "The seventh he filled with poison of a dragon serpent (saying) 'cause to perish the soul of life.'"

165. Luckenbill, *Ancient Records*, 2:224, 228.

166. Ibid., 229. See also the "Treaty of Esarhaddon with Baal of Tyre," *ANET*, 534.

167. In the Epic of Creation (*Enuma elish*) tablet VI line 81 the text states that the "seven gods of destinies were confirmed forever for rendering judgment." It is this

God's Glory Revealed 147

the *Sebetti* in this particular text are depicted as fierce warriors, as are the figures in Ezekiel 9. Interestingly, the account of "Erra and Ishum" has been found in both Assyria (Nineveh, Assur, and Sultantepe) and Babylonia and dates to no earlier than the eighth century BCE, a period close enough to be relevant to Ezekiel. Part of the text reads,

> 23. Different is the divine nature of the Sebitti, unrivalled warrior;
>
> 24. Their birth was strange and full of terrible portents.
>
> 25. Anyone who sees them is smitten with terror, for their breath is lethal;
>
> 26. People are petrified and cannot approach them.
>
> 27. Ishum is the door bolted before them.
>
> 28. When Anu, king of the gods, impregnated Earth,
>
> 29. She bore the Seven Gods for him and he named them Sebitti.[168]

The text extends for some 750 lines where these gods are seen as attendants to the warrior god Erra (see tablet III, lines 80–100). While a direct one-to-one parallel cannot be conclusively affirmed, it is indeed possible that Ezekiel could have drawn upon this motif.[169]

When considering the two possibilities (i.e., the astral deities versus the *Sebetti*) it seems more likely that in light of their purpose of destroying the people of Jerusalem, the second choice, i.e., the *Sebetti* are a closer parallel. The texts just noted seem to make the *Sebetti* the best choice when considered with the themes and motifs similar to Ezekiel's vision. Furthermore, there is no other text in the OT that matches this number of prosecuting warrior angels/gods from which Ezekiel could have drawn.[170] It is interesting that Ezekiel, being in

---

grouping of seven in the role of judgment that points to our pericope and the possible parallels with Ezekiel and the ANE. See "Epic of Creation," *COS* 1.111: 401.

168. "Erra and Ishum," *COS* 1.113:405.

169. The parallels of this poem and Ezekiel are taken to the extreme in Bodi's, *Ezekiel and the Poem of Erra*. Bodi's position has received mixed reviews. For a negative review, see Moore, review of Daniel Bodi, 519–20. For a more irenic perspective, see Postgate, review of Daniel Bodi, 137.

170. The destroying angel motif found in the OT is generally a singular figure. Examples of this can be seen in Exodus 12:23—the death angel in Egypt; 2 Samuel

Babylon where this myth circulated, is the first to use this motif. That is not to say that Ezekiel borrowed directly from the Erra epic, but that the motif of the seven gods makes sense here.

While dealing with these parallels, it seems appropriate to look at the work of Bodi which deals with the similarities between the *Poem of Erra* and Ezekiel, especially in relation to the *Sebetti*. Bodi, following Frankena,[171] suggests that Ezekiel fashioned many of his motifs after the *Poem of Erra*.[172] On the micro level, some borrowing may have occurred and Bodi seems to have added much to the debate and analysis of Ezekiel in light of ANE literature. His insights certainly help shed light on the symbolism and motifs present in Ezekiel 9.

First, Bodi moves away from the "astral deities" of Gunkel and opts for the *Sebetti* as noted above. He further points out that in both accounts (i.e., the *Poem of Erra* and Ezekiel 9) the setting is one of judgment. The main deity in each text passes judgment against the people due to their lack of proper cultic observance.[173] In Ezekiel idolatry is what brings judgment and in the *Poem of Erra* it is neglect of the cult. Second, Bodi points out that in each case the seven warrior deities are under the direct commands and control of the god in charge and are assigned the task of killing the "guilty." However, in the *Poem of Erra* all the people are targeted by the *Sebetti* while in Ezekiel the seven are limited to only the truly guilty persons and not the righteous.[174] Already one can see the motif of justice in Ezekiel's account as opposed to the capricious nature of the deities so prevalent in ANE literature. Third, Bodi notes the variant tradition of the LXX which states that the seventh figure in Ezekiel's vision had a "girdle of sapphire around his waist" (ζώνη σαπφείρου ἐπὶ τῆς ὀσφύος αὐτοῦ) instead of the

---

24:16—the sin of David's census; and 2 Kings 19:35—Jerusalem's deliverance from Sennacherib. See also comments by Taylor, *Yahweh and the Sun*, 149–50 esp. n. 4.

171. Bodi, *Poem of Erra*, 69–94, gives a detailed analysis of the linguistic similarities between Ezekiel and the *Poem of Erra*. This is in addition to similarities in content and themes. He asserts that there are at least 12 key parallels that have caused him to believe that Ezekiel relied on the *Poem of Erra* for thematic and linguistic concepts, which the prophet implemented and developed in his prophecy. Several of these will be noted throughout this monograph.

172. See also the work of Frankena, *Kanttekeningen*, and his comparison of Ezekiel with the *Poem of Erra*.

173. Bodi, *Poem of Erra*, 108.

174. Ibid., 108. Bodi (108–9) points out that the only salvation from the *Sebetti* was to chant praises to Erra (Erra V 53).

"writer's kit" as stated in the MT. This he uses to further bolster his *Sebetti* parallel as opposed to Nabu, the scribal god.[175] Bodi's insight concerning the LXX helps alleviate some of the problem of the seventh figure being more of a recorder than a warrior, but in the context of the overall chapter it does little to alleviate the lack of a complete one-to-one parallel. The seventh figure still places a mark upon those who are righteous even in the LXX tradition thus causing the MT to perhaps be the better reading. Here it appears that Bodi, in trying too hard to fit the ANE text into a direct one-to-one connection, has faltered in his presentation. Therefore, it seems better to allow Ezekiel the room to adapt these motifs as he does in ch. 9, a fact already noted above.

In light of our earlier discussions in ch. 1 above it is highly likely that Ezekiel had access to at least some of these ANE texts such as the *Poem of Erra*. Interestingly, tablets containing the text of the *Poem of Erra* were commonly buried in houses as a talisman by the Babylonians, as noted also in the text itself.[176] This particular section of the text reads,

> In the house where this tablet is placed,
> Even if Erra becomes angry and the Sebitti storm,
> The sword of judgment shall not come near him,
> But peace is ordained for him.[177]

Concerning this magical talisman angle, Ezekiel removes any possibility for this type of sympathetic "magic" to be invoked by the Israelites for their salvation.[178] For Ezekiel's audience, salvation is to come from the hand of Yahweh alone and that through his appointed servant as seen in ch. 9. Here we see that it is only the righteous who are marked for salvation. They play only a passive role—Yahweh will not be co-

---

175. Ibid., 109–10.

176. Ibid., 109. See also Reiner, "Plague," 148–55, esp. 148. Reiner points out that the Erra Epic was often used (in whole or in part) as a talisman worn by an individual or hung on the door of one's house. The amulets containing a condensed version of the epic, usually from tablet III or V, were used to ward off plague. So too Langdon, *Semitic*, 137–38. See also Marquès-Rivière, *Amulettes*, 82–99 (see esp. 89–93). Marquès-Rivière notes that the talisman were often buried in the foundations of homes and buildings of the Babylonians and that clay plaques were placed on the doors of homes to ward off evil spirits.

177. "Erra and Ishum," *COS* 1.113: 416.

178. Frankena, *Kanttekeningen*, 21. See also Brichto, *Problem of "Curse,"* 7–9.

erced by an act of magic from those who are destined to be judged.[179] Finally, in drawing his concluding parallels between the *Poem of Erra* and the book of Ezekiel, Frankena points out that one of the purposes of the *Poem of Erra* appears to have been to serve as an explanation of why Babylon (in the past) could have been destroyed while their great god Marduk was present. Similarly, the completed book of Ezekiel also seems to be an explanation as to why Jerusalem was destroyed while the God of the universe resided within its walls.[180] Once again, the parallels are striking but to what degree one can say with certainty that Ezekiel had only the *Poem of Erra* in mind when fashioning his book is impossible to determine. The motifs appear to be too ubiquitous to pinpoint them to one specific text. Just the same, the motif of the seven is compelling.

Ezekiel's "Seven" and the Sebetti Paralleled

So what are we to conclude about the motif of the seven in Ezekiel especially in light of the above texts? It seems logical to agree with Bodi and Frankena, at least in a general sense, that there may indeed be a parallel between Ezekiel 9 and the *Sebetti*. Ezekiel's mysterious seven "men" are a close parallel with those of the *Poem of Erra* and the other ANE texts especially as they relate to the function of judgment. In Ezekiel, however, the seven men are divided into two uneven groups. Six, with weapons in hand, are assigned the role of destruction and one is given the role of marking the righteous for mercy. The six figures[181] with the weapons of destruction were to stay by the bronze altar and wait for the seventh to mark those who would be spared (9:4). The key moment for the enactment of the judgment was the departure of

---

179. Frankena, *Kanttekeningen*, 21. Interestingly, Frankena points out that the Hebrew word for "mark" is *tav*: hence he suggests that the mark placed on the righteous people's foreheads was the Hebrew letter "T". So too Fechter, "Priesthood in Exile," 694. This would be more like our "X" seeing how the proto-Hebrew script rendered the *tav* closer to the English *x* rather than the English *t*.

180. Frankena, *Kanttekeningen*, 24.

181. In the Vassal-treaty of Esarhaddon the seven warrior gods appear in the curse section of the text. Line 464 says, "May the seven gods, the warrior gods, cause your downfall with their fierce weapons;" cf. "Vassal-treaties of Esarhaddon," *ANET*, 539. And in the god list of the Treaty between Ashurnirari V of Assyria and Mati'ilu of Arpad col. vi, line 6, we read, "be adjured by the Seven warrior gods;..." cf. "Treaty between Ashurnirari V of Assyria and Mati'ilu of Arpad," *ANET*, 533.

God's Glory Revealed 151

Yahweh from his sanctuary. The figures that would carry out the judgment waited for the appointed time to strike down the inhabitants of Jerusalem. The slaughter was to begin in the sanctuary where the sin of idolatry had pervaded the city as the epicenter of evil. Those who were supposed to have the greatest knowledge of the Law would suffer first.[182]

At the same time, the nameless designation of these seven figures as only "men" (אֲנָשִׁים) and the "ones who have charge over the city" (פְּקֻדּוֹת הָעִיר) seems closer to the nameless *Sebetti* who act at the behest of the gods in Babylon. Whereas these figures are known throughout Mesopotamian literature as being the gods (as a group) who execute vicious judgment at the bidding of the higher gods, in Ezekiel's case, Yahweh is seen as the one who summons the "executioners" to their task and has authority over them.

Another vital aspect to this vision and the seven is the fact that they come "from the direction of the upper gate which is facing north" (מִדֶּרֶךְ־שַׁעַר הָעֶלְיוֹן אֲשֶׁר מָפְנֶה צָפוֹנָה 9:2). The implication of the north, already mentioned above in relation to Yahweh's association with Babylon, lends more credence to the stance that these figures are to be seen as coming as the representation of Babylon.[183] Moreover, they "had charge over the city" (9:1), a fact that can be equated with the political situation at the time. Babylon did have charge over the city and Jeremiah had made it all too clear that Jerusalem would be controlled and conquered by Babylon "from the north." The first deportation and the ensuing control over the city by puppet kings enthroned by Nebuchadnezzar exemplified the subjugation of the city by Babylon. While they may rebel against Nebuchadnezzar (against Jeremiah's warnings), in essence Jerusalem was in the full charge of Babylon at the direction of Yahweh.

We must also consider the possibility that Ezekiel is playing off the wording of Jeremiah 22:7.[184] Here Jeremiah mentions that the palace of the king of Judah would be given into the hands of the "destroyers" (מַשְׁחִתִים), each one with "his weapons" (כֵּלָיו) in his hands. In both Jeremiah and in Ezekiel the same verbal root (i.e., שָׁחַת) and noun (כְּלִי)

---

182. Niehaus, *God at Sinai*, 274.

183. So too, Steinmann, *Ézéchiel*, 33.

184. The belief that Ezekiel is dependent upon the work of Jeremiah is in no way new. Cf. Vieweger, *Die literarischen*.

are used in combination.[185] It is clear that some of Jeremiah's prophecies did reach the exiles in written form according to Jeremiah 29:28 and 51:60–61 and no doubt were read by Ezekiel.[186] While Jeremiah seems to be using his particular terminology to speak of those who will destroy the palace of the king[187] and not the entire city, Ezekiel may have been picking up on the terminology and investing it with Babylonian imagery for his own message against the entire city. Thus, we can postulate that Ezekiel is borrowing a set of terms from Jeremiah which his older contemporary used in a setting of woe to the king of Judah. Ezekiel then added Babylonian "coloring" to it for the purpose of striking fear into the hearts of the people who would understand what the plight of the entire city would be once they were given into the hands of the "seven."[188]

Finally, the appearance of the Nabu-type figure (i.e., the scribe of the gods)[189] functioning in the role of marking the faithful of Jerusalem may be seen by some as a corruption of the *Sebetti* motif previously noted (e.g., Bodi). However, it seems that Ezekiel here is using some literary license with the concept of the *Sebetti*. The very mention of these seven gods would have conjured fear in the minds of the people, especially those in exile who had heard about the *Sebetti* from Babylonian legends. These gods were to be feared for their wrathful vengeance. However, Ezekiel has tempered his message with the grace of Yahweh to his people; a common theme often appearing immediately after a

---

185. Albeit Ezekiel uses שַׁחַת in the nominal form as opposed to Jeremiah's participial form. The dating of the oracle here in Jeremiah 22:7 is not covered by May in his article "Chronology of Jeremiah's Oracles" and as such points to the difficulty in placing exact dates on many of the oracles in Jeremiah.

186. In Jeremiah 51:60 it explicitly states that Jeremiah wrote a scroll to those in Babylon telling of the destruction of the city. Interaction between the exiles and Jerusalem appears to have been a common occurrence; see also Ezekiel 33:21. See May, "Chronology," 218 n. 6, for a list of scholars who see Ezekiel's words as playing a vital role in Jerusalem before it fell.

187. Alexander, *Ezekiel*, 511.

188. Block, "Gog in Prophetic Tradition," 165–66, esp. 165 n. 39, suggests that Ezekiel appears to have known about many of Jeremiah's prophecies.

189. Foster, *Before the Muses*, 702–3, in the "Names of Nabu," Nabu is given the name "The Bearer of the Tablet of Divine Destinies." See also similar titles given to Nabu in the annals of Shalmaneser IV in Grayson, RIMA 3/241, lines 3–5. Also Cheyne, "Ezekiel's Visions," 529, points out that it is hard to deny the parallels with Nabu and the figure presented in Ezekiel 9 although he rightly expresses caution in a pan-Babylonian concept for every similarity in Ezekiel.

message of disaster (e.g., 6:8; 11:17–20; 16:59–63; 17:22–24; 20:40–44). Further, as a priest, Ezekiel may have taken issue with employing the number seven, the number associated with Yahweh's rest, in such a caustic fashion. He therefore assigns the destruction of the city to "six" of the "men" (a number directly connected to humankind), and allowed the seventh figure to be a picture of God's mercy/rest. Yahweh would indeed send disaster upon his people but a remnant would be spared. Where the Babylonian *Sebetti* rained terror on people at will with no mercy shown, Ezekiel divests them of their independence and puts them under the direct control of Yahweh, who converts the role of one of the seven, to that of saviour.[190] Nevertheless, this reprieve is only temporary because in 10:2 this same "savior"/judge turns and joins in the judgment on Jerusalem by casting coals over the city causing it to burn. Not only does this mesh with Yahweh's dual role as judge and savior, but it also aligns well with Nabu's multifaceted role as presented in the "Hymns of Nabu." In this text we find Nabu as the "Incorruptible Judge" and enforcer of justice[191] and in the next line he is called "The Seven" (i.e., the *Sebetti*).[192] Thus, in this Akkadian text Nabu played the double role of judge and executioner as does the Nabu-type figure depicted in Ezekiel 9 and 10:2.

Chapter 11: Temple Abandonment

The abandonment of the temple by Yahweh in 11:22–23 serves as the climax of the first eleven chapters of the book and sets the stage for what is to follow. The people of Judah are left to the judgment and

---

190. Even this particular envoy of Yahweh appears to take on a destructive role in 10:2; however, this is only after all the righteous had been marked. For a discussion on individual responsibility in this chapter, see Joyce, "Ezekiel and Individual Responsibility," 318–19. While Joyce argues against individual responsibility in Ezekiel, he does admit that this theme does appear to be present in ch. 9. He quickly avers, however, that the corporate element is what is to be focused on. This seems like special pleading in this case. Ezekiel does appear to include an element of individual responsibility as will be demonstrated in ch. 3 below. See also, Kaminsky, *Corporate Responsibility*, 155–78. Kaminsky (178) argues that the corporate and individual responsibilities addressed in Ezekiel's oracles are complementary and not contradictory. The individualistic attitudes of ch. 18 build upon or offer a commentary on the older view with the purpose of enlightening the present situation.

191. Foster, *Before the Muses*, 702–3. See also the "Epic of Creation" tablet VII, line 39 in Foster, *Before the Muses*, 478.

192. Ibid., 702–3.

wrath of their hostile Suzerain who has lost patience with his people's sinful nature, thus removing his hand of protection from them. Yahweh will turn his face from them and in effect they will suffer the consequences of abandonment by their god (e.g., 8:6).

This is in no way a new concept for those who lived in the ANE. Mesopotamian examples of temple and city abandonment by the gods are numerous and parallels can be drawn. There is little doubt that Ezekiel was more than familiar with this concept, even if the people of Judah refused to see it as a viable outcome for their city and temple—indeed inviolability was soon to be challenged. Yahweh's glory had once filled the tabernacle in the wilderness (and later the temple in Jerusalem cf. 2 Kgs 8:10–11) for the sole purpose of bringing blessing and protection to his people in a way unknown to them before, but now his glory would depart. Niehaus sums up the final state of Jerusalem when he comments, "Now by contrast his glory cloud and radiance fill the place because he has come to loose judgment . . . he has chosen to abandon his temple and people. He has come to bring the greatest of all covenant curses—the absence of God."[193] It is this decisive act that Ezekiel uses as a literary climax to the rest of his message at least until the point of restoration in chs. 25–48. The unfolding of the next chapters will be the picture of a nation bereft of their covenant Provider and Protector—their Suzerain.

The disaster that follows for Jerusalem is thus the direct result of this departure. Ezekiel's presentation of the covenant-curse framework serves to highlight this catastrophic end to the nation. The message of the first eleven chapters anticipates the departure of Yahweh. Moreover, the constant rehearsal of the covenant breaches in the intervening chapters is the clear indictment of the nation. When reading the text, one naturally expects some great moment of truth and climax to be visited upon Judah by Yahweh for their sin. It is in this vein that we hear this crescendo in the text of 11:21,

וְאֶל־לֵב שִׁקּוּצֵיהֶם וְתוֹעֲבוֹתֵיהֶם לִבָּם הֹלֵךְ דַּרְכָּם בְּרֹאשָׁם נָתַתִּי נְאֻם אֲדֹנָי יְהוִה

"'But as for those whose hearts go after their detestable things and abominations, I shall bring their conduct down on their heads,' declares the Lord God" (NASB).

193. Niehaus, *God at Sinai*, 274.

In light of the lengthy list if covenant violations in the preceding chapters, especially those of ch. 8, this verse serves as the final indictment before the departure of Yahweh. Following immediately after this verse of indictment, the first great covenant curse is enacted in 11:22–23.

‎²²וַיִּשְׂאוּ הַכְּרוּבִים אֶת־כַּנְפֵיהֶם וְהָאוֹפַנִּים לְעֻמָּתָם וּכְבוֹד אֱלֹהֵי־יִשְׂרָאֵל עֲלֵיהֶם מִלְמָעְלָה ²³ וַיַּעַל כְּבוֹד יְהוָה מֵעַל תּוֹךְ הָעִיר וַיַּעֲמֹד עַל־הָהָר אֲשֶׁר מִקֶּדֶם לָעִיר

> 22 "Then the cherubim lifted up their wings and the wheels beside them, and the glory of the God of Israel was over above them. 23 And the glory of the Lord went up from over the midst of the city and it stood over the mountain which is to the east of the city (i.e., the Mount of Olives)."

This verse reveals to the reader the final act of Yahweh before he allows his vengeance to be unleashed on Jerusalem. As he stands outside the accursed city, he is about to oversee, as the presiding Judge, the destruction prophesied in chs. 4–9.

Summary

To summarize then, in Ezekiel's vision in chs. 8–11 we read of Yahweh's graphic revelation to Ezekiel of the extent of Judah's covenant infidelity. Judah had "rebelled" against their suzerain by "walking after" other gods. Through the mode of a visionary experience, the prophet is allowed to survey the extent to which the nation had fallen into sin by walking after these foreign gods (cf. Ezek 8 and 20:16). The horror of the sight would have been overwhelming for a prophet-priest like Ezekiel (cf. 9:8 and 11:13). There can be little doubt that the viewing of these abominations was reason enough for Ezekiel to use the most forceful means possible to point out the seriousness of the covenant breaches that had been made by the house of Israel. How long this abomination of idolatrous worship had been going on in Jerusalem is not made clear in the text, but we can assume by Ezekiel's reaction that the nation had slipped further into idolatry since the prophet's departure from the capital and temple five years earlier. Sadly, Yahweh's departure from Jerusalem would not be attributable to a sacking army as was all too common in the ANE;[194] rather, Yahweh would leave on

---

194. The ANE perspective of the gods leaving their temples, while appearing to be of their own volition, was in essence linked to the removal and/or the destruction of

his on accord, sending a clear message to the people that he was responsible for what was about to happen.

ANE Parallels

The ANE understanding of the gods' roles in history,[195] their pervading presence behind disastrous events,[196] and the attacks of invading armies are well attested in ANE literature.[197] Many times this was understood as the gods' way of righting wrongs done to them and/or their temples.[198] Indeed, to neglect a deity (e.g., through lack of offerings) brought punishment through misfortune and suffering. Lambert even goes so far as to state that "as a doctrine it is not questioned in any known cuneiform text."[199] Generally this "punishment" by the gods was directly related to the breaking of treaties by either a vassal or a suzerain[200] or the misrule of a king.[201] This was due in large part to the

---

their carved images/idols by the invading army. In the case of Yahweh, no image stood in the temple and therefore such a forced removal was impossible. See also Block, "Divine Abandonment," 37–38.

195. Labat, *Caractère Religieux* 35–39, gives an informative discussion on the interrelationship of the gods with kings in Mesopotamia and Assyria. He looks at how the gods appointed them and directed them in conquering foreign lands. Further, he gives an overview of how rulers such as Ashurbanipal and Shalmaneser III reacted to the foreign gods and their temples when they conquered Babylon and how the ANE texts give, generally, a positive picture of the reception of the conquerors by these gods.

196. See the "Plague Prayers of Mursilis II," *ANET*, 395–96. For biblical precedents for this, see 2 Samuel 21 and the curse of famine upon Israel in the days of David due to Saul's mistreatment of the Gibeonites.

197. On this topic, one of the most notable texts from the ANE which relates to the Bible is the Mesha Inscription (ca. 820 BCE) in which Mesha, the king of Moab, notes that their enslavement to Israel was due in part to the anger of Chemosh with his land.

198. Albrektson, *History and the Gods*, 101, points out that the text, "Curse of Akkad," was more of an explanation of why the enemy hordes of the Gutians were able to sack Akkad. The conclusion is that the god Enlil was upset that the ruler of Akkad had attacked and destroyed Ekur, "Enlil's shrine in Nippur." See also the *Erra Epic* for similar motifs.

199. Lambert, *Babylonian Wisdom Literature*, 15.

200. Some believe that Sennacherib's untimely death at the hands of his son was due in part because of the gods' anger over his treatment of Babylon and its temples.

201. See the Hittite text of the "Proclamation of Telipinus" (dated to the seventeenth century BCE) in Sturtevant and Bechtel, *A Hittite Chrestomathy*, 175–93. In

ANE understanding that the judgment of the gods on people, rulers, and nations was based on a universal law of justice and a moral order that was a vital part of Mesopotamian religion.[202]

For those of the ANE, the devastation brought upon cities by raiding hordes was "but a cloak" for the work of the gods and their desire to punish a particular city/nation.[203] At the same time one must keep in mind that destruction of a state was not always due to the weakness of a god[204] per se, but rather was primarily a belief in the wrath of the deity or deities against their own cities. This concept can be seen in Nabonidus' (555–539 BCE) belief that Sennacherib's sacking of Babylon was not due to the weakness of Marduk, but rather to the express will of the gods. The text states,

> (But he) [i.e., Sennacherib] acted (thus against the country only)
>
> according to the wrath(ful will) of the gods.

---

this text the gods repay the treasonous acts of the usurper Zidantas. The text reads, "And then the gods avenged the blood of Pisenis. And the gods made Ammunas, his (i.e., Zidantas') son, his enemy; and he killed Zidantas, his father" (187). The gods then in turn avenge the death of Zidantas at the hands of his son and refuse to bless Ammunas and prosper the rule of the new king (cf. pages 187 and 191, col. 2 lines 48–49). See also the comments of Speiser, "Ancient Mesopotamia," 55–60, esp. 56.

202. Albrektson, *History and the Gods*, 109. Albrektson (109) goes on to note that this understanding of universal justice and a moral order rules out the capricious actions of the gods. While he may be correct in noting that this concept is in later literature in the ANE, it seems apparent that there does appear to be capricious acts perpetrated by the gods, especially if one views the earlier texts such as Atrahasis and the Gilgamesh Epics.

203. Ibid., 28.

204. The passage in 2 Kings 18:33–35 seems to be a clear example where an ANE ruler/spokesman believed in the weakness of the gods of the lands, which Sennacherib had conquered. The Rabshakeh claims, "Has any one of the gods of the nations delivered his land from the hand of the king of Assyria? 'Where are the gods of Hamath and Arpad? Where are the gods of Sepharvaim, Hena and Ivvah? Have they delivered Samaria from my hand? 'Who among all the gods of the lands have delivered their land from my hand, that the LORD should deliver Jerusalem from my hand?'" (NASB). Yet in the same encounter the Rabshakeh identifies that it is Yahweh who sent Sennacherib against Jerusalem to destroy it (18:25). There seems to be a theological tension in the text on this key point. Did the Assyrians believe that the nations' gods were too weak to stop them or did they believe the nations' gods had sent them to destroy these foreign lands? This may very well be an attempt by the DtrH to belittle foreign gods while emphasizing the universal role Yahweh played in the fate of not only Israel and Judah, but also all nations.

> The princely Marduk did not appease his anger,
>
> for 21 years he established his seat in Ashur.
>
> (But eventually) the time became full,
>
> the (predetermined) moment arrived,
>
> and the wrath of the king of the gods,
>
> the lord of lords calmed down;
>
> he remembered (again) Esagila and Babylon, his princely residence.[205]

In this sixth-century text, the role the gods played is clear: Babylon fell because Marduk and the gods were angry with their city. Moreover, the only reason Sennacherib was victorious was because the gods supported his attack. This motif is carried into the period contemporaneous with Ezekiel in a text found in Harran dating to the period of the Neo-Babylonian and Persian periods.[206] The text is purportedly written by Adad-Guppi, the mother of Nabonidus. In the opening lines of the stele we read ". . . in the sixteenth year of Nabopolassar, king of Babylon, Sin, the king of the gods, became angry with his city and its people were transformed into ruin."[207] Here we can see that the relationship the gods had with their nations is much like the relationship between Israel and Yahweh as presented by the biblical prophets. In the context of judgment then, Albrektson concludes, "Thus desolation is not interpreted as a sign of divine wrath in general or of the power of the invaders' gods: it is understood as the wrath of the stricken nation's own deity, it is held to reveal the god's judgment upon his own people and his own abode."[208] Beyond this, however, there was an even more

---

205. "Nabonidus' Rise to Power," *ANET*, 309.

206. The first discovery of this text came in 1906 by H. Pognon and a similar one was found in 1956 by D. S. Rice.

207. "The Adad-Guppi Autobiography," *COS* 1.147:478. See also "The Mother of Nabonidus," *ANET*, 560. For the full text and translation with commentary, see Gadd, "Harran Inscription of Nabonidus," 35–92. See also the text from the Persian era where the gods are said to have become angry with Nabonidus for bringing them to Babylon. "Babylon and Assyrian Historical Texts," *ANET*, 315.

208. Albrektson, *History and the Gods*, 113. We see this as the cause of the destruction of Babylon by the god Erra. Dalley, *Myths from Mesopotamia*, 290, notes one text where it states that the "black-headed" people despised their gods, thus bringing the wrath of Erra upon them.

ominous picture presented in certain ANE texts, that being not only temple abandonment[209] by a nation's god(s) but also that that same deity would be leading the enemy's attack (a concept we introduced at the beginning of this chapter). In this case the outcome was certain defeat.

In Ezekiel's day, the people of Judah stood out as somewhat defiant of this ANE understanding as they hid behind their belief in the inviolability of the city of Jerusalem and its temple. Ezekiel's uphill battle (along with that of Jeremiah's) was to convince the people that their thinking was wrongheaded. As we demonstrated above, Ezekiel actually takes the ANE understanding of abandonment of the deity to an all new level through his imagery and presentation of his message. It is through his opening visions that Ezekiel begins to lay before the people of the exile the truth behind not only Yahweh's concept of covenant curses and their enactment, but also the ANE concept of divine punishment. Because of their history of incessant sinning, Ezekiel sets about to correct the error in Judah's presumptuous thinking that they were above any retribution from their God.

Thus, Judah was about to get a "history" lesson on the effects of covenant curses, a lesson long embraced and understood by other ANE cultures, vassal states, and their suzerains. Indeed, the "history," or should we say experience, of other ANE cultures had revealed that a defeated nation understood such a setback as divine disfavor and abandonment. This indeed was a lesson Judah would soon learn.

The ANE Curse of Temple Abandonment

Our brief survey of texts thus far has yielded an appreciation for the importance within the ANE mindset of keeping the gods placated in order to receive blessings from them. This, we have noted, was often directly related to the keeping of treaties and covenants between vassals and suzerains where treaties were witnessed by the gods of both parties. Any breach of the covenant thus initiated the curses of the treaty at the behest of the gods. In this regard, there are numerous texts that point out the devastating effects of the curses of treaties, par-

---

209. For a detailed chart on all the relevant ANE texts that deal with the removal, repair and/or return of divine images to their temples from the period of the Kassite ruler Agum-kakrime (ca. 1590 BCE) to the Persian ruler, Cyrus II (559/538–530 BCE), see Kutsko, *Between Heaven and Earth*, 157–69.

ticularly temple abandonment. Thus, the departure of the god(s) from their homeland/temple ensured the destruction of the offending party, nation, or city.

The picture presented in Ezekiel's vision of the departure of the Lord would have been just as devastating for those who heard the message in and of itself. Yet when coupled with the curse motif that is clearly evident in the text, one begins to get the true picture of the dread that must have befallen those who first heard the prophet's message, especially prior to the fall of the city.

In the ANE, covenanted kings and their vassals were bound to uphold the stipulations of sworn-to treaties. The suzerain was required to protect the vassal and the vassal was to remain loyal to the suzerain. Breach of these promises by either party caused the enactment of the curses of the treaty by the gods. One of the main curses placed upon either of the offending parties was the abandonment by the gods from the one who had broken covenant. Beyond the destruction of the offending party's homeland, exile served as a fitting punishment for offending the earthly suzerain and the gods who witnessed the treaty *and* the offense. This reality can be seen in the curse section of the Treaty of Esarhaddon with Baal of Tyre.[210] In col. iv the text reads "May Melqart and Eshmun deliver your land to destruction, your people to be deported; from your land . . ."[211] Here we can see the parallels with the biblical text in Deuteronomy 28:26, 63–68.

As for the former curse of abandonment, it was at this point that the offending side was left open to the attack of the gods (viz., through war, famine, pestilence etc.). Cogan bolsters this position when he notes that often the "[m]isfortunes suffered at the hands of an enemy were rationalized as being abandonment by one's own gods."[212] There are numerous examples of temple abandonment that are relevant to our curse motif in Ezekiel 8–11.

---

210. Frankena, "Vassal-Treaties," 150, notes that the colophon of this and several other of the Esarhaddon treaties contain the date of 16th Iyyar 672 BCE. Frankena (150–51) suggests that this date appears to have been a significant period when Esarhaddon was passing on the royal succession to Ashurbanipal his son. Other important dates that appear from the same time frame include the 12th of Iyyar 672 BCE—the gathering of the Assyrian people to swear allegiance to Ashurbanipal and the 18th of Iyyar 672 BCE—the dedication of the royal residence of Ashurbanipal in Tarbis (see Borger, *AfO Beiheft* 9, 71–73, §43–44).

211. "Treaty of Esarhaddon with Baal of Tyre," *ANET*, 534.

212. Cogan, *Imperialism and Religion*, 11.

The Curse of Agade

From the late third to early second millennium in Sumerian literature, the concept of the gods abandoning their cities, ruler/nation, and shrines can be found in various texts. In the *Curse of Agade* (2000 BCE), set within the reign of Naram-Sin, (the grandson of Sargon I) the goddess Inanna removes herself from the city of Agade at the command of the chief god Enlil. The result is the abandonment of the city by the rest of the gods as well and the ensuing destruction of Agade by the Gitians. The abandonment lines in the text read,

> 60. She withdrew her dwelling from the city,
>
> 61. Like a young woman abandoning her woman's domain,
>
> 62. Holy Inanna abandoned the sanctuary Agade.[213]

Lamentation over the Destruction of Ur

Also common during this period of Sumerian literature was the genre called city laments.[214] One text from this genre which addresses our motif of abandonment is the *Lamentation over the Destruction of Ur*.

> The lord of all the lands has abandoned (his stable),
>
> his sheepfold (has been delivered) to the wind;
>
> Enlil has abandoned ... Nippur,
>
> his sheepfold (has been delivered) to the wind.
>
> His wife Ninlil has abandoned (her stable),
>
> her sheepfold (has been delivered) to the wind.
>
> Ninlil has abandoned their house Ki[ur], her sheepfold (has been delivered) to the wind.
>
> The qu[ee]n of Kesh has [ab]andoned (her stable),
>
> her sheepfold (has been delivered) to the wind
>
> Ninmah has [aba]ndoned their house Kesh,

---

213. Cooper, *Curse of Agade*, 52–53. See also "Curse of Agade," *ANET*, 648.

214. Michalowski, *Destruction of Sumer and Ur*, 4–8. Note also, Green, "Eridu Lament, 127–67, and Green, "Uruk Lament," 253–79; Kramer, "Lamentation over the Destruction of Nippur," 89–93.

her sheepfold (has been delivered) to the wind.[215]

The text goes on to list over fifteen deities that have left Ur and abandoned their cult centers. The repercussions of this abandonment, a curse against a people beyond measure, was the subjugation of a nation/state to the horrors of war, exile, and death.

The Tukulti-Ninurta Epic

In the Middle Assyrian period, Tukulti-Ninurta I (1243–1207 BCE) tells of his troubles with the rebellious vassal, the Kassite king, Kashtiliash IV (1232–1224 BCE). In a text describing that rebellion, Tukulti-Ninurta I relates how the gods depart their temples in the land of Kashtiliash IV (i.e., Babylon), thus leaving Kashtiliash to the curse of the treaty and the judgment of the gods (by means of Tukulti-Ninurta I). The text reads,

> 32. . . . impious Cassite king . . .
>
> 33. Against the oath-breaker[216] Kaštiliaš the gods of heaven [and earth]
>
> 34. They showed [. . .] against the king of the land and the peop[les . . .]
>
> 35. They were angry with the *overseer*, their shepherd, and [. . .]
>
> 36. The Enlilship of the Lord of the Lands was distressed and [. . .] Nippur,
>
> 37. So that he did not approach the dwelling of Dûr-Kurigalzu [. . .]
>
> 38. Marduk abandoned his lofty shrine, the city of [. . .]
>
> 39. He [cu]rsed his beloved city Kâr[. . .]
>
> 40. Sin left Ur, [his] town[217] [. . .]

---

215. "Lamentation over the Destruction of Ur," *ANET*, 455. See also Kramer, *Lamentation over the Destruction of Sumer and Ur*, 17–21; "Lamentation over the Destruction of Sumer and Ur," *COS* 1.166:535–36; and Michalowski, *Destruction of Sumer and Ur*.

216. Niehaus, *God at Sinai*, 137 interprets the word as "covenant-breaker."

217. Ibid., 137, Niehaus renders this "cult center," while Foster renders it "holy place" (*Before the Muses*, 301).

41. With Sippar and Larsa Ša[maš . . .]

42. Ea [. . .] Eridu, the House of Wisdom [. . .]

43. Ištaran was angry [. . .]

44. Anunitu does not approach Akkad [. . .]

45. The mistress of Uruk forsook [. . .]

46. The gods were wrath [. . .]47. . at the dec[ree . . .[218]

Here it is clear that the departure of the gods was directly related to their wrath against the covenant partner who had breached the treaty.[219] Tukulti-Ninurta I is in this case presenting, albeit from a biased perspective, the departure of all the gods of Babylonia, which left the land open to his attack and implementation of the curses of the treaty. Interestingly enough, normally one looks to the conquered nations (e.g., Ezekiel's presentation in chs. 1–11) for texts that reflect divine

---

218. Lambert, "Three Unpublished Fragments," 42–45. See also translations by Foster, *Before the Muses*, 300–301; Niehaus, *God at Sinai*, 137; and Machinist, "Literature as Politics,"458.

Machinist notes that the *Tukulti-Ninurta Epic* and the *Sumerian Lament* both have the abandonment motif in common. He posits that although there are several centuries between these two texts it is very possible that the linking literature has not yet been unearthed that will show how these two became related. However, Lambert, "Three Unpublished Fragments," 42, notes that according to the text of Tukulti-Ninurta, literature from the royal archives and libraries was a part of the plunder brought back to Assyria from Babylon (see discussion in ch. 1 above). It is perhaps most probable to see in the later text of the *Tukulti-Ninurta Epic* a direct borrowing of the earlier laments of Babylon (no doubt from these looted libraries and archives) as a means of enriching Assyrian literature and culture. Further, Cogan, *Imperialism and Religion*, 11, appears to be incorrect when he notes that it was only during the Neo-Assyrian Empire that this motif of divine abandonment was first used by the conqueror, rather than the conquered, "in order to justify his ravages." The Middle Assyrian period under Tukulti-Ninurta makes Cogan's position untenable, and as Machinist correctly points out, the motif may be traced even earlier than this (so too Niehaus, *God at Sinai*, 139–40 n. 99). Machinist asserts that the abandonment motif was more implicit in early Assyrian literature. While the motif is explicit in the *Epic of Tukulti-Ninurta* and in the Sumerian Laments, earlier victors did "paint" their success in battle through the aid of the enemy's gods. This was done, however, without explicitly pointing out temple abandonment as the cause. See Machinist, "Literature as Politics," 464.

219. Harvey, *Plaidoyer*, 121, notes this fact as well when he posits that "Les dieux de Kaštiliaš entrent en fureur, parce que le roi cosséen a violé le traité qui le lie à l'Assyrie; ils quittent les villes."

abandonment as an explanation for their defeat, but here we can see the conqueror (viz., Tukulti-Ninurta) using it as a means to justify his victory over a foreign kingdom and his ravaging of their wealth.

Treaties in the Annals of Sennacherib

Archaeologists have also found Assyrian inscriptions dating to the reign of Sennacherib (704–681 BCE) that depict a similar picture. In the text we will look at below the gods abandoned seven rebellious cities on the border of Kutmuhu (i.e., the upper Euphrates). Here we see that the gods' abandonment implies their disapproval of the rulers of these cities in favor of Assyria and the rule of Sennacherib.[220] The text reads,

> 12. At that time the cities of Tumurra,
>
> 13. Sharim, Halgidda,
>
> 14. Kibsha, Esâma, Kûa, (and)
>
> 15. Kana, which are on the border of Kutmuhu
>
> 16. and, like the nest of the eagle,
>
> 17–18. are situated upon the peaks of Mt. Nipur;
>
> 19. who from days of old, in (the time of) the kings, my fathers,
>
> 20. were strong and proud, not knowing
>
> 21. the fear of (Assyrian) rule,-in the time of my rule,
>
> 22. their gods deserted
>
> 23. them and left them
>
> 24. empty[221]

The concept of the gods leaving the people "empty" pointed to the protective vacuum left when the gods deserted them and gave them over to their own devices and the wrath of the king of Assyria. In the case of Judah, the protective vacuum left when Yahweh deserted his temple was all too real and was felt immediately as the nation quickly

---

220. Niehaus, *God at Sinai*, 138.

221. Luckenbill, *Annals of Sennacherib*, 64. Cogan, *Imperialism and Religion*, 11, translates this phrase as, "Their gods abandoned them, rendering them helpless."

experienced the power of Babylon through privation resulting from the two-and-a-half-year siege that followed.

Sennacherib's Fifth Campaign

Next, in records of Sennacherib's fifth campaign, we find the account of the subjugation of Cilicia (698 BCE) due to the forsaking of the gods. Column iv lines 61–65 state that

> 61. In the company of Shulmu-bêl, the governor of Rimusi,
>
> 62. Kirua, prefect of Illubru,
>
> 63. a slave, subject to me, whom the gods forsook,
>
> 64–65. caused the men of Hilakku (Cilicia) to revolt, and made ready for battle.[222]

Scholars have pointed out that the Akkadian term $^{am}ardu$ in line 63 (here translated as "slave") is best understood as "vassal" in the context.[223] This being noted, what is pictured here is a confrontation of Sennacherib with a rebellious vassal who does not have the support of his gods because they have forsaken the nation.

The Esarhaddon Inscriptions

Later, the Assyrian ruler Esarhaddon (680–669 BCE) sought to remove the blame of Babylon's destruction by his father Sennacherib and place it upon the people themselves.[224] According to the popular belief of Esarhaddon's day, Sennacherib's destruction of cult sites in Babylon had raised the ire of not only the people of Assyria and Babylon (because the temple of Marduk in Babylon was sacred to both cultures) but also the anger of the gods. It was perhaps the untimely death of Sennacherib at the hands of his own son, what some felt was a direct

---

222. Luckenbill, *Annals of Sennacherib*, 61.

223. Niehaus, *God at Sinai*, 139 n. 95. For an example of such a rendering see *CAD* vol. AII, 248, definition 6. In texts from Ras Shamra and Alalakh one texts reads, *atta RN qadu mātika ARAD-di*—"(Now) you, Niqmepa, and your land are my vassals."

224. For a detailed discussion on Esarhaddon's "apology" for usurping the throne of Assyria, see commentary by Tadmor, "Autobiographical Apology," 38–47; and Porter, *Images, Power and Politics*, 77–118.

refection of the wrath of the gods, which caused Esarhaddon to rebuild Babylon and record a text about the event. In an effort to deflect the wrath of the gods and the people, Esarhaddon had a series of texts recorded that suggest that the destruction of the original temple and the defeat of Babylon was due to the anger of the gods and goddesses (especially Marduk) with their own people. Two of the texts read as follows.

> The lord of the gods, Marduk, was
> angry. He planned evil; to wipe out
> the land, to destroy its inhabitants . . .
> an evil curse was on his lips.[225]

The second text reads,

> 43–44. The gods and goddesses who dwell in it (i.e., the temple of Esagila)
>
> 45–46. Fled like birds and went up to heaven
>
> 17. The protective gods [. . . ran] off and withdrew.[226]

In the texts we can see Esarhaddon's desire is to present Assyria as being on the side of the gods with Babylon being clearly in the wrong. Thus, in order to appease the pro-Babylonian group in Assyria and the gods, especially Marduk, Esarhaddon took pains to rebuild Babylon and present Assyria in a more positive light.[227] However, in his annals that remained in Assyria, he attributes the vast destruction of Babylon to the evil acts of the people of the city, their moral depravity, and the anger of the gods.[228] These motifs can be seen in the following texts,

> 18b. Formerly,
>
> 19. under the reigns of the earlier kings,
>
> 20. there was in Sumer and Akkad
>
> 21. evil forces, the people
>
> 22. who lived there (with their mouth)

---

225. Cogan, *Imperialism and Religion*, 12.
226. Ibid., 12. See also Brinkman, "Through a Glass Darkly," 39.
227. Introduction to "Esarhaddon," *COS* 2.120:306.
228. Porter, *Images, Power and Politics*, 103–5. For a comparative analysis of the multiple recensions and various texts, see Brinkman, "Through a Glass Darkly," 39.

God's Glory Revealed 167

23. always answered "yes" and "no" to one another

24. and they spoke lies

25. They pushed away and neglected their gods

26–28a. Their goddesses left their divine orders and rode (away) . . .

28b. On the possessions of (the temple)

29. Esagila—the place of the gods,

30. a place forbidden (for laypersons), they laid their hands

31. and silver and gold and precious stones they give

32. to Elam as a purchase price (as assistance to Assyria)[229]

In another recension of the text even more emphasis is placed on the sin of the people in Babylon at least from an Assyrian perspective. This recension reads, "[When] in the reign of a form[er king, there were] evil [omens, all the shr]ines . . .Violence (and) murder was inflicted upon their bodies, and they oppressed the weak—they give them to the strong. Within the city there was oppression (and) accepting bribes, and daily without ceasing they stole one another's goods. The son in the marketplace has cursed his father, the slave [has disobeyed?] his master, [the female slave] does not listen to her mistress."[230] In these last two texts the destruction of the city is attributed to the departure of the gods due to cultic offences, plundering of the temple treasury, and ethical depravity. In Ezekiel's case, ch. 8 is vital in the presentation of cultic offences that also led to the departure of Yahweh. Moreover, even before this, the stripping of the treasures of the house of the Lord to pay tribute (2 Kgs 18:15–16) or to hire foreign armies (2 Kgs 16:8) was all too common and raised the ire of Yahweh because of a lack of faith. The moral depravity, which (is said to have) plagued Babylon, sounds eerily familiar when juxtaposed to the indictments of the prophets against the nation of Israel (e.g., Ezek 18:12; 22:9; 22:12; Amos 2:6–16). Moral depravity, although not the only aspect of the

229. Translation from Borger, *Asarhaddons*, 12–13, §11, recs. A, B, D, esp. 2–4. See also similar translations by Porter, *Images, Power and Politics*, 101 and Lambert, *Babylonian Wisdom Literature*, 4–5. See also commentary on the text by Brinkman, "Through a Glass Darkly," 36–57.

230. Translation from Porter, *Images, Power and Politics*, 101–2.

nation's sinfulness, also attributed to bringing about the covenant curses. As can be seen in the ANE texts above, social morality was a key part of the structure of any society along with cultic respect. Israel had failed on both counts—a holy God cannot dwell in the midst of an unclean people.

Finally, we find similar references to the abandonment of the gods of smaller kingdoms surrounding Assyria during Esarhaddon's reign, which led to their demise as well. One such text from the Annals of Esarhaddon reads,

Sanduarri, king of Kundu and Sissu . . . (was one) whom the gods had forsaken.[231]

The Texts of Ashurbanipal

During the reign of Esarhaddon's son, Ashurbanipal (668–627 BCE) the abandonment motif is also present in texts. Again, one text reads,

> Nanā, who for 1,635 years was angry,
> went to stay in Elam, a place not fit
> for her. But at the time that she and
> the gods, her fathers, spoke my name for
> rule of all the countries, she entrusted me
> with the return of her divinity.[232]

Of course there is a high degree of probability that this text is no more than propaganda (as were most annalistic records as noted above); yet it still offers us a glimpse into the thinking of the ANE rulers and populace concerning defeat and conquest in the period leading up to Ezekiel's message.

A final text from this period concerning the land of Arabia stresses this theme once more. We read, "To the goddess x x [, beloved of (?) Telḫunu, priest]ess of the land of [Arabia], Who, angered at Hazail, king of Arabia [] Handed him over to Sennacherib, my own grandfather, and caused him defeat. She (i.e., the goddess) determined not to

---

231. Cogan, *Imperialism and Religion*, 13. See also Borger, *Asarhaddons*, 49, § 27, esp. 6, lines 20–22. Kutsko, *Between Heaven and Earth*, 106, also makes note of this passage in the context of divine abandonment.

232. Cogan, *Imperialism and Religion*, 14.

remain with the people of Arabia and set out for Assyria."[233] Here the text tells of the conscious choice of the goddess to leave her people and support the enemy because of her anger with her home nation. In this case the goddess Telḫunu of Arabia is instrumental in the defeat of her own land. Whether Arabia had been a vassal of Assyria at this time is not made clear in the text but their defeat is nonetheless attributed to divine abandonment.[234]

Having given ample extra-biblical evidence of the curse of divine abandonment, we will now turn briefly to evidence within the biblical text itself.

OT Precedent for Being Abandoned by the Deity (2 Kings 18:33–35)

In 2 Kings 18 we find the encounter between the representative (i.e., the cup bearer) of Sennacherib and three of the leaders of Jerusalem. Here we see at least two aspects of treaty curse language being presented. In the Rabshakeh's speech to Hezekiah's leaders, the list of those nations whose gods had forsaken them is rehearsed before all those within earshot with the intended purpose of striking fear into the hearts of the people (2 Kgs 18:33–35). The use of the Hebrew language by the Rabshakeh is employed purposely in order to remind the soldiers on the wall of the treaty and its curses. Furthermore, the threat that they would eat their own excrement and drink their own urine can be linked to other treaty curses of the period.[235] The "negotiations" of the Rabshakeh are purposeful and direct. The fear of deity abandonment and being left to the anger of the suzerain is being invoked to instill

233. Translation of K.3405 Text (obverse) from Cogan, *Imperialism and Religion*, 16–17.

234. For a detailed discussion of Sennacherib's campaigns on the southern front of the Assyrian Empire, see Levine, "Sennacherib's Southern Front," 28–58. Levine, 48, suggests that the attack on Arabia took place in 691 BCE sometime during the sixth and seventh campaigns of Sennacherib which he combines. According to the later Prism of Esarhaddon (cf. col. iv, lines 1–31) the Arabians were vassals of Assyria and rebelled but were re-subjugated by Esarhaddon. However, at what time they first were subjugated is not clear. See also Thompson, *Prisms of Esarhaddon and Ashurbanipal*, 20–21.

235. Hillers, *Covenant*, 44–45, points out a line from an Assyrian treaty written about 50 years prior to the incident in our pericope. He notes that one of the lines reads, "May tar and pitch be your food, may the urine of an ass be your drink."

fear. His warning is clear: breaking their oath to Sennacherib would bring the curses of the treaty upon their heads. Indeed, the Rabshakeh even suggests that it was the Lord who had sent Sennacherib to destroy Judah (18:25). In this instance, the fact that one's own god would fight on the side of the enemy can be seen as a common understanding and an effective means of forcing compliance.

In Isaiah 36 the same encounter is presented. Hillers and others have argued that the confrontation of the Rabshakeh and the Hebrew leaders is nothing other than the picture of treaty curse warnings.[236] Because the Rabshakeh asserts that Yahweh sent the king of Assyria against Hezekiah (36:10), there can be little doubt that Yahweh's name must have been invoked in the original treaty. Yahweh's name was no doubt included as a part of the list of gods that witnessed the treaty and would, by association, enforce the curses.[237] In the mind of the Rabshakeh, Yahweh had deserted the people because they had broken the treaty agreed upon in his name. Hillers asserts that the interactions recorded in this event ". . . permits us to conclude that the Israelites were thoroughly, even uncomfortably, familiar with what a treaty involved."[238] Finally, we can see in this event a clear link to the thinking of Ezekiel, especially in ch. 17.[239] In this chapter Ezekiel indicts Zedekiah for treaty violations against Nebuchadnezzar. He had taken a vow to submit himself to Nebuchadnezzar before Yahweh and now Yahweh was going to hold him accountable for that oath (17:18–20).[240]

236. Ibid., 44.
237. Ibid., 43–45.
238. Ibid., 45.

239. Ibid., 44. See also Frankena, *Kanttekeningen*, 13, for comments on the breaking of the treaty oaths between Zedekiah and Nebuchadnezzar and their probable Babylonian context.

240. The reason that Hezekiah apparently escapes judgment from the Lord for breaking covenant with Sennacherib is not clear in the text. It is possible, according to 2 Kings 19, that Isaiah's words from the Lord appear to trump the treaty curse. Sennacherib had blasphemed the Lord and would therefore pay with his life. On the other hand, Tadmor, "Treaty and Oath," 149–52, avers that the kings of Israel and Judah up until the period of Zedekiah, were never in a vassal treaty (i.e., an *adê* agreement) with any of the Assyrian kings. Rather he posits that Judah and Israel had an *ardūtu* (i.e., one of yearly tribute and service to the king and his gods) agreement instead. He concludes that it was only Zedekiah who actually swore an oath (i.e., an *adê* agreement) in a vassal treaty with Nebuchadnezzar. Cf. also Mendenhall, "Puppy and Lettuce," 30 n. 16, who points out Zedekiah's implied taking of an oath in the name of Yahweh before Nebuchadnezzar.

Conclusion

In the opening chapters of Ezekiel, the prophet has a vision that serves to set the stage for what is to follow in the rest of his prophecies. Graphic imagery and symbolism laced with Babylonian and ANE meaning greet the reader within the first few verses of ch. 1 and serve to "educate" the prophet's audience about the nature of their God and the plight that would soon befall them. As with the experience of Isaiah in ch. 6 of his book, Ezekiel witnesses the awesome splendor of the God whom he serves—a scene that leaves him speechless for seven days (Ezek 3:15). The imagery of the vision with its descriptive language makes it clear that the deity with whom "the house of Israel" has broken covenant is fearsome, holy, and all-powerful. For Ezekiel's audience it was clear that they, as a nation, were being indicted for covenant violations and were in dire straits. It is for this reason that the literary buildup to the departure scene in chs. 8–11 marks the turning point in the book and allows for a tidal wave of indictments and curses to play themselves out within chs. 13–24 (see ch. 3, below, for my treatment of Ezekiel 12). The departure of Yahweh in ch. 11 thus fulfills the first and perhaps greatest treaty curse, namely, temple/divine abandonment. The ANE literature and treaties surveyed above make it abundantly clear that the picture Ezekiel is painting for his hearers was well known and the implications crystal clear. The curse of temple abandonment would allow for the invasion and exile of Jerusalem and its inhabitants. It is therefore no surprise that a prophecy of impending exile in ch. 12 follows immediately on the heels of ch. 11.

Structurally, the framework of the book finds its first and second "peaks" in the visions of chs. 1–3 and 8–11 respectively. Up until this point in the prophecy, these two visionary sequences drive the narrative while the rest of the prophecies, although still playing an important role, are muted in comparison. These peaks served as vivid mental pictures along the literary road of Ezekiel's message of warning and covenant indictment. The housing of the covenant curses in these visions, coupled with the symbolism of the ANE, served their purpose to warn the house of Israel of the realities that lay ahead.

However, Ezekiel had another means by which he could deliver his message, that being the use of metaphor. Within the twelve chapters containing the oracles of indictment (i.e., chs. 13–24), two stand head and shoulders above the rest. The extended metaphors of chs. 16 and 23 serve as a fitting reminder that Yahweh will also use the "standards" of the surrounding nations to judge his people who had broken covenant with not only their heavenly Suzerain, but also their earthly suzerain.[241] Here the ANE curses for covenant violators play out in the most graphic detail of the entire OT. It is to these chapters we now turn.

---

241. The use of the phrase וָאֶתְּנֵךְ בְּנֶפֶשׁ שֹׂנְאוֹתָיִךְ ("and I gave you over to the desire of the ones who hate you") in 16:27 (cf. also 16:37) seems to imply what is explicit in 23:24. Wong, *The Idea of Retribution*, 54, notes that the use of the phrase נתן בנפש in Psalms 27:12 and 41:3 connotes that the protection of Yahweh has been removed. This is clearly the implication here in ch. 16.

3

The Awesome Deity's Judgment
(Ezekiel 16 & 23)

HAVING SET THE STAGE WITH THE DEPARTURE OF THE *KĀBÔD* OF Yahweh in ch. 11, Ezekiel now brings many indictments, in covenant-lawsuit style, against the nation.[1] In this process he sets into prophetic motion the oracles against the wayward "house of Israel." As noted in our last chapter, throughout chs. 4–11 Ezekiel concisely enumerated the many sins of the people and their guilt in those sins. From chs. 12 to 24 the expansion of these covenant infractions is presented. The prophet in many cases links these infractions with the curses of the Sinai covenant and curses all too familiar in the ANE. Among their many shortcomings both spiritual and moral, Israel's sins included: child sacrifice (e.g., 16:21; 23:39; 20:26, 31), worship of idols (chs. 14, 23), following their own laws (20:24–26) and playing the spiritual and political harlot (chs. 16 and 23).[2]

In this chapter we will bring into sharper focus the particularly heinous sins as presented in chs. 16 and 23.[3] We will start by exploring the uniqueness of chs. 16 and 23 and then place these chapters within their literary context and identify common motifs across the oracular chapters of 12–24. Second, we will examine the particular punishment meted out to Israel and Judah for their sin of spiritual adultery. On the surface level, some see in the OT law no clear parallels for the treatment of the unfaithful wife as portrayed in these chapters or a

1. Cf. Wilson, "Ezekiel's Dumbness," 96 n. 3.

2. For an in depth discussion on the use of the metaphor in chs. 16 and 23 of Ezekiel, see Galambush, *Jerusalem*, and Durlesser, *Metaphorical Narratives*, 103–43.

3. Cf. Jer 3:6–14 for similar motifs perhaps borrowed by Ezekiel. The inclusion of ch. 23 is mainly due to similarity in content, theme(s), and metaphor. For all intents and purposes, ch. 16 serves as the essence of the covenant breach message in this section.

modern justification for it.[4] For this reason, we will give an overview of competing interpretive views of various scholars (viz., feminist positions and OT and ANE scholars) to see if the actions of Yahweh are justified, or conversely, constitute acts of brutality far exceeding the crime. Third, we will examine the language employed by Ezekiel to see if it fits better within the context of ANE marriage/divorce contracts and/or treaty curses and the punishment for individuals who were politically unfaithful to their suzerain.[5] Finally, we will look at literary works from the ANE that may have influenced Ezekiel's structural organization of ch. 16.

In the following discussion I will attempt to demonstrate that these two chapters appear to form the backbone of chs. 12–24 and the third "peak" in the structural framework of the book. Apart from their obvious length and placement in the text I will also examine the literary, linguistic, and thematic correlations which will help establish this premise. While the linguistic and thematic issues will be handled throughout this chapter, the literary form, i.e., the genre of the chapters, seems the most appropriate place to start.

The Uniqueness of Chapters 16 and 23

M. G. Swanepoel begins his essay on Ezekiel 16 by noting that the chapter is "surely one of the most gripping units in the book of Ezekiel."[6] Ezekiel's use of the extended metaphor or allegory is one of a kind in the OT.[7] Similarly, Boadt asserts that Ezekiel was one of the

4. Day, "Imagined Demise," 285–309.

5. Hillers, *Treaty-Curses*, 58–59. Cf. also Magdalene, "Treaty-Curses," 341–46.

6. Swanepoel, "Ezekiel 16," 84. For a structural analysis of ch. 16, see Swanepoel, "Abandoned Child," 93. Zimmerli, *Fiery Throne*, 98–99, points out that Ezekiel's use of this metaphor and imagery goes well beyond the former prophets Isaiah, Hosea, and Jeremiah.

7. I understand that a metaphor is normally defined as a literary means of comparison whereby a "resemblance" or "trait" of one object is used to illuminate something about another (e.g., Herod the "fox," cf. Luke 13:32) resulting in a desired effect, usually emotional. Similarly, allegory is usually understood as a literary device in which a tangible object or entire narrative account, unrelated to that which is being described, is used to illuminate or equate something of meaning about an abstract reality (e.g., Gal 4:22–31) and/or real thing. Often an allegory can be defined as an "extended metaphor." In this chapter, I use the term "metaphor" and "extended metaphor" (i.e., allegory) somewhat interchangeably without necessarily adhering to the strictest definitions of the terms. While the marriage metaphor finds immediate

first prophets of the OT to develop the extended metaphor and the allegory to the extent present in several texts (e.g., 15:1-6; 16:1-43; 17:1-22; 27:1-36; 28:12-19; 31:1-18) to which we may include not only ch. 23 but also ch. 19 and the pericope of 24:1-13.[8] As Durlesser correctly notes, Ezekiel's use of the metaphor allowed him to use "graphic, bawdy, perhaps even offensive, narrative style [to push] the metaphor of Israel as an adulterous woman to its creative limits."[9] In both chs. 16 and 23 the metaphor is the vehicle used to explicate the message of Israel's infidelity to the Sinai covenant. Thus, it appears that here the "metaphor is not an incidental ornament of biblical language, but one of its controlling modes of thought."[10]

These two chapters serve in a cohesive manner to focus the reader on the heart of the issue regarding the punishment of the nation—what Zimmerli calls "historical-theological summaries"[11] and Koch calls "a summing-up of a century and a half of critical prophecy."[12] Beyond these unique metaphorical presentations, however, lies the imagery and iconographic links to the land in which Ezekiel found himself. In this vein, Power contends that Ezekiel 23:14b-15 is "one of the few explicit biblical acknowledgments of the ancient Near East."[13] As we have been arguing throughout, Ezekiel's use of these images allowed him to formulate his message of covenant disloyalty in a distinctly Ezekielian style.

Broken covenant due to spiritual and political infidelity drives the message of this section and is most easily heard in these chapters. This is evidenced by the strong covenant language not only explicit in the linguistic presentation but also in the metaphor itself.[14] Moreover,

---

relevance in ch. 16, ch. 23 can be seen more as an allegory (i.e., Oholah and Oholibah = Samaria and Jerusalem respectively). In the case of ch. 16, however, the metaphor of the unfaithful wife is extended to the point of allegorical proportions. Therefore, my use of "metaphor" and "allegory" will be based upon these understandings. See further the definitions of Wong, *Retribution*, 34-35.

8. Boadt, "Ezekiel," 2:715.
9. Durlesser, *Metaphorical Narratives*, 135.
10. Frye, *Great Code*, 54; or Lee, *Collected Works of Northrop Frye*, 19:72.
11. Zimmerli, *Fiery Throne*, 52.
12. Koch, *Prophets*, 2:102.
13. Power, "Iconographic Windows," 1.
14. See Wong, *Idea of Retribution*, 35-50, for a forceful analysis equating marriage to covenant in this metaphor.

with the exception of ch. 20, these two chapters are the longest of this entire oracular section. It appears that the metaphor of ch. 16 (with many parallels with ch. 23) serves a distinct role in the course of the indictments and covenant-curse presentation.[15]

At the same time the presentation of the sin of spiritual and political infidelity against Yahweh within these chapters must be understood within the setting of the broken covenant and the punishment appropriate to the crime as it relates to the Law and ANE treaties and marriage contracts. While the sensibilities of twenty-first century thinkers may be troubled by the imagery, Ezekiel has a purpose for this harsh language. He is speaking to a people who refuse to acknowledge their guilt and responsibility for their sin. Furthermore, the regular appearance of the elders at Ezekiel's house (e.g., 8:1; 14:1; 20:1) serves as an appropriate setting for Ezekiel's scathing words. Ezekiel used cutting terminology in order to shock[16] and awaken the elders and the people from their lethargy (cf. 33:30–33). Ezekiel needed to use whatever literary means necessary to bring to the forefront the desperate condition of the people in Jerusalem and in Babylon. This desperate condition is echoed in the themes present not only in these two extended metaphors but also in the surrounding context.

Another aspect of the uniqueness of these chapters is the central role they play in the oracular section of chs. 12–24. This uniqueness is evident in the content of their message. For example, ch. 16 by itself serves as a microcosm of the entire book. The chapter covers the basic history of Israel in relation to the establishment, breach, and renewal of the covenant. In relation to the overall book, Ezekiel's mes-

---

15. Kaufmann, *Religion of Israel*, 432, insists that chs. 16 and 23 are the products of Ezekiel's "exuberant imagination that have no historical worth." However, while one can agree that there may be an inflated picture of the sins of the nation in these chapters for the purpose of rhetorical impact, to dismiss, wholesale, the message of the "historical" presentation in these chapters would be to miss the reality of the long history of Judah and Israel's sin. Kaufmann seeks to apply the message found in chs. 16 and 23 to the immediate period of the exile and the few years prior to the fall of Jerusalem. However, the message of Ezekiel extends much farther into the past than the immediate setting—a reality clearly seen in ch. 20.

16. Cf. Biggs, *Book of Ezekiel*, xviii–xix. Also, Hillers, *Treaty-Curses*, 66–67, points out the disgrace men would feel in the ANE for being compared to a woman or being effeminate. This was also a common treaty-curse for those (commonly warriors) who broke covenant with their suzerain. While Magdalene, "Treaty-Curses," 348, notes that the "provocative language" gets our attention, there can be no doubt that it served the same function for those of the sixth century.

sage begins with a nation in a covenant relationship who has sinned against its God, moves to the harsh reality of the punishment of the nation when breach of covenant relationship occurs, and ends with a picture of restoration. In this vein, Fishbane notes of ch. 16 that "the movement of Ezekiel's prophecy is from sin to judgment to restoration: from marriage to adultery (false alliances) to punishment to remarriage (covenant renewal). This sequence recalls Hosea 2, which also utilizes the allegorical pattern of marriage–adultery–remarriage in order to condemn the nation for covenant unfaithfulness; and it similarly recalls the reflex of that pattern found in Jeremiah 2–3."[17] Also, Fishbane's tripartite breakdown of ch. 16 as a presentation of sin, judgment, and restoration accurately summarizes the book of Ezekiel while expressing the role that the covenant played in the relationship between Israel and her God. At the same time the link between the marriage metaphor and the earlier works of Hosea and Ezekiel's contemporary, Jeremiah, places Ezekiel firmly within the prophetic tradition, while linking former covenant motifs with covenant and curse language, both implicit and explicit, in chs. 16, 23, and the entire book.

Beyond these unique literary and thematic aspects, the extended nature of chs. 16 and 23 begs the question as to the purpose of their present location in the text. Obviously Ezekiel and/or editor(s) wanted to draw the reader's attention to this section of the prophetic message by means of the vivid imagery and harsh language. Indeed, this appears to be exactly the purpose. The appearance of the extended metaphors in 16 and 23 fall between the two vision sequences on each end of the overall prophecy. The chariot throne visions of chs. 1–3 and 8–11 create the first bookend to Ezekiel while the restoration visions in chs. 37 and 40–48 complete the couplet. Thus, chs. 16 and 23 form the heart and soul of the prophet's message while summarizing the very content of the prophecy.

But, how are these two chapters to be heard within the context of the surrounding oracles of doom? A brief look at the literary and structural context of chs. 16 and 23 may shed some light on their importance. We will begin with a survey of the chapters surrounding these metaphors and then move into a more detailed analysis of chs. 16 and 23.

17. Fishbane, "Sin and Judgment," 138.

Literary Context of 16 and 23

Chapter 12: The "Rebellious House" Motif: A Fitting Inclusio to Chapters 1–12

With the close of ch. 11 the future of Judah appears grim—exile and destruction awaited the "rebellious house" of Israel. The curse of exile naturally followed the breach of the covenant (Deut 28:49, 63–65; Lev 26:33, 38, 39, 43) and was to be expected especially in light of similar ANE curse parallels. For example, in the treaty between Ashur-nirari V and Mati'ilu[18] (ca. 750 BCE) we read, "If Mati'ilu sins against (this) treaty made under oath by the gods (*adê tamîti ilāni*) then, just as this spring lamb, brought from its fold, will not return to its fold, will not behold its fold again, alas Mati'ilu, together with his sons, daughters, officials, and people of his land [will be ousted] from his country, will not return to his country, and not behold his country again."[19] It is therefore not surprising that after the vision of temple abandonment in 11:22–23 that ch. 12 immediately tells of the imminent enactment of the curse of exile.

Structurally, the recurrence of the phrase "rebellious house" (בֵּית מְרִי) and the word "rebellious" from the verbal root מָרָה ("to be rebellious against") is telling of the flow of Ezekiel's thought process from the commissioning chapters of 1–3 until Ezekiel's sign act of the covenant curse of exile depicted in ch. 12. It is in chs. 2, 3, and 12 where these linguistic links, in whole or in part, appear most frequently. The appearance of the phrase "rebellious house" in 17:12 (part of the allegorical trilogy of chs. 15–17) and in 24:3 (the concluding chapter of the oracles against Judah) helps extend the motif like a thread throughout these foundational sections of the book.[20] However, it is the clustering of these terms in chs 2, 3, and 12 which show the significance of the terms to the structural thought process of the prophet. The stressing of the term "rebellious" to describe Judah's nature in ch. 2 (cf. 2:3, 5, 6, 7, 8) and the recurring phrase "rebellious house" in the commissioning of Ezekiel in ch. 3 (cf. 3:9, 26, 27) is picked up again in ch. 12 after the

---

18. Also known as Mati'el, the king of Arpad in the Sefire treaties (ca. 754 BCE).

19. "Treaty between Ashurnirari V of Assyria and Mati'ilu of Arpad," *ANET*, 532, with parenthetic insets from Tadmor, "Treaty and Oath," 135.

20. The concept of the rebellious nature of Israel is briefly picked up again in 44:6, thus extending this motif to the restoration chapters as well.

departure of Yahweh from his temple (cf. 12:2, 3, 9, 25).[21] Thus, the linguistic concentration of particular terms/phrases in chs. 2, 3, and 12 serves as a fitting inclusio to the call of the prophet and the prophet's enactment of the curse of exile. At the same time the concentration of these linguistic concepts highlight the curses of temple abandonment and exile and sets the stage for the foreboding outpouring of God's judgment and curses in chs. 13–24. Finally, the transitional nature of ch. 12 functions much in the same way as ch. 33 does in the restoration chapters (see ch. 4, below). One could argue then that ch. 12 serves as a structural conclusion to the first eleven chapters while bridging the oracular section of 13–24.

This "bridging" effect can be best seen whereby ch. 12 links chs. 1–11 and 13–24 through similarities in genre forms (i.e., sign acts) and themes. The rhetorical use of the "sign acts" genre in 12:3–7 and 12:17–20 harks back to the sign acts of chs. 4 and 5 while looking forward to the final sign act in 24:15–27. Thematically, the presence of the prophecy against the "prince of Jerusalem" (i.e., Zedekiah—12:10–13) finds its parallel in chs. 17 and 19 while the sword motif in 12:14 and 16, which had been introduced in chs. 5 and 6 (cf. 5:1, 2, 12, 17; 6:3, 8, 11, 12), mirrors in miniature its later extrapolation in ch. 21. These themes found in ch. 12 bring cohesiveness to the indictments and their oracular fulfillments. Finally, ch. 12 ends with two brief oracles that confirm that the end of the nation is imminent (vv. 21–28), a reality that finds examples both before and after this pivotal chapter. Nevertheless, as of ch. 12, one is left in expectation as to how exactly this would play itself out.

We may conclude then, that the prophet has used the transitional nature of ch. 12 not only as an inclusio with chs. 1–3 but also as a means to link the previous material to what follows. Further, ch. 12 summarizes the curses to come—exile being the next greatest curse after temple abandonment. Nevertheless, simple mass migration of the people of Judah from Jerusalem to Babylon was not the entirety of what the prophet envisioned. Many would suffer the harsh realities of the covenant curses (e.g., ch. 9). These curses would be based not only on the curses of the Sinai covenant but also on the ANE curses enacted due to the broken covenant with Nebuchadnezzar (cf. ch. 17)—those

---

21. The verbal root מָרַד ("to rebel") is used only in 2:3 while the root מָרָה is used exclusively in the phrase "rebellious house" throughout these chapters.

most responsible being the leadership of the nation as noted in chs. 13 and 14.

Chapters 13 and 14: Judah's Leadership Indicted for Covenant Unfaithfulness

Immediately after the promise of exile in ch. 12, chs. 13 and 14 highlight the sins of the leadership of the people, both spiritual (ch. 13) and civic (ch. 14).[22] These chapters illustrate the depravity of those who were supposed to lead the people and call the nation to repentance. As depicted in the prophet's vision in ch. 9, judgment had to start from the top down (cf. 9:6).

It should not be surprising that at this key juncture in Ezekiel once again we see the judgment imagery likened to "violent storm winds" (רוּחַ סְעָרוֹת—cf. 13:11, 13) which was introduced in 1:4 and later poured out upon Jerusalem in chs. 9–12.[23] Interestingly, in the entire OT, it is only in these two verses in Ezekiel that סְעָרָה is used in the plural as a metaphor for judgment against the house of Israel.[24] One can speculate that this plurality is reflective of the ongoing motif of Yahweh's union with Babylon as the means of bringing destruction upon Judah.

The spiritual depravity of both the prophets (13:1–16) and prophetesses (13:17–23) followed by the presentation of the intense idolatry of the elders of the people in 14:1–11[25] is tempered only by the mentioning of the righteous men, Job, Daniel, and Noah (14:12–20).[26] The nation's leadership had become so depraved that even if these

---

22. Brueggemann, *Covenanted Self*, 93, comments that the prophets had tried to legitimize the dysfunction of the nation's leadership by giving "false assurance." Indeed, the reality of the nation's plight was being overlooked for a false belief in the inviolability of the city and temple.

23. Petter, "Book of Ezekiel," 146–47. Interestingly, in Amos 1:14 סְעָרָה is used in the oracle against Ammon where exile of this foreign nation is also in view.

24. The plural construct form of סְעָרָה is used in Zechariah 9:14, but here Yahweh is combining forces with Ephraim and Judah to fight Israel's enemies. This use of סְעָרָה in the plural reinforces my position that Yahweh is joining forces with Babylon in Ezekiel 13.

25. Cf. also Mosis, "Ez 14,1–11," 161–94.

26. Cf. also Jer 15:1 where Moses and Samuel are used in a similar context. See Dressler, "Ugaritic Dnil," 152–61, for an argument in favor of identifying Ezekiel's Dan'el with the Daniel of the biblical text. For a refutation of Dressler's position, cf. Day, "Daniel of Ugarit," 174–84.

three were in the city they would only be able to save themselves.[27] Yahweh's judgment would be complete and be effected upon the corrupt leadership and the nation. Those who were righteous would save only themselves—each person was accountable before God and would not be spared on account of the righteous merits of another (cf. chs. 9 and 18).[28]

The word of the Lord given to Ezekiel in the final three verses of ch. 14 serves as vindication for the coming judgment of the land. Ezekiel himself would witness the waywardness of the arriving exiles from Jerusalem and see firsthand just how depraved the nation had become. These chapters thus follow the normal pattern of prophetic judgment; Yahweh would initiate his punishment and curses upon the nation from the top down. The unleashing of the next series of curses upon the entire nation is thus ready to be presented in chs. 16 and 23. The mini allegory of the useless charred vine in ch. 15 fittingly brings the reader's focus back once again from the leadership of the nation to the entire population of the land.

Chapters 15–17: A Trilogy of Metaphors on Covenant Unfaithfulness

The brief eight verses of ch. 15 begin a trilogy of allegorical and metaphorical chapters that deal specifically with Judah's unfaithfulness to the covenant.[29] While covenant language is explicit in chs. 16 and 17, the brevity of ch. 15 is in no way diminished by the lack of the mention of the term "covenant." This allegory of the charred vine

---

27. For a redaction-critical study of ch. 14 focusing on the "Priestly case-law" as the possible grounds for the indictment of Judah's leadership, see Zimmerli, "Die Eigenart," 1–26.

28. Again Joyce, "Ezekiel and Individual Responsibility," 319–20, avers that this has nothing to do with individual responsibility even though he acknowledges the presence of the motif. He notes the "basic ideal" of individual responsibility as being present but that it is not "innovating" in this respect.

It seems to me that if Ezekiel is presenting the "ideal," even in the case of general judgment, is he not in some way "innovative" in applying the motif in the first place? Once again, as noted in our discussion of ch. 9 above, Joyce's analysis seems founded more on a preconception of a late development of individual responsibility as opposed to what the text is actually presenting.

29. For a discussion of ch. 15 as either a parable, allegory, or metaphor, see Simian-Yofre, "La métaphore," 234–47.

sets the context for the chapters that follow; the nation as a whole is beyond saving—they are worthless (15:4). In 15:8 the verb מָעַל ("to act unfaithfully" or "treacherously") implies the concept of covenant "unfaithfulness"[30] just as we see explicitly in 17:20.[31] We can assume that this trio of chapters thus plays a key role in presenting covenant infidelity as a focal point of Ezekiel's message at this juncture of his work. Chapter 16 is by far the most explicit in this regard and the most extensive both in length and in descriptive language. For the moment we will set ch. 16 aside and return to it when we address ch. 23 at the end of our study of chs. 13–24.

Ezekiel's mentioning of the broken covenant in ch. 17 (especially verse 13) follows after the clear covenantal language of ch. 16 (i.e., 16:8, 59, 60, 62).[32] Moreover, 17:12 points to the enactment of the covenant curses of Deut 28:36. The king of Judah was taken into exile in fulfillment of the curse of the Sinai covenant as well as a result of treaty violation with Nebuchadnezzar.[33] Judah's leadership and her people were unable to keep covenant with anyone, let alone their ultimate Suzerain, Yahweh. Even though the people of Judah were obliged to keep their oath with Yahweh, this in no way dismissed them from keeping their vows to foreign rulers. Yahweh had brought Babylon against Judah as an instrument of divine punishment and as Jeremiah had warned, they

---

30. See also a similar use of the verb in 39:23, 26.

31. Cf. also 14:13; 18:24; 20:27; 39:23, 26.

32. For a discussion on the use of *māšāl* in Ezekiel, see Polk, "Paradigms, Parables," 564–83, esp. 573–83. I cannot agree with Polk (581), that the author seeks to switch focus from the historical/political to the "theological plane" in this chapter. The switch to the breach of the Sinai covenant still falls within a political purview even though a "theological plane" may be included inferentially. The immediate context of ch. 16 and the political intrigues seem to bolster this conclusion.

33. For a literary analysis of the references to covenant in ch. 17, see Wong, *Idea of Retribution*, 57–66. Frankena, "Vassal-Treaties," 130, notes that in the treaties of Esarhaddon (viz., the Treaty with Ba'al of Tyre), it was a common practice to include the native deities of the vassal as well in the witness list of the treaty. If this were the case with Zedekiah, then Yahweh's name would have been invoked as well. Frankena therefore suggests an implicit curse from Yahweh in favor of the earthly suzerain in Ezek 17:19 and Isa 36:10. It is possible that this may have fueled Ezekiel's criticism of Zedekiah in this case. Interestingly, the Chronicler seems to be aware of an oath made in the name of Yahweh between Nebuchadnezzar and Zedekiah (cf. 2 Chron 36:13). See further the comments by Koch, *Prophets*, 2:85; Wong, *Idea of Retribution*, 61; and Stevenson, *Vision of Transformation*, 103–4, who also note the possible use of Yahweh's name in the covenant with Nebuchadnezzar.

must adhere to the punishments meted out or suffer the consequences. Those living in Judah were once again showing their true colors in their unwillingness to heed the warnings of Yahweh's prophets to keep their cultic and secular oaths.

Furthermore, the allegory of the eagle and the cedar tree in ch. 17 must be seen as a backdrop for the central message of Ezekiel especially in light of ch. 16 and the curses which accompany military defeat.[34] In 17:19–21 the heart of the message becomes clear: what was implicit in the visions and oracles now becomes explicit. Judah was guilty of breaking covenant with her Suzerain. It was this sin that would be the most serious of all her broken oaths.[35] The heart of the text (i.e., verse 19) which is directed at Zedekiah as the corporate "head" of the nation reads,

לָכֵן כֹּה־אָמַר אֲדֹנָי יְהוִה חַי־אָנִי אִם־לֹא אָלָתִי אֲשֶׁר בָּזָה וּבְרִיתִי אֲשֶׁר הֵפִיר וּנְתַתִּיו בְּרֹאשׁוֹ

"Therefore, thus says the Lord, Yahweh, as I live surely my oath which he has despised and my covenant which he has transgressed I will bring upon his head."

The language of this verse resonates linguistically with 16:59 and the motif of "despising" (בָּזָה) the covenant (so too 17:16, 18). While death, destruction, and exile at the hands of the Babylonians would be a just recompense in light of the breach of the covenant with Babylon, Judah must also understand that this was only a symptom of a greater illness, chronic disobedience to their covenant with Yahweh.[36] It is for this reason that Ezekiel's message in the first 24 chapters of his book focuses on the covenant breaches and the ensuing fallout of punishment (i.e., curses of the treaty) and exile. Chapter 17 serves as a fitting reminder that what was presented in ch. 16 (and 23) was based upon a common failure within the leadership and by extension, the nation as

---

34. For a discussion on the metaphor of Ezekiel 17, see Davis, *Swallowing the Scroll*, 95–104.

35. Greenberg, *Ezekiel 1–20*, 321–22, also notes this connection and comments that the text shifts from the earthly to the divine in verse 19.

36. Wong, *Retribution*, 62–66, 77, points out the three main punishments in the ANE for vassal rulers who break covenant. These include, the death penalty (which happened to Zedekiah's sons), removal from one's land (i.e., exile), and being made blind (cf. Ezekiel 12 as well). See further the ANE treaties of Ashurnirari V of Assyria and Mati'ilu of Arpad, and Sefire I A 35–40.

a whole. They had failed to live up to treaty and covenant agreements at every level. This failure would be their undoing.

Chapter 18: Hope for the Individual in the Midst of Covenant Unfaithfulness

Chapter 18 stands out as a message of hope on the heels of the condemnatory allegorical trilogy of 15–17.[37] The harsh treatment of the nation in ch. 16 especially, is softened by a message of hope to the individual.[38] This chapter presents what appears to be the personal responsibility of the individual to live a righteous life and in so doing choose life instead of death (cf. Deut 24:16). Zimmerli correctly notes that this chapter is not focused simply on the "doctrine of individual recompense" but rather on the concept that the individual could change his ways and accept the knowledge of Yahweh and live by his Law in order that life may ensue.[39] No longer did one need to be tied to the "sins of the fathers" but could rather, with this extension of grace, live free from those old ways and cling to the Law of the Lord for the hope of life. For so long, the concept of generational sin had dictated the lives of the Israelites, but now Ezekiel's new message focused on the individual (cf. also 33:10–20). While the destruction of the city and land may have been a foregone conclusion, on a personal level, change could be effected if each person turned away from sin and lived righteously before their God. A similar message of hope is found in ch. 9 in the midst of the nation's judgment at the hands of the seven executioners (cf. 9:4). The upright in heart, marked for their righteous living, would escape the judgment of Yahweh.

---

37. For an in depth analysis and exegesis of ch. 18, see Matties, *Ezekiel 18*. For a similar handling of the chapter from an ethical perspective, see Alaribe, *Ethics of Responsibility*.

38. So too Driver, *Introduction*, 284; Kaufmann, *Religion of Israel*, 440; Wilson, "Prophecy in Crisis," 167; Steinmann, *Ézéchiel*, 41; van Zyl, "Solidarity," 38–52; McConville, "Priests and Levites," 14; and Mozley, "Visitation," 120. Mozley (125) sees Ezekiel as reinterpreting the older law and making it "obsolete." Robinson, *Corporate Personality*, 8–9, argues that one cannot remove the individual aspect from the prophetic message even though corporate responsibility may have been the general focus. For an opposing view, cf. Joyce, "Individual Responsibility," 185–96; and Lindars, "Ezekiel and Individual Responsibility," 452–67.

39. Zimmerli, *I Am Yahweh*, 113.

On a side note, contrary to Fishbane's assumption that this chapter was *only* for the exiles,[40] the tenor of the message best reflects clear links to chs. 9 and 14 and the conditions in Jerusalem prior to its destruction as presented in chs. 16 and 23. At least portions of Ezekiel's message may have been heard among those in Jerusalem before the final destruction occurred (see discussion in ch. 2, above). It is true that the righteous people in the exilic community may have felt that the exile was unjust, but Ezekiel was setting the record straight. The destruction forecast in chs. 16 and 23 was punishment for covenant violation; those who had already escaped by means of the exile *had* received the mercy of God, not vice versa (cf. 33:23-29).[41] Therefore the call to live a righteous life was a means for individual Israelites in both communities, who did not embrace the idolatrous ways of their leaders or the covenant violations of their king (as depicted in chs. 16, 17, and 23), to save themselves from the coming wrath.[42] Once again, in the midst of the curses, hope is present.

Chapter 19: The Covenant Unfaithfulness of Judah's Kings

Chapter 19, in the form of a lament, returns to the plight of the kings of Judah (i.e., the offspring of Josiah) which thematically resonates with ch. 17. Also, the use of vine imagery in 19:10-14 recalls the same motif in ch. 15 (see also 17:6-8) along with the use of the motif of fire to consume its shoots and fruit (compare 19:14 to 15:4-7). While ch. 19 deals with the kings of Judah and ch. 15 the nation as a whole, the message is still one of sin and covenant unfaithfulness.[43] Moreover,

---

40. See Fishbane, "Sin and Judgment," 142.

41. Wong, *Idea of Retribution*, 250-51, correctly points out that Ezekiel's message sought to thwart the argument from the people that God was "unjust" (18:25, 29). Ezekiel is showing that every judgment they received in the course of the exile reflected the justice of God based upon the covenant stipulations. Indeed, even the punishments placed upon the surrounding nations reflected a "poetic justice" of sorts based upon how those nations had treated the house of Israel (see further my discussions in ch. 4, below).

42. One could argue that this message to the individual was one of the enduring qualities of Ezekiel's book. It was a message to every generation, not just the exilic one.

43. The inclusion of Babylon in v. 9 causes one to conclude that the actions of vv. 6-7 must have constituted treaty violation. Indeed, in the life of both Jehoiachin (cf. 2 Kgs 24:9) and Zedekiah, rebellion against Babylon and Yahweh brought about their exile.

the use of allegory here in ch. 19 fits well with that which precedes (chs. 15–17) and follows it (ch. 23). At the same time the sandwiching of ch. 18 dealing with personal responsibility between two allegories on kingship (i.e., chs. 17 and 19) allowed the prophet to address not only the responsibility of the average Israelite, but also the individual responsibility of the kings. Each had a choice to lead the nation in the proper direction despite the actions of their predecessors, a message directed at Zedekiah in light of the rapid succession of rulers in Jerusalem. While the city/nation would suffer destruction for a lifetime of sin (cf. 2 Kgs 23:26–27) with no possibility for a reprieve (as was granted in Josiah's day—2 Kgs 22:20), when it came to the individual, even for the king, salvation still proved to be a vital part of the prophet's message. In this regard Ezekiel's message echoed that of Jeremiah, "submit to Babylon and live" (cf. Jer 38:17–26).

Chapter 20: Israel's History of Covenant Unfaithfulness

In the midst of the harsh covenant indictments of chs. 16, 17, and 23, Ezekiel seeks to vindicate the curses that have befallen the nation by rehearsing Israel's long history of rebellion. Chapter 20 reiterates a history rife with idolatry and rebellion, a picture that was played out in full view for Ezekiel in chs. 5–8 but here is expanded to include the nation's entire history.[44] In this chapter Ezekiel focuses upon the punishment of the nation for following their own statutes (חֻקִּים), ordinances (מִשְׁפָּטִים), and practicing idolatry (20:18)—any of which constitute a breach of covenant.

Also, the difficulties with ch. 20 as being somehow "contradictory" to what precedes and follows it has often been pointed out.[45] The theme of individual responsibility in ch. 18 appears at first glance to be at odds with the concept of cumulative guilt in ch. 20. However, such is not the case when understood within the context of Ezekiel's message both within the chapter and in the overall presentation of the nation's sin. Those who suggest that the sins of the fathers were visited upon a later, "innocent" generation, viz., the exilic generation, fail to

---

44. For a discussion on Ezekiel's apparent revision of history, see Peterson, "Ezekiel's Perspective."

45. For example, Fishbane, "Sin and Judgment," 143–44, asserts that the theological message of ch. 20 is "diametrically opposed to the teaching of chapter 18" (143).

see the importance of the longsuffering of Yahweh throughout their generations. This reprieve often came in the form of Yahweh's desire to withhold punishment so his name would not be profaned among the nations (20:9, 14, 22, 29). However, in every case the sins of the fathers, i.e., their propensity for idolatry, caused the next generation to follow suit even when Yahweh offered a better way that would lead to life (20:11, 13, 21). The point Ezekiel was making was that Yahweh's longsuffering had not worked as a deterrent but rather had only caused each succeeding generation to be more profane.

The consummation of the nation's guilt came during the exilic generation when the city was destroyed and the people exiled. This was not due, as some posit, to "bad laws"[46] given to the nation by Yahweh, but rather was the culmination of systemic evil epitomized by the generation of Manasseh and thereafter (cf. Jer 15:4). While space and focus does not allow for a detailed exposition of the chapter, it is vital to point out that all that was about to come upon the nation was due to covenant infidelity from the nation's earliest history until Ezekiel's day. Covenant loyalty is the central focus of the chapter, which is driven home by the comments of 20:37. "And I will cause you to pass under the rod, and I shall cause you to enter into the bond of

---

46. For generations scholarship has wrestled with this small phrase וְגַם־אֲנִי נָתַתִּי לָהֶם חֻקִּים לֹא טוֹבִים וּמִשְׁפָּטִים לֹא יִחְיוּ בָּהֶם in v. 25. Most render the phrase as "therefore I gave them bad laws and ordinances by which they could not live." This translation has pitted Ezekiel against the Law of Moses, Deuteronomy in particular (e.g., see Crenshaw, "Theodicy," 247). However, I propose the following interpretation, "therefore I gave *them over* to (their own) bad laws and ordinances by which they could not live." Yahweh's act of giving the nation "over to" their own sinful "laws and ordinances" would be their undoing. In the context this is the only rendering that makes sense of the prophet's fluctuating use of the masculine חֻקִּים and the feminine חֻקּוֹת in the chapter (cf. 20:11, 13, 16, 18, 19, 21, 24). The lexigraphical shift in this term helps to bring into sharp contrast the laws of the fathers and the laws of Yahweh. Interestingly, the Targum of Ezekiel follows this line of thought in many ways. Cf. Levey, *Targum of Ezekiel*, 63. See further the use of לָהֶם with the meaning "to their" in Ezekiel 39:13 and the idea of Yahweh "giving over" the people to their own ways in Psalm 81:13 (see also the use of the verb נתן "to give" in Ezek 23:24). Betts, *Ezekiel the Priest*, 105, like me, rejects the notion that the Mosaic Law is being implied here. For a canonical approach to this passage which focuses on the elevation of the Priestly Law and the denunciation of the Deuteronomic Law (i.e., 20:25–26), see Hahn and Bergsma, "What Laws Were 'Not Good'?," 201–18. In this article the authors suggest that Yahweh gave the bad laws of Deuteronomy in order to bring about the covenant curses, namely, the exile. Earlier, Heider, "Further Turn," 721–24, argued that Ezekiel is in a way reinstituting the tenth plague formerly used against Egypt as a means of punishing his own people.

the covenant." Here the "rod" (שֵׁבֶט) is none other than the curses that the people would endure which included, divine abandonment, war, plague, famine, and ultimately, exile.

Chapter 21: *The Sword as a Means to Punish Covenant Unfaithfulness*

In chapter 21 we see a shift in the way the author presents judgment on Jerusalem. In light of what has preceded, no reason needs to be given for the destruction that follows, only the reality that judgment has arrived in the form of the "sword" obviously wielded by Babylon.[47] It is interesting to note that Nebuchadnezzar's use of belomancy, haroscopy, and divination in 21:21 brings forth a positive response from the gods of Babylon to attack Jerusalem.[48] However, as we noted in ch. 2 above, it is Yahweh who controls the gods of the Babylonians and he is the one who dictates the outcome of Jerusalem. Yahweh himself relinquishes the sword into the hand of the Babylonian aggressors.[49] This motif of judgment by the sword fits well within the context of chs. 16 and 23 especially in light of the punishments noted in both chapters which are directly related to the use of the sword by Israel's paramours (16:40; 23:47 see below).

Throughout the OT the sword motif is often used to represent punishment both human and divine (e.g., Exod 5:3; 17:13; 18:4; 22:24). This is especially pertinent due to the close relationship of the motif of the sword to the curses in Leviticus (cf. 26:7, 8, 25, 36, 37) and Deuteronomy (cf. 28:22). Harvey adds insight to the use of the sword here by noting, "Si bien que la justice appliquée dans le *rîb* ne se présente pas comme une vengeance mais comme une réponse aux exigences du droit: Yahvé ne s'y venge pas lui-même, mais revendique le droit juré dans l'alliance: l'épée ne venge pas Yahvé, elle venge l'alliance

---

47. Renz, *Rhetorical Function*, 85.

48. Maarsingh, "Schwertlied," 355. So too Power, "Iconographic Windows," 26. The use of haroscopy can also be seen in the accounts of Nabonidus. Cf. Gadd, "Harran Inscription," 63, col iii, lines 12–14.

49. Petter, "Book of Ezekiel," 151–52. Also, in the annals of Shalmaneser we find him saying, "I pointed the weapons of Aššur, my lord, against them (and) defeated them." Cf. Grayson, RIMA 3/22. Here the weapons/sword used in battle to defeat the enemy is attributed to the deity.

(Lev 26,25)."⁵⁰ Thus one could argue that Yahweh, while sovereign over the process, is merely allowing the curses of the covenant to run their course. It just so happens that the sword is the ANE instrument of choice for enacting many of the curses directly related to military conquest.

In another sense, this chapter also creates some theological tension within this section of Ezekiel due to the presence of verses such as 21:8–9 [Heb].

8 וְאָמַרְתָּ לְאַדְמַת יִשְׂרָאֵל כֹּה אָמַר יְהוָה הִנְנִי אֵלַיִךְ וְהוֹצֵאתִי חַרְבִּי מִתַּעְרָהּ וְהִכְרַתִּי מִמֵּךְ צַדִּיק וְרָשָׁע

9 יַעַן אֲשֶׁר־הִכְרַתִּי מִמֵּךְ צַדִּיק וְרָשָׁע לָכֵן תֵּצֵא חַרְבִּי מִתַּעְרָהּ אֶל־כָּל־בָּשָׂר מִנֶּגֶב צָפוֹן

8. "And say to the land of Israel, thus says Yahweh, "behold I am against you and I will stretch forth my sword from its sheath and I will cut off from you the righteous and the wicked. 9. Because I will cut off from you the righteous and the wicked therefore my sword will go forth from its sheath against all flesh from the south to the north.""

In these two verses, which appear to contradict our discussions of chs. 9, 14, and 18 where the salvation of the righteous is promoted, we see the magnitude of the judgment and curses against the nation. Fishbane has pointed out the problems of the contradictions between these verses and ch. 18,⁵¹ a problem that the authors of the LXX tried to remedy by removing the term "righteous" (δίκαιος) and replacing it with the term "transgressor" (ἄδικον). Again the scope of this book does not allow for an in depth discussion on the apparent theological "contradictions" within the work of Ezekiel. Nevertheless, besides the obvious possibilities of the time span between these oracles and the particular focus they may have had before they were compiled in their present form, a couple of points can be offered to help alleviate the tensions especially in light of the curse motif.

First, the focus of the oracle is against the "land of Israel" (לְאַדְמַת יִשְׂרָאֵל) which fits well within the boundaries of the figurative language and allegories of this section and the curse of exile and punishment in general (e.g., chs. 16, 20, 23 speak in general terms for Jerusalem and

---

50. Harvey, *Plaidoyer*, 168.
51. Fishbane, "Sin and Judgment," 145–46.

the nation). If in fact Ezekiel is speaking figuratively about the "land of Israel," then the concept of the sword (i.e., war or punishment in general) cutting all people off from the land is very appropriate. This does not contradict the plight of the righteous in a general sense but rather points out the obvious plight of all those who are exposed to war—that being the loss of life and exile from the land. This links back to ch. 14 and the fact that even though righteous men such as Daniel, Job, and Noah were in the land, the land still would be "desolate" (שְׁמָמָה 14:16) and destroyed by the judgment of war (cf. 14:17–18). Exactly who dies and who are exiled is not discussed. The general terms only inform us of the plight of the nation as a whole; both the good and the bad will suffer.[52] In chs. 9, 14 (vv. 10–20 specifically), and 18 we do not see the righteous being saved to remain in the land necessarily, although this is one possibility as was the case with Jeremiah and many of the poor people (cf. Jer 39:9–14; 52:16), but rather that they would be saved to go into exile (as seen with Daniel and his three companions and Ezekiel himself). This would allow for the offspring of the righteous to return to the land after the exilic period.

Second, even if some of the righteous were killed or affected by the curse on the land, this in no way belittles the message to the larger group of the righteous who were exiled or scattered in the land. Concerning this difficult aspect of ch. 21 Bodi comments, "in the destruction, looting and indiscriminate killing which accompanied the conquest of cities . . . the killing of innocent victims was inevitable. This is the predicament of any war. In the religious descriptions of historical events, the innocent victims might be identified with 'the righteous' ones."[53] This is perhaps part of the intent of Ezekiel in chs. 9, 14, and 18. Moreover, in this case the sin of Achan (Joshua 7) appears pertinent to the discussion.[54] Being under the curse of God affected all the people because of the nature of the covenant. Even the righ-

---

52. The sign act of ch. 5 speaks of three different outcomes for the nation: 1) exile, 2) siege, and 3) war. In ch. 5 the specifics of how the people would be judged are defined in more particular terms as opposed to the general terms in ch. 21. One must be careful not to push the theological message of Ezekiel into too narrow of a mould. Context must help define the theological message being presented. For example, Maarsingh, "Schwertlied," 353, suggests the possibility that the use of the "righteous" and the "wicked" here is a merismus.

53. Bodi, *Poem of Erra*, 270.

54. Cf. Mozley, "Visitation," 115–16, for a brief discussion on the purpose behind the punishment of Achan's entire family.

teous were affected in the short term because of Achan's sin, but the righteous in the broader sense of the term survived to conquer the land. Therefore, one must be careful not to skew Ezekiel's theological positions based upon certain terms and sweeping motifs. It is in the context of the curses that Ezekiel's theological stance seems to make the most sense. Covenant violation by the unjust, however large their numbers, affected everyone within the nation. Those were the cold hard facts of covenant violation as noted throughout the Pentateuch and in particular, Deuteronomy 28 and Leviticus 26.

Chapters 22–24: A Trilogy concerning the Covenant Unfaithfulness of Jerusalem

In chapters 22–24 we see a series of indictments against the city of Jerusalem as though it, as an inanimate object, could be responsible for its sin. In chs. 22 and 24 (we will deal with ch. 23 alongside of ch.16, below) Ezekiel characterizes Jerusalem as the "city of blood" (עִיר הַדָּמִים) and representative of the nation as a whole (cf. 22:2; 24:6, 9). He points out in ch. 22 that the "city" had shed innocent blood (22:2–6, 9, 12, 13, 27), oppressed the weak and was unjust (22:7, 12, 24–25, 29), had committed cultic impurity (22:8, 26) and sexual immorality (22:9–11), had false prophets and profane priests in its midst (22:25–28), and had a lack of integrity in business (22:12–13).[55]

---

55. Anbar, "Une nouvelle allusion," 352. Anbar seeks to make a connection between the lack of rain in both Ezek 22:24 and the lack of the deluge in the *Poem of Erra*. In the *Poem of Erra*, the city of Sippar was not flooded because it was an "eternal city, a religious center" ("*une ville éternelle un centre religieux*") as was Jerusalem. Bodi also follows this line of thinking and cites the rabbinic interpretation which states that the Flood had not covered the land of Israel. See *Midrash Bereshit Rabba*, 37, as cited by Bodi, *Poem of Erra*, 112 n. 10. Bodi has devoted four pages (i.e., 113–16) to develop this parallel which seems very tenuous. Such a remote connection, while possible, is not plausible in this context. This entire chapter is one of indictments and judgment. Perhaps one should see it more as expressing the fact that the nation, so dependant upon water, would not receive rain as a just punishment for its sin. The blessing of rain was promised to a faithful Israel (cf. Lev 26:4; Deut 11:14; 28:12). Therefore, Lev 26:19 is the curse opposite the blessing of Lev 26:4 while the curse of Deut 11:17 counters the blessing in Deut 11:14. Finally, in the curse list of Deuteronomy, 28:24 seems to point to the rain "as dust," which implies a lack of it as one of the curses in breaking covenant. This interpretation seems best especially in light of the context of verse 23. In the context of the overall chapter here in Ezekiel 22, indictments highlight each segment. It is the final verse (i.e., 22:31) that points to how the rest of the text needs to

Further, comments concerning the sexual impurity of the people in the city noted in 22:9–11 (a direct link to Lev 20:10–18), aptly introduces the imagery of the nation's lewd behavior addressed in ch. 23 while harking back to the language of ch. 16. In 22:15 exile, which had been introduced in ch. 12, once again becomes the punishment of choice, a recurring warning from the curses of Deuteronomy 28 and Leviticus 26. Also, in 22:30–31 we see an allusion to the account of Sodom and Gomorrah where Abraham sought for ten righteous people but could not find them. Here the depraved condition of the city is presented; a state that will cause them to be consumed in the fire of God's wrath, the same end meted out to Sodom and Gomorrah in Abraham's day. Interestingly, once again this allusion draws us back to ch. 16 and the mention of Sodom there (16:46, 48, 49, 53, 55, 56). The representative nature of Jerusalem as a wanton transgressor was the epitome of what the nation had become at the level of the individual. Thus this chapter serves as an appropriate introduction to the "Oholibah" allegory of ch. 23 and as a link back to the themes of the extended metaphor of ch. 16.

Finally, ch. 24 describes an oracle against the city pictured in allegorical fashion by means of the boiling pot in which the priests would cook sacrificial meat to be offered to the Lord.[56] In this case the "offering" would be the inhabitants of the land. In vv. 6, 11, and 12, the oracle points to the "rust"/ "scum" (חֶלְאָתָה) as the defiling agent (cf. also 22:18–22).[57] The rust of the "pot" (i.e., Jerusalem) denotes all the vileness that affects and pollutes the people. This in turn can be none other than the covenant violations of the people themselves especially those sins enumerated in ch. 22. At the same time the punishment of the city and its inhabitants and the melting of the very pot itself in the fire, points to the finality of Yahweh's purging and the completion of the curses. Nothing would remain of the city; it would be totally destroyed. Further, as previously noted, the phrase "bloody city" (עִיר הַדָּמִים) found in vv. 6 and 9 reflects similar language as found in 22:2 (see also 7:23). The theme of the sin of the people associated with "blood" or the shedding of innocent blood resonates throughout the

---

be heard. Because of their evil, curses have followed them and the wrath of Yahweh is upon them—no rain would fall upon them in the rainy seasons.

56. For a detailed form-critical discussion of 24:1–14, see Block, "Ezekiel's Boiling Cauldron," 12–37. See also Odell, "Genre and Persona," 626–48.

57. The use of purgation imagery parallels that found in 22:18–22.

oracles against Judah. This adds to the imagery depicting the covenant violations that were present in the city and the reason that the curses were about to be poured out upon the city and its inhabitants.

At the end of the chapter (cf. 24:15–27) the prophet's use of the sign act (a rhetorical device first introduced in ch. 4) brings the oracular section of chs. 4–24 full circle. This final sign act closes out this block of indictments against the nation. The sad but fitting nature of the sign act (i.e., the death of Ezekiel's wife) depicts the reality of Yahweh's relationship with Jerusalem. The marriage metaphors of chs. 16 and 23 presented the "death" of the marital relationship (i.e., the covenant) between Yahweh and Israel. Here, Ezekiel's own loss of the marital covenant through his wife's death appropriately shows the state of Yahweh's relationship with his "wife." Neither Ezekiel nor Yahweh would grieve the loss of their relationships. Yahweh's grief had run its course long before; now judgment would take its place. Ezekiel's inability to grieve the loss of his wife in the presence of the people represented the soon-coming reality of the curse of exile as presented in chs. 16 and 23. Those in exile would not be present in Judah to grieve the loss of both their beloved city and families. Chapter 24 thus shows that the curses upon the nation are complete and that Yahweh will be made known (24:24) to the remnant by means of these judgments.

Conclusions from the Oracles of 13–24

A few conclusions can be drawn from this brief overview of the oracular section against Judah and Jerusalem. First, there can be little doubt that the venting of the wrath of Yahweh against his people must be seen in the light of the covenant curses depicted in Leviticus 26 and Deuteronomy 28. Fishbane aptly concludes that, "a dominant feature of Ezekiel 4–24 is that YHWH will vent his wrath against Israel for her sins. Repeatedly such terms as "my anger" ('*appî*), "my fury" (*ḥᵃmâttî*), and "my zeal" (*qinā'tî*), recur through the sin-judgment chapters (cf. 5:13; 8:18; 14:19; 16:38; 20:33; 22:21–22), together with a panoply of stereotyped dooms (like, "sword," "pestilence," and "famine") drawn from the curses for covenant malfeasance found in Leviticus 26 and Deuteronomy 28."[58]

---

58. Fishbane, "Sin and Judgment," 147.

Second, many of these curses were also found in treaties from Ezekiel's time period—treaty curses he was no doubt familiar with. As will be developed below, these curses served as a vehicle to push the oracles to their intended end—that being the punishment of Israel for covenant breach and unfaithfulness to her heavenly Suzerain.

Third, unlike the hope which Jeremiah often presented, the judgment of Israel was a foregone conclusion in Ezekiel's mind. Yes, Ezekiel did offer a glimmer of hope to the individual (e.g., chs. 9, 14, and 18) but this would in no way stop the preordained destruction of the city and nation. What concerned him the most was presenting to the exilic community, and those remaining in Jerusalem, the reason for their present hardships (i.e., the curses of the covenant) and a solid theological understanding for their plight. They were to suffer the consequences of their actions through what Fishbane calls the "legal nexus" which is depicted by terms found throughout the oracular section.[59] Thus, because they had transgressed the Law, the punishment (i.e., the curses) would follow. Ultimately, this portion of the prophet's message served, if for no other reason, to reeducate the exiles by means of the implementation of the curses. This reeducation would include coming to the "knowledge" of who Yahweh was and understanding their covenant obligations to him (this concept will be developed in ch. 4).[60]

Chapters 16 & 23: A Summary Exposition

After looking at the content of the surrounding chapters, it is apparent that while themes and genre connect all these oracles, chs. 16 and 23 still appear to stand out in this section mainly due to their graphic content and curse depictions. Clearly, Ezekiel strategically placed these extended metaphors within this body of oracles for maximum effect. Yet, at the same time, we have noted that similar motifs, literary style, and genre forms (i.e., metaphors, parables, and allegory) help bring cohesiveness to the entire section. The next step needed in our assessment of the oracular section is to do a summary of the content of these two chapters before moving into a discussion of the parallels between these chapters and the OT and ANE texts.

---

59. Ibid., 148.
60. Ibid., 147–48.

Chapter 16 [61]

In ch. 16, Ezekiel presents the history of Israel by means of a metaphor of a female infant and her growth into adulthood.[62] The chapter is also steeped in the "legal reality" of the ANE and the legal expressions of the OT classical prophetic period.[63] Adopting the abandoned child motif, Ezekiel begins the metaphor with the child's (i.e., Israel's) ignoble birth from an Amorite father and a Hittite mother (16:3) and stresses the hopelessness of the future of the child after being cast out to the elements (16:4–6). Yahweh then passes by in the time of the infant's need and provides for her and enters into covenant with her when she was at marriageable age.[64] After the establishment of the covenant, Yahweh provides lavish marriage gifts on his bride (16:7–14).[65]

---

61. Kamionkowski, *Gender Reversal*, 92–133, effectively argues that the metaphor of ch. 16 also presents the idea of "gender ambiguity." She states, "in Ezekiel 16, chaos emerges not only as a result of cultic and social crimes but also as a result of the subversion of gender order . . . Ezekiel believed that chaos began when female Israel started playing the role of a male—by acting as a sexually independent individual" (133). Also Greenberg, "Notes," 34, points out the strong possibility of Ezekiel's borrowing the marriage motif from Hosea and Jeremiah and developing it with a "biography." This biography, he asserts, was extended to include "room not only for a descent into vice, but for the repeated, even-more-depraved actions of a woman, portrayed as a nymphomaniac."

62. Baumgartner, *Zum Alten Testament*, 368, notes that the prophet created an "allegory" around an already existing history as opposed to creating "history" through an allegory. Cf. also Robinson, *Corporate Personality*, 5, who sees chs. 16 and 23 as a perfect example of corporate personality being depicted in the metaphor of the unfaithful wife.

63. Malul, "Adoption of Foundlings," 98. Malul does acknowledge the difficulty in comparing many of the legal terms found in Ezekiel with other ANE legal material due to the separation of time (i.e., up to 1000 years apart). Malul studies the legal procedure in the ANE for adopting a child that has been abandoned to the elements.

64. Ibid., 97–126, esp. 104–5. In verse 8 Ezekiel's use of the Hebrew term כָּנָף ("skirt") is telling of the marriage relationship/covenant. This same term is used of Boaz's stretching of his "skirt" (כְּנָפֶךָ) over Ruth and entering a marriage covenant with her (cf. Ruth 3:9).

65. Driver and Miles, *Assyrian Laws*, 193–98, point out the giving of ornaments (*dumāqi*—Akk) as a bridal gift as early as the Middle Assyrian period (cf. also Gen 24:53). So too Greengus, "Marriage Contract," 516, 523. If a marriage was dissolved, the bride had to return these gifts. Wilcke, *Ancient Near Eastern Law*, 64–65, gives examples from the early Dynastic and Sargonic periods of Mesopotamia. On a side note, Galambush, *Jerusalem*, 95, notes the similarities in the language used for describing the clothing of the wife in Ezekiel's metaphor and similar terms used for the clothing of the priests and the temple curtains and veil elsewhere in the OT. Cf. Exod

But soon after the "girl's" marriage to Yahweh, she plays the harlot both spiritually (i.e., with idols vv. 16–21) and politically with foreign liaisons (i.e., Egypt [v. 26], Assyria [v. 28] and Babylon [v. 29]).[66] She takes the gifts that Yahweh had given to her and squanders them on her lovers getting nothing in return (16:15–31). Yahweh then declares her an unfaithful wife and a harlot and warns of impending punishment (16:32–38). The punishment enacted upon the unfaithful wife is then described. These punishments included being beaten, stripped, stoned, and cut with swords (16:39–43)—we will return to these punishments shortly. Interestingly, the robing of the young girl at the beginning of the chapter is juxtaposed with the disrobing of the harlot toward the end of the chapter. This stripping of unfaithful Jerusalem appears as a just punishment for her sinful acts. Next, Yahweh then likens his unfaithful wife to her Hittite mother and her sisters Samaria and Sodom. However, Yahweh tells her how her sins exceed even her "sisters'" sins (16:44–52). It is particularly noteworthy that references to Sodom throughout the OT prophetic corpus many times are associated with curses from God for covenant violations. This understanding is reinforced by its first appearance in such a format in Deuteronomy 29:22–28 (Heb).[67] Finally, restoration is promised for both her and her sisters as a means of showing Yahweh's goodness (16:53–63) and no doubt as a means of offering hope for the righteous.

To summarize then, as noted at the beginning of this chapter, the marriage metaphor can be linked closely to that of Hosea and Jeremiah as the covenantal bond between Israel and Yahweh. Central to this presentation is the motif of covenant which controls the content and

---

26:36; 27:16; 28:39; 35:35; 36:37; 38:18, 23; 39:29 for רקם and Exod 25:4; 26:1, 31, 36; 28:5, 6, 8 for שׁשׁ. Most of the time these terms are used together when referring to the tabernacle and the priests' garments.

66. These liaisons must be seen in the context of treaty making; first with Egypt, then with Assyria and Babylon. This concept was also present in Isaiah's prophecy against Judah in Isaiah 7–8 (Assyria) and later in chs. 30–31 (Egypt). Judah had hopped from one "man" to the next and had played the harlot through these detestable (in Yahweh's eyes) foreign alliances. Cf. Durlesser, *Metaphorical Narratives*, 135–36.

67. Hillers, *Treaty-Curses*, 74–76, points out that while the curse of Sodom and Gomorrah does not appear in the treaty curses outside of the OT, it is important to remember that the language of Deut 29:19–28 falls within covenant curse material. Also other OT prophets make the connection (as maledictions) between the cities of the plain and this form of a curse, see Isa 1:9; Jer 20:16; 49:17–18; 50:39–40; Hos 11:8; Amos 4:11; Zeph 2:9 and Lam 4:6.

general direction of the metaphor. Verse 8b identifies the entrance of Yahweh into a covenant (בְּרִית) with the young woman. From this point on the metaphor painstakingly moves in the direction of a negative assessment of the woman's treatment of her Husband and the breach of the covenant, indeed to the point of an outright indictment by Yahweh that she had "despised (בָּזָה) the oath (אָלָה) [what scholars have noted as the curses of the covenant][68] by breaking (פָּרַר) the covenant (בְּרִית)" (v. 59b).[69] However, in two of the concluding four verses Yahweh reaffirms his resolve to restore the covenant for his name's sake (vv. 60, 62).[70] Following this line of thinking, one can even see many of the aspects of the vassal-treaty format within chs. 16 and 23. Durlesser lists them as follows:

1. The covenant maker, Yahweh, is identified in 16:1.

2. An historical introduction is offered in 16:3–14, in which a list is offered of the "prior beneficial acts done by the great power on behalf of the smaller one."

3. . . . the primary demand in the covenant is for loyalty. The primary focus of both Ezek 16 and 23 is the failure of one party to be loyal to the other.

4. The vassal treaties of the ancient Near East and the covenant between Yahweh and Israel included lists of blessings and curses. In 16:59b, the narrator declares that his wife has, "held in disdain the words of the curse formula for the breaking of the covenant."[71]

It is from this covenantal perspective that the metaphor must be analyzed.

Chapter 23

In chapter 23 we find the allegory of two sisters, Oholah—Samaria, and Oholibah—Jerusalem (23:1–4).[72] By understanding the immedi-

---

68. Durlesser, *Metaphorical Narratives*, 118.

69. The series of verbs in this verse recalls our discussion in ch. 1 dealing with covenant terminology both in Ezekiel and the ANE.

70. Cf. Durlesser, *Metaphorical Narratives*, 108–9.

71. Ibid., 142.

72. Cf. also Jeremiah 2–3 for similar imagery.

ate literary context, it should not at all be surprising that the focus of ch. 23 is more on political unfaithfulness whereas ch. 16 emphasized Jerusalem's idolatrous liaisons with other countries.[73] The focus on political unfaithfulness with the surrounding nations in ch. 23 appropriately prepares the reader for the oracles against the nations in chs. 25–32. However, judgment must begin at home therefore Jerusalem and Samaria would not be passed over.

Starting with Oholah, Yahweh tells of how she had always played the harlot with Assyria and with Egypt in her early days. For this infidelity she was judged (i.e., exiled by Assyria—23:5–10). Ezekiel juxtaposes Judah and Israel's sins in these opening verses for the purpose of comparison and as justification for the punishment and exile of both. Next, Ezekiel turns to Oholibah and describes her unfaithful acts with Assyria and Babylon; when she no longer found enjoyment in these liaisons she turned to her old lover, Egypt (23:11–21).[74] For these acts of infidelity Yahweh plans to enact judgment upon her at the hands of her lovers who will strip her and leave her bare and destitute (23:22–35). He will allow them to punish her by the "customs" (מִשְׁפָּטִים) of their land (v. 24—a key point in the treaty curse motif). Ezekiel then is told to present the sins of the two sisters as a legal basis for their punishment. These sins include, idolatry, child sacrifice, temple defilement, and foreign alliances (23:36–44). As with ch. 16, her punishment will be the punishment of adulteresses and women who shed blood. This entails being stripped, stoned, and cut with swords.[75] Further, her children will be killed and her houses burned (23:45–47).[76] Finally,

---

73. Renz, *Rhetorical Function*, 88.

74. The language of v. 20 symbolically has Jerusalem longing for sexual relations with the Egyptians. The invoking of the physical reproductive aspects of the donkey and horse shows the perverse nature of Jerusalem's lust. This perversion even suggests bestial desire, something forbidden in Lev 18:23; 20:15–16 and deserving of the death penalty. Cf. Galambush, *Jerusalem*, 116 n. 70.

75. Westbrook, "Adultery," 561, points out that two punishments are being meted out here: one for murder (i.e., the killing of children in child sacrifice) which brought lapidation and quartering and one for adultery where stripping and sending away seemed to be the norm in the ANE. So too Lafont, *Femmes*, 85–88.

76. The metaphorical presentation of Judah as the unfaithful wife who is deprived of all her adornments and wealth would have made her destitute and impoverished. In order for a single woman in the ANE to survive in such a situation they would often indenture their children as a means of survival and/or paying mounting debts (cf. 2 Kgs 4:1; Neh 5:5). In the case of the metaphor in Ezekiel, even Judah's children would be killed thus leaving her completely without hope for a "backup" means of survival.

a warning goes out to "all women" (i.e., surrounding cities)[77] not to commit such acts. In the prophet's final assessment, all of Judah's sins are reduced to their lowest common denominator, namely her acts of idolatry (23:48–49).[78]

Common Motifs within the Extended Metaphors of Chapters 16 & 23

Based upon the summaries of chs. 16 and 23 immediately above, a few common motifs and intersecting themes need to be pointed out.

1. In both chapters idolatry, cultic/temple impurity and foreign alliances are the key sins.[79]

2. In both accounts Jerusalem and Samaria are presented as female characters in a marriage relationship with Yahweh (16:8 and 23:4) who are unfaithful to their "husband."

3. Their punishment will include stripping, beating, stoning, and cutting with swords.[80]

---

77. Contra Darr, "Ezekiel's Justifications," 18; and Joyce, *Ezekiel*, 133, who suggest that actual women are being addressed here. Also, Childs, *Introduction*, 368–69, sees this as a "re-use" of the original allegory in which the meaning of the oracle is "detached" and applied to the women/wives in the exile (cf. Zimmerli, *Ezekiel*, 1:492 for a similar interpretation). However, Galambush, *Jerusalem*, 20–23, gives several ANE examples of cities being addressed as females (cf. also Darr, "Ezekiel," 188). She argues that it was a common understanding that the "capital city" of a given nation was married to the god of that city (23) (cf. also Schöpflin, "Composition," 109). Galambush, ibid., 129, correctly notes that the language used to describe Jerusalem in chs. 1–24 is reflective of the language used of the unfaithful wife in chs. 16 and 23 (cf. 5:7–17; 6:6–10; 7:19–22; 22:1–5; 24:3–14). It is therefore most probable that the appearance of it here may very well be a warning to every "woman" (i.e., "city") in Judah. Indeed, Galambush's insight into the parallel between the death of the prophet's wife in 24:15–24 and the fall of Jerusalem is further evidence of this rhetorical device (140–41). See also Steinmann, *Prophete*, 136, for a similar conclusion.

Beyond this, there appears to be evidence, at least inter-textually, that cities in general were classed as female (e.g., Sodom, Gomorrah in Ezekiel 16; Jer 49:18; 50:40; Tyre—Isa 23:15–18).

78. Fishbane, "Sin and Judgment," 139, points out that v. 49 should be understood as the ultimate purpose for the harsh judgment on Jerusalem. They were to return to a "covenantal" knowledge of their God.

79. Levey, *Targum of Ezekiel*, 11, points out that harlotry equals idolatry and must be seen as the main sin of Judah here in chs. 16 and 23.

80. It appears that Ezekiel is using a combination of punishments both from the

4. This punishment will come at the hands of their "lovers" and by the foreign nations' standards (implicit in 16:27, 39 and explicit in 23:24) yet under the control of Yahweh.[81]

These four parallel motifs are vital in understanding the purpose of Ezekiel's inclusion of these chapters in his work. For this reason we will analyze each parallel concept noted in the above list in order to determine their value to the overall message and interpretation of the metaphors.

Under #1 above the sins of idolatry and cultic/temple impurity must be understood in the light of Judah's foreign alliances. Most of Judah's idolatry and temple impurity is directly related to her intrigues with other nations and the influence of their idolatrous practices. This is in no way a new problem in the history of the nation. The book of Judges is rife with examples of the cycle of sin and idolatry due to forbidden international cavorting. Moreover, in 2 Kings 16:10–15 Ahaz, the king of Judah, builds an Assyrian-styled altar in Jerusalem for the priests of Yahweh to use.

Under #2 above, female/wife imagery is highlighted. While it is understandable why some feminists find the metaphor demeaning to the female gender, especially when one considers Ezekiel's use of misogynous terms, we still must ask the hard question as to why he used such language. A few reasons come to mind in light of the historical and theological setting. First, we know biblically that Yahweh is almost always depicted in masculine terms thus making the female counterpart the obvious choice in the metaphor. Second, as noted earlier, cities in the ANE and in the Bible are most often depicted as female. Third, Hosea (cf. 2:2) had used the metaphor of the wife with particular effectiveness long before in his analogy of Israel's relationship with her God. On account of this and the ease with which the metaphor would have been understood, the marriage motif would have resonated with

---

Law and from the ANE curses and legal system. According to Deut 22:20–24 the penalty for adultery was stoning as was the penalty for child sacrifice (Lev 20:2). However, as will be demonstrated below, stripping, cutting with swords, and beating appear to be ANE punishments for adultery, divorce, and covenant violation. Lemos, "Shame and Mutilation," 240, also notes the non-Israelite nature of Ezekiel's invoked punishments. See further, McKeating, "Sanctions," 61.

81. V. 24b of the Targum of Ezekiel reads, "And I will place before them [i.e., the nations] the matter of just punishment and they shall call you to account according to their laws." Cf. Levey, *Targum of Ezekiel*, 72.

those listening to or reading the oracles (i.e., a predominantly male audience). Finally, the marriage metaphor, with the female in many ways being subservient to the male, would have best resonated in an ANE patriarchal society. Any other metaphor would have failed to communicate the desired message of the prophet. Moreover, the marriage metaphor allowed for the full gamut of the feelings of love, betrayal, retribution, and restoration to play out in the minds and emotions of the recipients of the oracle.[82]

Before we deal with the last two motifs from our list above it appears appropriate at this juncture to consider the feminists' concerns with these texts.

Interpretive Issues Surrounding the Metaphor

Among many feminist scholars the female motif in these chapters has created a heated debate as to their validity and value within Scripture.[83] However, much can be learned about the purpose of their inclusion by Ezekiel when placed within the framework of covenant curses as presented in our ongoing discussion. It seems appropriate to consider some of these issues surrounding these two chapters and see if some of the interpretive tension can be alleviated. We must stress from the outset that one needs to be sensitive to the concerns of individuals who find the harshness of the language of these texts troublesome. Indeed even the Jewish scribes had an issue with Ezekiel's language in these

---

82. Taylor, "Betrothed by God," 50–56, points out the value of the marriage metaphor based on Hosea's use of it. Cf. also Patterson "Metaphors of Marriage," 689–702, esp. 689–98 and McKenzie, *Covenant*, 57–58.

83. For a discussion of the different stages of feminist studies and the different methodological approaches to the Bible (with a focus on Gen 2–3), see Milne, "Patriarchal Stamp," 17–34. For a detailed bibliography and discussion of the state of feminist scholarship on Ezekiel at the turn of the century, see Patton, "Should Our Sister Be Treated Like a Whore?" 221–38. Cf. also the concise feminist perspective as outlined by Kamionkowski, *Gender Reversal*, 18–20. It must also be noted that "feminist" studies today have evolved from a long tradition of female authors and commentators on the Bible. Nevertheless, these earlier traditional female scholars of the Bible did not have an ardent feminist perspective as one sees in some realms of feminist scholarship today. For example neither Trimmer, *A Help to the Unlearned*, 445, 448, nor Baxter, *Ezekiel, Son of Man*, 150–63, 205–12, mention the harshness of the metaphor. For further study on early female biblical interpreters see, deGroot and Taylor, *Women Interpreters*; and Taylor and Weir, *Let Her Speak for Herself*.

chapters.[84] There is no question that Ezekiel intended these texts to be harsh but understanding them in their ANE context is vital for proper exegetical and theological insight and application.[85]

Some feminist scholars such as Katheryn Pfisterer Darr[86] and Corrine L. Patton[87] are careful with these and other troubling texts. They understand the value of these pericopes as they appear even if the language and message are abrasive to modern sensibilities.[88] At the other extreme, feminist authors such as Mary Shields[89] and Fokkelien van Dijk-Hemmes[90] have failed to give a clear picture of Ezekiel's message often due to poor exegetical work[91] and/or a total misunderstand-

---

84. The graphic sexual language also created a dilemma for the Jewish Targumists. They either eliminated the entire sixteenth chapter of Ezekiel or reworded troubling phrases. McNamara, "Interpretation," 176, gives a good example of this rewording when he says, "For example, 'Your breasts were formed, and your hair had grown; yet you were naked and bare' (v. 7b) becomes 'and because of the good deeds of your forefathers, the time had come for the redemption of your congregation, because you were enslaved and oppressed.'"

85. Biggs, *Book of Ezekiel*, xviii, correctly points out and lists the multiple places in the OT where women are portrayed in a very positive light despite the fact that the OT is mainly patriarchal.

86. Darr, "Ezekiel's Justifications," 97–117. However, I cannot agree with Darr (cf. 114) when she refuses to accept that the Babylonian captivity and destruction of Jerusalem was the plan of God for judgment on sin. She appears to have missed the covenant-violation language that permeates ch. 16 and the overall message of Ezekiel. Furthermore, the metaphor allows Ezekiel to use the relevant curses of the ANE in a forceful manner to present his message.

87. Patton, "Should Our Sister Be Treated Like a Whore?" 221–38. See also the work of Weems, *Battered Love*.

88. For a concise discussion on the role of feminists' interpretation within biblical scholarship, see Tolbert, "Defining the Problem," 113–26.

89. Shields, "Multiple Exposures," 5–18.

90. Dijk Hemmes, "Metaphorization of Women," 162–70. Dijk-Hemmes analyzes the prophetic marriage and relational metaphors, especially here in Ezekiel 23, in light of pornographic terminology and categories.

91. For example, Dijk Hemmes, "Metaphorization of Women," 167 n. 9, compares the account of Oholah and Oholibah in Ezekiel with Dinah's (Gen 34:2) and Tamar's (2 Sam 13:14) rapes because the same verb שכב ("to lie down") appears in all three accounts. She insists that this is proof that Oholah and Oholibah were innocent/passive because the use of the verb שכב suggests that a rape occurred, as it did in the former two accounts. This, however, does not hold up under close scrutiny. In both of these earlier accounts, the verb ענה ("to humble" in the Piel stem) follows or precedes the verb שכב to qualify the author's intended use of שכב in the text. The verb ענה clarifies for the audience that a forced act occurred. However, this verb does not appear in the Ezekielian text (i.e., 23:8). Thus, her understanding that Ezekiel is presenting the idea

ing of the ANE context of the metaphor.[92] Other feminists such as Cheryl Exum,[93] Carol Dempsey,[94] and Linda Day,[95] attack these and other OT texts as promoting abuse.[96] They see within the metaphor the steps of abuse associated with modern-day psychoanalysis of victims and their abusers.[97] My issue here with these authors' perspectives on the metaphor in chs. 16 and 23 is not their concern with the harshness of the language, for that is understandable, but rather what they do with the texts (i.e., their interpretive grid). For example, they often equate Yahweh as being no better than a modern-day wife abuser.[98] From this vantage point they do everything in their power to discredit the value of these texts and, in many cases, desire to excise them completely from the prophetic corpus. Once again, as we will demonstrate below, Ezekiel's message and metaphor must be placed within its proper historical context of the covenant curse format.

On the other hand, there are those feminist scholars who see the value of the metaphor although they reject the punishments meted out for the "adulteress" and the "harlot." They assert that these punish-

---

that raped victims are responsible for their own misfortunes is totally misguided and is being read into the text.

92. Shields, "Multiple Exposures," 5–18, accuses Yahweh of "spousal abuse" and removes the blame from Jerusalem and places it upon Yahweh. She has totally misunderstood the metaphor and the purpose of the shock value Ezekiel was enacting by it.

93. Exum, "Prophetic Pornography," 122, shows her true colors and desires when she admits she does not desire to create a canon within a canon but rather to take away "canon" and the authority of the Bible. Brenner also promulgates this attitude in her work on Jeremiah. See Brenner, "Prophetic Propaganda," 256–74. Brenner (257) seeks to remove the title "prophecy" from the prophetic corpus and assign it the title "poetry" because, she asserts, "poetic authority is easier to undermine than so-called prophetic authority."

94. Dempsey, *Prophets*, 98–103, and Dempsey, "'Whore' of Ezekiel 16," 57–78.

95. Day, "Rhetoric," 205–30, totally misreads the metaphor and the purpose of Ezekiel's message in light of the rest of the OT and the context of the covenant at Sinai. Day is one of the most radical and extreme in her analysis of the text and her accusations against Yahweh. Her conclusions are so extreme that they border on the absurd and have nothing to contribute to sound Ezekielian scholarship, especially in light of ANE covenant curse motifs.

96. See also Carroll, "Whorusalamin," 67–82.

97. So too Keefe, *Woman's Body*, 150.

98. For a discussion of how Ezekiel 16 and 23 should be understood in the light of modern-day spousal abuse, see Peterson, "YHWH, the 'Abusive Husband'?"

ments are no more than inexcusable depictions of rape.[99] While we can never be totally sure of the exact punishments for adultery and/or harlotry in every situation and culture in the ANE,[100] Ezekiel's metaphorical presentation of stripping, beating, cutting and even death by stoning were the accepted reality of his day based upon covenant curse formulations and marriage laws (we will explore this concept in detail below).[101]

While many feminist authors have dealt with this difficult and controversial metaphor, often drawing improper conclusions, the purpose here is not to be exhaustive but rather to try to come to a better understanding of why Ezekiel used this terminology and how it is to be understood in light of the rest of his message. From this perspective F. Rachel Magdalene seems to move the feminists' interpretations in the proper direction.[102] Magdalene begins to alleviate the interpretive issues when she suggests that in order to understand properly these metaphors, one must look to the treaty curses of those nations surrounding Judah (i.e., her "lovers"). Indeed, the treaty curse connections (and marriage contracts) do shed light on the two remaining motif parallels and intersecting themes of chs. 16 and 23, which we listed above. Nevertheless, before we mount an in depth discussion

---

99. Day, "Imagined Demise," 285–309. Day gives an excellent presentation of modern-day analogies for the metaphor here in Ezekiel but insists the punishment presented in the metaphor is not equal to the actual punishment for the broken law. As an example she uses the analogy of the "raping" of the forest by lumber companies. The lumber company may have broken the law against clear cutting, but the punishment is not equivalent to that of a rapist as presented in the metaphor. While her argument may have validity to a certain degree, there seems to be some merit in the punishments depicted by Ezekiel in these chapters, in light of the ANE covenant curses and general ANE treatment of adulteresses.

100. Roth, "'Prestations,'" 245–46, points out the dearth of written material on women in the ANE. In most cases the only reason they are mentioned at all is if their lives in some way intersect a man's "economic world." See further, Kornfeld, "L'Adultère," 92–109 and Westbrook, "Adultery," 542–80, esp. 542–69.

101. For a brief overview of the often, arbitrary manner in which punishment for adultery was rendered in the ANE, see VerSteeg, *Early Mesopotamian Law*, 119–21.

102 Magdalene, "Treaty-Curses," 326–52. Also, the work of Patton has returned the focus of passages such as chs. 16 and 23 to an ANE context within the confines of the horrors of war and exile. While I do not agree with Patton's assumptions that Ezekiel's use of the "hand" (יָד) of God and the term "flesh" (בָּשָׂר), more often than not, speak of sexual exploitation, her perspective on the horrors of war for the defeated foe is helpful to our discussion. Cf. Patton, "Should Our Sister Be Treated Like a Whore?" 233–38.

of ANE curses and marriage contracts which find parallels in Ezekiel 16 and 23, a couple of pressing issues need to be dealt with. First, we need to address the concerns of the feminist camp that chs. 16 and 23 glorify and promote the "rape" of women. And second, we need to look at how the OT prophetic authors used similar language as seen in Ezekiel. It is my hope that these excursus-style discussions will aid us in our understanding of Ezekiel's use of the harsh and retributive language found within the marriage metaphor.

"Rape" in an ANE Context

From a cursory reading of the marriage metaphors in Ezekiel (and other OT texts) it appears that chs. 16 and 23 do promote "rape" as an acceptable means of punishment for adulteresses and harlots. However, the ANE understanding of rape was narrowly defined as that which violated the property of a husband or a father (or brother who was a protector of a sister). In these cases the father, brother, or the husband had the right to retaliate for the lost "property" value (i.e., the woman would no longer be a virgin fetching a high bride price), spousal privilege, etc.[103] If one views Ezekiel's usage of the stripping and humbling of the metaphorical female in chs. 16 and 23 from the perspective that Israel and Judah are "harlots" or "prostitutes" as opposed to "wives" then the designation of "rape" in the technical sense no longer applies.[104] On this Magdalene draws an interesting conclusion. She notes, "Prostitutes are not victimized by rape in the ancient understanding of that word because male property right is not violated in such sexual assaults. Sexual assault perpetrated against such women would not be viewed as rape because the woman was not under the dominion of another male. Moreover, prostitutes were righteously subject to sexual humiliation at the hand of God because they acted

---

103. Magdalene, "Treaty-Curses," 334–38. For a detailed discussion of the concept of rape in the ANE, see Magdalene, "Treaty-Curses," 334–41. Magdalene helps to clarify the difference between modern definitions of rape and ANE understandings of the concept in an androcentric culture.

104. Ezekiel appears to equate the actions of adulterous Judah to those of a wanton prostitute. His use of זָנָה ("harlot") no less than 15 times in these two chapters makes the connection clear. Cf. 16:15, 16, 17, 26, 28, 30, 31, 34, 35, 41; 23:3, 19, 30, 44. Moreover, Wong, *Idea of Retribution*, 55–56, correctly points out that in ANE law there was no punishment for a man who went to a "prostitute" who was actually a married woman if he had no knowledge of the latter fact.

outside those roles determined as morally responsible for women."[105] In this sense, because Israel and Judah had acted outside the covenant stipulations and had breached the covenant by whoring after other gods and seeking foreign alliances, they stood accused, in the eyes of the prophets and Yahweh, of spiritual and covenantal prostitution and harlotry (see also Exod 34:15–16; Lev 20:5; Deut 31:16). By committing such acts against God, they had removed themselves from the protection of their "husband," Yahweh. Thus, they would receive the punishment as deemed acceptable by ANE standards for such acts. On this point, Magdalene goes on to note that regarding retribution for harlotry, "the punishment must, therefore, be both sexual and public. The woman is not violated; she is chastised through sexual savagery. To the mind of ancient peoples, these types of acts are not abusive."[106]

Therefore as twenty-first century readers, whether feminist or otherwise, our first priority is to understand the text we are reading from this ancient Near Eastern context. While this approach may not alleviate the immediate harshness of the language for us, it is the appropriate starting point for processing the information in the text and in understanding why the authors used the language that they did. "Rape" or "sexual abuse" while detestable in any age, was not as "cut and dry" as it is today. For the ancients, it was a fact of daily life that countries were conquered and re-conquered on almost a yearly basis. And as such, the horrors of war due to territorial aggression or to enforce treaty compliance were a living, palpable reality. As for the "rape" of the metaphorical woman in Ezekiel's prophecy it is best understood within this ANE context. Whereas some women of the ANE found themselves as prostitutes not of their own volition (i.e., it was their only means of survival), Judah knew full well about the harsh realities that awaited her as a spiritual prostitute. Even though she understood the horrors of war and ANE treaty curses she still chose to remove herself from under the protection of her "Husband." In so doing, she received the due recompense of her error from an ANE perspective—public stripping and abuse. Finally, and I cannot stress this enough, Ezekiel is *not* depicting an actual rape, but is speaking metaphorically as a means of describing a spiritual reality. This perspective will also help shed light on other examples within the prophetic corpus.

105. Magdalene, "Treaty-Curses," 340.
106. Ibid., 341.

The OT Motif of Prostitution as a Curse for Covenant Infidelity and Sin

Before we proceed to investigate the texts themselves, a note of clarification needs to be made. First, as we will shortly discover, in the OT we see both *individuals* and *cities* cursed/shamed as "prostitutes" for their harlotries/covenant unfaithfulness. Second, both ANE texts and the OT present the curse of humbling the wives of treaty breakers and unfaithful vassals. As we will show, some treaty curses warn of the ill treatment of treaty breakers' women/wives much in the same way prostitutes were often misused or shamed. However, many times there is a blurring between those who actually break the treaty and those who receive the punishment (e.g., Amos 7:10–17, esp. v. 17). In some cases the punishment involves the humbling of the unfaithful nation's/covenant violator's women as mere prostitutes; at other times the curse seems directed at the soldiers/men themselves. In the case of the OT prophetic corpus the curse of metaphorical public stripping and shaming (also common for those who are unfaithful to a marriage covenant) often appears as a punishment directly aimed at the actual perpetrator of spiritual "harlotries" (i.e., Israel or Judah).

With all these apparent conflicting motifs is there any common ground? I believe the answer is in the affirmative. Even though there seems to be a confusion of the details in different situations, one reality remains constant—sexual violation and shaming, whether as a prostitute or a "casualty" of war, remained an effective deterrent and punishment in ANE treaties and covenants and OT prophetic texts. For the men in these situations, the loss of their wives to the enemy threatened the purity of their family line and the rights of the husband. For the women, the horrors of being humbled and treated like a prostitute was an all-too-real possibility in times of war (a reality of war even today).[107] These concerns being noted we now turn the texts themselves.

---

107. Fishbane, "Sin and Judgment," 149, notes the metaphoric nature of the punishments presented in chs. 16 and 23. He, however, has failed to see the direct connection of the curse motif and the possibility that the very enactment of the curse/punishments depicted in this "metaphoric" picture may in fact have happened literally to some within the community at the point of Babylon's military entrance into the city.

Cites and Individuals Cursed as Prostitutes

Beginning with the OT appearances of cities being equated with prostitutes, Isaiah deals directly with this concept in his prophecy against Tyre. In Isaiah 23:15–18 the prophecy reads,

15 וְהָיָה בַּיּוֹם הַהוּא וְנִשְׁכַּחַת צֹר שִׁבְעִים שָׁנָה כִּימֵי מֶלֶךְ אֶחָד מִקֵּץ שִׁבְעִים שָׁנָה יִהְיֶה לְצֹר כְּשִׁירַת הַזּוֹנָה

16 קְחִי כִנּוֹר סֹבִּי עִיר זוֹנָה נִשְׁכָּחָה הֵיטִיבִי נַגֵּן הַרְבִּי־שִׁיר לְמַעַן תִּזָּכֵרִי

17 הָיָה מִקֵּץ שִׁבְעִים שָׁנָה יִפְקֹד יְהוָה אֶת־צֹר וְשָׁבָה לְאֶתְנַנָּה וְזָנְתָה אֶת־כָּל־מַמְלְכוֹת הָאָרֶץ עַל־פְּנֵי הָאֲדָמָה

18 הָיָה סַחְרָהּ וְאֶתְנַנָּהּ קֹדֶשׁ לַיהוָה לֹא יֵאָצֵר וְלֹא יֵחָסֵן כִּי לַיֹּשְׁבִים לִפְנֵי יְהוָה יִהְיֶה סַחְרָהּ לֶאֱכֹל לְשָׂבְעָה וְלִמְכַסֶּה עָתִיק

> 15. "And it will come to pass in that day that Tyre will be forgotten for seventy years according to the days of one king, and at the end of seventy years, Tyre will be as the song of the harlot. 16. Take [your] harp and go about the city as a forgotten harlot, be happy to play stringed music, sing many songs in order that you may be remembered. 17. And it will come to pass at the end of seventy years that Yahweh will remember Tyre and she will return to the hire of a prostitute and she will commit harlotries with all the kingdoms of the land over the face of the earth. 18. And her merchandize and her harlot's wage will be set apart for Yahweh, and it will not be stored up nor will it be hoarded for her gain will be sufficient food and choice attire for the ones who dwell in the presence of Yahweh."

In the context, Tyre is likened to a harlot and her "wages" (i.e., her merchandize) will be given to Yahweh (i.e., tribute to the house of the Lord and his people).[108] It is possible that her "harlotries" with the nations may be directly related to the spread of idolatry through her vast commercial links as a hub of the ANE marine trade. This can be readily seen in the spread of her pagan religion and practices (e.g., child

---

108. See also 1 Kgs 5:1–12 and the contextual theme of foreign nations (viz., Ethiopia, Egypt, and Assyria) supporting the people of Israel (cf. also Isa 18:7; 19:18–25). Delitzsch, *Isaiah*, 273–74, also points out that the seventy-year span mentioned here has to be a reference to the rule of the Neo-Babylonian Empire. Thus, the return of the Judeans under the edict of Cyrus was perhaps the period when Tyre supported the building of the temple with raw materials (cf. Ezra 3:7).

sacrifice) to port cities like Carthage, which was a colony of Tyre.[109] On the other hand, Isaiah may be connecting Tyre's plight to the actual occupation of prostitution readily available in any port city both then and now.[110] Nevertheless, the precedent for a city being likened to a prostitute has a biblical basis outside of Ezekiel.

Next, Amos uses the curse of becoming a prostitute as a punishment for unfaithfulness to the Law. While Amos's focus is on the individual and not a city per se, the curse has direct implications on our text because of the similar context of cursing those who have broken covenant with the Lord. In Amos 7:17 the prophet curses the wicked priest, Amaziah, because of the priest's opposition to the prophetic word and proper worship. Amos prophesies that Amaziah's wife will become a prostitute in the city—a public humiliation for a priest. The setting of Amos in the period before the Assyrian exile of 722 BCE helps shed light on Amos' usage of the curse. Treaties with Assyria, the dominant world power, would have been well known in public readings and thus would have been readily adaptable to the prophetic cause. A possible parallel to this passage in Amos is presented in the Vassal-Treaties of Esarhaddon. In the curse section of the treaty, the concept of the wives of the vassal being humbled by the enemy is presented. The text reads, "May Venus, the brightest among the stars, let your wives lie in the embrace of your enemy before your eyes."[111]

While Amos uses prostitution as a curse from God, the curse in the Esarhaddon account has a similar outcome in the context of military conquest. The humbling of the covenant breaker's women like prostitutes was an effective means of instilling fear in the hearts of the people signing treaties. What this text shows is that the degradation of females to the level of a prostitute was an effective deterrent and curse both biblically and extra-biblically. Nevertheless, while this text in Amos exemplifies the curse of becoming a prostitute, it falls short of Ezekiel's depiction in that it lacks the specific description of the actual punishment enacted against prostitutes and adulteresses.

---

109. Vaux, *Ancient Israel*, 446, makes the direct link between Tyre and Carthage and the rituals of child sacrifice. See also Stager, "Rite of Child Sacrifice," 1–11, and Stager and Wolff, "Child Sacrifice at Carthage," 31–51.

110. Grogan, *Isaiah*, 147; and Delitzsch, *Isaiah*, 270.

111. "Vassal-treaties of Esarhaddon" *ANET*, 538.

The OT Punishment of a Prostitute or Adulteress

At this point we can now return to our list of the four parallel motifs between chs. 16 and 23 which we last addressed on pages 199–200 above. Judah's punishment of being stripped, beaten, stoned, and cut with swords (i.e., motif #3) at the hands of her lovers (i.e., motif #4) is troubling to say the least. However, the third motif finds validity and precedent throughout the prophetic corpus and more importantly, in an ANE milieu. Because the city had behaved as a prostitute and adulteress, it will suffer the humiliation and punishment as such. In the case of motif #4, Yahweh's decision to allow this punishment to come at the hands of Judah's lovers added insult to injury yet was appropriate in light of the sin itself. Moreover, the fourfold mode of punishment matches many of the curses enacted by the rulers of Babylon and Assyria against countries that had violated treaties. More importantly, these punishments also reflect similar stipulations and curses used in marriage and divorce contracts from the region of Mesopotamia. Before we address these ANE parallels we need to examine the presence of motif #3 in the prophetic corpus.

Magdalene has traced the stripping motif and the metaphor of the adulterous wife in the OT prophetic texts.[112] Starting from her overview I will begin with those instances generally agreed to as the farthest removed from Ezekiel chronologically; then I will move forward to his immediate time frame in order to assess the development of the concept. We begin then with Hosea 2:4–5 [Heb] and 2:11–12.[113]

4 רִיבוּ בְאִמְּכֶם רִיבוּ כִּי־הִיא לֹא אִשְׁתִּי וְאָנֹכִי לֹא אִישָׁהּ וְתָסֵר זְנוּנֶיהָ מִפָּנֶיהָ
וְנַאֲפוּפֶיהָ מִבֵּין שָׁדֶיהָ
5 פֶּן־אַפְשִׁיטֶנָּה עֲרֻמָּה וְהִצַּגְתִּיהָ כְּיוֹם הִוָּלְדָהּ וְשַׂמְתִּיהָ כַמִּדְבָּר וְשַׁתִּהָ כְּאֶרֶץ צִיָּה
וַהֲמִתִּיהָ בַּצָּמָא

> 4. "Contend with your mother, contend, for she is not my wife and I am not her husband, let her put way her harlotries from before her and her adulteries from between her breasts; 5. lest I strip her naked and expose[114] her as in the day she was born

---

112. Magdalene, "Treaty-Curses," 328–34.

113. Gordis, "Hosea's Marriage and Message," 9–35.

114. The verb is to be understood as "to put" or "to place on exhibit." Therefore I have followed the NASB, which translates this verb as "expose."

and I will set her as a wilderness and make her as a drought-laden land and I will kill her with thirst" (NASB).

In this context, harlotry practiced by the female (Israel) brings about the stripping of the "woman" by Yahweh. Further on we read in 2:11–12 [Heb],

11 לָכֵן אָשׁוּב וְלָקַחְתִּי דְגָנִי בְּעִתּוֹ וְתִירוֹשִׁי בְּמוֹעֲדוֹ וְהִצַּלְתִּי צַמְרִי וּפִשְׁתִּי לְכַסּוֹת אֶת־עֶרְוָתָהּ

12 וְעַתָּה אֲגַלֶּה אֶת־נַבְלֻתָהּ לְעֵינֵי מְאַהֲבֶיהָ וְאִישׁ לֹא־יַצִּילֶנָּה מִיָּדִי

11. "Therefore I will turn and seize my corn in its time and my wine in its season and I will take away my wool and my flax [used] to cover her nakedness. 12. And now I will uncover her shamelessness in the eyes of her lovers and no man will be able to deliver her from my hand."

Again the implication of the text suggests the stripping of the "woman" (Israel) because of unfaithfulness and harlotry with other lovers. In the prophet Nahum we see similar terminology although it is directed at the Assyrians.[115] Nahum 3:5–6[116] reads,

5 הִנְנִי אֵלַיִךְ נְאֻם יְהוָה צְבָאוֹת וְגִלֵּיתִי שׁוּלַיִךְ עַל־פָּנָיִךְ וְהַרְאֵיתִי גוֹיִם מַעְרֵךְ וּמַמְלָכוֹת קְלוֹנֵךְ

6 וְהִשְׁלַכְתִּי עָלַיִךְ שִׁקֻּצִים וְנִבַּלְתִּיךְ וְשַׂמְתִּיךְ כְּרֹאִי

5. "Behold I am against you declares the Lord of hosts and I will remove your skirts over your face and I will cause the nations to see your nakedness, and the kingdoms, your shame. 6. And I will cast abominable things upon you and make you vile, and I will make you a spectacle."

In this case Assyria's spiritual harlotry (verse 4) which has caused the nations to stumble (no doubt Israel and Judah primarily) is the reason for the public shaming of Nineveh. The common thread in these passages so far has been the practice of harlotry in the spiritual sense.

---

115. For a discussion of the many curses found in Nahum that are parallel to other ANE curses, see Cathcart, "Treaty-Curses," 179–87. For the curse of stripping, see his comments on pages 183–84. Cf. further, Cathcart, "Aramaic Inscriptions," 179–87.

116. Hillers, *Treaty-Curses*, 66–67, asserts that Nahum 3:13 reflects a separate curse of warriors becoming like women.

Moreover, the use of the motif against a foreign nation causes one to assume that the metaphor was understood beyond Israel.

Next, Jeremiah uses a similar indictment against Judah as Nahum had used against Nineveh. In 13:22b[117] and verse 26 we read,

22b בְּרֹב עֲוֺנֵךְ נִגְלוּ שׁוּלַיִךְ נֶחְמְסוּ עֲקֵבָיִךְ
26 וְגַם־אֲנִי חָשַׂפְתִּי שׁוּלַיִךְ עַל־פָּנָיִךְ וְנִרְאָה קְלוֹנֵךְ

> 22b. "... on account of your great iniquity, I have removed your skirts, and your heels[118] suffer violence.... 26. Therefore I, myself, will strip off (i.e., lift up) your skirt over your face and your shame will be seen."

In this instance, Yahweh appears to be the key actor in the scene against Jerusalem as the metaphor reveals a very explicit confrontation where Jerusalem's "nakedness" is once again revealed. The euphemism "heels" no doubt in the context has a sexual understanding and suggests that the act of baring Jerusalem's "heels" will cause them to be "humbled" sexually. As we will demonstrate below, this metaphor is characteristic of ANE military actions against a defeated foe. The women were especially vulnerable to the sexual hostilities of the enemy. This is a vital part of treaty curses.

Finally, Magdalene draws attention to a passage from Isaiah where Babylon is brought low for its treatment of Israel and Judah. In Isaiah 47:1–3[119] we read,

1 רְדִי וּשְׁבִי עַל־עָפָר בְּתוּלַת בַּת־בָּבֶל שְׁבִי־לָאָרֶץ אֵין־כִּסֵּא בַּת־כַּשְׂדִּים כִּי לֹא תוֹסִיפִי יִקְרְאוּ־לָךְ רַכָּה וַעֲנֻגָּה
2 קְחִי רֵחַיִם וְטַחֲנִי קָמַח גַּלִּי צַמָּתֵךְ חֶשְׂפִּי־שֹׁבֶל גַּלִּי־שׁוֹק עִבְרִי נְהָרוֹת
3 תִּגָּל עֶרְוָתֵךְ גַּם תֵּרָאֶה חֶרְפָּתֵךְ נָקָם אֶקָּח וְלֹא אֶפְגַּע אָדָם

> 1. "Go down and sit in the dust virgin daughter of Babylon, sit on the earth with no throne daughter of the Chaldeans, for no longer will you be called tender and delicate. 2. Take millstones and grind meal, remove your veil strip the skirt, uncover the leg, cross over the rivers. 3. Let your nakedness be uncovered,

---

117. See also Nahum 2:7–8 [Heb] for similar language.

118. The noun in this case most likely means "buttocks."

119. See also 3:17–26 for a detailed description of the stripping process of the "daughters of Zion," which appears to cross over into city imagery by v. 26. Also, I am following Magdalene and the generally accepted late dating of Isaiah 40–66.

your reproach be seen, I will take vengeance, and I will not spare[120] a man."

In these verses the context moves away from spiritual harlotry and focuses more on the misuse of Yahweh's people. Punishment thus is meted out in a similar fashion as would be to one taken captive in battle. Isaiah is presenting the nation of Babylon, as a whole, humbled and humiliated, no doubt later in their history at the hands of Persia. For their hubris, idolatry (which caused Yahweh's people to stumble), and their general harsh treatment of Yahweh's people, the nation is metaphorically humbled (cf. the message of Habakkuk 2).

Enough examples have been given from the biblical text to conclude, at least in the world of the prophets, that stripping, violence, and even death were acceptable punishments for those who committed spiritual "adultery"/"harlotry." We also see these punishments used as a valid punishment for foreign powers that had misused Israel in some way. The problem arises when we try to find legal basis for these acts of retribution within the Mosaic Law code.[121] With the exception of stoning for adultery and fornication (Deut 22:21–24),[122] nowhere do we find these types of punishment prescribed.[123] While Ezekiel's use

---

120. The verb is difficult to translate here. Normally it has the connotation to "entreat," "make intercession," or "encounter." In this instance I am following the rendering adopted by the NASB.

121. McKeating, "Sanctions," 58, does note that nowhere in "Jewish narrative literature of the biblical period" do we find the actual death penalty enacted for adultery. He goes on to discuss the probable reasons for its inclusion in the law codes at a "later" date (64–65). Nonetheless, it is interesting that in Proverbs 6:32–35 we see the right of the husband to punish a wife's paramour; this appears to be pointing to the application of the death penalty as the right of the husband.

122. Jeremiah does note divorce as a means of punishing adultery, albeit in a metaphorical context, cf. Jer 3:8.

123. Contra Alexander, *Ezekiel*, 857–58; and Patterson "Metaphors," 695, who aver that the punishments noted here in Ezekiel are from the Mosaic Law. Scholars generally appeal to the laws of Deuteronomy or Leviticus for the punishment of stoning here in ch. 16 but they never address the "cutting by swords." For example, Driver, *Introduction*, 283, suggests that Ezekiel is listing the punishment for adulteresses but Driver gives neither an explanation of what this entails nor where it is found. McKeating, "Sanctions," 62, notes the difficulty with finding parallels between Ezekiel's list of punishments for adultery and the Law. However, once Ezekiel's references are understood within his ANE curse context these punishments make perfect sense. This conclusion seems to be implied by Joyce, *Ezekiel*, 162; and Lafont, *Femmes*, 87, as well.

of the metaphor is consistent with the OT prophetic usage this does not explain the origin of these punishments. Perhaps the reason the prophets used the imagery can be directly connected to the political and social realities of the period in which they lived and prophesied.[124] Therefore the ANE context of covenant violation and curses associated with such acts seems a fitting place to look for answers to the origins of these punishment motifs. Ezekiel himself gives this insight by noting in 23:24 that Yahweh would judge Judah "according to the customs" of her foreign lovers.

ANE Parallels for the Punishment of Prostitutes and Adulteresses

As just noted, the humiliation of spiritual prostitutes/adulteresses by stripping[125] and beatings finds biblical precedent outside of the Pentateuch but how is it related to extra-biblical material? Common retaliatory motifs similar to those found in the OT texts noted above appear in the curse sections of ANE treaties and marriage contracts. These texts can shed light on our passages in Ezekiel, especially as they relate to the public humiliation of the offending party (cf. 16:37–38; 23:10, 29).

ANE Punishment for Adultery[126]

To begin with, although violence and butchery by means of a sword were common during war, the phrase to be "cut by swords" (Ezek

---

124. Johnston, "Rhetorical Allusions," 418–22, suggests just such a scenario. Westbrook, "Adultery," 560, avers that it is possible that the Assyrian exile may be in view and therefore Israel would have been "stripped" of her possessions and sent away into exile.

125. Fishbane, "Sin and Judgment," 138, makes the connection with the robing of the infant earlier in the chapter. Thus, the removal of Israel's "robes" is another curse-like reversal of an original blessing.

126. Kornfeld, "L'Adultère," 97, queries, "A Babylone, l'adultère était-il un péché contre la divinité? Oui, si l'on croit différents textes religieux, et surtout la littérature de conjuration." It appears that Babylonians may have perceived adultery to be a sin against not only society and the husband/wife but also against the deity—at least indirectly. In the ANE the king established the law given to him by the gods. He was also the representative of the gods when he enacted justice. Cf. Loewenstamm, *Comparative Studies*, 147, for examples from Mesopotamian literature where adultery is presented as a sin against the gods.

16:40) appears nowhere in curse material as an explicit means of punishing violators of a treaty. However, there is a clause that was included in some Neo-Babylonian marriage contracts of Ezekiel's period that prescribed death by "iron dagger" (*patar parzilli*)[127] for a woman caught in adultery.[128] Roth translates an example of this curse/punishment from the text BM 65149 lines 10–11 as, "Should ᶠKaššā be found with another man, she will die by the iron dagger."[129] Of special note is the negotiated nature of this clause in the marriage contract. The wife agreed to the terms of the contract knowing full well that if she committed adultery the punishment was spelled out in clearly defined terms in this particular clause.[130] In similar fashion, Israel had entered into covenant with Yahweh knowing full well about the curses of the Law and what would happen if they were "unfaithful" to the covenant. Thus, because indictment for spiritual adultery drives the metaphor (i.e., Judah the "wife" cheated on her "husband" Yahweh), combined with the fact that Ezekiel is in the heart of Neo-Babylonian culture, it is not surprising that he included this punishment for the nation's adultery against its Suzerain.

---

127. Roth, "Iron Dagger," 187, discusses the issues surrounding the translation of this phrase. Also Roth, *Babylonian Marriage Agreements*, 46, 49, presents two particular cases where Nebuchadnezzar's reign is given in the dating sequence of the marriage agreement thus placing these practices within the time frame of Ezekiel. Lafont, *Femmes*, 80, avers that death by the iron dagger/sword was implemented by the husband.

128. Cf. Tetlow, *Women, Crime, and Punishment*, 1:110. So too Westbrook, "Adultery," 562 and Roth, "Iron Dagger," 186–206. Roth, "Iron Dagger" 187–88, notes that there are a total of 43 known extant marriage contracts from the Neo- and Late-Babylonian periods (for a detailed treatment of these texts, see Roth, "Prestations," 245–55). Twenty-four are dated to the late seventh and sixth centuries. Of the latter 24, ten of these contracts contain the clause we are dealing with and date between 635–523 BCE. For a list of these texts, see Roth, "Iron Dagger," 187 n. 3.

129. Roth, "Iron Dagger," 189. Cf. also idem, *Babylonian Marriage Agreements*, 38, 40, 45, 48, 70, 93, 99, for further examples. It should be noted that several other means of punishment for adultery stretching back to the Old Babylonian Period included drowning, impalement, and throwing off a wall. See discussion in chs. 1 and 2 in Tetlow, *Women, Crime, and Punishment*, vol.1, and comments by Kornfeld, "L'Adultère," 96–99. Stuart, "Curse," 1:1219, notes the curse related to the ordeal by water in Num 5:18–27 as a means of determining the innocence of a woman accused of adultery. This may reflect aspects of the Babylonian punishment by drowning.

130. Roth, "Iron Dagger," 190–92.

In a similar vein, throughout the ANE from the Hittite period until the Late Assyrian period[131] the mutilation of women was the punishment of choice for crimes against society and men, especially for adultery.[132] We see evidence of this in Middle Assyrian Laws (1363–1057 BCE) where one of the punishments for adultery was mutilation of both parties involved. For the woman, it may have involved the cutting off of her nose or ears while the complicit male could be castrated and have his face slashed.[133] Amazingly enough, in Ezek 23:25 we see the punishment of mutilation by the removal of the adulteress's nose and ears. This statement comes on the heels of the threat from Yahweh to judge the nation by the "standards" or "customs" of Judah's paramours. It is important to note that mutilation of one caught in the act of adultery appears in the legal material of every dominant culture of the ANE.[134] Ezekiel's mentioning of the Hittites and Amorites in conjunction with Israel's heritage in 16:3 along with their liaisons with Assyria and Babylon shows the range of cultures that influenced Israel. Thus, punishments for adultery long-held within these cultures were fitting to his message in chs. 16 and 23.

---

131. Tetlow, *Women, Crime, and Punishment*, 1:166–67. So too Driver and Miles, *Assyrian Laws*, 389. For a discussion on Sumerian practices, see Finkelstein, "Sex Offenses," 355–72.

132. Tetlow, *Women, Crime, and Punishment*, 1:205–19. Ibid., 1:213, does note that by the Late Babylonian period the practice of mutilation was relaxed in favor of restitution, compensation, and fines. This does not diminish the validity behind Ezekiel's use of the centuries-old practice common throughout the ANE. Ezekiel appears to be using a well-established punishment as a means of evoking fear in the hearts of his listeners. Cf. also Greengus "A Textbook Case," 41–42 esp. 41 n. 25, who points out the use of mutilation of an adulteress as early as the Old Babylonian period.

133. Tetlow, *Women, Crime, and Punishment*, 1:135, 137. Tetlow also notes that the cutting off of fingers, breasts, the removal of eyes, and pouring hot tar over the head of a convicted woman were common punishments of the Middle Assyrian period. So too Kornfeld, "L'Adultère," 102; and Lafont, *Femmes*, 82–85, esp. 82. See also "Middle Assyrian Laws," *ANET*, 181–82; and MacDonald, *Position of Women*, 43. Driver and Miles, *Assyrian Laws*, 381–85, also note mutilation as a punishment for women who were caught stealing. Finkelstein, "Sex Offenses," 372, points out the use of mutilation as a punishment for both the man and woman caught in adultery.

134. Cf. the work of Tetlow, *Women, Crime, and Punishment*; and Wong, *Idea of Retribution*, 56.

Stripping as a Sign of Divorce

As queried earlier, the origin and use of the stripping motif in the classical prophets and here in Ezekiel finds no clear legal nexus in the OT. However, several scholars have noted the ANE practice of stripping or removing garments as a sign of divorce.[135] It appears that if a man sought to divorce his wife for some fault, he could remove the gifts of the marriage contract (i.e., garments, shelter, and food) from the wife when she left. Often this was termed going out "empty."[136] The only thing she could take were those things she brought into the marriage. In the case of Israel, Ezekiel makes it clear that *all* her gifts came from Yahweh. Additionally, the concept of symbolically "cutting the hem of a garment" (*sissiktam batāqum*) was a means of dissolving a marriage[137] as was a public declaration of dissolution.[138]

Kamionkowski points out one Old Babylonian text where a "woman declares to her husband: 'you are not my husband' and then leaves naked."[139] In another marriage contract from the kingdom of Ḫana from the period of Hammurabi the custom of stripping and publicly humiliating a wife for divorcing her husband is presented.[140] The text states, "And if his wife Bitti-Dagan says to her husband Kikkinu

---

135. Westbrook, "Adultery," 561; Wong, *Idea of Retribution*, 55; Kruger, "Hem of the Garment," 82; Block, *Ezekiel 1–24*, 502 n. 231; and Gordon, "Hos 2:4–5," 277–80. Cf. also Gordon, "Status of Women," 163, for a brief discussion on the relationship between stripping and divorce at Nuzi.

136. Tetlow, *Women, Crime, and Punishment*, 1:58, 66, 129, 173. The texts dealt with by Tetlow cover a period from Hammurabi to the Middle and Late Assyrian periods. See also "Middle Assyrian Laws," ANET, 183 lines 37–38; and Driver and Miles, *Assyrian Laws*, 405, 425.

137. Malul, *Studies in Mesopotamian Legal Symbolism*, 153, 197–208. Cf. also Kamionkowski, "Savage Made Civilized," 127; and Greengus, "Marriage Contract," 515 n. 44. Gordon, "Status of Women," 157, points out that a dowry consisting of monies from both the groom and from the bride's family was often sewn into the hem of the bride's garment as a means of economic protection in the case of widowhood.

138. Cf. Kuhl, "Neue Dokumente," 102–9. See also Gordon, "Status of Women," 162, for an example from Nuzi.

139. Kamionkowski, "Savage Made Civilized," 127. So too Kuhl, "Neue Dokumente," 103–4; and Greengus, "Marriage Contract," 517.

140. Malul, *Studies in Mesopotamian Legal Symbolism*, 122–23. Malul also lists four wills from Nuzi where a wife who leaves her dead husband's house to marry another man will be stripped naked by her sons and sent away. Cf. also Gordon, "Hos 2:4–5," 278; Greengus "Textbook Case," 33–44; and idem, "Marriage Contract," 505–32.

'You are not my husband!' she shall go out naked; they will cause her to go up to the roof of the palace."¹⁴¹ Here we see a similar custom of stripping and public display as seen in Ezekiel and the classical prophets.

It is very possible then to assume that Ezekiel's use of the stripping motif may have been representative of an acceptable practice in the ANE when initiating divorce proceedings. In this case, Yahweh had every right to demand the return of the gifts and garments he had lavished on his bride (cf. 16:39; 23:26).

ANE Treaty Curses

The Treaty between Ashurnirari V and Mati'ilu

In the treaty curse material a couple of texts stand out as particularly relevant to our present discussion. First, in the treaty between Ashurnirari V (755–745 BCE) of Assyria and Mati'ilu of Arpad, similar terminology concerning the curse of becoming a prostitute is directed at Mati'ilu and his soldiers. The text reads, "If Mati'ilu sins against this treaty with Ashurnirari, king of Assyria, may Mati'ilu become a prostitute. His soldiers' women, may they receive [a gift] in the square of their cities (i.e. publicly) like any prostitute . . . may Mati'ilu's (seed) be that of a mule, his wives barren, may Ishtar, the goddess of men, the lady of women, take away their "bow," cause their [steri]lity . . . may they say, "Woe, we have sinned against the treaty with Ashurnirari, king of Assyria."¹⁴²

---

141. Westbrook, "Adultery," 559.

142. "Treaty between Ashurnirari V of Assyria and Mati'ilu of Arpad," *ANET*, 533. Of special interest is the fact that as early as the Hittite Empire, soldiers were forced to swear allegiance to the king with a curse that if they broke covenant with their king they would become like a woman. See Tetlow, *Women, Crime, and Punishment*, 1:193–94; and Beal, "Hittite Military Organization," 1:547–48. The applicable part of the ceremony is as follows: "They [i.e., the one hearing the oath for the king] bring in women's clothing, and a spindle and distaff (symbols of womanhood); and they break an arrow (symbol of manhood). You speak to them (the troops) as follows: 'What is this? Women's garments, which we have here for your oath. Whoever breaks these oaths and does evil to the king and the queen and the royal princes, let these oath-gods change him from a man into a woman. Let them change his soldiers into women. Let them dress them like women and cover their heads with kerchiefs like women. Let them break your bows, arrows, and (other) weapons in your hands and replace them with spindle and distaff.'" Cf. also "Soldiers' Oath," *ANET*, 353–54. See further the work of Kamionkowski, *Gender Reversal*, 58–91; and Holloway, "Distaff," 370–75.

Here the breaking of the treaty would bring the curse of causing the king and the women of his warriors to become prostitutes.[143] Also, they would receive their "gifts" (i.e., rewards) in the city square. What the implication is of someone receiving a "gift in the square" is not spelled out for us. One thing we can be certain of is that in the context we can safely assume that it was not a pleasant experience. It is possible that it may very well connote the punishment of a prostitute as depicted in Ezekiel (i.e., beating, stripping, and cutting with swords).[144] While it is true that the cursing of a city as a prostitute is not pictured here, obviously the fear of such an outcome, even against a person, had the desired effect in the treaty curse formula.

At the same time, while the treaty of Ashurnirari is addressed to king Mati'ilu, it also affects his nobles and warriors and their families. In Ezekiel, the prophet's indictment of the "city" in the metaphor clearly includes the king, nobles, and the people. The prophet often blurred the lines between the identification of these entities (cf. Ezek 4; 9:4, 8; 11:15; 12:10; 24 etc.). While this first ANE treaty curse example finds some parallels with Ezekiel's metaphor there is another treaty with curses closer to those found in Ezekiel 16 and 23.

Inscriptions of Bar-ga'yah and Mati'el from Sefire

In the "Inscriptions of Bar-ga'yah and Mati'el from Sefire" (ca. mid-eighth century in Old Aramaic,[145] some time prior to the defeat of Arpad by Tiglath Pileser III in 740 BCE),[146] at the beginning of the

---

Both discuss the motif of men becoming like women in the Bible and the ANE.

143. Curses focused on sexual violation seem to have had a wide usage in the ANE. In a text from the funerary temple of Thothmes III in Deir el-Bahri, Egypt we read, "an ass shall violate him, an ass shall violate [his] wife." Cf. Nordh, *Ancient Egyptian Curses*, 90.

144. On the other hand, there is also the valid argument that in the case of Ezekiel 16 and 23 the punishment is being meted out on the guilty for their actions whereas in the ANE text part of the punishment seems to be directed at the innocent women for the actions of their husbands. Some of this tension can be alleviated if we recognize the corporate nature of chs. 16 and 23. While the metaphor is depicting Jerusalem (as a whole) as an unfaithful wife, the punishment for covenant unfaithfulness meted out affects even the innocent (cf. Ezek 21:1–5) as also seen in the Ashurnirari treaty. Furthermore, as we have noted above with the account of Achan, the breaking of the covenant and/or God's commands affects even the innocent.

145. The Sefire steles were found 15 miles southeast of Aleppo in Syria.

146. From the introduction to "The Inscriptions of Bar-ga'yah and Mati'el from

curse sections we find the cities of Arpad pictured as "daughter-cities," a direct parallel with Ezekiel's metaphor.[147] Further on we encounter the curses that would befall Mati'el and his nobles if the treaty was broken. The curses have a central theme of becoming like, or receiving the punishment of prostitutes. The curses read,

40 [י]נזר עגלא זנה כן ינזר מתעאל וינזרן רבוה [ואיך זי יע]
41 [רר ז]נ[ה] כן יעררן נשי מתעאל זנשי עקרה זנשי ר[בוה ואיך ז]
42 [י תקח גברת שעותא זא] וימחא על אפיה כן יקחן [נשי מתעאל ו][148]

[Just as] 40. this calf is cut in two,
so may Mati'el be cut in two,
and may his nobles be cut in two!
[And just as] 41. a [har]lot is stripped naked,
so may the wives of Mati'el be stripped naked,
and the wives of his offspring, and the wives of [his] no[bles]!
And just as this 42. wax woman is taken] and one strikes her on the face,
so may the [wives of Mati'el] be taken [and . . .].[149]

Here, in Joseph Fitzmyer's translation,[150] the parallels with Ezekiel are striking. The threat of being mutilated by a sword alongside the curse of prostitution and being stripped naked resembles the "cutting with swords" (Ezek 16:40 and 23:47) and the stripping of the metaphorical

---

Sefire," COS 2.82:213. Cf. also, Fitzmyer, *Aramaic Inscriptions of Sefire*.

147. "Inscriptions of Bar-ga'yah and Mati'el from Sefire," COS 2.82:214, stele I face A line 35.

148. Fitzmyer, "Aramaic Inscriptions of Sefire I and II," 181.

149. "Inscriptions of Bar-ga'yah and Mati'el from Sefire," COS 2.82:214. Cf. also, Fitzmyer, *Aramaic Inscriptions of Sefire*, 14–17. For further commentary, see Crawford, *Blessing and Curse*, 190–91 and Johnston, "Nahum's Rhetorical Allusions," 427.

150. So too Hillers, *Treaty-curses*, 58–59. For a different rendering rejected by Hillers and Fitzmyer, see Dupont-Sommer and Starcky, *Les Inscriptions*, 18, 58, as noted by Hillers, *Treaty-curses*, 59. The key debate focuses on the reconstruction of the text where the verb ʿrr "to strip" is used as opposed to ʿbd "to serve" or "to be a slave." Fitzmyer, "Aramaic Inscriptions of Sefire I and II," 201, points out that ʿbd does not carry the meaning "to be a slave" or "to serve" in Aramaic. Fitzmyer's and Hillers's translations embrace the former rendering which appears to make the most sense in the context. Moreover, scholarship has generally accepted this rendering. The Aramaic verb ʿrr thus carries the same meaning as the more common Hebrew verb pšṭ found in both cases in Ezekiel.

city of Jerusalem in 16:39 and 23:26. Moreover, the notation regarding the striking of the prostitute in the face further adds to the violence inflicted on the one who broke the treaty. The Sefire treaty curses of beatings, stripping, and being cut with swords presented in the context of covenant/treaty violation accords well with our Ezekielian texts. In Ezekiel's case, however, he has developed the metaphor and curse so that the harsh treatment of the "city" in the curse format is drawn out over a longer sequence of verses. Again, the granting of literary license to Ezekiel is important to allow for the personalizing of the curse to the particular situation at hand.

We can conclude then that Ezekiel, as did the prophets mentioned above, borrowed language common to ANE treaty curses and marriage/divorce contracts. The period of Assyrian and Babylonian domination would have given ample opportunity to adopt such language. The punishment for covenant/treaty violation likened to that of the treatment of prostitutes and unfaithful women would have elicited fear and analogous concepts in the minds of Ezekiel's readers and listeners. While I may not agree with all of Magdalene's assumptions about Ezekiel's use of the metaphor, her assessment is appropriate to conclude this part of our discussion.

> In spite of our modern disdain for such texts, the images contained within these texts were not only acceptable to the men of ancient Israel, they meaningfully conveyed the message to return to the fold of the Israelite covenantal relationship with God. The public stripping or rape of the female cities of Israel and Judah is a perfect medium to convey the message that Israel has breached its covenant with God and that the natural consequences, well known to all because treaties were publicly announced documents, will flow therefrom. In a patriarchal system where God is the chief patriarch, he has total access to the females of his underlings, including its cities. Given the nature of the ancient Near Eastern treaties and their curses, the public sexual humiliation or rape of the underlings' cities/women is an appropriate response to any perceived actual violations of existing agreements between God and his people. God's threat of sexual violence will seem quite real in the ancient setting and will evoke compliance with the covenant.[151]

---

151. Magdalene, "Treaty-Curses," 347.

A Final Note: The Possible Dependence of Chapters 16 & 23 on ANE Literature and Art[152]

Having studied the literary context and ANE treaty and marriage contract parallels with chs. 16 and 23, what can be learned about the metaphor's possible connections to Mesopotamian literary or genre forms? A cursory reading of the texts as we have them enables one to spot obvious ANE coloring and depictions. In this regard, Dussaud points out that the depictions used by Ezekiel in the descriptions of the Babylonian and Assyrian officers in 23:12–15 stems from art works available in the exile and in daily life in Babylon.[153] Also, as noted in the *Inscriptions of Bar-ga'yah and Mati'el from Sefire* above, the designation of the cities by the term "daughter" or with female language was a common practice and easily adapted by Ezekiel. On a broader literary scale the studies of Joseph Coleson and Brian Lewis suggest that ch. 16 may have been influenced in part by common ANE literary works.

Coleson has posited that the motif of the abandoned child in ch. 16 is commonly found in the ANE as seen in the *Sargon Legend*.[154] Moreover, Lewis has shown that the abandonment motif was a common literary feature that presented a god, king, or cultural hero who, after suffering abandonment as a child, would ". . . rise above the crowd to shape the lives and thought of the common man."[155] While no instance, out of Lewis's 72 different cross-cultural examples,[156] represents the motif as referring to a nation or city *per se* as presented in Ezekiel 16, the designation of Israel as a great "child" is relevant. Israel as a nation was to be seen, at least in the eyes of the Israelites, as the

---

152. Due to the numerous suggestions of scholars in this regard only a couple will be developed to show possible ANE connections. For a comparison between the actions of Yahweh's treatment of Israel and the seducing of Enkidu by Shamhat in the Gilgamesh Epic, see Kamionkowski, "The Savage Made Civilized," 131–34.

153. Dussaud, "Les Visions," 302. See also Keel, *Symbolism*, 239–40, for depictions of wall drawings of horsemen.

154. Coleson, "Israel's Life Cycle," 237–50. See also "The Birth Legend of Sargon of Akkad," COS 1.133:461.

155. Lewis, *Sargon Legend*, 149.

156. Ibid., 152–95. Lewis offers examples of abandoned individuals who later become hero figures over a wide range of languages and cultures including, Hebrew, Greek, Akaddian, Latin, Chinese, Turkish, Irish, English, Icelandic, etc. These range from ANE periods such as the *Legend of Sargon* to the modern story of Superman.

chosen nation of Yahweh with whom he had made covenant. It is quite possible that Ezekiel is drawing on the greatness expected from the abandoned child motif[157] in an effort to apply it to Israel (see also the story of Moses in Exodus 2).[158] Thus, it would have led the reader to understand the important role they had been expected to live up to yet had failed at so miserably. The detailed development of the beauty of the child/woman and the adornments given to her by Yahweh further develops the notion of greatness and high expectations.

Following the work of Lewis, who presents seven key components of the child abandonment motif,[159] Coleson suggests that Ezekiel had this particular motif in mind when he presented the allegory of the life of Israel as a woman's "life cycle." Moreover, he asserts that beyond the Moses and Sargon accounts, Ezekiel may have drawn on the Canaanite tale of the birth of El's children.[160] However, Ezekiel seems to have used the abandoned child motif in a unique way. In the ANE it was common for unwanted female babies to be abandoned to the elements. However, even in those cases the child was given as much of an opportunity to survive as was possible until a third party could rescue it (e.g., Moses and Sargon were sheltered in a basket ark). In Ezekiel's presentation even this provision is missing—the infant is unwanted and unloved still having her umbilical cord uncut and not being rubbed with disinfecting salt (16:4). The imagery is reflective of the total dependence that Israel had on Yahweh from its inception. Note, however, that Lewis's seven parts of the motif are obviously not followed in detail but the motif is nonetheless relevant to the overall chapter in Ezekiel. Ezekiel appears to have used the basic model to begin with but modified it to fit the life of the nation. What this sug-

---

157. So too Swanepoel, "Ezekiel 16," 96.

158. See also the Babylonian Talmud version of the birth of Moses (*Sotah* 12a–13b), Joshua the son of Nun (*Rab Peʿalim* 12a), and Abraham (*Shevet Musar* ch. 52), as noted by Lewis, *Sargon Legend*, 153–55.

159. Ibid., 211, 244–50. Lewis presents these as such:
1. Explanation of Abandonment
2. Infant of Noble Birth
3. Preparations for Exposure
4. Exposure
5. Infant Protected and Nursed in an Unusual Manner
6. Discovery and Adoption
7. Accomplishments of the Hero

160. Coleson, "Israel's Life Cycle," 250 n. 8.

gests is the possibility that Ezekiel used the popular motif as a starting point for the metaphor and as a literary hook to those in exile who would have known the story of Moses' birth and, no doubt, the legend of Sargon. From this perspective, the natural development of the motif beyond the infant into adulthood would have been a natural progression. The development and nurturing of the "woman" to a place of prominence among the nations lends naturally to the greatness of the "hero" in the motif. Thus it was but a small step for Ezekiel to present the "marriage" (covenant) of the "woman" (Israel) to Yahweh and to connect that act to the covenant at Sinai (16:8). Clearly the use of the term "covenant" six times in Ezekiel 16 (vv. 8, 59, 60 [2 times], 61, 62) reinforces this conclusion. Once again, it is but a small step to anticipate the punishment for "marriage" infidelity through the curses initiated by the broken covenant.

Conclusion

We can determine from the context and length of chs. 16 and 23 that the extended metaphors played a key role in the fashioning of the framework of the book of Ezekiel. The prophet's use of the marriage metaphor in these chapters as a picture of Israel's covenant relationship is clear.[161] The covenant breach and the ensuing curses along with the harsh and stirring language in these two chapters serve as the centerpiece of the oracles of doom (i.e., chs. 13–24) after the departure of the glory of the Lord in ch. 11. The discussion above on ch. 12 concluded that the "rebellious house" motif in chs. 1–3 and ch. 12 forms a mini inclusio to the first and greatest curse of temple abandonment. Methodologically, Ezekiel chose the child abandonment and marriage motifs as a means to shame the exiles and the inhabitants of Judah into understanding the gravity of their sin before a loving, covenant God. The irony lies in the fact that it was not only the curses of the Mosaic Law that Ezekiel invoked, but also the curse standards of ANE treaties and marriage contracts. It was the combination of these two bodies of curses which prevailed upon Judah in the final analysis of their destruction and exile. While the language remains harsh and troubling even today, we still must read these chapters in light of ANE covenant curse and marriage contracts. Some feminists may cringe at such a

---

161. So too the conclusion of Wong, *Idea of Retribution*, 57.

prospect but the fact still remains that Judah had degraded *herself* to the level of a prostitute from an ANE understanding and as such had removed herself from the protection of her "Husband."

Furthermore, as an unfaithful wife who played the harlot, Yahweh had every right to enact the proceedings of divorce and punishment according to ANE customs. The stripping, beating, and cutting with swords, served as fitting punishments for a "wife" who had left her husband and played the harlot with numerous lovers. Her political and spiritual adultery would cost her her freedom. However, to add insult to injury, it would be her lovers who would carry out the punishments against her on behalf of Yahweh. Nevertheless, as had been the case with Habakkuk's complaint, these same nations would not go unpunished. They would end up in far worse circumstances in the hands of a sovereign God. Ezekiel's effective use of the curse motif would now be turned against the very nations that had been previously used to punish the house of Israel. It is this curse reversal that takes center stage in the restoration chapters of 25–39 (we will deal with chs. 40–48 in ch. 5). However, three chapters stand out among this grouping of oracles highlighted by the third vision, and the fourth "peak" in Ezekiel's framework; the valley of dry bones in ch. 37 and the Gog and Magog oracles of 38–39.

4

The Awesome Deity's Love

The Covenant Curses Reversed

(Ezekiel 37 Juxtaposed with 38–39)

In the second half of the book of Ezekiel (i.e., the exact midpoint of the book), the tenor of the prophet's message changes. It appears that the only remaining message for the prophet to give was one of hope and redemption after the period of cursing. As we showed in ch. 2 above, the curse of temple abandonment, depicted in Yahweh's departure from his throne, left the nation to the fate of exile and the curses of a broken covenant as outlined in Deuteronomy 28 and Leviticus 26. Moreover, in our previous chapter we showed how the extended metaphors of 16 and 23 told the people how this would happen, viz., by the "standards of the nations." In this vein, the sign act of 24:15–27 brought a close to the chapters of doom and foreboding. The plight of the house of Israel was sealed and destruction, inevitable. In light of this pivotal event in the life of the nation, I hope to demonstrate that the tide of Ezekiel's message shifts at this point from one of cursing to one of hope beginning with the punishment of the surrounding nations (cf. chs. 25–32).

As we noted in our structural section in ch. 1, the framework of Ezekiel seems to be tightly connected to the visions of the prophet. In this chapter we will explore the fourth vision (i.e., 37:1–14) which represents the fourth "peak" of our proposed framework along with its literary context. This vision seems to depict the reversal of a common ANE curse, viz., a nation cursed in battle whose warriors and inhabitants had been left unburied. However, in the context of curse-reversal, Ezekiel appears to be telling his audience that restoration will not only come to the covenant nation but that the pain and curses that they once suffered will be placed upon those nations who had misused them. For this reason, as part of our central focus in this chapter, we will examine the relationship between the vision of ch. 37 and the battle scenes of chs. 38–39 to see if we can perhaps detect an intended purpose for this order here in the final form. However, before addressing this central topic, is seems appropriate to deal with some literary concerns as they relate to Ezekiel's use, or should we say non-use, of terminology related to such a hope.

A Message of Hope

Ezekiel's literary technique for presenting the "awesome Deity's love" through the hope of restoration does not follow what one would normally expect from a prophet speaking words of hope and compassion.[1] Indeed, the prophet does not explicitly use the word "love" (אָהַב) when speaking of Yahweh's feelings for his people even in the restoration chapters.[2] Some have noticed this lacuna and have also commented about the lack of other words of "divine favor."[3] Words such as redemp-

---

1. Schwartz, "Dim View." In his thesis, Schwartz insists that the restoration was a part of the nation's punishment. For a refutation of Schwartz's position see Ganzel, "Restoration," 1–22.

Kaufmann, *Religion of Israel*, 440–41, comes to the same conclusion as Schwartz. Kaufmann avers that the people's desire to be absorbed into the nations and become like them (cf. 20:32–44) proves that the exile was not a severe punishment for many people. Indeed, many desired to stay in exile. One has to admit, that there seems to be some validity to this position based upon the small number of Israelites who returned to Judah in 538 BCE.

2. Schwartz, "Ezekiel's Dim View," 53. Schwartz points out that the only appearance of אָהַב in the book is in chs. 16 and 23 where it is used to describe Israel's and Judah's "illicit affairs" (cf. 16:33, 36, 37; 23:5, 9, 22). Zimmerli, "Special Form," 525–26, also notes this idea.

3. There are passages that seem to go against the concept of a merciful God in Ezekiel. For example, in 15:7 we read "and I set My face against them. *Though* they have come out of the fire, yet the fire will consume them. Then you will know that I am the LORD, when I set My face against them" (NASB). Zimmerli, *I Am Yahweh*, 93, points out the "merciless" nature of such passages. Here again a note of caution must be given. While it is true that many passages in Ezekiel do appear harsh, the overall context of the message must be held in view here. The curses of the covenant were not pleasant at the moment of initiation and do seem "merciless" when Yahweh's fury rages. However, once Yahweh's fury has subsided we can conclude that the intended effect has been achieved and Yahweh's compassion is once again offered. The remnant being renewed now exhibit a burning desire to keep the covenant with their God. This is nowhere more evident than during the post-exilic period and later when the "love

tion (גָּאַל), comfort (נָחַם), forgiveness (סָלַח), graciousness (חֵן), compassion (רַחֲמִים), and lovingkindness (חֶסֶד) are absent from Yahweh's words to his people even in chs. 33–48.[4] Furthermore, there appears to be no mention of the exiles' repentance but only Yahweh's unilateral declaration that he will restore them for the sake of his name (36:22).[5] While on the surface this may appear to create a problem, understanding Ezekiel within the context of ANE covenant curses gives one a better appreciation for this alleged absence of Yahweh's love.

First, Yahweh's goal, as presented in Ezekiel, was to punish his people for their sin and in so doing, demonstrate his power and authority over all nations including Israel. Even the restoration of Israel was for that one purpose (cf. 39:21–29). In order to demonstrate to all nations, including his own, his sovereignty and that he is the one with whom Israel had broken covenant, Yahweh needed to act independently of all terrestrial influence, even the cries of his people.[6] This is demonstrated foremost in Yahweh's departure from his throne by his own volition (cf. 11:23). It should not be surprising that restoration would also involve Yahweh's similar independent actions.

Second, it was a common ANE belief that a curse, once enacted, took on a life of its own with no way to recall it. This belief made the curse section of treaties and inscriptions from the ANE an effective deterrent. In Ezekiel's case, the prophet desired to show that both the curses of the Law and those of the ANE were under Yahweh's sovereign control rather than the whims of the gods or some magical force. Yahweh alone could enact them and he alone could reverse them as he saw fit. Therefore, by demonstrating his sovereignty to do so, Yahweh

---

of the Law" took center stage. Although ultimately taken to the extreme in Jesus' day, the covenantal Law did become rooted in the people's everyday life after the horrors of the exile.

4. Schwartz, "Dim View," 53–54. Note however, רָחַם ("to be compassionate" in the Piel) is present in 39:25 but Schwartz and many others see it as a secondary addition.

5. Cf. Robson, *Word and Spirit*, 25. However, Kaufmann, *Religion of Israel*, 442, concedes that 18:31 seems to suggest some form of repentance on the part of the people at least for their part in their striving for the "new heart." Cf. also the discussion by Delorme, "Conversion," 115–44.

6. That is not to say that he does not hear the prayers of his people but rather that in the case of the exile (and the return), Yahweh would not cease his action even though there were righteous people in the nation calling out for a reprieve (cf. chs. 3, 14, 18, 20). Also, it appears that Yahweh's *apparent* lack of concern for his people is exactly what Habakkuk is addressing.

would reveal his power to all nations.[7] The demonstration of Yahweh's power would first come through the exile of Israel and then by its restoration through the reversal of the curses; not necessarily from the influence of a contrite nation.

Finally, a note of caution must be given to those who suggest that Yahweh did not show compassion or *ḥesed* to his covenant people through the restoration process. The absence of particular words of compassion does not negate Yahweh's demonstration of his undying love. Yahweh demonstrated his love for his people by restoring all that the people held dear, viz., temple, land, and king, along with abundance, provision, and prosperity (cf. ch. 5 below). These are hallmarks of Yahweh's love which were present at the inception of the covenants with Abraham and the nation at Sinai. While the purpose of Ezekiel was to show the power of Yahweh as the sovereign Suzerain, he nonetheless demonstrated through curse reversal the awesome love of Israel's longsuffering and forgiving God.[8] Interestingly, it is this love and forgiveness that is developed in the vision of ch. 37.

Symbolic Vision of a Nation Cursed in Battle[9]

Perhaps one of the best-known pericopes in the OT is the valley of dry bones vision in Ezekiel 37:1–14.[10] The ghastly imagery[11] and stimulating mental picture is rivaled perhaps only by Ezekiel's opening vision of Yahweh's glory.[12] The "other worldly" encounter of Ezekiel

---

7. See also Exod 32:11–14; Num 14:13–24, and Deut 9:28 for a similar theological outlook.

8. Renz, *Rhetorical Function*, 113, correctly points out that the finished book of the prophet Ezekiel, in and of itself, served the purpose to "evoke a certain response which can be understood in terms of repentance."

9. Zimmerli, "Special Form," 521, suggests that Ezekiel developed this vision from Prov 17:22; "A joyful heart is good medicine, But a broken spirit dries up the bones" (NASB). However, the narrow connection between the two seems unlikely as a basis for an entire vision to be developed.

10. Cf. Vawter and Hoppe, *New Heart*, 165. For a detailed discussion on the structure and redaction history of this passage, see Allen, "Structure," 127–42.

11. Childs, "Enemy from the North," 187–90, posits that the use of "quaking /rattling" (רַעַשׁ) in Ezek 37:7 is part of the chaos tradition. He sees this as being amplified by the clear depictions in chs. 38–39.

12. For example, Eichrodt, *Ezekiel*, 506, points out the importance of this vision and ranks it with the *kābôd* visions of 1–3; 8–11; and 40–43 for its "dramatic power."

with the Lord, coupled with his transport to a barren valley of dry bones, evokes immediate interest in those who read it. Questions like, "What is the purpose of this vision?" or "What is a priest doing in the midst of a valley of bones?" immediately come to mind. These are legitimate questions but other issues seem more important in light of the author's apparent rhetorical argument. As early as 6:1-7, 13 (cf. also 34:8), Ezekiel suggested that as a result of Israel's idolatry and covenant unfaithfulness, their bodies would be left unburied (see also Jer 8:1-3; 34:20).[13] It is therefore no surprise that the devastating display depicted in this chapter is often directly linked to the curse of Israel's broken covenant with Yahweh. In the curse lists of Deuteronomy (cf. 28:26) and Leviticus (cf. 26:30) we see the curse which appears here in Ezekiel.[14] The similarity in covenant/treaty language found in the Leviticus and Deuteronomy passages and here in Ezekiel further supports our premise of covenant indictment by the prophet. In the light of our ongoing discussion of Ezekiel's use of curses from the Law and the ANE, it appears that once again the curse motif could be behind the imagery of this pericope.[15]

As ch. 37 ends, the remaining prophecies take on a marked shift from the curses that dominated chs. 3-24 to renewal and restoration with the promise of a unified kingdom—something that had not been a reality for almost 400 years (cf. 37:15-23). This unified kingdom would also experience the restoration of their greatest king to the throne (i.e., David—37:24-25). Where Zedekiah had been unfaithful to the treaty of Nebuchadnezzar and Yahweh's covenant in ch. 17, in the last days the new "prince" (vv. 24-26) would be faithful to Yahweh alone. This earthly ruler would take his rightful place in the city of renewed hope and reversed curses. This reversal is highlighted by vivid depictions of a renewed covenant, abundance, peace, and safety. While the king's role may fade as chs. 40-48 unfold, he is, nonetheless, a vital part of the restoration and reversal motif.[16] Finally, the new covenant,

---

13. Irwin, "Molek Imagery," 94 n. 3, points out that the scattering of one's bones (as seen in Pss 53:5; 141:7 and Ezek 6:5) was an example of Yahweh's "harshest judgment."

14. Cf. Odell, *Ezekiel*, 449-50; and Fensham, "Dry Bones," 59-60.

15. So too Block, *Ezekiel 25-48*, 377-78. Block asserts that the picture is that of the common ANE covenant curse of leaving an enemy unburied. This was an acceptable end for those who had broken "contracts and treaty oaths."

16. This will be developed further in the next chapter. Cohn, *Cosmos*, 150, 162, aptly points out in ch. 37 the link to the ANE motif of the exalted nation with a

which is addressed in 37:26 (see also 34:25), points to the completeness of Yahweh's work in Israel. In this vein, Fensham correctly points out that the only solution to covenant breach "... is the forming of a new covenant between God and his obedient remnant" (cf. Jer 31:31; Ezek 34:25; 37:26).[17]

Contextually, the unveiling of national restoration and the hope of a utopian existence in ch. 37 appears tempered (albeit negatively) by chs. 38–39 as the tide seems to change once again and the picture of hope falters. The depiction of Gog and Magog and the nations coming against Israel challenges the very existence of the re-born nation. This threat stands in stark relief against the backdrop of peace and security pictured in ch. 37. Nevertheless, as will be demonstrated below, Ezekiel has a greater rhetorical purpose in mind by including chs. 38 and 39. Here Ezekiel juxtaposes ch. 37 with 38 and 39 to show a reversal of the effects of the covenant curse epitomized in the vision of the unburied dead seen in ch. 37.[18] Whereas in ch. 37 Israel is depicted as an unburied army, in chs. 38 and 39 the enemies of Yahweh and Israel are cursed with non-burial. In this reversal of the curse, the prophet drives home the reality of Yahweh's protection and assurance of the new covenant promises.

The comparison of the motif of the scattered corpses in these three chapters is not new. Christopher Seitz posited the question as to whether these three chapters had parallels intended by the author(s).[19] He queries, "Is this a valley of the slain of Israel, whose reconstruction is to be contrasted with that of the mysterious Gog (39:11–20), whose hosts are picked clean of flesh by scavenger birds in another, equally mysterious valley?"[20] Unfortunately Seitz stopped short of answering his own question. In light of the ongoing discussion I believe the answer is a definite yes; these are intended parallels to which we will return shortly.[21]

---

divinely appointed king. This, he notes, was common throughout Mesopotamia and Egypt during the period of Ezekiel.

17. Fensham, "Maledictions," 9.

18. Taylor, "Ezekiel," 418, appears to allude to the contrasting picture of the two scenes without explicitly making the connection to ch. 37.

19. Seitz, "Ezekiel 37:1–14," 53–54. See also Matthews, *Ezekiel*, 140, where he also notes the similarities in the picture presented in ch. 37 and 39:11–16.

20. Seitz, "Ezekiel 37:1–14," 54.

21. Launderville, *Spirit and Reason*, 334, notes the similarities between these two scenes. Also, Power, "Iconographic Windows," 541, notes that "the vision of ch. 37

Interpretively, the vision of 37:1–14 has not only a metaphoric meaning but more importantly, has literal implications. First, the metaphor of spiritual deadness and loss of hope, which Yahweh ultimately interprets for the prophet in vv. 11–14, serves as a fitting object lesson for the prophet to apply to the reality of his immediate situation of the exile. Second, it is a picture of the literal devastation and human carnage brought about by the enacted treaty curse of unburied bodies, which perhaps reflected the results of the war against Nebuchadnezzar in 586 BCE. Following this, chs. 38–39, often noted for their apocalyptic nature, show the final battle between God and the enemies of Israel. As noted above, the focus in these two chapters is the reversal of various curses found throughout Ezekiel's message, but more specifically, the curse of the unburied dead in ch. 37. Where Israel had been the one cursed and lying unburied for the fowls of the air and beasts of the field to pick at their bones, now the nations will experience the effects of this curse—they will be food for the beasts. Yahweh is the one fighting for, and protecting, his people and fulfilling the promises as found in Deut 30:3–7.[22]

The Curse of Being Left Unburied: The ANE Perspective

Before discussing in detail the parallels between chs. 37 and 38–39, we must first understand the historical context of these chapters. In the ANE, boundary stone markers, building and tomb inscriptions, and treaty curse lists betray the wide use of the motif of being left unburied.[23] In light of this prolific use, one is faced with the challenge of understanding its intended purpose. The curse of being left unburied was not a random imprecation but rather a reality of life based upon a

---

with its evidence of previous death and destruction foreshadows the fate that awaits the enemies of God. The mighty empire will fall, as Israel had once fallen, but there will be no reversal of the fate of the nations." Stavrakopoulou, "Use and Abuse," 15, notes the sharp contrasts in the two pericopes. She states that the "'anti-ideal' in one is inverted in the other" but she fails to recognize the curse-reversal motif that is present. See also Power's comments on page 549 along similar lines as those of Stavrakopoulou.

22. We will return to this shortly.
23. Fensham, "Dry Bones," 59. Cf. also, Gevirtz, *Curse Motifs*, 171–90, esp. 171–72.

host of common fears of the average person of the ANE.[24] These fears were rooted within their philosophy of the afterlife.[25]

People in Mesopotamia believed that once a person died proper burial, with appropriate mortuary rites, was required.[26] This had to be done in order for their spirit (Akk. *etemmu*) to take its place among the dead. A properly buried body enabled the person's *etemmu* to be eternally connected to the community of the dead and the living. The living regularly honored the dead and in so doing forged the communal relationship between the two spheres.[27] If one's body was left unburied or destroyed in some way, be it by fire or animals, then the deceased could not be "integrated into the structured community of the dead . . ."[28]

However, the fear of being cut off from this "structured community" went beyond just being left unburied after death. The disinterring or destruction of one's bones cut the individual off from this cosmic

---

24. Richardson, "Death and Dismemberment," 200. Cf. also, Fensham, "Dog," 504–7, esp. 506.

25. The Israelites had no less of a strong desire for proper burial which seemed to focus on being buried with their ancestors on land owned by the family or clan (e.g., Abraham—Genesis 23; Jacob—Gen 50:4–7; and Joseph—Gen 50:24–26; Exod 13:19). See further, Brichto, "Kin, Cult, Land, and Afterlife," 1–54, esp. 8–11, 48. Stavrakopoulou, "Use and Abuse," 3, notes, "If interment in the family tomb is presented in the Hebrew Bible as the socially 'ideal' response to a corpse, non-burial or disinterment can frequently signal the 'anti-ideal.'" For a discussion of the concept of non-burial and its implications in later Judaism and the time of Christ, see Fletcher-Louis, "'Leave the Dead,'" 39–68, esp. 57–68.

26. Cf. also, Stavrakopoulou, "Use and Abuse," 1–16, esp. 1–3. Stavrakopoulou (1) states, ". . . the methods and means of dealing with a corpse constitute a process effecting and maintaining the transformation of the deceased from a social person into a non-living entity, enabling the living community to negotiate and reframe their relationship with that individual." See further, Chesson, "Remembering," 109–39, esp. 120–23; and Gnoli and Vernant, *La mort*. In this compendium see especially the essay by Cassin, "Le mort," 355–72.

27. Abusch, "etemmu," in *DDD*, 309–12.

28. Ibid., 309. Stavrakopoulou, "Use and Abuse," 4, points out that the refusal of the living to grant the deceased proper mortuary rites leads to the "disruption or fracture of the changing social relationship between the deceased and the living: in being abandoned, the corpse remains culturally and symbolically unplaced, rendering the individual's transition into post-mortem existence neither wholly effected nor settled, and marking at once the estrangement of the living from their dead and the isolation of the dead from their living." She goes on to note that disturbing the corpses of the departed in the ANE was a punishable offense through curses often found on grave inscriptions throughout the ANE and Mediterranean.

two-tiered community.[29] Interestingly, Josiah desecrated the bodies of the false priests at Bethel in the same manner (cf. 1 Kgs 23:15–20) which was prophesied about in 1 Kings 13:1–5.[30] Perhaps it was this event that fueled Ezekiel's prophecy in 6:1–7.

It is safe to say that premature death, lack of proper burial, or destruction or desecration of one's body was one of the "most dreadful sanctions of Mesopotamian society."[31] This reality is what made it an effective curse in treaties and inscriptions. Furthermore, the fear of improper burial was based primarily upon the fact that while other curses may have depended on the actions of an individual *while* he/she was alive this particular curse was invoked *after* the death of a person when he/she had no means of recourse. The individual was at the mercy of those who killed him/her (i.e., in battle) or those who were responsible for caring for his/her body. If in fact the person's family or enemy refused to give a proper burial, or if the person was disinterred, then the deceased could become associated with the demonic realm and, in worst case scenarios, become a demon (Akk. *udug/utukku*). The societal fear associated with demonic activity served as a two-way protective mechanism in their afterlife-belief system. If the living refused to give a proper burial to their deceased kinfolk then the deceased could return to haunt them.[32] This check and balance provided a level of assurance to those who died.

29. Abusch, "etemmu," in *DDD*, 310.

30. So too Stavrakopoulou, "Use fand Abuse," 5. While the act of Josiah was to desecrate the illegal altars, he also was sending a message to other individuals who would try and lead Israel astray in such a manner. If anyone attempted to lead Israel into false worship at the high places they would be cut off from the community of the living and the dead.

31. Abusch, "etemmu," 310. Also, Cohn, *Cosmos*, 56, has pointed out that most people in Mesopotamia believed that the improper burial of a person could cause the deceased to return and "bring physical or mental sickness upon his kin." Stavrakopoulou, "Use and Abuse," 6, avers that disinterment and mutilation of a corpse could cause the deceased to "harass or threaten the living."

32. Abusch, "etemmu," 310. Scurlock, *Magico-Medical Means*, 178–677, lists 352 full or partial texts (with transliterations and translations) dealing with the vast array of incantations and prayers to ward off ghosts and to heal ghost-induced illnesses. For a discussion of the various symptoms of such illnesses, see Scurlock's ch. 2, pages 5–20. See also Foster, *Before the Muses*, 658–59, 990–91. For further reading see Cooper, "Fate of Mankind," 19–33, esp. 27–30; and Scurlock, "Ghosts," 77–96. The use of curses and divination to ward off evil spirits that cause sickness also appears in Egyptian curse literature. Cf. Nordh, *Aspects*, 103.

This safety mechanism, however, appears not to have applied to those guilty of offences such as those delineated in treaties and inscriptions. Indeed, the enactment of this curse on an offending party in these situations would not only cut the individual off from the realm of the living but also cause that person's soul to wander for eternity unable to interact with the living or the dead.[33] This understanding of Mesopotamian afterlife enables us to appreciate the effectiveness of this particular curse as it appears in ANE literature and inscriptions. Furthermore it may also shed some light on its use in Ezekiel and the OT. It is to this application that we now turn.

The OT Curse of Unburied Dead

One of the curses of the Mosaic Law for unfaithfulness to the covenant was the curse of being left unburied, found specifically in Deut 28:26 and Lev 26:30.[34] In the OT the curse appears most frequently within the context of battle, conquest, and treaty/covenant violations.

Canonically, this curse first appears in an Egyptian context for unfaithfulness to the pharaoh.[35] In Gen 40:19, Joseph foresees this curse as the plight of the pharaoh's chief baker. This example aside, in the OT we see the curse used predominantly in military and treaty contexts.

---

33. Abusch, "etemmu," 311. Ibid., 311–12 also notes the *Maqlû* ("burning") ceremony performed at the time of the return of the spirits during the month Abu. This was when witches were burned so they could not enter the cosmic realm of the netherworld or have relationship with the living. Launderville, *Spirit and Reason*, 336–37, also notes that the *Maqlû* ceremony was used as a means of assuring that the *etemmu* returned to the netherworld after the celebration. The person performing this ritual (i.e., the exorcist or "cosmic gatekeeper") would recite the words "My city Zabban, my city Zabban. Concerning my city Zabban, it has two gates: one for sunrise and another for the sunset. . . . As I cleanse you, may you cleanse me" (*Maqlû* I:42–44, 48–49). Zabban (see also cognates in Hebrew and Ugaritic, viz., Ps 48:3—Ṣāpôn and in Ugaritic *Zaphon* [home of Baal—Mt. Casius] from Ugaritic *ṣpn*) was the gate between the cosmic boundary of the living and the netherworld that was situated on the horizon where the "cosmic travelers and ghosts" could pass unhindered. Cf. also, Abusch, *Mesopotamian Witchcraft*, 264 and Robinson, "Zion and Ṣāpôn," 118–23.

34. Cf. also, Stavrakopoulou, "Use and Abuse," 3.

35. In Egypt, the pharaoh was considered the earthly representation of the god Horus. It is probably safe to assume that the chief baker, as well as other close attendants, had to swear some form of oath to the pharaoh.

1 Samuel 17: David and Goliath

The curse of giving someone's body to the fowls of the air and the beasts of the field in a setting of battle was not only a means of evoking fear in your opponent, but also a common reality for those who died in battle. In the account of David and Goliath, the curse uttered by Goliath against David is the same as that found in the Mosaic Law (cf. 1 Sam 17:44). Five things in the 1 Samuel 17 account stand out as noteworthy. First, Goliath calls down a curse upon David in 17:43. The text reads, "and the Philistine cursed (קלל) David by his gods." The curse is then described in the following verse as giving David's carcass to the birds and beasts for food. Here we see a direct link between this curse in the context of battle and the role of the gods to fulfill it. Second, it must have been a "time-honored" curse because it appears, at least textually, to have been prevalent well before the time of David. Third, it was obviously a popular means of cursing an enemy because it is the only curse that Goliath invokes against David. Fourth, from the text we can determine that it was a curse known and used across cultures. Fifth, the curse is immediately reversed by David (i.e., placed on Goliath) and expanded to include the entire Philistine army (cf. 17:46). David, as the representative of Yahweh and the rightly anointed king of Israel (cf. 1 Sam 16), could speak on Yahweh's behalf to reverse the curse and place it upon the enemies of God and Israel. By its very nature, albeit on a micro scale, this account is a very close parallel to that depicted in Ezekiel 37–39. Thus, we can conclude from the David and Goliath pericope that the curse appears to be an appropriate means of evoking fear in a lower status individual or nation to comply with the demands of the higher ranked party. There is one further note of interest in this account that is relevant to our discussion. In 1 Samuel 17:46–47 David notes that the purpose of the defeat of Goliath and the reversal of the curse is in order that "all the earth (and the "assembly" of Israel—v. 47) may know that there is a God in Israel." The recognition formula (see below) played a key role in the purpose for David's victory that day.

1 Samuel 31: Saul and his Sons

In the account of the death of Saul and his sons, we see the curse of corpse exposure and desecration after a defeat in battle. The Philistines' decapitation of the fallen Israelite leader (v. 9) and his sons (implicit) followed by the display of their headless cadavers on the walls of Beth-Shan (v.10) point to the animosity between the two rival nations. The curse of being left unburied is apparently only remedied when the brave men of Jabesh-gilead steal the bodies of Saul and his sons under the cover of darkness and return them to their homeland (vv.11–13). After a brief cremation ceremony, the bones of the fallen are then placed in a grave in Jabesh-gilead. By these acts we can assume the abating of any lingering effects of the curse.[36]

2 SAMUEL 21:1–14: DAVID AND THE GIBEONITES[37]

In this account, the land of Israel is suffering from three years of famine and David inquires of the Lord to find out the reason why this is so (v. 1). The Lord informs him that the famine is due to a curse brought upon the land because of Saul's treatment of the Gibeonites (v. 1). David summonses the Gibeonites and asks how he may make restitution for Saul's actions. The Gibeonites respond by asking for seven sons of Saul to be slain (v. 2). David acquiesces to their demands and they kill the men and hang them "in the mountain" for the beasts of the field and the fowls of the air (vv. 3–9).[38] But Rizpah, the concubine of Saul and mother of two of the men who were killed, makes a vigil and watches over their bodies for the duration of the harvest keeping the birds and animals away from the corpses (v. 10). David, upon hearing of her actions, goes and takes the bones of these men and those of Jonathan and Saul, who were buried in Jabesh-gilead, and gives them a proper burial (vv. 11–14).

---

36. Stavrakopoulou, "Use and Abuse," 5, sees in this account the Philistines' desire to desecrate the bodies of their enemies and to refuse proper burial and passage into the afterlife. Thus, "the public dishonouring of the corpse and the absence of mortuary rituals ... mark the deliberate social dislocation of the dead." See also the treatment of Jezebel's corpse in 2 Kgs 9:34–37.

37. For a discussion on the nature of Joshua's treaty with the Gibeonites in Joshua 9 and 10 see, Fensham, "Treaty between Israel and the Gibeonites," 96–100.

38. Brichto, "Kin, Cult, Land, and Afterlife," 36–37, suggests that this displaying of the bodies of Saul's kinfolk was to cause Saul not to have rest in the afterlife. The Gibeonites, no doubt, followed the belief that one's continued earthly existence in the afterlife rested upon the continuation of his/her family line. The killing of Saul's descendants would thus end Saul's "rest" in the afterlife. This idea is also developed by Robinson, *Corporate Personality*, 3–4.

Again, several important points of reference between Ezekiel's account and that of this pericope need to be pointed out. First, the 2 Samuel 21 account is set within the context of a broken covenant (compare Josh 9 to 2 Sam 21:2). Saul broke the covenant made between Joshua and the Gibeonites thus causing the famine (2 Sam 21:2). The just punishment for that broken covenant was the "sacrifice" of those responsible for the breach; in this case seven male descendants of Saul serve in proxy. Thus, the curse is removed from the land and placed upon Saul's descendants represented by leaving the bodies of the seven men unburied (cf. Deut 21:23). Similarly, as we noted above, Ezekiel's vision appears to present a battlefield full of slain warriors who were punished for a broken covenant with Yahweh. Interestingly, Saul's offspring had suffered for Saul's breach of covenant with the Gibeonites in the same way these warriors in Ezekiel's vision had suffered the consequences of the nation's (Ezek 4–24) and Zedekiah's (Ezek 17) breach of covenant. Second, Rizpah sought to avoid the full force of the curse by keeping the beasts and fowls away from the bodies of her sons and kindred, something totally lacking in Ezekiel's account (although the vision of Ezekiel does offer hope through the restorative acts and power of Yahweh). Finally, as also noted in the David and Goliath pericope, the cross-cultural connection of covenant violation, curse, and unburied bodies finds support in the actions of the Gibeonites who were a remnant of the Amorite nation.

1 Kings 14:1–15: Ahijah Curses the House of Jeroboam

In the narrative of the prophet Ahijah's cursing of the house of Jeroboam, we find in verse 11 that the prophet curses Jeroboam's offspring with the plight of dying and being left unburied as food for the dogs and birds. This account also has interesting connections with Ezekiel's message. First, verse 11 enumerates the curses to fall upon Jeroboam's house because he had broken covenant with Yahweh and had caused Israel to fall into idolatry through idol worship at Dan and Bethel. The sin of idolatry as with Ezekiel's day (cf. Ezek 6:1–7, 13) brings this curse, as well as others, upon Jeroboam and the nation respectively. Second, in each case the prophet of Yahweh announces the curse. In Ezekiel's case the curse is announced in 6:1–7, 13 and is fulfilled, implicitly, in ch. 37, albeit with a positive outcome.[39]

1 Kings 16:4 and 21:24; 2 Kings 9:10, 36: The Fate of the Kings and Queens of Israel

As with the narrative of Jeroboam, both Baasha and Ahab receive the same curse as Jeroboam for their part in leading the nation of Israel astray into idolatry. Furthermore, Jezebel, as the enemy of the prophets of Yahweh and the promoter of Baal worship, would suffer the same fate (2 Kgs 9:10, 36). The Deuteronomistic historian appears to be using this particular curse as the curse of choice in rebuking and punishing kings and queens who thwarted true Yahweh worship.

Psalms 79:2 and 83:11 [Heb]: Asaph Laments the Curse

Psalm 79 is an exilic psalm of Asaph in which he laments the destruction of Jerusalem and the curse of non-burial, which the enemies of Israel had inflicted upon God's people. The context matches very closely that depicted in Ezekiel 37. The psalmist also recognizes the scene of the unburied dead as punishment from Yahweh for their sin. The author goes on to plead for Yahweh to vindicate his name against the nations responsible, and to forgive Israel for their sins. Finally, in verse 11 of Psalm 83, another psalm of Asaph, he seeks for God's help against the nations surrounding Israel who plot their demise. The psalmist calls for their armies to be cursed like Midian, Sisera, and Jabin whose bodies were left like "dung" (דֹּמֶן) upon the ground.

Isaiah 5:25; 18:6: Judah is the Recipient of the Curse

Isaiah used the same curse when he prophesied a similar fate for the nation of Judah (Isa 5:25). Later, in the metaphor of the grapevine of ch. 18, Cush is encouraged by the promise that Assyria will be devas-

---

39. While the context of 6:1–7, 13 appears to be focused only on the high places, in v. 3 we see the inclusion of the valleys and ravines. This inclusion of a diverse topographical range allows for a broader interpretation of the curse of unburied dead. In the context of ch. 6 we can assume that any unburied body left in the land can be directly related to the curse due to their idolatry whether on the high places or in the temple (cf. chs. 8–11).

tated on the mountains (Isa 18:6).[40] Their bodies will be given to the beasts of the field and fowls of the air, which will feed on their corpses for an extended period of time. Again, the important parallel is the cross-cultural appeal of this curse.

JEREMIAH 7:30–34; 8:2; 9:21 [HEB]; 12:9; 14:16; 15:1–5; 16:1–6; 19:1–7; 22:19; 25:33; 34:17–22; 36:30

The numerous appearances of the curse in Jeremiah depict, in various ways, what is described in Ezekiel. The similar outlook can perhaps be accounted for by the contemporaneous nature of these prophetic oracles to the final generation before the fall of Jerusalem. A quick overview of these occurrences will help illuminate the prophetic sentiment of the exilic age. Jeremiah's prophecy in 7:33[41] has parallels with the 2 Samuel 21 pericope where Rizpah keeps the birds and beasts of the field away from the bodies of her deceased loved ones. In Judah's case, none would be available to offer even this posthumous relief from the curse. In 12:9 one finds the general call to the beasts and birds to feed upon Judah's corpses while 14:16 stresses this curse as the plight for those who fall in the streets. In a more forceful depiction, 15:1–5 presents this curse from three different perspectives in a four-part disaster about to fall upon Judah. After the "sword" has done its work (the first curse), the dogs, birds, and beasts will feed upon those who fell in battle and conquest, thus rounding out the four modes of punishment. Ironically, the curse of being left unburied and eaten by the animals comprises the last three.

Next, as touched on in Psalm 83:11 above, the harsh comparative language of 8:2, 9:21, and 16:1–6 enables the reader to feel the animus of Yahweh, through the prophet, against his people. Their bodies will become as "dung" (דֹּמֶן) and none will lament their passing (cf. also 25:33). Also, in 19:1–7 Jeremiah draws the direct parallel between the curse of unburied bodies and the people's idolatry, especially child-sacrifice. Furthermore, the prophecy against Jehoiakim that he would be thrown outside of the city gate and "be buried with the burial of a donkey" (22:19) is proof that even kings would not escape this curse (see also Jer 36:30). Finally, in 34:17–22, Jeremiah's use of the curse linked directly to covenant breach as it relates to the responsibilities

---

40. Delitzsch, *Isaiah*, 230, notes that the nation being judged here is Assyria.
41. Cf. Brichto, "Kin, Cult, Land, and Afterlife," 37–40.

of the leadership of Judah, adds a legal nexus to the appearance of the curse. Here it is directly tied to the breach of the Mosaic covenant.

The plethora of appearances of this particular curse in Jeremiah and Ezekiel points to the imminent destruction of Jerusalem and the carnage that will follow. Whereas Jeremiah's presentations come prior to the fall of the city, Ezekiel's span both the pre-fall and post-fall realities of a nation under the curse of Yahweh. Thus we can say that the stressing of this curse by Jeremiah, in the same period of Ezekiel, brings poignancy to the picture presented in Ezekiel's vision.[42]

Ezek 6:1–7; 34:8—Judah Cursed; The Nations Cursed—29:5; 30:11; 32:4–5; 35:8; 39:4–5, 17–20

As already noted, Ezekiel 6:1–7, 13 (cf. also Jer 8:1–3) appears to present the curse of non-burial in direct relation to idolatrous practices.[43] Also, in 34:8 the presentation of the nation of Israel becoming "food for all the beasts of the field" due to the improper actions by their "shepherds" (i.e., kings and leaders) has both metaphorical and literal fulfillment. Literally, we know the nation did end up as depicted here and in 6:1–7, 13, and 37:1–14. However, metaphorically, the lack of strong leaders had also allowed the nation to become "prey" for those nations who wished to exploit it through treaties and alliances that Yahweh had never sanctioned. Furthermore, the nation suffered because of their leaders' broken covenants with both earthly (cf. Ezekiel 17) and divine suzerains. This covenant curse truly was a reality for Judah in ways they had never imagined as dwellers within the "inviolable" city of Jerusalem. Nevertheless, Ezekiel did not just reserve the

---

42. As we have pointed out at various intervals, the prophecies of Ezekiel and Jeremiah have many motifs in common, this being yet another. It seems likely that they corresponded during the period prior to the fall of Jerusalem. Also, when dealing with the time period in question, Wittstruck, "Influence of Treaty Curse," 100–102, argues that Daniel's sequence of beasts in Daniel 7 are dependent on the ANE treaty-curse sequence of devouring animals as found in Sefire I A 30–31 and especially Sefire II A 9 from the eighth century BCE. Whether or not the sequence is based on these texts remains to be determined; however, the biblical links with ANE treaty curses is definitely nothing new in scholarly circles.

43. Petter, "Book of Ezekiel," 163–65, esp. 165 n. 68, suggests that the constant reiterating of the destruction of the people by sword, famine, and pestilence points to a land littered with corpses even to the point of them being stacked one on top of the other.

curse for Israel; he effectively uses it throughout his oracles against the nations.

As part of the curse reversal, Ezekiel uses the motif explicitly in the oracles against the nations (viz., Egypt and Edom) and in the Gog-Magog account of chs. 38–39. Ezekiel's use of the curse primarily against Egypt in chs. 29–32 (cf. 29:5; 30:11; 32:4–5) serves to stress the animosity felt against this particular nation of oppression both in Israel's youth (ch. 20) and as a political and cultic paramour later in her history (chs. 16 and 23).[44]

Ezekiel's presentation of the curse in ch. 39 matches very closely that envisioned by Jeremiah (Jer 25:15–38—esp. v. 33).[45] As just noted above, both prophets preached the same message of divine retribution against the nations in the last days. Ezekiel's use of this curse has a particularly emotive forcefulness both in the vision of ch. 37 and in the reversal of that curse against the nations in 39:4–5, 17–20. Based upon the prophetic use of the curse a few basic conclusions can be drawn. First, the curse was often used in relation to broken covenants both secular and cultic especially for Israel. Second, the prophets (viz., Jeremiah and Ezekiel) used the curse effectively and with increased frequency throughout the period leading up to the full exile of Judah, perhaps reflective of the increase in treaty relations between surrounding countries. Third, this well-known curse was used over a long period of time by different nations to evoke fear and submission in subservient persons or nations.[46] In light of this last conclusion it seems appropriate to look at extra-biblical examples where this curse is found.

ANE Imperial Writings and Treaty Parallels

It is no surprise that scholars have long noted the possible ANE covenant curse link to the mass array of unburied bones lying in the valley

---

44. We will return to this below.

45. Cf. 7:30–34; 8:2; 9:21 [Heb]; 12:9; 14:16; 15:1–5; 16:1–6; 19:1–7; 22:19; 25:33; 34:17–22; 36:30.

46. Cf. Gen 40:19—Egyptian; 1 Sam 17:43–44; 31:9–10—Philistine; 2 Sam 21:3–9—Gibeonite.

envisioned by Ezekiel (e.g., Wright,[47] Block,[48] Hillers[49]). There is little doubt that the scene is that of a battlefield, something all too common in the ANE of this period. In this vein, Herrmann notes that "in 9 erfahren wir auch, daß die Leichname die Körper von Getöteten sind; das heißt, sie sind gewaltsamen Todes gestorben. Das Totenfeld ist nicht ein Friedhof, sondern ein Schlachtfeld!"[50] Moreover, Brownlee goes so far as to identify the slain as the soldiers of Zedekiah (cf. Ezek 17:21).[51]

With the ever-increasing vying for hegemony over the Fertile Crescent, Egypt, Hatti, Assyria, and Babylon often engaged in battles that marred the landscape with very similar pictures of reality. For example, in the annals of Shalmaneser III we find the following description of a battle; "I felled their fighting men with the sword . . . piled up their (bodies) in ditches, [filled the extensive] plain with the corpses of their warriors, (and) with their blood I dyed the mountain red like red wool."[52] Later on at the famous battle of Qarqar (853 BCE) the same picture emerges with Shalmaneser noting, "I filled the plain with their spread out (lit. "I spread out") corpses (and) <felled> their extensive troops with the sword . . . The plain was too small to lay the (incredible number of) their bodies (lit. "lives") flat."[53] We could list dozens of examples from the Assyrian annals alone but suffice it to

---

47. Wright, *Message of Ezekiel*, 304. Ibid. goes on to note that the scene depicted in 37:1–14 is that of a people under curse even in death and that divine judgment had played the key role.

48. Block, *Ezekiel 1–24*, 228–29.

49. Hillers, *Treaty-Curses*, 68–69.

50. Herrmann, *Ezechiel*, 235. So too Biggs, *Ezekiel*, 117; and Baumgartner, *Alten Testament*, 361, who calls it a "Schlachtfeldsagen."

51. Brownlee, *Ezekiel 1–19*, xxxi. This conclusion is also implied by Streane, *Book of the Prophet Ezekiel*, 290; and Sweeney, "Ezekiel," 746. Note that Ezek 17:21 seems to imply the vast loss of life of Zedekiah's soldiers where מברח ("fugitives") can possibly be emended to מבחר ("choice men"). See discussion on the possibility of a metathesis with this word by, Wong, *Retribution*, 63 n. 184.

52. Grayson, RIMA 3/9–10. See also Grayson, RIMA 2/20, col iv lines 18–21 and col iv lines 89–94 which deal with similar terminology during the reign of Tiglath Pileser I. For a discussion on the mutilation of corpses in the ANE, see Richardson, "Death and Dismemberment," 189–208, esp. 196–200; Bahrani, *Rituals of War*; and Lemos, "Shame and Mutilation," 225–41.

53. Grayson, RIMA 3/23–24. This type of brutality was copied by the brief rule of his son Shamshī-Adad V; cf. Grayson, RIMA 3/186, lines 37–44a, and the earlier reign of Ashurnasirpal II; cf. Grayson, RIMA 2/197, lines 50–53; 199, lines 85–93.

say that such carnage was a common theme in most ANE empires. Although obviously hyperbolic in many cases, it is still no wonder that treaties made between these dominant powers and their vassals often turned to this curse as a means of controlling through fear. Hillers comments that in the treaties of the period it was this particular curse that caused the most distress.[54] He notes, "being left unburied as food for carrion-eaters . . . [was] a most horrible malediction, given the ancients' dread of such a fate."[55] A few examples should suffice to reinforce this conclusion.

The Prism of Esarhaddon

On the *Prism of Esarhaddon*, Esarhaddon (680–669 BCE) recounts how he defeated the remote desert land of Bâzu and left his defeated foes unburied. The text reads, 6. "the corpses of their warriors unburied I gave to the wolf to eat."[56]

The Vassal Treaties of Esarhaddon

The *Vassal Treaties of Esarhaddon* that were found in 1955 in a structure to the north of the temple of Nabû at Nimrod, have added much to the discussion of treaties in the later periods of the kingdoms of Israel and Judah. These treaties were made before Esarhaddon's death in order to solidify the successful transition of the Assyrian throne to his son Ashurbanipal and the throne of Babylon to his son Samash-shum-ukîn.[57] In this compendium of treaties, under the curse section, on lines 425–427, the text reads, "May Ninurta, leader of the gods, fell you with his fierce arrow, and fill the plain with your corpses, give your flesh to the eagles and vultures to feed upon."[58] Also, later on in the curse section of this treaty the same curse is reiterated in different

---

54. Launderville, *Spirit and Reason*, 336, comments that in Mesopotamia this was the most feared outcome of a person's life.

55. Hillers, *Covenant*, 137.

56. Thompson, *Prisms of Esarhaddon and Ashurbanipal*, 23, col. v, line 6.

57. Frankena, "Vassal-Treaties," 123–24.

58. "Vassal-treaties of Esarhaddon," *ANET*, 538, line 425. See also Frankena, "Vassal-Treaties," 145. Frankena notes that this curse closely parallels that found in Deut 28:26. Frankena also posits that Deut 28:20–57 parallels the curse section of Esarhaddon's Vassal-Treaties lines 414ff.

terms on lines 483–484, "... may the earth not receive your body for burial, may the bellies of dogs and pigs be your burial place...."[59] It is also noteworthy that in this same treaty the very first thing mentioned after the interlude of warnings from Esarhaddon on behalf of his son Ashurbanipal, the crown prince (i.e., lines 513–518), is the line, "May Palil, lord of first rank, let eagles and vultures eat your flesh" (lines 519–520).[60]

This particular curse was obviously a popular means to threaten individuals and nations during this period. The unburied bodies of warriors and victims of the battle must have been a disturbing picture for those of the ANE for it to be invoked several times in one list of curses as a threat to the one who broke treaty with Esarhaddon and his sons.

The Poem of Erra and Ishum and the Gilgamesh Epic

Beyond these curses in Esarhaddon's treaties, we also find references to this curse in other literature of the ANE. Even in the telling of stories and poems the threat of being left unburied puts the onus of the curse on the one reading the tale. One finds an example of this in the text of "Erra and Ishum," tablet IV lines 96–97, where the wrath of the gods is poured out on humanity for those who fail to obey the deity. The text states,

> 96. Yet shall I put the son to death and his father shall bury him.
>
> 97. Afterwards I shall put the father to death, and he shall have nobody to bury him.[61]

The wrath of the deity (i.e., Erra) is demonstrated by the horror of leaving individuals with no one to bury them. We also see the threat of unburied dead in the Epic of Gilgamesh.[62] Even though these examples are not from the treaty genre, the curse still has its desired effect of instilling fear and dread.

---

59. "Vassal-treaties of Esarhaddon," *ANET*, 539.
60. Ibid., 539.
61. "Erra and Ishum," *COS* 1.113:414.
62. Cf. "Epic of Gilgamesh," *ANET*, 83, tablet V lines 40–43.

Kudurru Inscriptions and other Engravings[63]

Other forms of inscriptions that often invoked this curse were *kudurru* (i.e., boundary marker) inscriptions and stone tablet engravings.[64] During the period of Nabû-Mukin-Apli (979–943 BCE) of the eighth dynasty in Babylon, we find a *kudurru* curse inscription which reads,

> 20) May Gula, the great lady,
>
> 21) cause there to be a wasting sickness in his body,
>
> 22) so that, as long
>
> 23) as he lives, dark and light blood like water
>
> 24) he may pass, and [his corpse]
>
> 25) may she de[prive] of burial![65]

Also, on a stone tablet engraving describing Nabû-Aplu-Iddina's (888–855 BCE) re-endowment of the sun temple at Sippar the following curse is given to those who dare violate the deed or attempt to destroy the record,

> 50) may his name perish,
>
> 51) may his seed be destroyed,
>
> 52) through oppression and hunger
>
> 53) may his life come to an end,
>
> 54) may his corpse be cast aside,
>
> 55) and may he have no burial![66]

In these first two examples, the threat of a horrific death by various means is followed by the ultimate curse of having one's body left unburied and cast by the wayside with the implication that the beasts and birds will consume and desecrate their corpses. However, there

---

63. For a general discussion on the curses related to the defacing of monuments and related texts see, Gevirtz, *Curse Motifs*, 51–66.

64. King, *Babylonian Boundary-Stones*, x–xi, suggests that the boundary stone curses were probably of Kassite origin and were used especially in hostile areas where a particular king or ruler may not have had the ability to defend properly private property. See also comments in Anderson, "Social Function," 231.

65. King, *Babylonian Boundary-Stones*, 62. See also the Eshmunazar inscription, Crawford, *Blessing and Curse*, 180.

66. King, *Babylonian Boundary-Stones*, 127.

are other examples that explicitly state the fate of someone's body if they failed to adhere to a particular law or written ordinance.

In two different tax exemption tablets, dated 657 BCE, from Ashurbanipal (668–627 BCE) to two men by the names Balṭaya (chief of fodder supplies) and Nabû-šarru-uṣur (a chief eunuch) we find the threat of the curse against any person who disturbed their graves.[67] In each of these texts the same phrase appears; "May the dogs tear apart his [i.e., the intruder's] corpse as it lies unburied."[68]

Interestingly, in several of these land grants and tax exemption tablets from the reign of Assurbanipal, this same phrase appears at the end of each curse section. It is apparent that this was a stock curse phrase used repeatedly during this period, which is a little over 50 years removed from Ezekiel's day. Again, the curse of having one's body devoured by dogs (cf. 2 Kgs 9:10, 36) must have been an effective means of coercing compliance.

We can conclude that the threats and covenant curses in the ANE and the OT that included the curse of non-burial had a wide and varied usage. It was not only used to depict the reality of war, but was also used in imperial writings, on boundary markers and other engravings, and in varied genres of literature in the ANE. Ezekiel also uses it effectively in various genre forms including oracles and visions. The prophet utilizes it as a curse against his own nation as well as a means of cursing foreign aggressors. Indeed, it is the latter use that highlights the restoration chapters of his book. But where did Ezekiel find a precedent for curse reversal, especially as it relates to foreign nations? It is to this we now turn.

Deut 30:3–7—The Transition from Cursing the House of Israel to Cursing the Nations

For Ezekiel his appropriation of this curse against the "house of Israel" for idolatry and covenant unfaithfulness (6:1–7, 13) and later as a means of hope (37:1–14), had both treaty-style implications as well as theological import. Furthermore, in these restoration chapters the

---

67. See further, Gevirtz, "West Semitic Curses," 137–58, esp. 148–49.

68. Kataja and Whiting, *State Archives*, 26, 28. The first text has some lacunas present but the second is complete (see pages 34–35 where it appears twice). Cf. also, Gevirtz, *Curse Motifs*, 79–85, esp. 85.

prophet uses the curse as a means of bringing judgment to the nations when he reversed it and placed it upon those that had misused Yahweh's people (cf. 35:15; 36:4–8).[69] The prophet may very well have had a textual precedent for this view from the promises found within Deuteronomy, particularly, 30:3–7.[70]

> And the Lord your God will restore you from your captivity and he will have compassion on you and he will gather you again from among the peoples where the Lord your God has scattered you. If your outcasts are at the ends of the heavens, from there the Lord your God will gather you and from there bring you back. And the Lord your God will bring you back to the land which your fathers possessed and you will posses it and he will do good to you and he will multiply you more than your fathers. And the Lord your God will circumcise your heart and the heart of your descendants, to love the Lord your God with all your heart and with all your soul in order that you might live. *And the Lord your God will place all these curses upon your enemies and all the ones who hate and persecute you.* (italics mine)[71]

Here in Deuteronomy we find the hope of restoration for the people of God after a period of exile among the nations. More importantly, however, is the promise that the curses, which have plagued the nation of Israel, will be placed upon her enemies.[72] Interestingly enough, this reversal comes after the promise of a new "heart" has been given to the people of God. No passage better exemplifies this picture in Deuteronomy 30 than that painted by Ezekiel in the restoration chapters (viz., 33–39) leading up to the temple vision in chs. 40–48.[73] The promise of a new heart in 36:26 followed by the promise

---

69. Cf. Wong, *Idea of Retribution*, 196.

70. I am not attempting here to defend the dating primacy of textual witnesses but rather desire to point out that the concept of this style of curse reversal must have been present at least during the period of the exile.

71. Wong, *Idea of Retribution*, 245, correctly notes that, "when a punishment inflicted on an offender is like the offence, there is retributive justice. Thus, by forging correspondences between punishment and offence, Ezekiel not only creates a link between these two, but also appeals to the fundamental idea that justice is done when punishment is like the offence."

72. In "The Lamentation over the Destruction of Sumer and Ur" we see a similar reversal of fortune on nations surrounding Sumer for their evil practices no doubt against Sumer. See Michalowski, *Destruction of Sumer and Ur*, 67–68.

73. Johnston, "Nahum's Rhetorical Allusions," 417, 434–35, suggests that Nahum's prophecy against Assyria appears to reflect a similar reversing of the curses once

of the gathering and restoration of Israel from the far reaches of the earth in 37:1–22 matches the restoration sequence laid out in this pericope found in Deuteronomy 30. Throughout Ezekiel 34–37 the Deuteronomic sequence unfolds as Ezekiel offers a ray of hope to the exiles. It is only the reversal of the curses onto the nations that remains to be fulfilled. However, this is not absent from the picture Ezekiel paints in the restoration chapters.

Ezekiel's vision of the valley of dry bones catches the reader's attention that something of fundamental importance is taking place in the text. As noted in our introductory remarks of this chapter, the curse of unburied bodies was a feared and defiling end for those of the ANE. Here the curse is adopted and positioned at this key juncture in Ezekiel's message. The vision of ch. 37 highlights this curse. Remarkably though, this same vision shows the reversal coupled with the promises of restoration and blessings. The vision of ch. 37 thus anchors this section of restoration oracles within the larger framework of Ezekiel's message and anticipates the total restoration and return of the temple of the Lord (37:28). Therefore as anticipated by the ongoing rhetorical argument, the final "peak" of the framework stands on the immediate horizon in chs. 40–48. But, as will soon be demonstrated, one final barrier stood in the way of this ultimate utopia, the complete annihilation of the enemies of Israel by Yahweh. Chapters 38–39 display this last shift of the reversal motif. However, before we tackle this message of punishment of the nations by means of the curse reversal, we must consider the OT and ANE precedents for the reversal of curses.

The Precedent for Curse Reversal in the OT and ANE [74]

It is important to realize the uniqueness of the reversal motif as found in the OT as compared to the glaring absence of it in ANE texts. While in the prophets there is always a distant hope that God will reverse the harshness of the curses of the Law, the ANE treaties offer no such abeyance, and the few cases of curse reversal are not found in a treaty

---

threatened against Judah by Assyria—what he calls "poetic justice." He proposes that it was this motif within Nahum's prophetic word that may have prompted Josiah to rebel against Assyrian domination.

74. This section follows closely the conclusions of Wolf, "Transcendent Nature," 319–25.

format.[75] For example, in later times, during the Neo-Assyrian period (ca. 912–612 BCE), the curse list of treaties became elongated and any hope of blessings was eliminated altogether.[76] Therefore, by the time of the recording of the Deuteronomistic History and the classical prophets in the OT, promises of curse reversal and restoration with abundance and blessing found within these texts was unlike any ANE treaty or "prophecy."[77]

Therefore, one can search in vain to find a similar picture of curse reversals in ANE texts as seen in OT texts. Some of the reason for this seems to be due in part to the ANE understanding of the certainty of enacted curses. Fensham points out that the curses of ANE treaties had a life of their own once they were enacted. Individuals believed that an inherent magical force insured that the curse would be fulfilled as promised at the behest of the gods. The OT curses of the Law stood apart from these ANE treaty and boundary marker curses in that the OT curses were controlled by an external force viz., Yahweh, who could exhibit *ḥesed* at will (e.g., 2 Sam 16:12).[78] Thus, the reversal of the curses within the context of a given prophet's message must be understood in the light of Yahweh's greater plan for his people and his covenant love.

Throughout the OT we find several texts that seem to indicate that individuals believed they could remove or void a curse by destroying its source. We see this in Abishai's desire to kill Shimei after he cursed David (2 Sam 16:9)—Solomon seems to follow up on this desire when he ultimately had Shimei killed (1 Kgs 2:46). Jeremiah also warned that his death at the hands of those who opposed his message would not remove the curse of exile that had emanated from Yahweh,

---

75. Ibid., 320. Wolf notes that one way the ancients reversed their curses was by making a blessing override the curse. He cites the Gilgamesh Epic as an example; "In the Gilgamesh Epic the doomed hero Enkidu curses the city of Erech and the woman who has introduced him to civilization, but he changes this curse to blessing when Gilgamesh points out the benefits of civilized society." Cf. also, Evans, "'A Plague,'" 81–85.

76. Wolf, "Transcendent Nature," 319. Wolf comments that many times the curses themselves were enough to keep the vassal in an unhappy political union.

77. Perhaps with the exception of the brief notes of blessing in the Akkadian *ex eventu* prophecies which will be covered in ch. 5 below.

78. Fensham, "Common Trends," 174. See also comments by Brueggemann, "On Coping with Curse," 175–92, esp. 180–87.

who was "indestructible" (Jer 26). Despite the warning, Jehoiakim still tried to cancel the pronounced curse by burning Jeremiah's scroll as he read it (cf. Jer 36:23). In Amos 7:12 Amaziah seeks to send Amos back to Judah and thus remove his words of cursing from Bethel. Similarly, in 2 Kings 22:11 and Jeremiah 36:24 the idea of rending one's garments seemed to ward off or postpone the curses of the covenant. In the former account, Josiah's actions do exactly that while in the latter case, Jehoiakim refuses to do so and receives the punishment of the curses. Finally, it appears that a curse could be overridden by speaking forth a blessing as found in Judges 17:2 (Micah and his mother) and Exodus 12:32 (pharaoh and Moses and Aaron).[79]

In these latter two biblical examples, we see a rapid shift from cursing to blessing through the timely intervention of the individual who had originally uttered the curse (i.e., Micah's mother in Judges and Moses in Exodus). In the prophetic texts this rapid shift is no less present whereby a prophet may utter a message of hope and blessing on the very heels of a curse (e.g., Ezek 11:17–20). Fensham, as does Wolf, points out that nowhere in the ANE treaty curses and *kudurru* inscriptions does one find such a rapid shift from curses to blessing as seen in the prophetic corpus.[80] In the classical prophets curse reversal and blessing is often portrayed in grandiose terminology that reflects the elevated status that Israel experienced at the hand of their covenant God. Isaiah's prophecies are a clear example of this. The author of Isaiah depicts the miraculous intervention of Yahweh on behalf of his people when he prophesies the return of the remnant from exile. In his prophetic discourse, wild beasts will do no harm, deserts will flow with streams, rugged places are made passable, Exodus imagery is instituted, and Yahweh will lead them as in the days of Moses (Isa 35:8–10; 40:3–4; 43:19; 52:12 respectively).[81] Curse reversals also in-

---

79. Blank, "Blasphemy," 93–95. Cf. also Wolf, "Transcendent Nature," 320, who notes Numbers 22–24 and the attempted cursing of Israel by Balaam at the behest of Balak; however, Yahweh made Balaam bless Israel instead. Wolf (321) also points out the indirect reversal of Jacob's cursing of Levi and Simeon for their treachery against Shechem (Gen 49:5–7). During the exodus, the tribe of Levi is given a blessing beyond the curse when the tribe of Levi is rewarded with priestly duties after they vigorously defended the covenant following the Golden Calf incident (cf. Exod 32:25–29—see also Josh 21:1–42). For comments on Judges 17, see J. V. Morris, "Curse," 547–48.

80. Fensham, "Common Trends," 174; and Wolf, "Transcendent Nature," 319–25.

81. Cf. Wolf, "Transcendent Nature," 320–24. Compare also Isaiah 32:9–14 to 32:15–16. Isaiah even presents a picture of true abundance for the animals (Isa 30:23–24; 32:20).

cluded the promise of the rebuilding of the city of Jerusalem, its walls, and the temple.[82] We see the fulfillment of these blessings in Isaiah 44:28; Amos 9:4; Jeremiah 31:38-40 and Ezekiel 37:26-27 and chs. 40-43. Finally, the return of the Davidic king is noted not only in Ezekiel 34:23 and 37:24-25, but also in Isaiah 9:7; 11:1; 16:5 and later in Jeremiah 30:21; 33:15, 21-22.[83]

Also in the prophetic corpus, the reversal of the ravages of war, exile, pestilence, famine, disease and general cursing are prevalent (e.g., Jer 31:13, 16-17; 32:37; compare Hos 1:9 to 2:23).[84] In this vein, after incessantly prophesying doom and curse, Amos can speak of the plenty to be reaped in the period of restoration (Amos 9:13), and Jeremiah can look forward to abundant harvests (compare Jer 12:10-11 to 31:12). Hosea also hoped for the return of plenteous crops (compare Hos 2:12 to 21-23)[85] and Joel, as did Ezekiel, saw Yahweh's provision of an abundance of water and rain as the measure of fertility in the land (Joel 3:18). The restoration of the people of Israel to their geographic homeland after exile and apparent loss of nationhood was a means by which Ezekiel depicted the blessing of Yahweh on his people. This blessing was a visible sign to the nations that Israel was indeed the chosen nation of Yahweh—a fact further bolstered by the promise of peace and safety from all outside attackers (cf. chs. 38-39).

As for the punishment/cursing of surrounding nations which we introduced above, Ezekiel uses this motif in a unique way. It is only Ezekiel who actually uses the curse visually (i.e., in a vision—ch. 37). He then reverses and transfers the curse to other nations (cf. chs. 25-32; 35-36 and 38-39). As we will demonstrate, Ezekiel's approach goes beyond the normal oracular and woe sections of the prophets (e.g., Amos 1:3—2:3). Ezekiel uses the oracles against the nations as a means of offering hope to the people of Yahweh and as a lesson to the surrounding nations that Yahweh is sovereign over their outcome as

---

82. Wolf, "Transcendent Nature," 324.

83. Ibid.

84. Ibid.," 321. Galambush, "This Land is my Land," 73, correctly notes that the curse of wild animals, pestilence, fire, famine, etc. is directly related to the destruction of order and the "takeover of chaos." Here in the restoration chapters order is restored on a grand scale to a level beyond anything before attained.

85. Wolf, "Transcendent Nature," 325 n. 13, points out the reversal of the threats found in Hosea 2:2-13 in light of the blessings in 2:14-23.

well.[86] It is for this reason that Ezekiel targets certain nations that had either broken covenantal relations with Israel and/or had oppressed the nation of Israel beyond measure—a reality revealed clearly in chs. 25–32.

Ezekiel 37–39 in the Context of Chapters 25–32[87]

The intervening chapters between the end of the indictments on the house of Israel (i.e., 4–24) and the "restoration chapters" (i.e., 33–48)[88] deal with oracles against the nations in typical prophetic fashion.[89] Before restoration could be fully realized for Israel though, the wrongs of the past, perpetrated by Israel's neighbors, had to be righted. Indeed, the taunts of her neighbours only compounded the hardships that Judah encountered in exile. Instead of her neighbours "mourning" with her in her time of trouble, they gloated over her demise and reveled in her misery while seeking how they could profit from her misfortune. Therefore, Yahweh begins the restoration process by consoling Judah through "redressing injustices" done to her by bringing similar curses upon those nations which had troubled her for so long.[90]

The seven[91] nations identified in Ezekiel's indictments and laments are: Ammon, Moab, Edom, and Philistia (ch. 25), Tyre and its

86. So too Petter, "Book of Ezekiel," 174–77, esp. 174. See also Davis, "And Pharaoh," 227–28.

87. Scholars often assert that chs. 25–32 are later additions or due to later "canonical ordering." See Childs, *Introduction*, 366. However, contra de Jong, "Ezekiel," 13, who posits that these chapters serve as an "interlude," these texts play a integral part in the shift from judgment to restoration where the nations now receive the brunt of Yahweh's wrath. For a brief discussion on the literary connections between the oracles in chs. 25–32 and the rest of the book, see Boadt, "Rhetorical Strategies," 196–99.

88. While these chapters are traditionally labeled the "restoration chapters," I contend that chs. 25–32 can to be included under this label as well.

89. As previously noted, Amos, in similar fashion, indicted the nations surrounding Israel because of their general display of injustice and their egregious mistreatment of the people of God. Also, I do not seek to claim any dating primacy of one text over the other by this statement, but rather that there appears to be a common theme within the prophets to indict the nations around Israel. Among other reasons, Hayes, "Oracles," 81–92, esp. 81–87, suggests that the oracles against the nations were similar to earlier declarations of war, preparations for battle (e.g., Balaam—Num 22–24; 1 Kgs 20:26–30; 2 Kgs 13:14–19), or lament rituals.

90. Petter, "Book of Ezekiel," 176. As noted in ch. 1 above, chs. 25–48 play a key part in the restoration motif in Ezekiel's message.

91. See Boadt, *Ezekiel's Oracles*, 8.

king (chs. 26–28),[92] Egypt, her pharaoh, and her allies (chs. 29, 30, 32), and Assyria (ch. 31).[93] The purpose of these chapters in this location of Ezekiel's message is instrumental to the overall presentation of the prophet's structural framework and rhetorical argument. With the bulk of the indictments against the people of Yahweh complete, the tide begins to turn as the prophet zeroes in on these particular nations.[94] Ezekiel's indictment of these nations, which were either blood relatives (e.g., Edom, Moab and Ammon) or covenant partners (e.g., Tyre—cf. 1 Kgs 5:12; Amos 1:9), fits well within Ezekiel's covenant context.[95] The remaining nations had either oppressed Israel and Judah with severe bondage, led them into idolatry (e.g., Egypt and Philistia),[96] or forced oppressive treaties upon them (e.g., Assyria).

For example, the extensive treatment of Egypt, her pharaoh, and her allies is representative of the rancor felt by the prophet and Yahweh

---

92. For a study on the mythological motifs in ch. 27, see Geyer, "Cosmic Ship," 105–26. For parallels between Ezekiel 27 and two ANE texts (i.e., a Sumerian hymn and *Enki and the World Order*), see Petter, "Book of Ezekiel," 188–89. For a comparison of Ezek 28:12–19 and Genesis 2–3, see Lind, *Yahweh Is a Warrior*, 124–25. For a similar comparison with Genesis (esp. 1:26) based upon the emendation of חוֹתֵם תָּכְנִית ("seal of perfection") to the appositional phrase, חוֹתָם תַּבְנִית (you were a "seal, likeness") in Ezek 28:12, see Callender, "Primal Man," 2:606–25.

93. Even though this oracle is addressed to Egypt and her pharaoh, the message tells of Assyria's downfall.

94. Joyce, *Ezekiel*, 43; and Greenberg, *Ezekiel 21–37*, 618, see the order of the dates for the oracles against Tyre and Egypt (26:1 and 29:1 respectively) as problematic and suggest redactional emendation after the fact. However, if Ezekiel was presenting his oracles in the order of covenantal importance or closeness, then the apparent "misordering" of the oracles makes sense. Tyre actually had a covenant relationship with Israel and had broken it. Egypt did not have a covenant in the same sense.

On the other hand, Davis, "And Pharaoh," 228, suggests that one of the reasons these oracles are included was due to the fact that these nations were "rebels" with Judah against the God-ordained power of Babylon. However, this does not appear to be the case at least for Edom. Furthermore, Ammon and Moab, who apparently rebelled *after* the fact, were defeated only in 581 BCE (cf. Josephus, *Ant.* 10:181 and Lods, *Prophètes*, 185). Christensen, "New Israel," 256, points out that Edom actually allied with Nebuchadnezzar against Judah.

95. There is also the possibility that Ezekiel's oracles against Tyre may reflect its role in introducing the rival Baal worship into Israel through Ahab's marriage to Jezebel who was from that country (1 Kings 17–21). See, further, Boadt, "Mythological Themes," 226–27.

96 Batto, *Slaying the Dragon*, 163, points out that Egypt was "the source of Israel's 'original sin' acquired in its youth" (cf. Ezek 20:7–8 and 23:3, 19, 27); so too Mendenhall, "Ancient Orietal," 38.

for Egypt's influence on the covenant people. Because Egypt had enticed the people of God to commit whoredoms and covenant infidelity unlike any other nation (cf. chs. 16 and 23),[97] special attention is given to her. Interestingly the prophet chooses an "exodus-style" curse to fulfill his needs. Egypt would be cursed with desolation and scattering for 40 years (cf. 29:12), a punishment that was once placed upon Israel (cf. Num 14:20–25 and Ezek 4:6). Similarly, Assyria had been cruel and overbearing beyond the commands of the Lord (Isa 10:12) and, as with Egypt, had led the nation astray cultically (cf. Ezek 23:5–7). Furthermore, in the past, Assyria in particular had defied the God of Israel (2 Kgs 18–19; Isa 36–37).

Finally, the Philistines also played a vital role in opposing Yahweh and his people. The Philistines had been a constant threat to not only the very existence of Israel but also her greatest king, David.[98] Yahweh had chosen David as a young man to be king over Israel (cf. 1 Sam 16) yet the first and last real military threat to his life came at the hands of the Philistines (1 Sam 17 and 2 Sam 21:16). Indeed, David appears in Ezekiel as the ideal king to rule in the period of Israel's renewal (explicitly in 34:23–24; 37:24–25 and implicitly in chapters 44–48). Therefore, Yahweh would vindicate his people and restore the land by beginning with the punishment of the nations for their treatment of his covenant people and desecration of the Promised Land. Motifs previously used to denote judgment against the people of Yahweh are now turned against the nations who had wreaked havoc on Israel and Judah. In this regard, Ezekiel's motif of choice was that of the sword.

---

97. For a detailed treatment of the oracles against Egypt in chs. 29–32, see Boadt, *Ezekiel's Oracles*. For a discussion of the common motifs within the oracles against Egypt and the Gog and Magog oracles, see Boadt, "Rhetorical Strategies," 198; and Nobile, "Beziehung," 256–58. While Nobile (256) proposes that 39:6–16 are editorial insertions because they break the flow from vv. 4–5 and v. 17, there is really no reason to believe such is the case if in fact the author was continuing to explain the degree of carnage that was going to ensue. It seems appropriate that after the description of this extended carnage and the reasons given for it that the animals and beasts *then* could feed.

98. The constant vying for hegemony in Israel and the coastal plain brought David into constant conflict with the Philistines as can be seen throughout 1 and 2 Samuel. Indeed, it was the Philistines who threatened to destroy the Davidic dynasty before it even began. This would have jeopardized the continuation of the Davidic covenant.

The Motif of the Sword Turned against the Nations

The sword motif is a fundamental link between the oracles of punishment against the house of Israel and the oracles against the nations. Beyond the extended use of the motif against the house of Israel in ch. 21 and its presence in the metaphors of chs. 16 and 23, the effects of the sword (i.e., war, pillaging, and punishment) appear in similar fashion being wielded against the nations.

With the exception of ch. 27,[99] this motif appears in some form in every chapter of this section.[100] However, the building of the tension and anger against the nations crescendos in ch. 32 against the nation of Egypt and her pharaoh.[101] As noted in ch. 3 above, Israel's political harlotry with the most detested nation of the ANE (at least for Israel) becomes a special focus of the prophet. Yahweh had entered into covenant with Israel immediately after their deliverance from the land of bondage yet the nation of Egypt had long been a rival suitor for the political and cultic affections of Yahweh's beloved people (cf. 23:3). For this reason, Ezekiel spares no animus in this final indictment where the sword motif appears in 16 of the 32 verses of ch. 32. Indeed, the final 13 verses of ch. 32 all contain this motif in some form.[102] Furthermore, the appearance of the nations of Meshech and Tubal in 32:26 and all the "chiefs of the north" (32:30) helps to link these chapters to the ultimate destruction of Yahweh's enemies in chs. 38–39. Along with this link though, we also see in ch. 32 Egypt, Assyria, Edom, and Elam all descending to Sheol. The motif of the sword and the picture of the slain going down to the "pit" (בוֹר— 32:18, 23, 24, 25, 29, 30; 31:14, 16; 26:20) sets the stage for the return of the nation of Israel from the grave (ch. 37:12–14) while preparing the reader for what is to unfold in chs. 38–39.[103]

---

99. For a discussion of the Tyrian metaphors in chs. 26–28, see Newsome, "Maker of Metaphors," 188–99. Cf. also Good, "Ezekiel's Ship," 79–103; and Durlesser, "Ship of Tyre," 79–93 (as cited by Block, *Ezekiel 25–48*, 51); and Corral, *Ezekiel's Oracles*.

100. Cf. 25:13; 26:6, 8, 11; 28:23; 29:8; 30:4, 5, 6, 11, 17, 21, 22, 24, 25; 31:17, 18; 32:10, 11, 12, 20 (twice), 21–32.

101. This chapter also includes references to Assyria, Edom, Elam, Sidon, Meshech, and Tubal.

102. Interestingly, within this oracular section, it is ch. 30 that ranks second in appearances of the motif (9 times) which also focuses on Egypt.

103. So too Power, "Iconographic Windows," 527.

This judgment on the nations is "accented," however, by one pervasive literary motif, namely, that all the nations, including the house of Israel, would come to the knowledge of Yahweh. For Israel, this would be nothing less than a reeducation process; for the nations it would be vindication for Yahweh's judgment on them and a means of teaching them the sovereignty of Israel's God.

The Motif of the "Knowledge of Yahweh"—A Sign of Covenant in the OT

The punishments meted out on the nation of Israel had not merely served to reprove but also to rehabilitate the nation through a reeducation process. For Ezekiel, a reversal of the curses would only come after a period of renewed "knowledge" of their Suzerain. Robert Dentan comments, "Yahweh had entered into a uniquely intimate personal relationship with Israel; [. . . this included] the importance of knowing certain theological facts: that Yahweh is the God of Israel (Deut 29:6; 1 Sam 17:46; Ezek 6:7; etc.), that he is the only God there is (Deut 4:39), that he has a definite moral character (Ps 119:75; Jonah 4:2), that he has done mighty acts for his people (Judg 2:10; Ps 78:4; Mic 6:5), that his will has been revealed in formulas that can be learned (Pss 78:5f.; 119:125)."[104] Due to Israel's lack of "knowing" Yahweh through these various aspects, the house of Israel was faced with the prospect of a reeducation process that would not be pleasant (chs. 1–24). It was this process of reeducation that caused Ezekiel to use the "recognition formula"[105] as readily as he did. On the other hand, Ezekiel's use of the

---

104. Dentan, *Knowledge of God*, 38, 39.

105. Zimmerli, *Erkenntnis*, called this the Erkenntnisformel ("formula of acknowledgement") as pointed out by Rendtorff, "Concept of Revelation," 41. Zimmerli, *I Am Yahweh*, 5–6, notes that this formula is normally in the shortened form "I am Yahweh" but is only found as such once in Ezekiel (cf. 38:16). He links the use of the phrase to the Holiness Code of Leviticus. In *Fiery Throne*, 88, Zimmerli also points to the parallels in Exod 20:2 and the revelation of Yahweh to Israel as the one who brought them out of bondage and entered into covenant with them. The formula as it appears in Ezekiel is a lengthened form found predominantly in Ezekiel. Cf. also Drewermann, *Ezechiel* ch. 2, "Ich Jahwe Bin," 69–97.

Zimmerli, *I Am Yahweh*, 1–28, covers primarily the shortened form "I am Yahweh" and its origins. Here I draw out the peculiarity of the lengthened form as a means of showing the desire for Ezekiel to stress the need for the covenant community to come to a renewed knowledge of their Suzerain. A similar "recognition formula" also appears in ANE texts. An example can be found in the "Akkadian Oracles and

formula in the oracles against the nations served another purpose altogether. In chs. 25–39 the nations' acknowledgment of Yahweh would not be restorative in nature, but rather retributive.

Knowledge Equals Covenant

Huffmon has written a concise, but definitive, article in which he has posited that the terminology and concept of the knowledge of one's suzerain (i.e., "to know") was equal to observing a treaty or covenant. He gives examples from Hittite literature,[106] the Amarna Letters[107] and letters to Esarhaddon,[108] as well as the OT, to bolster his position. In several of the OT covenant stories we see examples of "mutual legal recognition."[109] For example, in Genesis 18:19 the covenantal relationship of Abraham and Yahweh is epitomized in Yahweh's statement, "for I know him" (כִּי יְדַעְתִּיו). Later, in 2 Samuel 7:20, David's covenantal relationship with the Lord is acknowledged in David's statement, "for you have known your servant, O Lord God" (יָדַעְתָּ אֶת־עַבְדְּךָ אֲדֹנָי יְהוִה). Examples of a direct covenant link and Israel's responsibility to "know" her God can best be seen in Hosea 13:4–5; verse 4 reads

וְאָנֹכִי יְהוָה אֱלֹהֶיךָ מֵאֶרֶץ מִצְרָיִם וֵאלֹהִים זוּלָתִי לֹא תֵדָע וּמוֹשִׁיעַ אַיִן

Prophecies," *ANET*, 450, line 16, "Fear not, Esarhaddon! I, the god Bel, speak to you," and line iii 15, "I am Ishtar of Arbela, O Esarhaddon king of Assyria."

Twice Ezekiel uses a variation of the phrase that is directly linked to his call and his message; "then they will know that a prophet has been among them" (2:5; 33:33). In each case the message delivered by Ezekiel, at the instruction of Yahweh, will be proof of Ezekiel's call and of the validity of Yahweh's word through him.

106. King Suppiluliumas to his vassal Ḫuqqanas, "And you Ḫuqqanas know only the Sun (ᵈUTU^ši-pat . . . šāk) regarding lordship; also my son, (of) whom I, the Sun say, 'This one everyone should know (šakdu),' . . . you, Ḫuqqanas, know him (apūn šā[k])!" Cf. Huffmon, "Treaty Background," 31–33.

107. In a letter from Abdi-Ashirta, king of Amurru, to his suzerain, pharaoh Amenophis III, Abdi-Ashirta says, "May the king my lord know me (*lu-ú yi-da-an-ni*) and put me under the charge of Paha(m)nate, my royal governor." Cf. Huffmon, "Treaty Background," 32.

108. A letter to Esarhaddon, speaking about the Cimmerians, "They are nomads, they know neither an oath by the god(s) nor a sworn agreement [treaty]" (*zēr ᴸᴼḫalqātî šunu [mā]mēti ša ili u adê ul idû*). Cf. ibid., 33.

109. Ibid., 34.

"For I am Yahweh your God from (the time of your sojourn in) the land of Egypt, and you will *know* no god except me, for there is no savior except me."

Huffmon has pointed out that here the knowledge of the Lord was in essence the equivalent to covenant.[110] This concept meshes well with my belief that Ezekiel used the term in order to emphasize the need to bring Israel back to the covenant knowledge of her God.

Interestingly, Hosea[111] had long before noted the inherent problem with the people's failure to have a proper knowledge of their God (Hos 4:6).[112] In any covenant relationship knowing the responsibilities of each of the parties was vital to success. The nation as a whole had failed to understand the scope of their sin, which was directly connected to their lack of knowledge of the laws of the covenant and, by extension, Yahweh (cf. Ezek 7:26; 22:26 compare Lev 10:10–11).[113] The resulting punishment and curses they were to experience became the only legitimate action Yahweh could take to bring his people to their knees.

In this vein, it is clear according to Fishbane that the house of Israel "will, in the future, have the knowledge, which is now lacking, that YHWH is a god of power who fulfills his doom predictions as announced."[114] He continues that for those of the exilic community (and generations to come) the prophecy of Ezekiel would be a means of educating the nation that the exile was not due to an impotent deity, "but is rather because a providential and powerful Judge has left his shrine and land in revulsion of the abominations performed there."[115]

---

110. Ibid., 34–35. Other texts include Deut 9:24; 1 Sam 2:12; Jer 12:3; Hos 2:22; 4:1; 8:2 and Isa 19:21 (here dealing with the future conversion of Egypt).

111. Zimmerli, *I Am Yahweh*, 87–88, notes that while Hosea speaks a lot about the knowledge of God he does not actually mention the formula. Jeremiah mentions it once in 24:7, while "Deutero-Isaiah" and Joel are the only books that show "any clear influence of the formula."

112. Huffmon, "Treaty Background," 37, links this passage with a lack of knowledge of the covenant obligations the priests were to instruct the people in.

113. Mein, "Ezekiel as a Priest," 201–3.

114. Fishbane, "Sin and Judgment," 149. Also, Seitz, "Ezekiel 37:1–14," 55, bolsters this understanding when he notes that "Ezekiel is a man of extremes. Over and over again he speaks of Israel coming to knowledge of God only by means of affliction and severe punishment."

115. Fishbane, "Sin and Judgment," 149.

Therefore, judgment was required in order that the people/nation would come to a renewed understanding of Yahweh and hopefully, be obedient to the covenant. Yahweh was acting within covenant guidelines to effect change in the lives of his covenant community. Short of total annihilation, an option not available to Yahweh based on the previous promises to the patriarchs, Yahweh therefore enacted the covenant stipulations as found in Deuteronomy and Leviticus. Thus, he acted, in an ANE legal manner, to bring his covenant people back into proper relationship with their Suzerain.[116] Following typical suzerain protocol, Yahweh could therefore invoke military action, the horrors of war, exile, famine, siege and the like, which were common in the treaty curses of the ANE of the period. Conversely, as the God over all the earth, these same curses were available for him to use against the nations.

The Recognition Formula: A Theological Lesson

The recognition formula, presented as, and "you/they[117] will know[118] that I am Yahweh"[119] also plays an important role in the presentation

---

116. Contra Zimmerli, *I Am Yahweh*, 88, who does not see the personal restoration of the individual as the primary concern in Ezekiel's use of the formula. However, in the context of the overall message of Ezekiel, it seems clear that bringing about a personal knowledge of Yahweh in the lives of the Hebrew people was a vitally important part of Ezekiel's use of the phrase.

117. The verbal form of ידע ("to know") can vary between the third person masculine plural and the second person singular and plural (masculine and feminine—Isa 49:23). Zimmerli, *I Am Yahweh*, 30, noting Mandelkern's concordance, points out that of the 947 verbal occurrences of the stem for the verb "to know," 99 appear in Ezekiel (first among all the OT books) with the Psalms running a close second at 93. Ezekiel's use of this term appears most frequently in conjunction with the recognition formula.

118. On two occasions in Ezekiel the verb ראה ("to see") appears with a similar meaning as ידע ("to know"). These include 20:48 and 39:21. Bodi, *Poem of Erra*, 302–3, argues that a similar motif appears in the *Poem of Erra* (V 61) as, "may the people of the world see it and glorify my name" (*nišī dadmê limurama lišarba šumī/ē*) [see also similar wording in I 75]. He posits that it served the same function in the Akkadian poem as it does here in Ezekiel, that being, to educate the nations concerning the might of Erra. Although there may be a possible link between the two texts on thematic grounds, perhaps such common linguistic formulae can best be attributed to Ezekiel's use of an already existent OT motif. It is my position that Ezekiel's use of ANE symbolism and motifs is best reserved for connections more obvious and plausible which can best be explained by looking to the book's Mesopotamian setting in more general terms.

119. See also comments on divine self-revelation in Gunkel, *Genesis*, 263.

of the curse and the restoration/reversal motifs in the second half of the book. This phrase, or a slight variation of it, appears no less than 63 times in Ezekiel alone.[120]

Ezekiel uses the formula consistently until 39:28.[121] Only 13 of the first 39 chapters fail to use the recognition formula in some form.[122] The importance of its regular appearance throughout the book points to a fundamental problem that had developed in the life of the nation of Israel: they had failed to maintain a proper knowledge of Yahweh. One could easily argue that it was this lack of knowledge that brought about the covenant curses in the first place (cf. Jer 4:19–22). In this vein Rendtorff's comment reinforces my position when he avers that "in Ezekiel, the formula of acknowledgement is exclusively connected with the words of judgment."[123] Rendtorff goes on to temper this "ex-

---

120. While I will focus on the clear passages where the formula is used (i.e., "then they/you will know that I am the Lord,") there are, nonetheless, several variations of this formula in Ezekiel. For example, "To make myself known to them" 20:5, 19; "I am the Lord your God" 20:7, 19; they will "know the Lord has spoken" 5:13; 17:21; 37:14; they will "know the Lord does the smiting" 7:9; 21:2; 22:22; they will "know I have not done this in vain" 14:23; they will "know the Lord is with them" 34:30; they will know "the Lord has heard" 35:12; and the nations will know "that the Lord has rebuilt the ruined places" 36:36.

121. See comments in footnote 156, below.

122. These include: 1–5; 8–10; 18; 19; 21; 27; and 31. The absence of the formula may be stylistic or have a different explanation. For example, in the first three chapters this omission is understandable because of the calling of the prophet (chs. 1–3). However, even in the sign act chapters of 4 and 5 we see that these chapters serve as a means of establishing exactly what the nature of the judgment against the nation would be on a broad scale. The note in 5:8–9 sets the stage for the particular indictments and curses that follow. Thus the formula does not fit the genre and immediate purposes of the prophet. It is for this reason that 6:7, 10, 13, 14 repeat the recognition formula as the basis for what is coming upon the nation. In chs. 8–10 the focus is a visionary picture of the sin of the people. In this case no action by Yahweh (perhaps with the exception of the vision of ch. 9) is present. The departure scene in 11:22–24 is prefaced with the formula twice in vv. 10 and 12. Here, as the vision of chs. 8–11 ends, all the prophet had seen in the vision is for the purpose of bringing Judah to the knowledge of the Lord. Chapter 18 focuses on individual responsibility for sin and serves more as an excursus in the middle of the nation-centered indictments. Chapter 19 is a short lament for the princes (i.e., kings) of Judah and the loss of a Davidic leader in Judah. Chapter 21 is the "song of the Sword" and while the rigid formula is absent it is implied in 21:5. As with ch. 19, ch. 27 is a lament and does not lend itself to the formulaic phrase. Finally, ch. 31 is an allegory of Assyria's fall as a lesson to Egypt. In this allegory, as in chs. 16 and 23, the insertion of the phrase would break the flow. Perhaps it is for this reason that the formula in chs. 16 and 23 is placed at the very end.

123. Rendtorff, "Concept of Revelation," 44. Rendtorff stresses the appearance of the formula as a means of Yahweh's "self-vindication." While this is definitely a part of

clusive" connection of the phrase to judgment by pointing out that the promise of restoration is also closely associated with the formula especially in the later chapters of Ezekiel.[124]

Returning to our immediate focus on the nations, the phrase also occurs within the framework of judgment on Israel's enemies (e.g., the Ammonites in 25:3-5).[125] The use of the phrase against the nations shows the importance of the prophetic message in bringing the various nations to the knowledge of Yahweh as well. Many times this lack of knowledge was directly related to their hubris and their ill treatment of Yahweh's people. Ezekiel appears to be using it in a twofold manner: first to vindicate the enacted judgment for a particular nation's sins, and, second, to heighten the anticipatory nature of the curse reversal developed fully in chs. 35-39. Part of the nations' procurement of this knowledge of Yahweh would come at their expense through the reversed curses, while the house of Israel would benefit from the promised blessings when this reversal was enacted.

It must be pointed out, however, that Ezekiel's stressing that the nations come to the knowledge of Yahweh rests more on a theological premise than a restorative or salvific motivation for the nations, a fact readily apparent in chs. 38-39. As prophets such as Habakkuk had struggled with the apparent "free pass" given to Babylon and other enemies of Israel, Ezekiel sought to remedy a misunderstood theological concept within the nation and especially those in exile. Indeed, the people of Judah would suffer exile at the hands of nations far worse than they, but in the grand scale of Yahweh's plan even those nations would come to a "knowledge" of Yahweh, much to their chagrin, through harsh judgment. Contextually it appears that the nations' knowledge of Yahweh would not be in a covenantal sense, but rather much in the same manner that Nebuchadnezzar and Darius came to acknowledge the power and supremacy of the God of Daniel (cf. Dan 2-6). Thus, the predominant use of the recognition formula in the oracles is for the sole purpose of bringing the people, whether Hebrew or Gentile, to a knowledge of Yahweh as sovereign Lord. The difference

---

the reason it is used here, the concept of the reeducation of Israel plays just as much a part, if not more so. To bring Israel back into covenant and back into their homeland would, by extension, vindicate the claims of her God and his power (chs. 36-39).

124. Ibid., 44.
125. Zimmerli, *I Am Yahweh*, 32-33.

for the Israelites would be the restorative nature and the future hope of complete reconciliation with their covenant God.

Chapters 37–39 in Context: The Recognition Formula, Restoration, and Curse Reversal in Chapters 33–39

Chapter 33: The Fall of Jerusalem—An Interlude

The fall of Jerusalem recorded in ch. 33 marks a key turning point in Ezekiel. Much like ch. 12, ch. 33 serves a transitional function within the book. Chapter 33 picks up once again on the judgment motif against the house of Israel last seen in chs. 4–24 while acting as an interlude between the past indictments and curse reversals against the nations in chs. 25–32 and those yet to come in chs. 35–39.[126] In similar fashion the watchman (צֹפֶה)[127] motif of 3:17–21 is resumed here in 33:1–9.[128] Where 3:17–21 had a legal nuance (a fitting correlation to our ongoing theme of covenant curses in chs. 4–24), 33:1–9 has a "military" tone.[129] This change in nuance for the watchman motif meshes well with the retributive and war-like presentation of Yahweh against the nations, especially in chs. 35 and 38–39.

The primary focus of the prophet at first glance appears to change from the nations to Judah but upon closer examination of the context we see merely a momentary reprieve from the prophet's pronouncements of judgment on the nations in order to bring clarification on a couple key points. First, this interlude announcing the fall of Jerusalem served as a justification of the prophet's message (he was correct about the judgment on the nation so he will no doubt be correct about the

---

126. The curse reversal vis à vis Judah and the nations is more implicit in the oracles against the nations in chs. 25–32. In chs. 35–39 the presentation becomes more explicit with linguistic comparisons in chs. 35–36 and then more striking parallels using visual aspects in chs. 37–39.

127. For a discussion of the nuances of being a "watchman" or "guard" here and in 2 Kgs 6:8–23, Exod 18:13–27 and 2 Chronicles 19, see Simian-Yofre, "Wächter," 151–62.

128. Ezekiel served as a watchman to the exiles, not to Judah directly—Jeremiah served in that capacity. So too the conclusion of Renz, *Rhetorical Function*, 81; and Power, "Iconographic Windows," 527.

129. Wilson, "Ezekiel's Dumbness," 96. The appearance of the sword motif in 33:3 also resonates with its ubiquitous use in the oracles against the nations in chs. 25–32 (see above).

restoration) and a climax to the long period of judgment on the geographical region of Judah (33:21, 30–33). Second, those who remained in the land after the fall of Jerusalem would not inherit the land even though they thought they had survived Yahweh's wrath and were blessed by him (33:23–29).[130] On the contrary, those remaining in the land are now likened to the surrounding nations. Therefore, as with the surrounding nations, Yahweh would finish his judgment upon them in order that they may know who Yahweh truly was (33:29).

In the same chapter we also see the marked shift from the homeland to the exilic community as Yahweh pleads with the exiles, much in the same manner as he had in ch. 18, to choose life and not death (33:10–20). Chapters 33 and 34 serve as a final word of warning to the individual (33:7–20) and a final rebuke to Judah's leaders (34:1–22). Ezekiel closes the door on those left in Israel and turns his message to those in exile; *they* were the future of the nation, not the ones left in the land of Israel. It would be the exiles who would return and begin again after 70 years of exile.[131]

Chapter 34: A Covenant of Peace Promised [132]

In ch. 34 the full power of Ezekiel's message of Yahweh's restoration begins with Yahweh's promise to eliminate the rule of the evil shepherds[133]

---

130. See also Petter, "Book of Ezekiel," 135; and Block, *Ezekiel 1–24*, 347, for parallels with 11:15 and the attitude of the exiles at that time.

131. Based upon a possible first exile in the early reign of Nebuchadnezzar (ca. 605/4 BCE).

132. Boadt, "Salvation Oracles," 13–14, argues convincingly for the thematic unity between 34:16–38 and ch. 20.

133. Besides the numerous occurrences of this designation in the Bible (e.g., David—1 Sam 16; Ps 78:70–72; Cyrus—Isa 44:28, Yahweh—Pss 23; 77:22 [Eng]; 78:52–53; 80:1 [Eng]; 95:7; 100:3), the use of the term "shepherd" (רֹעֶה) as a designation for rulership in the ANE was a common idiom stretching from Mesopotamia to Egypt. For example, see "The Laws of Hammurabi," *COS* 2.131:336: "I am Hammurabi, the shepherd, selected by the god Enlil." In Egypt one of the objects carried by the pharaoh was the shepherd's crook. Cf. Wright, "Good Shepherd," 44. For a detailed list of Egyptian iconography and texts, see Durlesser, *Metaphorical Narratives*, 10–15. Also in a text from the reign of Shalmaneser III, dating to about 856 BCE we read of Shalmaneser the "pious one, who ceaselessly provides for the Ekur, faithful shepherd who leads in peace the population of Assyria." Cf. Grayson, RIMA 3/7. We also have texts where Shalmaneser says, "When Aššur, the great lord, chose me in his steadfast heart (and) with his holy eyes and named me for the shepherdship of Assyria" Cf.

by leading his "sheep" himself through his servant David (34:1–24).[134] Ezekiel's oracles against flawed leadership (cf. 8:7–15; 11:1–3 and chs.13, 17, and 19) are replaced by a message of hope for future godly rule.[135] The promise of a covenant of peace (בְּרִית שָׁלוֹם) followed by the recognition formula (34:27, 30)[136] highlights the shift from judgment to the restorative acts of Yahweh. The language of vv. 25–31 echoes that of Micah 4:4 and Lev 26:4–13[137] with the hope of rest, peace, and plenty under the rule and safety of Yahweh their Shepherd.[138] Moreover, the covenant language (i.e., "my people" עַמִּי and "house of Israel" בֵּית יִשְׂרָאֵל) of verse 30 amplifies the new reality that the prophet wants

---

Grayson, RIMA 3/13–14. In the period of Gudea on a statue of the king an inscription reads, "when Ningirsu had directed his meaningful gaze on his city, had chosen Gudea as the legitimate shepherd in the land, and when he had selected him by his hand from among 216,000 persons." Cf. Edzard, RIME 3/1, 32, Statue B, col iii, lines 6–11; page 41, Statue D, col i, lines 11–16; page 69, Cylinder A, col i, lines 26–28 and col xi, line 1. Tiglath-pileser I is also called a shepherd of his people in his annals. See Grayson, RIMA 2/13, col. i lines 30–34 and similar terminology for Adad-nārārī II in Grayson, RIMA 2/147, lines 5–10. Also much earlier in the Ur III Period during the reign of Šū-Sîn we see a similar designation for the ruler. Cf. Frayne, RIME 3/2, 317, col. x, lines 11–12; and further on page 357. See further, Niehaus, *Ancient Near Eastern Themes*, 34–50. For a discussion on the concept of god-king connections in Assyria and Babylon, see Labat, *Caractère Religieux*.

134. Whether or not Ezekiel is borrowing from his older contemporary Jeremiah (cf. Jer 23:1–4) cannot be known for certain; nevertheless, his message resonates with a promise of divinely appointed kingship reconstituted and overseen by Yahweh himself.

135. Mein, "Unprofitable Shepherds," 493–504, forcefully argues that the picture being presented in ch. 34 must be interpreted in light of actual ANE shepherding contracts. The shepherds were not allowed to abuse the sheep, and they had to provide the owner of the sheep with a reasonable return from the flock in milk, wool, and offspring. Because the evil shepherds of Israel had failed to treat the "sheep" of Yahweh properly, Yahweh himself would come and take care of them thus showing his prerogative for dominance, ownership, and control more so than his desire to show love for the sheep. Mein's position helps shed light on the metaphor but to what degree the oracle fails to show Yahweh in "loving" terms is debatable especially in light of 34:12–16.

136. Boadt, "Salvation Oracles," 10, connects these verses and v. 31 to Lev 26:12.

137. Renz, *Rhetorical Function*, 107, rightly points out the Leviticus 26 connection. This is vital in connecting the restoration oracles with curse reversals. See also Boadt, "Salvation Oracles," 9–11.

138. Petter, "Book of Ezekiel," 179–85, argues that ch. 34 serves as a pattern for the remaining chapters. This indeed seems to be a valid assumption especially considering the role chs. 4–7 played as an overview for the rest of the oracles of judgment on Judah (see my ch. 2 above).

his readers to know regarding their relationship with their Suzerain—Yahweh viewed them not as the once "rebellious house" of earlier days but as his renewed covenant people.[139] The "house of Israel" would now begin to see their covenant God work on their behalf against all those who had oppressed and had taken advantage of them in their greatest moment of despair. No one nation had been guiltier of this very act than their brother, Edom.

Chapters 35 and 36: Edom and the House of Israel Juxtaposed[140]

Ezekiel's juxtapositioning of the material in chs. 35 and 36 dealing with Edom and the house of Israel, respectively, highlights Yahweh's anger against those who had misused Israel.[141] Indeed, by focusing on the renewal of the land of promise, the oracles against Edom become the exemplar for Yahweh's vindication of his punishment against the nations who have invaded the land (cf. 36:5–7). This chapter further serves as a means to set the tenor of curse reversal in the remaining fourteen chapters. Ezekiel chooses the one nation that was closest to Israel, relationally, to transfer the curse to. The purpose is clear: Edom should have known better and had compassion on his brother (cf. Ps 137:7; Lam 4:21–22; Amos 1:11–12). The centuries-long struggle boils to the surface in full view for Ezekiel's audience. The words of Yahweh in the last verse of ch. 35 reinforce this reversal motif.

כְּשִׂמְחָתְךָ לְנַחֲלַת בֵּית־יִשְׂרָאֵל עַל אֲשֶׁר־שָׁמֵמָה כֵּן אֶעֱשֶׂה־לָּךְ שְׁמָמָה תִהְיֶה
הַר־שֵׂעִיר וְכָל־אֱדוֹם כֻּלָּהּ וְיָדְעוּ כִּי־אֲנִי יְהוָה

---

139. Cf. also Eichrodt, *Ezekiel*, 484.

140. For a detailed form-critical and literary analysis of these two chapters, see Simian, *Die theologische Nachgeschichte*. Note also the summary of Irwin, "Exegetical Study," 72, where he states that "the parallel structure of the message makes it clear that what will be done in a negative sense to Edom will be done in a positive sense to Israel."

141. Wevers, *Ezekiel*, 5, asserts that the only reason chs. 35 and 36 are placed together is due to the mention of Edom in both chapters. Also, Cooke, *Ezekiel*, 372, suggests that ch. 35 was "inserted to sharpen the threats in 36:1–7." Siegman, *Book of Ezechiel* 2:16, calls this chapter a "footnote to Jerusalem's fall." However, contrary to these stated opinions, the linguistic complexity of these oracles betrays a much deeper purpose than a mere surface comparison.

"Because you rejoiced over the inheritance of the house of Israel because of its *desolation*, thus I will do to you; you will be a *desolation*, O Mount Seir, and all Edom, all of it. Then you will know that I am the Lord" (italics mine).

Here it is clear that the judgment enacted against Edom will include the curses once placed upon Israel. Ezekiel appears to be using this as the prototypical response of Yahweh against Israel's enemies in general.[142] Furthermore, the use of the word שְׁמָמָה ("desolation") for both the desolation of Israel and the judgment of Edom in this one verse reinforces the intent of the prophet in his use of the reversal motif.

Another area of contact between these two chapters includes the use of the alpine motif to address both nations.[143] In 35:4, 9, 12, and 15 the phrase "Mount Seir" (הַר שֵׂעִיר) is used as a metaphor for Edom. This metaphorical connection is mirrored in the prophet's use of the phrase "the mountains of Israel" (הָרֵי יִשְׂרָאֵל) as a designation for the nation of Israel in ch. 36 (cf. 36:1, 4, 6, and 8—also "heights" in verse 2).[144] Moreover, within the oracle against Edom in ch. 35 the author uses this exact terminology found in ch. 36 to address Israel (cf. 35:12). Also, Edom's taunt and desire to possess the land of his brother (35:10–12) is revisited in 36:2 where Edom is addressed only as "the enemy" (הָאוֹיֵב) who sought to "possess" the "everlasting heights" of Israel. Finally, it should be no surprise that in 36:5 Edom is the only nation noted by name—a clear link to the previous chapter and its content.[145]

---

142. Boadt, "Salvation Oracles," 11, also suggests Edom is representative of all the nations. He posits that because Edom actually occupied the southern portion of Judah as their own, Edom was the most culpable in their abuse of Israel (cf. Isa 14:24–27 for a similar case with Assyria). Renz, *Rhetorical Function*, 108–9, also argues that Edom is representative of the nations as a whole but suggests, what I feel correctly, that the remnant of Israelites in the land are being amalgamated into the "nations" and thus being judged for their unjust claims on the land. While this latter aspect does seem to find validity in the prophet's presentation here and in ch. 33, rhetorically, there seems to be a much deeper covenantal purpose in chs. 35 and 36 which Renz and others have missed.

143. See also Gosse, "Ézéchiel," 511–17.

144. Cf. also Cassuto, "Book of Ezekiel," 239.

145. The use of "all Edom" (אֱדוֹם כֻּלָּהּ) in both places lends further credence to the parallels.

Another point of contact is the notation that the mountains will be the place of judgment as seen in 35:8. In this verse, bodies are left unburied (cf. also 32:5–6; 39:4, 17) a setting anticipatory of 37:1–14 and reminiscent of 6:1–14.[146] In 35:8 the slain of Edom will not only be left upon the mountains, but also upon the hills, and in the valleys and ravines. The same topographical designations and parameters are used in ch. 36 as places of blessing and not cursing for Israel (cf. 36:4, 6, 8–12) thus paralleling the scene of devastation in ch. 35 but in a reversed context. We can assert then, that the prophet's use of the quartet of the terms "mountains" (הָרִים), "hills" (גְּבָעוֹת), "ravines" (אֲפִיקִים), and "valleys" (גֵּאָיוֹת) in both oracles is obviously intended to point out the reversal comparisons. As for Israel, Ezekiel's paralleling of these topographical limits closely resembling those found in 6:3, draws attention to the reality that the prophet wanted to prove once and for all that the curses were indeed being reversed.[147] Israel had suffered both the literal and metaphoric punishment of the Lord through the curse of being cast, unburied, over the farthest stretches of the land. Now hope for new life was in sight—a picture that aptly unfolds in ch. 37.

On a larger scale, motifs in ch. 36 also serve as a means of bridging chs. 37–39 with those prior to ch. 36. The shift in focus in ch. 36 to include all the nations (36:5) helps set the stage for the international scene of chs. 38 and 39. The focus on the alpine motif in ch. 36 as a place of blessing (e.g., 36:8–12) is a reversal of the use of the mountains as a place of punishment for both Israel and the nations throughout the entire book.[148] In this vein, the use of both of the phrases "mountains of Israel" and "mountains" here in ch. 36 recalls the same terminology in 6:3–4, and 13 while looking forward and connecting the motif with the picture of hope in 37:22. The difference is that in ch. 6 judgment

---

146. Gosse, "Ézéchiel," 511–13 and Batto, *Slaying the Dragon*, 157. Gosse and Batto suggest, as do I, that the curse that we see in ch. 6 once placed upon Israel is now reversed here in ch. 36 and placed upon Edom in ch. 35. However, Gosse (513) correctly points out that while the curses may be the same in many respects, the "motivation" for the curses is totally different. Israel's was due to idolatry, Edom's was due to their hatred for, and mistreatment of, the covenant nation of Israel. Again, while this is a valid point, within the context of curse reversal, broken covenant alliances (civic and familial) seem to be also a vital part of Ezekiel's motivation.

147. Gosse, "Ézéchiel," 514–16.

148. Cf. 7:7–9; 19:9; 31:12; 32:5–6; 33:28; 34:6; 35:8; 38:8, 20, 21; 39:2, 4, 17. Boadt, "Rhetorical Strategies," 191, also draws parallels with the mountain imagery here and in ch. 6.

(pictured as the curse of being left unburied) took place upon the "mountains of Israel" for idolatry while in chs. 36 and 37 the curse is reversed and the mountains are now a place where blessings abound.[149]

Returning to our discussion concerning Yahweh's purpose in reversing the curse, the use of the recognition formula four times in ch. 36 (36:11, 23, 36, 38) reinforces this paradigm shift not only against Edom, but also for the nations in general. Two of the occurrences of the recognition formula are for the benefit of the nations so that they might know that the God of Israel was responsible for both the judgment and blessing of Israel (vv. 23, 36). On the other hand, two of the occurrences appear to be for the benefit of his covenant people themselves (vv. 11, 38). Note, however, that within the context of ch. 36 the reason for Yahweh's beneficent actions on Israel's behalf does not rest upon *their* actions, but rather it would be for the sake of Yahweh's holy name, which they had profaned (36:21, 22).[150] In similar fashion Yahweh had shown his loving kindness to Israel in the wilderness (cf. Ezek 20:9, 14, and 22) despite Israel's rebellious nature. Interestingly, here in ch. 36 once the people receive their new heart they will desire to follow Yahweh's ordinances and laws. This is the opposite situation in which the people found themselves in Ezekiel 20.[151] In a display of reversed spiritual inclinations, the waywardness that had once plagued the children of Israel is now removed from their hearts and replaced with obedience, blessing, and prosperity. The cleansing of Israel from the "filthiness of their idols," the giving of a new heart and spirit (36:26–27), and their desire to follow the statutes (חֻקִּים) and the

---

149. Gosse, "Ézéchiel 35–36, 1–15," 511–17, suggests there is a transfer of the "maledictions" of ch. 6 to Edom in ch. 35. On the other hand, Renz, *Rhetorical Function*, 110 n. 129, argues against such a transferal of the curse motif. Renz suggests that the absence of the "sword," "famine," and "pestilence" motifs mitigates against such a connection. However, in Gosse's defense, Renz has failed to connect the ubiquitous sword motif against Edom earlier in 25:12–14 with the oracle against Edom here in ch. 35. Ezekiel has already made that connection of destruction and now moves to a reversal of the curses with the prominent alpine motif.

150. Cf. Delorme, "Conversion et pardon," 129, where he notes, "Le ton veut humilier et ne trahit aucune pitié. Aucun rappel des promesses faites aux patriarches, aucune allusion à la 'fidélité' de Yahvé. Yahvé prend sur lui d'agir d'une facon toute spontanée, sans aucun mérite de leur part."

151. In ch. 20, the main problem, apart from Israel's idolatry, was the nation's desire to follow their own statutes (חֻקִּים) and ordinances (מִשְׁפָּטִים). The mention of these motifs here in ch. 36 points to a reversal of a former way of life and thinking.

ordinances (מִשְׁפָּטִים) of Yahweh offered the nation hope in their time of greatest despair.[152]

To summarize, before the nations as a nebulous whole (i.e., those in chs. 38–39) would experience the curses once used against Israel, Ezekiel chose the nation of Edom to exemplify Yahweh's displeasure with the nations' treatment of his people and land. Judgment would begin with the closest blood relation of Israel, Edom. In Judah's time of need Edom had oppressed them as much as the foreign nations.[153] Therefore, what Edom would lose, Israel would gain in the form of blessings as depicted in ch. 36.

Chapters 37 and 38–39: Israel and the Nations Juxtaposed—A Theological Lesson[154]

As with our comparative analysis of chs. 35 and 36, the restoration motif presented in chs. 37 and 38–39 rests once again upon a juxtaposition of the two blocks of material. The recognition formula sets the tone and the basis for the motive behind the content. While the reversal of the curse of the unburied is a key part of the larger visual framework on which the message hangs (see below), it is not, in and of itself, the driving force of the message theologically. The importance for both Israel and the nations to come to a proper knowledge of Yahweh is the theological message that drives the visionary sequence (e.g., 37:13, 14, 28).[155] The curse is reversed and placed upon the conglomerate of

---

152. Beyond this, Ezekiel's use of the metaphor of flocks of sheep in 36:37–38 links this chapter with the shepherd imagery of ch. 34.

153. Obadiah devoted his entire, albeit brief, book to this lack of filial care.

154. For a discussion of Ezekiel's use of rhetoric in ch. 37, see Fox, "Ezekiel's Vision," 1–15.

155. One may argue that the concept of Yahweh's ability to deliver his people from the devastating effects of exile is also an important theological point in ch. 37. We see this in the argument made by Oylan, "'We are Utterly Cut off,'" 43–51. Here Oylan suggests that the despair of the exiles is reflected in the statement "we are completely cut off" found in 37:11. He asserts that this encompassed an entire range of feelings associated with being dead in Sheol, where the individual could not praise Yahweh, experience his covenant loyalty, his faithfulness, or return to the covenant land. The sum total of this expression reflected a feeling of abandonment by their God. If Oylan's assumptions are correct then this makes the restoration motif in these final chapters even more appropriate to the situation. The "dead" and hopeless exiles were about to witness, through prophetic insight, the greatest reversal of devastation ever experienced by the nation.

nations attacking Israel in order that they may "know" that Yahweh is the ruler of heaven and earth (cf. 38:14, 16, 23; 39:6, 23).[156]

Chapters 37 and 38–39: Gog and Israel Juxtaposed [157]

The vision of the valley of dry bones sets forth the desperate situation in which the exilic community finds itself. The curse of unburied bodies has come to fruition as prophesied in 6:1–7, 13 and from the description of the parched state of the bones, the exile has been ongoing for some time.[158] Furthermore, with Greenberg we can assert that the picture in ch. 37 is that of a nation cursed in battle whose transgressions are being "rescinded."[159] The hope of restoration depicted in the final verses of ch. 37 presents the restored nation not only geographically and covenantally, but also politically. Israel will be a unified country once again with an established monarchy and David as her king. Furthermore, the final three verses anticipate the temple vision of chs. 40–48. Thus, it is only the removal of any residual military threats that is remaining to be dealt with. The removal of this threat is needed before any utopian existence can ensue in a totally renewed and peaceful land as envisioned in chs. 37 and 40–48. Chapters

---

156. The absence of the recognition formula in chs. 40–48 is telling, to say the least. Some may posit that authorship issues arise from this lacuna. However, the fact that the nation of Israel has experienced the blessing and grace of their Suzerain and, by association, has come to a knowledge of who he is, appears fulfilled by the end of ch. 39. All that remains for this renewed community is the rebuilding of the temple and the return of their God (chs. 40–43). From this point in the narrative and beyond, the details of what the renewed covenant required and would be like are extrapolated. This covered not only the rules for the temple and the prince, but also the priests and the division of the land. Through this portion of his prophecy, Ezekiel makes it clear that when leadership performed their proper roles, the people would know what was required for a right relationship with their Suzerain. For example, false prophets are denounced in 13:2–4, 9, 16 and 22:25, 28; priests are reprimanded in 22:26 and the king and princes are judged in 7:27; 17:12; and 34.

157. Block, "Gog in Prophetic Tradition," 157 and idem, "Gog and the Pouring out of the Spirit," 257–70 esp. 263–70, has argued, I feel correctly, for a structural ordering of 38 and 39 whereby Ezekiel has presented two "panels" with four "frames," each followed by a conclusion. For a detailed exposition of these two chapters, see Cooper, *Gog's Armies*.

158. This vision is not dated, whereas many others are.

159. Greenberg, *Ezekiel 20–37*, 748, goes on to point out that along with this curse motif from the ANE, the "despairing metaphor" (i.e., "our bones are dried up") also appears to be a reason for the visionary experience.

38–39 present just such a scenario. On this Cook notes, "The preceding chapters of Ezekiel have dealt with Israel's restoration, describing future reversals of wrongdoings and wrong situations. These chapters of Ezekiel, however, lack a central reversal: Prior to Ezekiel 38–39, the enemies of Israel are not finally done away with, and God's holiness is not yet vindicated. In other words, the restoration chapters have not described any reversal of Israel's destruction in 586 BCE. This is now supplied by the Gog prophecy."[160]

Therefore, the setting of chs. 38 and 39 in the land of Israel is clearly in a period after the return when restoration has been effected upon the land and the destruction of 586 BCE reversed. Indeed, 38:8 makes it clear that this vision is for a later period after the land of Israel has been "restored from the sword" (מְשׁוֹבֶבֶת מֵחֶרֶב). Irwin correctly notes that the reversal of the destruction by the sword, the return from exile, and the restoration of the land (i.e., the mountains) here in verse 8 all point to curses from Leviticus 26 which have been overturned.[161] He continues "this tripartite description of the mountains of Israel finds its significance when it is seen as a picture of a land recently freed from the punishment meted out to an idolatrous people."[162] Yahweh will bring Gog and his cohorts into a restored land and against a restored people living in safety for the sole purpose of bringing his curses against them.

The implied curse of the unburied dead in the vision of the valley of dry bones and the explicit picture of the curse in ch. 39 is the closest and most vivid connection between chs. 38–39 and 37 yet it is not the only one to be drawn. The parallels between the two pericopes are striking. For example,

1. Yahweh commands Ezekiel to "prophesy" (הִנָּבֵא) during each account (37:4, 9, 12; 38:2, 14; 39:1)—for good in the former, for evil in the latter

---

160. Cook, *Prophecy and Apocalypticism*, 104. Childs, *Introduction*, 367, notes that the "eschatological hope" in these chapters resonate with the hope presented in Joel 3 and Zechariah 14 where the destruction of Israel's enemies plays a key part of the restoration motif.

161. Irwin, "Exegetical Study," 35–36. For a study of the sacrifice imagery found in the Gog oracle, compared to the Molek cult as evidenced in Isa 30:27–33 and Jeremiah 7, see Irwin, "Molek Imagery," 93–112.

162. Irwin, "Exegetical Study," 35.

2. Both tell of a future event (37:11–28; 38:8)

3. Chapter 37 depicts a re-gathered nation living peacefully and securely (לָבֶטַח) in the land whereas 38:8, 11 and 14 reports that the nebulous hordes desire to undo this utopian existence (cf. also 39:26)

4. Yahweh attacks those who live "securely" (לָבֶטַח) among the nations (39:6) in the same way the nations desired to attack Israel who lived "securely" in their new land (34:25, 27, 28)[163]

5. Both mention that Israel is re-gathered from the nations (37:21; 38:8, 12)[164]

6. Both refer to the place of resettlement as the "mountains of Israel" (הָרֵי יִשְׂרָאֵל) (37:22; 38:8; 39:2, 4, 17)

7. Leadership in both pericopes rests on one king (David—37:24 and Gog—38:2; 39:1)

8. Both use the term "prince" (נָשִׂיא) as a designation for their leader (37:25; 38:2, 3; 39:1, 18)

9. Both Israel (cf. ch. 37) and Gog and his allies (cf. chs. 38–39) are left unburied

10. In both cases the picture is that of bodies strewn about a valley (37:1–2; 39:11, 15)[165]

11. Both accounts speak of a mass grave/graves (37:12–13; 39:11)

12. The bodies of Gog and his allies are placed in a mass grave while Israel's are removed from the grave (39:11; 37:12)[166]

---

163. Even though the Hebrew term לָבֶטַח does not appear in ch. 37, I believe that the connection between the "covenant of peace" in 37:26 and 34:25 allows for the connection to be made.

164. In ch. 37 the term for "nations" is גּוֹיִם whereas in ch. 38 both עַם and גּוֹיִם are used. These terms appear to be used interchangeably for stylistic reasons.

165. Many scholars have commented on the importance of the identification of the valley in ch. 39. Most point to the Hebrew phrase גֵּי הָעֹבְרִים ("the valley of the ones who pass over") as important in identifying its location. Stavrakopoulou, "Use and Abuse," 12, suggests that it is the "valley of the dead" where the dead pass to the underworld. See also Irwin, "Molek Imagery," 98–105, for a discussion of the various topographical options.

166. Stavrakopoulou, "Use and Abuse," 13, suggests that Gog and his allies are to be buried and then disinterred for the purpose of further corpse abuse through the scavenging of the fowls of the air and the beasts of the field. While this is possible, it is

13. The Hebrew term עֶצֶם ("bone[s]") appears throughout (37:4, 5, 7, 11; 39:15)

14. In each pericope the Hebrew verb עָבַר ("to pass over") is used with definite interpretive nuances (37:2; 39:11, 14, 15)[167]

15. The picture in ch. 39 shows the decomposition and exposure of bodies while ch. 37 shows the reversal of this process[168]

16. The motif of a "great assembly and a mighty army" (קָהָל גָּדוֹל וְחַיִל רָב) in 38:4 and 15 parallels the "exceedingly great army" (חַיִל גָּדוֹל מְאֹד־מְאֹד) of 37:10[169]

17. Meteorological terms are used to describe the acts of Yahweh. He uses the "wind" (רוּחַ) to bring life in ch. 37 whereas the approach and attack of Gog and his allies are likened to a "storm" (שׁוֹאָה) and "cloud" (עָנָן) (cf. 38:9, 16) bringing destruction

18. Both accounts end with hope for Israel (37:22–28; 39:25–29)

19. Chapters 37 and 38 (cf. also 39:6) both end with the recognition formula "then they/the nations will know that I am the Lord" (וְיָדְעוּ כִּי־אֲנִי יְהוָה)

---

highly unlikely in light of the diligence undertaken by the Israelites to mark the location of the scattered bones and insure their burial. Stavrakopoulou (3, 9–16) goes on to note that the erecting of the mass grave in ch. 39 points to a similar picture in ANE sources where a defeated foe becomes a spectacle and the grave mound a memorial to the greatness of the conqueror. Here Yahweh is the victor, and the mass grave becomes a "memorial" to the final defeat of the enemies of Yahweh and Israel.

167. Ezekiel *passes over* the valley and views the loss of life, whereas in ch. 39 the armies of Gog *pass through* the valley to bring death and destruction. Also, they *pass over* to Sheol in this valley? Finally, appointed Israelites *pass through* the land looking for the deceased.

168. In ch. 37 the desecration of the bodies by wild animals is never presented; it is only implicit. Unlike Jeremiah, Ezekiel never explicitly uses this part of the curse against Israel, but rather reserves it for the nations alone (cf. 29:5; 32:4–5; 39:17–20). In 33:7 however, while Ezekiel uses the curse for those who are left in the land after the destruction of Jerusalem, it appears that he sees those who remain in the land as cursed and no better than the surrounding nations. For Ezekiel, it is the remnant in exile that will one day inherit the land again.

169. In ch. 37, in an act of curse reversal, the Spirit gives life to these bones, which in turn form an "exceedingly great army" not ready for battle, but rather ready to participate in a life of peace and security. Conversely, in chs. 38 and 39 the "great army" serves one function, i.e., to participate in a war against Yahweh's people. Nevertheless, Ezekiel is quick to point out that the ultimate purpose for the forming of the great army in ch. 38 is so that Yahweh may pass "judgment" (שָׁפַט) on the nations.

20. The eponym, Jacob, is mentioned in both accounts (37:25 and 39:25)

21. Both Gog (38:4-8; 39:2) and Israel (37:12, 21) are drawn to the land of Israel, one for resettlement the other for destruction

22. Both accounts mention the outpouring of the Spirit (37:14; 39:29).

Beyond these parallels, we see in ch. 37 that the tenor of the message is restoration, peace, and safety while in 38–39 it is judgment, war, and danger for all involved. Interestingly, in 37:26 Ezekiel uses the phrase "covenant of peace" (see also 34:25) to describe the new covenant between Israel and her God. Ironically, the picture presented in chs. 38 and 39 is far from a peaceful setting. Thus it seems apparent that the motif of peace and safety in ch. 37 is definitely contrasted by the picture of chaos and destruction displayed in chs. 38–39.

Another connection between these three chapters is the concept of the defilement of the land. In 39:11-16 we see the defilement of the land by the unburied bodies of Gog and his hordes. After the battle, an extended period of time is allotted for the burial of the dead in order to cleanse the land. The opposite picture is presented in ch. 37 where the need for cleansing of the land is not addressed due to the fact that the revivification of the bodies removes the demand for such a task. From this perspective, Ezekiel, as a priest, is not defiled by his direct visionary presence in the valley of dry bones because of the reversal of the defiling principle involved with dead bodies. However, because no revivification will take place for the fallen enemies of Yahweh, cleansing of the land is required.

Finally, the "Day of the Lord" imagery in 39:6-8 heightens the picture of Yahweh's ferocity as his curse includes the sending of fire upon the nations in areas where they appear to dwell in safety (39:6). Ezekiel's depiction of this final battle in "Day of the Lord" terminology serves as a fitting end to the judgment of the nations. Nevertheless, the prophet does not end the chapter on a harsh note against the nations, but rather reserves this space for a message of hope for Israel much like that of ch. 37. Once again Ezekiel returns to the recognition formula in 39:22 and 28 in order to bolster his reason for the culminating battle against the nations. In the last nine verses of the chapter, the prophet reiterates many of the promises of the last half of ch. 37, especially the gathering of the nation from exile (v. 27) and the security they will feel in their restored land (v. 26). Thus it is not surprising that, in a fitting manner, Ezekiel finishes the oracles against Gog and Magog by presenting Yahweh's promise to never hide his face from the house of Israel again (vv. 23, 29) and by promising the Spirit's blessing upon the nation.[170] The motif of the hidden face of God forms an inclusio here in 39:23-29 with 7:22. Whereas in 7:22 Yahweh had turned his face from his people, here in ch. 39 he allows his face to shine once more upon a cleansed and renewed people and land—a reality revealed in chs. 40-48.

Chapters 37 and 38–39: Ezekiel's Rhetorical Strategy

Rhetorically, Ezekiel's visions have played an important role up to this point. We see two visions in the opening eleven chapters (i.e., chs. 1–3 and 8–11) and two in the closing twelve chapters (i.e., 37 and 40–48). A host of indictments and prophetic material highlighted by extended metaphors appear between these two blocks. As I have shown with the vision in ch. 37, and will demonstrate in ch. 5 with the vision of chs. 40–48, rhetorically, these final two visions play just as much of an important structural role as the two opening visions do. As I have noted above, however, chs. 37 and 38–39 also appear to fit together not only thematically but also theologically and rhetorically. Yet scholars do not always agree with this position. Many see these two chapters as well as chs. 40–48 as late additions to the text. For this reason it seems appropriate to look briefly at some of the issues concerning authorship. In so doing I hope to further establish the vital role these chapters play in the book, and the strong possibility that they can be attributed to either Ezekiel or someone very close to the compiling process.

Ezekielian Authorship[171]

The often tedious argument of authorship has not been the focus of this book and is well beyond its scope. Methodologically, it is the unity

---

170. Compare 39:29b to 37:1–14 and the life-giving aspects of the Spirit of Yahweh. So too Block, "Gog and the Pouring out of the Spirit," 267–68. Block (268–69) correctly notes the outpouring of the Spirit (39:29b) as proof of a reestablished covenant relationship. His reference to Isa 44:1–5 helps bolster this conclusion.

171. For a complete discussion on the history of scholarship surrounding the

and organization of the final form of Ezekiel cast within a Babylonian setting that has informed our conclusions. Yet, one must still reckon, to a certain degree, with those who suggest that many of the final chapters of Ezekiel (viz., chs. 38-48) are later additions and do not reflect the thought or influence of the original prophet.

Ezekielian authorship of chs. 38 and 39 has been challenged by scholars such as Cooke,[172] Eichrodt,[173] Pfeiffer,[174] Hanson,[175] Ahroni[176] and Wilson.[177] While we can appreciate the depth of the arguments that many authors have developed and adopted in this vein, there appears to be just as many scholars who have come to the exact opposite

---

authorship of Ezekiel (with a focus on chs. 38-39), see Fitzpatrick, *Disarmament of God*, 2-48.

Harrison, *Introduction*, 823-32, notes that the first real challenge to Ezekiel's authorship came with Spinoza (1632-1677) in the seventeenth century and again about a century later with G. L. Oeder (1771—posthumously). Throughout the nineteenth century, however, the consensus returned to Ezekielian authorship. As late as 1913 the unity of the book caused most scholars to agree with the earlier understanding of Ezekielian authorship of the entire work. However, by 1924 Hölscher, based on an assumption of poetic style for the prophets, challenged the general consensus in his work, *Hesekiel der Dichter und das Buch* in which he propounded that only sixteen passages were original to Ezekiel, along with five short sections of prose. Nevertheless, by the 1950s the tide began to shift once again with scholarly works such as Howie's *Date and Composition of Ezekiel*. As of the 1970s Harrison (832) concluded that "the intense critical studies of thirty-five years have largely cancelled themselves out, and while they contributed to the understanding of much of the book, they have left the general position much as it was prior to 1924."

172. Cooke, *Ezekiel*, 372.

173. Eichrodt, *Ezekiel*, 520-21. One can also look to the earlier period of the twentieth century when the general rule was to isolate this section as non-Ezekielian. Scholars such as William A. Irwin and Hugo Gressmann proposed removing this section from the pen of Ezekiel on the basis of genre and content. See Gressmann, *Der Messias*, 118-34, esp. 124 and Irwin, *Problem of Ezekiel*, 172-80. Irwin (173) does suggest that at least 38:1-4a is Ezekielian.

174. Pfeiffer, *Introduction*, 562.

175. Hanson, *Dawn of Apocalyptic*, 234.

176. Ahroni, "Gog Prophecy," 1-27, esp. 2. Ahroni (15) argues that these chapters cannot be from Ezekiel's era because they are too apocalyptic with a future-looking perspective of God's kingdom. However, this does not make sense in light of his assessment that chs. 40-48 fit with the rest of Ezekiel. These final nine chapters are clearly eschatological in flavor and follow nicely after the establishment of the utopian peace of chs. 38-39.

177. Wilson, *Prophecy and Society*, 286.

conclusion (e.g., Astour,[178] Zimmerli,[179] Niditch,[180] Cook,[181] Block,[182] and Boadt[183]). Again, much of the debate swirling around the authorship of these chapters is the issue of the appropriateness of the message in the overall context of Ezekiel and his period. The fact that these chapters reflect an apocalyptic flavor supposedly places them out of reach for a sixth-century author such as Ezekiel.[184] However, many are now viewing Ezekiel from a thematic and literary perspective and are coming to the conclusion that these chapters are more integral to the overall structure of the book than once thought, a reality I demonstrated above.[185] Because this best reflects my methodological approach, a few conclusions will be made to reinforce this position.[186]

178. Astour, "Ezekiel's Prophecy of Gog," 567.
179. Zimmerli, *Ezekiel* 2:302-4.
180. Niditch, "Ezekiel 40-48," 208-24.
181. Cook, *Prophecy and Apocalypticism*, 87-103.
182. Block, "Gog and the Pouring Out of the Spirit," 269-70, seems to be implying this from his conclusions in this study.
183. Boadt, "Salvation Oracles,"1-21, argues forcefully for the unity of chs. 33-39 and the strong possibility of Ezekielian authorship.
184. Boadt, "Mythological Themes," 212-13; and Boadt, "Ezekiel," 2:711-22. In the latter work Boadt (717) says that "Many critics have pointed to the use of apocalyptic imagery in Ezekiel 38-39. Often they take this as proof that these must be later insertions into the text. However, most of the language is tied to the ancient imagery of the cosmic battle of the gods in creation, which was seen in early Israelite traditions of God as the divine warrior." Cf. also, Erling, "Ezekiel 39-39," 104-14.
185. For example, see the discussion of the literary links of these chapters to the rest of the book by Fitzpatrick, *Disarmament of God*, 74-81. Batto, *Slaying the Dragon*, 156, points out that the author of Ezekiel often employs the literary technique in the structure by using "a pattern of suspension, resumption, and/or reversal of themes" (e.g., the motif of dumbness in 3:17-27 is noted again in 24:25-27 and culminated in 33:21-22). This concept is also seen here in these chapters against the nations. The oracles start in 25-32 and are suspended until 35 and finalized in the Gog oracles of chs. 38-39 where the power of the nations is reversed and destroyed. Also, Irwin, "Molek Imagery," 106, points out that these two chapters serve as a "logical conclusion to the 'night messages'" of the prophet and are a vital structural conclusion to the "stages of Israel's restoration."
186. The discovery of Greek papyrus 967, in which chs. 38 and 39 come before ch. 37, does seem to create some difficulty in understanding the intent of the compilers of the LXX and their reason for the switch (if in fact they are responsible for it). Furthermore, their exclusion of 36:23c-38 begs the question as to why the MT included this pericope while opting for a different ordering. Perhaps Boadt, "Salvation Oracles," 16 n. 22, is correct when he points out that 39:25-29 would have served as an appropriate introduction to ch. 37 if it were placed before ch. 37. Thus, 36:23c-

First, beyond the obvious problem concerning the lack of scholarly consensus on the authorship of these chapters, the use of literary criticism has added much support for the position of Ezekielian authorship for these chapters. Many Ezekielian scholars are beginning to allow for the possibility that at least portions of these chapters should be attributed to the original author if not the majority.[187] Second, the thematic and structural positioning of these chapters is vital in understanding their placement in the book and the role they play in the overall message being presented. Levenson has noted that there is no thematic reason why chs. 38–39 could not have originally preceded chs. 40–48 based upon the motif of restoration that precedes chs. 38–39 (i.e., chs. 33–37).[188] Further, the work of Susan Niditch on chs. 40–48 and their parallels with ANE motifs has also added to the argument for the literary unity of this section.[189] Third, Cook's work on form critical aspects of the text and the literary unity of the restoration chapters in relation to the rest of the book reinforces my conclusions thus far. In this regard he notes that while Zadokite insertions may be

---

38 would not have been needed in the Greek text. Also, Block, "Gog in Prophetic Tradition," 156, argues that placing chs. 38–39 within the oracles against the nations (chs. 25–32) would only be possible if the final form were "adjudged irrelevant." In light of Block's assessment we can postulate that the compilers of the LXX may have opted to move the Gog-Magog oracles *closer* to the oracles against the nations of chs. 25–32 and 35 for thematic/practical purposes only.

On the other hand, Freedman and Overton, "Omitting the Omissions," 107, may be correct when they note that the omission of 36:23b–38 may be due to haplography. They go on to note that the inclusion of vv. 24–34 in the Ezekielian text found at Masada (almost 200 years older than Papyrus 967) lends credence to the MT. Whatever the reason, the placement of chs. 38–39, either before or after ch. 37, does not hinder our assumption that the curse motifs of 37 and 38–39 are being juxtaposed.

187. Cook, *Prophecy and Apocalypticism*, 87 n. 10, points out that form-critical work by scholars such as Astour and Hossfeld, *Untersuchungen zu Komposition*, 403–4, has aided in the change of thinking about the authorship of this section. Hossfeld points out the *Kernelelement* which is clearly Ezekielian has been developed by an Ezekielian school over time. On the other end of this developing spectrum, Astour, "Ezekiel's Prophecy of Gog," 567, notes that based upon the style and imagery content of these chapters, within the context of the overall section and those parts which are traditionally assigned to Ezekiel, there is no reason not to assign these to him as well.

188. Levenson, *Program of Restoration*, 15, argues for the thematic unity of these chapters based upon the theme "assault on Zion by the kings of the nations."

189. Niditch, "Ezekiel 40–48," 208–24. Even though Niditch focuses on chs. 40–48, her assessment of the unity of the entire restoration section adds much to the literary unity debate.

present, this in no way removes it from the exilic period.[190] Cook goes to great lengths to show the literary unity of chs. 38–39 with the rest of the book. He devotes five pages of his book to list the various Hebrew phrases and terms that are characteristic of not only these chapters, but of the rest of Ezekiel's work.[191] He concludes that the "idioms, style, and theology of Ezekiel 38–39 match what are common elsewhere in the book."[192]

Finally, if in fact many of the forms, themes, motifs, and ANE parallels are consistent throughout Ezekiel, including these chapters, it is nonsensical to excise them from Ezekiel or his "school" within a sixth-century setting. It appears that in taking a position for sixth century authorship, whether Ezekielian or from his "school," places one on firm scholarly ground. This position being noted, we will examine some of the key motifs that help link these chapters to the rest of the book.

Motifs That Link Chapters 38 and 39 to the Rest of Ezekiel

Many points of contact exist between chs. 38–39 and what precedes them.[193] One similarity is our ongoing discussion of the reversal of

---

190. Cook, *Prophecy and Apocalypticism*, 87. He goes on to note that if this is in fact the case then what is pictured in these chapters is the earliest example of a "priestly elite" inspired apocalyptic text.

191. Ibid., 98–103.

192. Ibid., 103. Block, "Gog in Prophetic Tradition," 157, offers a convincing structural analysis of these two chapters based upon matching literary panels. Block lists them as such.

Panel A: The Defeat of Gog	38:2–23
Frame 1: The Conscription of Gog	38:2–9
Frame 2: The Motives of Gog	38:10–13
Frame 3: The Advance of Gog	38:14–16
Frame 4: The Judgment of Gog	38:17–22
Interpretive Conclusion	38:23
Panel B: The Disposal of Gog	39:1–24
Frame 1: The Slaughter of Gog	39:1–8
Frame 2: The Spoiling of Gog	39:9–10
Frame 3: The Burial of Gog	39:11–16
Frame 4: The Devouring of Gog	39:17–20
Interpretive Conclusion	39:21–24

193. Cf. Fitzpatrick, *Disarmament of God*, 74–81.

Israel's experienced curses and their placement upon the enemies of Israel, viz., Gog and his allies. For example Cook comments, "Now these enemies will be destroyed in Gog as the final reversal associated with Israel's restoration. This destruction is depicted in Ezekiel 38–39 by means of judgment language that recalls expressions used previously in Ezekiel against Israel. For example, the Gog passage contains reversals of the prophecies against Israel in Ezekiel 5 . . . and Ezekiel 13. . . . It may therefore be concluded that the Gog passage has an important place in the restoration message of the book as the account of the reversal of the successful invasion of God's land demonstrating God's true power."[194] Moreover, prior to these chapters, the judgment and the destruction of the house of Israel had served as an example before the nations. Now in chs. 38–39 this example motif is reversed and it is the exposure of the nations' evil against Israel and Yahweh that comes into focus as a lesson to all peoples.[195]

The "Center of the World" Motif

The "center of the world" (i.e., טַבּוּר הָאָרֶץ) motif appears in both 5:5 and 38:12.[196] In the first appearance of the motif, Yahweh is reminding Israel of her privileged position at the center of the nations.[197] Because of their sin, this privileged position would be removed and judgment passed. However, in 38:12 Israel is once again restored to her prestigious centralized position among the nations. Here we see the revived and prosperous land of Israel being attacked, in mythological propor-

---

194. Cook, *Prophecy and Apocalypticism*, 104.

195. See also the great battle seen in 2 Esdras 13:1–58 and motifs developed in 1 Enoch 62:2 and the *Psalms of Solomon* 17:27, which appear to be dependent upon Ezekiel 38–39. Cook, *Prophecy and Apocalypticism*, 117–18, also points out the use of "hand" (יָד) as the symbol/instrument of God's judgment (found in 39:21) against both Israel and the nations, cf. 13:9; 14:9, 13; 16:27; 35:3–4.

196. Here it is literally the "center of the nations" (בְּתוֹךְ הַגּוֹיִם). While the phraseology may be different, the concept remains the same.

197. Most scholars assert that locating Jerusalem as the "navel" of the earth was for the purpose of emphasizing it as the geographic center of the nations. For example, see Zimmerli, *Ezekiel* 1:174; and Taylor, *Ezekiel*, 86. Taylor notes that Jerusalem is "theologically . . . the centrepiece of God's favour in the world and the object of His covenant-love." Josephus, *War* 3:52, also calls Jerusalem "the navel of the country" (ὀμφαλὸν τὸ ἄστυ τῆς χώρας). See also Jubilees 8:19–20a and Bodi, *Poem of Erra*, 219–26.

tions, by her enemies on every side.[198] The region that is un-walled with its people living in peace becomes the central focus of the nations. When attacked by these nebulous enemies it is at this point that the curse of annihilation that once threatened Israel in ch. 5 is reversed and placed upon those surrounding nations because Yahweh is now protecting his land.

The "Wrath of God" Motif

It really goes without saying that the wrath that was once placed upon the nation of Israel is now directed, full force, against Gog and his allies. Verse 18 of ch. 38 makes this point clear when Yahweh says "my wrath will rise up in my anger" (תַעֲלֶה חֲמָתִי בְּאַפִּי) against Gog. The doubling of the emotive words here, "wrath" (חֵמָה) and "anger" (אַף), brings a forcefulness to this motif. Irwin points out that the language here is reminiscent of 36:17–18 and the anger that once burned against Israel for her idolatry.[199] Moreover, in 38:19 the presence and wrath of God will bring a "great quaking" (רַעַשׁ גָּדוֹל) upon the earth (so too 38:20—the beasts of the air and field will "quake" before God) as a means of displaying the wrath of Yahweh against Gog and his allies (cf. also Judg 5:4; Job 39:24; 41:29; Ps 68:9; 1 Kgs 19:11–12; Isa 29:6; Jer 8:16; 49:21).[200] This language also harks back to that used in the theophanic throne vision of 3:12–13 where the terror of Yahweh is presented as approaching from the north.[201] Interestingly, the only other appearance of רַעַשׁ in Ezekiel (with the exception of 12:18) is in 37:7 where the power of Yahweh's Spirit begins to restore/reverse the curse of the fallen soldiers of Israel—yet another parallel between these three chapters.

---

198. Cf. Childs, "Enemy from the North," 187–98.

199. Irwin, "Exegetical Study," 40. Irwin (40 n. 71) goes on to point out that 36:23 and 38:16 as well as 36:4, 34, and 38:8 all find parallels in the punishment meted out for idolatry in Leviticus 26.

200. In all these cases the word רַעַשׁ is used to refer to God's anger or foreboding presence. Once again this provides support for the ominous foreboding we see in the opening vision of Yahweh in chs. 1–3.

201. Ibid., 40–41.

The "Sword" Motif

The sword[202] motif once used by Yahweh to punish Judah because of her sin (e.g., 5:2, 12, 17; 6:1–3, 8; 11:8; 12:14; 14:17; 21; 23:25) is now wielded against the nations here in 38–39—a similar picture depicted in chs. 25–32.[203] In 38:21 the author describes the annihilation of Israel's enemies as complete and utter destruction by the use of the sword (חֶרֶב).[204] Interestingly, this term appears for the last time in 39:23 (i.e., in relation to Israel) as a culmination and fulfillment of the curse reversal begun in ch. 25. Thus it is clear that the plight of the nations will mirror that which was once perpetrated against the house of Israel.

The "Directional" Motif

Another vital link between chs. 38–39 and the rest of Ezekiel can be seen in the direction from which the invasion comes, viz., the north (צָפוֹן—1:4 compare to 38:6 and 39:2). In ch. 2 we noted that the imagery of Yahweh coming from the north was an important link with the nation of Babylon. Yahweh himself, in the guise of Nebuchadnezzar and the armies of Babylon, brought upon Judah retribution for the covenant breaches. However, no longer is Yahweh depicted as coming from the north in fury, but rather we see him drawing the nations from the "north" with "hooks in their jaws." Here the presence of Yahweh is established *in* his land ready to fight for his people and avenge himself on the enemies of Israel. Therefore the directional term צָפוֹן is vital for the curse reversal. Ezekiel is now showing the exiles that there was no need to worry about Yahweh being at the vanguard of any future attack because he would be their defense from *within* the renewed community of faith and the newly restored land.

---

202. For Mesopotamian similarities in the sword motif especially in Ezekiel 21, see Maarsingh, "Das Schwertlied," 350–58 and Heintz, "Langage métaphorique," 55–72.

203. The sword motif does not appear in ch. 39 in relation to the nations, but it is implicit as the source of the carnage.

204. Cook, *Prophecy and Apocalypticism*, 118.

Theophanic Terminology

Next, in 38:9 we see terminology and imagery that is very close to that of Ezekiel's vision of Yahweh's chariot-throne in ch. 1. Verse 9 of ch. 38 reads,

> וְעָלִיתָ כַּשֹּׁאָה תָבוֹא כֶּעָנָן לְכַסּוֹת הָאָרֶץ תִּהְיֶה אַתָּה וְכָל־אֲגַפֶּיךָ וְעַמִּים רַבִּים אוֹתָךְ

> "And you will go up like a storm, you will come like a cloud to cover the earth, you and all your armies and many peoples with you."

Here the approach of the enemy from the north is likened to a "storm" (שֹׁאָה found in Ezekiel, only here) and a "cloud" (עָנָן).[205] The imagery recalls the earlier theophany where Yahweh's chariot-throne is seen coming from the north in a windstorm (סְעָרָה) and cloud (עָנָן) bringing judgment upon Israel (cf. 1:4).[206] Clearly one could argue that Ezekiel is purposefully seeking to present a reversal of the Yahweh-driven destruction of chs. 1–24 when he employs the "storm" and "cloud" language here in ch. 38.[207] The difference for Israel however, is that she was to fear the former appearance because of its association with her wrathful Suzerain, while the latter is merely humankind's attempt to thwart God's plan. Ezekiel uses the imagery in the latter instance as a means to demonstrate the strength of Israel's Suzerain over any perceived threat. Indeed, under the new order of reversed curses, the restored protection from the Lord in the renewed land will be unparalleled in a land rife with the benefits of the renewed blessings.

---

205. The term used for "storm" (שֹׁאָה) here in 38:9 is also used in Zeph 1:15 in the imagery of the "day of the Lord." In Zephaniah, as in Isa 47:11, the context is Yahweh's wrath against the inhabitants of the earth and Babylon respectively.

206. As Petter, "Book of Ezekiel," 154, points out, the use of the term סְעָרָה is used predominantly in conjunction with the actions of Yahweh on the earth (see also Pss 107:25, 29; 148:8; Job 40:6; Jer 23:19; 30:23; Ezek 13:11, 13). The use of the term in Isa 54:11, Jer 30:23, and Jonah 1:4 all are in relation to a God-sent storm of some kind or his controlling of it.

207. As we saw in the earlier discussion of the imagery in Ezekiel 1–3, the coupling of the storm with the cloud imagery is telling of the destruction about to be unleashed on the city. See also Petter, "Book of Ezekiel," 143.

The "Spoils of War" Motif

Ezekiel makes it clear that after this Yahweh-fought battle is complete, the spoils (שְׁלָלִים) and plunder (בִּזָּה) of the war are to be the property of the covenant people. Here Ezekiel reverses the picture of despoiling found in chs. 16 (cf. 16:39) and 23 (cf. 23:26, 46).[208] In 39:10 the Lord states that,

וְשָׁלְלוּ אֶת־שֹׁלְלֵיהֶם וּבָזְזוּ אֶת־בֹּזְזֵיהֶם נְאֻם אֲדֹנָי יְהוִה

"... and they will despoil the ones who despoiled them, and they will plunder the ones who plundered them declares the Lord."

Those who had been used to "judge" (cf. chs. 16 and 23) and despoil Judah in the past at the command of the Lord will ultimately be judged and their fortunes will be given into the hand of Yahweh's renewed people. Thus, the house of Israel in this new era will be blessed in the same way as they were when they left Egypt (Exod 3:22), namely, through the gaining of their oppressor's wealth by the direct command of the Lord.

The Number "Seven" Motif

Many scholars see the inclusion of the oracles against "seven" nations in chs. 25–32 as a sign of completion or as a means of bringing to memory the seven nations that were in the land of Canaan before the conquest (cf. Deut 7:1).[209] This motif also finds parallels in the seven nations mentioned in Amos 1:1—2:5 and Jeremiah 46:1—49:33. The Gog oracles highlight once again this particular number of enemies of Israel (i.e., Meshech, Tubal, Persia, Ethiopia, Put, Gomer, and Beth-togarmah).[210] It appears that Ezekiel either harmonized the number of enemies in the Gog pericope with the oracles of chs. 25–32 or he

---

208. Wong, *Idea of Retribution*, 196–245, 251, points out that Ezekiel often uses the same word to show that the "consequence of an action bears some similarities to the act"—what Wong refers to as 'like for like' (251).

209. See Boadt, *Ezekiel's Oracles*, 8.

210. Nobile, "Beziehung," 256–57. Nobile assumes that this is the work of a redactor who had the oracles of chs. 25–32 before him when he wrote and was trying to harmonize the two accounts.

may have simply been working from the concept of seven being the number of completion. Either way, the motif draws attention to the oracles against the nations and brings validity to the literary connections in these chapters.

We can conclude then that the Gog oracles serve as a fitting conclusion or "climax" to the preceding chapters and are thematically and linguistically linked to other portions of Ezekiel.[211] Moreover, this climax, bearing theological overtones, allows chs. 38–39 to serve the needs of the prophet to do away with every enemy of Yahweh and Israel before the fulfillment of the prophecy in chs. 40–48.

A Final Note: Possible Historical and Literary Settings for Chapters 38 and 39

Part of the focus of this book has been the ANE influences on Ezekiel in areas of literature, imagery, symbolism, and historical circumstances that may have shaped the prophet's message. As with previous chapters, I will conclude this chapter by looking at the possible ANE influences on Ezekiel's mindset in fashioning chs. 38–39.[212]

The debate as to the identity of Gog has spawned volumes of articles and entire books on the subject.[213] The identity of this figure, while mysterious and tantalizing is really beyond the present scope of this study. Moreover, the mythological and apocalyptic flavor of the oracles causes one to take a cautious approach when assigning any great significance to names and places. The general concept of judgment appears to be of greater importance here. For this reason, perhaps the work of Michael Astour on these two chapters may prove fruitful.[214]

Astour contends that the mysterious Gog was a name used by Ezekiel originating from the dynastic leadership of the Anatolian region during the Medo-Lydian war of 590–585 BCE. According to Astour, the Gog oracle must have been written some time after the

---

211. Ibid., 257.

212. Kaufmann, *Religion of Israel*, 446, suggests that the motif behind the Gog and Magog chapters is the Red Sea crossing and the attack by pharaoh's "hordes" (cf. Exod 14:2–4, 8, 17–31).

213. E.g., Bøe, *Gog and Magog*.

214. Boadt, "Mythological Themes," 225, also adheres to Astour's conclusions. Boadt (225 n. 75) points to the numerous copies of the text found both at Nineveh and Sultantepe.

end of this war. Astour posits that Nebuchadnezzar's role in bringing about the conclusion of the war through negotiations as well as a possible journey by Ezekiel to the "great international emporium of Tyre" may have helped inform Ezekiel about Anatolian affairs.[215] Ezekiel then adapted the name of the founder of the dynasty of Lydia, Guggu (Assyrian or Gyges in Greek),[216] because the dynasty of Guggu was from the remotest regions of Anatolia in the north. Moreover, the harshness of his name resonated with Ezekiel's purpose to present the northern hordes as "bellicose."[217]

From this historical reality Astour argues that Ezekiel did not rely on the actual historical event when fashioning his oracle but rather the Cuthean Legend of Naram-Sin.[218] The poem tells of a beast-like horde bred and set apart by the gods for the invasion of the south lands. This horde, which invades the land of Mesopotamia, was from the northern reaches beyond western Anatolia. In the account, the Mesopotamian king, Naram-Sin, being already forewarned by the gods not to attack this invading horde, in an act of pride goes out to stop the invading hordes but is unable to thwart them. Astour avers that Ezekiel eliminated this section dealing with the defeat of the king due to its theme of hubris, which was not needed in the idealic setting of Israel at this juncture in his prophecy. After a period of contrition and intercession, the gods, with Enlil at their head, step in and defeat the hordes on behalf of the king—a similar picture of Yahweh's intervention in chs. 38–39. Thus, Astour posits that Ezekiel took the concept of the mythic battle and modernized the place names and characters with the actual historical event in Anatolia and applied it to the enemies of Israel and Yahweh.[219]

Astour's assumptions, while seemingly tenuous at first glance, do present at least the plausibility of borrowing by Ezekiel from the litera-

---

215. Astour, "Ezekiel's Prophecy of Gog," 271 n. 23, suggests that the lapse in Ezekiel's prophecies between January 588 and January 585 may be due in part to this journey to Tyre. See also Allen, "Some Prophetic Antecedents," 19.

216. Koch, *Prophets*, 2:117, also identifies Gog with Gyges of Lydia.

217. Astour, "Ezekiel's Prophecy of Gog," 270.

218. Ibid., 272. For a transliterated text and translation, see Gurney, "The Sultantepe Tablets," 93–113, esp. 98–109. Cf. also, Foster, *Before the Muses*, 344–55. Foster presents the Old and Middle Babylonian versions, but the Late Assyrian is by far the longest and most complete covering 175 lines. For a refutation of Astour's use of the Cuthean Legend, see Longman, *Fictional Akkadian Autobiography*, 125–26.

219. Astour, "Ezekiel's Prophecy of Gog," 272–79.

ture, imagery, and historical events readily available during his day.[220] One need only look at the oracles of chs. 25–32 to see political situations and intrigue that may have been the seed for the oracles of doom against Egypt and Tyre. There can be no doubt that the positive identification of a direct reliance on the Naram-Sin poem is questionable, but that does not mean that it can be ruled out completely. Astour's assessment may very well be correct in light of Ezekiel's possible use of other Babylonian imagery and literature as has been noted in my previous chapters. At the same time, one can never overlook the fact that Ezekiel may have borrowed from the Hebrew writers of the past as a basis for portions of his imagery and themes; however, there still remain key aspects of Ezekiel's imagery that defy direct links to the OT. It is these symbols that perhaps can be best found in the ANE of his day.[221]

One other possible point of contact between chs. 38 and 39 and ANE literature may come from the region of Ugarit. Cook points out that "the image of becoming glutted and drunk on the fat and blood of the slain enemy (Ezek. 39:19–20) has been adapted by Ezekiel from the divine-warrior myth."[222] This motif, prevalent in the OT,[223] is also found in the Ugaritic texts, particularly the *Baal Cycle*. While the Ugaritic myths are from the western section of the Levant in modern-day Syria, they no doubt had a wide geographical influence, especially as can be seen in the parallels between the biblical and West Semitic texts. For example, Baal imagery can be found throughout many regions of Canaan and beyond.[224] In the *Baal Cycle* myth, the depiction of gore and blood, much like a modern horror flick, plays a prominent

---

220. For a negative critique of Astour's article, see Irwin, "Exegetical Study," 15–16.

221. For example, passages such as Isa 14:24–27 and chs. 24–27 (cosmic battle myths); Pss 46, 48, 76 (enemies attacking Mt. Zion); Zeph 1:7; Jer 12:9–13 and 46:10 (Yahweh's sacrificial-meal language), may have inspired the prophet. Cf. further, Zimmerli, *Ezekiel* 2:296–304.

222. Cook, *Prophecy and Apocalyptic*, 89.

223. The OT appearances of this motif (e.g., Deut 33:1–3, 26–29; Judg 5:4–5; Ps 68:8–9 [Heb]; Hab 3:3–7 etc.) do not have the same level of gore and blood as presented here in Ezekiel 39. It appears that this particular aspect may have been developed from other ANE literature where gore and blood played a greater role to elicit fear in the general populace.

224. Irwin, "Baal and Yahweh in the OT," 31–94, devotes an entire chapter to the occurrences of Baal in extra-biblical literature. He points out texts from Byblos, Phoenicia, Syria, and Egypt where Baal is mentioned.

role in eliciting fear of the gods in the heart of the reader. A clear example of this can be seen in *CAT* 3.2.27–29. The text reads,

27) *kbrkm . tġll . bdm . ḏmr*

28) *ḫlqm . bmm . mhrm*

29) *ʿd . tšbʿ. tmtḫṣ. bbt*[225]

27) as knee deep she [i.e., Anat] plunges in warrior blood

28) her loins in the gore of soldiers

29) until satiated with fighting in the house[226]

Interestingly, Cook points out that the Ugaritic verb *šbʿ* "to satiate" is parallel to the Hebrew verb שָׂבַע which is found in 39:19–20 (see also Jer 46:10).[227] Just as Anat revels in the victory and gore until she has her fill, so too Yahweh, the "Divine Warrior," revels in his victory by allowing the birds and beasts to be satiated on the blood and gore of the fallen warriors.

On the other hand, John McLaughlin suggests that the Ugaritic text, *CAT* 1.114 exhibits closer parallels with Ezekiel 39:17–20 than Cook's suggestion.[228] *CAT* 1.114.1–4a reads

1. *il dbḥ . b bth . mṣd . ṣd . b qrb*

2. *hklh . ṣh . l qṣ . ilm . tlḥmn*

3. *ilm . w tštn . tštn y<n> ʿd šbʿ*

4. *trṯ . ʿd . škr*

El slaughtered game in his house,
Beasts in the midst of his palace;
He invited the gods to the carving:
"Eat, O gods, and drink,
Drink wine to satiety,
New wine to drunkenness."[229]

225. Text reproduction from Peckham, *Baal Epic* (unpublished class notes)

226. Author's translation.

227. Cook, *Prophecy and Apocalyptic*, 89.

228. For McLaughlin's full discussion concerning the validity of Cook's proposal, see McLaughlin, *The marzēaḥ in the Prophetic Literature*, 205–12. McLaughlin avers that the picture in Ezekiel 39 is that of a *marzēaḥ* feast where Yahweh is presiding over the event as does El in the Ugaritic text.

229. Text and translation from ibid., 24.

While there may be some thematic and surface literary connections between these two Ugaritic texts and ch. 39, due to the tenuous nature of the links, it is best to withhold solid affirmation at this juncture. Because of so many OT appearances of the "divine warrior" motif it is hard to draw any solid conclusions on direct borrowing from any one ANE text. What we can conclude is that literature, traditions, and/or historical settings of the period *may* have influenced Ezekiel's literary methodology and his use of certain imagery.[230]

Conclusion

The curse of being left unburied resonated across cultures of the ANE including that represented by the OT authors. Because it was one of the most feared outcomes for the individual, it became an effective curse in a variety of settings. Ezekiel's use of the curse, no doubt influenced by earlier prophetic oracles and ANE usage, allowed the prophet to warn his audience of one of the outcomes of a broken covenant with Yahweh. In ch. 37 the vision of the dry bones presents just such an outcome but Yahweh makes it clear that all hope is not lost. This chapter, one among a series of restoration-centered oracles, is juxtaposed with chs. 38–39 and the scene depicting the futile attempt of the nations to possess Israel after the utopian period of restoration. Here we find out that a restored Israel will be protected by her God now that she has a renewed knowledge of her Suzerain and a new covenant of peace. But before the prophet offered this picture of hope he systematically addressed the nations either surrounding Israel or directly involved in her present dire situation (i.e., chs. 25–32). Throughout the oracles against the nations (i.e., chs. 25–32) curses once laid upon the unrepentant people of Yahweh are now placed upon all Israel's enemies both great and small. It is with this backdrop that the prophet presents the juxtaposed chapters of 35 and 36 focused on Edom and Israel, followed by the unforgettable vision of ch. 37 juxtaposed with the invasion of Gog and his hordes in chs. 38–39.

---

230. Ibid., 210. McLaughlin correctly notes that while the Ugaritic literature presented here was buried in the "sands of time" with the destruction of Ugarit in 1200 BCE, (some 600 years before Ezekiel's day) the "traditions" no doubt prevailed within the common culture and mindset for centuries afterward.

5

The Awesome Deity Returns
(Ezekiel 43; 48:35)

The Restoration of the Covenant—Treaty Curses Reversed

Introduction

SILVIO SERGIO SCATOLINI APÓSTOLO SAYS IT BEST WHEN HE SUMMArizes the essence of the closing chapters of Ezekiel by noting, "While the initial visions capture the 'Israel-that-was,' Ezekiel 40–48 projects the vision of the 'Israel-to-come.'"[1] Indeed, the last nine chapters end the book of Ezekiel with the vision of the new temple, the return of the glory of Yahweh, the priests' tasks in the temple, a revised law code, the overall role of the prince, and the division of the land.[2] The unifying theme of this section is clearly the restoration of all the institutional positions present at the height of the Davidic and Solomonic monarchies (i.e., temple, priests, and prince). While general observations and comment will be made on portions of many of these chapters, the focus of this chapter is the vision of the return of the Lord as seen in ch. 43 and the last statement of the book found in 48:35b.

Ezekiel's vision of the glory of the Lord found in chs. 1–3 and 8–11 returns, albeit in muted form, in ch. 43.[3] This final appearance

---

1. Apóstolo, "Imagining Ezekiel," 13.

2. Levenson, *Program of Restoration*, 42–44, suggests that the structural pattern found in chs. 40–48 is based upon Numbers 27–36.

3. For a discussion on the connections of the *kābôd* in chs. 8–11 and 40–48 and how these chapters relate to ANE imagery where Yahweh is battling chaos by means of his "hypostasis" (i.e., his *kābôd*), see. Strong, "God's *Kābôd*," 69–95.

of Yahweh's glory is not in judgment but rather to take up residence in the new temple. Ezekiel's visionary sequence comes to an end with this final vision, which represents our proposed final "peak" in the framework of Ezekiel's message. Moreover, the final statement of 48:35b, i.e., "The Lord is there," serves as a fitting end to the book as a literary and theological whole. Almost from the very beginning of Ezekiel we see the glaring absence of Yahweh's protection of his people, and, after ch. 11, the absence of his very presence. As we noted in ch. 3, above, because of the people's continued life of sin and idolatry, the curses had been implemented after the departure of the Lord in Ezekiel 11. Yet, even though the glory had departed in these early chapters of Ezekiel, in this fitting end to the prophetic oracles and visions, Yahweh's glory returns marking a complete reversal of the covenant curses once leveled against the house of Israel. In this vein, Haran points out that, "the glory's entrance into the temple is particularly contrasted with the departure in the visions of doom, and it appears to complete the cycle which began with those visions."[4] Thus this bookending of visions serves a dual function: first, it emphasizes the reversal of the curses and draws the prophecy to a fitting conclusion; second, it demonstrates that the covenant had been renewed and the people's sin expunged.

This last vision sequence builds for three chapters before reaching its apex with the return of the glory of Yahweh in 43:1–5. From this point forward the minutia of details concerning the responsibilities of the prince and the priests and the division of the land is interspersed with notations of blessings and curse reversals.[5] No matter how one views these final chapters, it is the return of the Lord in 43:1–5 that highlights all that surrounds it. There can be little doubt that the reason for this rests in the rhetorical strategy of the prophet. When Yahweh's glory departed in ch. 11 the anticipation of utter chaos was expected and indeed did play out as planned. The report of the destruction of the temple in 33:21 and the final exile and destruction of the nation had proven that the curses of the covenant had come to fruition—Yahweh certainly had abandoned his people and his earthly abode had been destroyed as promised.

---

4. Haran, "Law Code," 52. So too, M'Fadyen, "Ezekiel," 519.

5. For a discussion on the role of the *naśi'* in chs. 40–48, see Stevenson, *Transformation*, 119–23.

As noted in our previous chapter it is in the midst of the "valley" of this curse cycle, that Ezekiel's message of curse reversal is introduced. Beginning with the oracles against the nations in chs. 25–32 Ezekiel paints a picture of future hope which steadily builds from that point forward, reaching a momentary plateau in chs. 37 and 38–39. Yet, as can be seen from our conclusions in ch. 4, above, one vital piece of the idyllic pre-exilic picture remained unfulfilled, that being the rebuilding of the temple and the earthly return of Israel's Suzerain. It is for this reason that Yahweh gives the prophet an extended description of the new temple in the first three chapters of his final vision thus preparing the reader for the return of the Lord's glory.

However, we cannot stress enough that the vital link between these final nine chapters and the preceding restoration chapters still lies within the context of covenant renewal. In 34:25–31; 36:26–32; 37:26–28 and 39:25–29 it is apparent that the covenant (defined as a "covenant of peace" in 34:25 and 37:26) has been renewed in some eschatological fashion. Therefore we should not be surprised that immediately following the establishment of this "covenant of peace" that we find that the new temple is constructed, followed by the return of Yahweh's glory. Clearly the curses of the former covenant have been reversed. What follows is the promise of new life for the remnant of Israel and an overview of the laws required to govern exactly how that new life would play out before a holy God.

Covenants, Temple Construction, and Giving of the Law

OT Precedents

The combining of the motifs of covenant initiation, temple construction, and law giving is not new to Ezekiel. There are at least five instances where this combination occurs in whole or in part throughout Israel's history and pre-history. The first time appears with Noah after the flood. In Gen 8:20–22 and 9:1–17 the Noahic covenant is established, laws are given and a "temple," albeit an altar, is built. Second, during Jacob's encounter with the Lord at Luz (Genesis 28), the covenant of Abraham is passed on to Jacob. Once Jacob awakens from his dream he sets up a pillar and renames the place the "house of the Lord," i.e., Bethel (28:16–19). After the encounter is over, the "law" of tithing and blessing is established (vv. 20–22). The third appearance happens during the period of the exodus generation. The people of Israel under the leadership of Moses are given the Law in the wilderness and ratify the Sinai covenant (Exodus 19–24). This is immediately followed by the instructions for the first "temple" in chs. 25–31. Despite the interlude of the sin with the golden calf (chs. 32–34), the people faithfully follow Yahweh's instructions given to Moses concerning the tabernacle's construction (cf. chs. 35–40). Fourth, in Joshua 24, Joshua renews the covenant of God with the people and then proceeds to write the words of the Law in a book. Following this act, he sets up a large stone of witness "beside the sanctuary of the Lord" (בְּמִקְדַּשׁ יְהוָה) at Shechem (24:25–27). Obviously this temple/sanctuary was one in the same as the wilderness tabernacle but its "construction" or establishment at Shechem was still required. Fifth, the establishment of the Davidic covenant in 2 Samuel 7 is directly tied to David's desire to build Yahweh a temple. While the giving of the Law had preceded the construction of the temple by centuries, its renewal is addressed before and after the temple construction in 1 Kgs 6:12 and ch. 8.[6] Even though David wanted to build the temple immediately, it was delayed at the command of the Lord until after Solomon came to the throne (1 Kings 6). These OT examples offer a fitting parallel to what Ezekiel was witnessing in the final chapters of his work. Beyond the OT, this combination of motifs, in whole or in part, is also well established in the ANE.

ANE Precedents

While there are some parallels between ANE and OT motifs of covenant, law giving, and temple construction they are not an exact one-to-one parallel with Ezekiel or the rest of the OT. Some of the differences stem from the relationship between treaty and covenant (see my discussion in ch. 1, above). Despite the subtle nuances between these designations, it is still true that treaty forms were basically a covenant with stipulations, i.e., "laws" governing the relationship between a suzerain and a vassal. The only real connection to temples is the practice of placing copies of the treaty in the temples of each of the participants. Thus we can posit that the main difference between

---

6. One could argue that the stipulations of the Davidic covenant could be considered "law" albeit for the lineage of David, not the nation per se.

the blended motifs of covenant making, law giving, and temple construction in the ANE and the OT perhaps has more to do with the unique biblical use of the suzerain-vassal treaty format to define the relationship between Israel and her God. ANE suzerain-vassal relations did not require temple construction, it was understood that each participant would indeed have a "temple" for their respective gods. In the OT because the covenant was not between two earthly parties, but rather between Yahweh and the people of Israel, the building of a temple was required to house not only the covenant itself but also the very presence of their God—a common ANE practice. These distinctions about covenant making being noted, there are, nonetheless, parallels between Ezekiel's presentation and ANE texts regarding the building of temples and the giving of laws.

Lindquist has effectively argued that temple construction and law are closely related in the Hebrew and ANE traditions. In the Gudea Cylinders (ca. 2112–2004 BCE),[7] the Code of Uru-kagina (ca. 2351–2342 BCE), and the Code of Hammurapi (ca. 1792–1750 BCE), similar connections can be made which point to the link between temple construction and law giving.[8] He goes on to note that in the ANE it is the building of a temple that turns "chaos" into "cosmos." He concludes that temple construction "is the very capstone of universal order and by logic and definition creates the conditions under which law is possible."[9]

Linquist's argument closely resembles the picture of the "chaos" of chs. 38–39 which is transformed into the "cosmic" ordered world of the new temple and land of Israel in chs. 40–48 of Ezekiel. However, the defeat of chaos in Ezekiel's visions is not dependent upon temple construction; temple construction flows *out of* an established peace through the sovereign control of Yahweh. Moreover, in the OT it is only in Ezekiel's account where the chaos of international warfare interrupts the order of the motifs of covenant-law-temple construction.[10] In Ezekiel the motifs follow the order of covenant–chaos–temple

---

7. For a more recent compilation of the Gudea Cylinders and fragments, see Edzard, RIME 3/1.

8. Lindquist, "Temple, Covenant, and Law," 296–97.

9. Ibid., 299.

10. One could argue that the Golden Calf incident was a form of "chaos" that interrupted this flow. The problem is, however, that the "chaos" here is not international in scope but rather internally focused.

construction-law whereas in the Pentateuch and Joshua we see these motifs ordered as covenant–law–temple construction–chaos.[11] In light of Ezekiel's ongoing rhetorical argument it appears that the prophet is showing once again that it is the sovereign hand of Yahweh that first defeats "chaos" and then brings forth his plan of temple construction and law—God does not need the involvement of human agencies to fight his battles, to build a temple, or to institute "cosmic peace" (we will develop this in more detail below).

Therefore we can see that in Ezekiel 38–48 the defeat of "chaos" in the form of the amassed enemies against the peaceful land of Israel does indeed bring about cosmic order, hallmarked by restoration and the full reversal of the curses. This "cosmic order," which we will call the blessings of "curse reversal," flourishes after the construction of the new temple (apparently by Yahweh himself). This is closely followed by the laws of the sanctuary (43:10–12)[12] and the establishment of the laws for the priests in ch. 44.

In this regard, the stressing of the statutes (חֻקּוֹת) of the house of the Lord (43:11, 18; 44:5) appears to have close affinity with the Law/Torah of the Lord in a general sense.[13] In rigidly following the commands of the Lord, the priests will be able to teach and instruct the covenant community in the holiness and otherness of the Lord (44:24). Moreover, unlike before, with the established new covenant (34:25; 36:26; 37:26) and the giving of a new heart to the people they will be able to keep the commands and laws of the Lord. It appears that Ezekiel, himself a priest, is most concerned with the laws that are associated with the cult and laws for the priesthood and prince as opposed to a detailed law code for the lay person. One can assume that

---

11. It could be argued that Joshua's covenant renewal before beginning the conquest of Canaan (Joshua 5) and Moses' establishment of the covenant in the wilderness at Sinai both anticipate the invasion of Canaan which is a representation of "chaos."

12. For a discussion on the "Law of the Temple," see Tuell, *Law of the Temple*, 42–67.

13. The discrepancies between Ezekiel's view of the Law and the Pentateuch are beyond the scope of this paper. However, I am aware that Jewish tradition states that Hananiah ben Hezekiah ben Garon, head of the school of Shammai from the period of Jesus (i.e., the generation before the fall of the city), toiled over the two bodies of literature to try to harmonize them. Cf. Moore, *Judaism*, 1:246–47. For the Jewish sources see *Shabbat* 13b; *Hagigah* 13a; and *Menahot* 45a. In his article "Ezekiel the 'Prophet like Moses'?" McKeating attempts to explain the differences based upon Ezekiel's role as a second Moses figure.

Ezekiel envisions a return, at least in some way, to the Law of Moses based on the presentation of the renewed sacrificial system in these closing chapters.[14] Whatever the final form of this covenant and Law envisioned by Ezekiel is, it is not clearly spelled out for the reader. However, one important message resonates in the context: the community would be revived and the curses reversed. With a new covenant, temple, and renewed Law and with all the curses long since past, restoration reaches its apex in the land of Israel.

In our final assessment of Lindquist's proposal, it does appear that ANE motifs may have been adapted by Ezekiel and modified to suit the ongoing theological argument. However, Ezekiel could just have easily used motifs present in early Israelite traditions—traditions common throughout ANE cultic and legal circles. At the same time, while covenant, law, and temples were important to most cultures of the ANE, Yahweh could indeed act independently of such restraints, including an earthly temple. Yahweh was sovereign over all nations, gods, and kingdoms. He did not need a geographical base from which to operate; his abode was in the heavens as depicted in all three visions of the *kābôd* of the Lord. Yet, even while in his sovereign heavenly abode, Yahweh sought to dwell in the midst of his people. Therefore, the building of a temple and the return of the Lord are vital in bringing the curse reversal full circle. The curse of temple abandonment needed to be reversed in order for the "cosmos" to be at rest and equilibrium regained.

The Return of the Presence of Yahweh (43:1–5) Brings Blessings

A Restored Temple

As touched on in the introduction above, the physical return of the Lord's presence to dwell among his people depends upon the construction, or at least the presence of, the temple. It is no surprise, therefore, that the very next visionary revelation (i.e., "peak") after the valley of dry bones vision of ch. 37 is the extended vision of the tem-

---

14. Ezekiel's exclusion of all the furniture in the holy place except for a wooden table (41:22) does create problems for an exact return to the status quo. Scholars have struggled with what this is supposed to represent.

ple.¹⁵ It appears that the temple was not to be made by human hands, although 43:10–12 may imply this.¹⁶ The detailed blueprint for the temple given to Ezekiel on a "very high mountain" (הַר גָּבֹהַּ מְאֹד 40:2) in the land of Israel harks back to a similar situation in Exod 19:3 and 24:12–18 where Moses is given exact details for the construction of the wilderness tabernacle on Mount Sinai (cf. Exodus 25–40).¹⁷ This

---

15. Some scholars feel that the temple "construction" is not an earthly reality but rather is representative of the heavenly realm of Yahweh. See Tuell, "Divine Presence," 97–116.

16. See Liss, "'Describe the Temple,'" 122–43. Liss argues that Ezekiel's temple is only a literary device that served as the ultimate separation of the holy and the profane. As a literary device, it was used to present *tôrâ* to the people because only a fictionalized temple would be safe from defilement as had happened in the past. The literary temple replaced reality and became a "literary utopia" which could always contain the *kābôd* of the Lord without the fear of losing it ever again (esp. 141–43). Liss's argument has many strong points. However, exactly what portions of the vision the prophet meant to be taken as only "literary," as per Liss, and what portions are to be actually realized in a future utopian state within reality are not made clear. For this reason, while a "literary utopia" makes the most sense to a present-day mind, a concrete fulfillment of that "literary utopia" in the future may in fact be what the prophet had envisioned. This seems to be the case especially in light of the reality of the exile and the curse reversals prevalent in the text. This seems to be supported by the desire of many in Judah to rebuild the temple after the exile which is most notable in the books of Haggai and Zechariah.

17. Noted also by Block, *Ezekiel: Chapters 25–48*, 499–500 and Betts, *Ezekiel the Priest*, 74. Talmon and Fishbane, "Structuring of Biblical Books," 138, 149, posit that Ezekiel used an actual blueprint of a temple that he found in the "archives" (what archives they do not say) and invested it with theological import for his vision. Stevenson, *Transformation*, 4–5, 19–36, 116, argues that the idea of a "blueprint" genre here in 40–48 is misguided. She argues that Ezekiel's vision was primarily for the purpose of defining "spaces" or gradations of separation of the holy from the profane, not to give a literal blueprint for the temple. Therefore the problematic absence of "vertical" measurements in this picture of the temple would be solved. While Stevenson's argument makes sense in many respects, the fact that Ezekiel is indeed seeing the plans for a rebuilt temple is hard to pass off in light of the connection to the destruction of Solomon's temple seen in the notation of 40:1.

Also, Milgrom, "Whence the Unique Features," 1–17, proposes that the temple was fashioned after the Temple at Delphi. He bases this conclusion on five similar features of the two temples. Milgrom (1) notes that in Ezekiel's temple we see: "1. It is located on the southern slope of a high mountain (Ezek 40:2), 2. The raised inner court has no barrier wall (40:27–37), 3. There is no laver structure for the priestly ablutions, 4. The temple is devoid of all sacred objects (except for a wooden table, Ezek 41:22), 5. A spring runs beneath the temple building and surfaces outside the sacred precincts (Ezekiel 47) . . . [in the temple at Delphi we see]: 1. Delphi is located on the southern slope of Mt, Parnassus, 2. The raised inner court has no barrier wall, 3. There is a spring for ablutions 'Cassotis,' but no laver, 4. There are no sacred objects in

mountain motif here in Ezekiel is certainly used to recall the wilderness event and the establishment of the presence of the Lord in the people's midst after the ratification of the covenant in Exod 24:1–11. However, in Ezekiel, the renewed covenant seems to be an established fact at this point in the book and therefore only temple construction and Yahweh's return are needed for the full force of the curse reversal and covenant blessings to unfold.

The Chronological Setting[18]

In 40:1 we see another example of the dating sequence so prevalent in the book of Ezekiel which is used to set the following vision within a chronological context of the exile. The generally accepted date here in 40:1 is March/April 573 BCE.[19] In the same verse we are told that a second Spirit-aided journey to the city of Jerusalem takes place as depicted earlier in chs. 8–11.[20] A couple of important factors need

---

the temple, 5. A spring runs beneath the temple and surfaces outside the sacred precincts." While Milgrom's assertions are possible, it seems highly unlikely based upon Ezekiel's constant attack on idolatry throughout his book. I do agree, however, with Milgrom's comparison of Ezekiel's three-stepped temple (cf. 40:6, 26, 31, 37; 41:7 etc.) with that of a Babylonian ziggurat where the upper level was reserved for the deity (6). Indeed, if in fact Ezekiel is proving to the exiles that the numerous ziggurats used for the worship of other deities in Babylon were nothing compared to the eschatological "ziggurat" temple where Yahweh is the only deity, then such a comparison seems plausible. Interestingly, Wiseman, *Nebuchadrezzar and Babylon*, 68–73, points out that during the reigns of Nabopolassar and his son, Nebuchadnezzar, they restored the "ancient temple-tower (*ziggurat*) named Etemenanki ('The Building which is the Foundation of Heaven and Earth') [which] dominated the city" (68). Could it be that this event helped shape Ezekiel's vision?

18. For a detailed discussion of several proposed explanations of the date here in 40:1, see Liss, "'Describe the Temple,'" 127–32.

19. Stevenson, *Vision of Transformation*, 164, concludes that the tenth day in Ezekiel's dating sequence corresponds with the Babylonian New Year ceremony called *akitu* where Marduk takes possession of his temple.

20. Contra Stevenson, *Vision of Transformation*, 104–8, who suggests that Jerusalem is not the city being seen in Ezekiel's final vision. It is true that Jerusalem is not mentioned by name in the closing chapters, but the geographic notation on the destruction of Jerusalem in 40:1 makes it implicit that Ezekiel is seeing a reconstructed Jerusalem. Indeed this is the only logical conclusion to a complete reversal of the fortunes of the city. Note also that both 40:1 and 48:35 end with the adverb "there" (שָׁם), no doubt, referring to the city of Jerusalem. Compare also Isa 2:2–4 and Mic 4:1 for a similar elevated status of Jerusalem in the eschaton (explicit in Isa 2:1, 3, and Mic 4:2).

to be addressed in relation to the role played by these introductory remarks. First, the last date (textually) assigned to one of Ezekiel's prophecies is in 33:21 when Jerusalem fell. Thus, the mention of the date here in 40:1 appears to be for the purpose of making a connection back to this earlier vision. The mentioning of the destruction of Jerusalem here in 40:1 by the phrase, "after which the city was smitten" (אַחַר אֲשֶׁר הֻכְּתָה הָעִיר), bolsters this conclusion. Second, beyond the chronological link, the mode of transport to the city of Jerusalem (i.e., by the Spirit of the Lord) causes one to go back to the events leading up to the moment of the visionary destruction of the city in chs. 8–11. In this earlier case, the departure of the glory of Yahweh had made possible the sacking of the city. Therefore, these temporal and literary links help alert the reader to another pivotal point in the framework of the entire book. We are immediately aware that what is to follow (viz., chs. 40–48) will be directly related to these two events. As Greenberg puts it, "past disaster and future restoration are again counterpoised."[21] In this case, what we see in these closing chapters is the reversal of the momentous event of Jerusalem's destruction and the culmination of the entire prophetic announcement of Ezekiel. Jumping forward to 48:35 we can now begin to appreciate Ezekiel's final words which encapsulate the reversal of the curses—curses epitomized by the destruction of Jerusalem, the temple, and temple abandonment. Ezekiel's choice of the phrase, "and the name of the city from that day *forward will be* the Lord is there" (וְשֵׁם־הָעִיר מִיּוֹם יְהוָה שָׁמָּה) proves once and for all that the city and temple has been rebuilt and Yahweh has claimed the restored nation as his own.[22]

The Return of Yahweh's Glory

The entrance of Yahweh's *kābôd* into his temple in order that he may dwell in the midst of his people is in no way a new concept within the biblical witness.[23] Upon the completion of Solomon's temple Yahweh's

21. Greenberg, "Design and Themes," 190.

22. Ibid., 202. Greenberg notes that this is to rename Jerusalem (which Ezekiel calls "polluted of name" 22:5) to that which reflects the glory and name of Yahweh.

23. Stevenson, *Vision of Transformation*, 164, correctly points out, "The vision of the Kabod YHWH coming to take possession of the House of YHWH is YHWH's claim as power holder of the territory and the renewal of YHWH's claim to kingship." Indeed, the focus here in the closing chapters is the sovereignty and supremacy of Yahweh as the King and Leader of Israel.

kābôd filled the temple to such a degree that the priests could not perform their duties (1 Kgs 8:10–11). The Exodus generation experienced a similar event when Yahweh first chose to dwell among his people. After the completion of the tabernacle, Yahweh's glory fills the tabernacle to such an extent that even Moses could not enter (cf. Exod 40:34–35). On these parallels Greenberg states that "according to the priestly view, the climax of the Sinai event was the provision made for God's residence among the Israelites in the tabernacle. 'Let them make me a sanctuary,' says God to Moses before showing him the design of the tabernacle, 'that I may dwell in their midst' (Exod. 25:8; 30:45). Agreeably, the culmination of the series of blessings promised Israel for keeping the terms of the covenant reads: 'I will set my tabernacle in your midst . . . I will walk about in your midst, and I will be your God and you shall be my people' (Lev. 26:11–12). In terms unmistakably related to this priestly ideal, Ezekiel first proclaims God's resolve to reestablish his presence again in Israel, then sets out his blueprint for doing so."[24] We must add to Greenberg's conclusions the fact that Ezekiel's presentation of Yahweh's plan for restoration rests upon a reversal of all that has gone before, especially the pivotal events of the departure of God's glory and the curses placed upon Israel which included temple destruction. In order for restoration to be complete, these two impediments had to be reversed; hence the first two areas of focus in chs. 40–48 rest upon the rebuilt temple and the return of the glory of Yahweh.[25] The difference, however, between the return of the glory of God in Ezekiel and the earlier biblical accounts is the eternality evident in Ezekiel's vision. Ezekiel's revelation of the return of Yahweh is truly utopian in its presentation because, according to Ezekiel's plan of restoration and curse reversal, Yahweh will never depart from his temple again.

But beyond the eternal presence of Yahweh depicted in these closing chapters, Ezekiel envisioned a utopian existence in a renewed land as a reunited people (ch. 37). Moreover, the conditions that led to the covenant breaches and the curses that followed would be erased. Due to Yahweh's tangible presence and the placing of his law upon the people's hearts (cf. 36:26–27) the nation would no longer turn to their

---

24. Greenberg, "Design and Themes," 182–83.

25. For a discussion on the concept of theophany and restoration of Yahweh's glory, see Matthews, "Theophanies," 307–17.

idols. And the surrounding nations would no longer contribute to this spiritual infidelity nor would they be a physical threat (cf. chs. 38–39). Thus the natural conclusion was the establishment of proper worship and the peaceful existence of Israel in her rejuvenated and productive land. Indeed, the framework and rhetorical strategy of Ezekiel comes full circle with the return of the Lord to his temple.

With the exception of the loss of the Ark to the Philistines for a brief period (cf. 1 Sam 5), Israel had never experienced the absence of the presence of the Lord up until this point in her history; therefore Ezekiel was on new literary ground in his visionary presentation. For this reason it is most likely that motifs from the ANE may have informed his understanding as to the best way to present such a revolutionary concept to the exilic community.

ANE Literature Parallels with Temple (Re)construction and Enthronement of the Gods

In this closing vision of Ezekiel, the prophet devotes what amounts to three chapters in our English Bibles to describing the details of the new temple and how it is constructed (cf. 40:1—43:1). In ANE studies temple (re)construction is often directly connected to the motif of the "temple hymn." This common motif in ANE literature is characterized by the juxtaposing of a cosmic temple archetype with earthly temple realities.[26] G. B. Gray has also pointed out that Babylonian literature appears to support the idea that plans for temples on earth were given by the gods and that the temples (in some cases) were to be seen as symbols of the cosmos which was an "anti-type."[27] Moreover, Diane Sharon avers that the ubiquitous nature of the "hypothetical" pattern for temple building and its function throughout ANE cultures was, no

---

26. Sharon, "Biblical Parallel," 99–109. She also gives a concise list of scholars who deal with this very topic. Because a detailed investigation in this regard is beyond the present scope of this book, notation of a consensus of these parallels will have to suffice (cf. 104 nn. 35 and 36).

27. Gray, "Heavenly Temple: II," 530. See also part 1 of this article: Gray, "The Heavenly Temple: I," 385–402. Gray points out the parallels between Ezekiel's presentation/vision of the temple and the dream of Gudea of Lagash in ancient Babylon who ruled sometime during the third dynasty of Ur ca. 2112–2004 BCE. Also, Bodi, *Poem of Erra*, 47 n. 56, gives a detailed bibliography of the history of scholarship on the interpretation and translations of the Gudea cylinders. For a more recent, fully translated text, see "Cylinders of Gudea," *COS* 2:155:417–33 and bibliography on page 433.

doubt, known by Hebrew writers. She sees this especially prevalent in both Solomon's temple construction (1 Kgs 5:1—9:9) and Hezekiah's renovations of the temple in 2 Chronicles 29-31.[28] At the same time one needs to be cautious in applying direct parallels due to the, sometimes, speculative nature of the links. It is also possible that the temple plan presented in Exodus 25-31 may very well have spawned what is being presented in Ezekiel's vision. This caution and possible biblical parallel being noted, the key aspect that seems to push one in the direction of ANE borrowing, beyond Ezekiel's obvious Babylonian setting, appears to be the cosmic nature of these closing chapters of Ezekiel which is unattested elsewhere in the OT. Thus, we can, with caution, suggest that Ezekiel perhaps used common ANE temple motifs to add to his already long list of symbols and images that inundate his work. For example, one facet Ezekiel may have borrowed is the specific steps involved in temple building throughout the ANE.

From the period spanning the Old Babylonian Era to the Persian period, temple (re)construction is closely linked to the purposes of the gods.[29] In cases where a particular king sought to build a temple for a god, careful planning was undertaken which involved several key steps. These could include: 1) rest from one's enemies granted by the gods (this step is normally implicit); 2) the king's decision to build or the revelation to do so given by the gods; 3) the god's approval; 4) the giving of a divine pattern from the gods or divine approval of an earthly pattern; 5) site preparation; 6) solemn rituals to find original foundations (steps 5 and 6 are sometimes combined); 7) the gathering of raw materials; 8) the laying of a new foundation or the preparation of an old one (the latter is the normal occurrence); 9) the actual construction; and 10) the dedication of the temple with all the accompanying rituals.[30] We find many of these even in the OT where David and Solomon share in different steps of the list above (cf. 2 Sam 7; 1 Kgs 5-6; 8).[31]

---

28. Sharon, "Biblical Parallel," 105.

29. See the overview given by Boda, "Dystopia," 211-49.

30. Ibid., 217. This list can vary depending on how particular scholars see the process unfolding. See Hurowitz, *Exalted House*, 64 and Ellis, *Foundation Deposits*, 5-34, as noted by Boda, "Dystopia," 217 nn. 15 and 16; and Labat, *Caractère*, 177-201.

31. For a similar application of the steps as they apply to Haggai and Zechariah's building project, see Boda, "Dystopia," 231-38.

In the case of Ezekiel, many of these steps are missing completely (e.g., material gathering, decision to build, approval of Yahweh, site preparation, construction etc.). Interestingly, the steps that are missing can be directly connected to the steps which would normally be undertaken by the king (i.e., human involvement). The reason for these missing steps may have something to do with step six above. In this vein, Mark Boda points out that one of the main concerns of temple builders of the ANE was to find the exact foundation of the original temple before starting the rebuilding process in order to have continuity with the present and the past both in worship and in construction practices.[32] This concept is clearly lacking here in Ezekiel which reinforces my opinion that Ezekiel's temple perhaps was not intended to be made with human hands.[33] Furthermore, the shear size of Ezekiel's temple in no way resembles that of Solomon's day so the foundations would not align.[34] A few key issues seem to be in play here if indeed Ezekiel was familiar with the ANE pattern for temple construction, yet knowingly omitted several of the key steps.

First, whereas David and Solomon (and later Hezekiah) had been instrumental in preparing and (re)building the first temple, Yahweh, through his prophet Ezekiel, may have sought to remove any vestige of human involvement on theological grounds. Ezekiel envisions a completed temple devoid of human agency in the preparation and construction process. After the detailed description of the temple in chs. 40–42 the only thing lacking was the presence of Yahweh and the dedication and rituals that follow. Second, the reason for this lacuna of human agency may be the result of the prophet's belief that the sin and idolatry that had pervaded the first temple had desecrated it beyond use (cf. 43:6–9). Third, in light of our second reason above, the ANE desire for continuity in worship from a past era to the present age would not have been acceptable by Yahweh due to the continuous idolatrous state of the house of Israel that culminated in their exile and the destruction of the first temple (exemplified in Ezekiel 8). We can conclude from this perspective alone that what Ezekiel was envision-

---

32. Ibid., 240.

33. See a similar conclusion by Stevenson, *Vision of Transformation*, 123.

34. Ibid., 114 n. 18. Stevenson (27) does note the close size of the inner three rooms (i.e., the vestibule, nave, and inner room) of the temple proper but the overall temple complex appears much larger.

ing was far greater than what had come before. Indeed, it was a new era highlighted not only by the "new covenant of peace," curse reversal, and holiness, but also by a new temple unlike Moses' tabernacle or Solomon's temple.

Before we move on with our examination of what the restored land would look like, a few more ANE connections may shed light on Ezekiel's vision of the completed temple. One ANE text which has remarkable similarities is the *Dream of Gudea* from Lagash.

THE DREAM OF GUDEA[35]

Researchers of the Ezekielian temple vision often note its parallels with the *Dream of Gudea*. The account tells of a king of Lagash named Gudea (2125 BCE) who is given a dream by the god Ningirsu concerning the construction of a temple. One particular scholar who has studied this text at length is Diane Sharon. She has noted several parallels between Ezekiel's vision and Gudea's dream. Interestingly, she notes that the dream of Gudea is given after a "seventy- or eighty-year domination of Sumer by a people known as the Gutians," a tantalizing link with Ezekiel's setting in the "seventy-year" exile.[36] Sharon suggests that there are seven key aspects to the pattern found in both the dream of Gudea and that of Ezekiel 40–48. She lists them as

1. The annunciation to the seer in a vision or a dream of the divine desire to have a temple built;
2. The precise blueprint received in an altered state of consciousness at the hand of a divine "architectural assistant";
3. The concern throughout with purification, consecration, and ritual/cultic renewal;
4. The installation of the divine majesty into the completed edifice;
5. The assignment of specific duties to designated temple personnel;

---

35. See also the "Cylinders of Gudea," *COS* 2:155:417–33; and Edzard, RIME 3/1, Cylinder A, pages 68–88. Also during the reign of Nabonidus we find a similar account where Nabonidus has a dream and is told to build a temple for Sin as "quickly" as possible. Cf. Gadd, "Harran Inscription," 56–57, col. 1, lines 11–12.

36. Sharon, "Biblical Parallel," 100. Cf. also, Cooper, "Curse of Agade," esp. 57–61, text 4. For a brief history of this period, see the introduction to "Curse of Agade," *ANET*, 646.

6. The ultimate consecration of the temple for service to the divinity; followed finally by

7. The divine blessing in the form of abundance expressed in water imagery.[37]

On the macro level, while the order of the above list may not follow the exact presentation of Ezekiel, there are clear connections between the two that appear to have validity (e.g., the dream, blueprint, the installation of the god in his temple followed by cultic regulations and earthy abundance).

On a micro level, Sharon has also made some interesting connections between these texts. She notes that the theophanic storm imagery of Ezekiel's vision in chs. 1–3, 8–11 and 43 has many points of contact with the appearance of Ningirsu in Gudea's dream. For instance, Gudea offers a chariot of lapis lazuli[38] to the god, where lapidary adornment in Ezekiel's vision is also mentioned (Ezek 1:26). Also the men who accompany both Gudea and Ezekiel in their respective dreams/visions are described using terms for copper. Finally, a seven day feast/consecration follows the installation of the god/ Yahweh (Ezek 43:25–26).[39]

Blessing Parallels

In the *Dream of Gudea*, the concept of blessing is presented as a result of the construction of the temple by the earthly ruler. The text reads, "When you, O true shepherd Gudea, will effectively start (to build) my House for me . . . then I will call up to heaven for a humid wind so that surely abundance will come to you from above and the land

---

37. Sharon, "Biblical Parallel," 104.

38. Lapis lazuli apparently was a common gift to the gods across cultures. Several lines in a Hittite votive text from the reign of Hattušili (thirteenth century BCE), king of Hakpiš, and son (?) of Muršili II, note such gifts. Cf. de Roos, *Hittite Votive Texts*, 85. See especially his translation of texts KUB15.5 and KUB 48.122. According to the text, "The Apology of Hattusilis," Hattušili III is said to be the (youngest) son of Muršilis II and grandson of Suppilulyumas "the great king, king of the land of Hatti." According to Sturtevant and Bechtel, *Hittite Chrestomathy*, 65, col. 1, lines 1–4, the succession was as follows: Muršilis II, Muwattallis II, Urhitesupas (i.e., Urshi-Teshus/Muršilis III), Hattušili III (1267–1237 BCE).

39. Sharon, "Biblical Parallel" 106–7. In the Gudea account the being is called Ninuruda ("Lord of Copper") while in Ezekiel the man in 40:3 is described as "like the appearance of copper" (כְּמַרְאֵה נְחֹשֶׁת).

will immediately (or: under your reign) gain in abundance. When the foundations of my House will be laid, abundance will surely come at that same time: the great fields will 'raise their hands' to you, dykes and canals will 'raise the neck' to you, water will—for your profit—(even) rise to 'hills' where it never reaches (in other years). Under your rule more fat (than ever) will be poured, more wool (than ever) will be weighed in Sumer."[40] Here we see the abundance that is promised to Gudea for his service in the construction of the temple for Ningirsu. The apparent role played by the king to effect blessing on the land while prominent in the Gudea text is downplayed in Ezekiel in the person of the "prince." In Ezekiel the prince plays only a minor role, which is more passive in nature. This passivity by the prince is clearly to show that the reversal of the curses and granting of blessing is effected by the hand of Yahweh and no one else. Ezekiel's message once again is clear and to the point. In this renewed land, Yahweh, the Suzerain of the house of Israel, will be the provider of the blessings because of his great love for his people, not because someone has built a temple for him.

Nonetheless, points of contact such as those noted here and above by Sharon lead one to query as to whether these are due to coincidence, direct borrowing, or part of a larger genre related to the belief in divine involvement in temple construction in the ANE. There must have been at least the possibility that Ezekiel may have been acquainted with this text or possibly the genre. Sharon correctly notes that Ezekiel's role as a literate priest and his unquestionable interest in cultic aspects may have led him to study Babylonian cultic texts as well (see ch. 1, above). The fact that Sumerian texts were preserved by later Babylonian scribes is proof of their enduring qualities and importance to the literary world even into the time of Ezekiel.[41] She concludes, "It is as though the authors of both texts hope against hope that if all proceeds as revealed, if every cubit is measured, if every molded brick is perfect, then the divinity will be mollified, disaster will be averted, and abundance and blessing will flow from the cosmic center."[42]

Sharon's conclusions fit well within the ANE perspective as to why the rigid details of temple construction were followed to the letter by

---

40. Edzard, RIME 3/1, Cylinder A xi lines 1–17, as quoted by Boda, "Dystopia," 241. For a full rendering of the text, see Edzard, RIME 3/1, 69–88.

41. Sharon, "Biblical Parallel," 108–9.

42. Ibid., 109.

kings. Rulers of the ANE who proceeded to build temples did indeed "hope against hope" that the deity would be "mollified," and pleased with their efforts. But Ezekiel's presentation suggests much more than this mere hope of blessing and restoration. We can be assured that Ezekiel is not standing on the sidelines wringing his hands hoping that all will be done correctly so that Yahweh may return to bless his people. On the contrary, as we have noted throughout these last two chapters, Yahweh, at least in a visionary sense, had already reversed many of the curses and was blessing his people already. The act of temple construction and return of Yahweh was merely the outward tangible expression of that reality, a reality that would be expanded once Yahweh returned. Thus, the presence of Yahweh in his temple, as with the belief system of other ANE cultures, brought ultimate blessing. For Ezekiel, however, it was the proper culmination of an extended period of cursing that once again brought his message full circle to picture the magnificent presence of the Suzerain of Israel among his people (48:35).

Separation of the Holy and the Profane

Another possible ANE connection is the separation of the holy and profane in temple precincts. Ezekiel spends an extended amount of time defining the layout of the temple where gradations from holy places to the most holy place demonstrate the need for the separation of the holy and the profane (cf. 42:20). This is further developed in the separation of the people's and the prince's portion of the land from that of the Lord and the priests and Levites (compare 43:7–9 to 45:7).[43] In this vein, Toy avers that the granting of land for the priests in the restored Jerusalem and Israel found in chs. 40–48 has a direct connection to the similar practice in Babylon.[44] Toy's assumption may be correct because the practice of granting blocks of land to the priests

---

43. For an insightful linguistic and thematic discussion on the interpretation of Ezek 44:6-16 as a message of hope as opposed to judgment, see Duke, "Punishment or Restoration," 61–81. Duke presents a forceful argument challenging the oft-held assumption that Ezekiel is handing down a further judgment on the Levites here in this pericope. Duke's conclusions, based upon the prevailing motif of restoration in chs. 40–48, lend credence to his linguistic argument and translation of these verses. See further discussions on this passage by Cook, "Innerbiblical Interpretation," 193–208. Here Cook argues that Ezekiel 44 is based upon Numbers 16–18 and was written during the post-exilic period by an Ezekielian Zadokite group.

44. Toy, "Babylonian Element," 66.

near the temple is absent from the Bible with the exception of it here in Ezekiel. On the other hand, Ezekiel may be drawing upon the picture presented in Numbers 3 where the tribe of Levi is divided by clans and placed around the tabernacle during the wilderness wanderings. This practice ensured a separation of the holy from the profane (i.e., the rest of the tribes). In Ezekiel's case, the levels of separation between the holy and the profane, which highlight the degrees of holiness around the new temple, allow for an atmosphere of blessing and abundance after Yahweh returns to "energize" the new temple and land. Therefore, once the temple is complete and Yahweh returns to rejuvenate the land, it is no surprise that abundant waters flow from his temple to bring life to the most barren region of Israel, viz., the Dead Sea (ch. 47).[45]

The Poem of Erra

A text that has been scrutinized throughout this monograph, thanks to the comprehensive work of Daniel Bodi, is the *Poem of Erra*. In this text, also known as "Erra and Ishum," tablet V line 1 informs us that the warrior-god Erra, after unleashing his anger and wrath upon the people and beasts of the earth, sits down in "his dwelling" and rests.[46] As we can see, the theme of divine vengeance followed by a period of repose is present in the text—arguably a similar picture as that in Ezekiel. While the capriciousness of Erra is evident throughout the poem, in Ezekiel the vengeance of Yahweh is justified against both Israel and the nations. Finally, in both of these texts, after the deity rests in his dwelling place/temple there is a time of abundance and great wealth.

If Ezekiel was familiar with this text, as scholars such as Bodi suggest, then such a parallel is not farfetched. However, we must also temper these types of parallels with the reality that common themes and motifs such as these were prevalent over an extended period of time in the ANE. One can just as easily say, contra Bodi, that the motifs were well known through knowledge of a variety of texts and artwork in Ezekiel's day. As I have been arguing throughout, it appears

---

45. Levenson, *Program of Restoration*, 29–32, points out the Edenesque picture here in Ezekiel, which is related to Near Eastern concepts of water bringing life.

46. "Erra and Ishum," COS 1.113:415. See also Foster, *Before the Muses*, 880–911; and Dalley, *Myths from Mesopotamia*, 282–315. For the transliteration, see Cagni, *Das Erra-Epos*.

that narrowing Ezekiel's dependence to one or two motifs or pieces of literature is by far too restrictive on an author who obviously was well aware of many themes and motifs from both the OT and the ANE. Indeed, it is Ezekiel's uniqueness that makes his work stand out from both the OT and the ANE texts.[47]

Akkadian Prophecies[48]

The Akkadian prophecies are classified as *vaticinia ex eventu*[49] prophecies written in the Akkadian language which "predict" the rise and fall of kings of a given period without naming said ruler.[50] Within these prophecies are similar motifs as those found in Ezekiel (explicitly in 37:24–28 and implicitly in chs. 43–48). In some of these texts, the con-

---

47. We will return to this concept in our conclusions and implications in ch. 6, below.

48. The following are the catalogue listings for the four texts that have been viewed for this section.

A=KAR421 also listed under VAT19179
B=6 fragments K7127, 7204, 7861, 11026, 11357 and BM33726
C=K4495, 4541, 15508 and is also listed under VAT14404
D=ASS13348

These cataloguing numbers are based upon those given by Grayson and Lambert in their 1964 article and may not reflect a more modern numbering system. A few of these texts are published in this particular article for the first time. They go on to note that the texts were found in the following locations:

A and D were found in Aššur
B was found in both Aššurbanipal's (669–627 BCE) library and in Babylon
C was found in both Aššur (Sargon II's time 722–705 BCE) and Nineveh in Aššurbanipal's library. See Grayson and Lambert, "Akkadian Prophecies," 7. The dates of these texts are hard to ascertain with certainty but scholars have placed them in the following periods based upon internal historical indicators. See also Grayson and Lambert, "Akkadian Prophecies," 9.

A=Twelfth century BCE, during the Kassite period of Marduk-apla-iddina (1170–1157 BCE)
B=Approximately in the first dynasty of Babylon (1650–1530 BCE)
C=Sometime in the thirteenth century BCE within the reign of Tukulti-Ninurta I (1243–1207 BCE)
D=Early second millennium BCE

49. That is "prophecies" from the event or written after the event.

50. For a discussion dealing with the concept of "prophecy" in the ANE, see Sparks, *Ancient Texts*, 216–43 and Ringgren, "Prophecy," 1–12. Note especially his discussion of the Akkadian Prophecies on pages 8–11.

cept of a coming king who will restore the fortunes of the land and rebuild the temples of the gods is a common theme. While they are not seen as "prophecies" in the biblical concept of the word, they do, nonetheless, exhibit a common understanding within the ANE of the granting of blessings by the gods after the establishment of a king and the construction of a temple. This attitude prevailed over a long period of time as can be seen in the similar temple (re)construction ideals presented above in the Gudea account which is a much earlier text than the *Akkadian Prophecies*.

Grayson and Lambert note that these *vaticinia ex eventu* prophecies are worded in "vague terms" so that only those who lived during the reign of a given king (who was being inferred) would be able to know who the "prophecy" was really talking about.[51] Many times this was done for the purpose of gently coercing a particular king, through literary patronization, to restore temples and support the cult. Interestingly, the kings who were most supportive of the cult, restored temples, and returned the gods to their abodes, are given glowing reports and the gods bless them with abundant rain and crops. An example of this progression of temple (re)construction and blessing can be found in text D column i lines 4–23[52] according to Grayson and Lambert's ordering.

> 4. That prince will become powerful and [will not have a r]ival
>
> 5. The city will prosper (its) scattered will be reassembled/he will reassemble
>
> 6. Ekur, Egalmah, and the (other) temples
>
> 7. He will make splendid/will be made splendid like the *splendid gem* Ningal,
>
> 8. Gula, KURnuni/atu[m]
>
> 9. he will . . .
>
> 10. The temples, their luxurious abodes,
>
> 11. he will . . .
>
> 12. That prince will feed the land the yield of his vegetation.

---

51. Ibid., 10.
52. D=ASS13348 dated to the early second millennium BCE.

13. His days will be long

14–17 lacuna

18. The temples he will make splendid/will be made splendid like the *splendid gem*.

19–20. He will . . . all the gods

21. The scattered land he will reassemble/will be reassembled

22. He will make its (the land's) foundations firm

23. The gate of heaven[53]

While the text is very broken up and choppy, the apparent blessing is clearly seen. The establishment of a good king will bring about the return of exiles; will bring order to the land; and abundance will be the norm. Implicitly we see that the king's restoration of the temples assures these blessings from the deities. What can be seen in these "prophecies," as far as motifs related to Ezekiel are concerned, is the direct relationship of the utopian picture of abundance and peace when a ruler restores gods to their temples and temples to their former glory. In this regard, Ezekiel is blatant in his removal of the human element so prevalent in the ANE prophecies (see discussion above).[54] Whereas in the ANE texts the king is responsible for undertaking the restoration of the temples and returning deities to their rightful abodes, Ezekiel shows it is Yahweh who controls his own movements. Ezekiel is clearly pointing out who is in control of all the eschatological events for Israel and the temple.

Finally, in Ezekiel's account the sending of David to be prince over the people of Israel serves as a stabilizing factor (cf. 37:24–28). He not only gives political leadership but will also rule over a land where peace and safety prevail and there is wealth and plenty—a reality also reflected in the Akkadian texts. However, in Ezekiel the prince fades to a supporting role, and Yahweh becomes the motivator and director of the restoration and blessing of the land.

---

53. Grayson and Lambert, "Akkadian Prophecies," 22.

54. The prophecies of Haggai and Zechariah maintain the human element in temple construction, which is unseen here in Ezekiel.

The Marduk Prophecy[55]

The *vaticinia ex eventu* prophecy of Marduk is again very close to the *Akkadian Prophecies*. We see this in the motifs of a coming earthly king who will effect great prosperity in the land of Babylon as people are gathered from exile and the land brings forth abundance. In the *Marduk Prophecy* this is witnessed by the promise of abundant fish, agricultural produce, and clement weather with proper clouds for rain all of which is closely connected to the restoration of temples. The return of Marduk to his temple allows the "prince" to "experience the goodness of god."[56] The most notable similarity between the *Marduk Prophecy* and Ezekiel's vision is the control of the god Marduk over what is taking place. The first person references to the deity closely resembles that of Ezekiel's vision in chs. 40–48 where Yahweh is overseeing all that unfolds. Also, the futuristic/prophetic aspect of the prophecy matches the prophetic tenor of Ezekiel's message as well.

The Uruk Prophecy[57]

The message of the *Uruk Prophecy* is very similar to that found in the *Marduk Prophecy*. After a series of evil kings, a good king comes and restores the gods to their temples and brings prosperity to the land. Part of the text reads, "He [the good king] will rebuild the temples of Uruk and restore the sanctuaries of the gods. He will renew Uruk. The gates of Uruk he will build of lapis lazuli. He will fill the rivers and fields with abundant yield."[58] Here abundance, temple restoration, and general order are the hallmark of this good king's rule. Even though the prophecy is somewhat harder to date than perhaps other Akkadian

---

55. Generally dated to the reign of Nebuchadnezzar I (1125–1104 BCE). Cf. Clifford, "Roots of Apocalypticism," 13. For translations and discussion see also Longman, *Akkadian Autobiography*, 132–42, 233–35; "The Marduk Prophecy," COS 1.149:480–81 and Foster, *Before the Muses*, 388–91.

56. Arnold and Beyer, "Marduk Prophecy," 216. See also "Marduk Prophecy," COS 1.149:480–81.

57. For an overview and discussion, see Longman, *Fictional Akkadian Autobiography*, 146–49, 237–38.

58. Arnold and Beyer, *Readings from the Near East*, 217; and Hunger and Kaufman, "Akkadian Prophecy," 371–75.

prophecies, most scholars place it between 720 BCE[59] and 562 BCE.[60] These dates allow for at least the possibility of it being known by Ezekiel. We can be somewhat assured that if such prophecies were common in the time of Ezekiel, who was a prophet himself, he would have been familiar with them or at least their general themes. We can ascertain that the utopian rule of the good kings in these "prophecies" does match the return of David/the prince in Ezekiel 34, 37 and 40–48.

We may conclude that these five literary examples from Babylon (*The Dream of Gudea* included here) have many themes and motifs in common with Ezekiel's final prophecies of restoration and blessing. Ezekiel's unique presentation proves that he was not a slave to the common genres of his period, but may very well have seized on themes and motifs present in the common literature where he lived. However, the presentation of Ezekiel far exceeds that of the ANE literature because of his strong theological bent that informed his final message (e.g., monotheism).

This being noted, the overarching motif of the gods being returned to their temples does deserve closer scrutiny due to the climactic nature of this same event here in chs. 40–48. This concept was prolific in the ANE and may very well have informed Ezekiel's choice of particular motifs and the general layout and framework for his prophetic message to the exiles. There can be little doubt that such a well-known concept of temple restoration and proper return and enthronement of the gods was known in the cultural heartland of the ANE. Furthermore, it is possible that the exiles themselves may have worked on temple restoration in Babylon as slaves in a foreign land.

---

59. Goldstein, "Uruk Prophecy," 43–46, argues for the period of Marduk-apla-iddina II who was a puppet king of Assyria and ruled in Babylon. He was a benefactor of Uruk. He ruled from 721–710 BCE at which time he was forced to leave Babylon by Assyria because of his rebellion.

60. Hunger and Kaufman, "Akkadian Prophecy," 371–75, date the text to the reign of Amel-Marduk, the son and co-regent of Nebuchadnezzar II (605–562 BCE). They base their conclusion upon lines 11–19 of the prophecy that speaks of the world domination of a ruler and his son in Babylon and their benevolence to Uruk. For example, line 16 of the reverse side of the tablet points to this world domination; "After him his son will arise as king in Uruk and become master over the world" (Hunger and Kaufman translation). Hunger and Kaufman see the text as propaganda by a priest or diviner for the unpopular son of Nebuchadnezzar II. On the other hand, Lambert, *Jewish Apocalyptic*, 11–12, argues that the lineage used by Kaufman and Hunger is off and inconsistent, and opts for Nabopolassar and his son Nebuchadnezzar II as the last two benevolent kings to Uruk.

ANE Examples of the Return of the Gods to Their Temples

As we saw above in ch. 2 the motif of the *departure* of gods from their temples is a ubiquitous motif throughout the ANE. Similarly, we can also find numerous ANE literary examples of the *return* of the gods to their temples after a period of punishment or exile exercised against a people or nation.[61] The difference in the two motifs, however, is the focus on the blessings of the gods when they return to their abodes. Furthermore, the strength and stability of a particular nation and its ruler allowed such a policy to flourish. Once a ruler gained hegemony over his rivals, the practice of reversing the damage done to temples and their gods was often undertaken (e.g., Esarhaddon's work on Babylon after Sennacherib's destruction in 689). We pointed out this concept as the first of the ten steps in temple construction above, viz., temples were (re)built after a ruler gained rest from his enemies. While the political motivation behind such actions cannot be overlooked, the belief that such acts appeased the gods, both foreign and domestic, also played a key role. This motivation can be seen in Cyrus' decree to allow the return of the Jewish exiles to Jerusalem in 538 BCE (cf. Ezra 1:1–4). It is clear that Cyrus' decree also allowed for the return of the cult objects and the rebuilding of the temple. Although Cyrus is said to have been prompted by Yahweh, which no doubt he was (cf. Isa 44:28), he nonetheless was clearly following standard ANE precedent. It should be noted, however, that many times these acts of beneficence flowed out of a polytheistic ideology. Conquering kings, as a rule, did not want to offend any great deity, but rather sought their approval—a hedging of their bets, so to speak.

Interestingly, this picture of hegemony and then restoration is presented in Ezekiel 38–48. Yahweh, the ultimate King, destroyed the threat from all the nations surrounding his land and gained hegemony over the nations. However, instead of restoring other nations' temples and gods, (something unacceptable to the sovereign Lord), he restores his own temple and brings abundance and blessing to his land of Israel.

---

61. See appendix in Kutsko, *Between Heaven and Earth*, 157–69, for a detailed listing of the texts containing this motif, as well as the removal and repair of gods in the ANE from the period of the Kassite ruler, Agum-kakrime (ca. 1590 BCE) to the Persian ruler, Cyrus II (559/538–530 BCE). See also Hurowitz, *Exalted House*.

Neo-Assyrian Policy under Esarhaddon

The reign of Esarhaddon, and for that matter Ashurbanipal,[62] marked an increase in the restoration of temples and the return of the gods to their sanctuaries. In the annals of Esarhaddon (the *Uruk A* recension) line 16 we read, "(he, Esarhaddon) restored the temple of Ashur and constructed again Esagila and Babylon (and) renewed Eanna."[63] In the *Ashur-Babylonian* text lines 36–37 we find a similar comment about the restoration of the gods. "(Esarhaddon) the priest who purifies the images of the great gods, builder of the temple of Assur, restorer of Esagila and Babylon, who returns the captive peoples (the gods of the lands[64]) to their places, and settles them (there) for all time (*lit.*, in lasting abodes)."[65]

Esarhaddon's and Ashurbanipal's policy of temple reconstruction and returning gods and goddesses to their temples extended beyond the region of Babylon. Concerning this philanthropic policy Kutsko notes, "Several accounts exist of these efforts, indicating the political effectiveness of the policy."[66] He goes on to point out the numerous texts that betray this policy in the annals of Esarhaddon whereby gods/statues were returned to the cities of Nineveh, Der, Erech, Larsa, and Sippar-Arur.[67] Moreover, this policy of returning gods and temple repair can be traced also to the reigns of Nabopolasar[68] and later Cyrus.[69]

In Ezekiel's vision it is Yahweh who builds his own temple and restores and "repairs" his own people in the exile and then returns them to their land of birth and promise. Because John Kutsko has done extensive research on this motif it seems appropriate to do a brief excursus on his hypothesis and a few of his conclusions.

---

62. See Thompson, *Prisms of Esarhaddon and Ashurbanipal* 1:29–34, cols. i–iv.

63. Borger, *Asarhaddons*, 74, § 47, *Uruk rec.* A, line 16.

64. Luckenbill, *Ancient Records*, 2:258, opts for the translation "returns the captive peoples"; however, in Borger's transliteration and translation, Borger opts for "national gods" (i.e., Landesgötter) in the reconstruction of the text. See Borger, *Asarhaddon*, 80, § 53, *AsBb*A, line 37.

65. Luckenbill, *Ancient Records*, 2:258.

66. Kutsko, *Between Heaven and Earth*, 116–17.

67. Ibid., 117. For a series of texts relating to this topic, see Borger, *Asarhaddon*, 78–91, § 53 and Luckenbill, *Ancient Records*, 2:242–64.

68. Grayson, *Chronicles*, 88, Chronicle 2, lines 16–17.

69. "Cyrus," *ANET*, 315–16.

Excursus: John Kutsko's "The Image of God"[70]

The work of Kutsko and some of his conclusions, especially in relation to the concluding chapters of Ezekiel, shed light on the unity of the restoration chapters of Ezekiel. His connection of temple abandonment by the gods in ANE literature and the restoration motif is directly related to some of the conclusions I have been presenting throughout.

Kutsko argues for a direct Mesopotamian link between Ezekiel's message against Israel's idolatry, and the symbolism of the exile, repair, and restoration of idols/images as found in ANE texts.[71] He posits that in the same way kings such as Sennacherib, Esarhaddon, Ashurbanipal, and Cyrus "exiled" foreign gods of conquered lands and then later repaired, restored, and returned the "images of the gods and goddesses" (ṣalam ilil ilāni-Akk) to their homelands, so too Yahweh exiled, "repaired," and restored his people. According to Kutsko, this ANE motif is applied directly to Israel's idolatry. Part of Kutsko's thesis rests on the assumption that Ezekiel stresses the belief that Israel embodies the image of God; what Kutsko posits comes from Ezekiel's familiarity with the "image of God" (ṣelem ʾĕlōhîm) motif of the so-called Priestly writer of Genesis 1.

Kutsko notes that in Ezekiel 11 the people of Israel are exiled because of their sinful idolatry while in chs. 36 and 37, they are depicted as being "repaired" and returned to their land. Thus, the restoration/recreation of Israel in the image of God and the repatriation of the nation finds its roots in Mesopotamian literature reflecting this motif. Moreover, Kutsko draws many linguistic parallels when comparing the sin of Israel to her idols (e.g., Israel had a "heart of stone," representative of their "stone" idols—cf. Ezek 20:32–34). This stony heart, however, was replaced with a "living heart" (i.e., a heart of flesh) as noted in Ezekiel 36:26. Therefore, Kutsko sees in the restoration motifs of chs. 36–37 a direct parallel to the ANE literature concerning the repair and restoration of the gods. In Israel's case, Yahweh had exiled them and then restored and "repaired" the people's hearts before they were returned to their land. This was essential in order for them to be

---

70. The following analysis is a broad overview and summation of portions of Kutsko's book, *Between Heaven and Earth*. See also Kutsko, "Ezekiel's Anthropology," 119–41.

71. In this endeavor, Kutsko in particular juxtaposes chs. 11 and 20 to chs. 36 and 37.

repatriated to Israel as a changed people—a picture clearly presented in chs. 36–48.[72]

While this portion of Kutsko's work focuses more on the chapters of Ezekiel covered in ch. 4, above, his use of the motif of the return and restoration of the gods fits best within our discussion of chs. 40–48. This being noted, Kutsko certainly makes some interesting parallels between the Mesopotamian motifs and the text of Ezekiel. Moreover, his insights into the Hebrew text of Ezekiel 20 and 36 are thought-provoking to say the least. However, to what degree this "repairing" of the idols motif as found in Mesopotamian literature serves as a background to larger portions of the book of Ezekiel and the "repairing" of the Israelites' hearts is not as clear.

It is very possible that this may have been a sub-theme in the mind of Ezekiel especially when it comes to chs. 40–48. Kutsko's conclusion that Yahweh is "repairing" the hearts of his people is correct. Theologically, Yahweh is obviously using prophets like Ezekiel to "repair" the hearts and sinful mindset of his people, something that would not happen overnight. Also, the exile would be the means by which Yahweh brought about a shift in the way the house of Israel viewed idolatry. For all intents and purposes the exile had its intended effect by removing the idolatrous practices of the people when they returned to their land.

There are, however, a couple points where I depart from Kutsko's thinking. First, the vision and covenant-curse framework, which I have been arguing throughout, makes the most sense of the entire work of Ezekiel from beginning to end. Second, the reversal of the curse imagery depicted in 37:1–14 appears to be juxtaposed to the curse imagery found in chs. 38–39, as I noted in ch. 4. In this vein, Kutsko does next to nothing with chs. 38–39 in his presentation of the ANE motifs of exile, repair, and repatriation of the gods. This creates a problem especially as it relates to the parallel imagery of the unburied bodies as found in 37:1–14 and 39:17–20. What is more, chs. 38–39 best lay the groundwork for chs. 40–48 and the atmosphere of peace and safety from all Israel's enemies. Thus, it appears that Kutsko's presentation perhaps functions better as a sub-theme to the greater vision and covenant-curse framework. Nevertheless, his insights add much to the discussion and aid in our understanding of the "image of

---

72. Kutsko, *Between Heaven and Earth*, 124–49.

God" motif and the probable ANE parallels present in Ezekiel. Finally, Kutsko's argument in relation to Ezekiel's use of Mesopotamian motifs only strengthens my assertions as I have been contending all along.

Summary

We can conclude therefore that the ANE motifs of temple repair and the restoration of gods to their sanctuaries indeed find affinity with Ezekiel's presentation in the closing chapters. The motifs of abundance, blessing, temple restoration and the repatriation of gods when a righteous king reigns have their parallels here in chs. 40–48. The disconnect comes, however, in the realm of the theological perspective as well as the eschatological ideals presented in Ezekiel's vision. Theologically, Yahweh is in control, not a human ruler. Moreover, eschatologically Ezekiel's vision was never fulfilled as envisioned and therefore perhaps awaits a final enactment.

Curses Reversed: A Restored Prince and Land

The motifs of a restored king, land, blessing, temple repair, and return of the gods find ample support in ANE texts as touched on above.[73] As part of Ezekiel's program of restoration, the restoration of these particulars also plays an important role in what Ezekiel saw as the ultimate fulfillment of curse reversal.

The King/Prince Restored [74]

We have demonstrated throughout these last two chapters that the restoration of Israel to nationhood in their own land followed by abundance and blessing is directly connected to covenant curse reversals. The coming of David to rule over the restored nation is representative of the utopian ideal Ezekiel envisioned in the eschaton.[75] David's role as leader, while apparently vital as noted in 34:23–24 and 37:24–25,

---

73. Block, "Divine Abandonment," 40.

74. For an in-depth discussion on the roles played by all levels of leadership in Ezekiel's renewed Israel, see Duguid, *Leaders of Israel*.

75. Boadt, "Mythological Themes," 220, suggests that Ezekiel's use of *naśi'* here harks back to the idealized rule of the *naśi'* in Numbers 2 and 7.

does not equate to a central functionary in the final nine chapters. Interestingly we do not even see David's name mentioned again after ch. 37; instead we see only the general term "prince" (נָשִׂיא) used, especially in chs. 45, 46, and 48.[76] Some see this as evidence of later editorial work and/or multiple authorship.[77] There can be no question that the absence of David's name does cause one to wonder why. The scope of this study will not allow for an in-depth analysis as to why such an omission was made. Moreover, it does not serve as a major detraction in light of the numerous other connecting themes and motifs. Nevertheless, there are a few possible reasons for this lacuna. First, the ongoing rhetorical argument of Ezekiel focuses on Yahweh as "King"/ Suzerain over the nation of Israel. In these closing chapters Ezekiel appears to be more concerned with the restoration of Yahweh as the rightful *king* whereby the temple and the land take secondary "billing."

76. Tuell, *Law of the Temple*, 103–20, esp. 115–16, suggests that the "prince" in these closing chapters is a reference to the Persian-appointed governors of Judah beginning during the reign of Darius I. He bases his assumptions upon the references to the role of the prince as one who assures just weights and measures in 45:10-12 along with the secondary role played by the prince in these closing chapters. Tuell avers that the prince is under the "great king" of Persia (i.e., Darius I). It appears that Tuell's position is based upon a "reworking" of some of the dating issues surrounding chs. 40–48 suggested by Messel, *Ezechielfragen*, 21–30, 127–33. Two problems immediately arise from Tuell's assessment. First, by his own admission (113), the weight system used by Ezekiel or his followers could have been based upon Babylonian measurements that assigned 60 shekels per mina as noted in 45:10-12 which was later adopted by the Persians. Ezekiel could therefore have been using the well-known measurement from his day in his prophecy to show that established leadership (as was the case in Babylon) should guarantee order in business. Second, Tuell suggests that the message of the chapters dealing with the prince was reflective of the actual role played by the Judean governors under Darius I, the "great king." This conclusion flies in the face of the ongoing message of peace, safety, freedom, and the like portrayed not only in these chapters but more importantly, in chs. 34–39. Indeed, the purpose of the opening chapters of this final vision is to establish Yahweh as the final king over his people in a renewed land. To suggest that this prophecy in some way reflects Persian hegemony over Judah would be to deny the very tenor of the eschatological hope present in the text. Moreover, beyond the obvious equating of David with the "prince" in 34:24 and 37:25, it appears that the enthroning of Yahweh in this renewed city and temple serves as a clear picture of the kingship of Yahweh over the land and people. Therefore the substitution of the term *melek*/"king" with *naśî*/"prince" in the final vision makes perfect sense based upon the general message being set forth. The Davidic prince was under the King, Yahweh. Finally, it is perhaps misguided to feel the need to find an actual historical event for an explanation of these closing chapters that clearly have an eschatological bent throughout especially in light of chs. 40–43 and 47:1–12.

77. Cf. Duguid, *Ezekiel*, 11–31, 142–43, who argues against a *naśî* strand.

One should not forget that the prince does play a key role in these restoration chapters but he takes on a nondescript quality. Again this may be for the purpose of elevating the return and kingship of Yahweh. Second, in the earlier chapters where David is mentioned (i.e., 34:23, 24; 37:24, 25) it is in the context of the "covenant of peace." It is possible that where covenants are in play a defined leader needed to be named. In this vein, David was the ideal king and these chapters dealing with covenant seem to be reminiscent of an earlier ideal age. Third, in 37:25 (the last appearance of David's name), David *is* linked directly to the "prince" where the term *naśi'* is actually used. This may in fact be for the very purpose of making the connection to the prince in the closing chapters. Fourth, there is definitely a span of time between the three appearances of the term in the noted prophecies. Therefore the change between these earlier chapters and the use of "prince" in chs. 40–48 may have more to do with the purpose and direction of the prophet as opposed to multiple authorship. Finally, the focus in the closing chapters is more on cultic aspects like those found in Leviticus whereas chs. 34 and 37 seem to have more of a social and civil tone. This cultic bent can be seen in the separation of the holy and profane in the removal of the kings' bones from the presence of the temple, and by extension, Yahweh (cf. 43:7–9). It is possible that Ezekiel did not want to link David's name with the kings who started the practice of being buried near the temple.

To summarize, Ezekiel's primary purpose throughout is for the nation in exile to understand that Yahweh has always been its true Suzerain and King and any earthly ruler must be subservient to that reality. It is this focus of the prophet, which solidifies our assumption that the visions, especially those dealing with the glory of Yahweh, are the primary driving force of the overall message and framework. We can be assured, however, that any restoration and curse reversal was not seen as complete in Ezekiel's eyes without the recognition of the Davidic covenant (cf. 2 Samuel 7) and the restoration of Israel's greatest king. Where chs. 17 and 19 had warned about, and mourned, the fall of the last Davidic king, Zedekiah (cf. also 21:30–32 [Heb] and 34:1–16), the restoration of the Davidic line would be highlighted by Israel's greatest king, David himself.

The Land and Priesthood Restored

THE LAND[78]

The motifs of the restoration of the land and the promise of abundance, themes clearly reflected in the ANE literature that we covered above, find fertile ground in the final chapters of Ezekiel. In a general sense, where the pollution of the land had been used as a metaphor for the corruption of the nation of Israel (cf. 7:2; 8:17; 9:9; 12:19–20; etc.), now the land will reflect the blessings and abundance of Yahweh. Furthermore, the desolation of the land and the destruction of Jerusalem showed that Judah's sin had had an adverse affect even on inanimate objects. However, Ezekiel remedies the curse on the land in these closing chapters and restores Jerusalem to a level of splendor far exceeding its previous state (cf. 36:35; 45:2, 4).[79] The renaming of the city "Yahweh is there" completes this restoration of both land and city.[80]

Also we see a restoration of the mountains. The motif of the cursing of the mountains is prevalent throughout the book of Ezekiel both for Israel and the nations (e.g., chs. 6, 17, 35–36, 38–39). For Israel this entailed having the mountains defiled by the corpses of her idolaters. Here in the closing chapters, however, we see a return of the glory of the Lord and the building of his temple on the mountain of Israel. Boadt correctly points out that "Ezekiel never refers to the home of the temple as Mt. Zion . . . The new mountain of the temple in 40–48 . . . instead becomes a new Mt. Sinai."[81] But this does not negate the fact that Mount Zion is indeed the mountain being renewed and recast into the eschatological home of Yahweh and his temple. As I noted at the

---

78. Tuell, *Law of the Temple*, 153–74. Tuell develops an impressive explanation for the divisions of the land in Ezekiel 47–48 in which he connects the borders of the land in Ezekiel's vision to the Persian-period province of Abar-Nahara. While Tuell's research and comparisons are impressive and detailed, one is still left wondering if the divisions could not just as easily be coordinated to the Babylonian-era borders or an idealized eschatological depiction of the land as presented in Num 34:1–12 or Josh 15:1–4. Cf. also, Galambush, "Castles in the Air," 158–63, for a discussion on the renewal of the land in Ezekiel 40–48.

79. There is textual evidence supporting the purification of the land especially the priests' portion which is called "holy" (cf. 45:1, 4; 48:12). We also see in the re-division of the land an implicit renewal and an explicit reordering (cf. ch. 48, see also the cleansing of the land in 39:11–16).

80. Galambush, "This Land Is My Land," 80–86.

81. Boadt, "Ezekiel," 2:721.

beginning of this chapter, the implications of 40:1 seems to betray the prophet's focus on Jerusalem, viz., Mt. Zion, in these closing chapters.

On a grander scale, the large swaths of land allotted to the prince, tribes, and the priestly class in chs. 45 and 48 exemplify the reality of a renewed land and possessions in the Land of Promise—what some see as a "new Joshua event."[82] In these closing chapters the land is not depicted as needing to be possessed and conquered but rather, in light of the context of chapters 38–39, all foreign armies and influences are absent in Ezekiel's utopian kingdom where Yahweh rules supreme. Clearly this is a fitting conclusion to a curse-laden book where physical exile from the land was the capstone of the covenant curses.

The Abundance of Water and Food

Another predominant picture of curse reversal and abundance is the use of water imagery especially as it relates to the temple. Niditch points out that "the river imagery has Edenesque qualities—all is provided in an ultimate fulfillment of the Deuteronomic blessings. In contrast to the implications of the Eden narrative in Genesis 2–3, but in tune with Genesis 1, this easy fecundity coexists with hierarchy, with social structure, and in fact is made possible by a proper orderliness of human relationships within the world demarcated by the temple and its environs."[83] The harmony of these social, cultic, and hierarchical orders in the restored land is thus further highlighted by the harmony of the fructifying qualities of the river flowing from the temple which brings abundance to the land.[84] Also, the presentation of the new Israel in "Edenesque" terms serves well to highlight the prophet's utopian presentation, something already noted in 36:35 (i.e., "garden of Eden"). In these final chapters, the river in Ezekiel's vision is the source of life (see also Ps. 46:4 and Isa 8:6–8) in the New Jerusalem and, as Niditch comments, these types of "idealized sources of life are common in Near Eastern and other mythologies."[85]

82. Zimmerli, *Fiery Throne*, 55.

83. Niditch, "Ezekiel 40–48," 217.

84. Allen, "Antecedents," 18, posits that this is possibly the little Gihon spring that seems to have cultic importance, according to 1 Kgs 1:33, 45 and Ps 110:7.

85. Niditch, "Ezekiel 40–48," 217. Cf. also Levenson, *Program of Restoration*, 28–29. In a similar vein, Bodi, *Poem of Erra*, 310, points out that the "oracle of bliss" with which the *Poem of Erra* ends (V. 33–37) presents the Tigris and the Euphrates as

However, the water imagery in Ezekiel serves a much greater purpose. The reversal of drought and barrenness epitomized by the blossoming of the Dead Sea and its environs exemplifies the lengths to which the curses once placed upon Israel will be reversed. Ezekiel 34:26–27 and ch. 47 help paint this picture for us where a well-watered land enables abundant crops to grow in the desert and fish to inhabit the streams.

Food Production and Availability

Closely associated with the river imagery of ch. 47 is also the practical aspect of food and water availability for the average person. Indeed, the reversal of curses dealing with the lack of food and water plays an important role in these final chapters. In 4:16–17, God tells Ezekiel that the people will be forced to limit their daily intake of water and food because of the siege and war. In 47:1–5 we see this reversed with water so plentiful in the renewed land that there is water to swim in and a river that cannot be crossed. Also, while famine once prevailed and food was scarce (cf. 4:16; 5:12, 16–17; 7:15, 19; 12:16; 14:13, 21), in 47:12 plenty is the norm in the period of restoration (cf. also Joel 2).[86] Fish, an important part of Israel's former economy and diet, will be in abundance and offer a means of employment for many (47:9–10) even to the level of marine stocks equaling the "Great Sea." Finally, where the charred trees and vines served as a negative metaphor for the nation (cf. 15:6; 19:12–13) in 47:7 and 12 we see them as a source of abundant food and for healing.

It is worth noting that as a general rule, the first thing devastated in a time of war is the arborous aspects of the land (cf. Deut 20:20). Even today Israel is attempting to reforest the mountains surrounding Jerusalem, mountains which have been stripped by centuries of war, siege, and exploitive deforestation. In Ezekiel's day this would have been no different. The landscape around Jerusalem after Nebuchadnezzar's two-and-a-half-year siege must have been devastating to view for those remaining in the land and those departing into exile. Yet even

---

restoring the fertility of the land. In this case the restoration motif is accented by the life-giving properties of these two important rivers in Mesopotamia.

86. 2 Baruch 29:4–6 picks up on the motif of the plenteous amount of food in the end times.

this destruction is renewed. Trees that took years or even generations to come to a level of satisfactory production find instant fruitfulness in the renewed land beside the river issuing from the temple.[87] The year-round production of the trees for both food and medicinal purposes completes the curse reversal.

THE PRIESTHOOD RESTORED

Finally, Ezekiel's obsession with the Zadokite priesthood and proper worship appears to betray a particular bias for one segment of the priestly family.[88] While many times this becomes the focus of debate among scholars, something well beyond our present topic, it nonetheless shows a reversal of the curse that fell upon all levels of leadership within the nation (cf. chs. 13, 14, esp. ch. 8 and 22:26).[89] Apparently the Zadokites had in some way remained faithful to Yahweh even during the exile and Ezekiel sought to highlight that qualification. What his exact purposes are for doing so may never be known. What is important to point out here is the fact that in this restored land, there would be a thriving priesthood devoted to the service of Yahweh and his new earthly abode. What had been corrupted by the priesthood of the past will be restored and the sins of those overseeing the cultic system, expunged.

---

87. As pointed out earlier, the *Dream of Gudea* has many parallels with the temple construction and restoration of the land. Here we find a close parallel with the same text. During the dream of Gudea, trees appear in Gudea's renewed kingdom "all at once from above." These include ebony trees, cypress, *zabalum*, *ḥalub*, cedars, etc. Cf. Edzard, RIME 3/1, Cylinder A, col xii, lines 1–6.

88. Niditch "Ezekiel 40–48," 119, also points out that several scholars argue that the "virulently pro-Zadokite" sections of Ezekiel 40–48 (i.e., 44:10–31 and 48:11) are from the prophet himself. Niditch, however, still posits that 44:10–14 are later insertions but tempers this position by stating that vv. 10–31 still may contain original material. For further discussion, see Greenberg, "Design and Themes," 181–208 esp. 196, 208; Haran, "Law Code," 61, 65; McConville, "Priests and Levites," 3–31; and Duguid, "Putting Priests in Their Place," 43–59. For an opposing view to that of Niditch on Ezek 44:10–14, see Duke, "Punishment or Restoration," 61–81.

89. For a discussion on the key role played by the priesthood in chs. 40–48, see Fechter, "Priesthood," 673–99.

Conclusion

What we may conclude from this section is that the restoration chapters of Ezekiel present ultimate blessings on the land through the reversal of the curses of the Law. Indeed, the utopian picture presented in the final chapters of Ezekiel go beyond the blessings of Deuteronomy and Leviticus and suggest that in the future the people of Israel will experience blessings unmatched in their history. Obedience to their Suzerain and a reversal of the curses of the Law enables the restored nation to dwell in the land and perform their function as intended from the outset, namely, to be a light to the Gentile nations (cf. Isa 49:6; 60:3). Wolf perhaps says it best when he comments, "With the raising up of the righteous king, the restoration of Israel will be consummated. Once again Jerusalem will become the center of a prosperous kingdom, filled with people enjoying plentiful crops, a city safe and secure. In spite of the harsh realities of judgment, a gracious YHWH delights in reversing the curses that covenant disobedience had made necessary. Indeed, in a concrete sense Israel's restoration consists of a transcendent reversal of these divine curses—a miraculous and marvelous healing of the effects of transgression. As a result of this reversal, Israel's final state will surpass in glory any to which she had attained formerly."[90]

Ezekiel's Message Comes Full Circle in 48:35b

35b וְשֵׁם־הָעִיר מִיּוֹם יְהוָה שָׁמָּה

"Now the name of the city from *that* day *forward will be* Yahweh is there."

The seemingly odd appearance of this last phrase in 48:35b, especially after an entire chapter dealing with the division of the land, can be accounted for on the basis of the prophet's rhetorical argument.[91] The presentation of the curse motif, as we have attempted to demonstrate

---

90. Wolf, "Transcendent Nature," 325.

91. Abegg et al., *Dead Sea Scrolls Bible*, 407, suggest that this phrase is the answer to the fundamental question being addressed by Ezekiel's prophecy to the exiles, "has God abandoned us?" However, this understanding seems somewhat simplistic in light of the complex indictments and curses being leveled against the nation and exiles throughout the entire prophecy, not to mention the detailed rhetorical argument that is in play.

throughout, helps us to understand the importance of its presence here. While the final vision of chs. 40–48 appears, at first glance, to be a self-contained unit, in essence it is an integral part of the overall covenant curse reversal format. This final vision has been masterfully woven into the larger message and rhetorical argument of Ezekiel with this final phrase serving as a fitting conclusion.

The first covenant curse to be enacted was the removal of Yahweh's presence from the city and his people—a picture of the sealed fate of Judah. Yahweh's glory had departed through the eastern gate of the city and stood over the Mount of Olives. From this vantage point Yahweh had served as the presiding Judge over the curses that would fall upon the city and nation. This departure of the glory of the Lord due to Judah's sin and idolatry had made the nation vulnerable to attacks from the surrounding nations and paved the way for the curses of the Law. Thus, the unfolding of the prophecy by means of a visionary experience and oracular speeches from Ezekiel proved to the people once and for all that Yahweh's word was to be understood as accurate and sure and the curses of the Law something to be feared. Furthermore, the nation had come to realize that Yahweh's prophet Ezekiel was certainly to be trusted because his word had indeed come to pass as warned (33:33).

At the same time, as assuredly as the curses came upon the nation after the departure of the Lord according to the word of Ezekiel, so too the blessing of the Lord would come upon the people and land when Yahweh's glory returned. In this regard, in 43:7 and 9 Ezekiel had pointed out that as part of the blessings of the return of the Lord, Yahweh would dwell "among the children of Israel forever" (בְּתוֹךְ בְּנֵי־יִשְׂרָאֵל לְעוֹלָם), terminology reminiscent of the Exodus generation (cf. Exod 29:45). Therefore, this final address in the book serves as a final assertion that the curses *had* indeed been reversed and the nation liberated from its oppressors. As in the day of Noah when the Lord used the rainbow as a sign of the covenant never again to destroy the world by a flood (cf. Gen 9:13), so too in Ezekiel's day a sign would be given beyond the renewed covenant, namely, the very presence of the Lord. Where the city of Jerusalem had showcased the horrors of Yahweh's wrath in the past, in the restored nation, the city would epitomize the finished work of curse reversal and the blessings of Yahweh (cf. also Isa 62:4–5). The Lord would be there; the very name of the city would reflect this reality once and for all.[92]

A Final Note: The Unity of Ezekiel's Message in 40–48 and ANE Motifs[93]

In light of the unity of themes and rhetorical argument presented above, we can conclude that the motifs found in these closing chapters of Ezekiel are further evidence of an organized framework and intentionality in how the book unfolds. It also adds to our understanding of how we are to view the purpose of chs. 40–48 in the context of the final form of the book.[94] Recently, scholars have begun to see these unifying factors and are challenging the oft-held, historical-critical opinion that these chapters form a separate addition to Ezekiel.[95] One can see this older historical-critical bias in the work of scholars such as Eichrodt when he notes, "In the series of chapters with which the book of Ezekiel ends we meet with a part separated from the rest so as to form a self-contained whole. In it, a number of pieces of different types have been put together, representing contrary tendencies."[96]

---

92. Vawter and Hoppe, *A New Heart*, 210, suggest that this new name was "necessary" because Jerusalem had been renamed "polluted" earlier in 22:5. However, the use of "polluted" in 22:5 seems to be interpretive in the context as opposed to an actual name.

93. Zimmerli, *I Am Yahweh*, 114–15, notes that there is no reason not to assign good portions of chs. 40–48 to Ezekiel. He goes on to note, however, that later strands are to be assigned to an "Ezekielian school." Cf. also the conclusions of Stevenson, *Vision of Transformation*, 125–42, and her outline of these chapters on page 134, and Allen, "Prophetic Antecedents," 15–28, esp. 16. Allen asserts an exilic date for these chapters.

94. See also Paranuk, "Literary Architecture," 61–74, for a discussion on the literary and thematic unity of these chapters with chs. 1–3 and 8–11.

95. For example, Talmon and Fishbane, "The Structuring of Biblical Books,"139; Boadt, "Mythological Themes," 211–31; Zimmerli, *Ezekiel* 2:345, 547–53; Fohrer, *Hauptprobleme*, 95; Niditch, "Ezekiel 40–48," 211; Clements, "Ezekiel Tradition," 129.

Stevenson, *Vision of Transformation*, 7, posits that cutting and dissecting the text into pieces is like taking a patchwork quilt and removing the scraps piece by piece. She goes on, "For the text of Ezekiel 40–48, the issue is not that someone pieced together scraps, but that someone wanted a quilt."

96. Eichrodt, *Ezekiel*, 530.

It is this type of scholarly opinion that I have sought to confront by this monograph.[97] The book of Ezekiel, especially as we have presented it throughout, betrays an overarching mindset and organization second to none.[98] The oft-misunderstood concept that it represents "contrary tendencies" is exactly the opposite of what we have found through our study. The unity of these closing chapters in light of what comes before makes it clear that thematic and literary unity along with the rhetorical argument of Ezekiel causes a "slice and dice" perspective to be untenable.[99] Niditch rightly concludes that "If one puts aside redactional considerations . . . and treats the temple vision from the perspective of composition-criticism, some fascinating conclusions can be reached about the place of chaps. 40–48 in the Book of Ezekiel as it now stands. In the composition of the work, the temple vision has been located in a logical, esthetically, and traditionally appropriate place."[100]

---

97. Niditch, "Ezekiel 40–48," 211, notes that the arguments for multiple or later authorship of these chapters based on style of language is not consistent. She gives multiple examples where similar terms and phrases appear in passages that have been deemed both as "genuine" and "non-genuine" to Ezekiel. This assumption is also held by Greenberg in his work on these chapters. He concludes that those who seek to dissect the text without first considering the ANE context and style of writing that was common before and during Ezekiel's period do a disservice to the text and totally misunderstand the literary presentations of this period. See Greenberg, "Design and Themes," 183–89. Greenberg is particularly critical of the work of Harmut Gese, *Verfassungsentwurf*; Zimmerli, *Ezechiel* 2; and Wevers, *Ezechiel*. Greenberg (189) calls much of their style as "exhibiting an isolationism all too prevalent in European biblical scholarship," a similar conclusion reached by Cassuto, "Arrangement," 227–28.

98. Levenson, *Program*, 10, notes the unity between the visions of chs. 1–3, 8–11, and 40–48. See also a similar conclusion by Sweeney, "Ezekiel," 747.

99. The concept of diversity within these sections is not necessarily a new concept. Josephus (*Ant.* 10:79) noted that Ezekiel had written two books. According to Fishbane, "Sin and Judgment," 132, these books represent, 1) the oracles of doom (chs. 1–24) and 2) the temple construction (chs. 40–42). However, these two books noted by Josephus may reflect the biblical book of Ezekiel and Pseudo Ezekiel found at Qumran.

100. Niditch, "Ezekiel 40–48," 221. Niditch continues, "It is the culmination of an extremely ancient mythic pattern employed by Ezekiel elsewhere in the book, that of the victory and enthronement of the deity. The essential action motifs or plot events of this traditional theme often consist of: 1) a challenge to the deity, (2) a battle, (3) a victory, (4) a procession, (5) the enthronement/building of a 'house,' and (6) a feast. This pattern appears with variations in the Babylonian *Enuma elish* which depicts Marduk's victory over Tiamat, and the Canaanite epic of Baal and Anat, which tells of Baal's victory over the Sea and of his temporary defeat by and eventual victory over Death."

Niditch goes on to draw strong parallels between chs. 38–39 and chs. 40–48. Her presentation of the hubris[101] of the nations against God (38:10–13) and their defeat in the ensuing battle (39:1–10) followed by the establishment of peace and order (39:11–16) are thematically linked to chs. 40–48. Here she points out that the feast of 39:17–20 and the procession of 39:25–29 set the stage for the final aspect of the building of a "house" viz., the temple and cosmic order of the vision of 40–48.[102] This self-contained cosmological order according to Niditch is the clue for linking these sections together. She suggests that the building of Marduk's palace was vital in the order of creation for these early Mesopotamian thinkers (see *Enuma elish* 6.50–72).[103]

From this we can assume then that it is very possible that the symbolism and imagery of the ANE, which we have been presenting throughout, may have once again played a key role in how Ezekiel fashioned his closing vision. The pertinent motifs, which are ubiquitous in the literature we surveyed above, served as a ready-made pool of literary exemplars to draw upon. Finally, while methodological stances such as those adopted by Niditch (cf. also Greenberg footnote 97 above) may not have always been an acceptable way of viewing an OT book, an increasing number of scholars are beginning to see the validity in the canonical and literary approaches as an acceptable means of discussing the unity of particular biblical books. Building on the work of scholars such as these allows us to conclude quite assuredly that Ezekiel's message in these final chapters clearly presents a unified focus on curse reversals.

---

101. For a detailed linguistic study of the occurrence of this motif in Ezekiel, in Classical Greek, and in Akkadian literature, see Bodi, *Poem of Erra*, 123–61.

102. Niditch, "Ezekiel 40–48," 221. See also the role of the "feast" in 45:21, 23, 25.

103. See also Greenberg, "Valid Criteria," 123–35.

6

Conclusions and Implications

Conclusions and Implications

General Conclusions

THE PURPOSE OF THIS WORK HAS BEEN TO UNDERSCORE THE IMPORtant role the visions and extended metaphors of Ezekiel play in the message of the prophet as they relate to the overall framework of the final form and their relationship to an ANE setting and the curse motif (cf. diagram on p. 89 above). The visions and metaphors (i.e., the "peaks" or highpoints of the book) move the entire prophetic message toward a logical conclusion as demonstrated in our previous chapter. In chapter 1 we established the ANE and OT precedents for Ezekiel's message and the importance his new exilic home played in shaping his thought processes and visions. Ezekiel's message stands out from his contemporaries and those who came before him mainly due to the influence of the region of Babylon. Throughout we have seen the numerous motifs and themes in Ezekiel which find their parallel primarily in Mesopotamian and Assyrian literature and treaties. The use of the curse motif as a means of fashioning many of his indictments seems a foregone conclusion in light of the prevalence of treaty curses during this ever-shifting political period. Therefore it is safe to conclude that Ezekiel's methodological approach to his prophecy and his unique presentation must be understood as being predominantly influenced by his new home in Babylon.

In chapter 2 we showed that the house of Israel had failed to grasp the awesomeness and omnipotence of their Suzerain with whom they had broken covenant. The misplaced trust of the nation in the inviolability of the temple and city of Jerusalem as well as in foreign alliances had to be corrected. Therefore, the extended description of the theophanic appearance of Israel's Suzerain served a fitting introduction to the prophet's message, as Ezekiel painted a one-of-a-kind picture of Yahweh's glory and splendor. Replete with ANE symbolism and imagery pregnant with meaning for his audience, the prophet made it clear that this deity was not a god to be taken lightly. The theophany represented the reality that their offended Suzerain was coming in judgment and in vindication of his holy name so that Israel and the nations would know that he alone is the one true God and Master of the fates of both Israel and the nations.

Also in chapter 2 we explored the possible meanings behind the visionary symbolism and the fulfillment of the first and greatest curse upon the nation; that being the departure of Yahweh from his earthly abode. The numerous examples of similar phenomena from ANE literature and treaty material bolstered the presupposition that Ezekiel's message was bound to curse language found not only in Deuteronomy 28 and Leviticus 26 but also similar curse language which was ubiquitous throughout the ANE. The departure of Yahweh and his symbolic appearance in the vanguard of the Babylonian attack sealed the fate of Jerusalem and the nation. The use of a foreign nation to punish the house of Israel and implement the covenant curses is elucidated in chapter 3 of this monograph. However, it must be pointed out that in chs. 38–39 (cf. ch. 4 above) Ezekiel makes it clear that no nation could touch Yahweh's covenant people unless it was at the behest of Yahweh himself. Any attempt to attack Israel on any other terms would elicit immediate retribution by Yahweh against all foreign invaders.

Our discussion in chapter 3 dealing with the extended metaphors of chs. 16 and 23 showed that these chapters serve as a centerpiece to the oracles of judgment against the house of Israel. While the curses of the Law do not mention many of the particular punishments leveled against the rebellious house of Israel in these chapters, the text itself gave us a clue as to the possible mindset of Ezekiel. Judah and Israel had played the harlot with foreign lovers and had broken covenant with their Suzerain by going after foreign alliances as opposed to trusting in him. For this reason, Yahweh would allow his wayward vassal to suffer punishment by the "standards" of her paramours. Thus, Ezekiel invoked stripping, beating, stoning, and cutting with swords as the appropriate curse and punishment for unfaithful Israel. We also saw that many of these punishments were also used against rebellious vassals and unfaithful wives in ANE contexts. Finally, the highlighting of the oracles against Judah with the metaphors of chs. 16 and 23 allowed Ezekiel to cluster indictments related to covenant infidelity around common motifs and curses.

In chapter 4 we discovered once again that Ezekiel chose a vision as the means to present the next "peak" in the framework of his overall message. The vision of the valley of dry bones served as an appropriate picture of one of the most feared outcomes for an individual living during Ezekiel's era—the curse of non-burial. The reversal motif in chs. 25–39 are accentuated by the vision of chapter 37 and the imagery of chs. 38–39. The ultimate reversal of the curse of unburied bodies after a battle in ch. 37 is juxtaposed with the exact same curse being enacted upon the invading armies from the north in chs. 38–39. Israel will no longer need to fight for herself, her Suzerain will have the final say as he turns the sword of vengeance away from Israel (ch. 21) and lashes out against all the nations who oppose him and his people. Furthermore, within this same grouping of nations, Ezekiel chose particular nations upon which to place the same curses; curses that had once beset Israel. Edom, Egypt, Ammon, Moab, Philistia, Assyria, and Tyre are all implicated in some way for their treatment of the covenant people and for their role in broken covenants and causing the house of Israel to go astray.

Finally, as we pointed out in chapter 5, the ultimate reversal of the curses is fulfilled in the final vision depicting the rebuilding of the temple and the return of the Lord to his earthly abode. Abundance, blessing, and fecundity under Davidic rule and proper cultic practices are the hallmarks of the renewed land. Just as Yahweh earlier had overseen the destruction of his city and temple, so too will he oversee the restoration of his land so that the house of Israel would know that Yahweh is her true Suzerain. The final "peak" in the framework of Ezekiel's rhetorical structure once again relies on a vision—one spanning nine chapters depicting a utopian existence for Israel living at peace in a restored land. Ezekiel's message comes full circle as the greatest of the covenant curses, namely the departure of one's god, is reversed and the city of Jerusalem once more becomes the earthly dwelling place of Yahweh with the city being renamed, "Yahweh is there" (יְהוָה שָׁמָּה).

We may conclude that it seems very probable that Ezekiel had an intended purpose in placing his four visions and two metaphors at key junctures in his book. Moreover, Ezekiel's use of the curse motif, coupled with this metaphor and visionary framework, enabled the prophet to link present realities in the exile with known ANE and OT punishments for treaty/covenant violations. It is apparent that the evidence appears to point in this direction. The message found in Ezekiel, no doubt delivered to a primarily oral and aural society, is housed in visions, symbols, and metaphors in order to highlight key aspects of the prophet's message. This structural framework thus allowed the prophet to group large portions of material around memorable focal points that would not only warn his exilic generation of what was coming but also educate future generations about the holiness and sovereignty of their heavenly Suzerain.

Theological Conclusions

As pointed out in chapter 2 above, Ezekiel is often preoccupied with conveying the gravity of the nation's sin to the exilic community and those still in Judah before it fell. Obviously the exilic community needed to understand why they were in Babylon and how Babylon's gods seemingly appeared stronger than Yahweh. However, Ezekiel's theological presentation had an even greater focus.

To begin with, Ezekiel's calling and ministry in distant Babylon debunked the theological misconception that Yahweh could only operate and be worshipped in Jerusalem and Judah. Moreover, the theological reeducation of the people regarding the sovereignty and holiness of Yahweh harks back to the same educational process undergone by the wilderness generation. Yahweh's appearance in theophanic form had caused the nascent nation to understand the awesomeness and otherness of the God with whom they were entering into covenant at Sinai. In similar covenant-enactment fashion, Ezekiel's theological message started with a theophanic appearance of their Suzerain, only this time it was for the opposite purpose. They were not entering into covenant; they were being judged by the covenant curses spelled out in Deuteronomy 28 and Leviticus 26.

The appearance of Yahweh in his theophanic glory in Exodus 20:19–20 was for the sole purpose of placing the fear of their Suzerain in the hearts of the people. This, in turn, was supposed to cause them not to sin against him. Over the centuries since that incipient event the people had failed to remember the awesomeness of their Suzerain. This lack of fear of their God is the theological motive behind Ezekiel's presentation of the glory of the Lord in chs. 1–3. The proper response of the people should have been immediate fear and compliance, but instead they had mistaken the presumed presence of Yahweh in Jerusalem as an acceptance of their sinful behavior. Ezekiel's theological message could not be clearer in these opening chapters. Because the people refused to fear and keep the statutes and ordinances of the covenant, Yahweh would reeducate the nation by harsh punishments defined in the curses of the Law.

Ezekiel's presentation that Yahweh alone was to be worshipped and feared reaches a visionary apex in chs. 8–11 with an outright denunciation of the false worship present in the temple. Moreover, when Yahweh is seen leaving the temple in Jerusalem and leading the attack on his own nation, the death knell is sounded against the false theological concept of trusting in the inviolability of Jerusalem. Thus, the importance of Ezekiel's presentation of Yahweh being over every god, even those of the Babylonian juggernaut, challenged the perception that Babylon's gods were more powerful than Yahweh. One might say that Ezekiel's theological message returned the nation to a pre-exodus period when they had learned the power of their God while "exiled" in the foreign land of Egypt—then by means of the ten plagues. Finally, before the promise of the new covenant could be enacted (cf. chs. 34, 36, and 37), the house of Israel had to return to the classroom of history. They needed to be schooled in who Yahweh was. Not only was he their benefactor in the past but he could also be their worst adversary when they refused to acknowledge their sin (cf. ch. 20).

As noted in my third chapter, Ezekiel placed the nation of Israel not in the hands of a loving God but rather in the hands of her foreign paramours (cf. Ezek 23:24). The blessed and idyllic days of Hezekiah and Josiah were long past. Moreover, the theological understanding that Yahweh would protect his city when their backs were against the wall no longer had relevance for the exilic generation. The irony that the curses germane to these particular foreign nations were now falling upon the house of Israel once again bolstered the reality that the covenant nation was devoid of their divine Suzerain. Through this presentation, Ezekiel challenged the people's premise that Yahweh needed the military aid of other nations to protect his people. Indeed, Israel would come to realize that alliances with foreign powers had been the root of her spiritual and military problems. Idolatrous influences from these pagan nations had caused the people to violate the covenant. These covenant violations in turn had brought upon the nation the curses of the Law.

Finally, the recurring message of hope and restoration takes center stage in chs. 4 and 5 above. Here Ezekiel takes the opportunity to highlight this pair of theological exigencies by two final visions. The reversal of the curses and the destruction and punishment of the nations served as a reminder that Yahweh honored his covenant even though Israel refused to do so. After the appropriate period of punishment, the *ḥesed* of Yahweh once again shined forth on a nation beaten and battered due to their sin and punishment. Yahweh's love is reflected in the reversal of the harsh curse of the defeated army of Israel lying dead and unburied on the battlefield. The theological reeducation of the house of Israel draws to a close as the nation witnesses their Suzerain once again taking his place as protector and deliverer. Israel would be restored and reunited according to Yahweh's word through the prophet in ch. 37. Israel's theological perspective, now refocused by means of a new heart, would finally recognize the truth of the prophet's words and the reality of the blessings of her God even when she did not deserve it. Yahweh's grace and mercy are enacted not because the nation merited it but rather because Yahweh sought to bring honor to his name.

The final act of temple reconstruction and Yahweh's return would usher in untold blessings to the restored land. Theologically, Ezekiel's message comes full circle by presenting a utopian existence for Israel in her rejuvenated land in the future. Ezekiel's message is clear: even though the people were in exile now, they could look forward to a future in their own land with their Suzerain once more dwelling in their midst. Ezekiel's visionary sequence could not be complete without the recognition that beyond punishment, grace and restoration abounds. A renewed heart, temple, and land overseen by a renewed priesthood and Davidic prince were the utopian end desired by every exile in a foreign land of oppression. It is thus not surprising that after the extended presentation of covenant curses and woe, Ezekiel ends his message on the powerful theological note that in this renewed land of hope and blessing, the name of the city would be "the Lord is there."

Implications

The clearest implication that flows out of my presentation and conclusions above is the intentionality behind the compilation of the final form. When all is considered, the compiler of this rhetorical argument appears to have had an intended focus. That is not to say that additions could not have been made, but rather that those additions could not have affected the basic structural and rhetorical presentation of the curse-vision-metaphor combination.[1] In this regard, most important in the discussion is the role that chs. 38–39 and 40–48 play in the restoration emphasis of the final form. Chapters 40–48, especially, are needed in order to show the complete and final reversal of the curse of temple abandonment, exile, and destruction of the land and its productivity. This conclusion challenges the belief that the book reflects an accretion of material over an extended period of time with input from a multiplicity of authors.[2] Thus, scholars who suggest that chs. 38–39 can only be from a later hand, or those who suggest that chs. 40–48 are a post-exilic addition fail to grasp the complex, yet straightforward message inherent in the overall book.[3] Finally, Ezekiel's obvious use of ANE imagery suggests that authorship issues fit best within a Babylonian rather than a Palestine setting. One need not search for a later period in Israel's history when such influences could have produced a book such as Ezekiel; the exile itself matches all the required criteria. Curses, ANE symbolism, covenant violation, and an unrepentant vassal are all seeds that find fertile ground in the land of Babylon and the imagination of a "Yahweh-alone" prophet.

One final implication can be drawn from our focus on Ezekiel's use of the imagery and symbolism of the ANE. The numerous parallels between Ezekiel's visions and later apocalyptic writings causes one to wonder what influence Ezekiel's work had on these later writers and whether Ezekiel could be classed as the "proto-apocalyptic" forefather of the later apocalypticists. While there is neither time nor space within this discussion to cover the possible connections (see appendix, below) suffice it to say that one is left with the notion that there is yet

---

1. Boadt, "Mythological Themes," 215–16, comes to the same conclusion. He suggests that while some minor editing may have taken place by Ezekiel's followers, the vast majority of the material reflects a single mind.
2. Ibid., 215.
3. For example, Zimmerli, *Ezekiel* 1:74.

another entire monograph's worth of study on the implications of such a link.

Why Did the Book of Ezekiel Survive the Exilic Period?

Finally, one must also answer the question as to why Ezekiel's message, so focused on an exilic setting, survived as Scripture. In his concluding remarks, Renz presents a similar question with a less than satisfactory response. Renz proposes that Ezekiel's message encouraged the exilic community to jettison its past for a renewed future as presented by the prophet. He continues, the "initial fulfillment" of Ezekiel's vision (namely the return of the people) during the post-exilic period allowed this "exilic" message to survive beyond its immediate purpose.[4] While there can be no doubt that this was true, what Renz fails to point out is the eschatological impetus of the message. Indeed the post-exilic temple of Haggai and Zechariah's day, for example, was in no way equal to what Ezekiel had envisioned. But this neither thwarted the importance of the message nor the role played by Ezekiel's prophetic visions.[5] It was Ezekiel's grandiose picture of the renewed temple, nation, and its institutions that fueled many of the writers of the post-exilic and New Testament eras to look for a futuristic fulfillment.

In this vein, the eschatological hope offered by the visions of Ezekiel inspired not only the apocalypticists, but also those at Qumran, the New Testament writers, and possibly later zealots during the first Jewish revolt of 66–70 CE.[6] While space does not permit a detailed analysis of each, suffice it to say that John the Revelator's use of Ezekiel to fashion his message of hope serves as ample proof of the later eschatological interpretation of Ezekiel. John's Gog and Magog oracles of Revelation 19:17–21 and 20:7–10, the new Temple/Jerusalem imagery

---

4. Renz, *Rhetorical Function*, 246.

5. Mackay, "Zechariah," 197–210, suggests that Zechariah is the first "expositor" of Ezekiel 40–48 as reflected in his post-exilic prophecy. For a similar conclusion, see Plöger, *Theocracy*, 88–96 and Tuell, "Haggai-Zechariah," 263–86, esp. 268–72.

6. A fragment of Ezek 37:1–14 was found under the floor of the synagogue at Masada during recent excavations. It has been posited that during the Jewish revolt of 66–70 CE the remaining survivors at Masada were believed to have read Ezekiel 37:1–14 as the Romans beat upon their walls in 73 CE.

of ch. 21, and the Edenesque river imagery of ch. 22 share many affinities with the final 11 chapters of Ezekiel.

Finally, it is hard to dispense with the reality that Ezekiel's message fits best in one historical milieu, that being the exilic period of 597–539 BCE.[7] It goes without saying that the overall message of judgment (chs. 1–24) served Ezekiel's purpose well as a means of upbraiding those who held the false belief of an early return to Jerusalem. At the same time his message of hope would have been a means of encouragement for the post-fall community from both the prophet's immediate generation and the "second generation" of exiles.[8] It also seems fitting to conclude that the strong "Yahweh-alone" tenor of the book functioned as an effective tractate against a syncretistic worldview and those who hoped for the nation's slow amalgamation into the Babylonian empire.[9] The most logical conclusion remains, however, that Ezekiel's early visions and message of chs. 1–24 must have been preached or delivered prior to the fall of Jerusalem in 586 BCE. The symbolism and potency of the message would have served that historical situation well. Indeed, this portion of Ezekiel served as a fitting way to explain the "why" of the exile. As for the final visions and message of hope, this message has enduring qualities for any generation facing hardship and privation.

7. Boadt, "Mythological Themes," 214, suggests a date before the rebuilding of the second temple in 520 BCE. and possibly as early as 562 BCE. He suggests that if the second temple had been constructed, "Ezekiel's" temple would not have been described as such in 40–48. Moreover, in Ezekiel we see no mention of the monumental fall of Babylon or the death of Nebuchadnezzar in 562.

8. Jer 26:17–24 shows the scope and poignancy of the message of a prophet from one generation to the next. The fact that the elders of the people are rehearsing the prophecies of Micah and Uriah to the leadership of Jerusalem (both religious and civil) shows that the message of the prophets held sway at all levels of the population and the administration. The popularity of the messages in these two cases had a folklore-like appeal that reached to several levels of society. This account helps prove the high degree of plausibility that Ezekiel's message was well known at all levels of the exilic community. Cf. Carley, *Book of the Prophet Ezekiel*, 71.

9. Cf. Bickermann, "Babylonian Captivity," 1:342–58, esp. 352–8 and Steinmann, *Ézéchiel*, 11. Smith, *Palestinian Parties*, 66–68, points out the continued practice of idolatry both in the Egyptian Diaspora and the Babylonian captivity within biblical (cf. Jer 44:15–19; Ezek 14:3–9; 20:31) and archeological evidence (see esp. p. 68 of Smith). See also Lang, "Yahweh-Alone," 13–59 and Wright, *Old Testament against Its Environment*, 9–41, esp. 20–29. For further study see, Smith, *Early History of God*; Assmann, *Of God and Gods*; Becking et al., *Only One God*, and Oeming and Schmid, *Der eine Gott*.

Appendix

Ezekiel and Apocalyptic

As early as 1856, E. Meyer presented Ezekiel as full-blown apocalyptic which was then "by-passed until Daniel."[1] By this assertion Meyer identified the obvious genre gap in the canonical record.[2] In trying to explain this gap, R. North concluded that "first-Zechariah" and Daniel's dream-riddles have more historical perspective and less cosmic myth than is typical of later apocalyptic—thus suggesting the transitional nature of these works.[3]

---

1. As noted by North, "Prophecy to Apocalyptic," 67. See further, Schmidt, *Die jüdische Apokalyptik*, 34; and Dürr, *Die Stellung des Propheten Ezechiel*, 10.

2. Scholars are divided on when this shift in thinking took place. Some point to the influx of Persian and Greek literature and thought as the watershed moment. Both Persian dominance and the later Hellenistic period of Alexander the Great paved the way for this cross-pollination of literary style and apocalyptic thinking. Hanson, in *Dawn of Apocalyptic* (esp. 228–40), asserts that Ezekiel does show a developmental stage in early apocalyptic thought but that it lapsed during the Persian period with the post-exilic writings like Ezra and Nehemiah. The three hundred-year span between Ezekiel and the full-blown apocalypses of the third century BCE and onward does create a challenge due to the lag time between Ezekiel and this period when little change occurred in writing styles (viz., the birth of full-blown apocalyptic). Daniel, a book that has its own dating issues, cannot be appealed to for final proof because of the controversy surrounding its provenance and date. Thus, one is left with the dilemma of where Ezekiel fits into the schema of later apocalyptic writing. It is noteworthy however, that rarely will an apocalyptic scholar exclude the possibility that the symbols and imagery of Ezekiel in some way directly influenced later works. Terms such as "nascent," "incipient," and "proto-apocalyptic" have been used to describe Ezekiel's visions in relation to apocalyptic of the later period. While one may never be able to prove conclusively why the later genre developed when it did and why Ezekiel's "proto-apocalyptic" forms lay dormant for centuries, one can still readily acknowledge that when these later writers sought a starting point for their visionary experiences, Ezekiel was a fertile field of ready-made images and symbols from which they harvested.

3. North, "Prophecy to Apocalyptic," 70.

It is obvious that due to the hybrid nature of these proto-apocalyptic texts, exact categorization often eludes scholars. This is exactly the problem in categorizing Ezekiel. Ezekiel's use of "typical" mythic symbolism with an apocalyptic flavor mixed with historical realities makes Ezekiel closer in some respects to Daniel and "first-Zechariah." On the other hand, the book's prophetic core also finds close affinity with the pre-exilic prophets. One can see in Ezekiel a genre in the making whereby the book of Ezekiel marks a clear shift in style from classical prophecy in the strictest sense of the word, and full-blown apocalyptic of a later period. Like Daniel and Zechariah, Ezekiel's work thus resembles a hybrid of sorts. This is reinforced by the conclusions of S. B. Frost.

Frost notes that, "Ezekiel has laid the ground-plan of apocalyptic. Others may come and build thereon according to their fancy, but the elevation cannot escape from the peculiarities of the original plan."[4] It is this uniqueness that sets Ezekiel apart, a uniqueness due primarily to the Babylonian setting of the book. While Frost sees two authors at work, one in Jerusalem and one an exile in Babylon (see my discussion in ch. 1, above), it does not affect the conclusions about Ezekiel's distinct "Babylonian" style. Frost picks up this concept in his attempt to explain the parallels between Zechariah and Ezekiel. When comparing his "Babylonian-Ezekiel" with Zechariah Frost states that the writer of the vision sequence in Zechariah "brought much of the new 'Ezekiel-style' to Palestinian soil."[5] This "Ezekiel-style," which reflected a Babylonian influence, is clearly recognized by many scholars like Frost. Indeed it is the distinctiveness of this "Babylonian style" that has led many, such as Frost, to conjecture a second author for the book of Ezekiel stationed in Babylon with the exiles. Therefore we can begin our discussion by referring back to many of our conclusions in ch. 1, above. Ezekiel's "Babylonian style" makes him a prime candidate for the origins of apocalyptic thought in the exilic period. But what do apocalyptic scholars have to say about Ezekiel as "proto-apocalyptic"? It is to this we now turn.

---

4. Frost, *Old Testament Apocalyptic*, 92.

5. Ibid., 96. Frost relies heavily upon the conclusions of Herntrich in his assessments of a "Babylonian-Ezekiel" and the term "Ezekiel-style." See Herntrich, *Ezechielprobleme*.

D. S. Russell makes no qualms about pointing out the importance of the book of Ezekiel to the apocalyptic genre. He calls it an "important source of influence . . . whose language, imagery and religious insight left their mark on the whole field of apocalyptic thought."[6] He points out the increased and expanded role that the "transcendence of God," "individualism" and "individual responsibility" (cf. Ezek 18:3-32) plays in light of previous prophetic works. These motifs become fully developed in later apocalyptic works and can be seen as a backdrop of New Testament writings as well, especially that of Revelation. Ezekiel's use of visions (1:4—3:15), catalepsy (3:25-27) and his inspired ecstatic messages (3:12), to name a few, all appear in greater frequency in later works of apocalyptic. Because of this many scholars such as Russell trace the roots of apocalyptic back to Ezekiel. Although Russell does not use the term "bridge" when speaking of Ezekiel in relation to later apocalyptic works, his belief that Ezekiel is the link between the two is evident.

Klaus Koch in his laying out of the question of "What is Apocalyptic?" stops short of pointing out the bridge that exilic prophecy plays in joining and elucidating later full-blown apocalyptic books. He states that "what is plain in the prophets—a transparently simple image—is heightened into the grotesque by the apocalyptic writers and is now incomprehensible without interpretation."[7] There can be no doubt that Koch's explanation is true but he does nothing to aid in the clarification and explanation of the process from the former to the latter. He notes portions of Daniel (e.g., 7:7-28) as "being relatively easily understood"[8] but with the vast amount of scholarly attention given to Daniel as apocalyptic this conclusion is not at all surprising. Moreover, the interpretive dimension inherent within the text of Daniel itself (e.g., 7:15-28) does make Daniel easier to interpret than most, later apocalyptic works. Nevertheless, Koch does add to the discussion by pointing out the transitional nature between the prophetic and apocalyptic use of symbolism and imagery. Based upon his unique use of symbols and imagery, Ezekiel once again falls within these two eras of literature in a definitive manner.

---

6. Russell, *Method and Message*, 89.
7. Koch, *Rediscovery*, 26.
8. Ibid., 26.

Paul Hanson's conclusions are representative of many who work in the field of apocalyptic. Because of this representative nature, Hanson's work needs to be considered at some length due to his sometimes erroneous methodology and the conclusions that he draws.[9] Hanson asks the question that if "the prophecies of Second Isaiah can be called proto-apocalyptic, can the same be maintained for the message of Ezekiel?" Hanson hedges his negative response to his own query by, in some ways, negating his conclusion. He consistently affirms the value of the symbols and forms found in Ezekiel and their use by later apocalyptic writers. He also notes that "the connections between the book of Ezekiel and later apocalyptic writings are unmistakable: the bizarre imagery, the form of the vision, and the device of divine interpretation (later developing into the figure of the *angelus interpres*) live on in later apocalyptic compositions."[10] Hanson even concludes that the "element of waiting for Yahweh's intervention" in the midst of turmoil (i.e., exile and destruction) does bring "the prophecy of Ezekiel close to the orientation of apocalyptic."[11] However, he quickly veers away from this observation by positing that the editorial work on the book by later "hierocratic" editors moves the book in a direction away from the "future thrust" and "causes us to refrain from applying the designation *proto-apocalyptic* to the message of Ezekiel."[12]

Hanson's observations of a hierocratic perspective present in the book of Ezekiel appear valid from a straightforward reading of the text. Indeed, Ezekiel does appear to push an agenda of restoration of the nation to pre-exilic norms in cultic and political life while full-blown apocalypses of a later period tend to break with all forms of the past in favor of a new heavenly order. Hanson does acknowledge the presence of "apocalyptic forms and motifs" in Ezekiel.[13] However, he concludes that their influence on later apocalyptic forms is more in the arena of a hierocratic eschatological agenda in many ways reflective of Ezekiel's biases toward the exilic priesthood.[14] Thus the problem with

9. For a concise assessment of Hanson's changing positions on apocalyptic eschatology, see Allen, "Some Prophetic Antecedents," 16–17. For a negative critique of Hanson's hierocratic tradition, see Renz, *Rhetorical Function*, 243–45.

10. Hanson, *Dawn of Apocalyptic*, 234.

11. Ibid., 235.

12. Ibid.

13. Ibid., 232.

14. Kaufmann, *Religion of Israel*, 443, insists that a "hierocracy" of priests is not what Ezekiel has envisioned but rather a "visionary kingdom of God."

Ezekiel and Apocalyptic

Hanson's conclusions lies in how the later apocalyptic writers actually used Ezekiel's message, especially his symbols and forms. There can be no doubt that these forms and symbols are clearly developed in later apocalyptic tradition. Nevertheless, Hanson focuses too much on one aspect of the apocalyptic definition, viz., eschatology. Moreover, Rowland argues forcefully that "eschatological teaching" is not an "essential feature of an apocalypse."[15] The reality is that Ezekiel's *symbols* play a greater role in later apocalyptic thought than does his eschatological outlook, that is if you eliminate chs. 38–39 as do most who hold a view like Hanson.

At the same time even if we do accept the importance of the eschatological element of Hanson's argument do his conclusions reveal the entire picture presented by Ezekiel and his use of ANE symbolism and motifs? In his attempt to discard Ezekiel's form of apocalyptic symbols as only serving a hierocratic setting, Hanson has failed to consider fully the *ideal* eschatological setting and hope presented in some of the visions of Ezekiel (e.g., chs. 34, 36–48). Hanson has "fudged" his conclusions by conveniently choosing to attribute the clearly idyllic, or should we say apocalyptic, eschatological defeat of the powers of evil found in Ezekiel 38–39 to a later literary period. He does this by suggesting that chs. 38–39 served as a later reinterpretation of chs. 36–37 when the post-exilic community failed to be instituted as envisioned by Ezekiel.[16] However, Zimmerli (as does Cook[17] among others) goes to great lengths to show that there is no historical validity in denying Ezekiel's writing of the Gog oracles late in his ministry (see my discussion in ch. 4, above).[18] Zimmerli even goes on to note that what is present in the Gog oracles are the "first steps" in apocalyptic.[19]

Moreover, when these oracles are understood in the context of restoration and hope as we discussed in chs. 4 and 5 above, a greater appreciation for their eschatological bent with an apocalyptic flavor is apparent. When ch. 37 is juxtaposed to 38–39, one cannot simply state that these chapters merely present a desire to return to the pre-exilic norms and ordered institutions. On the contrary, what appears to be

---

15. Rowland, *Open Heaven*, 389.
16. Hanson, *Dawn of Apocalyptic*, 234 n. 47.
17. Cook, *Apocalyptic Literature*, 95.
18. Zimmerli, *Ezekiel* 2:302.
19. Ibid., 304.

the case is a future utopian existence of Israel in complete safety from her enemies. Yahweh has provided this safety through an apocalyptic intervention or inbreaking. Israel's safety was not secured through the previous norms of human military conquest with the aid of Yahweh, but rather her safety is miraculously secured by the sole intervention of Yahweh himself. Furthermore, one cannot overlook the utopian form of the new temple and the new Israel as described by Ezekiel in chs. 40–48. While it is true that the old order of hierocratic forms are present, at the same time the common ANE imagery (e.g., water and temple) and utopian setting in the land with Yahweh as cosmic ruler cannot be downplayed and overlooked. Thus, Hanson's opinion that the prophecies of Ezekiel served only as an immediate remedy to a cultic tradition in limbo due to the exile does not make sense when the entire book is scrutinized. The book has an apocalyptic eschatological dimension colored by ANE symbolism that cannot be denied.

Hanson, himself, when comparing the apocalyptic value of Second Isaiah and Ezekiel goes on, in some ways, to contradict his previous statements about the validity of Ezekiel's contributions to later apocalyptic. He states that "In both the visionary form is pronounced, in both the future orientation toward a restoration to be inaugurated by Yahweh is apparent, in both images and symbols are applied to Israel's situation which would later be adopted by apocalyptic writers. These similarities could lead one to conclude that both the Zadokite-led hierocratic group and the visionary followers of Second Isaiah take their point of departure from the same future-oriented, visionary, or even apocalyptic view of Yahweh's relation to his defeated community, a view replete with forms and motifs which could easily develop into full-blown apocalyptic, given the right circumstances."[20] Finally, Hanson's conclusion that the hierocratic element of the *gôlāh* (i.e., the exiles) pushed Ezekiel's agenda away from the normal apocalyptic visionary future to one more rooted in the status quo of the pre-exilic period[21] seems contradictory when the Davidic figure is factored into the equation (34:23–24; 37:24–25). If Ezekiel's hierocratic goal was to return to a time when the priesthood was dominant then why not wish for a time prior to the monarchy when the priesthood had an almost exclusive role in leadership (e.g., the wilderness years and the period

20. Hanson, *Dawn of Apocalyptic*, 236.
21. Ibid., 237–40.

of Eli)? It appears that the visionary elements of Ezekiel may stress the vital role played by the cultic leadership but at the same time they also seem to be presenting a future of utopian bliss where the Davidic ruler is closer to Yahweh than ever before.

Cook sounds the death knell to Hanson's thesis when he points out (without naming Hanson directly) that "Many scholars think of priests as traditionalist and guardians of the status quo. They find it hard to imagine them prophesying about God overturning the present world. Ethnographic and cross-cultural studies of central priests in many cultures, however, show that they are fully capable of an apocalyptic imagination."[22] Therefore, while Ezekiel's message may have reflected aspects of a literal present reality that he saw as being restored in the future based upon the pre-exilic status quo, his work is still, nonetheless, proto-apocalyptic. This is particularly true when the prophet uses other-worldly mediators and radical visions unlike any of those seen in the classical prophetic texts.

Next, both Kvanvig and Rowland note that Ezekiel's translation by the Spirit of Yahweh (3:14; 8:3) serves as the intended backdrop for *1 Enoch* 14.[23] Rowland goes on to add the *Apocalypse of Abraham* (chs.17–21, esp. 18) to the list of influenced texts.[24] The latter has numerous parallels with Ezekiel 1–3 especially with the description of the chariot-throne and the four living creatures. Rowland also points out that text fragments from cave 4 at Qumran (4QS1) contained descriptions of the chariot-throne of God. Here Rowland readily admits that "the fiery character of Ezekiel's chariot-throne has contributed greatly to the descriptions of the heavens found in these apocalypses."[25]

Mitchell Reddish is quick to point out the portions of Ezekiel that are apocalyptic or proto-apocalyptic in "nature" (viz., chs. 40–48) and those portions (i.e., chs. 38–39) which reflect a movement from prophetic eschatology to the apocalyptic eschatological milieu.[26] Reddish's

22. Cook, *Apocalyptic Literature*, 95.

23. Kvanvig, *Roots of Apocalyptic*, 518.

24. Rowland, *Open Heaven*, 84.

25. Ibid., 84.

26. Reddish, *Apocalyptic Literature*, 29. Note also, Ladd, "Why not Prophecy-Apocalyptic?" 192–200, who sees a melding of prophetic and apocalyptic eschatology in both the prophets and in Jesus' ministry.

Reddish (28–29) lists fourteen non-canonical Jewish apocalypses, many of which borrow imagery and symbolism from Ezekiel. They include:

struggle with the designation of some of Ezekiel's work (and other OT works[27]) as apocalyptic is evident in his work. He notes that the chapters in question "are similar to the eschatological pronouncements of Jewish apocalypses in that they contain ideas of universal judgment, an eschatological banquet, and destruction of God's enemies. These passages (as well as others that have been noted by various scholars) probably should be seen as reflecting the beginning stages of apocalyptic literature in Israel. They provide *the* [italics mine] bridge between prophetic and apocalyptic thought."[28] Here, Reddish's struggle in the classification of Ezekiel and other OT passages is evident. He concludes, as do I, that Ezekiel *is* the most obvious bridge between the former prophetic works and the later Jewish apocalypses. Reddish goes on to conclude that one needs to "recognize that apocalypticism grew out of post-exilic prophecy within Israel, but was enriched by ideas and imagery borrowed, either directly or indirectly, from several traditions in the Hellenistic world. Persian, Babylonian, Egyptian, Greek, Roman, and Canaanite influences affected Jewish apocalypticism."[29] However, I would add, that it was the Babylonian influence on Ezekiel's work in the *exilic* period that shaped the apocalyptic thought of those who used his book later—not some later post-exilic "updating" of his work.

1. The "Book of the Watchers" (*1 Enoch* 1–36)—3rd century BCE
2. The "Book of the Heavenly Luminaries" (*1 Enoch* 73–82)—3rd century BCE
3. The "Animal Apocalypse" (*1 Enoch* 85–90)—2nd century BCE
4. The "Apocalypse of Weeks" (*1 Enoch* 93:1–10; 91:11–17)—2nd century BCE
5. *Jubilees* 23—2nd century BCE
6. *The Testament of Levi* 2–5—2nd century BCE
7. *The Testament of Abraham*—1st century BCE—2nd century CE
8. *The Apocalypse of Zephaniah*—1st century BCE—1st century CE
9. The "Similitudes of Enoch" (*1 Enoch* 37–71)—1st century CE
10. *2 Enoch*—1st century CE
11. *4 Ezra*—1st century CE
12. *2 Baruch*—1st century CE
13. *The Apocalypse of Abraham*—1st–2nd century CE
14. *3 Baruch*—1st–2nd century CE

27. Reddish, *Apocalyptic Literature*, 29, willingly concedes that, Isaiah 24–27 is indeed not "apocalyptic" in the generally accepted sense of the term; however he is not willing to jettison the importance of the effects these and other apocalyptic flavored passages had on the growth of later apocalyptic.

28. Ibid., 29.

29. Ibid., 33.

Stephen Cook weighs in on the debate swirling around the categorical placement of Ezekiel in the apocalyptic school by shrouding his proto-apocalyptic stance in what he calls "nascent apocalypticism."[30] At the same time however, he qualifies his respect for the position that the book of Ezekiel plays in the growth of apocalypticism when he reprimands scholarship for their unwillingness to acknowledge the role the book plays in the development of this genre. He notes that "with few exceptions, modern scholars have overlooked Ezekiel's role as the earliest known apocalyptic visionary in Israel."[31] Cook characterizes Ezekiel and some other OT authors (viz., Daniel, Zechariah, Joel, Isaiah, Malachi) as having an "apocalyptic imagination" in at least "an incipient form."[32] He concludes that it is hard for scholars to deny at least the incipient nature of these books when it comes to an apocalyptic imagination.

In a similar vein, the mythological aspects of the prophetic voice are in transition at this period as well. In addressing this change in the exilic and post-exilic prophetic texts Cook states, "they speak of mythological entities in a radically new way, not in the language of poetic hyperbole but of literal concrete reality."[33] His example of Ezekiel's presentation of the Gog and Magog oracle in chs. 38–39 is an excellent instance of this. He avers, "they embody cosmic chaos and collective evil. This is a qualitative change from earlier prophetic visions, where God's enemies are historical, geopolitical realities."[34] The historically based realities upon which many of the pre-exilic texts (both prophetic and wisdom) were fashioned are now seen as being in transition in the book of Ezekiel. While in some cases Ezekiel is addressing actual historical personages and events using symbolism and imagery (e.g., chs. 29 and 32), there is also the shifting of focus to faceless foes. These

30. Cook, *Apocalyptic Literature*, 95.

31. Ibid., 95.

32. Ibid., 28. On this topic, Hanson argues for the "inchoate or emergent" apocalyptic forms in passages such as those found in the "Isaiah Apocalypse" of 24–27, "second" (40–55 and perhaps 34–35) and "third" Isaiah (56–66), Zechariah 1–6; 12–14 and Ezekiel 38–39. See Hanson, *Old Testament Apocalyptic*, 35–38.

33. Cook, *Apocalyptic Literature*, 28.

34. Ibid., 28. Cook (29) goes on to give several examples from the social sciences of the late 19th–20th century people groups (viz., millennial and apocalyptic groups) where native prophetic elements changed their focus to a more apocalyptic style. He sees the sociological element as proof that changes on the same level could, and did in fact occur within the outlook of the exilic and post-exilic prophets.

foes have no physical national boundaries per se and are representative of all evil and those who oppose God and his people. This reality is the picture presented in Ezekiel 38–39. Cook admits that the intermediate texts of the exilic and post-exilic periods do not represent a "full-blown" apocalyptic imagination but are in many senses transitory between the former historically-based writers of the pre-exilic period and the later cosmic writers of the apocalyptic era.

Finally, Russell recognizes the role that ancient mythology and OT allusions and metaphors play in apocalyptic. He notes that "over the course of the years a pattern of imagery and symbolism was evolved—indigenous and foreign, traditional and mythological—which became part of the apocalyptists' stock-in-trade. The same figures, images and ideas appear in book after book; but because of the constant adaptation and re-adaptation of the old figures to convey new interpretations there is no guarantee that they will have the same meaning in two successive books."[35] While one can readily agree with Russell that OT forms and metaphors were drawn on consistently by successive authors (e.g., chariot imagery and accompanying cherubim), one must also be ready to admit that Ezekiel went beyond these motifs to add symbolism and imagery found nowhere else in the OT prior to the late exilic and post-exilic periods. It is not until the book of Daniel (i.e., full-blown apocalyptic) and Zechariah that some of Ezekiel's specific symbols reappear and are reinterpreted by these authors for their own use. What Ezekiel does with OT forms and symbols is something radically different. He adapts OT forms and motifs and adds symbolism beyond the norm—what could be classed as a foreign element. This "foreign" aspect is what is vital in Ezekiel's contribution to the later genre of apocalyptic and in understanding the message itself.

---

35. Russell, *Method & Message*, 122. Rowland, *Open Heaven*, 60, notes that the "major source" for later apocalyptic was the OT while at the same time not discounting the role that "mythological ideas" from other cultures may have played due to their availability and influence on practically all nations in the ANE. He then suggests that when dealing with just the biblical text and apocalyptic influence on later apocalyptic writers, Ezekiel and Daniel "provided much of the inspiration." He goes on to note that in order to fully appreciate and understand later apocalyptic, one must be willing to look at Isaiah 6; 1 Kgs 22:19; Ezekiel 1–3 and 40–48; as well as the first six chapters of Zechariah as vital in understanding aspects of apocalyptic such as later concepts of the heavenly world (199).

Implications: Is Ezekiel Proto-Apocalyptic?

As presented in ch. 1 above, one of my essential tenets is the belief that Ezekiel is radically different than his predecessors in his presentation of his prophetic oracles—this by means of his setting, visions, and imagery. As just touched on above, Ezekiel established a host of symbols that would later prove to be stock-in-trade for visionaries and mystics in full-blown apocalyptic discourse.[36] Yet, in light of these realities, one is hard-pressed to find one scholar, let alone a consensus, who will admit that Ezekiel is in fact one of *the* key transitional books (if not *the* transitional book) between OT prophetic style and later apocalyptic.[37] Ezekielian scholars are mostly silent on the topic and refuse to admit the "proto-apocalyptic" nature of Ezekiel. Interestingly enough, there are those within German scholarship on Ezekiel who do see Ezekiel as directly influencing the apocalyptic genre; however, those scholars also propound that Ezekiel is a pseudepigraph from the apocalyptic period.[38]

Much of the controversy surrounding the use of the term "proto-apocalyptic" for the book of Ezekiel stems from two key issues. First, scholars are hesitant to use this label to describe what appears to be a strictly prophetic account reworked over time by different authors to suit their needs. Second, to label Ezekiel as such would be to place it out of chronological sync with what most scholars say is the beginning of apocalyptic thought.[39] Yet it is exactly the style of writing found in Ezekiel that has caused many scholars to explain a number of the later apocalyptic motifs as being based on Ezekiel. Sadly, it is for this reason

---

36. James Barr is one who notes this connection but refuses to assign "apocalyptic" to any part of Ezekiel. See Barr, "Jewish Apocalypticism," 19. For a concise discussion on the rise of apocalypticism see Plöger, *Theocracy*, 26–52.

37. Boadt, "Mythological Themes," 230–31, does note a gradual shift in Ezekielian scholarship away from this reluctance. He attributes this to the new interaction between Ezekielian scholars and scholarship on the Psalms as well as ancient Near Eastern cultic parallels with many of the motifs of the prophets. These combine to show a much earlier "proto-apocalyptic" sentiment than once thought.

38. In Pohlmann's latest commentary on Ezekiel he notes this trend within scholarship led by individuals like Joachim Becker. Cf. Pohlmann, *Ezechiel*, 81–83. See also Becker, "Erwägungen zur ezechielischen Frage," 142–44. Becker, lists the characteristics of Ezekiel and how they align with later apocalyptic writings. The connections are so close for him that he insists Ezekiel is a pseudepigraph that was written during the post-exilic period and was influenced by the rising apocalyptic genre movement.

39. For example, see Wilson, *Prophecy and Society*, 299.

that one needs to work chronologically backwards[40] (i.e., starting with the ancient apocalyptists and scholars who deal with these works) in order to prove this point—something best reserved for another monograph. Suffice it to say that it appears as though Ezekielian scholars tend to avoid the matter entirely in an effort not to get bogged down in discussions dealing with the development of apocalyptic.

To conclude then, the book of Ezekiel stands out as a book with motifs distinct to itself. Chariot-throne imagery, the valley of dry bones, extended metaphors such as those found in chs. 16 and 23, the Gog-Magog chapters of 38–39 and the utopian temple and princely rule in 40–48 all add to this distinctiveness. Scarcely can one pick up a book on apocalypticism and not find, at some juncture, reference to the contributions of the book of Ezekiel to the genre, which became full-blown between the third century BCE and the second century CE.

---

40. The issue of starting with the later apocalyptic works and working backwards is needed in order to show that the apocalyptists of the third century and beyond must have viewed Ezekiel as different in some way from earlier authors—this is due in part to their constant borrowing from his symbolic expressions. It is unfortunate that most scholars today and of the past century have refused to designate any portion of Ezekiel as "apocalyptic" or "proto-apocalyptic" even though evidence seems to point in that direction. When scholars do encounter clear apocalyptic themes (viz., chs. 38–39) they quickly assign it to a later hand closer to the apocalyptists of the post-exilic period. However, when scholars start asking the hard questions as to where the mystics and visionaries of later periods got their symbols and ideas, inevitably the searching eye returns to Ezekiel, Isaiah 24–27, and Zechariah.

Interestingly enough, Ezekiel is one of the most common of the OT books where scholars look, yet even then they stop short, many times, in taking the leap and calling Ezekiel "proto-apocalyptic." Much of this reticence appears to stem from the entrenched historical critical approach in dating texts that "do not fit" to later hands or disciples of a given prophet. Understanding the incipient themes and symbolism in Ezekiel, which could very well be traced to the sixth century, may have enabled scholars to make a more defining link to the ANE at a much earlier period. Commentators on the Book of Ezekiel regularly pass over the issue in their books and the researcher is left to look to apocalyptic scholars and their research for answers. It is when these apocalyptic scholars are studied that an earlier period for these chapters can be posited than once believed. Ezekiel can clearly be seen as a transitional book between the prophets of the classical period and the visionaries of the apocalyptic period.

Note, however, that Block, "Gog in Prophetic Tradition," 156, rejects the designation of chs. 38–39 as "apocalyptic" as defined by Collins, "Towards the Morphology of a Genre," 9. Nevertheless, while a strict apocalyptic definition may not fit these chapters perfectly, due to the fact that motifs found in later apocalyptic thought are also found in these chapters may allow the definition of proto-apocalyptic to define their genre classification. Even Block, "Gog in Prophetic Tradition," 168, goes on to suggest that portions of ch. 38 are the "first step on the way to apocalyptic."

Concepts such as angelology, theophanic imagery, and eschatology can all be seen in transition in Ezekiel from the prophetic perspective of the classical prophets to the later full-blown apocalypses.[41] Much of this radical change from pre-exilic prophecy to later full-blown apocalyptic must have had some catalyst to change the mode of expression of later writers; Ezekiel appears to be that catalyst.

As we noted above, part of understanding the message of Ezekiel and his use of ANE symbols and thought is also to appreciate the cultural perspective from which he worked. It should not at all be surprising that Ezekiel stands out from the classical prophets in his presentation of his material especially when one takes into account that he is the first of all the OT prophets to live and write from a foreign land.[42] It appears that the "catalyst" that started this radical shift within Jewish literature may in fact have begun with the work of Ezekiel in a Babylonian setting.

At the same time, seldom would a scholar deny the role that pre-exilic prophets[43] played in shaping the book of Ezekiel and some aspects of the apocalyptic writers. Motifs from passages such as Exodus 19–25; 2 Kgs 2:11; Isaiah 6; Pss 29; 46:47; 74:13; Genesis 1, etc., all contain imagery reflected in Ezekiel and apocalyptic writings. However, Ezekiel has moved beyond simple theophanic imagery (e.g., Exod 19–25) and chariot-throne motifs (e.g., 2 Kgs 2) to present a new and expanded form of the older ideas. Furthermore, the shift from the pre-exilic prophets to the books of Zechariah, Daniel, and later Jewish and Christian apocalypses such as Revelation[44] is pronounced to say the

---

41. For a discussion on the development of OT eschatology, see Müller, *Ursprunge und Strukturen*.

42. Daniel excepted, based on dating issues.

43. When dealing with the roots of apocalyptic and its connection to mythology Collins, *Apocalyptic Imagination*, 20, points out that in more recent times apocalyptic is seen as the combination of ANE mythology (especially Canaanite) and OT prophecy. It may be true that Canaanite imagery plays a key role in later apocalyptic works, but just as true is the role that Mesopotamian mythological connections play in Ezekiel's visionary symbolism that are clearly developed in later apocalyptic works. It is for this reason that one must not be too quick to downplay the importance of the Mesopotamian mythological links to later apocalyptic works. Thus, the nuts and bolts of the later genre can be found, albeit in a somewhat rudimentary form, in the visionary experiences of Ezekiel.

44. For a detailed comparison of the development of angelology from Ezekiel to Daniel and Revelation, see Rowland, *Open Heaven*, 94–113. While apocalyptic sections of biblical texts other than Daniel and Revelation have been recognized by

least. In this vein, Hanson states that "the origins of apocalyptic cannot be explained by a method which juxtaposes seventh- and second-century compositions and then proceeds to account for the features of the latter by reference to its immediate environment. The apocalyptic literature of the second century and after is the result of a long development reaching back to pre-exilic times and beyond, and not the new baby of second-century foreign parents."[45] He concludes this thought by noting that one must look at the development of apocalyptic eschatology from prophetic and "other even more archaic native roots."[46] While Hanson's use of "native" here seems to intimate Hebrew roots, based upon our work above, one can also posit that many of these "roots" must have come from Mesopotamian, Canaanite, and Egyptian influence as well. However, it is Ezekiel who melds these cultural images in his own unique way and expands them, thus making them his own, while he is in the cultural center of the ANE. Indeed, there can be little doubt that Ezekiel's expansion of old ideas and introduction of new motifs must have been the literary spark that influenced many of the later writers. For clarification purposes an example seems in order.

One key area that has created a lot of debate within the realm of prophetic and apocalyptic eschatology is the perspective of history in each. Put simply, the prophets sought to show Yahweh's working within history while the later apocalyptists sought to show Yahweh's breaking into or overriding of history.[47] Yet it is true, as Schmithals points out that "the eschatology of apocalyptic, though undoubtedly radicalized in comparison with the OT, cannot be understood apart from its OT roots, . . . both [OT prophecy and apocalyptic] understand history as linear."[48] In this vein, it is within the book of Ezekiel that we see both the prophetic and apocalyptic view of eschatology blended

---

a wide range of scholarship, Paul Boyer goes further than most and lists a variety of biblical books that contain generally recognized apocalyptic themes and motifs. These include Ezekiel, Isaiah, Mark, 1 and 2 Thessalonians, 1 Corinthians and 2 Peter. Cf. Boyer, "Growth of Fundamentalist," 518.

45. Hanson, *Dawn of Apocalyptic*, 6.

46. Ibid., 6. Cf. also Osiek, "Apocalyptic Eschatology," 341–45.

47. H. H. Rowley comments on this by noting that in general terms "the prophets foretold the future that should arise out of the present, while the apocalyptists foretold the future that should break into the present." See Rowley, *Relevance of Apocalyptic*, 35.

48. Schmithals, *Apocalyptic Movement*, 77.

for the first time in the OT. Ezekiel made a conscious effort to depict history in a detailed linear fashion with a utopian end (as depicted in chs. 37–48). Ezekiel's eschatological view is only made possible by Yahweh's intervention/inbreaking in history (i.e., chs. 37–39).[49]

Much of this change in the concept of linear history can be attributed to Ezekiel's perspective of *salvation* and what it would entail for the exilic community *after* their time in exile. David Aune points out that pre-exilic prophetic perspectives attributed salvation to God working within the realm of established historical reality while the later apocalypses jettisoned this concept.[50] Ezekiel bridges this gap by presenting the hope of salvation for the nation both in a historically based setting, as appears to be the case in ch. 37 (i.e., a future return to the land which did indeed take place), yet also in a somewhat utopian futuristic setting as presented in chs. 38–48 (i.e., Israel has neither experienced peace and safety on all sides as presented in chs. 38–48, nor has she had a temple or land as described in the final vision).

Space does not permit me to present a detailed analysis of a one-to-one borrowing from Ezekiel to the later apocalyptic writers; however, one need only read modern apocalyptic scholars to find a plethora of examples. Suffice it to say that many apocalyptic scholars see in Ezekiel's visions the "nuts and bolts" of later apocalyptic thought. Indeed, we may conclude that by its very definition (i.e., apocalyptic) Ezekiel meets many of the requirements for this genre of literature.[51] Thus, while most Ezekielian scholars refuse to do so, I find no solid scholarly reason not to conclude that Ezekiel *is* indeed proto-apocalyptic both in perspective and in form. Whatever dating problems this conclusion may cause is not so much an issue for the text and Ezekiel, but rather is an issue for modern theories on the development of the apocalyptic imagination—it is this concept that most may have to rethink.

---

49. Isaiah 49–66 have flashes of a utopian end for Israel but in no way present a detailed program, as does Ezekiel. Also, Daniel's visions of 7–12 offer a very truncated presentation of the history of Israel and only a brief look into the future (ch. 12).

50. Petersen, "Eschatology (OT)," 2.595.

51. See the definition of apocalyptic by Collins, *Apocalyptic Imagination*, 5. See also the discussion of the problems in defining "apocalyptic" by Knibb, "Prophesy," 155–65; and Webb, "'Apocalyptic,'" 115–26, esp. 115–17. There are scholars who acknowledge the close ties of Ezekiel with later apocalyptic. For example, Batto, *Slaying the Dragon*, 158; and Muilenburg, "Ezekiel," 569.

Bibliography

Abegg, Martin G. Jr. et al., translators. *The Dead Sea Scrolls Bible: The Oldest Known Bible Translated for the First Time into English.* New York: HarperCollins, 1999.

Abusch, Tzvi. *Mesopotamian Witchcraft: Toward an Understanding of Babylonian Witchcraft Beliefs and Literature.* Ancient Magic and Divination 5. Leiden: Brill, 2002.

Ackroyd, Peter R. *Exile and Restoration: A Study of Hebrew Thought of the Sixth Century B.C.* OTL. Philadelphia: Westminster, 1968.

——— et al. editors. *The Major Prophets: A Commentary on Isaiah, Jeremiah, Lamentations, Ezekiel, and Daniel.* Interpreter's Concise Commentary 4. Nashville: Abingdon, 1983.

Ahroni, Reuben. "The Gog Prophecy and the Book of Ezekiel." *HAR* 1 (1977) 1–27.

Alaribe, Gilbert N. *Ezekiel 18 and the Ethics of Responsibility: A Study in Biblical Interpretations and Christian Ethics.* ATSAT 77. St. Ottilien: Erzabtei St. Ottilien, 2006.

Albrektson, Bertil. *History and the Gods.* CBOTS 1. Lund: Gleerup, 1967.

Albright, W. F. "King Jehoiachin in Exile." *BA* 5 (1942) 49–55.

———. "The Seal of Eliakim and the Latest Preëxilic History of Judah, with Some Observations on Ezekiel." *JBL* 51 (1932) 79–106.

Alexander, Ralph H. *Ezekiel.* EBC 6. Grand Rapids: Zondervan, 1986.

Allen, Leslie C. *Ezekiel 1–19.* WBC 28. Dallas: Word, 1994.

———. *Ezekiel 20–48.* WBC 29. Dallas: Word, 1990.

———. Review of *Ezekiel 18 and the Rhetoric of Moral Discourse*, by Gordon Matties. *JBL* 111 (1992) 523–25.

———. "Some Prophetic Antecedents of Apocalyptic Eschatology and Their Hermeneutic Value." *ExAud* 6 (1990) 15–28.

———. "Structure, Tradition and Redaction in Ezekiel's Death Valley Vision." In *Among the Prophets: Language, Image and Structure in the Prophetic Writings*, edited by Philip Davies and David Clines, 127–42. JSOTSup 144. Sheffield: JSOT Press, 1993.

Alt, Albrecht. *Essays on Old Testament History and Religion.* Biblical Seminar. Sheffield: JSOT Press, 1989.

Amsler, Samuel. "Zacharie et l'Origine de l'Apocalyptique." In *Congress Volume: Uppsala 1971*, edited by G. W. Anderson et al., 227–31. VTSup 22. Leiden: Brill, 1972.

Anbar, Moshé. "Une nouvelle allusion à une tradition babylonienne dans Ézéchiel (XXII 24)." *VT* 29 (1979) 352–53.

Anderson, Jeff S. "The Social Function of Curses in the Hebrew Bible." *ZAW* 110 (1998) 223–37.

Angel, Andrew R. *Chaos and the Son of Man: The Hebrew Chaoskampf Tradition in the Period 515 BCE to 200 CE*. T. & T. Clark Library of Biblical Studies. London: T. & T. Clark, 2006.

"Apocalypse." In *The Dictionary of Judaism in the Biblical Period*, edited by Jacob Neusner and William Scott Green, 46–47. Peabody, MA: Hendrickson, 1999.

Apóstolo, Silvio Sergio Scatolini. "Imagining Ezekiel." *JHScr* 8/13 (2008) 1–30.

Arnold, Bill T., and Bryan E. Beyer editors. *Readings from the Ancient Near East: Primary Sources for Old Testament Study*. Encountering Biblical Studies. Grand Rapids: Baker Academic, 2002.

Assmann, Jan. *Of God and Gods: Egypt, Israel, and the Rise of Monotheism*. George L. Mosse Series in Modern European Cultural and Intellectual History. Madison: University of Wisconsin Press, 2008.

Astour, Michael C. "Ezekiel's Prophecy of Gog and the Cuthean Legend of Naram-Sin." *JBL* 95 (1976) 567–79.

Auvray, Paul. *Ezéchiel*. Sainte Bible / traduite en français sous la direction de l'Ecole biblique de Jérusalem. Paris: Cerf, 1949.

———. "Le Poblème Historique du Livre d'Ezéchiel." *RB* 55 (1948) 503–19.

Bahrani, Zainab. *Rituals of War: The Body and Violence in Mesopotamia*. New York: Zone Books, 2008.

Balentine, Samuel E. *The Hidden God: The Hiding of the Face of God in the Old Testament*. Oxford Theological Monographs. Oxford: Oxford University Press, 1983.

Baltzer, Dieter. *Ezekiel und Deuterojesaja: Berührungen in der Heilserwartung der beiden grossen Exilspropheten*. BZAW 121. Berlin: de Gruyter, 1971.

Baltzer, Klaus. *The Covenant Formulary: In Old Testament, Jewish, and Early Christian Writings*. Translated by David E. Green. Philadelphia: Fortress, 1971.

Bardtke, H. "Der Prophet Ezechiel in der modernen Forschung." *TLZ* 96 (1971) 721–34.

Barker, M. "Slippery Words III. Apocalyptic." *ExpTim* 89 (1977–78) 325.

Barr, James. "Jewish Apocalypticism in Recent Scholarly Study." *BJRL* 58 (1975/76) 9–35.

———. "Some Semantic Notes on the Covenant." In *Beiträge zur Alttestamentlichen Theologie: Festschrift für Walther Zimmerli zum 70 Geburtstag*, edited by Herbert Donner et al., 23–38. Göttingen: Vandenhoeck & Ruprecht, 1977.

Batto, Bernard F. *Slaying the Dragon: Mythmaking in the Biblical Tradition*. Louisville: Westminster John Knox, 1992.

Bauckham, Richard. "A Quotation from 4Q Second Ezekiel in the Apocalypse of Peter." *RevQ* 15 (1991–1992) 437–45.

———. "The Rise of Apocalyptic." *Them* 3 (1978) 10–23.

Baumann, Gerlinde. "Connected by Marriage, Adultery and Violence: The Prophetic Marriage Metaphor in the Book of the Twelve and in the Major Prophets." In *The Society of Biblical Literature 1999 Seminar Papers*, 552–69. SBLSP 38. Atlanta: SBL, 1999.

Baumgartner, Walter. *Zum Alten Testament und seiner Umwelt*. Leiden: Brill, 1959.

Baxter, Elizabeth. *Ezekiel, Son of Man: His Life and Ministry*. 1902. Reprint, London: Christian Herald, 1914.

Beal, Richard H. "Hittite Military Organization." In *CANE*, edited by Jack M. Sasson, 1:545–54. 4 vols. New York: Scribner, 1995.

Becker, Joachim. "Erwägungen zur ezechielischen Frage." In *Künder des Wortes*, edited by Lothar Ruppert et al., 137-49. Würzburg: Echter, 1982.

———. "Ez 8-11 als einheitliche Komposition in einem pseudepigraphischen Ezechielbuch." In *EHB*, edited by J. Lust, 136-50. BETL 74. Leuven: Leuven University Press, 1986.

Becking, Bob et al., editors. *Only One God? : Monotheism in Ancient Israel and the Veneration of the Goddess Asherah*. Biblical Seminar 77. London: Sheffield Academic, 2001.

Beekman, John et al., editors. *The Semantic Structure of Communication*. Dallas: Summer Institute of Linguistics, 1981.

Bellefontaine, Elizabeth. "The Curses of Deuteronomy 27: Their Relationship to the Prohibitives." In *No Famine in the Land: Studies in Honor of John L. McKenzie*, edited by James W. Flanagan and Anita Weisbrod Robinson, 49-61. Missoula, MT: Scholars, 1975.

Bergren, Richard Victor. *The Prophets and the Law*. HUCM 4. Cincinnati: Hebrew Union College-Jewish Institute of Religion, 1974.

Berrigan, Daniel. *Ezekiel: Vision in the Dust*. Maryknoll, NY: Orbis, 1997.

Berry, George Ricker. "The Composition of the Book of Ezekiel." *JBL* 58 (1939) 163-75.

———. "The Glory of Yahweh and the Temple." *JBL* 56 (1937) 115-17.

———. "The Title of Ezekiel (1:1-3)." *JBL* 51 (1932) 54-57.

———. "Was Ezekiel in the Exile?" *JBL* 49 (1930) 83-93.

Bertholet, Alfred. *Das Buch Hezekiel erklärt*. KHC 12. Freiburg: Mohr/Siebeck, 1897.

Bertholet, Alfred, and Kurt Galling. *Hesekiel*. HAT 13. Tübingen: Mohr/Siebeck, 1936.

Betts, Terry J. *Ezekiel the Priest: A Custodian of the Tôrâ*. SBLit 74. New York: Lang, 2005.

Bickermann, Elias J. "The Babylonian Captivity." In *CHJ*, edited by W. D. Davies and Louis Finkelstein, 1:342-58. 4 vols. Cambridge: Cambridge University Press, 1984.

Biggs, Charles R. *The Book of Ezekiel*. Epworth Commentaries. London: Epworth, 1996.

Bird, Phyllis. "To Play the Harlot: An Inquiry into an Old Testament Metaphor." In *Gender and Difference in Ancient Israel*, edited by Peggy L. Day, 75-94. Minneapolis: Fortress, 1989.

Black, Jeremy et al., editors. *A Concise Dictionary of Akkadian*. 2nd (corrected) printing. Santag 5. Wiesbaden, Germany: Harrassowitz, 2000.

Blank, Sheldon H. "The Curse, Blasphemy, the Spell, and the Oath." *HUCA* 23 (1950-51) 73-95.

Blenkinsopp, Joseph. *Ezekiel*. Interpretation: A Commentary for Teaching and Preaching. Louisville: Westminster John Knox, 1990.

Bloch, Maurice, and Jonathan Parry, editors. *Death and the Regeneration of Life*. Cambridge: Cambridge University Press, 1982.

Block, Daniel I. *The Book of Ezekiel: Chapters 1-24*. NICOT. Grand Rapids: Eerdmans, 1998.

———. *The Book of Ezekiel: Chapters 25-48*. NICOT. Grand Rapids: Eerdmans, 1998.

———. "Bringing David Back: Ezekiel's Messianic Hope. In *The Lord's Anointed: Interpretation of Old Testament Messianic Texts*, edited by Philip E. Satterthwaite et al., 167-88. Tyndale House Studies. 1995. Reprint, Eugene, OR: Wipf & Stock, 2012.

———. "Divine Abandonment: Ezekiel's Adaptation of an Ancient Near Eastern Motif." In *The Book of Ezekiel: Theological and Anthropological Perspectives*, edited by Margaret S. Odell and John T. Strong, 15-42. SBLSymS 9. Atlanta: SBL, 2000.

———. "Ezekiel's Boiling Cauldron: A Form-Critical Solution to Ezekiel xxiv 1-14." *VT* 41 (1991) 12-37.

———. "Gog and the Pouring Out of the Spirit: Reflections on Ezekiel xxxix 21-9." *VT* 37 (1987) 257-70.

———. "Gog in Prophetic Tradition: A New Look at Ezekiel xxxviii 17." *VT* 42 (1992) 154-72.

———. "In Search of Theological Meaning: Ezekiel Scholarship at the Turn of the Millennium." In *Ezekiel's Hierarchical World: Wrestling with a Tiered Reality*, edited by Stephen L. Cook and Corrine L. Patton, 227-39. SBLSymS 31. Atlanta: SBL, 2004.

———. "Text and Emotion: A Study in the 'Corruptions' in Ezekiel's Inaugural Vision (Ezekiel 1.4-28)." *CBQ* 50 (1988) 418-39.

Bloome, Edwin C. "Ezekiel's Abnormal Personality." *JBL* 65 (1946) 277-92.

Boadt, Lawrence. "A New Look at the Book of Ezekiel." *TBT* 37 (1999) 4-9.

———."Ezekiel." In *ABD*, edited by David Noel Freedman, 2:711-22. 6 vols. New York: Doubleday, 1992.

———. *Ezekiel's Oracles against Egypt: A Literary and Philological Study of Ezekiel 29-32*. BibOr 37. Rome: Biblical Institute Press, 1980.

———. "The Function of the Salvation Oracles in Ezekiel 33-37." *HAR* 12 (1990) 1-21.

———. "Mythological Themes and the Unity of Ezekiel." In *Literary Structure and Rhetorical Strategies in the Hebrew Bible*, edited by L. J. Regt, et al., 211-31. Winona Lake, IN: Eisenbrauns, 1996.

———. "Rhetorical Strategies in Ezekiel's Oracles of Judgment." In *EHB*, edited by J. Lust, 182-200. BETL 74. Leuven, Belgium: Leuven University Press, 1986.

———. "Textual Analysis in Ezekiel and Poetic Analysis of Paired Words." *JBL* 97 (1978) 489-99.

Boda, Mark J. "From Dystopia to Myopia: Utopian re(visions) in Haggai and Zechariah 1-8." In *Utopia and Dystopia in Prophetic Texts*, edited by Ehud Ben Zvi and Michael Floyd, 211-49. Publications of the Finnish Exegetical Society. Helsinki: Finnish Exegetical Society/University of Helsinki, 2006.

Bodendorfer, Gerhard. *Das Drama des Bundes: Ezechiel 16 in rabbinscher Perspektive*. Herders Biblical Studies 11. Freiburg: Herder, 1997.

Bodi, Daniel. *The Book of Ezekiel and the Poem of Erra*. OBO 104. Freiburg: Universitätsverlag, 1991.

Bøe, Sverre. *Gog and Magog: Ezekiel 38-39 as pre-text for Revelation 19,17-21 and 20,7-10*. WUNT 2. Tübingen: Mohr/Siebeck, 2001.

Boer, E. A. de. *John Calvin on the Visions of Ezekiel: Historical and Hermeneutic Studies in John Calvin's "Sermons inédits," Especially on Ezek. 36-48*. Kerkhistorische bijdragen 21. Leiden: Brill, 2004.

Bogaert, Pierre-Maurice. "Les Deux Rédactions Conservées (LXX et TM) D'Ézéchiel 7." In *EHB*, edited by J. Lust, 21–47. BETL 74. Leuven, Belgium: Leuven University Press, 1986.

Borger, Riekele. *Die Inschriften Asarhaddons Königs Assyrien*. AfO 9. Graz, Austria: Weidner, 1956.

———. "Zu den Asarhaddon-Vertagen." *ZA* 54 (1961) 173–96.

Botterweck, G. Johanness, and Helmer Ringgren, editors. Translated by John T. Willis et al. 15 vols. Grand Rapids: Eerdmans, 1974–2006.

Boyer, Paul. "The Growth of Fundamentalist Apocalyptic in the United States." In *The Continuum History of Apocalypticism*, edited by Bernard J. McGinn, John J. Collins, and Stephen J. Stein, 516–44. New York: Continuum, 2003.

Brenner, Athalya. "On Prophetic Propaganda and the Politics of 'Love': The Case of Jeremiah," in *A Feminist Companion to the Latter Prophets*, edited by Athalya Brenner, 256–74. The Feminist Companion to the Bible 8. Sheffield: Sheffield Academic, 1995.

Breuer, Joseph. *Sefer Yehezkel: The Book of Yechezkel*. Translated by Gertrude Hirschler. New York: Feldheim, 1993.

Brichto, Herbert C. "Kin, Cult, Land, Afterlife: A Biblical Complex." *HUCA* 44 (1973) 1–54.

———. *The Problem of "Curse" in the Hebrew Bible*. Philadelphia: Society of Biblical Literature and Exegesis, 1963.

Bright, John. *A History of Israel*. Westminster Aids to the Study of the Scriptures. Louisville: Westminster John Knox, 2000.

Brinkman, John A. "Through a Glass Darkly: Esarhaddon's Retrospects on the Downfall of Babylon." *JAOS* 103 (1983) 36–57.

Brownlee, William H. *Ezekiel 1–19*. WBC 28. Waco: Word, 1986.

Brueggemann, Walter. *The Covenanted Self: Explorations in Law and Covenant*. Edited by Patrick D. Miller. Minneapolis: Fortress, 1999.

———. "On Coping with Curse: A Study of 2 Sam 16:5–14." *CBQ* 36 (1974) 175–92.

Brunner, Robert. *Ezechiel*. 2 vols. Prophezei : Schweizerische Bibelwerk für die Gemeinde Zürich: Zwingli, 1944.

Bultmann, Christoph. Review of *The Rhetorical Function of the Book of Ezekiel*, by Thomas Renz. *VT* 51 (2001) 419–20.

Buss, Martin J. Review of *Bundestheologie im Alten Testament*, by Lothar Perlitt. *JBL* 90 (1971) 210–12.

Cagni, Luigi. *Das Erra-Epos. Keilschrifttext*. Studia Pohl 5. Rome: Pontifical Biblical Institute, 1970.

Calès, J. "Rétribution individuelle, vie des justes et mort des pécheurs d'après le livre d'Ezéchiel." *RSR* 11 (1921) 363–71.

Callahan, Allen. "Perspectives for a Study of African American Religion from the Valley of Dry Bones." *NR* 7 (2003) 44–59.

Callender, Dexter E. Jr. "The Primal Human in Ezekiel and the Image of God." In *The Book of Ezekiel: Theological and Anthropological Perspectives*, edited by Margaret S. Odell and John T. Strong, 175–93. SBLSymS 9. Atlanta: SBL, 2000.

———. "The Primal Man in Ezekiel and the Image of God." In *The Society of Biblical Literature 1998 Seminar Papers*, 1:606–25. 2 vols. SBLSP 37. Atlanta: Scholars, 1998.

Calvin, John. *Calvin's Old Testament Commentaries: Ezekiel I–Chapters 1–12*. Translated by D. Foxgrover and D. Martin. Grand Rapids: Eerdmans, 1994.

Carley, Keith W. *The Book of the Prophet Ezekiel*. The Cambridge Bible Comentary: New English Bible. London: Cambridge University Press, 1974.

———. *Ezekiel among the Prophets: A Study of Ezekiel's Place in the Prophetic Tradition*. SBT, 2nd ser., 31. London: SCM, 1975.

Carlebach, Joseph. *Die drei grossen Propheten: Jesjas, Jirmija und Jecheskel*. Basel: Morascha, 1994.

Carmignac, J. "Description du phenomene de l'Apocalyptique dans l'Ancien Testament." In *AMWNE*, edited by D. Hellholm, 163–66. Tübingen: Mohr/Siebeck, 1983.

Carroll, Robert P. "Twilight of Prophecy or Dawn of Apocalyptic." *JSOT* 14 (1978–9) 3–35.

———. "Whorusalamin: A Tale of Three Cities as Three Sisters." In *On Reading Prophetic Texts*, edited by Bob Becking and Meindert Dijkstra, 67–82. Biblical Interpretation Series 18. Leiden: Brill, 1996.

Casson, David. "When Israel Loses Its Meaning: The Reconstruction of Language and Community in Ezekiel's Prophecy." In *The Society of Biblical Literature 2003 Seminar Papers*, 215–26. SBLSP 42. Atlanta: SBL, 2003.

Cassuto, Umberto. "The Arrangement of the Book of Ezekiel." In *Biblical and Oriental Studies*, 1:227–40. 2 vols. Translated by Israel Abrahams. Publications of the Perry Foundation for Biblical Research in the Hebrew University of Jerusalem. Jerusalem: Magnes, 1973.

Cathcart, Kevin J. "The Curses in Old Aramaic Inscriptions." In *Targumic and Cognate Studies: Essays in Honour of Martin McNamara*, edited by Kevin J. Cathcart and Michael Maher, 140–52. JSOTSup 230. Sheffield: Sheffield Academic, 1996.

———. "Treaty-Curses and the Book of Nahum." *CBQ* 35 (1973) 179–87.

Černý, Jaroslav, peleographer. *Ancient Egyptian Religion*. Hutchinson's University Library: World Religions. London: Hutchinson's University Library, 1957.

Chesson, Meredith S. "Remembering and Forgetting in Early Bronze Age Mortuary Practices on the Southeastern Dead Sea Plain, Jordan." In *Performing Death: Social Analyses of Funerary Traditions in the Ancient Near East and Mediterranean*, edited by Nicola Laneri, 109–39. UCOIS 3. Chicago: OIUC, 2007.

Cheyne, T. K. "Ezekiel's Visions of Jerusalem." *The Expositor* 6 (1908) 225–30.

Childs, Brevard. "The Enemy from the North and the Chaos Tradition." *JBL* 78 (1959) 187–98.

———. *Introduction to the Old Testament as Scripture*. Philadelphia: Fortress, 1979.

Christensen, Duane L. "A New Israel: The Righteous from among All Nations." In *Israel's Apostasy and Restoration: Essays in Honor of Roland K. Harrison*, edited by Avraham Gileadi, 251–59. Grand Rapids: Baker, 1987.

Christman, A. R. *"What Did Ezekiel See?": Christian Exegesis of Ezekiel's Vision of the Chariot from Irenaeus to Gregory the Great*. The Bible in Ancient Christianity 4. Leiden: Brill, 2005.

Clements, R. E. "The Chronology of Redaction in Ez 1–24." In *EHB*, edited by J. Lust, 283–94. BETL 74. Leuven, Belgium: Leuven University Press, 1986.

———. *Ezekiel*. Westminster Bible Companion. Louisville: Westminster John Knox, 1996.

---. "The Ezekiel Tradition: Prophecy in a Time of Crisis." In *Israel's Prophetic Tradition: Essays in Honour of Peter Ackroyd*, edited by Richard Coggins et al., 119-36. Cambridge: Cambridge University Press, 1984.

---. "The Interpretation of Prophecy and the Origin of Apocalyptic." *BapQ* (1989 Supplement) 28-34.

---. *Prophecy and Covenant*. SBT 43. London: SCM, 1965.

---. *Prophecy and Tradition*. Growing Points in Theology. Oxford: Blackwell, 1975.

---. "Woe." In *ABD*, edited by David Noel Freedman, 6:945-46. 6 vols. New York: Doubleday, 1992.

Clifford, Richard J. "The Roots of Apocalypticism in Near Eastern Myth." In *The Encyclopedia of Apocalypticism*, edited by Bernard McGinn et al., 1:3-38. 3 vols. New York: Continuum, 2002.

Cody, Aelred. *Ezekiel, with an Excursus on Old Testament Priesthood*. OTM 11. Wilmington, DE: Glazier, 1984.

Cogan, Morton. *Imperialism and Religion: Assyria, Judah and Israel in the Eighth and Seventh Centuries B.C.E.* SBLMS 19. Missoula, MT: Scholars, 1974.

Cohn, Norman. *Cosmos, Chaos, and the World to Come: The Ancient Roots of Apocalyptic Faith*. New Haven: Yale University Press, 1993.

Collins, John J. *A Commentary on the Book of Daniel*. Hermeneia. Minneapolis: Fortress, 1993.

---. "Apocalyptic Genre and Mythic Allusions in Daniel." *JSOT* 21 (1981) 83-100.

---. *The Apocalyptic Imagination: An Introduction to Jewish Apocalyptic Literature*. 2nd ed. Grand Rapids: Eerdmans, 1998.

---. *Daniel: With an Introduction to Apocalyptic Literature*. FOTL 20. Grand Rapids: Eerdmans, 1984.

---. "Early Jewish Apocalypticism." In *ABD*, edited by David Noel Freedman, 1:284-85. 6 vols. New York: Doubleday, 1992.

---. "From Prophecy to Apocalypticism: The Expectation of the End." In *The Continuum History of Apocalypticism*, edited by Bernard J. McGinn et al., 64-88. New York: Continuum, 2003.

---. "Towards the Morphology of a Genre." In *Apocalypse: The Morphology of a Genre*. edited by John J. Collins, 1-19. Semeia 14. Missoula, MT: SBL/distributed by Scholars, 1979.

Collins, Terence. *The Mantle of Elijah: The Redactional Criticism of the Prophetical Books*. The Biblical Seminar 20. Sheffield: JSOT Press, 1993.

Collon, D. "Mesopotamian Iconography." In *EncRel*, edited by Lindsay Jones, 7:4315-17. 15 vols. 2nd ed. New York: Macmillan, 2005.

Cook, Stephen L. *The Apocalyptic Literature*. Interpreting Biblical Texts. Nashville: Abingdon, 2003.

---. "Innerbiblical Interpretation in Ezekiel 44 and the History of the Priesthood." *JBL* 114 (1995) 193-208.

---. *Prophecy and Apocalypticism: The Postexilic Social Setting*. Minneapolis: Fortress, 1995.

Cook, Stephen L., and Corrine L. Patton, editors. *Ezekiel's Hierarchical World: Wrestling with a Tiered Reality*. SBLSymS 31. Atlanta, Ga.: SBL, 2004.

Cooke, G. A. *A Critical and Exegetical Commentary on the Book of Ezekiel.* ICC. Edinburgh: T. & T. Clark, 1936.
Cooper, David L. *When Gog's Armies Meet the Almighty: An Exposition of Ezekiel Thirty-Eight and Thirty-Nine.* 2nd ed. Los Angeles: Biblical Research Society, 1943.
Cooper, Jerrold S, compiler. *The Curse of Agade.* The Johns Hopkins Near Eastern Studies. Baltimore, Johns Hopkins University Press, 1983.
———. "The Fate of Mankind: Death and Afterlife in Ancient Mesopotamia." In *Death and Afterlife: Perspectives of World Religions*, edited by Hiroshi Obayashi, 19–33. Contributions to the Study of Religion 33. New York: Greenwood, 1992.
———. *The Return of Ninurta to Nippur.* AnOr 52. Rome: Pontificium Institutum Biblicum, 1978.
Cornill, Carl Heinrich. *Das Buch des Propheten Ezechiel.* Leipzig, Germany: Hinrich, 1886.
Corral, Martin Alonso. *Ezekiel's Oracles against Tyre: Historical Reality and Motivations.* BibOr 46. Rome: Pontifical Biblical Institute Press, 2002.
Costen, James H. "How Can These Bones Live? Ezekiel 37." *JITC* 24 (1996–1997) 51–65.
Craigie, Peter. *Deuteronomy.* NICOT. Grand Rapids: Eerdmans 1976.
———. *Ezekiel.* The Daily Study Bible. Edinburgh: St. Andrews Press, 1983.
Craven, Toni. *Ezekiel.* Collegeville Bible Commentary: Old Testament 16. Collegeville, MN: Liturgical, 1986.
Crawford, Timothy G. *Blessing and Curse in Syro-Palestinian Inscriptions of the Iron Age.* American University Studies Series 7. Theology and Religion 120. New York: Lang, 1992.
Crawley, Alfred E. "Cursing and Blessing." In *Encyclopaedia of Religion and Ethics*, edited by James Hastings, 4:367–74. 13 vols. Edinburgh: T. & T. Clark, 1959.
Crenshaw, J. L. "Theodicy and Prophetic Literature." In *Theodicy in the World of the Bible*, edited by Antti Laato and Johannes Cornelis de Moor, 236–55. Boston: Brill, 2003.
Cross, Frank Moore. *Canaanite Myth and Hebrew Epic: Essays in the History of the Religion of Israel.* Cambridge: Harvard University Press, 1973.
———. "Council of Yahweh in Second Isaiah." *JNES* 12 (1953) 274–77.
———. "Divine Warrior in Israel's Early Cult." In *Biblical Motifs: Origins and Transformations*, edited by Alexander Altmann, 11–30. Philip W. Lown Institute of Advanced Judaic Studies, Brandeis University. Studies and texts 3. Cambridge: Harvard University Press, 1966.
———. "Kinship and Covenant in Ancient Israel." In *From Epic to Canon: History and Literature in Ancient Israel*, 3–21. Baltimore: Johns Hopkins University Press, 1998.
———. "New Directions in the Study of Apocalyptic." *JTC* 6 (1969) 157–65.
Cunningham, Graham. *Deliver Me From Evil: Mesopotamian Incantations 2500–1500 BC.* Studia Pohl: Series Major 17. Rome: Pontificio Istituto Biblico, 1997.
Curbera, Jaime, and David Jordan. "Curse Tablets From Pydna." *GRBS* 43 (2002) 109–27.
Currid, John D. *Ancient Egypt and the Old Testament.* Grand Rapids: Baker, 1997.
Dalley, Stephanie. *Myths from Mesopotamia: Creation, the Flood, Gilgamesh, and Others.* World's Classics. Oxford: Oxford University Press, 1991.

Darr, Katherine Pfisterer. "Ezekiel." In *The Women's Bible Commentary*, edited by Carol A. Newsom and Sharon H. Ringe, 183–90. London: SPCK, 1992.

———. "Ezekiel's Justifications of God: Teaching Troubling Texts." *JSOT* 55 (1992) 97–117.

———. "Write or True? A Response to Ellen Frances Davis." In *Signs and Wonders: Biblical Texts in Literary Focus*, edited by J. Cheryl Exum, 239–47. SBLSS. Atlanta: Scholars, 1989.

Davidson, Andrew Bruce. *The Book of the Prophet Ezekiel*. Cambridge Bible for Schools and Colleges 22. London: Cambridge University Press, 1924.

Davis, Ellen S. "'And Pharaoh Will Change his Mind . . .' (Ezek 32:31) Dismantling Mythical Discourse." In *Theological Exegesis: Essays in Honor of Brevard S. Childs*, edited by Christopher Seitz and K. Greene-McCreight, 224–39. Grand Rapids: Eerdmans, 1999.

———. *Swallowing the Scroll*. Bible and Literature Series 21. Sheffield: Almond, 1989.

———. "Swallowing Hard: Reflections on Ezekiel's Dumbness." In *Signs and Wonders: Biblical Texts in Literary Focus*, edited by J. C. Exum, 217–37. SBLSS. Atlanta: Scholars, 1989.

Day, Linda. "Rhetoric and Domestic Violence in Ezekiel 16." *BibInt* 8 (2000) 205–30.

Day, Peggy L. "Adulterous Jerusalem's Imagined Demise: Death of a Metaphor in Ezekiel xvi." *VT* 50 (2000) 285–309.

———. "The Bitch Had It Coming to Her: Rhetoric and Interpretation in Ezekiel 16." *BibInt* 8 (2000) 231–54.

Day, John. "The Daniel of Ugarit and Ezekiel and the Hero of the Book of Daniel." *VT* 30 (1980) 174–84.

De Groot, Christina, and Marion Ann Taylor, editors. *Recovering Nineteenth-Century Women Interpreters of the Bible*. Atlanta: SBL, 2007.

Delitzsch, Franz. *Isaiah*. Translated by James Martin. 1866–91. Reprint, Peabody, MA: Hendrickson, 2001.

Delorme, Jean. "Conversion et pardon selon le prophète Ezéchiel." In *Mémorial J. Chaine*, 115–44. Bibliothèque de la Faculté Catholique de Théologie de Lyon 5. Lyon: Facultés Catholiques, 1950.

Dempsey, Carol J. *The Prophets: A Liberation-Critical Reading*. A Liberation-Critical Reading of the Old Testament. Minneapolis: Fortress, 2000.

———. "The 'Whore' of Ezekiel 16: The Impact and Ramifications of Gender-Specific Metaphors in Light of Biblical Law and Divine Judgment." In *Gender and Law in the Hebrew Bible and the Ancient Near East*, edited by Victor H. Matthews et al., 57–78. JSOTSup 262. Sheffield: Sheffield Academic, 1998.

Demsky, Aaron. "Education." In *EncJud* 6:381–98. Edited by Cecil Roth. 16 vols. Jerusalem: Encyclopaedia Judaica, 1972.

———. "Literacy in Israel and among Neighboring People in the Biblical Period." PhD diss., Hebrew University of Jerusalem, 1976.

Demson, David. "Divine Power Politics: Reflections on Ezekiel 37." In *Intergerini Parietis Septum (Eph. 2:14)*, edited by Dikran Y. Hadidian, 97–110. PittTMS 33. Pittsburgh: Pickwick, 1981. Reprint, Eugene, OR: Pickwick Publications, 2004.

Dentan, Robert C. *The Knowledge of God in Ancient Israel*. New York: Seabury, 1968.

Dhorme, P., and L. H. Vincent. "Les chérubins." *RB* 35 (1926) 328–58.

Dietrich, Manfried et al., editors. *The Cuneiform Alphabetic Texts from Ugarit, Ibn Hani, and Other Places*. 2nd, enlarged ed. Münster: Ugarit, 1995.

Dillard, Raymond, and Tremper Longman III. *An Introduction to the Old Testament*. Grand Rapids: Zondervan, 1994.

Djik Hemmes, Fokkelien van. "The Metaphorization of Women in Prophetic Speech: An Analysis of Ezekiel xxiii." *VT* 43 (1993) 162–70.

Dörfel, Donata. *Engel in der apokalyptischen Literatur und ihre theologische Relevanz: am Beispiel vom Ezechiel, Sacharja, Daniel und Erstem Henoch*. ThSt. Aachen: Shaker, 1998.

Dorsey, David. "Can These Bones Live? Investigating Literary Structure in the Bible." *EvJ* 9 (1991) 11–25.

Dressler, Harold H. P. "The Identification of the Ugaritic Dnil with the Daniel of Ezekiel." *VT* 29 (1979) 152–61.

Drewermann, Eugen. *"— auf das ihr wieder leben sollt": Die Botschaft des Propheten Ezechiel*. Zürich: Pendo, 2001.

Driver, Godfrey R., and John C. Miles. *The Assyrian Laws*. Ancient Codes and Laws of the Near East 2. Oxford: Clarendon, 1935.

Driver, S. R. *Introduction to the Literature of the Old Testament*. New York: Scribner, 1910.

Duguid, Iain M. *Ezekiel and the Leaders of Israel*. VTSup 56. Leiden: Brill, 1994.

———. "Putting Priests in Their Place: Ezekiel's Contribution to the History of the Old Testament Priesthood." In *Ezekiel's Hierarchical World: Wrestling with a Tiered Reality*, edited by Stephen L. Cook and Corrine L. Patton, 43–59. SBLSymS 31. Atlanta: SBL, 2004.

Duke, Rodney K. "Punishment or Restoration? Another Look at the Levites of Ezekiel 44.6–16." *JSOT* 40 (1988) 61–81.

Dundes, Alan, editor. *The Evil Eye: A Casebook*. Madison: University of Wisconsin Press, 1992.

Dupont-Sommer, André, and Jean Starcky. *Les Inscriptions araméennes de Sfiré (Stèles I et II), Extrait des Mémoires présentes par divers savants à l'Academie des Inscriptions et Belles Lettres, Tome XV*. Paris: Imp. nationale, 1958.

Durlesser, James A. *The Metaphorical Narratives in the Book of Ezekiel*. Lewiston, NY: Mellen, 2006.

Dürr, Lorenz. *Die Stellung des Propheten Ezekiel in der Israelitisch-Jüdischen Apokalyptik; ein Beitrag zur Erklärung des Buches Ezechiel und zur Israelitischen Religiongeschichte*. Münster: Aschendorff, 1923.

Dussaud, René. "Les Visions D'Ézéchiel." *RHR* 37 (1898) 301–13.

Eastman, Susan. "The Evil Eye and the Curse of the Law: Galatians 3.1 Revisited." *JSNT* 83 (2001) 69–87.

Edzard, Dietz Otto. *Gudea and His Dynasty*. RIME 3/1. Toronto: University of Toronto Press, 1997.

Eichrodt, Walther. *Ezekiel*. Translated by Cosslett Quin. OTL. Philadelphia: Westminster, 1970.

Eissfeldt, Otto. *The Old Testament*. Translated by Peter R. Ackroyd. Oxford: Blackwell, 1965.

Ellison, Henry Leopold. *Ezekiel: The Man and His Message*. London: Paternoster, 1967.

Enns, Paul P. *Ezekiel*. Bible Study Commentary. Grand Rapids: Zondervan, 1986.

Enns, Peter. "Abstracts of Recent WTS Doctoral Dissertations." *WTJ* 65 (2003) 357–62.
Eph'al, Israel. *The Ancient Arabs: Nomads on the Borders of the Fertile Crescent 9th–5th Centuries B.C.* Jerusalem: Magnes, 1982.
Erling, B. "Ezekiel 38–39 and the Origins of Jewish Apocalyptic." In *Ex Orbe Religionum*, edited by George Widengren, 104–14. SHR 1. Leiden: Brill, 1972.
Evans, Mary J. "'A Plague on Both Your Houses': Cursing and Blessing Reviewed." *VE* 24 (1994) 77–89.
Exum, J. Cheryl. "Prophetic Pornography." In *Plotted, Shot and Painted: Cultural Representations of Biblical Women*, edited by J. Cheryl Exum, 101–28. JSOTSup 215. Gender, Culture, Theory 3. Sheffield: Sheffield Academic, 1996.
Eybers, I. H. "The Book of Ezekiel and the Sect of Qumran." In *Studies on the Book of Ezekiel: Papers Read at the 4th Meeting Held at Bloemfontein 31 January—3 February 1961*, edited by A. H. van Zyl, 1–9. Pretoria: University of South Africa, 1961.
Fairbairn, Patrick. *An Exposition of Ezekiel*. Limited Classical Reprint Library. Minneapolis: Klock & Klock, 1979.
Fechter, Friedrich. "Priesthood in Exile according to the Book of Ezekiel." In *The Society of Biblical Literature 2000 Seminar Papers*, 673–99. SBLSP 39. Atlanta: SBL, 2000.
Feinberg, Charles L. *Jeremiah*. EBC 6. Grand Rapids: Zondervan, 1986.
———. *The Prophecy of Ezekiel: The Glory of the Lord*. Chicago: Moody, 1969.
Feist, Udo. *Ezechiel. Das literarische Problem des Buches forschungsgeschichtlich betrachtet*. BWANT 138. Stuttgart: Kohlhammer, 1995.
Fensham, F. Charles. "Common Trends in Curses in the Near Eastern Treaties and Kudurru-Inscriptions Compared with Maledictions of Amos and Isaiah." *ZAW* 75 (1963) 155–75.
———. "The Curse of the Dry Bones in Ezekiel 37:14 Changed to a Blessing of Resurrection." *JNSL* 13 (1987) 59–60.
———. "The Dog in Ex 11:7." *VT* 16 (1966) 504–7.
———. "Maledictions and Benedictions in Ancient Near Eastern Vassal-treaties and the Old Testament." *ZAW* 74 (1962) 1–9.
———. "Treaty between Israel and the Gibeonites." *BA* 27 (1964) 96–100.
Finegan, Jack. "The Chronology of Ezekiel." *JBL* 64 (1950) 61–66.
Finkelstein, S. S. "Sex Offenses in Sumerian Laws." *JAOS* 86 (1966) 355–72.
Fisch, S. *Ezekiel: Hebrew Text & English Translation*. Soncino Books of the Bible. London: Soncino, 1985.
Fishbane, M. "Sin and Judgment in the Prophecies of Ezekiel." *Int* 38 (1984) 131–50.
Fitzmyer, Joseph A. *The Aramaic Inscriptions of Sefire*. BibOr. Sacra Scriptura antiquitatibus orientalibus illustrata 19. Rome: Pontifical Biblical Institute, 1967.
———. "The Aramaic Inscriptions of Sefire I and II." *JAOS* 81(1961) 178–222.
———. "The Aramaic Suzerainty Treaty from Sefire in the Museum of Beirut." *CBQ* 20 (1958) 444–76.
Fitzpatrick, Paul E. *The Disarmament of God: Ezekiel 38–39 in Its Mythic Context*. CBQMS 37. Washington DC: The Catholic Biblical Association of America, 2004.

Fletcher-Louis, Crispin H. T. "'Leave the Dead to Bury Their Own Dead': Q9.60 and the Redefinition of the People of God." *JSNT* 26/1 (2003) 39–68.
Fohrer, Georg. *Die Hauptprobleme des Buches Ezechiel*. BZAW 72. Berlin: Töplemann, 1952.
Fohrer, Georg, and Kurt Galling. *Ezechiel*. HAT 13. Tübingen: Mohr/Siebeck, 1955.
Foster, Benjamin R. *Before the Muses: An Anthology of Akkadian Literature*. 3rd ed. Bethesda: CDL, 2005.
Fox, Michael V. "The Rhetoric of Ezekiel's Vision of the Valley of the Bones." *HUCA* 51 (1980) 1–15.
Fox, W. Sherwood. "Old Testament Parallels to Tabellae Defixionum." *AJSL* 30 (1914) 111–24.
Frankena, Rintje. *Kanttekeningen van een Assyrioloog bij Ezechiël*. Leiden: Brill, 1965.
———. "The Vassal-treaties of Esarhaddon and the Dating of Deuteronomy." In OtSt 14, 122–54. Leiden: Brill, 1965.
Fraser, A. D. "The Ancient Curse: Some Analogies." *CJ* 17 (1922) 454–60.
Frayne, Douglas. *Ur III Period (2112–2004 BC)*. RIME 3/2. Toronto: University of Toronto Press, 1997.
Freedman David Noel, and Shawna Dolansky Overton. "Omitting the Omissions: The Case for Haplography in the Transmission of the Biblical Texts." In *'Imagining' Biblical Worlds: Studies in Spatial, Social and Historical Constructs in Honor of James W. Flanagan*, edited by David M. Gunn and Paula M. McNutt, 99–116. JSOTSup 359. London: Sheffield Academic, 2002.
Freedy, Kenneth Stanley. "The Literary Relations of Ezekiel: A Historical Study of Chapters 1–24." PhD diss., University of Toronto, 1969.
Freehof, Solomon B. *Book of Ezekiel: A Commentary*. Jewish Commentary for Bible Readers. New York: Union of American Hebrew Congregations, 1978.
Fromaget, Michel. *Le Symbolisme des Quatre Vivants: Ezéchiel, Saint Jean et la Tradition*. Paris: Félin, 1992.
Frost, Stanley Brice. *Old Testament Apocalyptic: Its Origins and Growth*. The Fernley-Hartley Lecture 1952. London: Epworth, 1952.
Frye, Northrop. *The Great Code: The Bible and Literature*. New York: Harcourt Brace Jovanovich, 1982.
Fuhs, Hans F. *Ezechiel 1–24*. Die Neue Echter Bible: Kommentar zum Alten Testament mit der Einheitsübersetzung 7. 2nd ed. Würzburg: Echter, 1986.
Gadd, C. J. "The Harran Inscription of Nabonidus." *AnSt* 8 (1958) 35–92.
Gaebelein, P. W., Jr. "Marduk." In *ISBE*, edited by Geoffrey W. Bromiley, 3:244. 4 vols. Grand Rapids: Eerdmans, 1988.
Gager, John G., editor. *Curse Tablets and Binding Spells from the Ancient World*. New York: Oxford University Press, 1992.
Galambush, Julie. *Jerusalem in the Book of Ezekiel: The City as Yahweh's Wife*. SBLDS 130. Atlanta: Scholars, 1992.
———. "Castles in the Air: Creation as Property in Ezekiel." In *The Society of Biblical Literature 1999 Seminar Papers*, 147–72. SBLSP 38. Atlanta: SBL, 1999.
———. "This Land is My Land: On Nature as Property in the Book of Ezekiel." In *'Every City Shall Be Forsaken': Urbanism and Prophecy in Ancient Israel and the Near East*, edited by Lester L. Grabbe and Robert D. Haak, 71–94. JSOTSup 330. Sheffield: Sheffield Academic, 2001.

Ganzel, Tova. "The Descriptions of the Restoration of Israel in Ezekiel." Paper presented at the annual meeting of the SBL. Boston, MA, November 24, 2008.
Garaudy, Jean. *Ezechiel: Henry Mortenthau ist wieder da: der Maastricher Vertrag als apokalyptische Katastrophe*. Frankfurt: Haag & Herchen, 1994.
Garfinkel, S. P. "Studies in Akkadian Influences in the Book of Ezekiel." PhD diss., Columbia University, 1983.
Garscha, Jörg. *Studien zum Ezechielbuch: eine redaktionkritische Untersuchung von 1–39*. Bern: Lang, 1974.
Gelb, Ignace J. et al., editors. *CAD*. 21 vols. Chicago: Oriental Institute, 1956– .
Gerstenberger, Erhard S. "The Woe-Oracles of the Prophets." *JBL* 81 (1962) 249–63.
Gese, Hartmut. "Anfang und Ende der Apokalyptik, dargestellt am Sacharjabuch." *Theologie und Kirche* 70 (1973) 20–49.
———. *Der Verfassungsentwurf des Ezechiel (Kap. 40-48) Traditions-geschichtlich Untersucht*. BHT 25. Tübingen: Mohr/Siebeck, 1957.
Gevirtz, Stanley. "Curse Motifs in the Old Testament and in the Ancient Near East." PhD diss., University of Chicago, 1959.
———. "West Semitic Curses and the Problem of the Origins of Hebrew Law." *VT* 11 (1961) 137–58.
Geyer, John B. "Ezekiel 27 and the Cosmic Ship." In *Among the Prophets: Language, Image and Structure in the Prophetic Writings*, edited by Philip Davies and David Clines, 105–26. JSOTSup 144. Sheffield: JSOT Press, 1993.
Gnoli, Gherardo, and Jean-Pierre Vernant, editors. *La mort, les morts dans les sociétés anciennes*. Cambridge: Cambridge University Press, 1982.
Goldstein, Jonathan A. "The Historical Setting of the Uruk Prophecy." *JNES* 47/1 (1988) 43–46.
Good, Edwin M. "Ezekiel's Ship: Some Extended Metaphors in the Old Testament." *Sem* 1 (1970) 79–103.
Goodspeed, George Steven. *A History of the Babylonians and Assyrians*. New York: Schribner, 1909.
Gordis, Robert. "Hosea's Marriage and Message: a New Approach." *HUCA* 25 (1954) 9–35.
Gordon, C. H. "Hos 2:4–5 in the Light of New Semitic Inscriptions." *ZAW* 54 (1936) 277–80.
———. "The Status of Women Reflected in the Nuzi Tablets." *ZA* 43 (1936) 146–69.
Gosse, Bernhard. "Ézéchiel 35–36, 1–15 et Ézéchiel 6: La désolation de la montagne de Séir et le renouveau des montagnes d"Israël." *RB* 96 (1989) 511–17.
Gottwald, Norman K. *The Hebrew Bible. A Socio-Literary Introduction*. Philadelphia: Fortress, 1985.
Gowan, Donald E. *Ezekiel*. Knox Preaching Guides. Atlanta: John Knox, 1985.
———. *Theology of the Prophetic Books: The Death and Resurrection of Israel*. Louisville: Westminster John Knox, 1998.
Grabbe, Lester L. *Priests, Prophets, Diviners, Sages: A Socio-Historical Study of Religious Specialists in Ancient Israel*. Valley Forge, PA: Trinity, 1995.
———. "The Social Setting of Early Jewish Apocalypticism." *JSP* 4 (1989) 27–47.
Grabbe, Lester L., and Robert D. Haak, editors. *Knowing the End from the Beginning. The Prophetic, the Apocalyptic and Their Relationship*. JSPSup 46. London: T. & T. Clark, 2003.

Graetz, Naomi. "God is to Israel as Husband is to Wife: The Metaphoric Battering of Hosea's Wife." In *A Feminist Companion to the Latter Prophets*, edited by Athalya Brenner, 126–45. Feminist Companion to the Bible 8. Sheffield: Sheffield Academic, 1995.

Grassi, Joseph. "Ezekiel xxxvii: 1–14 and the New Testament." *NTS* 11 (1965) 162–64.

Gray, G. B. "The Heavenly Temple and the Heavenly Altar: I." *The Expositor* 5 (1908) 385–402.

———. "The Heavenly Temple and the Heavenly Altar: II." *The Expositor* 6 (1908) 530–46.

Grayson, A. Kirk. *Assyrian and Babylonian Chronicles*. TCS 5. Locust Valley, NY: Augustin, 1975.

———. *Assyrian Rulers of the Early First Millennium BC I (1114–859 BC)*. RIMA 2. Toronto: University of Toronto Press, 1991.

———. *Assyrian Rulers of the Early First Millennium BC II (858–745 BC)*. RIMA 3. Toronto: University of Toronto Press, 1996.

Grayson, A. Kirk, and W. G. Lambert. "Akkadian Prophecies." *JCS* 18/1 (1964) 7–30.

Green, M. W. "The Eridu Lament." *JCS* 30 (1978) 127–67.

———. "The Uruk Lament." *JAOS* 104 (1984) 253–79.

Greenberg, Moshe. "The Design and Themes of Ezekiel's Program of Restoration." *Int* 38 (1984) 181–208.

———. *Ezekiel 1–20*. AB 22. Garden City, NY: Doubleday, 1983.

———. *Ezekiel 21–37*. AB 22a. Garden City, NY: Doubleday, 1997.

———. "Ezekiel's Vision: Literary and Iconographic Aspects." In *History, Historiography and Interpretation: Studies in Biblical and Cuneiform Literatures*, edited by H. Tadmor and M. Weinfeld, 159–68. Jerusalem: Magnes, 1983.

———. "Notes on the Influence of Tradition on Ezekiel." *JANESCU* 22 (1993) 29–37.

———. "What Are the Valid Criteria for Determining Inauthentic Matter in Ezekiel?" In *EHB*, edited by J. Lust, 123–35. BETL 74. Leuven: Leuven University Press, 1986.

Greengus, Samuel. "A Textbook Case of Adultery in Ancient Mesopotamia." *HUCA* 40 (1969) 33–43.

———. "The Old Babylonian Marriage Contracts." *JAOS* 89 (1969) 505–32.

Gressmann, Hugo. *Der Ursprung der israelitisch-jüdischen Eschatologie*. Göttingen: Vandenhoeck & Ruprecht, 1905.

———. *Der Messias*. Göttingen: Vandenhoeck & Ruprecht, 1929.

Grogan, Geoffrey W. *Isaiah*. EBC 6. Grand Rapids: Zondervan, 1986.

Gruenwald, Ithamar. *Apocalyptic and Merkavah Mysticism*. ALGHJ 14. Leiden: Brill, 1980.

Gunkel, Hermann. *Creation and Chaos in the Primeval Era and the Eschaton*. Translated by K. William Whitney Jr. 1895. Reprint, Grand Rapids: Eerdmans, 2006.

———. *Genesis*. Translated by Mark E. Biddle. 1922. Mercer Library of Biblical Studies. Reprint, Macon: GA: Mercer University Press, 1997.

———. "Die Israelitische Literatur." In *Die Orientalischen Literaturen mit Einleitung*. edited by Erich Schmidt et al., 51–102. Die Kultur der Gegenwart 1/7. Berlin: Teubner, 1906.

———. "Die Schreiberengel Nabû im A.T. und im Judentum." *AR* 1 (1898) 294–301.

———. *Schöpfung und Chaos in Urzeit und Endzeit*. Göttingen: Vandenhoeck & Ruprecht, 1895.

Gurney, O. R. "The Sultantepe Tablets: The Cuthean Legend of Naram-Sin." *AnSt* 5 (1955) 93–113.

Hafemann, Scott J., and Paul R. House, editors. *Central Themes in Biblical Theology: Mapping Unity in Diversity*. Grand Rapids: Baker Academic, 2007.

Hahn, Scott. "Covenant in the Old and New Testaments: Some Current Research (1994–2004)." *CBR* 3 (2005) 263–92.

Hahn, Scott, and John Sietze Bergsma. "What Laws Were 'Not Good'? A Canonical Approach to the Theological Problem of Ezekiel 20:25–26." *JBL* 123/2 (2004) 201–18.

Hallo, William W., editor. *COS*. 3 vols. Leiden: Brill, 1997–2002.

Hallo, William W., and J. J. A. van Dijk. *The Exaltation of Inanna*. Yale Near Eastern Researches 3. New Haven: Yale University Press, 1968.

Halperin, David J. *Seeking Ezekiel: Text and Psychology*. University Park: Pennsylvania State University Press, 1993.

Hals, Ronald M. *Ezekiel*. FOTL 19. Grand Rapids: Eerdmans, 1989.

Hanson, Paul D. *The Dawn of Apocalyptic*. Philadelphia: Fortress, 1975.

———. *Old Testament Apocalyptic*. Interpreting Biblical Texts. Nashville: Abingdon, 1987.

Haran, Menahem. "The Law Code of Ezekiel XL–XLVIII and its Relation to the Priestly School." *HUCA* 50 (1979) 45–71.

Harper, Robert Francis. *Assyrian and Babylonian Letters Belonging to the K Collection of the British Museum*. New York: N. & N., 1977.

———. "Babylonian and Assyrian Imprecations." *BibWor* 24 (1904) 26–30.

Harrison, R. K. *Introduction to the Old Testament*. Grand Rapids: Eerdmans, 1969.

Harton, George M. "Fulfillment of Deuteronomy 28–30 in History and in Eschatology." ThD diss. Dallas Theological Seminary, 1981.

Harvey, Julien. *Le Plaidoyer Prophétique contra Israël Après la Rupture de L'alliance*. Studia 22. Bruges: de Brouwer, 1967.

———. "Le 'Ribpattern,' requisitoire prophetique sur le rupture de l'alliance." *Bib* 45 (1962) 172–96.

Hauser, A. *Recent Research on the Major Prophets*. Recent Research in Biblical Studies 1. Sheffield: Sheffield Phoenix, 2008.

Hawass, Zahi A. *Curse of the Pharaohs: My Adventures with Mummies*. Washington DC: National Geographic Society, 2004.

Hayes, John H. "The Usage of Oracles against Foreign Nations in Ancient Israel." *JBL* 87 (1968) 81–92.

Heider, George C. "A Further Turn on Ezekiel's Baroque Twist in Ezek 20:25–26." *JBL* 107 (1988) 721–24.

Heinisch, Paul. *Das Buch Ezechiel übersetzt und erklärt*. Bonn: Hanstein, 1923.

Heintz, Jean-Georges. "De l'absence de la statue divine au 'Dieu qui se cache' (Ésaïe 45/15) Aux origines d'un thème biblique." *RHPR* 59 (1979) 427–37.

———. "Langage métaphorique et représentation symbolique dans le prophétisme biblique et son milieu ambiant." In *Image et signification: Rencontres de l'École du Louvre II*, 55–72. Paris: La Documentation Française, 1983.

Hellholm, David, editor. *Apocalypticism in the Mediterranean World and the Near East: Proceedings of the International Colloquium on Apocalypticism, Uppsala, August 12–17, 1979.* Tübingen: Mohr/Siebeck, 1983.

Henderson, E. *The Book of the Prophet Ezekiel.* Andover: Draper, 1870.

Herntrich, Volkmar. *Ezechielprobleme.* BZAW 61. Giessen: Töpelmann, 1932.

Herrmann, Johannes. *Ezechiel übersetzt und erklärt.* KAT 11. Leipzig: Deichert, 1924.

Hillers, Delbert R. *Covenant: The History of a Biblical Idea.* Seminars in the History of Ideas. Baltimore: Johns Hopkins University Press, 1969.

———. *Treaty-Curses and the Old Testament Prophets.* BibOr 16. Rome: Pontifical Biblical Institute, 1964.

Himmelfarb, Martha. *Ascent to Heaven in Jewish and Christian Apocalypses.* New York: Oxford University Press, 1993.

Hoftijzer, Jacob. "Prophet Balaam in a 6th Century Aramaic Inscription." *BA* 39 (1976) 11–17.

Holladay, John Jr. "Assyrian Statecraft and the Prophets of Israel." *HTR* 63 (1970) 29–51.

Holladay, William L. *A Concise Hebrew and Aramaic Lexicon of the Old Testament.* Grand Rapids: Eerdmans, 1988.

Holloway, Steven W. "Distaff, Crutch or Chain Gang: the Curse of the House of Joab in 2 Samuel 3:29." *VT* 37 (1987) 370–75.

Hollis, F. J. "The Sun Cult and the Temple at Jerusalem." In *Myth and Ritual: Essays on the Myth and Ritual of the Hebrews in Relation to the Culture Pattern of the Ancient East,* edited by S. H. Hooke, 87–110. London: Oxford University Press, 1933.

Hölscher, Gustav. *Hezekiel, der Dichter und das Buch.* BZAW 39. Giessen: Töpelmann, 1924.

Hossfeld, Frank L. *Untersuchungen zu Komposition und Theologie des Ezechielbuches.* FB 20. Würzburg: Echter, 1977.

Houk, Cornelius. "בן־אדם Patterns as Literary Criteria in Ezekiel." *JBL* 88 (1969) 184–90.

Howie, Carl Gordon. *The Book of Ezekiel: The Book of Daniel.* LBC 13. Richmond: John Knox, 1961.

———. *The Date and Composition of Ezekiel.* SBLMS 4. Philadelphia: SBL, 1950.

Huffmon, Herbert B. "The Covenant Lawsuit in the Prophets." *JBL* 68 (1959) 285–95.

———. "The Treaty Background of the Hebrew *Yāda*'." *BASOR* 181 (1966) 31–37.

Hugenberger, Gordon Paul. *Marriage as a Covenant.* VTSup 52. Leiden: Brill, 1994.

Hultgård, Anders. "Forms and Origins of Iranian Apocalypticism." In *AMWNE,* edited by David Hellholm, 385–411. Tübingen: Mohr/Siebeck, 1983.

———. "Persian Apocalypticism." In *The Encyclopedia of Apocalypticism,* edited by Bernard McGinn et al., 1:39–83. 3 vols. New York: Continuum, 2002.

Hunger, Hermann, and Stephen Kaufman. "A New Akkadian Prophecy Text." *JAOS* 95/3 (1975) 371–75.

Hurowitz, Victor. *I Have Built You an Exalted House: Temple Building in the Bible in Light of Mesopotamian and Northwest Semitic Writings.* JSOTSup 115. Sheffield: Sheffield Academic, 1992.

Hurvitz, Avi. *A Linguistic Study of the Relationship between the Priestly Source and the Book of Ezekiel.* CahRB 20. Paris: Gabalda, 1982.

———. "Evidence of Language in Dating the Priestly Code: A Linguistic Study in Technical Idioms and Terminology." *RB* 81 (1974) 24–56.

Hyatt, J. Philip. "The Peril from the North in Jeremiah." *JBL* 59 (1940) 499–513.

Irwin, Brian. "An Exegetical Study of Ezekiel 38–39." M. Rel. thesis, Wycliffe College at the Toronto School of Theology, 1990.

———. "Baal and Yahweh in the OT: A Fresh Examination of the Biblical and Extra-Biblical Data." PhD diss., Wycliffe College at the Toronto School of Theology, 1999.

———. "Molek Imagery and the Slaughter of Gog in Ezekiel 38 and 39." *JSOT* 65 (1995) 93–112.

Irwin, William A. *The Problem of Ezekiel: An Inductive Study.* Chicago: University of Chicago Press, 1943.

Jacobsen, Thorkild. *Toward the Image of Tammuz.* HSS 21. Cambridge: Harvard University Press, 1970.

Jaspers, Karl. "Der Prophet Ezechiel: Eine pathologische Studie." In *Arbeiten zur Psychiatric, Neurologie und ihren Grenzgebieten: Festschrift für Kurt Schneider,* edited by Heinrich Kranz, 1–9. Willsbach: Scherer, 1947.

Jeremias, Alfred. *Das Alte Testament im Lichte des Alten Orients.* Leipzig: Hinrichs, 1906.

Jesse, Jennifer G. "Postliberal Theology in the Valley of Dry Bones. *Enc* 58 (1997) 19–39.

Jirku, Anton. *Altorientalischer Kommentar zum Alten Testament.* Leipzig: Erlangen, 1923.

Johnston, Gordon H. "Nahum's Rhetorical Allusions to Neo-Assyrian Treaty Curses." *BSac* 158 (2001) 415–36.

Jones, Lindsay, editor-in-chief. *The Encyclopedia of Religion.* 16 vols. 2nd ed. Detroit: Macmillan Reference, 2005.

Jong, Matthijs J. de. "Ezekiel as a Literary Figure and the Quest for the Historical Prophet." In *The Book of Ezekiel and its Influence,* edited by Henk Jan de Jonge and Johannes Tromp, 1–16. Aldershot, England: Ashgate, 2007.

Joyce, Paul. *Divine Initiative and Human Response in Ezekiel.* JSOTSup 51. Sheffield: JSOT Press, 1989.

———. *Ezekiel: A Commentary.* T. & T. Clark Library of Biblical Studies. LHB/OTS. New York: T & T Clark, 2007.

———. "Ezekiel and Individual Responsibility." In *EHB*, edited by J. Lust, 317–21. BETL 74. Leuven, Belgium: Leuven University Press, 1986.

———. "The Individual and the Community." In *Beginning Old Testament Study*, edited by John Rogerson, 74–89. Philadelphia: Westminster, 1983.

———. "Individual Responsibility in Ezekiel 18?" In *Studia Biblica 1978: Papers on Old Testament and Related Themes*, edited by E. A. Livingstone, 185–96. JSOTSup 11. Sheffield: JSOT Press, 1979.

Kalland, Earl S. *Deuteronomy.* EBC 3. Grand Rapids: Zondervan, 1992.

Kalluveettil, Paul. *Declaration and Covenant: A Comprehensive Review of Covenant Formulae from the Old Testament and the Ancient Near East.* AnBib 88. Rome: Biblical Institute Press, 1982.

Kaminsky, Joel S. *Corporate Responsibility in the Hebrew Bible*. JSOTSup 196. Sheffield: Sheffield Academic, 1995.

Kamionkowski, S. Tamar. *Gender Reversal and Cosmic Chaos: A Study on the Book of Ezekiel*. JSOTSup 368. London: Sheffield Academic, 2003.

———. "The Savage Made Civilized: An Examination of Ezekiel 16:8." In *'Every City Shall Be Forsaken': Urbanism and Prophecy in Ancient Israel and the Near East*, edited by Lester L. Grabbe and Robert D. Haak, 124–36. JSOTSup 330. Sheffield: Sheffield Academic, 2001.

Kapelrud, Arvid S. "The Prophets and the Covenant." In *In the Shelter of Elyon: Essays on Ancient Palestinian Life and Literature in Honor of G. W. Ahlström*, edited by W. Boyd Barrick and John R. Spencer, 175–83. JSOTSup 31. Sheffield: JSOT Press, 1984.

Kataja, L., and R. Whiting. *State Archives of Assyria Volume XII: Grants, Decrees and Gifts of the Neo-Assyrian Period*. SAA 10. Helsinki: Helsinki University Press, 1995.

Kaufmann, Yehezkel. *The Religion of Israel: From Its Beginnings to the Babylonian Exile*. Translated by Moshe Greenberg. Chicago: University of Chicago Press, 1960.

Kearney, Peter J. Review of *Bundestheologie im Alten Testament*, by Lothar Perlitt. *CBQ* 34 (1972) 524–28.

Keefe, Alice A. *Woman's Body and the Social Body in Hosea*. JSOTSup 338. Gender, Culture, Theory 10. Sheffield: Sheffield Academic, 2001.

Keel, Othmar. *Jahwe-Visionen und Siegelkunst: Eine neue Deutung der Majestätsschilderungen in Jes 6, Ez 1 und 10 und Sach 4*. SBS 84/85. Stuttgart: Katholisches Bibelwerk, 1977.

———. *The Symbolism of the Biblical World: Ancient Near Eastern Iconography and the Book of Psalms*. Winona Lake, IN: Eisenbrauns, 1997.

Keil, C. F. *Ezekiel*. COT 9. 1866–91. Reprint, Peabody, MA: Hendrickson, 2001.

King, Leonard W. *Babylonian Boundary-Stones and Memorial-Tablets in the British Museum*. London: Oxford University Press, 1912.

———. *Babylonian Magic and Sorcery: Being "the Prayers of the Lifting of the Hand."* London: Luzac, 1896.

Kitchen, K. A. *On the Reliability of the Old Testament*. Grand Rapids: Eerdmans, 2003.

Kittel, Rudolf. *Geschichte des Volkes Israel* Vol. 3 Part 1. Stuttgart: Kohlhammer, 1927.

Klein, Ralph W. *Ezekiel: The Prophet and His Message*. Studies on Personalities of the Old Testament. Columbia: University of South Carolina Press, 1988.

Kline, M. G. *The Treaty of the Great King*. Grand Rapids: Eerdmans, 1963.

Knibb, Michael A. "Prophecy and the Emergence of Jewish Apocalypses." In *Israel's Prophetic Tradition: Essays in Honour of Peter Ackroyd*, edited by Richard Coggins, et al., 155–80. Cambridge: Cambridge University Press, 1984.

Koch, Klaus. *The Growth of the Biblical Tradition: The Form-Critical Method*. New York: Macmillan, 1988.

———. "Is Daniel among the Prophets?" *Int* 39 (1985) 117–30.

———. *The Prophets*. Vol. 2, *The Babylonian and Persian Periods*. Translated by Margaret Kohl. 2 vols. Philadelphia.: Fortress, 1984.

———. *The Rediscovery of Apocalyptic*. Translated by Margaret Kohl. SBT 2/22. London: SCM, 1972.

Kohn, Risa Levitt. "Ezekiel, the Exile, and the Torah." In *Society of Biblical Literature 1999 Seminar Papers*, 501–26. SBLSP 38. Atlanta: SBL, 1999.

———. *A New Heart and a New Soul: Ezekiel, the Exile, and the Torah*. JSOTSup 358. London: Sheffield Academic, 2002.

König, Ed. "Die letzte Pentateuchschicht und Hesekiel." *ZAW* 28 (1908) 174–79.

Kornfeld, Walter. "L'Adultère dans l'Orient antique." *RB* 57 (1950) 92–109.

Kortner, U. H. J. "Weltzeit, Weltangst und Weltende." *TZ* 45 (1989) 32–52.

Kraetzschmar, Richard. *Das Buch Ezekiel*. Göttingen: Vandenhoeck, 1900.

Krahn, Cornelius. "'Can These Bones Live?': Ezekiel 37:3." *ML* 1/2 (1946) 3–4.

Kramer, Samuel N. "Lamentation over the Destruction of Nippur: A Preliminary Report." *ErIsr* 9 (1969) 89–93.

———. *Lamentation over the Destruction of Sumer and Ur*. AS 12. Chicago: University of Chicago Press, 1940.

Kroeze, J. H. "The Tyre-Passages in the Book of Ezekiel." In *Studies on the Book of Ezekiel: Papers Read at the 4th Meeting Held at Bloemfontein 31 January—3 February 1961*, edited by A. H. van Zyl, 10–23. Pretoria: University of South Africa, 1961.

Kruger, Paul A. "The Hem of the Garment in Marriage: The Meaning of the Symbolic Gesture in Ruth 3:9 and Ezek 16:8." *JNSL* 12 (1984) 79–86.

Krüger, Thomas. *Geschichtskonzepte im Ezekielbuch*. BZAW 180. Berlin: de Gruyter, 1989.

Kuhl, C. "Neue Dokumente zum Verständnis von Hos 2:4–15." *ZAW* 52 (1934) 102–9.

Kutsch, Ernst. *Die chronologischen Daten des Ezechielbuches*. OBO 62. Freiburg: Universitätsverlag, 1985.

Kutsko, John F. *Between Heaven and Earth: Divine Presence and Absence in the Book of Ezekiel*. Biblical and Judaic Studies from the University of California San Diego 7. Winona Lake, IN: Eisenbrauns, 2000.

———. "Ezekiel's Anthropology and Its Ethical Implications." In *The Book of Ezekiel: Theological and Anthropological Perspectives*, edited by Margaret S. Odell and John T. Strong, 119–41. SBLSymS 9. Atlanta: SBL, 2000.

Kvanvig, Helge S. *Roots of Apocalyptic: The Mesopotamian Background of the Enoch Figure and the Son of Man*. WMANT 61. Neukirchen-Vluyn: Neukirchen, 1988.

Labat, René. *Le Caractère Religieux de la Royauté Assyro-Babylonienne*. Paris: Librairie d'Amérique et d'Orient Adrien-Maisonneuve, 1939.

Ladd, George E. "Why Not Prophecy-Apocalyptic?" *JBL* 76 (1957) 192–200.

Lafont, Sophie. *Femmes, Droit et Justice dans l'Antiquité orientale*. OBO 165. Göttingen: Vandenhoeck & Ruprecht, 1999.

Lambert, W. G. *The Background of Jewish Apocalyptic*. Ethel M. Wood Lecture 1977. London: Athlone, 1978.

———. "Three Unpublished Fragments of the Tukulti-Ninurta Epic." *AfO* 18. Graz: Weidner (1957–58) 40–50.

———, editor. *Babylonian Wisdom Literature*. Oxford: Clarendon, 1960.

Landerdorfer, P. S. *Der Baal Tetramorphos und die Kerube des Ezechiel*. Paderborn: Ferdinand Schoningh, 1918.

Laney, J. Carl. "A Fresh Look at the Imprecatory Psalms." *BSac* 138 (1981) 35–45.
Lang, Bernard. *Ezechiel: Das Prophet und das Buch*. EF 153. Darmstadt: Wissenschaftliche Buchgesellschaft, 1981.
———. *Kein Aufstand in Jerusalem: Die Politik des Propheten Ezechiel*. SBB. Stuttgart: Katholisches Bibelwerk, 1978.
———. *Monotheism and the Prophetic Minority: An Essay in Biblical History and Sociology*. SWBA. Sheffield: Almond, 1983.
———. "No God but Yahweh! The Origin and Character of Biblical Monotheism." *Con* 177 (1985) 41–49.
———. "Street Theater, Raising the Dead, and Zoroastrian Connection in Ezekiel's Prophecy." In *EHB*, edited by J. Lust, 297–316. BETL 74 Leuven: Leuven University Press, 1986.
———. "Zur Entstehung des biblischen Monotheismus." *TQ* 166 (1986) 135–42.
Langdon, S. *Die Neubabylonischen Königsinschriften*. VAB 4. Leipzig: Hinrichs, 1912.
Langdon, Stephen H. *The Mythology of all Races*. Vol. 5, *Semitic*. Edited by Louis Herbert Gray. 13 vols. 1931. Reprint, New York: Cooper Square, 1964.
Launderville, Dale F. *Spirit and Reason: The Embodied Character of Ezekiel's Symbolic Thinking*. Waco: Baylor University Press, 2007.
Layard, Austen Henry. *Nineveh and Its Remains*. New York: Putnam, 1854.
Lee, Alvin A., editor. *The Collected Works of Northrop Frye*. Vol. 19, *The Great Code: The Bible and Literature*. Toronto: University of Toronto Press, 2006.
Lemaire, André. "Les formules des datation dans Ézéchiel à la lumiere de données épigraphiques recentes." In *EHB*, edited by J. Lust, 359–66. BETL 74 Leuven: Leuven University Press, 1986.
Lemaire, A. and J. M. Durand. *Les Insciptions Araméenns de Sfiré et l'Assyrie de Sham-shi-ilu*. Geneva: Librairie Droz, 1984.
Lemos, T. M. "Shame and Mutilation of Enemies in the Hebrew Bible." *JBL* 125 (2006) 225–41.
Lenormant, François. *Les Origins de l'histoire d'après la Bible et les traditions des peuples orietaux*. 3 vols. Paris: Maisonneuve & cie., 1880–1884.
Levenson, Jon D. "The Last Four Verses in Kings." *JBL* 103 (1984) 353–61.
———. *Theology of the Program of Restoration of Ezekiel 40–48*. Edited by Frank Moore Cross. HSM 10. Missoula.: Scholars, 1976.
Levey, Samson H. *The Targum of Ezekiel*. ArBib 13. Collegeville, MN: Liturgical, 1990.
Levine, Louis. "Sennacherib's Southern Front: 704–689 B.C." *JCS* 34 (1982) 28–58.
Levitt, Kohn. *A New Heart and a New Soul: Ezekiel, the Exile and the Torah*. JSOTSup 358. London: Sheffield Academic, 2002.
Levy, Abraham J. *Rashi's Commentary on Ezekiel 40–48*. Philadelphia.: Dropsie College for Hebrew and Cognate Learning, 1931.
Lewis, Brian. *The Sargon Legend*. Cambridge, MA: ASOR, 1980.
Lewis, Theodore J. "CT 13:33–34 and Ezekiel 32: Lion-Dragon Myths." *JAOS* 116 (1996) 28–47.
———. *Cults of the Dead in Ancient Israel and Ugarit*. HSM 39. Atlanta: Scholars, 1989.
Lewy, Immanuel. "Puzzle of Dt XXVII: Blessings Announced, But Curses Noted." *VT* 12 (1962) 207–11.

Lind, Millard C. *Ezekiel*. Believers Church Bible Commentary. Scottdale, PA: Herald, 1996.

———. *Yahweh Is a Warrior: The Theology of Warfare in Ancient Israel*. Christian Peace Shelf Selection. Scottdale, PA: Herald, 1980.

Lindars, Barnabas. "Ezekiel and Individual Responsibility." *VT* 15 (1965) 452-67.

Liss, Hanna. "'Describe the Temple to the House of Israel': Preliminary Remarks on the Temple Vision in the Book of Ezekiel and the Question of Fictionality in Priestly Literatures." In *Utopia and Dystopia in Prophetic Texts*, edited by Ehud Ben Zvi and Michael Floyd, 122-43. Publications of the Finnish Exegetical Society. Helsinki: Finnish Exegetical Society/University of Helsinki, 2006.

Little, Lester K. "Cursing." In *EncRel*, edited by Mircea Eliade, 4:182-85. 16 vols. New York: Macmillan, 1987.

Lods, Adolphe. *Les Prophètes d'Israël et les débuts judaïsme*. Paris: Albin Michel, 1935.

Loewenstamm, Samuel E. *Comparative Studies in Biblical and Ancient Oriental Literatures*. AOAT 204. Neukirchen-Vluyn: Neukirchener, 1980.

Lofthouse, William Frederick. *Ezekiel*. Edinburgh: T. C & E. C. Jack, 1907.

Loretz, O. "Eine sumerische Parallele zu Ez 23,20." *BZ* 14 (1970) 126.

Luckenbill, Daniel David. *Ancient Records of Assyria and Babylon*. 2 vols. 1926-1927. Reprint, New York: Greenwood, 1968.

———. *Annals of Sennacherib*. 1924. Reprint, Ancient Texts and Translations. Eugene, OR: Wipf & Stock, 2005.

Lundquist, John M. "Temple, Covenant, and Law in the Ancient Near East and the Old Testament." In *Israel's Apostasy and Restoration: Essays in Honor of Roland K. Harrison*, edited by Avraham Gileadi, 293-305. Grand Rapids: Baker, 1988.

Lust, J., editor. *Ezekiel and His Book: Textual and Literary Criticism and Their Interrelation*. BETL 74. Leuven: Leuven University Press, 1986.

Lyons, Michael A. *From Law to Prophecy: Ezekiel's Use of the Holiness Code*. LHB/OTS 507. T. & T. Clark Library of Biblical Studies. New York: T. & T. Clark, 2009.

Maarsingh, B. "Das Schwertlied in Ez 21,13-22 und das Erra-Gedicht." In *EHB*, edited by J. Lust, 350-58. BETL 74. Leuven: Leuven University Press, 1986.

———. *Ezechiël*. 3 vols. Nijkerk: Callenbach, 1985-1991.

MacDonald, Elizabeth Mary. *The Position of Women as Reflected in Semitic Codes of Law*. Toronto: University of Toronto Press, 1931.

Machinist, Peter. "Literature as Politics: The Tukulti-Ninurta Epic and the Bible." *CBQ* 38 (1976) 455-82.

Mackay, Cameron. "Zechariah in Relation to Ezekiel 40-48." *EvQ* 40 (1968) 197-210.

Macumber, Heather. "God's Protection and Rejection of Israel: The Harlot Metaphor in Ezekiel 16." MDiv thesis, Tyndale University and College, 2005.

Magdalene, F. Rachel. "Ancient Near Eastern Treaty-Curses and the Ultimate Texts of Terror: A Study of the Language of Divine Sexual Abuse in the Prophetic Corpus." In *A Feminist Companion to the Latter Prophets*, edited by Athalya Brenner, 326-52. The Feminist Companion to the Bible 8. Sheffield: Sheffield Academic, 1995.

Magnetti, Donald L. "The Function of the Oath in the Ancient Near Eastern International Treaty." *AJIL* 72 (1978) 815-29.

Malamat, Abraham. "Jeremiah and the Last Two Kings of Judah." *PEQ* 83 (1951) 81–87.

———. "The Last Kings of Judah and the Fall of Jerusalem." *IEJ* 18 (1968) 137–56.

Malul, Meir. "Adoption of Foundlings in the Bible and Mesopotamian Documents: A Study of Some Legal Metaphors in Ezekiel 16:1–7." *JSOT* 46 (1990) 97–126.

———. *Studies in Mesopotamian Legal Symbolism*. AOAT 221. Kevelaer: Butzon & Brecker, 1988.

Marquès-Rivière, Jean. *Amulettes, Talismans et Pantacles dans les Traditions Orientales et Occidentales*. 2nd ed. Paris: Payot, 1972.

Martinez, F. Garcia. "Apocalypticism in the Dead Sea Scrolls." In *The Continuum History of Apocalypticism*, edited by Bernard J. McGinn et al., 89–111. New York: Continuum, 2003.

———. "Encore l'Apocalyptique." *JSJ* 17 (1987) 224–32.

Mason, Rex. "The Prophets of the Restoration." In *Israel's Prophetic Tradition: Essays in Honour of Peter R. Ackroyd*, edited by Richard Coggins et al., 137–54. Cambridge: Cambridge University Press, 1982.

Matthews, I. G. *Ezekiel*. Chicago: The American Baptist Publication Society, 1939.

Matthews, Victor H. "Theophanies Cultic and Cosmic: Prepare to Meet Thy God!" In *Israel's Apostasy and Restoration: Essays in Honor of Ronald K. Harrison*, edited by Avraham Gileadi, 307–17. Grand Rapids: Baker, 1988.

Matthews, Victor H., and Don C. Benjamin. *Old Testament Parallels: Laws and Stories from the Ancient Near East*. New York: Paulist, 1991.

Matthews, Victor H., and James Moyer. *The Old Testament*. Peabody, MA: Hendrickson, 1997.

Matties, Gordon H. *Ezekiel 18 and the Rhetoric of Moral Discourse*. SBLDS 126. Atlanta: Scholars, 1990.

May, Herbert G. "The Book of Ezekiel." *IB* 6. Nashville: Abingdon, 1956.

———. "The Chronology of Jeremiah's Oracles." *JNES* 4 (1945) 217–27.

———. "The Departure of the Glory of Yahweh." *JBL* 56 (1937) 309–21.

———. "Three Hebrew Seals and the Status of Exiled Jehoiachin." *AJSL* 56 (1939) 146–48.

Mays, James Luther. *Ezekiel, Second Isaiah*. Proclamation Commentaries. Philadelphia: Fortress, 1978.

McCarthy, Dennis J. *Old Testament Covenant: A Survey of Opinions*. Growing Points in Theology. Richmond: John Knox, 1972.

———. Review of *Bundestheologie im Alten Testament*, by Lothar Perlitt. *Bib* 53 (1972) 110–21.

———. *Treaty and Covenant: A Study from the Oriental Documents and the Old Testament*. AnBib 21. Rome: Pontifical Biblical Institute, 1963.

———. *Treaty and Covenant: A Study in Form in the Ancient Oriental Documents and in the Old Testament*. New ed. Rome: Biblical Institute, 1978.

McConville, J. Gordon. "Priests and Levites in Ezekiel: A Crux in the Interpretation of Israel's History." *TynBul* 34 (1983) 3–31.

McKeating, Henry. *Ezekiel*. OTG. Sheffield: Sheffield Academic, 1995.

———. "Ezekiel the 'Prophet Like Moses?'" *JSOT* 61 (1994) 97–109.

———. "Sanctions against Adultery in Ancient Israelite Society, with some Reflections on Methodology in the Study of Old Testament Ethics." *JSOT* 11 (1979) 57–72.

McKenzie, Steven L. *Covenant.* Understanding Biblical Themes. St. Louis: Chalice, 2000.

McLaughlin, John L. *The marzēah in the Prophetic Literature: References and Allusions in Light of the Extra-biblical Evidence.* VTSup 86. Leiden: Brill, 2001.

McNamara, Martin. "Interpretation of Scripture in the Targumim." In *A History of Biblical Interpretation.* Vol. 1, *The Ancient Period.* Edited by Alan J. Hauser and Duane F. Watson, 167–97. Grand Rapids: Eerdmans, 2003.

McWilliam, Stuart. "The Valley of Dry Bones." *ExpTim* 63 (1952) 283–85.

Mein, Andrew. *Ezekiel and the Ethics of Exile.* Oxford Theological Monographs. Oxford: Oxford University Press, 2001.

———. "Ezekiel as a Priest in Exile." In *The Elusive Prophet: The Prophet as a Historical Person, Literary Character and Anonymous Author,* edited by Johannes C. de Moor, 199–213. OtSt 45. Leiden: Brill, 2001.

———. "Profitable and Unprofitable Shepherds: Economic and Theological Perspectives on Ezekiel 34." *JSOT* 31 (2007) 493–504.

———. Review of *The Rhetorical Function of the Book of Ezekiel,* by Thomas Renz. *JTS* 52 (2001) 733–35.

Meissner, Bruno Albert von. "Bemerkungen zu den Asarhaddoninschriften." *OLZ* 14/10 (1911) cols. 474–77.

Mendenhall, George E. "Ancient Oriental and Biblical Law." *BA* 17 (1954) 26–46.

———. "Covenant Forms in Israelite Tradition." *BA* 17 (1954) 50–76.

———. *Law and Covenant in Israel and the Ancient Near East.* Pittsburgh: Presbyterian Board of Colportage of Western Pennsylvania, 1955.

———. "Puppy and Lettuce in Northwest-Semitic Covenant Making." *BASOR* 133 (1954) 26–30.

———. "The Relation of the Individual to Political Society in Ancient Israel." In *Biblical Studies in Memory of H. C. Alleman,* edited by J. M. Myers et al., 89–108. Locust Valley, NY: Augustin, 1960.

———. *The Tenth Generation: The Origins of the Biblical Tradition.* Baltimore: Johns Hopkins University Press, 1973.

Mercer, Samuel A. B. *The Oath in Babylonian and Assyrian Literature.* Paris: Geuthner, 1912.

Merrill, Eugene. *Deuteronomy.* NAC 4. Nashville: Broadman & Holman, 1994.

Messel, Nils. *Ezechielfragen.* Oslo: I Kommisjon Hos Jacob Dybwad, 1945.

M'Fadyen, J. E. "Ezekiel." In *Peake's Commentary on the Bible,* edited by M. Black and H. H. Rowley, 501–21. London: Nelson, 1937.

Michalowski, Piotr. *The Destruction of Sumer and Ur.* Mesopotamian Civilizations 1. Winona Lake, IN: Eisenbrauns, 1989.

Milgrom, Jacob. *Leviticus 1–16: A New Translation with Introduction and Commentary.* AB 3. New York: Doubleday, 1991.

———. *Leviticus 17–22: A New Translation with Introduction and Commentary.* AB 3A. New York: Doubleday, 2000.

———. *Leviticus 23–27: A New Translation with Introduction and Commentary.* AB 3B. New York: Doubleday, 2001.

———. *Leviticus: A Book of Ritual and Ethics.* CC. Minneapolis: Fortress, 2004.

———. Review of *A Linguistic Study of the Relationship between the Priestly Source and the Book of Ezekiel,* by Avi Hurvitz. *CBQ* 46 (1984) 118–19.

———. *Studies in Cultic Theology and Terminology*. Studies in Judaism in Late Antiquity 36. Leiden: Brill, 1983.

———. *Studies in Levitical Terminology*. University of California Publications. Near Eastern Studies 14. Berkeley: University of California Press, 1970.

———. "Whence the Unique Features of Ezekiel's Sanctuary." Paper presented at the annual meeting of the SBL. Boston, MA, November 24, 2008.

Millar, W. R. *Isaiah 24–27 and the Origin of Apocalyptic*. HSM 11. Missoula, MT: Scholars, 1976.

Miller, J. E. "The Thirtieth Year of Ezekiel 1:1." *RB* 99 (1992) 499–503.

Miller, Patrick D. Jr. *Deuteronomy*. Interpretation: A Commentary for Teaching and Preaching. Louisville: John Knox, 1990.

———. *Sin and Judgment in the Prophets: A Stylistic and Theological Analysis*. SBLMS 27. Chico: Scholars, 1982.

Milne, Pamela J. "The Patriarchal Stamp of Scripture: The Implications of Structuralist Analyses for Feminist Hermeneutics." *JFSR* 5 (1989) 17–34.

Mitchell, Christopher Wright. *The Meaning of BRK "to Bless" in the Old Testament*. SBLDS 95. Atlanta: Scholars, 1987.

Moore, George Foot. *Judaism in the First Centuries of the Christian Era*. 3 vols. Cambridge: Harvard University Press, 1927–1930.

Moore, Michael S. Review of *The Book of Ezekiel and the Poem of Erra*, by Daniel Bodi. *JBL* 112 (1993) 519–20.

Morgenstern, J. "The Gates of Righteousness." *HUCA* 6/1 (1929) 1–37.

Morris, J. V. "Curse (in the Bible)." In *The New Catholic Encyclopedia*, edited by William J. McDonald, 4:547–48. 16 vols. New York: McGraw-Hill, 1967.

Morris, Leon. *Apocalyptic*. Grand Rapids: Eerdmans, 1972.

Mosis, R. "Ez 14,1–11—ein Ruf zur Umkehr." *BZ* 19 (1975) 161–94.

Moule, Samuel George. *Notes on Ezekiel*. Tunbridge Wells: Baldwin, 1940.

Mowinckel, Sigmund. *The Two Sources of the Predeuteronomic Primeval History JE in Gen. 1–11*. Oslo: Dybwad, 1937.

Mozley, J. B. "Visitation of the Sins of the Fathers upon the Children." In *Ruling Ideas in Early Ages and Their Relation to Old Testament Faith*, 104–25. London: Longmans, Green, & Co., 1962.

Muilenburg, James. "Ezekiel." *Peake's Commentary on the Bible*, edited by M. Black and H. H. Rowley, 568–90. New York: Nelson, 1962.

———. "Form Criticism and Beyond." *JBL* 88 (1969) 1–18.

Müller. H. P. *Ursprunge und Strukturen alttestamentlicher Eschatologie*. BZAW 109. Berlin: Töpelmann, 1969.

Mullo Weir, Cecil J. "Aspects of the Book of Ezekiel." *VT* 2 (1952) 97–112.

Naveh, Joseph. "A Paleographic Note on the Distribution of the Hebrew Script." *HTR* 61 (1968) 68–74.

Newsom, Carol. "A Maker of Metaphors: Ezekiel's Oracles against Tyre." In *Interpreting the Prophets*, edited by James Luther Mays and Paul J. Achtemeier, 188–99. Philadelphia: Fortress, 1987.

Nicholson, E. W. *Deuteronomy and Tradition*. Philadelphia: Fortress, 1967.

Niditch, Susan. "Ezekiel 40–48 in a Visionary Context." *CBQ* 48 (1986) 208–24.

Niehaus, Jeffrey J. "Amos." In *The Minor Prophets: An Exegetical and Expository Commentary*, edited by Thomas Edward McComiskey, 1:315–494. 3 vols. Grand Rapids: Baker, 1992.

———. *Ancient Near Eastern Themes in Biblical Theology*. Grand Rapids: Kregel, 2008.

———. "Covenant: An Idea in the Mind of God." *JETS* 52 (2009) 225–46.

———. *God at Sinai: Covenant and Theophany in the Bible and Ancient Near East*. Studies in Old Testament Biblical Theology. Grand Rapids: Zondervan, 1995.

Nitzan, Bilha. "Blessing and Cursing." In *EncDSS*, edited by Lawrence H. Schiffman and James C. Vanderkam, 1:95–100. 2 vols. New York: Oxford University Press, 2000.

Nobile, Marco. "Beziehung zwischen Ez 32,17–32 und der Gog-Perikope (Ez 38–39) im Lichte der Endredaktion." In *EHB*, edited by J. Lust, 255–59. BETL 74. Leuven: Leuven University Press, 1986.

Nordh, Katarina. *Aspects of Ancient Egyptian Curses and Blessings: Conceptual Background and Transmission*. Boreas Stockholm 26. Uppsala: Acta Universitatis Upsaliensis, 1996.

Norris, Richard A., Jr., editor and translator. *The Song of Songs: Interpreted by Early Christian and Medieval Commentators*. The Church's Bible. Grand Rapids: Eerdmans, 2003.

North, R. "Prophecy to Apocalyptic Via Zechariah." In *Congress Volume: Uppsala 1971*, edited by G. W. Anderson et al., 47–71. VTSup 22. Leiden: Brill, 1972.

Noth, Martin. *The Laws in the Pentateuch, and Other Studies*. Philadelphia: Fortress, 1967.

O'Connor, Kathleen M. "Jeremiah." In *The Women's Bible Commentary*, edited by Carol A. Newsome and Sharon H. Ringe, 169–77. London: SPCK, 1992.

Odell, Margaret S. *Ezekiel*. The Smyth & Helwys Bible Commentary. Macon: Smyth & Helwys, 2005.

———. "Genre and Persona in Ezekiel 24:15–24." In *The Society of Biblical Literature 1998 Seminar Papers*, 1:626–48. 2 vols. SBLSP 37. Atlanta: Scholars, 1998.

———. "You Are What You Eat: Ezekiel and the Scroll." *JBL* 117 (1998) 229–48.

Odell, Margaret S., and John T. Strong, editors. *The Book of Ezekiel: Theological and Anthropological Perspectives*. SBLSymS 9. Atlanta: SBL, 2000.

Oeming, M., and K. Schmid. *Der eine Gott und die Götter: Polytheismus und Monotheismus im antiken Israel*. Zürich: Theologischer, 2003.

Oppenheim, Leo. "The Eyes of the Lord." *JAOS* 88 (1968) 173–80.

Osiek, Carolyn. "Apocalyptic Eschatology." *TBT* 34 (1996) 341–45.

Osten-Sacken, Peter von der. *Die Apokalyptik in ihrem Verhältnis zu Prophetie und Weisheit*. Theologische Existenz heute 157. Munich: Kaiser, 1969.

Oswalt, John N. "Recent Studies in Old Testament Apocalyptic." In *The Face of Old Testament Studies: A Survey of Contemporary Approaches*, edited by David W. Baker and Bill T. Arnold, 369–90. Grand Rapids.: Baker, 1999.

Oylan, Saul M. "'We are Utterly Cut off': Some Possible Nuances of נגזרנו לנו in Ezek. 37:11." *CBQ* 65 (2003) 43–51.

Parker, Simon B. *Stories in Scripture and Inscriptions: Comparative Studies on Narratives in Northwest Semitic Inscriptions and the Hebrew Bible*. New York: Oxford University Press, 1997.

Parpola, Simo, and Kazuko Watanabe. *Neo-Assyrian Treaties and Loyalty Oaths*. SAA 2. Helsinki: Helsinki University Press, 1988.

Parunak, H. Van Dyke. *Linguistic Density Plots in Ezekiel*. 2 vols. The Computer Bible 27. Wooster, OH: Biblical Research Associates, 1984.

———. "The Literary Architecture of Ezekiel's *Marʾôt ʾĔlōhîm*." *JBL* (1980) 61–74.
Patterson, Richard D. "Metaphors of Marriage as Expressions of Divine-Human Relations." *JETS* 51 (2008) 689–702.
Patton, Corrine L. "Priest, Prophet and Exile: Ezekiel as a Literary Construct." In *The Society of Biblical Literature 2000 Seminar Papers*, 700–27. SBLSP 39. Atlanta: SBL, 2000.
———. "Should Our Sister Be Treated Like a Whore?" A Response to Feminist Critiques of Ezekiel 23." In *The Book of Ezekiel: Theological and Anthropological Perspectives*, edited by Margaret S. Odell and John T. Strong, 221–38. SBLSymS 9. Atlanta: SBL, 2000.
Peake, Arthur S. *The Roots of Hebrew Prophecy and Jewish Apocalyptic*. Manchester: Manchester University Press, 1923.
Pearson, Brook W. R. "Dry Bones in the Judean Desert: The Messiah of Ephraim, Ezekiel 37, and the Post-Revolutionary Followers of Bar Kokhba." *JSJ* 29 (1998) 192–201.
Peckham, Brian. *The Baal Epic*. Unpublished class notes. University of Toronto, 2005.
Perlitt, Lothar. *Bundestheologie im Alten Testament*. WMANT 36. Neukirchen-Vluyn: Neukirchener, 1969.
Petersen, David L. "Creation in Ezekiel: Methodological Perspectives and Theological Prospects." In *The Society of Biblical Literature 1999 Seminar Papers*, 490–500. SBLSP 38. Atlanta: SBL, 1999.
———. "Eschatology (OT)." In *ABD*, edited by David N. Freedman, 2:594–96. 6 vols. New York: Doubleday, 1992.
Peterson, Brian. "Ezekiel's Perspective of Israel's History: Selective Revisionism?" In *Prophets and Prophecy and Ancient Israelite Historiography*, edited by Mark J. Boda and Lyssa Wray Beal. Winona Lake, IN: Eisenbrauns, 2012.
———. "YHWH the 'Abusive Husband'?: A Closer Look at Ezekiel 16 and 23." *Peace and Safety in the Christian Home* (Spring 2010). Online: http://www.peaceandsafety.com/articles/97.
Pettazzoni, Raffaelle. *The All-Knowing God*. London: Methuen, 1956.
Petter, Donna. "The Book of Ezekiel: Patterned after a Mesopotamian City Lament?" PhD diss., University of Toronto, 2008.
Pfeiffer, R. H. *Introduction into the Old Testament*. New York: Harper, 1948.
Phillips, Anthony. "Prophecy and Law." In *Israel's Prophetic Tradition: Essays in Honour of Peter Ackroyd*, edited by Richard Coggins et al., 217–32. Cambridge: Cambridge University Press, 1984.
Plöger, Otto. *Theocracy and Eschatology*. Translated by S. Rudman. Oxford: Blackwell, 1968.
Pohlmann, Karl-Friedrich. *Das Buch des Proheten Hezekiel (Ezechiel) Kapitel 1–19*. Göttingen: Vandenhoeck & Ruprecht, 1996.
———. *Ezechiel: Der Stand der theologischen Diskussion*. Darmstadt: Wissenschaftliche Buchgesellschaft, 2008.
Polk, Timothy. "Paradigms, Parables, and *Mešâlîm*: On Reading the *Māšāl* in Scripture." *CBQ* 45 (1983) 564–83.
Porteous, Norman W. *Daniel*. OTL. Philadelphia: Westminster, 1965.

Porter, Barbara N. *Images, Power and Politics: Figurative Aspects of Esarhaddon's Babylonian Policy*. Memoirs of the American Philosophical Society 208. Philadelphia: American Philosophical Society, 1993.

Postgate, J. N. Review of *The Book of Ezekiel and the Poem of Erra*, by Daniel Bodi. *VT* 43 (1993) 137.

Power, Bruce. "Iconographic Windows to Ezekiel's World." PhD diss., University of Toronto, 1999.

Preuss, H. D. *Jahweglaube und Zukunftserwartung*. BWANT 87. Stuttgart: Kohlhammer, 1968.

Pritchard, James D., editor. *ANET*. 3rd ed. Princeton: Princeton University Press, 1969.

Rabinowitz, Chaim Dov. *Da'ath Sofrim: The Book of Yehezkel*. Jerusalem: Vagshal, 2001.

Rad, Gerhard von. *Old Testament Theology*. Translated by D. M. G. Stalker. 2 vols. New York: Harper & Row, 1962–1965.

Raitt, Thomas M. *A Theology of Exile: Judgment/Deliverance in Jeremiah and Ezekiel*. Philadelphia: Fortress, 1977.

Reddish, Mitchell G., editor. *Apocalyptic Literature: A Reader*. Peabody, MA.: Hendrickson, 1995.

Redford, D. B. "The Dates in Ezekiel in Relation to Biblical, Babylonian and Egyptian Sources." *JAOS* 90 (1970) 462–85.

Reiner, Erica. "Fortune-Telling in Mesopotamia." *JNES* 19 (1960) 23–35.

———. "Plague Amulets and House Blessings." *JNES* 19 (1960) 148–55.

Rendtorff, Rolf. "The Concept of Revelation." In *Revelation as History*, edited by Wolfhart Pannenberg, 23–53. Translated by David Granskou. New York: Macmillan, 1968.

Renz, Thomas. *The Rhetorical Function of the Book of Ezekiel*. VTSup 76. Leiden: Brill, 1999.

Reventlow, Henning Graf. *Wächter über Israel: Ezechiel und seine Tradition*. BZAW 82. Berlin: Töpelmann, 1962.

Richards, Sandra L. "Dry Bones: Spiritual Apprehension in August Wilson's Joe Turners Come and Gone." In *African Americans and the Bible*, edited by Vincent L. Wimbush, 743–53. New York: Continuum, 2000.

Richardson, Seth. "Death and Dismemberment in Mesopotamia: Discorporation between the Body and Body Politic." In *Performing Death: Social Analyses of Funerary Traditions in the Ancient Near East and Mediterranean*, edited by Nicola Laneri, 189–208. UCOIS 3. Chicago: OIUC, 2007.

Riesenfeld, Harold. *The Resurrection in Ezekiel XXXVII and in the Dura-Europos Paintings*. Uppsala universitets arsskrift 11. Uppsala: Lundequist, 1948.

Ringgren, Helmer. "Akkadian Apocalypses." In *Apocalypticism in the Mediterranean World and the Near East*, edited by David Hellholm, 379–86. Tübingen: Mohr/Siebeck, 1983.

———. "Prophecy in the Ancient Near East." In *Israel's Prophetic Tradition: Essays in Honour of Peter Ackroyd*, edited by Richard Coggins et al., 1–12. Cambridge: Cambridge University Press, 1984.

Robinson, A. "Zion and ṣāphôn in Psalm XLVIII 3." *VT* 24 (1974) 118–23.

Robinson, Henry Wheeler. *Corporate Personality in Ancient Israel*. 1936. Facet Books. Biblical Series 11. Reprint, Philadelphia: Fortress, 1967.

———. *Two Hebrew Prophets: Studies in Hosea and Ezekiel*. London: Lutterworth, 1948.
Robson, James. *Word and Spirit in Ezekiel*. LHB/OTS 447. New York: T. & T. Clark, 2006.
Rooker, Mark F. *Biblical Hebrew in Transition: The Language of the Book of Ezekiel*. JSOTSup 90. Sheffield: JSOT Press, 1990.
———. "Ezekiel and the Typology of Biblical Hebrew." *HAR* 12 (1990) 133–53.
Roos, Johan de. *Hittite Votive Texts*. Uitgaven van het Nederlands Instituut voor het Nabije Oosten te Leiden 109. Leiden: Nederlands Instituut voor het Nabije Oosten, 2007.
Rosenau, William. "Ezekiel 37:15–28: What Happened to the Ten Tribes?" *HUCA* 2a (Jubilee Volume 1925) 79–88.
Roth, Cecil, editor-in-chief. *Encyclopaedia Judaica*. 16 vols. Jerusalem: Encyclopaedia Judaica, 1972.
Roth, Martha T. *Babylonian Marriage Agreements 7th–3rd Centuries B.C.* AOAT 222. Kevelaer: Butzon & Bercker, 1989.
———. "Marriage and Matrimonial Prestations in First Millennium B.C. Babylonia." In *Women's Earliest Records: From Ancient Egypt and Western Asia*, edited by Barbara S. Lesko, 245–55. BJS 166. Atlanta: Scholars, 1989.
———. "'She Will Die by the Iron Dagger': Adultery and Neo-Babylonian Marriage." *JESHO* 31 (1988) 186–206.
Roth, W. "Between Tradition and Expectation: The Origin and Role of Biblical Apocalyptic." *Explor: A Journal of Theology* 4 (1978) 3–14.
Rowland, Christopher. *The Open Heaven: A Study of Apocalyptic in Judaism and Early Christianity*. London: SPCK, 1982.
———. "The Visions of God in Apocalyptic Literature." *JSJ* 10 (1979) 137–54.
———. *"Wheels within Wheels": William Blake and the Ezekiel Merkabah in Text and Image*: The Père Marquette Lecture in Theology 2007. Milwaukee: Marquette University Press, 2007.
Rowley, H. H. "The Book of Ezekiel in Modern Study." *BJRL* 36 (1953/54) 146–90.
———. *The Relevance of Apocalyptic: A Study of Jewish and Christian Apocalypses from Daniel to the Revelation*. New and revised ed. London: Lutterworth, 1963.
Ruiz, Jean-Pierre. *Ezekiel in the Apocalypse: The Transformation of Prophetic Language in Revelation 16,17–19,10*. European University Studies. Series XXIII Theology 376. Frankfurt: Lang, 1989.
Russell, D. S. *Apocalyptic, Ancient and Modern*. The Hayward Lecture. The Nordenhaug Memorial Lectures. Philadelphia: Fortress, 1978.
———. *Divine Disclosure: An Introduction to Jewish Apocalyptic*. London: SCM, 1992.
———. *The Method & Message of Jewish Apocalyptic, 200 BC–AD 100*. OTL. Philadelphia: Westminster, 1964.
———. *Prophecy and the Apocalyptic Dream: Protest and Promise*. Peabody, MA: Hendrickson, 1994.
Savignac, J. de. "La sagesse du Qôhéléth et l'Épopée de Gilgamesh." *VT* 28 (1978) 318–23.
Schaeffer, Claude F. A. *The Cuneiform Texts of Ras Shamra-Ugarit*. The Schweich Lectures of the British Academy, 1936 London: Oxford University Press, 1939.

Schiffman, Lawrence H., and James C. Vanderkam, editors. *Encyclopedia of the Dead Sea Scrolls*. 2 vols. New York: Oxford University Press, 2000.

Schmithals, Walter. *The Apocalyptic Movement: Introduction and Interpretation*. Translated by John E. Steely. Nashville: Abingdon, 1975.

Scholer, David M. "Feminist Hermeneutics and Evangelical Interpretation." *JETS* 30 (1987) 407–20.

Schöpflin, Karin. "The Composition of Metaphorical Oracles within the Book of Ezekiel." *VT* 55 (2005) 101–20.

Schroer, Silvia. "Toward a Feminist Reconstruction of the History of Israel." In *Feminist Interpretation: The Bible in Women's Perspective*, edited by Luise Schottroff et al., 85–176. Translated by Martin and Barbara Rumscheidt. Minneapolis: Fortress, 1998.

Schultz, Hermann. *Das Todesrecht im Alten Testament*. BZAW 114. Berlin: de Gruyter, 1969.

Schumpp, Meinrad. *Das Buch Ezechiel*. Heilige Schrift für das Leben erklärt X. Freiburg: Herder, 1942.

Schwartz, Baruch J. "Ezekiel's Dim View of Israel's Restoration." In *The Book of Ezekiel: Theological and Anthropological Perspectives*, edited by Margaret S. Odell and John T. Strong, 43–67. SBLSymS 9. Atlanta: SBL, 2000.

Scurlock, JoAnn. "Ghosts in the Ancient Near East: Weak or Powerful?" *HUCA* 68 (1997) 77–96.

———. *Magico-Medical Means of Treating Ghost-Induced Illnesses in Ancient Mesopotamia*. Ancient Magic and Divination 3. Leiden: Brill, 2006.

Sedlmeier, Franz. *Das Buch Ezechiel*. NSKAT 21. Stuttgart: Katholisches Bibelwerk, 2002.

———. *Studien zu Komposition und Theologie von Ezechiel 20*. SBB 21. Stuttgart: Katholisches Bibelwerk, 1990.

Seitz, Christopher R. "Ezekiel 37:1–14." *Int* 46 (1992) 53–56.

Setel, Drorah. "Prophets and Pornography: Female Sexual Imagery in Hosea." In *A Feminist Interpretation of the Bible*, edited by Letty M. Russell, 86–95. Philadelphia: Westminster, 1985.

Sharon, Diane. "A Biblical Parallel to a Sumerian Temple Hymn? Ezekiel 40–48 and Gudea." *JANES* 24 (1996) 99–109.

Shields, Mary E. "Circumcision of the Prostitute: Gender, Sexuality and the Call to Repentance." *BibInt* 3 (1995) 61–74.

———. "Multiple Exposures: Body Rhetoric and Gender Characterization in Ezekiel 16." *JFSR* 14 (1998) 5–18.

Siegman, Edward F. *The Book of Ezekiel: With a Commentary*. 2 vols. Pamphlet Bible Series 31 32. New York: Paulist, 1961.

Simian-Yofre, Horacio. *Die theologische Nachgeschichte der Prophetie Ezechiels: Form—und traditionskritische Untersuchung zu Ez 6; 35; 36*. FB 14. Würzburg: Echter, 1974.

———. "La Métaphore d'Ézéchiel 15." In *EHB*, edited by J. Lust, 234–47. BETL 74. Leuven: Leuven University Press, 1986.

———. "Wächter, Lehrer order Interpret?: Zum theologischen Hintergrund von Ez 33, 7–9." In *Künder des Wortes: Beiträge zur Theologie der Propheten*, edited by Lothar Ruppert et al., 151–62. Würzburg: Echter, 1982.

Skinner, John. *The Book of Ezekiel*. London: Hodder & Stoughton, 1895–96.

Smend, R. *Der Prophet Ezechiel*. 2nd ed. Kurzgefasstes exegetisches Handbuch zum Alten Testament 8. Leipzig: Hirzel, 1880.
Smith, Gary V. *The Prophets as Preachers: An Introduction to the Hebrew Prophets*. Nashville: Broadman & Holman, 1994.
Smith, James. *The Book of the Prophet Ezekiel: A New Interpretation*. London: SPCK, 1931.
Smith, Mark. *The Early History of God: Yahweh and the Other Deities in Ancient Israel*. 2nd ed. The Biblical Resource Series. Grand Rapids: Eerdmans, 2002.
Smith, Morton. *Palestinian Parties and Politics That Shaped the Old Testament*. 2nd, corrected edition. London: SCM, 1987.
Smith, Ralph L. *Old Testament Theology: Its History, Method, and Message*. Nashville: Broadman & Holman, 1993.
Sohn, Seock-Tae. "'I will Be Your God and You Will Be My People': The Origin and Background of the Covenant Formula." In *Ki Baruch Hu: Ancient Near Eastern, Biblical, and Judaic Studies in Honor of Baruch A. Levine*, edited by Robert Chazan et al., 355–72. Winona Lake, IN: Eisenbrauns, 1999.
Sparks, Kenton L. *Ancient Texts for the Study of the Hebrew Bible: A Guide to the Background Literature*. Peabody, MA: Hendrickson, 2005.
Speiser, E. A. "Ancient Mesopotamia." In *The Idea of History in the Ancient Near East*, edited by Robert C. Dentan et al., 35–76. New Haven: Yale University Press, 1966.
———. "'People' and 'Nation' of Israel." *JBL* 79 (1960) 157–63.
Spiegel, S. "Ezekiel or Pseudo-Ezekiel?" *HTR* 24 (1931) 245–321.
———. "Toward Certainty in Ezekiel." *JBL* 54 (1935) 145–71.
———. Review of *Hesekiel*, by Alfred Bertholet. *JBL* 56 (1937) 403–8.
Stade, D. B. *Biblische Theologie des Alten Testaments*. Tübingen: Mohr/Siebeck, 1905.
Stager, Lawrence E. "The Rite of Child Sacrifice at Carthage." In *New Light on Ancient Carthage: Papers of a Symposium*, edited by John Griffiths Pedley, 1–11. Ann Arbor: University of Michigan Press, 1980.
Stager, Lawrence E., and Samuel R. Wolff. "Child Sacrifice at Carthage—Religious Rite or Population Control: Archaeological Evidence Provides Basis for a New Analysis." *BAR* 10/1 (1984) 31–51.
Stalker, D. M. G. *Ezekiel*. Torch Bible Commentaries. London: SCM, 1974.
Stavrakopoulou, Francesca. "Ezekiel's Use and Abuse of Corpses." Paper presented at the annual meeting of the SBL. Boston, MA, November 24, 2008.
Steinmann, Jean. *Ézéchiel*. Connaître la Bible. Paris: Brouwer, 1961.
———. *Le Prophete Ézéchiel et les débuts de l'exil*. Lectio divina 13. Paris: Cerf, 1953.
Stevenson, Kalinda Rose. *The Vision of Transformation: The Territorial Rhetoric of Ezekiel 40-48*. SBLDS 154. Atlanta: Scholars, 1996.
Steymans, Hans Ulrich. *Deuteronomium 28 und die adê Thronfolgeregelung Asarhaddons: Segen und Fluch im Alten Orient und in Israel*. OBO 145. Freiburg: Vandenhoeck & Ruprecht, 1995.
Stiebert, Johanna. *The Exile and the Prophet's Wife: Historic Events and Marginal Perspectives*. Interfaces. Collegeville, MN: Liturgical, 2005.
Streane, A. W. *The Book of the Prophet Ezekiel*. 1st ed. 1892. The Cambridge Bible for Schools and Colleges. Reprint, Cambridge: Cambridge University Press, 1924.

Strong, John T. "God's *Kābôd*: The Presence of Yahweh in the Book of Ezekiel." In *The Book of Ezekiel: Theological and Anthropological Perspectives*, edited by Margaret S. Odell and John T. Strong, 69-95. SBLSymS 9. Atlanta: SBL, 2000.

Stuart, Douglas. "Curse." In *ABD*, edited by David Noel Freedman, 1:1218-19. 6 vols. New York: Doubleday, 1992.

———. *Hosea-Jonah*. WBC 31. Waco: Word, 1987.

———. "The Prophetic Ideal of Government in the Restoration Era." In *Israel's Apostasy and Restoration: Essays in Honor of Ronald K. Harrison*, edited by Avraham Gileadi, 283-92. Grand Rapids: Baker, 1988.

Sturtevant, Edgar H. and George Bechtel. *A Hittite Chrestomathy*. William Dwight Whitney Linguistic Series. Philadelphia: Linguistic Society of America, University of Pennsylvania, 1935.

Swanepoel, M. G. "Abandoned Child, Bride Adorned or Unfaithful Wife?" In *Among the Prophets: Language, Image and Structure in the Prophetic Writings*, edited by David Clines and Philip R. Davies, 84-104. JSOTSup 144. Sheffield: JSOT Press, 1993.

Sweeney, Marvin A. *I & II Kings: A Commentary*. OTL. Louisville: Westminster John Knox, 2007.

———. "Ezekiel: Zadokite Priest and Visionary Prophet of the Exile." In *The Society of Biblical Literature 2000 Seminar Papers*, 728-51. SBLSP 39. Atlanta: SBL, 2000.

Tadmor, Hayim. "Autobiographical Apology in the Royal Assyrian Literature." In *History, Historiography, and Interpretation: Studies in Biblical and Cuneiform Literatures*, edited by Hayim Tadmor and Moshe Weinfeld, 36-57. Jerusalem: Magnes, 1983.

———. "Treaty and Oath in the Near East." In *Humanizing America's Iconic Book: Society of Biblical Literature Centennial Addresses 1980*, edited by Gene M. Tucker and Douglas A. Knight, 127-52. SBLBSNA 6. Chico, CA: Scholars, 1982.

Tallqvist, K. *Der assyrische Gott*. Helsinki: Societas Orientalis Fennica, 1932.

Talmon, S., and M. Fishbane. "The Structuring of Biblical Books: Studies in the Book of Ezekiel." *ASTI* 10 (1975/76) 129-53.

Tarlin, Jan. "The Skull beneath the Skin: Light Shadow Reading in the Valley of Dry Bones." In *Self, Same, Other: Re-visioning the Subject in Literature and Theology*, edited by Heather Walton and Andrew Hass, 173-82. Playing the Texts 5. Sheffield: Sheffield Academic, 2000.

Taylor, Barbara Brown. "Betrothed by God." In *Gospel Medicine*, 55-62. Cambridge: Cowley, 1995.

Taylor, John Bernard. *Ezekiel: An Introduction and Commentary*. TOTC. Downers Grove, IL: InterVarsity, 1976.

Taylor, Marion Ann. "Ezekiel." In *The IVP Women's Bible Commentary*, edited by Catherine Clark Kroeger and Mary J. Evans, 396-421. Downers Grove, IL: InterVarsity, 2002.

Taylor, Marion Ann, and Heather Weir, editors. *Let Her Speak for Herself: Nineteenth-Century Women Writing on the Women of Genesis*. Waco, TX: Baylor University Press, 2006.

Tetlow, Elisabeth M. *Women, Crime, and Punishment in Ancient Law and Society*. 2 vols. New York: Continuum, 2004-2005.

Thiselton, Anthony C. "The *Supposed Power of Words* in the Biblical Writings." *JTS* 25 (1974) 282–99.
Thompson, Reginald Campbell. *The Prisms of Esarhaddon and Ashurbanipal Found at Nineveh, 1927–28*. London: British Museum Library, 1931.
Thomsen, Marie-Louise. "The Evil Eye in Mesopotamia." *JNES* 51 (1992) 19–32.
Tigay, Jeffery H. *Deuteronomy*. JPSTC. Philadelphia: JPS, 1996.
———. *The Evolution of the Gilgamesh Epic*. Philadelphia: University of Pennsylvania Press, 1982.
Tigchelaar, E. J. C. "L'Ange Qui Parlait a Zacharie, Est-Il un Personnage Apocalyptique?" *EstBib* 45 (1987) 347–60.
Tolbert, Mary Ann. "Defining the Problem: The Bible and Feminist Hermeneutics." *Semeia* 28 (1983) 113–26.
Toorn, Karel, van der et al., editors. *Dictionary of Deities and Demons in the Bible*. 2nd ed. Leiden: Brill, 1999.
Torrey, Charles Cutler. *Pseudo-Ezekiel and the Original Prophecy*. New Haven: Yale University Press, 1930. Reprint, New York: Ktav, 1970.
Towner, W. Sibley. *Daniel*. Interpretation: A Bible Commentary for Teaching and Preaching. Atlanta: John Knox, 1984.
Toy, Crawford H. "The Babylonian Element in Ezekiel." *Journal of the Study of Biblical Literature and Exegesis* 1 (1881) 59–66.
———. *The Book of the Prophet Ezekiel*. The Sacred Books of the Old Testament, pt. 12. Leipzig: Hinrichs, 1899.
Trible, Phyllis. "Feminist Hermeneutics and Biblical Studies: Emerging Trends in Biblical Thought; 4th in a Series." *ChrCent* 99 (1982) 116–18.
Trimmer, Sarah. *A Help to the Unlearned in the Study of the Holy Scriptures: Being an Attempt to Explain the Bible in a Familiar Way (1805)*. London: Bensley, 1805.
Tsevat, M. "The Neo-Assyrian and Neo-Babylonian Vassal Oaths and the Prophet Ezekiel." *JBL* 78 (1959) 199–204.
Tuell, Steven. "Contemporary Studies in Ezekiel: A New Tide Rising." In *Ezekiel's Hierarchical World: Wrestling with a Tiered Reality*, edited by Stephen L. Cook and Corrine L. Patton, 241–54. SBLSymS 31. Atlanta: SBL, 2004.
———. "Divine Presence and Absence in Ezekiel's Prophecies." In *The Book of Ezekiel: Theological and Anthropological Perspectives*, edited by Margaret S. Odell and John T. Strong, 97–116. SBLSymS 9. Atlanta: SBL, 2000.
———. *Ezekiel*. NIBCOT 15. Peabody, MA.: Hendrickson, 2009.
———. "Haggai-Zechariah: Prophecy after the Manner of Ezekiel." In *The Society of Biblical Literature 2000 Seminar Papers*, 263–86. SBLSP 39. Atlanta: SBL, 2000.
———. *The Law of the Temple in Ezekiel 40—48*. HSM 49. Atlanta: Scholars, 1992.
Tupper, E. F. "The Revival of Apocalyptic in Biblical and Theological Studies." *RevExp* 72 (1975) 279–303.
Turner, G. A. "Gate, East." In *ISBE*, edited by Geoffrey W. Bromiley, 2:409. 4 vols. Grand Rapids: Eerdmans, 1988.
Van Seters, John. *Prologue to History: The Yahwist as Historian in Genesis*. Louisville: Westminster John Knox, 1992.
VanderKam, James C. "Recent Studies in Apocalyptic." *WW* 4 (1984) 70–77.
Vaux, Roland de. *Ancient Israel*. Translated by John McHugh. 1961. Reprint, Grand Rapids: Eerdmans, 1997.

Vawter, Bruce. "Apocalyptic: Its Relation to Prophecy." *CBQ* 22 (1960) 33–46.
Vawter, Bruce, and Leslie J. Hoppe. *A New Heart: A Commentary on the Book of Ezekiel*. ITC. Grand Rapids: Eerdmans, 1991.
VerSteeg, Russ. *Early Mesopotamian Law*. Durham: Carolina Academic, 2000.
Vieweger, Dieter. *Die literarischen Beziehungen zwischen den Büchern Jeremia und Ezechiel*. BEATAJ 26. Frankfurt: Lang, 1993.
Vogt, Ernst. *Untersuchungen zum buch Ezechiel*. AnBib 95. Rome Biblical Institute Press, 1981.

———. "Die Vier 'Gesichter' (*pānîm*) der Keruuben in Ez." *Bib* 60 (1979) 327–47.
Wacholder, Ben Zion. "Deutero Ezekiel and Jeremiah (4Q384–4Q391) Identifying the Dry Bones of Ezekiel 37 as the Essenes." In *The Dead Sea Scrolls: Fifty Years after Their Discovery 1947–1997*, edited by Lawrence Schiffman et al., 445–61. Jerusalem: Israel Exploration Society in cooperation with The Shrine of the Book, Israel Museum, 2000.
Walmesley, Charles. "Ezechiel's Vision Explained: or the Explication of the Vision Exhibited to Ezechiel the Prophet, and Described in the first Chapter of his Prophecy, by Sig. Pasturini." In *Religion and Philosophy*, 3–73. London: Coghlan. In Eighteenth Century Collections Online. Gale Group. Online: http://galenet.galegroup.com/servlet/ECCO.
Waltke, Bruce K. "The Phenomenon of Conditionality within Unconditional Covenants." In *Israel's Apostasy and Restoration: Essays in Honor of Roland K. Harrison*, edited by Avraham Gileadi, 123–49. Grand Rapids: Baker, 1987.
Walton, John H. *Ancient Israelite Literature in Its Cultural Context*. Library of Biblical Interpretation. Grand Rapids: Zondervan, 1990.

———. *Ancient Near Eastern Thought and the Old Testament: Introducing the Conceptual World of the Old Testament*. Grand Rapids: Baker Academic, 2006.
Webb, R. "'Apocalyptic': Observations on a Slippery Term." *JNES* 49 (1990) 115–26.
Weems, Renita J. *Battered Love: Marriage, Sex, and Violence in the Hebrew Prophets*. OBT Minneapolis: Fortress, 1995.
Wehmeier, Gerhard. *Der Segen im Alten Testament: Eine semasiologische Untersuchung der Wurzel brk*. Theologischen Dissertationen 6. Basel: Reinhardt.
Weinfeld, Moshe. "Covenant Terminology in the Ancient Near East and Its Influence on the West." *JAOS* 93 (1973) 190–99.

———. *Deuteronomy and the Deuteronomic School*. Oxford: Clarendon, 1972.
Welch, Adam C. *Deuteronomy: The Framework to the Code*. London: Oxford University Press, 1932.
Wellhausen, Julius. *Prolegomena to the History of Ancient Israel*. Translated by J. Sutherland Black. 1883. Meridian Library 6. Reprint, New York: Meridian, 1957.
Westbrook, Raymond. "Adultery in Ancient Near Eastern Law." *RB* 97 (1990) 542–80.

———. *Old Babylonian Marriage Law*. AfO 23. Horn, Austria: Berger, 1988.
Westermann, Claus. *Basic Forms of Prophetic Speech*. Translated by Hugh Clayton White. Philadelphia.: Westminster, 1967.

———. *Blessing in the Bible and the Life of the Church*. Translated by Keith Crim. OBT 3. Philadelphia: Fortress, 1978.
Wevers, John W., editor. *Ezekiel*. The Century Bible. London: Nelson, 1969.

Wevers, John W., and Detlef Fraenkel. *Studies in the Text Histories of Deuteronomy and Ezekiel*. Abhandlungen der Akademie der Wissenschaften zu Göttingen. Mitteilungen des Septuaginta-Unternehmens 26. Philologisch-Historische Klasse, Series 3/256. Göttingen: Vandenhoeck & Ruprecht, 2003.

Wiesel, Elie. "Ezekiel." In *Congregation: Contemporary Writers Read the Jewish Bible*, edited by David Rosenberg, 167–86. San Diego: Harcourt Brace Jovanovich, 1987.

Wigoder, Geoffrey. "Blessing and Cursing." In *The New Encyclopedia of Judaism*, edited by Geoffrey Wigoder et al., 135–37. New York: New York University Press, 2002.

Wilcke, Claus. *Early Ancient Near Eastern Law: A History of Its Beginnings*. Rev. ed. Winona Lake, IN: Eisenbrauns, 2007.

Williamson, Paul R. *Sealed with an Oath: Covenant in God's Unfolding Purpose*. New Studies in Biblical Theology 23. Downers Grove, IL: Apollos/InterVarsity, 2007.

Wilson, Robert R. "An Interpretation of Ezekiel's Dumbness." *VT* 22 (1972) 91–104.

———. *Prophecy and Society in Ancient Israel*. Philadelphia: Fortress, 1980.

———. "Prophecy in Crisis: The Call of Ezekiel." *Int* 38 (1984) 117–30. Reprinted in *Interpreting the Prophets*, edited by James Luther Mays and Paul J. Achtemeier, 157–69. Philadelphia: Fortress, 1987.

Wiseman, D. J. *The Vassal Treaties of Esarhaddon*. Iraq 20, pt. 1. London: British School of Archeology in Iraq, 1958.

———. *Nebuchadrezzar and Babylon*. The Schweich Lectures of the British Academy 1983. London: Oxford University Press, 1985.

Wittstruck, Thorne. "Influence of Treaty Curse Imagery on the Beast Imagery of Daniel 7." *JBL* 97 (1978) 100–2.

Wolf, Herbert M. "The Transcendent Nature of Covenant Curse Reversals." In *Israel's Apostasy and Restoration: Essays in Honor of Roland K. Harrison*, edited by Avraham Gileadi, 319–25. Grand Rapids: Baker, 1988.

Wong, Ka Leung. *The Idea of Retribution in the Book of Ezekiel*. VTSup 87. Leiden: Brill, 2001.

Wright, Benjamin. "The Apocryphon of Ezekiel and 4Qpseudo-Ezekiel." In *The Dead Sea Scrolls: Fifty Years after Their Discovery 1947–1997*, edited by Lawrence Schiffman et al., 462–80. Jerusalem: Israel Exploration Society in cooperation with The Shrine of the Book, Israel Museum, 2000.

Wright, Christopher J. H. *Deuteronomy*. NIBC 4. Peabody, MA: Hendrickson, 1996.

———. *The Message of Ezekiel: A New Heart and a New Spirit*. The Bible Speaks Today. Leicester: Inter-Varsity, 2001.

Wright, G Ernest. "The Good Shepherd." *BA* 2 (1939) 44–48.

———. *The Old Testament against Its Environment*. SBT 1/2. London: SCM, 1950.

Würthwein, E. "Gott. II. In Israel." In *Die Religion in Geschichte und Gegenwart*, edited by Kurt Galling, 2:1705–10. 7 vols. Tübingen: Mohr/Siebeck, 1957–1965.

Yee, Gale A. "Hosea." In *The Women's Bible Commentary*, edited by Carol A. Newsom and Sharon H. Ringe, 207–15. London: SPCK, 1992.

Ziegler, Joseph. *Ezechiel*. Biblia. Würtzburg: Echter, 1948.

Zimmerli, Walther. "Die Eigenart der prophetischen Rede des Ezechiel." *ZAW* 66 (1954) 1–26.

---. *Erkenntnis Gottes nach dem Buche Ezechiel: eine theologische studie*. ATANT 27. Zürich: Zwingli, 1954.

---. *Ezekiel: A Commentary on the Book of the Prophet Ezekiel*. 2 vols. Hermeneia. Philadelphia: Fortress, 1979–1983.

---. *The Fiery Throne: The Prophets and Old Testament Theology*. Edited by K. C. Hanson. Fortress Classics in Biblical Studies. Minneapolis: Fortress, 2003.

---. *I Am Yahweh*. Translated by Douglas W. Scott. Edited by Walter Brueggemann. Atlanta: John Knox, 1982.

---. "The Special Form- and Traditio-Historical Character of Ezekiel's Prophecy." *VT* 15 (1965) 515–27.

Zucker, David J. *Israel's Prophets: An Introduction for Christians and Jews*. New York: Paulist, 1994.

Zyl, A. H. van. "Solidarity and Individualism in Ezekiel." In *Studies on the Book of Ezekiel: Papers Read at the 4th Meeting Held at Bloemfontein 31 January—3 February 1961*, edited by A. H. van Zyl, 38–52. Pretoria: University of South Africa, 1961.

Scripture Index

OLD TESTAMENT

Genesis

1	317, 323, 353
1:26	254n92
2–3	201n83, 254n92, 323
6:18	70n237
8:20–22	293
9:1–17	293
9:9	70n237
9:12	70n237
9:13	327
9:17	70n237
17:2	70n237
17:7	70n237
17:19	70n237
18:19	258
23	233n25
24:7	89
24:53	195n65
26:28	75n253
28	293
28:16–19	293
28:20–22	293
34:2	202n91
40:19	235, 242n46
49:5–7	251n79
49:9	124n81
50:4–7	233n25
50:24–26	233n25

Exodus

2	223
3:22	285
4:8–9	82n282
5:3	188
6:4	70n237
6:6	68
7:4	68
12:3	147n170
12:12	68
13:19	233n25
14:2–4	286n212
14:8	286n212
14:17–31	286n212
15	37n141
17:13	188
18:4	188
18:13–27	263n127
19–25	353
19–24	53, 55, 56, 58, 294
19:3	298
19:16	127
20	51, 52
20–24	48
20:2	257n105
20:3–4	103
20:18	101
20:19	102
20:19–20	334
21–23	51
22:24	188
23:27–30	138–39
24:1–11	299
24:7	52, 89n313
24:7–8	70
24:10	109n32
24:11	52
24:12–18	298
25–31	294, 303
25–40	298
25:4	196n65
25:8	301

Exodus (cont.)

25:16	52
26:1	196n65
26:31	196n65
26:36	196n65
27:16	196n65
28:5	196n65
28:6	196n65
28:8	196n65
28:38	68
28:39	196n65
29:45	327
32–34	294
32	46
32:11–14	229n7
32:12	251
32:25–29	251
32:30	145
30:31	145
30:33	145
30:45	301
34:15–16	206
34:25	129
35–40	294
35:35	196n65
36:37	196n65
38:18	196n65
38:23	196n65
39:29	196n65
40:34–35	301

Leviticus

2:5	64
5:1	68
5:4	46, 47n166
5:17	68
6:14	64
7:9	64
8:9	64
10:6	64
10:10	67
10:10–11	259
10:17	68
13:45	64
16:4	64
16:22	68
17–26	62, 65, 66, 67
17:16	68
18:6–19	68
18:19	67
18:23	198n74
19:8	68
20:2	200n80
20:5	206
20:9	68
20:10–18	192
20:11–13	68
20:15–16	198
20:16	68
20:17	68
20:19–21	68
20:23	68
22:16	68
25:18	67
26	41, 42, 43, 47, 56, 60, 61n200, 62, 63, 63n205, 67, 67n225, 69, 72, 98, 191, 192, 193, 226, 265n137, 272, 282n199, 332, 334
26:3	67, 68
26:4	191n55
26:4–13	67, 265
26:7	188
26:8	188
26:9	67, 70n237
26:11–12	301
26:12	265n136
26:17	67, 100n10, 122, 138
26:19	48n168, 67, 191n55
26:21	122
26:24	100n10, 122
26:25–26	67
26:25	188, 189
26:29	48n168, 141
26:30	67, 230, 235
26:33	100n10, 178
26:36	188
26:37	188

Scripture Index   395

Leviticus (cont.)
26:38   100n10, 178
26:39   68, 100n10, 178
26:42   67
26:43   100n10, 178
26:45   67

Numbers
2   117n59, 319n75
3   309
4:3   92n324
4:23   92n324
4:30   92n324
5:18–27   215n129
5:23   18
5:31   68
6:25   124n81, 129
6:25–26   98n5
7   319n75
8   92n324
9:13   68
14:13–24   229n7
14:18   68
14:20–25   255
14:34   68
16–18   308n43
16:24–26   46
18:1   68
18:23   68
22–24   253n89
24:9   124n81
25:12   67, 70n237
27–36   291n2
30:16   68
34:1–12   322n78

Deuteronomy
4:2a   53
4:26   73n246
4:27   62, 96
4:28   113n45
4:34   62
4:39   257
5–28   53
5–26   55
5:15   62
6:5   62
6:10–15   62
7:1–5   62
7:1   285
8:17–20   62
8:18   70n237
9:24   259n110
9:28   229n7
11:14   191n55
11:16–17   62
11:17   191n55
11:28   144
12:1–4   62
13:4   143
17:18   18
20:20   324
21:23   238
22:20–24   200n80
22:21–24   213
22:21   62
24:16   184
26–28   61
26:8   62
26:16   62
28   41, 42, 43, 47, 48n171, 53, 55, 56, 59, 60, 61n200, 69, 72, 98, 191, 192, 193, 226, 332, 334
28:12   191n55
28:15   61
28:20–57   244n58
28:22   188
28:23   48n168, 191n55
28:24   191n55
28:25   100n10
28:26   160, 230, 235, 244n58
28:29   96
28:36   62, 182
28:45   61
28:48   100n10
28:49   62, 100n10, 122, 178
28:53–57   48n168, 141
28:63–65   178

Deuteronomy (cont.)

28:63–68	160
28:64–65	100n10
28:64	62, 113n45
29:6	257
29:19–28	196n67
29:27	61
30	248, 249
30:3–7	232, 247, 248
30:19	73n246
31:11	89n313
31:16–18	100n10
31:16	206
31:24–26	18
31:28	73n246
32:11	124n81
33	52
33:1–3	288n223
33:2	129, 137
33:20	124n81
33:26–29	288n223
34	52

Joshua

5	296n11
6	139
7	46, 190
8	53
8:32–35	18
8:34–35	89n313
9	74n250, 237n37, 238
9:15	75n253
10	237n37
15:1–4	322n78
21:1–42	251
24	48, 49n175, 53, 56–58, 294
24:25–27	294
24:26	18

Judges

2:10	257
5:4	137, 282
5:4–5	288n223
11:24	113n45
17	251n79
17:2	251

Ruth

3:9	195n64

1 Samuel

2:12	259n110
4	139
5	302
11:1	74n250
15:23	98n3
16	236, 255, 264n133
17	255
17:43–44	242n46
17:43	236
17:44	236
17:46	236, 257
17:46–47	236
17:47	236
26:19	113n45
31	236
31:9–10	242n46
31:9	236
31:10	236
31:11–13	236

2 Samuel

6:2	120
7	294, 303, 321
7:20	258
13:14	202n91
16:9	250
16:12	250
21	156n196, 238, 240
21:1–14	237
21:1	237
21:2	74n250, 237, 238
21:3–9	237, 242n46
21:10	237
21:11–14	237
21:16	255
22:11	120
23:5	70n237
24:16	147–48n170

1 Kings

1:33	323n84
1:45	323n84
2:46	250
5–6	303
5:1—9:9	303
5:1–12	208n108
5:12	74n250, 254
6	294
6:12	294
6:23–35	120n68, 124
7	117, 123n79
7:27–39	117
7:29	124
8	294, 303
8:6–7	120n68
8:10–11	301
8:12–13	111n39
8:12	111n40
12:28–33	46
13:1–5	234
14:1–15	238
14:11	238
14:15–16	46
15:19	74n250
16:4	239
17–21	254n95
19:10	71
19:11–12	282
20:23	113n45
20:26–30	253n89
20:28	113n45
20:34	74n250
21:24	239
22:19	350n35
23:15–20	234

2 Kings

2	107, 107n26, 127, 353
2:1	130, 130n105
2:11	107, 130, 130n105, 353
4:1	198n76
5:17	113n45
6:8–23	263n127
8:10–11	154
9:10	239, 247
9:34–37	237n36
9:36	239, 247
13:14–19	253n89
16:8	167
16:10–15	200
17:4	45
17:15	71
18–19	101n14, 255
18	169
18:7	44n159
18:15–16	167
18:25	157n204, 170
18:33–35	157n204, 169
19–20	19n66
19	170n240
19:15	120
19:35	148n170
21:7	118n62
21:8–11	46
22–23	55
22:11	251
22:19–20	75
22:20	186
23:2	89n313
23:3	70n237
23:26–27	186
24:9	185n43
24:14–16	18

1 Chronicles

9:18	113n45

2 Chronicles

3:13	124
5:7	124
15:12	70
16:3	74n250
16:9	134
19	263n127
29–31	303
34	55
34:30	89n313
36:13	182n33

Ezra

1:1–4	315
3:7	208n108
4:23	89n313

Nehemiah

5:5	198n76
8:3	89n313
8:8	89n313
8:18	89n313
10:30	70, 75n253
13:1	89n313

Esther

3:14	89n313

Job

1:7	134
2:2	134
3:8	31n109
7:12	31n109
13:14	99n9
26:12–13	31n109
34:29	99n9
38:1	130n105
39:24	282
40:6	130n105, 284n206
41:1–34	31n109
41:29	282

Psalms

10:11	99n8
13:2	99n8
18:11 [Heb]	120
22:25	99n8
23	264n133
27:9	99n8
27:12	172n241
29	19n66, 108, 353
29:3	108
29:10	108
30:8	99n8
41:3	172n241
44:18	71
44:25	99n8
46	288n221
46:4	323
46:47	353
48	288n221
48:3 [Heb]	137n130
50:2	129
51:11	98n3, 99 nn. 8–9
53:5	230n13
55:8	130n105
67:1	129
68:8	137, 138
68:8–9 [Heb]	288n223
68:9	282
69:18	99n8
74:13	31n109, 353
76	288n221
77:22	264n133
78:4	257
78:5	257
78:52–53	264n133
78:70–72	264n133
79	239
79:2	239
80:1	264n133
81:13	187n46
83:11	239, 240
83:15	130n105
88:15	99n8
89:34	71
95:7	264n133
100:3	264n133
102:3	99n8
104:29	99n8
107:25	130n105, 284n206
107:29	130n105, 284n206
110:7	323n84
115:2–3	114, 114n48
119:75	257
119:125	257
137:4	113n45
137:7	266
141:7	230n13
143:7	99n8
148:8	130n105, 284n206

Proverbs

6:32–35	213n121
17:22	229n9
19:12	124n81
20:2	124n81

Isaiah

1–39	4n5
1	56n190, 73n247
1:9	196n67
1:15	98
1:25	98
1:41–46	73
1:48	73
2:1	299n20
2:2–4	19n66, 299n20
2:3	299n20
2:8–9	112
3:17–26	212n119
3:26	212n119
5:5	99
5:25	239
5:26–30	99
6	171, 350n35, 353
6:6–8	323
6:9–11	102
7–8	196n66
8:1	18
8:17	98
9:7	252
9:19–20	141n144
10:12	255
11:1	252
14:13	137n130
14:24–27	267n142, 288n221
16:5	252
18	239
18:6	239, 240
18:7	208n108
19:18–25	208n108
19:21	259n110
23:15–18	199n77, 208
24–27	288n221, 348n27, 349n32, 352n40
27:1	31n109
29:6	106n25; 130n105, 282
30–31	196n66
30:8	18
30:23–24	251n81
30:27–33	272n161
31:4	124n81
32:9–14	251n81
32:15–16	251n81
32:20	251n81
34–35	39n148, 349n32
35:8–10	251
36–39	19n66
36–37	101n14, 255
36	170
36:7	45
36:10	170, 182n33
40–55	39n148, 349n32
40–66	37n141, 212n119
40:3–4	251
40:24	130n105
41:16	130n105
43:19	251
44:1–5	276n170
44:28	252, 264n133, 315
47:1–3	212
47:11	284n205
49–66	355n49
49:6	326
49:23	260n117
49:26	141n144
50:6	99n8
51:9	31n109
52:12	251
53:3	99n8
54:8	99n8
54:11	130n105, 284n206
56–66	349n32
59:2	99n8
60:3	326
62:4–5	328
64:6	99n8

Jeremiah

1:1	122
1:13–15	136
1:14	122
1:15	122
2–3	177, 197n72
3:6–14	173n3
3:8	213n122
4:5–8	136
4:6	122
4:13–22	136
4:19–22	261
4:27–31	136
5:15	122
6:1	122
6:1–8	136
6:22–26	136
6:22	122
7	272n161
7:4	44, 101, 103
7:8–15	99
7:17–18	110n37
7:30–34	240, 242n45
7:33	110n37, 240
7:34	48n168
8:1–3	230, 241
8:2	240, 242n45
8:14–17	136
8:16	282
9:21 [Heb]	240, 242n45
10:22	122, 136
11:11	135
11:14	135
11:16	108
12:3	259n110
12:8	124n81
12:9	240, 242n45
12:9–13	288n221
12:10–11	252
13:10	102
13:22b	212
13:26	212
14:16	240, 242n45
15:1	180n26
15:1–5	240, 242n45
15:4	187
15:12	122
16:1–6	240, 242n45
16:9	48n168
19:1–7	240, 242n45
19:9	48n168
19:19	141n144
20:9	83
20:16	196n67
22:7	151, 151n185
22:19	240, 242n45
23:1–4	265n134
23:19	106n25; 130n105, 284n206
23:33	99
24	11, 13
24:6–7	13
24:7	259n111
24:8	99
25:9	122, 136
25:10	48n168
25:15–38	242
25:32	130n105
25:33	240, 242, 242n45
25:38	124n81
26	251
26:17–24	339n8
29	11, 13
29:12–14	13
29:15	13
29:24–28	14
29:28	152
29:29–32	13
30:2	18
30:21	252
30:23	106n25, 130n105, 284n206
31:12	252
31:13	252
31:16–17	252
31:31	231
31:38–40	252
32:37	252
33:11	48n168

Jeremiah (cont.)	
33:15	252
31:21–22	252
34:10	70
34:17–22	240, 242n45
34:18	70n237
34:20	230
36:6	120
36:6–23	89n313
36:20	13
36:23	251
36:24	251
36:30	240, 242n45
37:5	30
38:7	136n126
38:17–26	186
39:3	136n126
39:4	136n126
39:9–14	190
43:10	138n135
44	110n37
44:15–23	110
44:15–19	339n9
44:30	30
46:1—49:33	285
46:10	288n221, 289
46:24	136
47:2	122
48:40	122n77
49:5	122
49:17–18	196n67
49:18	199n77
49:21	282
49:22	122n77
49:35	48n168
49:36	130
50:3	122, 122n78
50:9	122n78
50:39–40	196n67
50:40	199n77
50:41	122n78
51	40
51:48	122n78
51:60	152n186
51:60–61	152
51:61	89n313, 120
52:15	87, 87n306, 120
52:16	190
52:28–30	20n70

Lamentations	
4:6	196n67
4:10	141n144
4:21–22	266

Ezekiel	
1–24	9n24, 72, 82, 83, 85, 92n322, 93n329, 199n77, 257, 284, 329n99, 339
1–12	12, 93, 94, 178
1–11	163, 179
1:1—11:25	93n326
1–5	261n122
1–3	1, 27, 82n282, 89–93, 97, 98, 101, 103, 106, 122–24, 141, 171, 177, 178, 224, 229n12, 261n122, 276, 282n200, 284n207, 291, 306, 328n94, 329n98, 335, 347, 350n35
1	61, 76n258, 91n319, 103n18, 116n53, 118, 123, 123n79, 124n83, 127, 284
1:1a	112
1:1–3	91n319, 92n323
1:2–3	140
1:3	137
1:4	136, 137, 138, 180, 283, 284
1:4—3:15	343
1:4–28a	112
1:10	124n83, 125n86
1:15–21	132n114
1:17	126
1:18	132
1:24	108

Ezekiel (cont.)

1:25	108
1:26–28	127
1:26	306
1:27–28	127
1:28—3:27	109
2	87, 178, 179
2:3	61, 110, 178, 179n21
2:4—3:11	12
2:5–8	61, 110
2:5	14, 178, 258n105
2:6	178
2:7	14, 178
2:8	178
3–24	230
3	112, 178, 179, 228n6
3:1	80
3:1–3	4
3:2	82
3:2—5:17	91n319
3:7	14
3:9	101, 110, 178
3:11	14, 120
3:12–13	282
3:12	343
3:14–15	80n274
3:14	347
3:15–16	92n324
3:15	11n38, 12, 22, 171
3:16	81n281
3:17–21	263
3:17	99
3:22	91n319
3:25–27	343
3:26–27	110
3:26	81, 178
3:27	81, 178
4–24	92, 193, 238, 253, 263
4–12	93
4–11	173
4–9	155
4–8	102
4–7	140, 265n138
4–6	102
4–5	82, 140
4	82n282, 87, 179, 193, 219, 261n122
4:1–3	15
4:1	34
4:4–6	68
4:4	64
4:6	255
4:16–17	324
4:16	324
5	82n282, 87, 179, 190n52, 261n122, 281, 282
5–8	186
5:1–3	15
5:1	179
5:2	179, 283
5:5–17	82n282
5:5–7	72, 281
5:6–11	110
5:7–17	199n77
5:7–8	41
5:8–9	261n122
5:8	138, 139
5:9	41n157
5:10	48n168, 68, 141
5:11	41n157, 62, 99
5:12	67, 122, 179, 283, 324
5:13	193, 261n120
5:15	68
5:16–17	324
5:16	111n39
5:17	67, 111n39, 122, 179, 283
6	10n33, 141, 179, 239n39, 268, 268n146, 268n148, 269n149, 322
6:1–14	268
6:1–7	230, 234, 238, 239, 239n39, 241, 247, 271
6:1–3	283
6:1	81n281, 82n282
6:2–3	141
6:3–6	67
6:3–4	268
6:3	179, 239n39

Scripture Index 403

Ezekiel (*cont.*)

6:4–6	110
6:5	141, 230n13
6:6–10	199n77
6:6	62, 141
6:7	141, 257, 261n122
6:8–10	141
6:8	153, 179, 283
6:9	41n157, 62, 110
6:10	261n122
6:11	41n157, 111n39, 122, 179
6:11–14	141
6:11–12	67
6:12	179
6:13	110, 230, 238, 239, 241, 247, 261n122, 268, 271
6:14	261n122
7	141, 141n145
7:1	81n281
7:2	322
7:3	41n157
7:4	41n157
7:7–9	268n148
7:8–9	41n157
7:8	141
7:9	261n120
7:15	67, 111n39, 122, 324
7:18–27	141
7:19–22	199n77
7:19	141, 324
7:20	41n157
7:22	99, 100, 276
7:23	192
7:26	259
7:27	271n156
8–11	1, 11, 14, 27, 42, 76n258, 82, 89, 90, 91, 91n319, 97, 98, 100, 103, 115, 140, 142, 143, 155, 160, 171, 177, 229n12, 239n39, 276, 291, 291n3, 299, 300, 306, 328n94, 329n98, 335
8:1—11:25	8n20
8–10	261n122
8	15, 103, 110, 110n37, 112, 141, 142, 143, 155, 167, 325
8:1–3	91n319
8:1	13, 20n72, 92n323, 176
8:3	110, 137, 347
8:5	110
8:6	41n157, 143, 154
8:7–15	265
8:9	41n157, 143
8:10–11	110
8:10	62, 110
8:12	136, 143
8:13	41n157
8:14	110, 111n40
8:15	41n157
8:16–17	111n39
8:16	111, 111n40
8:17	41n157, 322
8:18	72, 193
9–12	180
9–10	145
9	18, 112, 141, 145, 147, 148, 149, 150, 152n189, 153, 153n190, 179, 181, 181n28, 184, 185, 189, 190, 194, 261n122
9:1	151
9:2	137, 151
9:3	123n80, 146
9:4	41n157, 150, 184, 219
9:6	180
9:8	155, 219
9:9	136, 143, 322
9:10	72
10–11	122, 123
10	112, 118, 123, 123n79, 132n114, 134
10:1	109n32
10:2	153, 153n190
10:4	123n80
10:5	108

Ezekiel (cont.)

10:12	132
10:14	123, 124n83
10:15b	124n83
10:16	123n80, 126
10:18	123n80
11	95, 110, 142, 145, 153, 171, 173, 178, 224, 292, 317, 317n71
11:1–3	265
11:8	283
11:9	68
11:10	261n122
11:12	261n122
11:13	14, 155
11:14–21	82n284
11:14	81n281
11:15–16	13
11:15	11n41, 219, 264n130
11:16	62, 114, 126, 142
11:17–20	153, 251
11:18	41n157
11:20	62, 72
11:21	41n157, 154
11:22–24	261n122
11:22–23	153, 155, 178
11:23	103, 123n80, 228
11:25	120
12:1—24:27	93n326
12	87, 94n330, 102, 171, 173, 178, 179, 180, 183n36, 192, 224, 263
12–24	173, 174, 176
12:1–11	12, 15
12:1	81n281
12:2	179
12:3–12	11
12:3–7	179
12:3	179
12:5	15
12:8	81n281
12:9	179
12:10–13	179
12:10	219
12:14	179, 283
12:16	41n157, 67, 179, 324
12:17–20	179
12:17	81n281
12:18	282
12:19–20	322
12:21–28	11n41, 179
12:21	81n281
12:23	120
12:24	219
12:25	179
12:26	81n281
13–24	1, 93, 94, 171, 179, 182, 193, 224
13	46, 95, 180, 180n24, 265, 281, 325
13:1–6	180
13:1	81n281
13:2–4	271n156
13:5	141n146
13:9	271n156, 281n195
13:11	180, 284n206
13:13	180, 284n206
13:16	114, 271n156
13:17–23	180
14	46, 68, 110, 173, 180, 181, 185, 189, 190, 194, 228n6, 325
14:1–11	180
14:1	13, 20n72, 176
14:2	81n281
14:3–9	339n9
14:4	120
14:6–9	46
14:6	41n157
14:8	67
14:9	281n195
14:10–20	190
14:10	68
14:11	72
14:12–20	180
14:12–23	12
14:12	81n281
14:13	182n31, 281n195, 324
14:14	22n82

Ezekiel (cont.)

14:16	190
14:17–18	190
14:17	283
14:18	46
14:19	193
14:20	46
14:21	67, 324
14:23	261n120
15	181, 181n29, 185
15–19	79
15–17	178, 181, 184, 186
15:1–6	175
15:1	81n281
15:4–7	185
15:4	182
15:6	324
15:7	67, 227n3
15:8	182
16	1, 40, 42, 43, 46, 46n164, 49n174, 71, 81n281, 83, 89, 91, 91n319, 91n321, 110, 135, 141, 172, 172n241, 173, 173nn2–3, 174, 174n6, 175n7, 176, 176n15, 177, 178, 181–86, 188, 189, 191–95, 195n62, 197–99, 199n77, 199n79, 202n84, 202n86, 203, 203n98, 204, 204n102, 205, 207n107, 210, 213n123, 216, 219, 219n144, 222, 224, 226, 227n2, 242, 255, 256, 261n122, 285, 332, 333, 352
16:1–43	175
16:1	197
16:2	11n38, 41n157
16:3–14	197
16:3	195, 216
16:4–6	195
16:4	223
16:7–14	195
16:7b	202n84
16:8	70, 182, 199, 224
16:8b	197
16:15–43	73
16:15	205n104
16:16	205n104
16:17	205n104
16:21	173
16:22	41n157
16:26	205n104
16:27	172n241, 200, 281n195
16:28	205n104
16:30	205n104
16:31	205n104
16:33	227n2
16:34	205n104
16:35	205n104
16:36	41n157, 227n2
16:37–38	214
16:37	68, 227n2
16:38	193
16:39	200, 218, 221, 285
16:40	62, 188, 215, 220
16:41	68, 205n104
16:42	82n284
16:43	41n157
16:44–53	72
16:46	192
16:47	41n157
16:48	192
16:49	192
16:50–51	41n157
16:51–63	82n284
16:53–63	91n320
16:53–55	83n284
16:53	192
16:55	192
16:56	192
16:58	41n157
16:59–63	153
16:59	71, 182, 183, 224
16:59b	197
16:60	67, 182, 197, 224
16:61	224

Ezekiel (cont.)

16:62	67, 182, 197, 224
17	40, 45, 46, 46n164, 47, 71, 72, 74n250, 96, 134, 134n122, 170, 179, 182, 182n33, 183, 183n34, 185, 186, 230, 238, 241, 265, 321, 322
17:1–22	175
17:1	81n281
17:3	121n74
17:6–8	185
17:9	44n159
17:11–21	45, 71
17:11	81n281
17:12	178, 182, 271n156
17:13	70
17:14	71
17:15	71
17:16	71, 183
17:18–20	170
17:18	183
17:19–21	183
17:19	46n164, 73, 182n33, 183, 183n35
17:20	72, 182
17:21	243, 243n51, 261n120
17:22–24	82n284, 153
18	68, 83, 110, 141, 181, 184, 184n37, 186, 186n45, 189, 190, 194, 228n6, 261n122
18:1	81n281
18:3–32	343
18:6	62
18:6c	67
18:12–13	41n157
18:12	167
18:13	68
18:19–20	68
18:19	67
18:21	67
18:24	41n157, 182n31
18:25	185n41
18:29	185n41
18:31	228n5
19	124n81, 179, 185, 186, 261n122, 265, 321
19:6–7	185n41
19:9	185n43, 268n148
19:10–14	185
19:12–13	324
19:14	185
20	68, 91n319, 110, 176, 176n15, 186, 186n45, 189, 228n6, 242, 264n132, 269, 269n151, 317n71, 318, 335
20:1	13, 20n72, 92n323, 176
20:2	81n281
20:4	41n157
20:5	261n120
20:7–8	254n96
20:7	261n120
20:9	187, 269
20:11	187, 187n46
20:13	187, 187n46
20:14	187, 269
20:16	155, 187n46
20:18	68, 186, 187n46
20:19	187n46, 261n120
20:21	187, 187n46
20:22	187, 269
20:23	145
20:24–26	173
20:24	187n46
20:25–26	187n46
20:25	187n46
20:26	173
20:27	182n31
20:29	187
20:31	173, 339n9
20:32–44	227n1
20:32–34	317
20:32–33	96
20:32	11n41, 62
20:33–35	83n284
20:33	62, 193

Ezekiel (cont.)

20:34	62
20:37	70, 71, 187
20:39–44	82n284
20:40–44	153
20:45	81n281
20:48	260n118
20:49	80, 81n275
21	32, 134, 179, 188, 190, 190n52, 256, 261n122, 283, 283n202, 333
21:1–5	219n144
21:1	81n281
21:2	261n120
21:5	261n122
21:8–9	189
21:8	81n281
21:14–22	32n119
21:18	81n281
21:21	188
21:23–29 [Heb]	45, 71
21:26 [Heb]	15, 21, 21n78
21:28 [Heb]	71
21:30–32 [Heb]	321
21:31	64
22–24	191
22	191, 191n55, 192
22:1–5	199n77
22:1	81n281
22:2–6	191
22:2	11n38, 41n157, 191, 192
22:5	300n22, 328n92
22:6	191
22:7	191
22:8	191
22:9–11	191, 192
22:9	167, 191
22:10	67, 68
22:11	41n157
22:12–13	191
22:12	167, 191
22:13	191
22:15	192
22:17	81n281
22:18–22	192, 192n57
22:21–22	193
22:22	261n120
22:24–25	191
22:24	32, 191n55
22:25	271n156
22:26	67, 191, 259, 271n156, 325
22:27	191
22:28	271n156
22:29	191
22:30–31	192
22:31	191n55
23	1, 42, 43, 83, 89, 91, 91n319, 91n321, 110, 135, 141, 172, 173, 173nn2–3, 174, 175, 175n7, 176, 176n15, 177, 178, 181–83, 185, 186, 188, 189, 191–94, 195n62, 197–99, 199n77, 199n79, 202n90, 203, 203n98, 204, 204n102, 205, 207n107, 210, 216, 219, 219n144, 222, 224, 226, 227n2, 242, 255, 256, 261n122, 285, 332, 333, 352
23:1–35	91n320
23:1–4	197
23:1	81n281
23:3	205n104, 254n96, 256
23:4	199
23:5–10	198
23:5–7	255
23:5	227n2
23:8	202n91
23:9	227n2
23:10	68, 214
23:11–21	198
23:12–15	222
23:14b–15	175
23:18	68
23:19	205n104, 254n96
23:20	33, 33n120

Ezekiel (*cont.*)

23:22	227n2
23:22–35	198
23:23–24	137n129
23:24	172n241, 187n46, 198, 200, 214, 335
23:25	216, 283
23:26	218, 221, 285
23:27	254n96
23:29	68, 214
23:30	205n104
23:36–44	198
23:36	41n157
23:39	173
23:44	205n104
23:45–47	198
23:46	285
23:47	62, 188, 220
23:48–49	199
23:49	199n78
24	87, 173, 191, 192, 193
24:1–13	175
24:1	81n281, 92n323, 141
24:2	18
24:3–14	199n77
24:3	178
24:6	192
24:9	192
24:11	192
24:12	192
24:14	72
24:15–27	179, 193, 226
24:15–24	12, 199n77
24:15	81n281
24:19	120
24:20	81n281
24:21	67
24:24	193
24:27	82
25–48	1, 89, 93n329, 94, 154, 253n90
25–39	93n329, 225, 258, 333
25–32	12, 40, 41, 79, 92n322, 93, 198, 226, 252, 253, 253nn87–88, 263, 263n126, 263n129, 279n186, 283, 285, 285n210, 288, 290, 293
25:1—32:32	93n326
25	93, 93n329, 135, 253, 283
25:1	81n281
25:3–5	262
25:12–14	269n149
25:13	256n100
26–28	254, 256n99
26:1	81n281, 92n323, 254n94
26:6	256n100
26:8	256n100
26:7	122n78, 137n129
26:11	256n100
26:13	48n168
26:20	256
27	31n110, 254n92, 256, 261n122
27:1–36	175
27:1	81n281
28	31n110
28:3	22n82
28:7	122
28:11	81n281
28:12–19	175, 254n92
28:12	254n92
28:20	81n281
28:22	68
28:23	256n100
28:26	68
29–32	242, 255n97
29	31n110, 254, 349
29:1	81n281, 92n323, 254n94
29:5	31n109, 31n110, 241, 242, 274n168
29:6b–9a	12
29:8	256n100
29:12	255
29:14–16	45
29:15	71
29:16	71
29:17	81n281, 92n323

Ezekiel (cont.)

30	254, 256n102
30:3	141n146
30:4	256n100
30:5	256n100
30:6	67, 256n100
30:11	241, 242, 256n100
30:14	68
30:17	256n100
30:18	67
30:19	68
30:20–26	31n110
30:20	81n281, 92n323
30:21	256n100
30:22	256n100
30:24–25	40
30:24	256n100
30:25	138, 256n100
31	254, 261n122
31:1–18	175
31:1	81n281, 92n323
31:12	268n148
31:14	256
31:16	256
31:17	256n100
31:18	256n100
32	29, 30, 31, 31n110, 93, 254, 256, 349
32:1–16	8n20
32:1	81n281, 92n323
32:2–6	30
32:2b	31
32:3	31
32:4–5	241, 242, 274n168
32:4	31n109
32:5–6	29, 268, 268n148
32:6	30
32:10	256n100
32:11	256n100
32:12	256n100
32:17	81n281, 92n323
32:18	256
32:20	256n100
32:21–32	256n100
32:23	256
32:24	256
32:25	256
32:26	256
32:29	256
32:30	256
33–48	87, 92n322, 93, 228, 253
33–39	92n322, 248, 263
33–37	279
33–34	93n328
33	94n330, 263, 264, 267n142
33:1—39:29	93n326
33:1–9	263
33:1	81n281
33:2–7	99
33:3	263n129
33:5	68
33:7–20	264
33:7	274n168
33:10–20	184, 264
33:21	15, 92n323, 152n186, 264, 292, 300
33:22	81, 82
33:23–29	11n41, 12, 185
33:23	81n281, 83
33:24–33	83
33:24	114
33:26	41n157
33:28	67, 268n148
33:29	41n157, 264
33:30–33	80, 81n275, 176, 264
33:33	258n105, 327
34–39	320n76
34–37	249
34	46, 83, 264, 265n135, 265n138, 270n152, 271n156, 314, 321, 335, 345
34:1–24	265
34:1–22	264
34:1–16	321
34:1	81n281

Ezekiel (cont.)

34:6	268n148
34:8	230, 241
34:12–16	265n135
34:16–18	264n132
34:17–31	12
34:23–24	255, 319, 346
34:23	252, 321
34:24	72, 320n76, 321
34:25–31	67, 265, 293
34:25	67, 71, 231, 273, 273n163, 275, 293, 296
34:26–27	324
34:27	265, 273
34:28	273
34:30–31	72
34:30	261n120, 265
34:31	265n136
35–39	262, 263, 263n126
35–36	252, 263n126, 322
35	10n33, 12, 40, 93, 263, 266, 266n141, 267n142, 268, 268n146, 269n149, 270, 279n186, 290
35:1–15	93n328
35:1	81n281
35:3–4	281n195
35:4	267
35:8	241, 268, 268n148
35:9	267
35:10–12	267
35:12	261n120, 267
35:15	248, 266, 267
36–48	318, 345
36–39	262n123
36–37	317, 345
36	10n33, 266, 266n141, 267, 267n142, 268, 268n146, 269, 269n151, 270, 290, 317, 317n71, 318, 335
36:1–7	266n141
36:1	267
36:2	267
36:4–8	248
36:4	267, 268, 282n199
36:5–7	266
36:5	267, 268
36:6	267, 268
36:8–12	268
36:8	267
36:11	269
36:16	81n281
36:17–18	282
36:20–38	13
36:21	269
36:22	13, 228, 269
36:23	269, 282n199
36:23b–38	279n186
36:23c–38	278n186
36:24–34	279n186
36:26–32	293
36:26–27	269, 301
36:26	248, 296, 317
36:27	62, 67, 68
36:28	72
36:30	137n129
36:31	41n157
36:34	282n199
36:35	322, 323
36:36	261n120, 269
36:37–38	270n152
36:38	269
37–48	355
37–39	236, 253, 263, 263n126, 268, 273n164, 274, 355
37	1, 27n97, 82, 91, 95, 141, 177, 225, 226, 227, 229, 230, 231, 231nn18–19, 231, 232, 239, 242, 249, 252, 269, 270, 270nn154–55, 271–73, 273n163, 274, 274nn168–69, 275, 276, 278n186, 279n186, 290, 293, 297, 301, 314, 317,

Ezekiel, 37 (cont.)
    317n71, 320, 321, 333, 335,
        336, 345, 355
37:1–22   249
37:1–14   26, 42, 91n319, 141,
        226, 229, 231n21, 232,
        241, 243n47, 247, 268,
        276n170, 318, 338n6
37:2   274
37:4   272, 274
37:5   274
37:7   229n11, 274, 282
37:9   130, 243, 272
37:10   274
37:11–28   273
37:11–23   14
37:11–14   232
37:11   11n38, 270n155, 274
37:12–14   256
37:12–13   273
37:12   272, 273, 275
37:13   270
37:14   261n120, 270, 275
37:15–23   230
37:16   18
37:20   18
37:21   273, 275
37:22–28   274
37:22   268, 273
37:23   72
37:24–28   310, 312
37:24–26   230
37:24–25   230, 252, 255,
                   319, 346
37:24   273, 321
37:25   275, 320n76, 321
37:26–28   293
37:26–27   252
37:26   67, 71, 231, 273n163,
                   275, 293, 296
37:28   249, 270
38–48   277, 296, 315, 355
38–39   1, 37, 38, 40, 40n153,
            42, 80, 93, 94n330,
            122n78, 137n130, 225,
            226, 227, 229n11, 231,
            232, 242, 249, 252, 256,
            262, 263, 270–72, 275,
            276, 277n171, 277n176,
            278n184, 279, 279n186,
            280, 281, 281n195, 283,
            286, 287, 290, 293, 295,
            302, 318, 322, 323, 330,
            332, 333, 337, 345, 347,
            349, 349n32, 350, 352,
            352n40
38   231, 271n157,
            273n164, 274, 274n169,
            275, 277, 278n186, 284,
            288, 352n40
38:1–4a   277n173
38:1   81n281
38:2–23   280n192
38:2–9   280n192
38:2   272, 273
38:4–8   275
38:4   274
38:6   40n153, 122n78,
                   137n129, 283
38:8   268n148, 272, 273,
                   282n199
38:9   274, 284, 284n205
38:10–13   280n192, 330
38:11   273
38:12   273, 281
38:14–16   280n192
38:14   271, 272, 273
38:15   122n78, 137n129, 274
38:16   257n105, 271, 274,
                   282n199
38:17–22   280n192
38:18   282
38:19   282
38:20   268n148, 282
38:21   268n148, 283
38:23   271, 280n192
39   231, 242, 271nn156–57,
                   273n165,

Scripture Index

Ezekiel, 39 (cont.)
  274, 274nn166–67, 274n169,
    275–77,
  278n186, 283n202, 288,
    288n223, 289n228, 290
39:1–24   280n192
39:1–10   330
39:1–8   280n192
39:1   272, 273
39:2   122n78, 137n129,
    268n148, 273, 275, 283
39:3–20   141
39:3   48n168
39:4–5   241, 242, 255n97
39:4   268, 268n148, 273
39:6–16   255n97
39:6–8   275
39:9–10   280n192
39:10   285
39:11–20   231, 288
39:11–16   231n19, 275,
    280n192, 322n79, 330
39:11   273, 274
39:13   187n46
39:14   274
39:15   274
39:17–20   241, 242, 274n168,
    280n192, 289, 318, 330
39:17   255n97, 268,
    268n148, 273
39:19–20   289
39:21–29   228
39:21–24   280n192
39:21   260n118, 281n195
39:22   275
39:23–29   276
39:23–24   100
39:23   182nn30–31, 271,
    276, 283
39:24   99
39:25–29   274, 278n186,
    293, 330
39:25   228n4, 275
39:26 182nn30–31, 273, 276

39:27   276
39:28   261, 275
39:29   275, 276
39:29b   276n170
40–48   26, 27, 42,
  62, 65, 79, 82, 85n297,
  89, 91, 91n319, 92n322,
  93n329, 94n330, 177,
  225, 230, 248, 249, 271,
  271n156, 276, 277n176,
  279, 279n189, 286, 291,
  291nn2–3, 292n5, 295,
  298n17, 300, 301, 305,
  308, 308n43, 313, 314,
  318, 319, 320n76, 321,
  322, 322n78, 325nn88–
  89, 327, 328, 328n93,
  328n95, 329, 329n98,
  330, 337, 338n5, 339n7,
  346, 347, 350n35, 352
40:1—48:35   93n326
40–43   229n12, 252,
    271n156, 320n76
40:1—43:1   302
40–42   304, 329n99
40:1–2   91n319
40:1   92nn323–24, 298n17,
    299, 299n20, 300, 323
40:2   298, 298n17
40:3   306n39
40:6   299n17
40:26   299n17
40:27–37   298n17
40:31   299n17
40:37   299n17
41:7   299n17
41:18–20   124
41:18–19   117, 123n79
41:19   123n79, 124n81,
    124n83
41:22   297n14, 298n17
42:20   308
43–48   95, 310
43   112, 291, 306
43:1–5   91, 292, 297

Ezekiel (cont.)

43:1–4	112n41
43:2	129, 140
43:4	112
43:6–9	304
43:7–9	308, 321
43:7	327
43:8	41n157
43:9	327
43:10–12	296, 298
43:11	18, 296
43:18	296
43:25–26	306
44–48	255
44	296, 308n43
44:5	296
44:6–16	308n43
44:6–7	41n157
44:6	178n20
44:7	71
44:10–31	325n88
44:10–14	325n88
44:10	68
44:12	68
44:13	41n157
44:20	64
44:24	296
45	320, 323
45:1	322n79
45:2	322
45:4	322, 322n79
45:7	308
45:10–12	320n76
45:21	330n102
45:23	330n102
45:25	330n102
46	320
47–48	322n78
47	298n17, 309, 324
47:1–12	320n76
47:1–5	324
47:7	324
47:9–10	324
47:12	324
48	320, 322n79, 323
48:11	325n88
48:12	322n79
48:35	291, 299n20, 300, 308
48:35b	291, 292, 326

Daniel

1:4	20n71
2–6	262
7–12	355n49
7	37n141, 130, 241n42
7:7–28	343
7:9–28	130n106
7:9–10	107n26
7:15–28	343
9:11	75n253
9:17	129
12	355n49

Hosea

1:5	48n168
1:9	252
2	177
2:2–13	252n85
2:2	200
2:4–5 [Heb]	211
2:11–12 [Heb]	211
2:12	252
2:14–23	252n85
2:21–23	252
2:22	259n110
2:23	252
4:1	259n110
4:6	259
5:4–6	98
6:7	73n247
8:1	73n247, 122n77
8:2	259n110
11:8	196n67
12:1	74n250
13:4–5	258

Joel

2	324
2:20	122
3	272n160
3:18	252

Amos

1–2	12
1:1—2:5	285
1:3—2:3	252
1:9	254
1:11–12	266
1:14	130n105, 180n23
2:4–5	99
2:6–16	167
3	56n190, 73, 73n247
3:7	99
4:11	196n67
7:10–17	207
7:12	251
7:14	98n2
7:17	209
9:4	252
9:13	252

Jonah

1:4	130n105, 284n206
1:12	130n105
4:2	257

Micah

1:2–7	73
1:8–16	99
3:4	99
3:11	99
4:1–3	19n66
4:1	299n20
4:2	299n20
4:4	265
4:5	113n45
6	56n190, 73n247
6:1–8	73
6:5	257
6:16	99

Nahum

1:2	139n136
2:7–8	[Heb]n117
3:3	211n116
3:4	211
3:5–6	211

Habakkuk

1:8	122n77
2	213
3:3–7	288n223
3:3	137
3:13	138

Zephaniah

1:7	288n221
1:15	284n205
1:18	141
2:9	196n67

Zechariah

1–6	349n32, 350n35
4:10	134
9–14	37n141
9:14–15	137
9:14	106n25; 130n105, 180n24
11:9	141n144
12–14	349n32
14	272n160

~

NEW TESTAMENT

Mark	354n44

Luke

13:32	174n7

1 Corinthians	354n44

Galatians

4:22–31	174n7

1 and 2 Thessalonians	354n44
2 Peter	354n44

Revelation

12	37n141

Revelation (*cont.*)

12:3	31n109
17:1–14	31n109
19:17–21	338
19:20	31n109
20:7–10	338
21	339
21:1	31n109
22	339

APOCRYPHA

Ben Sira

49:8	106

2 Esdras

6:49–52	31n109

4 Ezra   348n26

PSEUDEPIGRAPHA

Apocalypse of Abraham

	348n26
17–21	347
18	347

Apocalypse of Zephaniah

	348n26

2 Baruch

	348n26
29:4–6	324n86

3 Baruch   348n26

1 Enoch

1–36	348n26
14	347
37–71	348n26
61:10	132
62:2	281n195
71:7	132
73–82	348n26
85–90	348n26
91:11–17	348n26
93:1–10	348n26

2 Enoch   348n26

Jubilees

8:19–20a	281n197
23	348n26

Psalms of Solomon

17:27	281n195

The Testament of Abraham   348n26

The Testament of Levi

2–5	348n26

OTHER ANCIENT SOURCES

ANET (by the page)

53	128n94
62	129n101, 133n117
64	133n117
66	129n101
83	245n62
109	104n21
181–82	216n133
183	217n136
309	158n205
315	158N207
315–16	316n69
353–54	218n142
395–96	156n196
447	132n110
450	258n105
455	162n215
517	130n102

ANET (cont.)

532	178n19
533	150n181, 218n142
534	146n166, 160n211
538	209n111, 244n58
539	150n181, 245n59
560	158n207
646	305n36
648	161n213

COS
(by volume, text, and page)

1.108:381–84	27n96
1.111:397–98	31n109
1.111:401	147n167
1.113:405	145n158, 147n167
1.113:414	245n61
1.113:415	309n46
1.113:416	149n177
1.133:461	222n154
1.147:478	158n207
1.149:480–81	313nn55–56
1.166:535–36	162n215
2.82.213	220n146
2.82:214	44n160, 220n147, 220n149
2.115:431	121n74
2.120:306	166n227
2.131:336	264n133
2.155:417–33	302n27, 305n35

Dead Sea Scrolls

4QS1	347

Herodotus

2:161	30n107
4:159	30n107

Josephus

Antiquities

10:79	329n99
10:98	20n70
10:181	254n94

War

3:52	281n197

Printed in Great Britain
by Amazon